The Armenian Events
of Adana in 1909

The Armenian Events of Adana in 1909

Cemal Paşa and Beyond

Yücel Güçlü

Hamilton Books
Lanham • Boulder • New York • Toronto • London

Copyright © 2018 by
The Rowman & Littlefield Publishing Group, Inc.
4501 Forbes Boulevard
Suite 200
Lanham, Maryland 20706
Hamilton Books Acquisitions Department (301) 459-3366

Unit A, Whitacre Mews, 26-34 Stannary Street,
London SE11 4AB, United Kingdom

All rights reserved
Printed in the United States of America

British Library Cataloging in Publication Information Available
Library of Congress Control Number: 2017953672
ISBN 978-0-7618-6993-1 (pbk. : alk. paper)
ISBN 978-0-7618-6994-8 (electronic)

∞™ The paper used in this publication meets the minimum
requirements of American National Standard for Information
Sciences—Permanence of Paper for Printed Library Materials,
ANSI Z39.48—1984

Contents

Acknowledgments		vii
Maps		ix
Introduction		1
1	Geographical and Economic Importance of the Province of Adana and Its Vicinity	37
2	Position of Armenians in Adana at the Turn of the Twentieth Century	61
3	Major Causes of the Outbreak, 1908–1909	95
4	Dimensions of the Disorder, April 1909	165
5	Responsibility for the Outrages	211
6	Reestablishing Order, May–August 1909	241
7	Cemal Paşa's Governorship in Adana, August 1909–June 1911	287
8	Post–1911 Adana and Cemal Paşa	363
Conclusion		431
Bibliography		439
Index		475
About the Author		499

Acknowledgments

Many people contributed to the conception and drafting of this book, and I gratefully acknowledge the help and kindness they showed me at various stages along the way. At Hamilton Books, Julie Kirsch, vice president and publisher, bravely set the ball rolling, while my editors, Emma Richard and Melissa McClellan, have since encouraged and advised me with the voice of experience and a sure touch. I am indebted to them for the confidence they have demonstrated in me.

My gratitude also goes to Michael Reynolds, associate professor in Princeton University's Department of Near Eastern Studies, who kindly read and offered invaluable corrections on an earlier draft of this work. He was generous with his specialist insights.

The research for the present volume was carried out in various countries in the course of the last five years. It could not have been complete without the patient and efficient assistance of the staffs of a great many archives and libraries in Turkey, Britain, France, and the United States. These include the Prime Minister's Office Ottoman Archive in Kağıthane/İstanbul, the Turkish General Staff Military History and Strategic Studies Directorate Archive in Ankara, The National Archives in Kew/London, Archives de Ministère des Affaires Etrangères in Courneuve/Paris, Centre des Archives Diplomatiques in Nantes, the National Archives and Records Administration in College Park, Maryland, the National Library in Ankara, Atatürk Library in Taksim/İstanbul, the British Library in Euston/London (including the Newspaper Collection at Colindale), the Library of Congress in Washington, DC, and the Houghton Library of the Harvard University in Cambridge, Massachusetts.

While in London, I had the good fortune of meeting Gül Tokay, visiting professor of diplomatic history at Richmond University in Surrey, who cheerfully shared advice and experience. I must express my deep thanks to her.

Sinan Kuneralp has been a steady source of close friendship, unflagging support, and incisive comment. He kindly took the time from his own work to discuss my ideas with me and give his advice.

For generously sending a diverse array of source materials and answering my various queries, I must acknowledge my colleagues Ayten Eler, Elvan Hacıefendioğlu, Özkan Duman, Ali Onaner, and İbrahim Yükseltan. I am greatly appreciative of all their efforts and dedication.

Conversations with Professor Gökhan Çetinsaya of Şehir University in İstanbul helped me think through the challenging historical period covered in the book. A decade of agreeing and disagreeing with him in various settings has sharpened my reflection upon a host of questions. He has been an invaluable source of advice and ideas.

Professor Edward Erickson deserves special mention. For many years, I have been privileged to benefit from his sage advice and friendship.

Professor Jeremy Salt has stood out for me as an inspiration and uplift. He has been a conscientious scholar. I treasure the long lunches with him.

Illustrations are reproduced by kind permission of the Turkish Historical Society. I wish to thank archivists Semiha Nurdan and Mustafa Sipahi, who were tireless in processing my photograph requests. They also provided valuable advice with interpretation of photographs.

I am indebted to the Turkish Historical Society for permission to reprint a map from Vedat Eldem, *Harp ve Mütareke Yıllarında Osmanlı İmparatorluğunun Ekonomisi* (Economics of the Ottoman Empire During the Years of War and Armistice) (Ankara: Türk Tarih Kurumu Basımevi, 1994). Also I am indebted to http://1914-1918.invisionzone.com/forums/index.php?/topic/251978-online-maps-of-turkey-before-1915 for two maps (from Cornucopia of Ottomania and Turcomania).

In addition to the above, I benefited from the guidance of the following individuals who were generous with their time: Mehmet Alkan, associate professor in İstanbul University's Faculty of Political Sciences; Kürşad Karacagil, assistant professor in İstanbul University's Institute of Principles of Atatürk and History of the Revolution; Mustafa Toker in Ankara University's Institute of the Turkish Revolution; and Ayhan Kaygusuz and Tuğba Dağlı in Şehir University.

One person who must be thanked for a different type of help is Kamil Dalyan. He chartered me through the shoals of cyberspace: he cheerfully took my calls to bail me out when my personal computer was playing tricks on me, he often came to my office to give me lessons in how to use it, and he went beyond the call of duty to print out the many drafts of the manuscript.

While it would be difficult to exaggerate the value of assistance I have received from all those I have mentioned, I am alone responsible for the text as it stands and such errors of fact and judgment as it may contain.

Maps

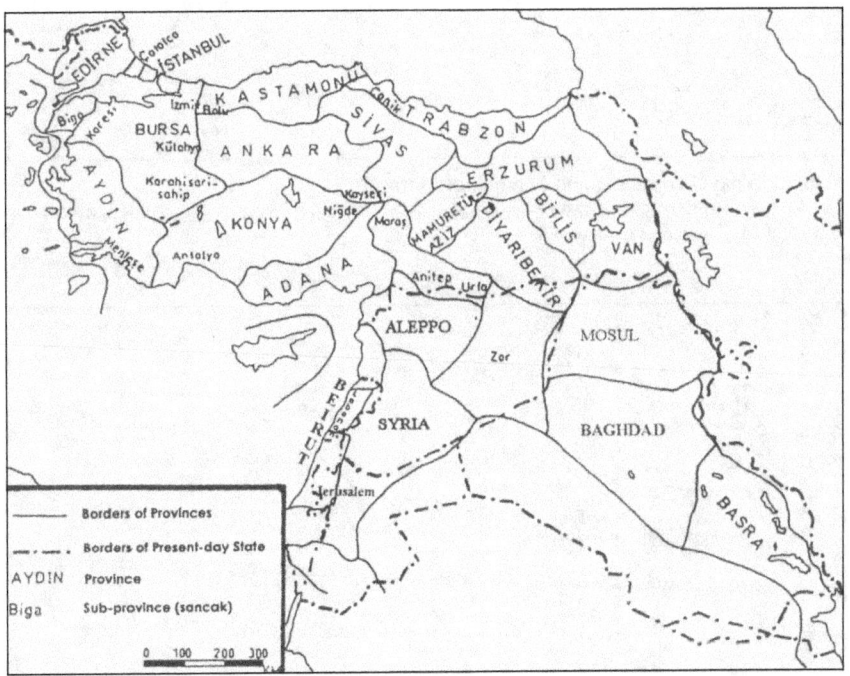

Map 1. Ottoman Provinces in 1914
Source: Vedat Eldem, Harp ve mütareke yıllarında Osmanlı İmparatorluğu'nun ekonomisi (Ankara: Türk Tarih Kurumu Basımevi, 1994).

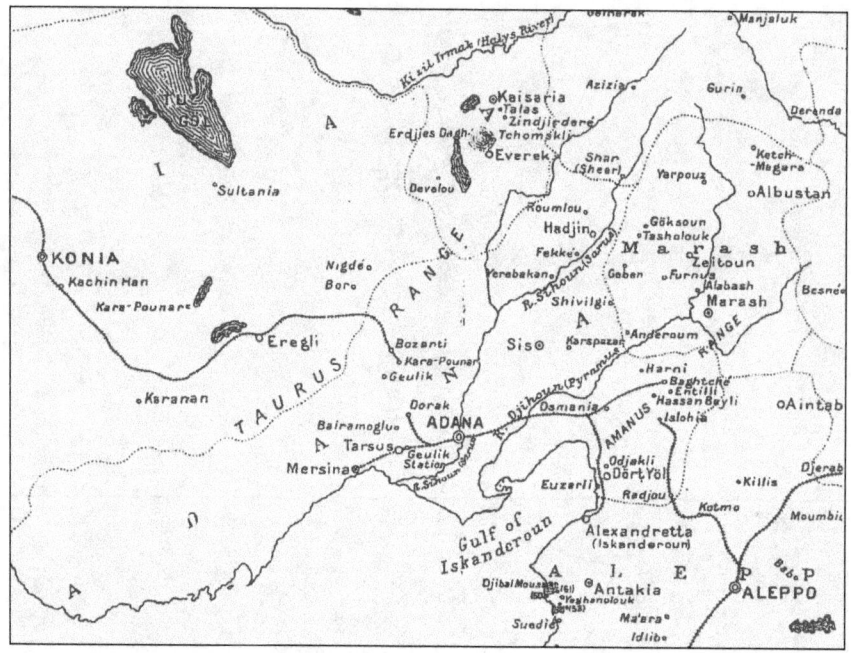

Map 2. Vilayet of Adana and Sandjak of Marash
Source: http://1914-1918.invisionzone.com/forums/index.php?/topic/251978-online-maps-of-turkey-before-1915 (from Cornucopia of Ottomania and Turcomania).

Map 3. Vilayet of Aleppo
Source: http://1914-1918.invisionzone.com/forums/index.php?/topic/251978-online-maps-of-turkey-before-1915 (from Cornucopia of Ottomania and Turcomania).

Introduction

The controversy on what actually happened between Turks and Armenians at Adana in south central Asia Minor[1] in 1909 has been going on for more than a century and shows no sign of resolution. It is hardly necessary to say that Armenian accounts of the Adana affair differ sharply from that by many Turkish historians. It is right that historians should look closely at the particular aspects of tragedies such as at Adana. What is needed is closer investigation of the local situation over a longer time period with a view to setting out what factors were peculiar to that region and contributed to the clashes which occurred, and also the marrying of local developments with national or even international events which impinged especially on the region. A series of detailed local studies might take consideration of the historical Armenian question beyond the state achieved by broad brush treatments, and link the national question with the social and economic changes which were taking place in Anatolia[2] at the time. Especially, one would like to see more studies of the city and province of Adana, which was one of the centers of the most active Armenian politics.[3]

Little has been written about the Adana events[4] of 1909. This lack is all the more apparent when considering the many books on various aspects of the Armenian question. We still do not know with exactitude the answers to basic questions such as how, when, and why the Adana affair came about, or who was primarily responsible. It may be difficult to get answers to these questions, because there are gaps in the documentary record and legitimate differences of opinion over the facts. Some of the key individuals who ordered or arranged the killings remain mysterious figures, whose personalities are difficult to fathom and whose exact roles in these events are unclear. Among them, remarkably, are Zachariah Bezdikian and Garabet Letchilian. As it turns out, this lacunae left by the bearers of secrets in our knowledge is more significant than it might seem. Many important exchanges between key actors were verbal and are not recorded—they can be reconstructed only from indirect evidence or later testimony. The Armenian organizations involved in the violence at Adana were extremely secretive and left virtually no paper trail. The affair is an under-studied and under-researched topic, long in need of fresh review and insight.

With the centenary of 1909 passed years ago, it is high time to stop regarding the Adana crisis as current affairs and the provincial governor Cemal Paşa[5] as our contemporary. Both the event and the man need to be placed in the historical context in which they belong. Only if this is done can Cemal Paşa's true significance be properly assessed.

It is to be noted here that the impulse to treat the history of the Ottoman Empire as a whole has gained significant momentum in the West during the last three decades for a number of reasons, not the least of which is the increasing distance between the present day and the Ottoman past, a distance making the Empire more suitable for objectification. Equally important factors contributing to the trend are the world history movement in Europe and America, where 623 years of Ottoman history find a suitable niche; the maturation of the discipline itself, which has evolved from the study of linguistics and palaeography to a more nuanced interpretation of events and culture as primary documents and secondary studies become numerous. In this period there has been a major discovery of Ottoman sources. The work of Halil İnalcık, Kemal Karpat, Ahmet Yaşar Ocak, Gökhan Çetinsaya, Tufan Buzpınar, Bernard Lewis, Stanford Shaw, Suraiya Faroqhi, Edward Erickson, Michael Reynolds, among others, has dramatically revolutionized Ottoman historiography.[6]

In spite of all we have learned about twentieth-century Ottoman Armenian history, many questions remain. Some concern the meaning, significance, or comparability of events already explored; others involve discussions of original motives or causes; and still others revolve around specific episodes not yet clearly illuminated in the historical record. Finally, there are disputes among scholars who have drawn contradictory messages from the same set of events or evidence. Some of the disputes also raise serious questions about how we do research and write history.

EARLIER RESEARCH

The historiography of the Adana affair began in 1909 and continues today. The 109-year-old historiography of the field is in its fourth narrative generation. The extant history is incomplete and there are gaps, holes, and niches that need to be filled in order to achieve a more complete understanding of what happened in Adana in 1909 and beyond. None treat the question in sufficient depth or at sufficient length to reveal the wider diplomatic, political, military, economic, social, and cultural contexts. Most of the authors clearly had difficulty thinking more broadly about their subjects.

British journalist Duckett Ferriman's *The Young Turks and the Truth about the Holocaust at Adana in Asia Minor, during April, 1909* is an ordinary survey written with a pronounced bias and without any attempt to put the Armenian question into a larger setting. This is not a correct account of the events of Adana. They need to be placed in a broader context of the restoration of the Ottoman Constitution on July 24, 1908, and its aftermath, of Armenian aspirations, of European policy. The author's viewpoint is distinctly limited. Due to the Armenian prism through which Ferriman looks at its subject, it is a blatantly anti-Turkish work replete with all the nineteenth-century stereotypes of the vicious Turk abusing the industrious Armenian community of the Empire. Ferriman's problems begin with his total failure to familiarize himself with even the rudiments of Ottoman history. Not a single footnote refers to a single study dealing with the history of the period in question. The text indicates little or no effort to consult much of the literature on the Turkish-Armenian conflict. On many topics, not even the standard histories in English had been consulted. In the best tradition of his nineteenth-century predecessors, Ferriman views the world solely in terms of that small segment of the Anatolian Armenian population. The resultant portrait is one of helpless, innocent Armenian victims of brutal Turkish massacres and exterminations. Covering, as it does, the time frame of 1908–1909, Ferriman's readers have every right to expect that he had taken the trouble to apprise himself of the basic outline of Ottoman history for that period. The author exclusively focuses on his topic without comprehension of the historical framework within which the events he purports to describe occurred. There is no bibliography, and the few references made to published material are extremely variable in quality and appropriateness, as well as being sloppily cited. It is also worth noting that the author is a traveler and not the erstwhile historian who, one imagines, would have produced a book on the subject. This, however, should not detract from the informational value of the work—although the title of the study erroneously posits the Adana events of 1909 a "holocaust."[7]

Originally published in Armenian in 2009 as the *Widespread Massacres of Armenians in Cilicia (April 1909)*, Hrachik Simonyan's *The Destruction of Armenians in Cilicia, April 1909* was brought into print in English three years after its initial appearance. In the inner cover page, it is mentioned that the book represents the forefront of Armenian language historiography on the Adana massacres of 1909 and was recommended for publication by the Center of Armenian Studies of Yerevan State University. But not only is the vast body of primary Ottoman source material totally ignored by Simonyan, his work never even acknowledges that he is aware of its existence. Not only would these have helped to confirm or disprove the veracity of many published accounts but they might have brought to light much additional information as well. There exists a great deal of source material in Ottoman Turkish and in various forms. But not a single source in this language is included. It is difficult to imagine how a study that deals with the events of Adana in 1909 can avoid all reference to records or publications of the government in question. Simonyan excessively relies for vital information on secondary materials. Otherwise the chief source for him is Armenian literature, which one cannot consider adequate for this kind of study. In the Prime Minister's Office Ottoman Archive (BOA) in İstanbul and in the Turkish General Staff Military History and Strategic Studies Directorate's Archive (ATASE) in Ankara, he undoubtedly would and should have found primary materials that would have made his work more substantial, original, and convincing. Reference to secondary works that do utilize Ottoman data is not sufficient. Given his failure to utilize primary Ottoman materials, and his almost complete reliance on Armenian language sources, Simonyan's work is yet another in the long line of Armenian distortions.[8]

This book is not intended to be comprehensive. There is no substantial discussion, for instance, of the rich array of primary sources available for this period, nor of the historiographical framework. Nor does the author seek to address in detail the wider socioeconomic, religious, or legal contexts for the Adana events of 1909.

Further, *The Destruction of Armenians in Cilicia, April 1909* has neither scholarly bibliography nor enough footnotes. The bibliographies to which Simonyan refers his interested reader are, with a few exceptions, unscholarly and addressed not to historians and the student of history, but to the general public. There is something to be said for compiling that kind of guide to sources in a book for popular consumption, but it certainly does not entitle the author to praise for his historical scholarship. This is a book that harks back to the "national histories" of a past age, histories in which nothing is entertained that might contend with the national vision. Opposing views are avoided. Today it is considered a better practice for historians to at least refer readers to books and articles with alternative views. This is one of the practices that separates history from propaganda.

Memoirs of persons who experienced historical events require the greatest caution of all.[9] Most memoirs are written too soon after the events they describe to be impartial and too early for pertinent records to be available for the settlement of controversial issues. They are marred by the narrowness of the author's view and by their lack of knowledge of all the facts that influenced decisions and actions other than their own.[10] Even when a period of three years has passed since the incidents described, as in the case of Hagop Terzian's *Cilicia 1909: The Massacre of Armenians*, the account can still be seriously affected by the same defects if the author relies only or even mainly on his own records and recollections. In Terzian's memoirs, originally published in Armenian in 1912, there are numerous examples of value judgments inadequately supported by the evidence provided, of general statements offered without substantiating evidence, and of assertions made as if they were historical facts when actually they may be either incorrect or subject to debate. It is obviously a reflection of personal bias, not of scholarly judgment. For some important statements, there are no references. Perhaps interpretive works resting on widely known and noncontroversial events and sources do not need documentation. With the Armenian events of 1909, however, the basic sequence of orders and actions is in dispute. The historian should read these tendentious memoirs only after a thorough steeping in authentic contemporary materials.[11]

The Adana Massacres and the Catholic Missionaries: An Account by Eye Witnesses, issued by the Society for the Propagation of the Faith, is an illustrated booklet which while relating incidents of the massacres in general, describes more in detail the scenes actually witnessed by the Jesuit missionaries in Adana and its vicinity, and by the Sisters of Saint Joseph, of Lyons, who had charge of their schools, orphanage, and hospital. It is, in fact, an appeal for the Jesuit Mission of Adana. The narrators see these events through the prisms of their own personal visions and are not always accurate or reliable, but they do serve to cross-check some other sources.[12]

A large volume of about four hundred pages of type, and illustrations and photographs and facsimiles, entitled *Aspirations et Agissements Révolutionnaires des Comités Arméniens Avant et Aprés la Proclamation de la Constitution Ottomane*, was published in İstanbul in 1917. It dealt with things that had to do with the Armenian situation. It harked back to Sasun, touched briefly on 1895–1896, and dwelled at length on later events in connection with the Young Turk revolution of 1908 and the attitudes and actions of the Armenian revolutionaries since the First World War began. It gave explanation of events, as well as details of the Armenian outrages and atrocities perpetrated on Muslims during the Russian advance and at other times wherever they could find opportunity. It gave photographic copies of Armenian letters and proclamations and other documents, and a lot of photographs to substantiate that the Armenians were plotting revolution. It gave the names of the Armenian National Defense Union in America and information about their actions.[13]

The twelve contributors to *1909 Adana Olayları:Makaleler* come from Turkey, the United States, Germany, Austria, Japan, and Israel. The articles were originally presented as papers at a symposium in Ankara in June of 2009. The symposium was organized by the editor Kemal Çiçek, a professor of history at Karadeniz Technical University, Trabzon, and hosted by the Turkish Historical Society. The venue and the host add particular interest to what is intrinsically an informative and valuable book. In a short introduction, the editor describes the development and transformation of the Turkish-Armenian relations between 1908 and 1909. With this collection, Çiçek and the contributors present a competent overview of and offer valuable insights on the Armenian events of Adana in 1909. Although somewhat uneven in its treatment of the subject, these articles are most useful in that they constitute an excellent stimulus for discussion and informed debate. As several of the contributors make plain in their papers, there is a lot more to be said. Çiçek's declared aim in producing this study is to stimulate further research. Without doubt, this book will succeed in doing so.[14]

Much has been done in the last three decades by the Directorate General of the Turkish State Archives to declassify material and make it readily available to the scholar and informed reader. The publication of *Osmanlı Belgelerinde 1909 Adana Olayları* in two volumes by Recep Karacakaya et al. deserves particular attention. The editors were given full access to all BOA documents and full control over selection for printing. The editors state that no documents were withheld or omitted for reasons of state or to avoid embarrassment to any individual or group. The primary aim of the project was to present material that would show what happened and why it happened at Adana in 1909. This was taken to mean the selection of papers that represented the senior level of government policy and decision making and the omission of the contributions by lower-level officials unless they happened to be the most revealing expression of a problem, position, or policy that is extant. Documents that had been published elsewhere were omitted unless they were considered necessary to explain an aspect of policy or policy making. First offered is an analytical list of documents, chronologically arranged, with date, document number, and the number of the page on which it is printed in the volume. A clear, concise, and accurate summary statement of the character and principal content of each document is given with the list. Footnotes are used for cross-references, references to documents not printed, further identification of individuals or documents, and an occasional editorial correction or other clarification. The volumes will be best used, as intended, as works of reference. The uninitiated will bog down in it, and the specialist will find more corroborative detail or confirmation of their general knowledge than surprises or material for startling new interpretations.[15]

Still, even the appearance of these two volumes containing 192 documents on 1,036 pages of text does not mean—despite their weight and size—that everything one always wanted to know about the Adana episode in 1909 can be found here. Partly this is because the conflict is not discreetly filed away in folders marked "Armenian Events of Adana in 1909" in the BOA but must be searched out in all sorts of unlikely places. Partly, too, this is because choices must be made about what to print. And finally, the editors of the Directorate General of Turkish State Archives' mandate does not extend to private collections, such as the papers of journalists and others like Hüseyin Cahit Yalçın.

1909 Adana Ermeni Olayları by Yusuf Sarınay and Recep Karacakaya is a brief and largely unsatisfactory study, based almost wholly on Turkish primary and secondary sources. No European, American, and Armenian materials have been employed, except two English-language books translated to Turkish. The introduction is a short chronological overview of Turkish-Armenian relations between 1902 and 1909, reduced to mere five pages. It does a major injustice to the complexity of a crucial period of Ottoman history, explaining neither why or how the Armenian troubles occurred in the country, nor how the Ottoman rulers dealt with that question. The succeeding sections on the outbreak of violence at Adana in 1909 and the establishment of order in the region are all simplistic in construction, simply rephrasing the words of, and frequently quoting, officials and other persons. The topics the authors pursue seem dictated more by what they have found in the archival material and not by any unifying structure or even scholarly exposition. Despite these shortcomings, the book is a treasure trove of information and data, and it can serve as a useful addition to the scant literature on this hitherto insufficiently researched subject.[16]

Fueled by yet another revival of popular and scholarly interest in the conflict, historians have grappled with an important shift in our understanding of the context of Adana events. Japanese historian Tetsuya Sahara's *What Happened in Adana in April 1909?*, although it exposes few fresh archival materials and is a reanalysis of the existing historical base, questions much of the previously received wisdom. The book seeks to use Turkish sources more fully to achieve more nuanced understanding of its subject. The author quotes the direct testimony of the participants, both Turks and American missionaries. There is no attempt to produce anything novel here, but the job is competently done and the judgments are generally sound enough. Sahara has not, by his own admission, broken much new ground for the scholarly community.[17]

No new consensus emerges from these books, but, taken as a whole, they move the debate forward in new ways. Historians have scoured archives, identified incriminating evidence, and built their cases, only to find other historians disputing their interpretations of particular documents, pointing to contrary evidence in other archives, and introducing mitigating circumstances. Even with this renewed interest in synthetic histories of the conflict, there remain ample opportunities, particularly in Turkey, to publish monographs on 1909.

The relative bounty of documentary sources, coupled with significant gaps in the record, means that there will always be scope for different interpretations of the Armenian events of Adana and Cemal Paşa. Further archival research may alter interpretations of specific issues but it is unlikely that a single source will establish a new consensus on the causes of the outbreak of violence in the region in 1909.

SUBJECT MATTER

The rather paucity of scholarly studies is not an accurate reflection of the intrinsic interest of the subject. The creation of broader and innovative narrations of this turbulent and controversial chapter in the twentieth-century Ottoman history will facilitate a better understanding of the Turkish-Armenian past. The present work attempts to fill a void existing in the field.

The purpose of this book is twofold: first, to give an accurate and reasonably complete narrative account of the Armenian events of 1909 and their aftermath in Adana and the developments leading up to and following them; and equally importantly, to provide an interpretive framework that makes it easier to comprehend this episode in Ottoman history. The survey covers a range of years far beyond the limits of 1909. The events and the creation of a new form of imperial citizenship are contextualized against the background of the multilingual and multireligious Ottoman Empire. A number of themes central to the study of the Ottoman provinces, notably the nature of provincial administration, local notables, educational life and their relationships to trends in the imperial capital, and transformations in the nineteenth and twentieth centuries are also treated. For the Turkish men who appear in the book, there is no biographical work in English. The study aims to introduce these individuals to an English-speaking audience. They are made flesh and blood.

It is also intended to introduce readers to the large amount of new research, which has taken the Ottoman history into many new and exciting areas. Consequently, the notes are designed to be as comprehensive as possible. It is hoped that the true significance of an episode will emerge from this volume and that, at the same time, it will go some way to demythologizing the popular memory of a crisis which is widely misunderstood.

The outbreak of the 1909 events in Adana can justly be described as the most complex series of happenings in the early twentieth-century Ottoman history, much more difficult to comprehend and explain than the Young Turk revolution of 1908, the Balkan Wars of 1912–1913, or the onset of the First

World War. The study is concerned less with why the Adana crisis broke out than with how it came about. Questions of why and how are logically inseparable, but they lead us in different directions. The question of *how* invites us to look closely at the sequences of interactions that produced certain outcomes. By contrast, the question *why* invites us to go in search of remote and categorical causes. The why approach brings a certain analytical clarity, but it also has a distorting effect, because it creates the illusion of a steadily building casual pressure; the factors pile up on top of each other pushing down on the events; local actors become mere executors of forces long established and beyond their control.

Some of the most interesting recent writing on the subject has argued that, far from being inevitable, this crisis was in fact "improbable"—at least until it actually happened. From this it would follow that the conflict was not the consequence of a long-term deterioration, but of short-term shocks to the local scene.[18]

This book utilizes many previously unavailable sources, but it is also a synthetic work bringing together arguments and findings from a number of scholars who have worked on the Second Ottoman Constitutional Period (1908–1918) and the Adana affair. It relies on scholarship by Tarık Zafer Tunaya and Abdurrahman Şeref Efendi. Studies by Nevzat Artuç, Hikmet Özdemir, Talha Çiçek, and others inform my own reconstruction of Cemal Paşa's biography and his deeds. Şevket Süreyya Aydemir's biography of War Minister Enver Paşa is invaluable for understanding the complex turbulence of the time. Hasan Babacan did extensive work of Grand Vizier Talat Paşa's biography. The names of other scholars whose work has informed my own can be found in the notes.

The work is composed of an introduction, conclusion, and eight intermediatory content chapters. After setting the stage by providing a brief background to the Adana affair of 1909, the introduction addresses the relevant historiography, that is to say the range of historical interpretations upon which studies from 1909 are based. This is important for two reasons. First, it is a concrete illustration of the dynamic quality in history. For those who practice history, history is dynamic rather than static, something continually subject to revision and reinterpretation. And the reason for this is not only because new documents come to light, but because new minds have been set to work. In fact, the documentation may remain relatively unchanged, what changes is the observer, the perspective. Second, the introduction also acknowledges a collection of debts which historians acquire from antecedents and peers.

Chapter 1 opens with an exposition of the geographical and economic importance of the province of Adana and its vicinity. This is followed by a broad demographical overview of the region. Chapter 2 takes up the position of the Armenians in Adana at the turn of the twentieth century, in which their linguistical and educational characteristics, their role in the economic and social life, and their schooling effort in the province are examined. Chapter 3 covers the major causes of the outbreak in 1908–1909. In this regard, it outlines the restoration of the Ottoman Constitution on July 24, 1908, elections and the inauguration of the new Parliament on December 17, 1908, identity of Ottomanism and the Committee of Union and Progress (CUP),[19] arming and boasting of Armenians of Adana after the reintroduction of the constitution, and the provincial governor's warnings and early dangers in October 1908–April 1909. Chapter 4 highlights the dimensions of the disorder in April 1909. Here an effort is made to discuss the beginning of the clashes in Adana, British vice-consul's role in the control of the fighting, end of the clashes in Adana on April 16, 1909, events in the vicinity of Adana and the province of Aleppo on April 16–24, 1909, provincial governor's dispatches to the Ministry of the Interior and the debate in the Chamber of Deputies in April–May 1909, resumption of the clashes on April 25, 1909, arrival of the foreign warships in Mersin, and government's effort to restore order. Chapter 5 explores the responsibility for the outrages. It traces the Armenians' unruly agitation; opinions of the Americans, Turks, and Armenians on the events; and Sultan Abdülhamid II's and Young Turks' alleged roles in the events. The focus in chapter 6 addresses the reestablishing of order in the district in May–August 1909. It looks, at length, at the measures taken by the government, report of the provincial governor on the events to the government of May 25, 1909, economic losses inflicted by the events, the debate in the Chamber of Deputies on May 1, 5, and 7, 1909, commission of inquiry to investigate the events, total casualties during the massacres, report of the courts martial of July 20, 1909, and the Young Turk-Dashnak cooperation. In chapter 7, a description and an analysis of Cemal Paşa's work of humanitarian relief and reconstruction when he was provincial governor in Adana is provided. Chapter 8 is devoted to a survey of post-1911 Adana and Cemal Paşa's governorship at Baghdad in 1911–1912. The author's conclusions and observations are given at the end of the study.

Time usually gives historians perspective on events. Historians and archivists will have to provide the concrete evidence to convince future generations of what happened. And because of the difficulties in obtaining evidence, a historian interested in broad questions and controversies about the Adana affair needs some of the techniques of the biographer. A historian who knows the subject well enough can manage to fill in at least some gaps in the documentary record by using their knowledge of the individuals involved in the decisions. A person may change their mind on an issue, but does not easily change their personality, methods, and values. They have to follow one individual over a long enough period of time to be able to isolate inconsistencies of personality and of method and use them to interpret or augment fragmentary evidence. In this way, a scholar can penetrate beyond the limitations of the historical record and still end up with a picture of the whole. So I am interested here in both Cemal Paşa and the Adana affair. But it is usually easier to see history through the lens of the individual, and there is no better vantage point overlooking the Adana affair than the life of Cemal Paşa.

The inquiry tries to offer new insights into Cemal Paşa and uncover new biographical and historical facts. Personalities in Ottoman history, even in the twentieth century, are crucial, often more so than issues. Leaders matter; biographies count. The essence of history is the human base. Individuals, not statistics or demographics, make events that form the past. Human agency shapes history fully as much as geography, climate, economics, and other impersonal forces.

History is largely made up of the biographies of the leaders. Contemporary documents are the stuff of which history, and therefore biography, is made, because, unlike memoirs, they have not been reinterpreted—consciously or unconsciously—after the event. The present study therefore contains brief biographical sketches of some Ottoman statesmen and officials who, by virtue of their positions, exercised influence on policy. Being a postmaster in the art of the biographical sketch, Ali Çankaya has a wealth of information to contribute to the historian and the genealogist. The specialists of the nineteenth- and twentieth-century Ottoman Empire will find the rich crumbs of evidence on many aspects of life of this period, personal and political, interspersed throughout the volumes of *Mülkiye Tarihi ve Mülkiyeliler*.[20]

The historian's job is important. Because the chronology is crucial to the historians' debates, I have taken care to lay out and to document even events that may not seem directly related to the Adana affair, particularly in chapters 2 and 3. No one would be as sensitive as the historian to the chronology.

The consistent misinformation of the Western world with regard to the Ottoman Empire has been of such longstanding as to take its place among the inherent traditions and almost ineradicable beliefs of whole nations. The few Westerners of importance who have tried to give faithful pictures of life in the Ottoman polity and realm have been outnumbered to the extent of being smothered. The age-old charge against the Turks is of course the Armenian accusations. A journalist not long after the First World War tabulated the reports of these massacres and showed that they totaled thirty-five million slain. As the whole Armenian population in the world at the time is known never to have exceeded three million, there is obviously a case of falsification somewhere. The Bryce reports have been proved to be without tangible evidence and to have been based entirely on hearsay.[21]

SOURCES

Contemporaneous documents, that is, the written record created at the time the events took place, are the most valuable sources. In the twentieth century, governments have generated vast quantities of documents, and modern methods of duplication have increased the chances that at least one of many copies survives. No record is probably more valuable and interesting to the student of history than a correspondence between people who were immediately connected with an important historical event and who discussed their problems freely in the assurance that their writings would never see the light of publicity. To this class undoubtedly belongs the government records. These records, however, are not the only surviving contemporaneous documents. Various civil society agencies also generated substantial records. One such example, the American Board of Commissioners for Foreign Missions (ABCFM)[22] (now the United Church Board for World Ministries) located in Boston has left us detailed correspondence and reports about its observations of events and its efforts to aid the natives. These contemporaneous records have been an essential source for historians attempting to reconstruct events. They possess an authenticity lacking in documents generated after the events they describe. Eyewitness accounts are an important third source for the study of past events. Obviously, the most valuable of these are diaries, notes, and letters composed at the time. The majority of eyewitness accounts are usually composed after the end of events. It is obvious that those written almost immediately after the events are more authentic, though not always accurate, than those composed many years later. Those composed immediately presented the undiluted (or sometimes diluted) memory of recent experience, whereas those produced much later have often only reflected popular views of the experience. Although such later accounts are often engrossing stories, they are the least reliable source for an accurate history of the events. Further, the few persons able to supply crucial information, because they had been in positions of influence or direct observers of crucial events, gave their accounts (whether correct or incorrect) mostly soon after the events.

There is no single archive which allows even the general outline of the subject to be seen as a whole. Our account has had instead to be pieced together from a diffuse variety of official and unofficial sources. Newly discovered or previously neglected sources of data are particularly used.

The study is based primarily on Ottoman government documents, British Foreign Office (FO) reports, French consular correspondence, United States foreign service records, ABCFM papers, memoirs and autobiographies of the protagonists of the period, the contemporary press, and the available secondary sources generated by writers on both sides of the conflict. The proceedings of the Ottoman Chamber of Deputies are utilized. American missionary documents and publications are extensively used. Benefit is made of a number of unpublished doctoral dissertations. Bound volumes and microfilm editions of journals are examined. Meticulous attention is paid to the historical detail, providing a reliable and lucid guide through the often tortous and tangled pathways of Ottoman society and politics in the first decade of the twentieth century.

The Ottoman archives, which came into being in the mid-nineteenth century, have always been agencies of the administration and have always been staffed with archivists who regarded themselves primarily as servants of the state. In time they recognized their responsibilities to the research scholar and thought of the papers in their custody as the treasure trove of the people, as something which should be used to bring back the past.

The BOA and the ATASE are in possession of a wealth of documentary information which appear to be unique in every historical sense. The materials in the BOA are of two types: (1) individual documents, including copies of reports and papers sent to the central government and decrees and orders sent by it to subordinate officials and subjects; and (2) registers of orders and decrees and of financial statements, budgets, cadastral surveys, and the like. These repositories, concerned with the planning, coordination, and administration of systems, methods, and procedures pertaining to service, preservation, reduction, transfer, and disposition of files and records, have been organized according to west European norms: collections have detailed inventories and are arranged by document number and date. The BOA stores the massive Ministry of the Interior files with their provincial reports broken down by year, region, and subject—a major source for political and economic trends. The Ottoman Ministry of Foreign Affairs records are organized by functional as well as some geographic divisions. Carbons of papers were sent upward through the bureaucracy or to other agencies according to their general importance. Reading the files provides insight into significant issues. Over the last three decades, a steady stream of formerly classified documents has been opened to public inspection. They are available to historians and other researchers responding to the continued public interest in the Ottoman past. Turkish sources have certainly not been used exhaustively for the purpose by the international scholarly community, but their great importance is universally recognized by now. It is impossible for Western researchers to study Ottoman and Turkish history without using Turkish sources and considering Turkish points of view when examining historical issues and problems. The days when a book on Ottoman history could be researched purely from British or American archives are over. The time has come for historians to catch up with new realities.[23]

It may legitimately be asked, however, whether in view of the present accessibility of Ottoman archives, there is really any place for the continuous use of European and American materials which may be biased, or uninformed, and generally suspect. The ambassadors and consuls who reported on the Ottoman Empire represented, after all, foreign interests. They often saw what they or their governments wanted to see. Their prejudices were sometimes reinforced by imperfect knowledge of Turkish or complete ignorance of it. They often employed dragomans from among the non-Muslim minorities and unreliable Levantines who had their own prejudices and personal interests. Ahmed Cevdet Paşa, a historian who combined scholarship with state service in the nineteenth century, accused such diplomats of living only in Frankish Pera and seeing Turkish İstanbul through a telescope.[24] The philologist and statesman Ahmed Vefik Paşa[25] cautioned Westerners that they should be aware of their shortcomings as observers: "To know this country you must do four things. First, you must learn the language; secondly, you must unlearn all your previous notions; thirdly, you must seek the truth, not facts in support of preformed conclusions; and lastly, you must stay among us for three or four years." Ahmed Vefik Paşa's standards are sound. Few Westerners met all of them. Westerners resident in the Ottoman Empire were also critical of their own ambassadors and consuls. In İzmir, for instance, British merchants asserted that "the training of the Consuls does not fit them to give diplomatic reports or political appreciations of Turkey. [. . .] Nobody here would think of asking Mr. Blunt's opinions on the subjects treated by him." Western sources, then, archival or not, must be used with prudence, and should not be used in isolation.[26]

Admitting all this, there are still good reasons for exploiting the Western archives. The basic one is inherent in the nature of historical research: the serious historian will survey all the evidence, including what may be biased and peripheral, before coming to conclusions. But there are other compelling reasons for using Western archives. So many of the great powers were concerned with affairs inside the Ottoman Empire that documents which appear to be purely diplomatic often concern internal Ottoman affairs. Foreign pressures sometimes determined the fall of ministries, or the issuance of edicts. The *Hatt-ı Hümayun* (Reform Edict) of 1856, for example, was a proclamation of domestic reform dictated largely by outside pressures. Much of this can be gathered from Turkish sources, but the full story requires consulting British, French, and Austrian archives. Some Westerners, further, did meet Ahmed Vefik Paşa's four conditions.[27]

Such men carried on the traditional triple task of the diplomat: vigilance, advice, and negotiation. All three aspects of the job produced information on the Ottoman Empire. Sometimes this concerned the vast and important minorities, who frequently had recourse to foreign embassies for support. Sometimes it was on political affairs in the capital, or in the provinces and the semi-independent subject states. Sometimes it was on economic conditions. More rarely, the diplomats inquired into the intellectual climate and social organization. Whatever the subject, they collected information and occasionally sought out statistics or attempted analyses which answer questions a modern historian might ask, but which to Turks of a century ago might have been unimportant and unrecorded. The diplomats reported faithfully conversations with leading personalities; the reports are often valuable in a period when among Turks the writing of diaries and memoirs was uncommon. The diplomats also were trained squirrels, acquiring and sending home local newspapers, clippings, documents, pamphlets, petitions, even books, some of which are of great use to the historian but remain unknown until they are encountered as enclosures to consular or diplomatic reports.[28]

Further advantages in the use of Western archival sources derive from the mechanics of Western reporting and filing practices. The ambassadors and consuls were trained to write immediately after the event, to date their dispatches accurately, and to number them in sequence. This is no mean advantage in straightening out exact dates of events in the Ottoman Empire. The diplomatic reports were usually concise, drained both of Ottoman verbiage and Western polemic. Further, the Western archives have been generally well preserved and well arranged. They are indexed; they are available. Usually they are easily read. Before the typewriter came into use in the 1880s, the embassy clerks wrote in a clear hand. In sum, then, Western archives do contain available and useful information which complements and serves as a check on Ottoman materials, and may in addition fill gaps in the Ottoman archives. These Western materials need to be used with caution and in combination with other sources, but they should not be disregarded.[29]

Extensive archives sources exist in the British National Archives (TNA) at Kew, London. Important FO reports and position papers are printed and circulated as "confidential prints," but selection is limited. Documents in the TNA are subject to Crown copyright. Quotations from them are made pursuant to the blanket waiver granted in Her Majesty's Stationery Office Guidance Note 3. The FO kept a close watch on the Adana affair. Those who examine the FO's raw files for those years will find little of importance omitted. The files of the TNA have been picked over by historians again and again, and yet there always seem to be new materials to be found. Each January 1 there is the rich crop of new TNA releases to be drawn upon. The FO series contain the correspondence arranged by date of receipt, which are entered on each document. FO 195 is the general correspondence that covers the years 1808 to 1962 comprising 2,722 volumes. FO 197 is the register of correspondence from 1823 to 1921 between the FO and the embassy and consulates in the Ottoman Empire with seventy-four volumes. FO 198 includes miscellaneous papers related to the Ottoman Empire and Turkey from 1775 to 1941 with 107 volumes. Accompanying these are minutes by various FO officials and drafts of replies, often in several forms, including the final draft of the outgoing dispatch. Those documents cited in this book are referred to by the designation used at the TNA, including the class and file number—which locates the file in which the original is to be found—and in the case of FO documents the archive designation originally applied to the item in the FO.

But some of the British records of the Armenian question are subjected to extended closure. The Public Records Act of 1958, and the Amending Act of 1967, specifies that records whose disclosure should involve a breach of good faith on the part of the government, or of persons who obtained the information in them, should not be disclosed. They were mainly those concerning information about individuals whose disclosure would cause distress or embarrassment to living persons or their immediate descendants, and those certain exceptionally sensitive papers which affect the security of the state. In 1970, the categories of records for which applications for closure for longer than thirty years were set out. They were similar to the categorization just described. They were (1) exceptionally sensitive papers, the disclosure of which would be contrary to the public interest whether on security or other grounds; (2) documents containing information supplied in confidence, the disclosure of which might constitute a breach of good faith; and (3) documents containing information about individuals, the disclosure of which would cause distress or embarrassment to living persons or immediate descendants. The Public Records Act also permit records (more than thirty years old) to be retained, with the Lord Chancellor's approval, for administrative or other special reasons. Under Section 3(4) of the 1958 Act, "blanket" approvals have been given for the retention of records concerned with intelligence and security.[30] These include many files on Ottoman Armenians in twentieth century. They are simply unavailable. It will be seemingly some time before these sensitive materials are opened to research. Should these documents ever see the light of day, then obviously the work of the British government at least in the pre-1914 period might have to be reevaluated.[31]

The French consular correspondence, deposited in the Ministry of Foreign Affairs archives in the northern Parisian suburb of Courneuve, deals mainly with matters of every day detail in the Adana affair. It is a potentially rich vein for study. The French records are sparser, in part because the inner organization of the Quai d'Orsay was less elaborate and systematic. They are mostly argumentative and prescriptive rather than being analytical and descriptive.

By a law from December 1980, the French government brought into force a thirty-year archival principle. That principle assured public access to state documents that are older than thirty years. In short, 2018 ought to bring the opening of archival material pertaining to 1988. However, certain significant exceptions were written into the law. Individual medical records remain closed 150 years from the birth of the subject, and personnel dossiers for 120 years. Certain court documents may be closed for one hundred years, as may census and survey findings of a family or individual character. Documents deemed sensitive to state security or national defense may be closed for sixty years, and of course exceptional restrictions may be imposed on private papers by their donors. These arrangements, on the whole, provide reasonably well for the student of the early twentieth-century history. It is true that some private papers remained closed or are subject to limited access. Nevertheless, what is not closed by law is theoretically open—theoretically, because in practice another kind of law may still intrude. This is the "in progress" law, one articulated in the familiar expression *en train de classement*, which is to say the documents are not closed to research, only to researchers. In fact, they are being organized, packaged, and inventoried for more efficient future use.[32]

Some valuable material for this work came from the Diplomatic Post Records in the United States National Archives and Records Administration (USNA), containing the incoming and outgoing communications of the diplomatic and consular offices in the Ottoman Empire. Both before the First World War and for a lengthy period after its outbreak, a neutral United States maintained significant diplomatic and consular establishments in the Ottoman realm and was therefore afforded a close and ubiquitous view of events. American diplomats in the sultan's land at the period were often well informed—even if the government in Washington did little with their reports except file them. The United States records, produced by relatively disinterested observers, provided useful, and possibly more sober, outside material at a time when the diplomats of the other major powers had become participants in the game. Many European officials entrusted Americans with information difficult or impossible to find elsewhere, and the Central Files of the Department of State in the USNA are as a result important for Ottoman-Armenian relations. Material from the USNA is cited with the appropriate record group number, entry number where applicable, folder name, and document name.[33]

There are no restrictions on the use of the Department of State records, although some material remains classified and has been withdrawn from files. The declassification teams have in fact screened the records, declassifying some of them (probably most), and simply removing from the files those that are not to be declassified. The researcher has no sure way of identifying or knowing what has been screened out during the declassification review. They can, of course, see the "out-cards" sticking in the files that are open for viewing. But the out-cards contain only brief notations, typically the file number and date of the removed document, the date on which it was removed, and the initials of the person who removed it.

The United States Department of State has been publishing selections of diplomatic correspondence under various titles from as far back as 1861; as the twentieth century expanded the role of the United States, the content of that which became Foreign Affairs of the United States series grew in overall significance and in bulk. This system is useful for the purposes of research but is not entirely satisfactory. Documents are selected by officials who are not accountable and readers never know what documents have been omitted. It is always possible to criticize the selection of documents illustrating policy and interest. Suffice it to say, for the moment, that serious students will always examine documents of this sort with caution, placing them in historical perspective. These documents should give a good introduction both to archival materials and to a vast literature which calls for wide reading and study.

In 1909 while the Americans had access to British documents, the British were reading the many American ones. At that date the American ambassador in İstanbul regularly saw the reports of the British vice-consul in Mersin. Materials at the USNA must be supplemented by important collections elsewhere.

The Western embassies and consulates in the Ottoman Empire operated according to the Capitulation agreements[34] and vigorously defended their protégés. The Capitulations were a complicated system of bilateral arrangements governing the relations of the Sublime Porte[35] with the outside world. They restricted Ottoman trading rights, its right to impose customs and harbor dues, and its right to export Ottoman goods. They gave to foreign nationals a wide range of extraterritorial privileges, including immunity from taxation and rights of consular jurisdiction.

Ambassadors, as supreme diplomatic agents of their states and with direct access to the Sublime Porte, exerted sufficient influence and pressure to ensure the implementation of the capitulations in the environs of İstanbul. Outside the Ottoman capital, consular offices became inextricably bound to the exercise and retention of these prerogatives. In addition to supporting their own country's official policy toward the Sublime Porte and communicating with their embassy, consuls promoted trade, interceded with Ottoman officials on behalf of fellow nationals, provided notary services, and adjudicated civil and criminal suits among their own countrymen. Consuls, in short, administered the duties and rights of extraterritoriality, serving as guardians, governors, and judges of their consular districts.[36]

The most important right gained in the Capitulations agreements was the privilege of each consul to serve as judge and jury for the subjects of his own sovereign, residing on Ottoman soil. Without spelling out the details of the consul's extraterritorial rights, a consul gained supreme power over the property, person, and even the life of his fellow nationals living within the territorial boundaries of his jurisdiction. Indeed, they attained a very influential position, thereby compelling the authorities to treat them with respect. The position of a Western consul in the Ottoman Empire, owing to the extraterritorial privileges and right to conduct trials, gave the post a special authority. As late Edward Mead Earle of Columbia University rightly remarks, "the Western consuls were exalted officials usurping the place of the Ottoman authorities, who often found themselves quite helpless under the most trying and exasperating circumstances."[37] Extraterritoral judiciature most clearly threatened to intrude into the every day government of the Ottoman Empire.[38]

The capitulations were an abuse of Ottoman sovereignty by nature, but they became worse in the nineteenth century as non-Muslim Ottomans became citizens of foreign nations and obtained protection under the Capitulations. Without the inconvenience of leaving the Empire, Ottomans became citizens of foreign governments by obtaining a document called *berat* (official warrant of approval). Armenian merchants often adopted foreign citizenship to obtain Western consular protection in their business transactions and held foreign passports instead of Ottoman ones. The attending privileges were sufficiently favorable to entice many Ottoman subjects to exercise this option. Muslims by law and choice did not change their religion or nationality. Only non-Muslims, therefore, enjoyed the benefits of the *berats* in trade and industry, which they already dominated. The protracted intercourse of these indigenous "foreigners" with the West not only brought them prosperity, but knowledge and skills in languages for them and their offspring, which widened an existing breach between them and Ottoman Muslims. It was little wonder that many Muslims not only resented the *berat* holders' unwarranted success but often regarded them as fifth column elements within the Empire.[39]

Just as İstanbul was the center for ambassadors to the Empire as a whole, Mersin became the center of activity for the consuls who served their countries' interests in south central Asia Minor, and who set their minds to the strengthening of their countries' diplomatic and commercial footholds in the area as part of the European powers' efforts to realize their ambitions in the Middle East.[40]

The contacts of the foreign consulates in Mersin with the Ottoman authorities were conducted at various levels—from local ones to the highest provincial instances and in İstanbul. The main contact of the consuls in Mersin was with the *mutasarrıf* (subdistrict governor). Most of the contacts were through correspondence, some of it in French, but mainly in Turkish. The consuls took an interest in all aspects of life in the region. The reports the consuls filed with the ambassador kept him informed about the events in their localities and especially the political, economic, social, and religious situations among the various elements of the population. They encouraged trade with their countries, strove for the improvement of the services they controlled (such as banking, mail, and sea transport), and showed exceptional interest in the daily life of the inhabitants. Consequently, the consular archives are first-class historical source for events and developments in the province of Adana, as elsewhere.[41]

Consular reports were by state officials who were responsible to their superiors for providing accurate information. Because they had official responsibilities in the cities, they were better placed than travelers in gaining access to the required data for their reports. Most of the time, there was mutual understanding and common interest between local Ottoman government officials and the foreign consuls. In addition to this, they constituted a part of the higher echelon of the cities and were usually in close contact with government officials. At the same time, they also had other, more remote sources for their information. They had informants in the countryside and in different towns in order to learn about the state of affairs in the region. Their reports were not written for the public and neither published nor publicized. Therefore there was no need for falsified or arbitrary estimates and criteria added for the purpose of attracting or convincing the general reader.[42]

Nothing struck the traveler in the Ottoman Empire more forcibly than the immense influence wielded in the provinces by strong and tactful foreign consuls, among whom, it is fair to say, British consuls were usually second to none. The presence of an efficient consul with a turn for diplomacy at the seats of local governments led to marked improvement in social conditions, such as the administration of justice, the prosecution of public works, security, and so forth. When a consul was backed by their ambassador, the consul was great for good in the district, could do much to reduce abuses, and could do something material to forward the interests of home commerce.[43]

Some of the reports written by the British consuls stationed in various towns and cities in the Ottoman Empire in the second half of the nineteenth century offer excellent information on the socioeconomic conditions in the country. Not all reports are of equal quality. Kemal Karpat, formerly professor of history at the University of Wisconsin, has found, after reading thousands of such reports, that the military men and the regular foreign service personnel provide the most factual, relatively objective, and comprehensive accounts, despite their tendency to look down upon all things not British. The least reliable reports, with notable exceptions, were written by agents recruited from among the local citizens.[44]

It is also worth pointing out that British documents must be read as carefully and critically as memoirs, newspapers, or secondary sources. British consuls communicated messages in a language sometimes coded with multiple layers of meaning.

Reports from the embassies and consulates of Western countries should be of more value had their authors been less dependent upon the translation/interpretation services of their local staffs, usually recruited from minority communities, hence too often individuals of compromised loyalties.

The correspondence between those in the field and their central headquarters at the ABCFM form a crucial archival basis for the historical construction of events in Adana between 1909 and 1911 and their contexts. The information contained in them is rich but widely scattered because most of the volumes are arranged chronologically and not by subject. The letters of American missionaries to Boston reflect the general atmosphere of the province of Adana with a wealth of detail which one would seek in vain in a purely official correspondence. These volumes were employed to provide some of the background information required for this study which could not be found elsewhere.

That the person of Cemal Paşa should be the subject of much ABCFM correspondence is not surprising. Not only was Cemal Paşa the leading figure in the province of Adana in 1909 to 1911, but he was also colorful in his own right. Both of these factors gave him sufficient reputation to justify considerable comment. What is surprising, however, is the uniformity of opinion that this correspondence produced. American missionaries on the whole found Cemal Paşa impressive, intelligent, and capable. Moreover, regardless of any bluster to the contrary, they also regarded him, much as William Nesbitt Chambers did, as inherently enlightened and progressive. Thus, for instance, Chambers observed in 1909 that Cemal Paşa was a good and upright administrator. He did not change this opinion in future years. Such also was the view of Thomas Davidson Christie, who had much to say that had a deep interest concerning the history of that period. Both of them were long resident in the province of Adana and much respected by every one who knew them.

The American mission schools in the Ottoman Empire up to 1908 worked almost entirely among the non-Muslims and thus were naturally better acquainted and sympathesized more with their problems and difficulties than with similar ones which the Muslims themselves might have had. This rather one-sided acquaintance was inevitably reflected in their accounts of conditions obtained in their field of work, accounts read in turn by their thousands of supporters in America. These reports, however, confined themselves strictly to events as they happened, not attempting to argue any theory of causes or prevention. Above all every field worker urged education for all classes and people—which became possible after 1908—as the only way to advance for the Empire. Teaching and "teachableness" were the basis of their work and of their hope.[45]

The documents of the ABCFM, of course, see Western encroachments and the processes of modernization and revolutionary upheaval through American eyes. They were often written in disturbing circumstances of conflict and rivalry, and they were inevitably one-sided in their critical comments on the activities of the Ottoman government and its organs. They were written by men thoroughly confident of their own moral and cultural superiority, and the missionaries were often frank and outspoken in their commentaries. At the same time, most of the men on the spot were remarkable for their fascination with what they saw, for their power of detailed observation, and for a capacity to understand through long years of experience Ottoman and other viewpoints fundamentally different from their own. The documents of the ABCFM, indeed, are valuable not only for the information they record about the waning years of the Ottoman Empire, but also for the unconsciously expressed values and assumptions of those agents that transmitted it. Obviously one must read them critically and in light of whatever other evidence may be available.

It is unlikely that these documents will sharply reverse cardinal historical judgments. They supply, however, a myriad of valuable details and insights.

During the last few decades, Turkish historians have engaged in a historiographical reassessment of the activities of the American missionaries in the Ottoman Empire. Their published works have more recently been less partisan in their approach to the missionary enterprise than were earlier works.[46]

Records of the ABCFM, including personal papers and photographs of individuals and organizations associated with it, is presently housed at the Houghton Library of Harvard University in Cambridge, Massachusetts, and formerly in the Divinity School library there. Some of these records are not well preserved and their quality varies tremendously. Many documents are faded and difficult to read without extraordinary effort. The text of some handwritten carbon copies is literally in the process of disappearing.

It should be noted that as of April 2012, the American Research Institute in Turkey became custodian of the library and archives of the Amerikan Bord Heyeti, historical descendent of ABCFM's administrative agency in Turkey. The library resources are located at the American Research Institute in Turkey's İstanbul Center in Arnavutköy and may be consulted by scholars. The archives are stored offsite and closed to researchers. Much of the materials are in boxes, and the finding aids are rather general.[47]

Armenian archives are not yet open for general inspection. Repositories of the Dashnak Party and the first Armenian Republic in Watertown, Massachusetts, together with those of the Catholicosate in Echmiadzin and the Armenian Patriarchate in Jerusalem,[48] are not available for general research.[49] They must be more extensively consulted than any of the European archives. Turkey opened the Ottoman archives for academic research many years ago. Armenian archives that remained closed, including those in the United States, should be available for examination by scholars. Openness would foster constructive change by creating an impartial forum to establish a more comprehensive narrative of the Adana events of 1909. Historians can benefit greatly from the release and systematic analysis of Armenian records, and the result can be a far greater understanding about the role of Armenian activities in the origins, outbreak, and outcome of the Adana episode and its aftermath. As a consequence, historians will be in a position to evaluate the period from new perspectives that have been overlooked or deliberately obfuscated.

The present inaccessibility of these files is, of course, a serious obstacle to scholarship which one can only hope will soon be removed.[50] American military historian Edward Erickson, therefore, asks the pertinent question: Why is it that the Turkish archives are open to scholars today and those of Armenia, the Armenian Revolutionary Federation in Watertown, Massachusetts, and the Armenian Patriarchate in Jerusalem closed?[51]

One of the interesting trends in Armenian-related publications is the appearance of a large number of "memoirs" authored by Armenians born in the Ottoman Empire who subsequently resettled in other parts of the world. While uneven in quality and value (some of the authors were infants at the time of their departure from the country), collectively such works provide the scholar with a glimpse into the conditions of the period. One point of observation. Children may remember evils done to their families, but they are unlikely to remember evils done by their families. Indeed, it is unlikely that they would have even been told. Can one imagine a report of someone who was ten years old in 1909 in which the survivor states, "My father went out and killed a number of the enemy and their families, then the enemy came and killed them and my mother?" Of course not. What a child of 1909 would remember was the sadness and terror in his or her own life. This would be true whether the memoirist was Armenian, Turkish, or from any other people who have suffered. In fact, comparable memoirs of Turks who clashed with Armenians in Adana in 1909 tell of Armenians killing Turks, not of Turks killing Armenians. The inherent difficulty in memoirs such as these, some written in 1909 and 1910, some written in the 1970s, is that they only tell one side of a complicated story. Armenian suffering is described in detail. Turkish suffering goes unmentioned.[52]

One must, nevertheless, become acquainted with literature presenting the Armenian viewpoint and allegations. It not only narrates personal suffering and large-scale massacres but, paradoxically, also frequently mentions organizations and operations of revolutionary guerrillas—the few damaging the image and status of the many Armenians—that caused the lawful government to initiate necessary measures. There are also references to widespread possession of arms and some mobilization of paramilitary methods. Nevertheless, it is standard practice for many Armenians today to cite inflated numbers of massacre victims, and importune the present government of Turkey to confess implication in the Ottoman action of more than four generations ago, deny that there were either Armenian criminal behavior or subversive operations necessitating anything like the measures to which the government resorted.

People are central to any story. Some are tough and resilient in crises; others fade into the background. Some people make wise decisions, but some act on mistaken assumptions.

It is gratifying that Cemal Paşa, while a refugee in Germany, set down enough of his experiences to provide notion of the Adana events of 1909 as it was viewed in high Ottoman circles. It is not very common to have firsthand information about the activities of individual Ottoman officials derived from their own writings. In this case, however, we are fortunate to have in our possession published memoirs written by the governor who was himself the chief representative of the Sublime Porte in the province of Adana for a period of almost two years. There are numerous documents, chiefly from the author's private and official correspondence. From his writing it is possible to learn much, not only about the main problems which Ottoman authorities encountered in Adana, and the way they handled them, but also about the workings of the Ottoman administration at the time. The work, being a synthesis of biography and history, is interesting and revealing throughout. The publication of an English translation of such a book is thus a great contribution to scholars studying the history of the Ottoman Empire in those turbulent years. This is especially so because Cemal Paşa proved to be a very keen observer and precise narrator. He observes, records, and comments on the unfolding, breath-taking developments as well as the behavior, reactions, and efforts of various individuals to affect and influence events in İstanbul, Adana, Berlin, Moscow, Kabul, and elsewhere. With unfailing care, precision, and, at times, passion, he helps us relive the past events. His memoirs have been widely praised and continue to be read and cited by historians.[53]

Personal records, however, are scarce in Cemal Paşa's case. Like many of his Ottoman contemporaries, he did not keep a personal diary and only fragments of his private correspondence have survived the First World War. His collection of letters does not cover the period of his governorate in Adana.

It must be noted that keeping a diary was an unusual event in Ottoman Turkey where the genre did not exist—Cavid Bey's *Meşrutiyet'in Ruznamesi*[54] being a major exception. Cavid Bey, a minister of finance and a leading member of the CUP, recorded from day to day what he saw and thought at the time of writing, and that record has not been altered. The record stands here as originally written. His diary faithfully records Turkey in the years of transition from the Second Constitutional Period to the Republic. It contains a storehouse of informative material. Vivid pictures of current events, political upheavals, wars, rumors of wars, diplomatic discretions and indiscretions, Machiavellian intrigues, and plots and counterplots unfold before the eyes of the reader. Perhaps the most useful revelations in Cavid Bey's diaries are the intimate and colorful behind-the-scene portraits he paints of the CUP: its main players, their maneuvering, and his impressions of many of them. Cavid Bey's diaries are important as a source for historians, and until recently have been accessed in their archival locations by only a handful of scholars. With the publication of *Meşrutiyet'in Ruznamesi*, many readers can add new depth and detail to their understanding of the inner workings of the unappreciated CUP.

The debates made in meetings of the Ottoman parliament between 1908 and 1922 form one of the principal sources for the understanding of the twentieth-century history of the Ottoman realm and polity. The records of the parliament in this period are of central importance for a comprehension of the ideas and practices of government and politics, while its legislation is a vital source for contemporary perceptions and practices in a wide range of social activities. These have proved invaluable to such specialists as have used them. But they contain much rich ore which could be mined usefully and interestingly by many more persons, in many more ways, to the betterment of scholarship.

Much information is also available in the pages of Ottoman and Western newspapers and periodicals that flourished during this period. Contemporary newspaper articles are valuable source. Even when factually wrong, they reflect the perception of events at the time and often provide the only reliable guide to their chronology, without which any interpretation of history is impossible.

Tanin, meaning the Echo, was the leading newspaper in the Ottoman Empire at the period which gained greatly in prestige and influence among the public, in the press, in parliament, and in government. In it appeared the most distinguished of journalists, among whom must be mentioned Hüseyin Cahid (Yalçın),[55] who was the master of a clear, concise style. He was deputy for İstanbul after the 1908 revolution and the editor of *Tanin*.[56] *İkdam* was one of the oldest and most widely circulated Turkish dailies of İstanbul. It served as the mirror of Ottoman opinion. Ahmed Cevdet (Oran), a journalist with a special interest in foreign affairs, was the proprietor of *İkdam*. His clear style and meticulous documentation (of the result of confidential sources of information) earned for his daily an important audience both at home and abroad.[57] Access to this trove of information came primarily from the National Library in Ankara and Beyazıt State, Atatürk, and Hakkı Tarık Us libraries in İstanbul. They are among the major depositories in Turkey that contain newspaper and review collections of varying size and importance.

The publications that cannot be found in one can generally be found in the other. The National Library is unparalleled, both for the depth of its collection and for the helpfulness of its staff.

Extensive use of newspaper sources are made and thus an overview of press reaction to, and discussion of, the Adana affair is presented. All journalists did not react to these events in the same way, and overall public reactions sometimes varied as well. Although most newspapers focused on the "Armenian problem" and urged the government to fix it, some journalists expressed sympathy for the Armenians and urged the government to recognize their humanity and their rights. Some were suspicious of Armenians and believed that all of their actions were full of menace, while some sought to balance their coverage and present both sides of the conflict as much as possible. By using both Ottoman and Western newspapers, the study tries to get as close to the events as possible. These news and comments shaped the public perception of the events and the people involved in them.

One final observation. There is no such thing as a perfectly informative and unbiased historical document. The work of the historian is to interpret the evidence.

METHODOLOGY

History can never be truthfully presented if the presentation is purely emotional. It can never be truthfully or usefully presented unless profound, patient, laborious, painstaking research has preceded the presentation. The vision of the true historian must be both wide and lofty. But it must be sane, clear, and based on full knowledge of the facts and of their inter-relations. Historical phenomena are always complex and full of nuances and subtleties. However, there are also proven facts and ascertainable verities. How can one take seriously opinions or interpretations of someone who does not have the facts straight? In scholarly works on the Ottoman Empire, contemporary sources can be used effectively if one knows the relevant historical facts and is able to separate facts from allegations, propaganda, and outright falsehoods. Political analyses, interpretations, and opinions have to be based on facts and not on misinformation.

No historian, however, can justify his or her work solely on the basis of providing the "essential facts." Writing history is not separable from interpreting it. Even the most positivist and meticulously factual approach to history cannot avoid interpretation, if only in the selection of facts deemed worthy of presenting.[58] In this book, I tried to present the interpretation that I believe is best suited to help us understand the Adana affair.

All interpretations are bound to generate some controversy as they provide a particular perspective that not everyone may share. That perspective is determined by the historian's values, particularly political values, which are usually, but not always, the values of the society or subgroup he or she lives in or identifies with. If the disagreement is about basic facts, it can usually be readily resolved. But more often the disagreements between historians involve the meaning and importance of those facts. The same facts may be evaluated quite differently by different historians. That is why there are still many historical issues on which serious historians disagree, even though the basic facts are known and accepted on all sides and the contending historians are genuinely committed to sound scholarly practices and the objective evaluation of the evidence. This is particularly true for questions of historical responsibility, all the more so if the events in question, large-scale killings, are universally condemned.[59]

A different method of approaching historical events, and more satisfactory, when possible, is to give a detailed and accurate description of events. The devil is in the details. Causes are thus often revealed, and how and why things happened explained. But in order to do this with any chance of success, it is essential to consult original documents from which reliable information can alone be obtained. In this respect we are in a particularly favorable position.

This book is an attempt to interpret events and policy from a wide-angle perspective and support those views by telescoping in on key events, decision makers, and their motivations. To accomplish this, the initial research effort focused on unpublished source materials. From the unpublished materials the research effort progressed to published collections, memoirs, and first-person accounts, and then secondary source materials. For example, rather than examining *Meclisi Mebusan Zabıt Ceridesi* (Proceedings of the Chamber of Deputies) first and then working back into the archives, this effort took the opposite approach by examining archival materials first followed by a later examination of *Meclisi Mebusan Zabıt Ceridesi*. The reader will find citations from the BOA that are in *Meclisi Mebusan Zabıt Ceridesi*, but those documents were first located at the BOA. Where the document was found first in *Meclisi Mebusan Zabıt Ceridesi*, then the citation is *Meclisi Mebusan Zabıt Ceridesi*. Why do it this way? By going directly to the raw materials, the historical significance uninfluenced by a previous judgment is determined. It can become possible to compare a broader segment of documents to ascertain what actually happened and why.

The book is organized according to a largely chronological structure. When available, the author has utilized original documents and correspondence, although if published versions of the same material are available they are sometimes cited to facilitate verification or further study. When several versions of an event are known, the present work stresses the earliest one, if possible an account contemporary with the event described, for the later versions are more likely to have been colored, intentionally or not, by subsequent developments, or to protect the subject or the writer.

I have sought to be helpful to professional scholars through the references and by treating selected controversial or little-known episodes as fully as possible. Hence the notes and index are intended to be elaborate. There are quotations from primary sources and notes to point the way for the future researchers. Quotations from contemporary sources are presented with original spelling, punctuation and grammar unchanged, though elisions are expanded and presented in parentheses. The notes provide a closer identification of relevant documents. In them a sufficient indication of the sources on which any given passage is based is given. At first mention in the notes, each work is provided with a full bibliographic description, while further mentions are by author-title citations. The purpose of the note references is not only to show the origins of quotations or to provide evidence for the author's conclusions, but also to aid the reader who wishes to pursue further the lines of thought developed here. Notes are also used for biographical purposes.

The book relies to an extent on secondary sources. I have tried to list in the bibliography all those that have been useful. Even though secondary books may be reliable, there is still a matter of probing, interpreting, and sometimes expanding the information that they report.

The bibliography appended to this volume does not reflect all relevant source materials or the full state of the research, and should not be seen as a comprehensive listing of all works on the subject. It records mostly those works to which references has been made in the notes, and those which I have found particularly useful in my studies of the period. Preference is given to sources in English, and after that those in Turkish and French. The bibliography enables the interested reader to "translate" the short citation into the full bibliographic record without searching for the first mention. Where non-English words are used, they are italicized unless in common usage and English translations are given immediately afterwards.

Because many of the accounts and other documents quoted in this book were not written for publication, words and punctuation necessary to make them comprehensible and easy to read have often been omitted by their authors. Alternatively grammar is faulty. I have taken the liberty of correcting punctuation wherever this has occurred, but when I have added a word to help the sense I have placed it in square brackets, and when I have omitted a word I have marked the omission by inserting three dots.

Several documents are too long to have been reproduced in full. Where I have omitted material from the original document, I have placed ellipses within brackets [...]. Ellipses without brackets are from the original document itself. In quotations outside actual documents, my occasional omissions of text are without brackets and original parenthetical comments appear without parentheses.

Translations generally are by the author unless otherwise noted or unless it is from an old publication which did not list the name of the translator.

My hope has been to present a total picture of the Adana affair on the basis of extensive primary and secondary sources that have not been synthesized previously. The picture that emerges is different from those offered by Armenian historians. I am aware that there are still many questions that are begging historians' further research. It is my wish that this book will help stimulate further discussion on various aspects of the subject under review here.

NOTES

1. The term Asia Minor is applied to the territory of present-day Asiatic Turkey, and is used synonymously with Anatolia.

2. The name Anatolia is traced from the Greek verb *anatillo*, to rise (i.e., rising of the sun equals east). It has actuated every Western power with ambitions to extend its commerce and sphere of influence, right down to the present day.

3. See M. E. Yapp's review of Salahi Sonyel's *The Great War and the Tragedy of Anatolia: Turks and Armenians in the Maelstrom of Major Powers*, Middle Eastern Studies, Vol. 37, No. 1 (January 2001), p. 238.

4. A precise name for the conflict that raged in the province of Adana in April 1909 has yet to be agreed upon. While recognizing that many factors were involved in the conflict, insofar as this study traces Turkish-Armenian relations from 1909 to 1911, it has adopted the terms "events" and "affair."

5. The spelling of Turkish names may present some difficulties to the English-language reader. Nevertheless, modern Turkish orthography (i.e., post-1928) rather than contemporary English spelling is used throughout the text except quoting from non-Turkish sources. Hence "Cemal Paşa" rather than "Jemal or Djemal Pasha" and "Hacin" for "Hadjin." Paşa, Bey, and Efendi are Ottoman civilian/military titles that are generally treated as part of a name. Neither word is a surname.

6. Yücel Güçlü, *Historical Archives and the Historians' Commission to Investigate the Armenian Events of 1915* (Lanham, MD: University Press of America, 2015), pp. 46–50; idem, "Review of Nesim Ovadya İzrail's *24 Nisan 1915 İstanbul, Çankırı, Ayaş, Ankara* (24 April 1915 İstanbul, Çankırı, Ayaş, Ankara)," *Belleten*, Vol. 79, No. 1 (April 2015), pp. 395–97; Virginia Aksan, "Review of Carl Brown's, ed., *Imperial Legacy: The Ottoman Imprint on the Balkans and the Middle East*," *The International History Review*, Vol. 23, No. 4 (November 1996), p. 894.

7. Duckett Ferriman, *The Young Turks and the Truth about the Holocaust at Adana in Asia Minor, during April, 1909* (London: n.p., 1913; republished Yerevan: The Armenian Genocide Museum-Institute, 2009).

8. Hrachik Simonyan, trans. Melissa Brown and Alexander Arzumanian, *The Destruction of Armenians in Cilicia, April 1909* (London: Gomidas Institute, 2012).

9. Ali Birinci, "Hatırat Türünden Kaynakların Tarihi Araştırmalardaki Yeri ve Değeri" (The Place and Value of Sources Like Memoirs in Historical Research), *Atatürk Araştırma Merkezi Dergisi*, Vol. 14, No. 40 (March 1998), pp. 611–20; Murat Hanilçe, "İkinci Meşrutiyet Dönemine Dair Hatırat Bibliyografyası Denemesi" (Essay on the Memoir Bibliography Relating to the Second Constitutional Period), *Bilig*, No. 47 (Fall 2008), pp. 147–66.

10. See, for instance, *Massacres d'Adana et nos missionaires, récit de témoins* (Lyon: Imprimerie Vve M. Paquet, 1909); *The Adana Massacres and the Catholic Missionaries: Account of Eye-Witnesses* (New York: Society for the Propagation of the Faith, 1910); Alexandre Adossidès, *Arméniens et Jeunes-Turcs: les Massacres de Cilicie* (Paris: P.V. Stock, 1910); Georges Brézol, *Les Turcs ont passé là... Recueil de documents, dossiers, rapports, requêtes, protestations, suppliques et enquêtes, établissant la vérité sur les massacres d'Adana en 1909* (Paris: [en vente chez l'auteur], 1911; republished Yerevan: The Armenian Genocide Museum-Institute, 2010). Georges Brézol was actually an Armenian man of letters born Boghos Kupelian.

11. Hagop Terzian, trans. Ara Stepan Melkonian and ed. Ara Sarafian, *Cilicia 1909: The Massacre of Armenians* (London: Gomidas Institute, 2009).

12. *The Adana Massacres and the Catholic Missionaries.*

13. *Aspirations et Agissements Révolutionnaires des Comités Arméniens Avant et Aprés la Proclamation de la Constitution Ottomane* (İstanbul: Matbaai Orhaniye, 1917).

14. Kemal Çiçek, ed., *1909 Adana Olayları:Makaleler* (Adana Events of 1909: Articles) (Ankara: Türk Tarih Kurumu Basımevi, 2011).

15. Recep Karacakaya et al., eds., *Osmanlı Belgelerinde 1909 Adana Olayları* (Adana Events of 1909 in Ottoman Documents), two volumes (Ankara: Başbakanlık Basımevi, 2010).

16. Yusuf Sarınay and Recep Karacakaya, *1909 Adana Ermeni Olayları* (Armenian Events of Adana in 1909) (İstanbul: İdeal Kültür Yayıncılık, 2012).

17. Tetsuya Sahara, *What Happened in Adana in April 1909?* (İstanbul: The İsis Press, 2013).

18. Ibid.

19. The subject of the CUP will be treated in chapter 3.

20. See Ali Çankaya, *Mülkiye Tarihi ve Mülkiyeliler* (History of the College of Administrative Sciences and Its Alumni), eight volumes (Ankara: Mars Matbaası, 1968–1969). An assessment of the work is in Ali Galip Baltaoğlu, *Atatürk Dönemi Valileri (29 Ekim 1923–10 Kasım 1938)* (Provincial Governors in the Atatürk Period [29 October 1923–10 November 1938]) (Ankara: Ocak Yayınları, 1998), pp. 47–48.

21. *The Treatment of Armenians in the Ottoman Empire 1915–1916: Documents Presented to Viscount Grey of Fallodon, Secretary of State for Foreign Affairs*, Parliamentary Papers Miscellaneous No. 31 (London: Joseph Causton, 1916; reprinted, Astoria, New York: J.C. and A.L. Fawcett, 1990).

22. ABCFM was organized by the General Association of Congregational Churches of Massachusetts in 1810 for the purpose of devising ways and means,

and adopting and prosecuting measures, for prompting the spread of the gospel in "Heathen lands." It was the largest American missionary organization operating in the Ottoman Empire, with 145 missionaries, eight hundred native workers, 114 churches, thirteen thousand converts, sixty thousand students, 132 higher-grade schools, and 1,100 lower-grade schools in 1900. See Edwin Munsell Bliss, Henry Otis Dwight, Allen Tupper, eds., *The Encyclopedia of Missions* (Detroit, MI: Gale Research Company, 1975), pp. 29–31. On ABCFM consult (in order of publication) also Rufus Anderson, *History of the Missions of the American Board of Commissioners for Foreign Missions to the Oriental Churches*, two volumes (Boston, MA: Congregational Publishing Society, 1872); William Strong, *The Story of the American Board: An Account of the First One Hundred Years of the American Board of Commissioners for Foreign Missions* (New York: Pilgrim Press, 1910); Julius Richter, *A History of Protestant Missions in the Near East* (Edinburgh and London: Oliphant, Anderson and Ferrier, 1910); David Brewer Eddy, *What Next in Turkey: Glimpses of the American Board's Work in the Near East* (Boston, MA: The American Board Press, 1913); Joseph Greene, *Leavening the Levant* (New York: The Pilgrim Press, 1916); Clifton Jackson Phillips, *Protestant America and the Pagan World: The First Half Century of the American Board of Commissioners for Foreign Missions, 1810–1860* (Cambridge, MA: Harvard University Press, 1969). The author of each of these surveys is a missionary official.

23. See Mustafa Küçük et al., *Başbakanlık Osmanlı Arşivi Katalogları Rehberi* (Guide to the Catalogs of the Prime Minister's Office Ottoman Archive) (Ankara: Başbakanlık Basımevi, 1995); Yusuf İhsan Genç et al., *Başbakanlık Osmanlı Arşivi Rehberi* (Guide to the Prime Minister's Office Ottoman Archive) (Ankara: Başbakanlık Basımevi, reprinted, 2010); and *Türkiye Cumhuriyeti Genelkurmay ATASE ve Denetleme Başkanlığı Yayın Kataloğu* (Publication Catalog of the Turkish General Staff Directorate of Military History and Strategic Studies and Directorate of Inspection) (Ankara: Genelkurmay Basımevi, 2005).

24. Together with Fuat Paşa, Ahmed Cevdet Paşa produced the first modern Ottoman grammar in 1840s. Having served in many different educational functions, he was made a vizier in 1865. As president of the Council of Judicial Ordinance from 1868 onwards, he was primarily responsible for the codification of Islamic law in the *Mecelle* (Ottoman Civil Code). Thereafter he served in the provincial administration and in central government. In the last twenty years of his life he was minister of justice five times, minister of education four times, minister of pious foundations three times, and minister of the interior and of trade, once each. He is the author of the most important nineteenth-century Ottoman history, the ten-volume *History of Cevdet* dealing with years 1774 to 1826. See Richard Chambers, "The Education of a Nineteenth-Century Ottoman *Alim*, Ahmed Cevdet Paşa," *International Journal of Middle East Studies*, Vol. 4 (1973), pp. 440–64.

25. Ahmed Vefik Paşa was ambassador in Paris, twice grand vizier, and president of the Chamber of Deputies in the Ottoman parliament of 1877. His literary and scholarly achievements were at least equal significance. His Turkish dictionary, the first serious attempt at one by a Turk, had an importance analogous to that of Dr Johnson's Dictionary in Britain; his translations of *Télémaque*, *Gil Blas*, and above all his brilliant

adaptation of a group of plays by Moliére opened new paths and revealed new vistas in Turkish literature. On Ahmed Vefik Paşa, see İbnülemin Mahmud Kemal İnal, *Osmanlı Devrinde Son Sadrazamlar* (The Last Grand Viziers in the Ottoman Era), Sect. 5 (İstanbul: Maarif Matbaası, 1940–1953), pp. 651–738. Though published more than seven decades ago, İbnülemin Mahmud Kemal İnal's work remains the standard in the field. It contains documents and other archival material together with an appropriate commentary. To date no one has made İnal's tome obsolete. İnal was a learned and scrupulous scholar and one of the most engaging figures in late Ottoman and early Republican history. He was a rather eccentric individual endowed with an exceptional memory, a volatile personality, and a seemingly unlimited capacity for work.

26. Roderic Davison, "European Archives as a Source for Later Ottoman History," in Kathleen Brown, ed., *Report on Current Research 1958: Survey of Current Research on the Middle East* (Washington, DC: The Middle East Institute, 1958), pp. 36–37.

27. Ibid., p. 37.

28. Ibid., pp. 37–38.

29. Ibid., p. 38; Mübahat Kütükoğlu, "Osmanlı İktisad Tarihi Bakımından Konsolosluk Raporlarının Ehemmiyet ve Kiymeti" (The Importance and Value of the Consular Reports Regarding the Ottoman Economic History), *İstanbul Üniversitesi Edebiyat Fakültesi Güney-Doğu Avrupa Araştırmaları Dergisi*, Vol. 11–12 (1983), pp. 151–66.

30. Nicholas Cox, "Thirty-Year Rule and Freedom of Information: Access to Government Records," in G. H. Martin and Peter Stufford, eds., *The Records of the Nations: The Public Record Office 1838–1988 The British Record Society 1888–1988* (Woodbridge: The Boydell Press, 1990), pp. 82–83.

31. See Yücel Güçlü, *Armenians and the Allies in Cilicia 1914–1923* (Salt Lake City, UT: University of Utah Press, 2010), p. 227fn13; idem, *The Holocaust and the Armenian Case in Comparative Perspective* (Lanham, MD: University Press of America, 2012), p. 12; idem, *Historical Archives and the Historians' Commission to Investigate the Armenian Events of 1915* (Lanham, MD: University Press of America, 2015), pp. 129–39.

32. Robert Young, *French Foreign Policy, 1918–1945. A Guide to Research and Research Materials* (Wilmington, DE: Scholarly Resources Inc., second and revised edition, 1991), p. 43.

33. *Guide to the National Archives of the United States* (Washington, DC: National Archives and Records Service, 1974). With this guide, researchers will at least know which record groups and collections at the National Archives and the Washington National Records Center might hold material related to their research.

34. The capitulations had been enjoyed by foreigners in the Ottoman Empire for centuries, some of them dating from 1453, when Sultan Mehmed II conquered İstanbul. They were granted in condescending benevolence when Sultan Süleyman the Lawgiver felt himself the greatest monarch on earth, when he was master of most of the cities famous in ancient history, when Athens, Nice, Jerusalem, Cairo, Baghdad, and Belgrade were tributary to him, when the Nile, the Euphrates, the Jordan, and the Danube flowed through his domains, when it was beneath his dignity to rise

to receive any sovereign of Christendom. Extraterritorial privileges which Western nationals enjoyed were granted voluntarily, actuated by the desire to give the foreigner justice, and the Ottoman Empire received no compensation. Although Genoa, Venice, and Florence had obtained earlier capitulations from the sultan, the French Treaty of Amity and Commerce of 1535 formed the basis in the Ottoman Empire for the capitulary regime under which other Western Powers later obtained analogous privileges. They remained a thorn in the Ottoman Empire's side until their unilateral abrogation on October 1, 1914. The foreign post offices, the international board of health, extraterritorial courts, and special and direct ways of dealing with non-Muslim communities and foreign residents in the Empire were thus suppressed; henceforth, it was declared all were to come under Ottoman law; there was to be no difference between Muslim and foreigner in their relations to the government. See İsmail Hakkı Uzunçarşılı, *Osmanlı Tarihi* (Ottoman History), Vol. 2: *İstanbul'un Fethinden Kanuni Sultan Süleyman'ın Ölümüne Kadar* (From the Conquest of İstanbul to the Death of Sultan Süleyman the Lawgiver) (Ankara: Türk Tarih Kurumu Basımevi, 1949), p. 498. Complete texts of the capitulary agreements are in Gabriel Effendi Noradounghian, ed., *Recueil d'actes internationaux de l'Empire ottoman: traités, conventions, arrangements, déclarations, protocoles, procès verbaux, firmans, berats, lettres patentes et autres documents relatifs au droit public extérieur de la Turquie*, four volumes (Paris: Librairie Cotillon, F. Pichon, Successeur, 1897–1903).

35. The Sublime Porte was originally the gateway to the palace where the sultan or his grand vizier conducted official business. The metonomy became official and the expression came to mean either the Ottoman government itself or the Empire. It is frequently abbreviated as "the Porte." See Mehmet Zeki Pakalın, *Osmanlı Tarih Deyimleri ve Terimleri Sözlüğü* (Dictionary of Ottoman Historical Expressions and Terms) (İstanbul: Milli Eğitim Bakanlığı Yayınları, 2004), pp. 136–39.

36. Theophilus Prousis, *British Consular Reports From the Ottoman Levant in an Age of Upheaval, 1815–1830* (İstanbul: The Isis Press, 2008), p. 16.

37. Edward Mead Earle, "The New Constitution of Turkey," *Political Science Quarterly*, Vol. 40, No. 1 (March 1925), p. 81. The author is thoroughly competent to deal with the subject.

38. John Spagnolo, "Portents of Empire in Britain's Ottoman Extraterritorial Jurisdiction," *Middle Eastern Studies*, Vol. 27, No. 2 (April 1991), p. 256.

39. İsmail Hami Danişmend, *İzahlı Osmanlı Tarihi Kronolojisi* (Annotated Chronology of the Ottoman History), Vol. 4 (İstanbul: Türkiye Yayınevi, 1961), pp. 409–10; Feroz Ahmad, "Ottoman Perceptions of the Capitulations 1800–1914," *Journal of Islamic Studies*, Vol. 11, No. 1 (2000), pp. 1–20; Emory Bogle, *The Modern Middle East: From Imperialism to Freedom, 1800–1958* (Upper Saddle River, NJ: Prentice-Hall, Inc., 1996), p. 6.

40. No unanimity has so far been reached on a definition of the Middle East, and even the name has not been universally accepted. Scholars, statesmen, and journalists refer to the area sometimes as the Near East, sometimes as the Middle East. The Near East is the older term. In addition to southwestern Asia, it comprises those areas of southeastern Europe which have in the past been under Turkish control. The term Middle East seems to be of more recent origin and owes its widespread acceptance

in modern times to its official use by the British. In this study the understanding of the Middle East encompasses Turkey, the Levant, Mesopotamia, Arabia, the Persian Gulf, and Iran. "Persia" is the mistaken nomenclature for the country that has always been known by its inhabitants as "Iran." The practice of using a name derived by the ancient Greeks from only one part of Iran, the modern province of Fars, was prevalent in the West. Since "Iran" was the name employed by the Ottoman Empire in its interaction with the country, it is, therefore, the name that appears here. For an unconventional notion of Near and Middle East, see Michelle Tusan, *Smyrna's Ashes: Humanitarianism, Genocide, and the Birth of the Middle East* (Berkeley and Los Angeles, CA: University of California Press, 2012), pp. 12–16.

41. This is discussed at length in Uygur Kocabaşoğlu, *Majestelerinin Konsolosları, İngiliz Belgeleriyle Osmanlı İmparatorluğundaki İngiliz Konsoloslukları (1580–1900)* (Consuls of Their Majesties, British Consulates in the Ottoman Empire in British Documents [1580–1900]) (İstanbul: İletişim Yayınları, 2004). Author's credentials for examining this subject are unreservedly valid.

42. Bülent Özdemir, "Being Part of the Cinderella Service: Consul Charles Blunt at Salonica in the 1840's," in Colin Imber, Keiko Kiyotaki and Rhoads Murphy, eds., *Frontiers of Ottoman Studies*, Vol. 2: *State, Province and the West* (London and New York: I. B. Tauris, 2005), p. 243.

43. David Fraser, *The Short Cut to India: The Record of a Journey along the Route of the Baghdad Railway* (Edinburgh and London: William Blackwood and Sons, 1909), p. 84.

44. Kemal Karpat, "The Social, Economic and Administrative Situation of the Sanjak of Kayseri in 1880: The Report of Lieutenant Ferdinand Bennet, British Vice-Consul of Anatolia (October, 1880)," *International Journal of Turkish Studies*, Vol. 1, No. 2 (Autumn 1980), p. 108.

45. Florence Billings, "The Causes of the Outbreak in Cilicia, Asia Minor, April, 1909," master's thesis, Columbia University, 1927, p. 7. Florence Billings was a Near East Relief worker in Turkey in 1919–1928. Her thesis examines the causes of the troubles between Muslims and non-Muslims in the Ottoman Empire, among them the expansionist and protective policies of Europe. For work done in the 1920s, when archives were closed and private papers at a premium, this was study of high quality. Not surprisingly, cross-checks with the existing archival evidence reveal that Billings's survey was a sound piece of historical research.

46. The following list of works is by no means comprehensive. Uygur Kocabaşoğlu, *Anadolu'daki Amerika Kendi Belgeleriyle 19. Yüzyılda Osmanlı İmparatorluğundaki Amerikan Misyoner Okulları* (America in Anatolia: American Missionary Schools in Nineteenth-century Ottoman Empire in Their Own Documents) (İstanbul: İmge Kitabevi Yayınları, 1989), pp. 219–22; Ömer Turan, *Avrasya'da Misyonerler* (Missionaries in Euroasia) (Ankara: ASAM Yayınları, 1992); idem, "Lozan Konferansında Amerikan Misyonerleri" (American Missionaries in the Lausanne Conference), in Yusuf Halaçoğlu, ed., *80. Yılında 2003 Penceresinden Lozan Sempozyum Bildirileri 6 Ekim 2003, Ankara* (Communications of the Lausanne Symposium at Its Eightieth Anniversary from the 2003 Window 6 October 2003, Ankara) (Ankara: Türk Tarih Kurumu Basımevi, 2005), pp. 205–39; Erdal Açıkses, *Amerikalıların Harput'taki Misyonerlik*

Faaliyetleri (Missionary Activities of the Americans in Harput) (Ankara: Türk Tarih Kurumu Basımevi, 2003); Şamil Mutlu, *Osmanlı Devletinde Misyoner Okulları* (Missionary Schools in the Ottoman State) (İstanbul: Gökkubbe Yayınları, 2005); Cemal Yetkiner, "At the Center of the Debate: Bebek Seminary and the Educational Policy of the American Board of Commissoners for Foreign Missions (1840–1860)," in Mehmet Ali Doğan and Heather Sharkey, eds., *American Missionaries and the Middle East: Foundational Encounters* (Salt Lake City, UT: University of Utah Press, 2011); idem, "After Merchants, Before Ambassadors: Protestant Missionaries and Early American Experience in the Ottoman Empire, 1820–1860," in Nur Bilge Criss, Selçuk Esenbel, Tony Greenwood, and Louis Mazzari, eds., *American Turkish Encounters: Politics and Culture, 1830–1989* (Newcastle upon Tyne: Cambridge Scholars Publishing, 2011), pp. 8–34; Özgür Yıldız, *Anadolu'da Amerikan Misyonerleri* (American Missionaries in Anatolia) (İstanbul: Yeditepe Yayınları, 2015); Gülbadi Alan, *Osmanlı İmparatorluğunda Amerikan Protestan Okulları* (American Protestant Schools in the Ottoman Empire) (Ankara: Türk Tarih Kurumu Basımevi, 2015).

47. Rıfat Bali, *Bir Kıyımın, Bir Talanın Öyküsü Hurdaya (S)Atılan Matbu ve Yazma Eserler, Evrak-ı Metrukeler, Arşivler* (The Story of a Destruction, a Plunder: Printed and Manuscript Works, Abandoned Documents, Archives That Are Sold or Thrown As Waste) (İstanbul: Libra Yayıncılık, second revised edition, 2015), pp. 102–3.

48. The Jerusalem Patriarchate is one of the four Hierarchical Sees of the Armenian Apostolic Church, along with the Catholicosate of All Armenians, Catholicosate of the Great Cilicia, and the Patriarchate of İstanbul.

49. On this point, see Mary Mangigian Terzian, *The Armenian Minority Problem 1914–1934: A Nation's Struggle for Security* (Atlanta, GA: Scholars Press, 1992), p. 257; Ara Sarafian, "Génocide arménien et la Turquie," *Nouvelles d'Arménie*, septembre 2008, p. 1; Bedross Der Matossian, "The Genocide Archives of the Armenian Patriarchate of Jerusalem," *The Armenian Review*, Vol. 52, No. 3–4 (Fall–Winter 2011), p. 22; Garabet Moumdjian, "From Millet-i Sadıka to Millet-i Asiya," in Hakan Yavuz with Peter Sluglett, eds., *War and Diplomacy: The Russo-Turkish War of 1877–1878* (Salt Lake City, UT: University of Utah Press, 2011), p. 336fn3; Vahakn Dadrian and Taner Akçam, *Judgment at Istanbul: The Armenian Genocide Trials* (New York and Oxford: Berghahn Books, 2011), p. 9fn8; Levon Thomassian, *Summer of '42: A Study of German-Armenian Relations During the Second World War* (Atglen, PA: Schiffer Publishing Ltd., 2012), p. 11.

50. Güçlü, *Armenians and the Allies in Cilicia 1914–1923*, pp. 5–8; idem, *The Holocaust and the Armenian Case in Comparative Perspective*, pp. 9–12; idem, *Historical Archives and the Historians' Commission to Investigate the Armenian Events of 1915*, pp. 119–28; idem, "Will Untapped Ottoman Archives Reshape the Armenian Debate?" *The Middle East Quarterly*, Vol. 16, No. 2 (Spring 2009), pp. 35–42; "Study the Armenian Genocide with Confidence, Ara Sarafian Suggests," *The Armenian Reporter*, December 20, 2008, p. 2; Matossian, "The Genocide Archives of the Armenian Patriarchate of Jerusalem," p. 20.

51. Edward Erickson, *Ottomans and Armenians: A Study in Counterinsurgency* (New York: Palgrave Macmillan, 2013), p. 229. See Yücel Güçlü's review of this

title in *Journal of Muslim Minority Affairs*, Vol. 34, No. 2 (June 2014), pp. 199–201. Edward Erickson is widely recognized as one of the foremost specialists on the Ottoman army during the First World War.

52. For an insightful and nuanced study on the subject, see Meline Toumani, *There Was and There Was Not: A Journey Through Hate and Possibility in Turkey, Armenia, and Beyond* (New York: Mark Smith/Metropolitan Books, 2014), pp. 21–36.

53. Djemal Pasha, *Memories of a Turkish Statesman 1913–1919* (New York: George Doran Company, 1922). Also in Turkish *Cemal Paşa Hatıratı, 1913–1922* (Memoirs of Cemal Paşa, 1913–1922) (İstanbul: Ahmed İhsan ve Şürekası, 1339 [1923]); and Cemal Paşa, Behcet Cemal, ed., *Hatıralar* (Memoirs) (İstanbul: Selek Yayınları, 1959). An excellent assessment of Cemal Paşa's memoirs in Turkish is in İnci Enginün, "Cemal Paşa'nın Hatıraları" (Cemal Paşa's Memoirs), *Hisar*, Vol. 17, No. 171 (March 1978), pp. 10–11. For a critical evaluation, see Talha Çiçek, *War and State Formation in Syria: Cemal Pasha's Governorate during World War I, 1914–1917* (London and New York: Routledge, 2014), p. 25. For reviews in English by Arnold Toynbee, Bernadotte Schmitt, and S.A. Korff, see respectively "Djemal Pasha; An Ottoman Apologia; Turkey and the West," *The Times*, October 6, 1922, p. 6; *Political Science Quarterly*, Vol. 38, No. 1 (March 1923), pp. 500–3; and *The American Historical Review*, Vol. 28, No. 4 (July 1923), pp. 748–50.

54. Cavid Bey, Hasan Babacan, and Servet Avşar, eds., *Meşrutiyet'in Ruznamesi* (Agenda of the Constitutionalism), four volumes (Ankara: Türk Tarih Kurumu Basımevi, 2014).

55. According to the law of July 2, 1934, all Turks assumed a family name. Hüseyin Cahid adopted the name Yalçın. When appropriate, new family names will be given in parentheses on the first appearance of the particular person.

56. For a comprehensive study on Hüseyin Cahid Yalçın and *Tanin*, see Hilmi Bengi, *Gazeteci, Siyasetçi ve Fikir Adamı Olarak Hüseyin Cahid Yalçın* (Hüseyin Cahid Yalçın As Journalist, Politician, and Intellectual) (Ankara: Atatürk Araştırma Merkezi, 2000). Also Yusuf Ziya Ortaç, *Portreler* (Portraits) (İstanbul: Akbaba Yayınları, reprint, 1963), pp. 37–43; Zekeriya Sertel, *Hatırladıklarım* (Those I Remember) (İstanbul: Remzi Kitabevi, reprint, 2000), pp. 227–34; Uygur Kocabaşoğlu, *"Hürriyeti" Beklerken İkinci Meşrutiyet Basını* (Waiting for the "Liberty": Press of the Second Constitutionalism) (İstanbul: İstanbul Bilgi Üniversitesi Yayınları, 2010), pp. 137–42; Mehmed Asım Us, Seval Şahin, ed., *Karikatür İkinci Meşrutiyet Döneminin Ünlü Simaları* (Caricature: The Important Faces of the Second Constitutional Period) (İstanbul: Kitap Yayınevi, 2008), pp. 63–67 and 185–86.

57. Kocabaşoğlu, *"Hürriyeti" Beklerken*, pp. 45–46; Us, *Karikatür*, pp. 106–10 and 189–90.

58. Roderick Stackelberg, *Hitler's Germany: Origins, Interpretations, Legacies* (London and New York: Routledge, 1999), p. 1.

59. Ibid., p. 2.

Chapter One

Geographical and Economic Importance of the Province of Adana and Its Vicinity

On the map of Ottoman territories, Adana appeared as a mere speck. The Ottoman Empire at the turn of the twentieth century could still claim the status of an imposing world power. Its territorial possessions, stretching across three continents, included the Balkans, Anatolia, and the Arab lands from the border of Tunisia in the west to the Iranian frontier in the east. This vast and diverse world boasted a large population, a variety of abundant sources, and important international routes and waterways. The great capital of İstanbul still displayed the pomp of an imperial nerve center which set trends in fashion and refinement and made the momentous decisions of peace and war.[1]

Some idea of what these lands might be expected to produce when fully opened up might be gained by glancing at some of Ottoman Empire's products even under present conditions. It provided a large percentage of the borax used in Europe and of the world's emery supply; it produced annually nearly a million tons of coal; until recently most of the chrome iron ore used was derived from Asia Minor; it had one of the largest, if not the largest, lead mines in Europe; and from mines being worked at the present time it obtained antimony, gold, mercury, copper, zinc, and other metals. Its figs, raisins, and canary seed were famous throughout the world. South Africa was its only rival in supplying mohair; among its other notable exports might be mentioned valonea, opium, wines, cotton, and tobacco. Yet it was no exaggeration to say that so far its resources had hardly been touched.[2]

Certain physical features of the province of Adana are the cardinal points upon which its fateful history has turned, and these must be carefully examined before a beginning can be made of understanding what has happened. Geography counts. It is about the political imagination as well as the location. It is also one of the most important constraints in the development of defense policy and strategy. Geography can shape the strategic calculations

of policy makers and strategic planners—apparently against their will—
toward the brink of armed conflict. The omission of geography from analysis
then results in an overly simplistic model of the strategic calculus, one that
focuses on either balances in military power or strategies. It is the influence of
geography on tactical and operational elements of the strategic calculus that
underpins, albeit subliminally, strategic calculations about the feasibility of
the use of military force because the geographical conditions will influence
policy makers' and strategic planners' perceptions of strategic vulnerabilities
or opportunities. The physical geography of a region generally changes very
slowly, though some features change at different rates than others. Applying
this concept of strategic geography to the province of Adana, one can identify
a great many examples of its continuing importance.[3]

LOCATION OF CILICIA

Adana is the principal city of Cilicia (Çukurova), a vast alluvial plain, one
of the most fertile regions of the world. Known from ancient times because
the Cilician Gates were the invasion route to Syria for conquering armies like
that of Alexander the Great—perhaps also because Cicero was its governor—
Cilicia is the triangle formed by the Mediterranean to the south, the Taurus
Mountains to the northwest, and the Amanus range to the east. Its mountains
surround a lowland like the seats of an amphitheater. It can be easily identified on any topographical map as the patch of green north of the Gulf of
İskenderun (Alexandretta). Adana plain was richer than the Delta of Nile, and
it was potentially a more wealthy and more fertile land than Palestine. This
plain, which has an approximate length of nearly 160 kilometers from west
to east, was traversed by the Baghdad railway, whose official title was *La
Société Imperiale Ottomane du Chemin de Fer de Baghdad*.[4]

İskenderun was a reclaimed marsh, cut off from Asia Minor and from
Syria by the huge crescent of Amanus range, with only one roadway out to
reach. With Syria it communicated through the Belen (Beilan) Pass, and with
Asia Minor by the Payas-Toprakkale road. Belen, fifteen kilometers inland
from İskenderun on the carriage road leading to Aleppo, nestles in the tops
of the mountains and occupies the Syrian Gates. The Amanus itself is shaped
like a bow, and its two tips lie on the sea. The southern tip is Domuzburnu
(Ras Khanzir), which descends in cliffs and bluffs to the water without leaving any beach at all. There is no way past it, and İskenderun is on this side
absolutely cut off. The northern horn of the hills rests on the sea from Babı
Yunus (Jonah's Pillar) to Dörtyol, and north of the latter point breaks away
the Mediterranean Sea again.[5]

A writer said in 1916:

Making liberal allowance for developments in Mesopotamia, there remains about 100.000 square miles of country, much of it the richest in the Turkish Empire, for which a port in the Gulf of Alexandretta will be the outlet, and have no rival. You see something of the importance of the Alexandretta Gulf port on the map, but you do not see half of it so. You need to be familiar with the country in order to understand the future of this North-eastern end of the Mediterranean. You need to have seen the agricultural possibilities of the Cilician Plain; of the Central parts of Anatolia; to have travelled in Northern Syria and seen wheat going to the horizon like prairie grass. You also need to realize what mineral riches are awaiting scientific mining and means of conveyance. There are copper deposits near Kharput and Diarbekir equal to any in the world. In the mountains of Albistan, peasants bring lumps of lead ore and lumps of magnetic iron and tell you what masses these samples come from. From a mineralogist's point of view, it is an almost unknown country. [. . .] If, at the present time, the Gulf of Alexandretta is the most vital spot in the Turkish Empire outside the capital, not less but more so will it be a vital point after the war. Its importance will increase with every year, and in view of the developments likely to take place between the Aegean and the Persian Gulf it is difficult to overestimate its future [. . .] Call Alexandretta of the future one of the greatest, perhaps the greatest, seaport in the Mediterranean, and you still will not have estimated its full possibilities.[6]

Armenian historian Hrachik Simonyan points out that there is no consensus among scholars regarding the name "Cilicia." Setting aside the mythological variants, many consider it probable that the name derives from the Hebrew word "khilkim" (kilki), which means "stone" or "rocky." Others believe that a Phoenician military commander named Cilix settled in this land and it was named Cilicia after him.[7] We are told by Herodotus that the original inhabitants of Cilicia were called Hypacheans, and that it was not until the arrival of Cilix, the son of Agenor king of Phoenicia, that they obtained the appellation of Cilicians. Cilix, it is related, set out in search of his sister Europa, who had been carried away by pirates; after seeking her in many countries by sea and land, disgusted and worn out by his want of success, and attracted by the fertility of the soil, he settled down on the coast of Asia Minor, and gave his name to the region about 1552 B.C.[8]

There is no single, agreed definition of the geographical boundaries of Cilicia. Geographers and historians use the term, yet frequently have different definitions of what they mean. The name Cilicia has changed and evolved over time. It is employed variously according to the historic context. On the political map of 1909, it meant the province of Adana and sanjak[9] of Maraş, which had once been part of Adana but had been transfered in the 1880s to the neighboring province of Aleppo.[10]

The sanjak of Maraş was subdivided into the kazas (lower subdivisions) of Maraş, Elbistan, Zeytun, Göksun, and Pazarcık. The town of Maraş is in mountainous country, being on the southern slope of the mountain range of the Ahır Dağ and having an altitude of about seven hundred meters. The slopes around the town had flourishing groves and orchards, and there was abundance of water. The town itself was built on terraces with narrow ill-paved streets; the houses were well constructed of stone and many had red-tilled roofs. The town was commanded by a ruined citadel, which was manned with artillery and garrisoned. Situated on a major trade route at one of the approaches to the Taurus Mountains, Maraş had been an important urban center since ancient times. The inhabitants were engaged mainly in weaving and in the manufacture of furniture from the fine wood of the forests nearby. The area had always been a settlement place for the Armenians, and they lived there as a minority with considerably good economic conditions. At the turn of the twentieth century, almost 60 percent of the merchants in Maraş were Armenians.[11]

The districts of Ayntab and Urfa to the east were also sometimes included in references to Cilicia. Ayntab was a city of some eighty thousand inhabitants, situated about forty kilometers from the Euphrates river at Birecik about 120 kilometers nearly due east from the north end of the Gulf of İskenderun, the nearest point of the Mediterranean Sea. Its population was a mixed one of Muslims and Christians.

Politically and historically, Cilicia derived its importance from being the highway between the nations of the East and West. It has been a crossroad linking empires, dynasties, cultures, and armies in both peace and war, and those who controlled access to its vital land and water trade routes wielded great power and influence.[12]

PAST OF CILICIA

Not much has been written about pre-1914 Cilicia in Turkish and Western languages. The early history of this part of the Ottoman Empire is less well known than of any other part of Asia Minor. For many years a tiny number of scholars worked on Cilicia and produced the studies in the field. Large areas still have not received proper scholarly attention and that will remain the case due to the demanding requirements in linguistic and palaeographic skills. Also, satisfactory biographies do not exist for numerous modern Cilician figures. Some scholars are giving economic and agricultural topics increased attention. Future bibliographies will reflect these trends. These developments are the result of increased awareness of the importance of Cilicia in understanding Turkey.[13]

During the last three decades a few significant books have been published by Turkish historians on the history of Cilicia, Cezmi Yurtsever's *Ermeni Terör Merkezi: Kilikya Kilisesi* being a notable case. The study is based in large part upon documents from the Ottoman archives and may be described as one of the first systematic and scholarly investigation of a crucially important subject. This effort deserves to be applauded, and it is hoped that preparations are now underway to translate Yurtsever's vigorously argued study into English.[14] It is a work which makes a serious attempt to sketch the history of Cilicia since the arrival of the Turks. Its introductory historical account briefly mentions the Armenian kingdom, concentrating instead on the Seljuks and the Turkification of the region. Armenians are mentioned as tax collectors in the nineteenth century, as revolting in Hacin, and leaders of a revolt in Zeytun which sparked an Armenian movement. In a detailed account of the Turkoman tribes, the author frequently indicates the centers of Armenian population. Yurtsever gives a broader perspective of Armenian history in the section on terrorism. He dwells on the history of the Armenian kingdom, making extensive reference to the *Encyclopedia of Islam*, and concludes that the kingdom cannot be considered a state, but rather a small principality like the Turkish feudal lordships of the time. He then discusses Armenian prosperity as merchants and bankers under the Ottomans, population figures, the revolts of Zeytun and Adana. This work presents a fairly objective account of the acts, and it turns out to be more sober than many contemporary studies.[15]

Cilicia seems never to have been firmly under the control of the great kingdoms of the ancient East. In the ninth century B.C. the Assyrian King Shalmaneser was obliged to conquer the Cilicians (Khilikku in Assyrian inscriptions) seven times. Three centuries later Cilicia suddenly appears as an independent kingdom and one of the four chief powers of Asia. In alliance with Nebuchadennazar II, it negotiated a peace between the Lydians and the Medes. Under the Iranian Empire, Cilicia was governed by tributary native kings who bore the title Syennesis. In 401 B.C. they made no opposition to the march of Cyrus and the ten thousand Greeks through their country, and Alexander the Great in 333 B.C. found the Cilician Gates open. These facts show that the Cilicians were always glad to cooperate with the enemies of Iran. After Alexander the Great's death, the region fell under the control of Seleucids. In 103 B.C. it became Roman territory. Soon afterwards the coast, particularly between the Lamas river and Cape Anamur, became the haunt of pirates. That rugged littoral furnished innumerable rockbound bays which they thought impregnable places of refuge. These pirates with one thousand galleys roamed the Mediterranean and, as allies of Mithridates, preyed upon Roman commerce. In 68 B.C. Pompey sacked their strongholds and completely subdued them. In the days when Cicero was pro-consul Cilicia supported a much larger population than it did in 1914. In the first century A.D. it became a rival of Athens and Alexandria as a seat of philosophical and liberal studies, and the first scene of the missionary labors of Paul of Tarsus was Cilicia.[16]

In the seventh century the district was invaded by the Arabs who held it until 965. The Seljuk invasion of eastern Anatolia in the eleventh century caused an exodus of Armenians southward, who under Prince Rupen founded in 1080 in the heart of the Cilician Taurus, not very far from the town of Hacin in the sanjak of Kozan (Sis), a small Armenian community. This gradually grew into the kingdom of Lesser Armenia, with its capital at Sis. Under its Armenian king, Leo II or the Great, circa 1200 A.D., its domains extended to the summit of the Taurus, including Maraş, and controlled the coast from İskenderun inclusive to the Manavgat Çay. This Christian kingdom gave considerable aid to the Crusaders and formed thriving commercial relations with Venice and Genoa, both of which cities emporia on the Cilician coast. The idea of Armenian independence was thus associated with this district.[17]

The position of the Cilician plain, lying between the great passes of the Cilician and Syrian Gates (Gülek and Belen Passes), has at all times exposed it to the ravages of hostile armies advancing northwards to Anatolia or southwards to Syria. Along it passed the Ten Thousand Greeks on their march to aid Cyrus; along it marched Alexander the Great to the battlefield of Issus; along it, centuries later, poured the hosts of the Crusaders on their mission of misdirected zeal.

One result of this position has been that the original population of the plain has entirely disappeared, and its place has been taken by semi-nomad tribes of Turkish descent. The description of the Turkish population's ancestry as Seljuk or Turkoman rather than Ottoman is correct insofar as these Turks entered the region fully four centuries before Sultan Selim I (r. 1512–1520) conquered it.

The Turkomans, whose natural instincts led them to a pastoral and predatory life, were sedentary or nomad according to local and climatic conditions. But they preferred a migratory life, oscillating with the season between the lowlands and mountains. These tribes, who dispersed in the plains, valleys, and mountains of this region, fed their flocks in the pasturages of the Ceyhan, Seyhan, and their tributaries in winter, and repaired to the uplands of Taurus in summer. Before 1864 many of the tribes were purely nomad, and in open revolt against the Porte. After some hard fighting, they were reduced to submission by Derviş and İsmail Paşas, and were settled in villages on the plain. The people were not allowed to leave their villages for the summer pasture grounds in the mountains for five years; numbers sickened and died, and the loss in camels, horses, and livestock was large. The tribes which were once strong in numbers, and rich in all that constituted the wealth of nomads, were now weak and poor. They lived by cultivating a few hectares of land in the plain, and on the produce of their flocks, which they were now allowed to take to summer pasture grounds in the mountains. The semi-nomad population was composed of Yörüks in the western districts; of Sırkıntılı Turkomans in the center; and of Cerid, Tecirli, Kayı, and Bozdoğanlı Turkomans in the east. Karalar tribe was one of those most important Turkoman groupings that was settled down in the Çimeli, Helvacı, Oymaklı, Yüzbaşı, and Kamışlı villages of the Yüreğir plain. A list of Turkoman tribes contained many names identical with those of powerful families who claim a remote ancestry. In addition to the ordinary population alluded to above, there was during harvest time a large floating population. The harvesters, men and women, were from Diyarbekir, Harput, Urfa, and sometimes even from Bitlis and Mosul. These people performed the long journey on foot, and after the harvest was finished they returned to their homes.[18]

PROVINCE AND CITY OF ADANA

At the turn of the twentieth century, the province of Adana—an area of about 37,350 square kilometers—comprised five sanjaks, from west to east: Silifke (İçili), Mersin, Adana, Kozan, and Cebelibereket (Osmaniye). These five sanjaks were again subdivided into nineteen kazas whose names were as follows: Silifke, Ermenek, Gülnar, Mut, Anamur, Mersin, Tarsus, Adana, Karaisalı, Kozan, Hacin, Feke, Karsı Bazar (Kadirli), Osmaniye, Bulanık (Bahçe), İslahiye, Yarpuz, Hassa, and Payas. The provincial boundaries for the most part followed some logical geographic divisions.[19]

The city of Adana, a few kilometers from the foothills of the Taurus, is at the crossroads of the main west-east and north-south communication lines. The Cilician plain is shut off from the interior plateau of Asia Minor by the great range of the Taurus. For trade purposes a road was built through the Cilician Gates. It is said that the rocky walls which form the Gates approached so close that, until İbrahim Paşa (the son of Mehmed Ali Paşa of Egypt) blasted a road for his artillery, a loaded camel could just pass between them. This road is one of the most famous in history, and it led directly to Tarsus. This locality was the birthplace of apostle Paul. The town lay on the west of the river Tarsus Çay, over which Cleopatra sailed for the last time when she brought her Egyptian army to help Antony. There is no uncertainty as to the site, for the town has never entirely disappeared in all its long history, and even the name Tarsus has been persistently attached to the place since 400 B.C. At the turn of the twentieth century it was comparatively small, but in Augustan times it covered a large area on both sides of the Tarsus Çay, with suburbs in the hills to the north (where the ruins of fine buildings and public works were still to be seen) and in Aulai, some kilometers to the south, then only a marsh.[20]

Its large open harbor and its railway connections made Mersin by far the most important part of the province of Adana. It was the natural point of exportation for Adana, Tarsus, and the western part of the Cilician plain and for regions fed by the roads leading to Tarsus and Adana from the north.[21] The handling of cargo at Mersin was greatly facilitated and expedited by an aerial railway which was constructed in 1912. It consisted of a single-rail line about five hundred meters in circumference running to the end of a pier and around a large warehouse and railroad yard. It was operated by electricity. A special powerhouse had been erected, equipped with a dynamo of sufficient energy to give power to the railway and furnish light for the railroad yard and buildings. Earlier all cargo had to be brought to and from vessels in lighters, and was then handled by porters, who gave the goods considerable rough treatment. The railway was intended to replace in a large measure the use of these porters, for trucks and hooks which would suspend from the rail would be lowered directly into the lighters as they lay alongside the pier. The cargo would then be transported to cars in the railroad yard or to the warehouse. As this railway was at the terminus of the Adana-Mersin Railroad, which was also the feeder of the new sections of the Baghdad Railroad, much cargo to and from the interior of Asia Minor would be spared some of the rough handling it had hitherto experienced at this port.[22]

Three rivers that once bore the classic names of Sarus (Seyhan), Cydnus (Ceyhan), and Pyramus (Tarsus Çay or Berdan), rise in the Taurus, Anti-Taurus, and Amanus Mountains, and make short passages across the plain to the sea. The importance of these rivers is not to be measured by their length, but by volume, which represents the winter snow from these great ranges and the summer rain of a wide catchment area. Emperors and empresses used to voyage up the Ceyhan in great sailing vessels; on the Tarsus Çay lay the port city of Cilicia, a center of Greek trade and influence; the Seyhan gave rise to a great scheme of land reclamation and harbor construction. But these glories belonged to a period of two thousand years old. In 1909 the three rivers whose banks were once lined with quays and wharfs flew unconstrainedly toward the sea, their waters rolled over muddy flats or were lost in swampy wastes, their navigable channels had become impassable ditches.[23]

The most striking geographical feature of the province of Adana is its large and fertile coastal plain. It extends from the Gulf of İskenderun on the east to the Lamas Su on the west. It is thus more than a 170 kilometers long from east to west. It varies in breadth from nearly one hundred kilometers on the east, at the Amanus range, to only a few kilometers at Mersin. The western part of the plain, in which lie the towns of Adana and Tarsus, is very fertile. The soil is a rich stoneless loam (great quantities of good soil are brought down from the Taurus and Amanus by the rivers) and produce an abundance of cotton and cereals. Along the coast were sandhills about three meters high, cane brakes, lagoons of saltwater and freshwater, and two permanent marshes, one southwest of Tarsus and the other eight kilometers southwest of Adana. The eastern part of the plain, in which lies Anazarba, was not so fertile and was only partially cultivated. It contained some cane brake and marshy land. Probably not more than 10 percent of the plain was at the turn of the twentieth century under cultivation.[24]

Cilicia was once of mighty strategic importance, for through it ran the only practicable road from Asia Minor into Syria, Mesopotamia, and the great old-time empires that lay therein and beyond.[25] In 1921 the French publicist René Pinon remarked that Cilicia was the most important strategic, economic, and political point of all western Asia because of its proximity to the sea as well as its position on the Baghdad railway.[26] A single glance at any up-to-date military map of the Ottoman Empire would reveal the significant fact that this view is true.[27]

Adana city is the capital of the province of Adana and is situated in the center of the Yüreğir plain which extends some thirty kilometers toward the Taurus Mountains that rise to a height of ten thousand feet to the north. After digging down for thirty feet to find solid ground for the foundations of the American Seminary building, the workmen uncovered a jar and a number of pieces of pottery. Even at this depth the soil was so soft that piles had to be driven. This would indicate that the site of Adana was an ancient one, covered deep by the ruins and the accumulations of the centuries. It was said that the place (the ancient Anatolia ad Sarum) was colonized by the Greeks in the dim past. The Seyhan river divides the city. It is spanned by an ancient stone bridge, the foundations of which must have been laid by the Iranians, and it was said that the Roman Emperor Justinian repaired it. The Ottoman government in trying to repair it found that the structure had taken on the consistency of rock.[28]

The provincial boundaries of Adana did not remain entirely fixed throughout the centuries. From time to time the government transferred a peripheral district from one province to the jurisdiction of another for political or fiscal reasons. Although Adana was the residence of the governor and the seat of the local government, the only resident consul was the representative of Iran, with all the other consuls—British, American, French, German, Austrian, Russian, Italian, Spanish, and Greek—living at Mersin. These powers did not at once proceed to appoint full consuls in Mersin but instead relied on consular agents, at first usually native Christians, later mostly their own officials. Most of the consular agents at İskenderun were business residents of the locality. There were Russian, French, and Austrian post offices in Mersin. In pursuance of the provisions of the treaty of 1783 the Russian mails were distributed by a special Russian post office in the consulate for many years. Other foreign post offices were subsequently established on the ground that those countries were entitled under their treaties with the Sublime Porte to the same privileges as were enjoyed by others. These arrangements, therefore, were longstanding and had been necessitated by the alleged absence of any security that the Ottoman government could efficiently replace the foreign post offices. The maintenance of foreign post offices in the realm deprived the Ottoman government of a certain portion of the postal revenues which would have otherwise accrue to it. The mails consigned to these foreign post offices, and distributed by them, often conveyed packets of watches and other valuable articles, which thus evaded the Ottoman customs duties. The Ottoman government stated since the turn of the twentieth century that they contemplated the eventual suppression of the foreign post offices in the country.[29]

NATURAL RESOURCES OF ADANA AND ADJACENT AREAS

Lieutenant Herbert Chermside writing to Patrick Henderson, the British consul at Aleppo, from Nergizlik (near İskenderun) on June 25, 1879, pointed out how enormously the gross revenue of the Adana province might be raised with an increased population, good government, and the development of the natural, irrigational, and mineral resources that would result from the attraction of foreign enterprise and capital. Chermside knew of no more favored district in the Ottoman Empire: excellent soil, abundant water and water power, easy facilities for developing communications, timber, coal, minerals, and all the necessary elements for the establishment of industries and manufactures were at hand.[30]

Lieutenant Colonel Sir Charles Wilson, the British consul general in Anatolia, reporting to the Earl of Dufferin, the British ambassador in İstanbul, from Adana on December 31, 1881, supplied the following information respecting the richness of soil of the Cilician plain, and the field which lay open for all kinds of agricultural pursuits. Much more than half the plain was at the time uncultivated, and served only as a winter pasture ground for the horses, cattle, sheep, and goats which were brought to it from all parts of Anatolia. If capital were available, the large area then occupied by marshes and morasses, or liable to inundation, might be drained, and many thousand square kilometers might be brought under cultivation by a simple scheme of drainage. Abidin Paşa, governor of Adana, took an interest in agriculture; he had lately purchased a large tract of marshy land which he proposed to drain, and he was at present in correspondence with a British firm respecting the introduction of steam ploughs, threshing machines, and traction engines into this province. Various projects were on foot for improving the communications of the province; roads had been commenced and were in course of construction; and by orders from İstanbul, a special examination had been made of the harbor of Ayas (Yumurtalık), a short distance east of Adana.[31]

In the early 1900s the city of Adana was considered the most prosperous city in Asia Minor, being the trade center of other provinces. Woodcutting from the magnificent forests in the mountains, small farms and pasturage in the foothills, truck gardening around the cities, home weaving of native wool, and the small trades and retail works of the bazaars all contributed to the prosperity of the province, but its mainstay was agriculture as the great crops of cotton and wheat from the central plain made the riches of the people. Agriculture depended upon labor (emigration), irrigation, and capital. The land was in holdings of about five hundred hectares, though one thousand hectares was common. The peasants were proprietors of the small holdings; the large ones were often rented out on shares to many renters. From year to year the fields were extended and worked by immigrants from the Caucasus, the Balkans, and Crete, as well as from the adjacent Anatolian provinces. There was a continual scarcity of labor. Various large schemes had failed because of sickness arising from the great marshes. "Ten times as much labor could be used." In harvest time and for cotton picking fifteen thousand to twenty thousand transient laborers came down from the hills, many of them nomadic Kurds, and many Armenians from the poverty-stricken mountain villages around Hacin and Kozan. These were coming at the time of the outbreak in April 1909 and account largely for the great number of dead in the plain.[32]

Cotton might be produced enough for the whole Ottoman requirements. Adana cotton had been renowned for centuries for its superiority over other Turkish cotton. Planting was done in March and picking in August. After supplying the home consumption the city exported annually between ninety thousand to one hundred thousand bales of cotton, principally to Britain. Several million bushels of wheat and flaxseed, which was the finest in the world, were also exported. A considerable amount of sheep skin and buffalo hides were shipped, and the city was the headquarters for wool that came from eastern Anatolia and the provinces on the coast of the Black Sea. At the beginning of the twentieth century the wool exportation of Adana was enough to supply France for a year. There were large forests in the Taurus and Anti-Taurus Mountains. The timber in these forests was of very great value. The city in summer time was deserted, as almost all of the inhabitants went to vineyards in the outskirts.[33]

Thirty years before 1909, the province of Adana had almost no dealings with the outside world, nor with parts of the Ottoman Empire other than those immediately adjacent. In 1909 there was a great production of cotton, a large proportion of it ginned, spun, and woven on the spot. A total of seventy thousand bales was the annual product, part of which was exported to Europe raw, the remainder in a manufactured condition being dispatched inland, wherever and as far as transport facilities offered. Besides cotton, Adana produced sesame, wheat, and barley in large quantity; oats, Indian corn, tobacco, etc., in small degree. There was a small crop of sugar cane where there might be a huge production, as soil and climate were especially favorable. Fruit of infinite variety and fine quality was grown in great quantity.[34]

Industrial life had gradually penetrated Adana. The first cotton-processing factories were founded by a French engineer, Justin Daudet, in 1864. The next year, James Kot, a British merchant, built three cotton-sorting factories in Adana, Tarsus, and Mersin. The French, the British, then the Germans, the Swiss, and the Austrian financiers invested heavily in the cotton business in Cilicia and constructed large factories and trade companies.[35]

As the cotton growing and wheat areas increased, so did the factories. The first cotton spinnery with twenty-seven thousand spindles came in 1880, and the first steam mill about the same time.[36] In the year 1884, Greek engineer Tripani imported a small machine for cotton ginning. This was the first effort of modern enterprise in Cilicia, and, incidentally, the beginning of the fortunes of the firm of Tripani Brothers (Constantine and Manolli), which in 1909 had established at Adana factories and machinery valued one hundred thousand Turkish liras.[37] But for one small German concern, which was only the beginning of a much larger project, the industrial machinery was owned and worked by Greeks, and the agricultural machines by Turks. One or two of the engines were German gas engines, but the great bulk were old-fashioned steam engines, built on the Clyde or the Midlands. Most of this machinery had been imported by the Tripani firm for their own account, or for others, and the total import might be said to be due to their initiation. Thus, though there was not a born Briton at Adana or Tarsus, British reputation for the manufacture of machinery seemed to remain undiminished.[38]

In 1908 there were fifty thousand spindles, twenty-two ginning factories, ten steam mills, sixty steam thrashers and reaping machines, and various factories for tiles and silks. The Germans had set up a factory for baling and processing cotton on the spot, and the only two things that stood in the way of industrial expansion were the lack of large irrigation works and of labor for the mills. These enterprises employed up to two thousand permanent workers and a few thousand more day laborers.[39]

As Western capital preferred to employ Christian managers, it was the Armenians that benefited the most. Although the Tripani Brothers, ethnic Greeks, owned the most important factories in Cilicia, many Armenians achieved success in the cotton trade and related businesses. At the end of the nineteenth century, they also dominated the local banks.[40]

As in all areas deficient in communications, fuel had been one of the grand difficulties in Cilicia. There were several workable coal mines in the district, but owing to the impossibility of obtaining concessions to exploit on reasonable terms, they remained untouched. For a long time wood from the foothills and mountain slopes was the only available fuel, its consumption, as it had to be sought for always farther and farther away, proving expensive and ineffective. Imported coal became at the opening of the Mersin-Adana railway. Cardiff briquettes landed at Adana costed forty-five shillings per ton, a price that handicapped manufacture in no small measure. It was now found that gas engines consuming anthracite were much more economical than steam engines, with the result that all new engines were of this type, while it was probable that the other type would have to be discarded in order to reduce expenses.[41]

A rough estimate of the total export and import trade of Mersin during the years 1904, 1905, and 1906 gave an annual average of one and a half million of Turkish liras. This very considerable figure, and the remarkable development in the cotton industry, was attained not, as might be imagined, owing to the fact that there was a large population engaged in exploiting the total cultivable area, but from the cultivation of some five-eighths of the land available. The upper plain of Cilicia lay almost fallow, not a third of it having been touched by the plough for many hundreds of years. There had been a steady increase of the area under cultivation in recent years, but production had not kept pace with cultivation: in fact, production had decreased, owing to inferior farming methods and the consequent exhaustion of the land. Shallow ploughing, ignorance in regard to the best rotation of crops, and so forth, had resulted in a deterioration of the soil that would be fatal in a region not so blessed by nature. Cilicia had an average rainfall of some twenty-five inches per annum. The presence of three well-filled rivers, some lakes, and large expanses of marsh, produced, in the great heat of summer, a prodigious humidity that caused great discomfort to human beings, but which promoted fertility in the vegetable world. No ill usage could seriously diminish Cilicia's powers of production.[42]

But the area suffered considerably, nonetheless, from the neglect of mankind. The deforestation on a grand scale, necessitated by the fuel requirements of the numerous factories established since the last two decades of the nineteenth century, had seriously affected the rainfall. Where moderate and regular showers were formerly induced by a richly wooded hill environment, there occurred in 1909 violent storms due to the accumulation in the adjacent mountains of moisture-laden clouds. These storms bursted suddenly, filled the rivers with rushing water that they could not accommodate, and resulted in floods that destroyed crops and property. In 1906 there occurred a flood that ruined two hundred thousand Turkish liras worth of grain. A succession of floods might end in the establishment of a permanent marsh. A curious feature of farming life in the neighborhood of Adana was that people living within one or two hours of the city were frequently completely isolated from it for many months of the year. The soft stoneless soil did not lend itself to the construction of good roads, and upon such tracks as existed traffic was impossible in and immediately after the rainy season. One of the great anxieties of the farmer was whether the roads would be good enough at the critical moment for the transport from the market of the seed for the ensuing crop. Deforestation was generally accepted as being responsible for much of the vagaries of the weather.[43]

The district of Aleppo was renowned for its fertility and the excellency of its soil. In its territory were comprised the plains of Antakya (Antioch), Amik, and Cum, and the luxuriant areas of Ayntab, Kilis, and Maraş, all of which were crossed by numerous more or less important rivers. The plain stretching from Antakya to Maraş was a very fertile region, perhaps one-third of which might be irrigated by the mountain streams from the Amanus or the great springs upon the plain which uniting form the Karasu river. The irrigable portion produced a fine quality of rice, and the nonirrigable portion grew large crops of wheat, barley, lentils, millet, and maize. The river known as the Aksu rising some one hundred kilometers northeast of Maraş makes a long detour to the south and finally empties into the Ceyhan river about fifteen kilometers southwest of that city. This stream also flows through a fertile plain nearly as large as the one between Maraş and Antakya and carries twice the water of Karasu. Forty-five kilometers north of Antakya, beyond the low but rugged range of mountains called the Karadağ is another plain of nearly the same size, known as Araban, not so well irrigated, but even more fertile, which debouches upon the Euphrates river on the east. Much larger than all these put together was the fertile region of which Aleppo was the center. This covered, roughly estimated, about four thousand to forty-five thousand square kilometers of which probably only about one-tenth could be easily irrigated, but the nonirrigable portion of which yielded fine crops of wheat, barley, millet, lentils, sesame, and olives. The land, through which the Baghdad Railway ran from Aleppo as far as Resülayn, presented another area nearly as large and fertile, and better watered than the one about Aleppo. The hill country lying between these plains, wherever there was a trickle of water, yielded all kinds of fruits and vegetables, and where there was soil without water grew the best of grapes and olives. Where there was not soil enough for vineyards or olive orchards, the pistachio nut, and the pine tree for timber, could be grown at a good profit.[44]

It was sad, however, to state that in a country so well endowed by nature agriculture was still conducted in a rudimentary manner: plowing with a sharp stick pointed with a bit of iron, harvesting with the sickle, and tramping out the grain with oxen or horses drawing a sort of sledge. Until 1911 no real energetic efforts had been made by anybody to introduce modern agricultural implements. The farmers were quite in contrast with their colleagues in the bordering province of Adana where the farm work was practically entirely performed by machinery. The area of land under cultivation in the present primitive fashion did not perhaps constitute a fifth of what was suitable for that purpose. Thousands and thousands of acres of a soil of an exceptional fertility extending to the east of Aleppo and crossed by the Euphrates remained uncultivated. The settled population of that region was very limited in proportion to the area of the land which could be utilized.[45]

In his overland journey from İskenderun to Ayntab in the autumn of 1911 the American missionary Francis Leslie was surprised at the evident fertility of the soil of much of the country through which he passed and more surprised to see so much of it untilled and the backward methods in use where the land was tilled. It appeared to him that that land ought to yield most abundant crops if it were only properly cultivated. Leslie's first impressions of the region was that it was a land of great industrial possibilities of which its inhabitants seemed quite unaware. Here were the natural resources required for that material prosperity as a basis on which to build a higher civilization.[46]

In discussing the question of agriculture, it might be mentioned that various endeavors had been made to establish European enterprise, all failing, however, owing largely to the difficulty of coming to terms with the authorities. A German company proposed to start a farm for the growing of beetroot and a factory for the making of sugar. They wanted various privileges and a monopoly, so the officials had probably reason in refusing a concession. Several British syndicates wished to start farming on a large scale and on scientific lines, but gave up their plans owing to the administrative difficulties. A French company wanted to drain the large lake near Tarsus, but could not get a concession. Sultan Abdülhamid II (r. 1876–1909) had estates aggregating some 150,000 acres in the upper plain, at present practically untouched. A British syndicate offered to rent this land and grow cotton upon it, but could not arrange matters. For permission to mine coal, iron, copper, lead, chrome, etc., there had been many applications, none of which had been successful.[47]

The condition of rivers watering the plain was of extreme importance to the welfare of Cilicia. In the entire absence of conservancy they were in a deplorable state, and simply served to flood the country at unseasonable times, and to augment the already large marsh land. The Seyhan during certain months of the year was navigable to lighters from the coast, and a few braved the difficulties of the channel. During the last decade of the nineteenth century steam launches used to come up to Adana, but that was impossible in 1909. The fact was that all three rivers in the region might be made available for shallow draught vessels, but, of course, at considerable expense. Much expenditure was out of the question under present conditions, but comparatively little money would render the Seyhan navigable, and decrease the liability to disastrous floods. There being a fair rainfall in Cilicia, the necessity for irrigation was not so great as in regions less blessed. Still there were seasons of the year when water would greatly add to the fertility of the land, and it seemed a pity that greater enterprise was not shown in this respect. It was generally agreed that pumps, of which numbers had recently come into use, were more practical than canalization, owing to the nearness of the water to the surface of the ground. As the utility of pumps became more generally recognized, it was probable that there would be much increase in their number, especially in the smaller kind that costed about a couple of liras.[48]

In Adana sunburned bricks were used in the construction of the buildings. The wooden buildings were two story and some three story with flat roofs, which were used as sleeping quarters in the summer by those who stayed in the city. Many of the Armenians went in for well-built cut stone houses, which were finished and even elegant in appearance. Summer lasted from the end of April to the middle or end of October and was intensely hot, as much as forty-five degrees centigrades being sometimes registered in the shade. April and November, separating seasons of inevitable discomfort, were the pleasant months of the year; and they resembled each other in a manner which was perhaps not often to be noticed in other localities. The wonderful verdure of November following close upon half a year of blazing sun was the more remarkable.

The group of administration buildings fronted on the Seyhan river and enclosed a courtyard covering 160,000 square meters. Two walled gateways, one facing the river and the other opposite, led under the buildings and admitted to the grounds.[49]

DEMOGRAPHY OF ADANA

There was a preponderant Turkish majority in the province of Adana. This majority was not the result of any war or the extermination of Armenians, or of the alteration of statistics. The population was emphatically Turkish.

The reports of British officials were not confined solely to the natural resources of Cilicia. Comparable information was supplied about the demography of the region. Lieutenant Herbert Chermside believed on June 25, 1879, that the population of the Adana province was 240,000. According to him, the rural population was almost exclusively Muslim, with the exception of five Greek villages near Silifke, one near Mersin, and the Armenian population of Kozan, and in the neighborhood of Hacin, in all thirty-five thousand Armenians and ten thousand Greeks.[50] In 1891 Admiral Woods, of the Ottoman navy, in a table of the populations of the Asia Minor gave the population of the Adana province as 378,698, of which 31,876 were Armenians.[51]

The last Ottoman census taken by the Directorate General for the Administration of Population Records of the Ministry of the Interior before the outbreak of the First World War indicates that 50,139 Armenians were living in the province of Adana, whose total population as of March 14, 1914,[52] was 411,023.[53] The Ottoman population figures are corroborated by Thomas Davidson Christie, president of St. Paul's College at Tarsus, who lived and worked in the region for more than twenty-five years and spoke Turkish and Armenian fluently. He wrote that there were about fifty thousand Armenians in the province of Adana, and that at least four-fifths of the population of that administrative division were Turks.[54]

Christie was a scholar and a linguist, and his ability received recognition when New York University conferred on him the degree of doctor of divinity in 1893 and Aberdeen University that of doctor of linguistics in 1904. His missionary interest was by no means confined to education; he was very fond of itinerating in the towns and villages and had the love and confidence of all classes of the people.[55]

Yale University professor David Magie, in his study of the population of Asiatic Turkey at the outbreak of the First World War, estimated the total population of the province of Adana at 520,000 of which seventy-five thousand were Armenians. He based his calculations mainly on the report for the year 1891 of the British consul in Mersin, which stated that Muslims constituted 328,760 souls among a population of 371,171.[56]

According to the 1912 figures of the Armenian Patriarchate of İstanbul, there were 407,000 Armenians living in Cilicia, constituting 43.4 percent of the total population,[57] but this number for the Armenians is clearly excessive. It should be remembered that the census figures arrived at in 1912 by the patriarchate were based on the estimate of the Armenian population on the civil status registers as regards births, deaths, and marriages. In these figures there was a wide margin of error and uncertainty. The patriarchate's figures were thus riddled with discrepancies and inconsistencies. It is noteworthy that on the grounds that they had owned Cilicia for centuries, constituted the ruling element there after the end of the Crusades and acted as the sovereigns of the region since 1516, Turks were in a better position in 1914 for having more accurate demographical figures than the patriarchate in 1912. The patriarchate's figures concerning the Armenian population of Cilicia should therefore be treated with much reserve. These estimates could expect little credence, given the absence of a census conducted according to modern techniques.[58]

When analyzing the figures presented by the patriarchate, Justin McCarthy, professor of Middle Eastern history and demographer at the University of Louisville, makes several interesting points, some of which raise other questions. He notes that the figures are round, which is never true of exact figures. He indicates that no specific rules from the patriarchate for collection of birth, death, and marriage records have been discovered; no Armenian parish records have come to light; and the patriarchate figures were not compiled on the basis of baptismal records.[59] McCarthy is a pioneer in the demographic study of the Ottoman Empire, the Caucasus, the Balkans, Russia, and Palestine.[60]

NOTES

1. For the background, see Enver Ziya Karal, *Osmanlı Tarihi* (Ottoman History), Vol. 8: *Birinci Meşrutiyet ve İstibdat Devirleri 1876–1907* (Periods of First Constitutionalism and Despotism 1876–1907) (Ankara: Türk Tarih Kurumu Basımevi, reprinted, 1995). I owe an immense amount to the richly detailed and comprehensive chapters of this splendid series.

2. "The Economic Future of the Near East," The Editorial, *The Near East*, as cited in "Turkey's Resources," *The Orient*, Vol. 4, No. 15 (April 9, 1913), p. 4.

3. Geoffrey Parker, *Geopolitics. Past, Present and Future* (London: Pinter, 1998) is a brief, fair survey of geopolitics and G. O. Tuathail, S. Dalby, and P. Routledge, *The Geopolitics Reader* (London: Routledge, 1998) is a useful introduction to key texts. Also D. Hooson, ed., *Geography and National Identity* (Oxford: Blackwell, 1994); P. J. Taylor, *Political Geography. World-Economy, Nation-State and Locality* (Harlow: Longman, 1989); and Bernard Loo, "Geography and Strategic Stability," *The Journal of Strategic Studies*, Vol. 26, No. 1 (March 2003), pp. 156–57.

4. Though hardly definitive, the most useful summary of the history of the Adana plain is Kasım Ener, *Tarih Boyunca Adana Ovasına (Çukurova'ya) Bir Bakış* (A Glance at the Adana Plain [Cilicia] Throughout History) (Adana: Bugün Matbaası, 1955). Also Türkiye Cumhuriyeti Genelkurmay Askeri Tarih ve Stratejik Etüt Başkanlığı Arşivi (Archive of the Turkish General Staff Directorate of Military History and Strategic Studies), Ankara (henceforth referred to as ATASE), Birinci Dünya Harbi Koleksiyonu (Collection of the First World War) (henceforth referred to BDHK), Headquarters of the Chief Command Third Division, Administrative and Miscellaneous Matters. Supply: Correspondence relating to Adana-Baghdad Railway, Box: 957, File: 1267, September 5, 1914–March 30, 1918; Foreign Office

Papers, The National Archives, Kew, London (henceforth referred to as FO) 371 R14745/177/44. Report on the District of Iskenderun compiled by Acting Consul General E. H. Peck and Lieutenant Commander J. D. Wylson, Consular Shipping Adviser, August 24, 1945; Georges Tsapalos et Pierre Walter, *Rapport sur le domaine imperial de Tchoucour-Ova (Vilayet d'Adana, Turquie d'Asie)* (Paris: Imp. L'Union Typographie, 1911–1912), p. 7; James Gidney, *A Mandate for Armenia* (Oberlin, OH: Kent State University Press, 1967), pp. 4–5.

5. ATASE, BDHK, Headquarters of the Chief Command First Division. Fourth Army Command, Operations: İskenderun Coast, Box: 175, File: 753, September 15, 1917–November 27, 1917; War Office Papers, The National Archives, Kew, London, 157/689. Notes on Alexandretta Supplied by Joseph Catoni and Samuel H. Kennedy, January 20, 1915; FO 371 R14745/177/44. Report on the District of Iskenderun compiled by Acting Consul General E. H. Peck and Lieutenant Commander J. D. Wylson, Consular Shipping Adviser, August 24, 1945.

6. "Alexandretta," *Levant Trade Review*, Vol. 6, No. 1 (June 1916), p. 90. *Levant Trade Review*, published in İstanbul partly in English and partly in French, was the organ of the American Chamber of Commerce for the Levant. This Chamber, started in 1911 through the instrumentality of the American consul general at İstanbul, Gabriel Bie Ravndal, strove to increase the volume of trade between America and the Near East.

7. Simonyan, *The Destruction of Armenians in Cilicia, April 1909*, p. 13. See also Niyazi Ramazanoğlu, *La Province d'Adana Aperçu Historique, Ethnographique et Statistique* (İstanbul: Société Anonyme de Papeterie et d'Imprimerie, 1920), p. 3; Bilge Umar, *Kilikia Bir Tarihsel Coğrafya Araştırması ve Gezi Rehberi* (Cilicia: A Historical Geography Research and Travel Guide) (İstanbul: İnkılap Kitabevi, 2000), pp. 2–3; Albrecht Goetze, "Cilicians," *Journal of Cuneiform Studies*, Vol. 16, No. 2 (1962), pp. 48–58.

8. William Burckhardt Barker, *Lares and Penates: Or Cilicia and Its Governors* (London: Ingram, Cooke, and Co., 1853), p. 14.

9. A sanjak is an Ottoman administrative unit meaning "county" or "subdistrict." It was the principal administrative subdivision of a province.

10. ATASE, BDHK, Headquarters of the Chief Command First Division, Miscellaneous Matters. Individual Reports and the Map of Anatolia, Box: 18, File: 89, April 16, 1915–March 6, 1915.

11. Tuncer Baykara, *Anadolu'nun Tarihi Coğrafyasına Giriş I Anadolu'nun İdari Taksimatı* (Introduction to the Historical Geography of Anatolia I: Administrative Division of Anatolia) (Ankara: Türk Kültürünü Araştırma Enstitüsü, 2000); Besim Atalay, *Maraş: Tarihi ve Coğrafyası* (Maraş: Its History and Geography) (İstanbul: Dizerkonca Matbaası, reprinted, 1973), p. 187; Ahmet Eyicil, "Maraş ve Zeytun Ermenileri" (Armenians of Maraş and Zeytun), in *Ermeni Araştırmaları 2. Türkiye Kongresi Bildirileri* (Communications of the Second Turkish Congress of Armenian Studies), Vol. 1 (Ankara: Avrasya Stratejik Araştırmalar Merkezi Ermeni Araştırmaları Merkezi, 2007), p. 319.

12. Umar, *Kilikia*, pp. 1–2; Vahé Tachjian, *La France en Cilicie et en Haute-Mésopotamie: Aux confins de la Turquie, de la Syrie et de l'Irak, 1919–1933* (Paris: Karthala, 2004), p. 37.

13. Eren Özalay, "Adana ve Çevresi Toplumsal ve Ekonomik Tarihi Konferansı" (Social and Economic History Conference on Adana and Its Vicinity), *Toplumsal Tarih*, No. 180 (December 2008), p. 9; Ahmet Ünal and Serdar Girginer, *Kilikya-Çukurova: İlk Çağlardan Osmanlı Dönemine Kadar Kilikya'da Tarihi Coğrafya, Tarih ve Arkeoloji* (Cilicia-Çukurova: Historical Geography, History and Archaelogy in Cilicia From the Early Ages to the Ottoman Era) (İstanbul: Homer Kitabevi, 2007), p. 16.

14. Cezmi Yurtsever, *Ermeni Terör Merkezi: Kilikya Kilisesi* (Center of Armenian Terror: Church of Cilicia) (İstanbul: Alper Yayınları, 1983).

15. See Clive Foss, "Armenian History As Seen By Twentieth Century Turkish Historians," *The Armenian Review*, Vol. 45, No. 1–2 (Spring–Summer 1992), pp. 42–43.

16. United States National Archives and Records Administration, College Park, Maryland (henceforth referred to as USNA), Inquiry Documents: Special Reports and Studies, 1917–1919, Document 85, Report on the Vilayet of Adana, O. J. Campbell, pp. 1–2. The Inquiry Documents have been reproduced in forty-seven reels of microfilm. In 1980, these reports were classified under the heading of "Special Reports and Studies, 1917–1919." These documents are of vital interest to scholars although usually there are no new major startling revelations.

17. Ibid., p. 3.

18. The principal account is Ahmed Cevdet Paşa, Cavid Baysun, ed., *Tezakir 21–29* (Communications 21–29) (Ankara: Türk Tarih Kurumu Basımevi, second edition, 1986), pp. 107–240. See also Faruk Sümer, "Çukurova Tarihine Dair Araştırmalar (Fetihten Onaltıncı Yüzyılın İkinci Yarısına Kadar)" (Research on the History of Cilicia [From the Conquest to the Second Half of the Sixteenth Century]), *Tarih Araştırmaları Dergisi*, Vol. 1, No. 1 (1963), pp. 1–19; Yusuf Halaçoğlu, *Onsekizinci Yüzyılda Osmanlı İmparatorluğunun İskan Siyaseti ve Aşiretlerin Yerleştirilmesi* (The Resettlement Policy of the Ottoman Empire and the Placement of the Tribes in the Eighteenth Century) (Ankara: Türk Tarih Kurumu Basımevi, 1988), pp. 132–35; Bekir Sami Bayazıt, *1865–1866 Kürtdağı, Cebeli Bereket Kozanoğulları İsyanı ve Güneydeki Aşiretlerin İskanları* (The Revolt of the Kozanoğlu Tribe of Kürtdağı and Cebeli Bereket in 1865–1866 and the Resettlement of the Tribes in the South) (Antakya: Kültür Eğitim Tesisleri, 1989), pp. 64–172; Ahmet Gökbel, *Anadolu'da Varsak Türkmenleri* (Varsak Turkomans in Anatolia) (Ankara: Atatürk Kültür Merkezi Yayınları, 2007), pp. 65–79.

19. ATASE, BDHK, Adana Supply Inspectorate of the Fourth Army First Division. Operations: Provincial Administrative Units, Box: 3321, File: 269, April 1, 1918–September 19, 1918.

20. For more on the province of Adana in the nineteenth and early part of the twentieth centuries, see William Burckhard Barker, *The Birth Land of St. Paul, Cilicia: Its Former History and Present State* (London and Glasgow: Richard Griffin and Company, 1853); Léonce Alishan, *Sissouan ou L'Arméno-Cilicie: Description Géographique et Histoire* (Venice: S. Lazare, 1899); Ramazanoğlu, *La Province d'Adana*; Meltem Toksöz and Emre Yalçın, "Modern Adana'nın Doğuşu ve Günümüzdeki İzleri" (The Birth of Modern Adana and Its Present-Day Traces), in Çiğdem Kafesçioğlu and Lucienne Thys-Şenocak, eds., *Essays in Honor of Aptullah Kuran*

(İstanbul: Yapı Kredi Yayınları, 1999); Meltem Toksöz, *Nomads, Migrants and Cotton in the Eastern Mediterranean: The Making of the Adana-Mersin Region 1850-1908* (Leiden and Boston, MA: E. J. Brill, 2010); Fraser, *The Short Cut to India*; Tsapalos et Walter, *Rapport sur le domaine imperial de Tchoucour-Ova (Vilayet d'Adana, Turquie d'Asie)*; Pierre Redan (pseudonym of Pierre-Jean Daniel André), *La Cilicie et le problème ottoman* (Paris: Gauthier-Villars, 1921); Tachjian, *La France en Cilicie et en Haute-Mésopotamie*. They offer valuable framework for further study.

21. Tülin Selvi Ünlü and Tolga Ünlü, eds., *İstasyon'dan Fener'e Mersin* (Mersin: From the Railway Station to the Lighthouse) (Mersin: Mersin Ticaret ve Sanayi Odası Yayınları, 2009).

22. Edward Nathan, "Aerial Cargo Railway at Turkish Port," *Levant Trade Review*, Vol. 2, No. 3 (December 1912), p. 240.

23. Süha Göney, *Adana Ovaları I* (The Plains of Adana I) (İstanbul: İstanbul Üniversitesi Coğrafya Enstitüsü Yayınları, 1976), pp. 60–66; Fraser, *The Short Cut to India*, pp. 74–75.

24. Göney, *Adana Ovaları I*, pp. 50–56; Vital Cuinet, *La Turquie d'Asie: géographie administrative, statistique descriptive et raisonnée de chaque province de l'Asie Mineure*, Vol. 2: *Les Provinces Arabes: Alep, Mossoul, Bagdad, Bassorah* (Paris: Ernest Leroux, 1890–1895), p. 1.

25. Yılmaz Kurt, *Çukurova Tarihinin Kaynakları I: 1525 Tarihli Adana Sancağı Mufassal Tahrir Defteri* (Sources of Cilician History I: Detailed Tax Register of the Sanjak of Adana Dated 1525) (Ankara: Türk Tarih Kurumu Basımevi, 2004), p. xix. This tome contains a rich mine of source material. Yılmaz Kurt, an expert archivist, has drawn on little-used Ottoman documents.

26. René Pinon, "Préface," in Redan, *La Cilicie et le problème ottoman*, p. vi.

27. See, for instance, ATASE, BDHK, Amanus Supply Line of the Fourth Army. Supply: Location Maps and Transport Reports, Box: 3315, File: 235, May 9, 1917–April 20, 1918.

28. William Nesbitt Chambers, "The Possibilities of Adana and the Cilician Plain," *Levant Trade Review*, Vol. 4, No. 2 (September 1914), p. 148.

29. M. Barré de Lancy, "Mersine et la province d'Adana," *Revue Technique d'Orient*, No. 19 (mars 1912), p. 16; F. Garelli, "Lettre d'Alexandrette," *Revue Commerciale du Levant*, No. 250 (31 janvier 1908), pp. 789–90; İbnüzziya Ahmed Reşit, "Memleketimizde Ecnebi Postahaneleri" (Foreign Post Offices in Our Country), *İstişare*, No. 16 (1908), pp. 721–28; Nesimi Yazıcı, "Osmanlı İmparatorluğunda Yabancı Postalar ve Atatürk Türkiye'sinde Postacılık" (Foreign Mail Posts in the Ottoman Empire and Postal Services in Atatürk's Turkey), *İletişim*, No. 3 (1981), pp. 137–79; Salih Kuyaş, "Posta Tarihi ve Kapitülasyon Postahaneleri I" (History of Postal Services and the Post Offices of the Capitulations I), *Tarih ve Toplum*, No. 1 (1984), pp. 49–83.

30. FO 424/85. Revenue of the Adana Province. Lieutenant Herbert Chermside (Nergizlik) to Patrick Henderson (Aleppo), June 25, 1879.

31. FO 424/132. Richness of the Cilician Soil. Lieutenant Colonel Sir Charles Wilson (Adana) to Earl of Dufferin (Istanbul), December 31, 1881.

32. Billings, "The Causes of the Outbreak in Cilicia, Asia Minor, April, 1909," pp. 23–24.

33. "Adana A Large Province," *The Boston Daily Globe*, April 20, 1909, pp. 1 and 6.

34. Fraser, *The Short Cut to India*, pp. 76–77.

35. Stephan Astourian, "Testing World-System Theory, Cilicia (1830–1890): Armenian-Turkish Polarization and the Ideology of Modern Historiography," doctoral dissertation, University of California at Los Angeles, 1996, pp. 166 and 524. The thesis of Stephan Astourian unfortunately remains unpublished. Also Charles Woods, *The Danger Zone of Europe: Changes and Problems in the Near East* (London: T. Fisher Unwin, 1911), p. 128; Sahara, *What Happened in Adana in April 1909?* pp. 51–52.

36. Billings, "The Causes of the Outbreak in Cilicia, Asia Minor, April, 1909," p. 28; Simonyan, *The Destruction of Armenians in Cilicia, April 1909*, p. 40.

37. Ottoman money had the advantage of being on the decimal system, with modifications. The standard coin of those days was the lira, a gold piece worth 4.40 United States dollars, or 18 British shillings and 2 pennies. This was divided into 100 piaster or kuruş, and the kuruş was equal to 40 paras. When accounts were kept in any wholesale way, it was almost invariably in gold currency.

38. Fraser, *The Short Cut to India*, pp. 77–78.

39. Billings, "The Causes of the Outbreak in Cilicia, Asia Minor, April, 1909," p. 28; Simonyan, *The Destruction of Armenians in Cilicia, April 1909*, p. 40.

40. Astourian, "Testing World-System Theory, Cilicia (1830–1890)," pp. 166 and 524; Woods, *The Danger Zone of Europe*, p. 128; Sahara, *What Happened in Adana in April 1909?* pp. 51–52.

41. Fraser, *The Short Cut to India*, p. 78.

42. Ibid., pp. 78–79.

43. Göney, *Adana Ovaları I*, pp. 24–49; Fraser, *The Short Cut to India*, p. 79.

44. F. D. Shepard, "Undeveloped Resources of Northern Syria," *Levant Trade Review*, Vol. 5, No. 2 (September 1915), pp. 199–200.

45. Lorenzo Manachy, "Report from Aleppo," *Levant Trade Review*, Vol. 1, No. 3 (December 1911), pp. 292–93.

46. ABCFM Papers, Houghton Library, Harvard University. Unit 5 (16.9.5) Reel 672. Vol. 26 Central Turkey Mission 1910–1919 Letters N-W ABC 16: The Near East 1817–1919. Letter from Francis Leslie to James Barton, Boston, Massachusetts, November 26, 1911, Aintab.

47. Fraser, *The Short Cut to India*, pp. 81–82.

48. Ibid., pp. 82–83.

49. Damar Arıkoğlu, *Hatıralarım Milli Mücadele, Çukurova'da Fransız İşgali ve Kanlı Savaşlar, Birinci Büyük Millet Meclisi, Yurtta Çeşitli İsyanlar, Yunanlıların Denize Dökülmesi, Atatürk'ten Hatıralar, Resimler Vesikalar* (My Reminiscences: The National Struggle, The French Occupation of Cilicia and the Bloody Battles, The First Term of the Grand National Assembly, Various Revolts in the Country, Pushing the Greeks into the Sea, Recollections from Atatürk, Pictures Documents) (İstanbul: Tan Gazetesi ve Matbaası, 1961), p. 39. The memoirs themselves are familiar to any

specialist in the period. Damar Arıkoğlu was well placed to write about major developments and personalities during the reigns of Sultans Reşat and Vahdettin and the leadership of President Kemal Atatürk.

50. FO 424/85. On the Province of Adana. Lieutenant Herbert Chermside (Nergizlik) to Patrick Henderson (Aleppo), June 25, 1879.

51. FO 424/169. On the Province of Adana. Thomas Jago (Aleppo) to the Marquis of Salisbury (FO), April 18, 1891.

52. All dates are given according to the Gregorian calendar. The lunar calendar, in use in the Ottoman Empire, was thirteen days behind.

53. Kemal Karpat, *Ottoman Population, 1830–1914: Demographic and Social Characteristics* (Madison, WI: University of Wisconsin Press, 1982), pp. 188–89. This volume is a detailed study that will have permanent value as a book of reference. It will serve as a stimulating and challenging model for further research in the field. See also *Tableaux Indiquant le Nombre de Divers Eléments de la Population dans l'Empire Ottoman au 1er Mars 1330* (İstanbul: Imprimerie Osmanié, 1919).

54. USNA, Inquiry Documents: Special Reports and Studies, 1917–1919, Document 97, Turkish Survey, Adana, Thomas Davidson Christie, p. 2.

55. On veteran Thomas Davidson Christie, see ABCFM, Evangelistic Work Personal Matter, Announcement by Fred Field Goodsell About the Life's Journey and Dead of Thomas Davidson Christie, 1921; James Harbord, "Mustapha Kemal Pasha and His Party," *The World's Work*, Vol. 15 (May 1920–October 1920), p. 191.

56. USNA, Inquiry Documents: Special Reports and Studies, 1917–1919, Document 1005, The Population of Asiatic Turkey at the Outbreak of the War, David Magie.

57. Shavarsh Toriguian, *The Armenian Question and International Law* (Beirut: Hamaskaine Press, 1973), p. 135.

58. The Armenian Patriarch of İstanbul's statistics are reproduced in Justin McCarthy, *The Arab World, Turkey and the Balkans (1878–1914): A Handbook of Historical Statistics* (Boston, MA: G.K. Hall and Company, 1982). Particularly instructive is a comparison of the 1914 population figures given by the patriarchate (pp. 90–93) with the equivalent Ottoman count (pp. 64–83) for the same provinces and districts. On the accuracy of Ottoman census counts see, Stanford Shaw, "The Ottoman Census System and Population, 1831–1914," *International Journal of Middle East Studies*, Vol. 9, No. 3 (October 1978), pp. 325–38; idem, "Ottoman Population Movements During the Last Years of the Empire, 1885–1914," *Journal of Ottoman Studies*, Vol. 1, No. 1 (1980), pp. 191–205; Kemal Karpat, "Ottoman Population Records and the Census of 1881/82–1893," *International Journal of Middle East Studies*, Vol. 9, No. 2 (May 1978), pp. 237–74; Servet Mutlu, "Late Ottoman Population and Its Ethnic Distribution," *Turkish Journal of Population Studies*, Vol. 25 (2003), pp. 3–41.

59. Justin McCarthy, *Muslims and Minorities: The Population of Ottoman Anatolia and the End of the Empire* (New York: New York University Press, 1983).

60. Howard Reed, "Perspectives on the Evolution of Turkish Studies in North America Since 1946," *The Middle East Journal*, Vol. 51, No. 1 (Winter 1997), p. 26.

Chapter Two

Position of Armenians in Adana at the Turn of the Twentieth Century

Although dispersed throughout the Near East, Armenians wherever they were living considered their homeland to be eastern Anatolia and, to a lesser degree, Cilicia. This became an important issue as the Armenian nationalist movement began to develop in the latter half of the nineteenth century.[1]

CREATION OF AN ARMENIAN PRINCIPALITY IN CILICIA, THE HUNTCHAK COMMITTEE, AND THE OCCURRENCE OF SASSOUN TROUBLES

According to George Bournoutian, a professor of eastern European and Middle Eastern history at Iona College in New Rochelle, New York, the Cilician period, culminating in the establishment of a new Armenian kingdom in 1199, represents a unique chapter in the history of the Armenian people. He argues that for the first time Armenians created an independent state in lands outside their historic homeland. It is also the first time that Armenians were in a region with direct access to the sea and came into close contact with the emerging nations in western Europe and the Roman Catholic Church. Surrounded by three mountain chains, Cilicia offered a secure enclave, as the narrow mountain passes were easily defended against invaders. The coastline and the navigable rivers, as well as a number of trade centers, Bournoutian contends, made the region ideal for those Armenians who were forced to leave eastern Anatolia in the eleventh century.[2]

Adana was a spiritual and economic center for Armenians in Asia Minor. Sis housed the seat of the Catholicosate of the Great House of Cilicia and the monastery of St. Sophia. The central rallying point for all Armenians was their church, and this ancient heritage to them was preserved intact by the Ottoman system of government. The Armenian Church came to define ethnic identity. It presided over the Armenian nation in the Ottoman Empire. The deputy of Adana, Ali Münif (Yeğena), highlights this fact in his memoirs in order to demonstrate the importance of Adana for Armenians and the ways in which the Church became a center of revolutionary activities for the Armenian committees. In addition, he mentions that during a congress of Gregorian Armenians, who had gathered in Paris in 1905, a decision was taken to establish Cilicia as an independent entity.[3] Yeğena, by previous knowledge of circumstances and persons, was able to discern the validity of reports and to determine whether false information was being given to him for the purpose of misleading or misinforming. French historian Gaston Gaillard agrees with Yeğena and states that as early as 1905 the Armenian committees had decided at a congress held in Paris to resort to all means in order to make Cilicia an independent country.[4]

Yeğena played a prominent role during the Second Constitutional Period and the Republic. After graduating from the College of Administrative Sciences at İstanbul in 1896, he and other members of his class vowed to support the constitutional movement in whichever province they were posted. In June 1908, he was in Macedonia when the Young Turk[5] insurrection broke out; he supported it secretly even though he was an official in the Hamidian bureaucracy and not a member of the CUP. During this period, he became acquainted with the Unionist (as members of the CUP were called) leadership who understood his value to the movement. Yeğena was member of the Ottoman Chamber of Deputies for Adana in 1908–1910. He was born there and had local roots. He was elected deputy for Aleppo in 1918–1919. After serving as mayor of Adana in 1922–1926, he became deputy for Mersin in 1927–1931, for Adana in 1931–1935, and for Seyhan between 1935 and 1950 in the Turkish Grand National Assembly (TGNA). He also acted as minister of public works in 1917 and 1918. It is important to note that the lack of attention to Yeğena does not stem from a paucity of source materials.[6]

Committees with charitable or economic purposes such as "The Association of Kindness" and "The Association of Benevolence," which were started in 1860 with a large capital to develop the natural resources of Cilicia, played a part in the Armenian movement. Risings, which may be traced back to 1545 and lasted until the relocation in 1915, were continually taking place in the mountainous area of Zeytun, about fifty kilometers northwest of Maraş. The town of Zeytun was built, one house above another, the flat mud roof of one house often serving as the dooryard of the next one above, upon the steep sides of a promontory. The houses were built of wood, and a torch applied to one in the lower tier would burn them all like a box of kindling. The place was commanded from the nearby hills on three sides, its only military advantage being its inaccessibility because of the bad mountain trails.[7] Rebellions were partly brought about by the feudal system of administration still prevailing in that region. Each of the four districts of Zeytun was governed by a chief who had assumed the title of "ishehan" or prince, a kind of nobleman to whom Turkish villages had to pay some taxes collected by special agents. The action of the revolutionary committees, of course, benefited by that state of things, to which the Ottoman government put an end only in 1895. The Armenians had already refused to pay the taxes and had rebelled repeatedly between 1782 and 1851, at which time the Turks, incensed at the looting and exactions of the Armenian mountaineers, left their farms and emigrated. But the leaders of the Armenian movement soon took advantage of these continual disturbances and quickly gave them another character. The movement was spurred on and eagerly supported by Armenians living abroad, and in 1865, after the so-called Turkish exactions, the Nationalist committees openly rebelled against the government and demanded the independence of Zeytun. Henceforth rebellion followed rebellion, and one of them, fomented by the Huntchak Committee, lasted three months in 1896. On this occasion a force of Armenians took the offensive and they defeated an Ottoman force in battle, ejected the Ottoman garrison from the citadel of Zeytun, captured four hundred Ottoman prisoners, and changing into Ottoman uniforms, looted and burned a neighborly Turkish town, thus obtaining a wide measure of control over the area. The Ottomans finally advanced with a large force on Zeytun, bombarding its citadel after the Armenians had evacuated it and setting it on fire. There is no evidence which justifies in describing these proceedings as excesses committed by the Ottoman soldiery. Meanwhile the Armenian community in İstanbul had appealed for mediation by the foreign ambassadors, and it was agreed with the authorities that all in the area should surrender their arms, with a view to an amnesty.[8]

The Huntchak Committee was founded in 1887, in Tiflis, by three Armenians—Rupen Kambour, Nishan Magavourian, and Hamayak Rooshbazian. Its first object was the publication of a newspaper of the same name, which, after appearing successively in Tiflis, Geneva, and Athens, was finally edited and printed in London. The same Huntchak press also flooded Europe and the Ottoman Empire with nihilistic literature of the most advanced school, of which the following may serve as a specimen (it is taken from the work of Viscomte des Coursous, who extracted it from the archives of the Court of Appeal at İstanbul):

> Before all else we are anarchists, with a fixed object as our program. We purpose bringing about anarchy in Anatolia, this is our essential aim. To attain it we have resolved to establish a national independent government there, and to stir up disturbances forthwith, with a view to obtaining wider political liberties.

The Statutes of the Committee also threw much light on the events of the time. Article 6 said: "The Committee shall name a chief spy chosen from among its members. This chief spy should either be in Government employ or else in close relations with an Armenian civil servant, so as to be in a position to reveal to the Committee the secrets and intentions of the Porte. He should be brave and discreet, and should have under his orders a brigade of ten men to warn the Committee of all danger. These secret agents should penetrate everywhere under various disguises. The Committee will only know their chief." Article 8 provided: "The Committee shall have a Chief Executioner, under whose orders shall be a detachment of aides. Their duty shall be to execute any whom the Committee shall order or designate as noxious. There are three degrees of punishment—reprimand, bastinado, and death. The sentence of death may be carried out by the knife or revolver, by strangulation or by poison. To blow up buildings three materials are to be used—dynamite, bombs, nitro-glycerine, or fire balls containing powder."[9]

The constitution of the Huntchak Committee goes on to provide in detail for the carrying out of its program, the attacking of mosques and barracks, the assaulting of governors and other government officials, resistance to tax collectors, forcible delivery of prisoners, and a mass of other revolutionary acts. In 1897 according to this committee, the only way of achieving political independence was by a revolutionary movement completely overthrowing the present form of administration in Ottoman Armenia and encouraging the people to rebel against the Ottoman government. The following means were to be employed: (1) Propaganda in order to disseminate Huntchak revolutionary ideas, particularly among the working classes, by means of books, newspapers, talks, and lectures, and to set up revolutionary organizations and action squads. (2) Terror in order to employ punitive terrorist tactics against Ottoman administrators, agents, informers, and traitors. Terror was to be used as a weapon defending the revolutionary organization and protecting the people against oppressors and corrupt administrators. (3) Organization of vigilante groups in order to hold in readiness a military force to protect the people from government troops and the attacks of savage tribes. In the case of a general revolt these bands would play a leading role. (4) General revolutionary organization in order to form a large number of revolutionary groups acting in close collaboration, with the same goals and objectives, employing the same tactics and organized from the same center. The strength and powers of all the various sections of the organization in Ottoman Armenia were set forth in the special statute listing the organization and activities of the Huntchak revolutionary party. (5) The organization of revolutionary squads. (6) The outbreak of war between the Ottoman Empire and any other country was the most opportune moment for the beginning of a general revolution.[10]

The man who gave the most explicit and true account of the Armenian revolutionary movement was Cyrus Hamlin, for many years identified with American missionary enterprise in the Ottoman Empire, and founder and first president of the Robert College at İstanbul. Few Americans at the time had acquired so scholarly a use of the Turkish language as had Hamlin.[11] On December 23, 1893, he published in *The Congregationalist* a truly prophetic statement, the perusal of which is absolutely necessary for an impartial understanding of the case. It deserves, for this reason, to be quoted at length:

> A very intelligent Armenian gentleman, who speaks fluently and correctly English as well as Armenian, and is an eloquent defender of the revolution, assured me that they have the strongest hopes of preparing the way for Russia's entrance into Asia Minor to take possession. In answer to the question as to how, he replied: "These Huntchaguist bands, organized all over the empire, will watch their opportunities to kill Turks and Kurds, set fire to their villages, and then make their escape into the mountains. The enraged Moslems will then rise and fall upon the defenseless Armenians, and slaughter them with such barbarities that Russia will enter, in the name of humanity and Christian civilization, and take possession." When I denounced the scheme as atrocious and infernal beyond anything ever known, he calmly replied: "It appears so to you, no doubt, but we Armenians are determined to be free. Europe listened to the Bulgarian horrors, and made Bulgaria free. She will listen to our cry when it goes up in the shrieks and blood of millions of women and children." I urged in vain that this scheme would make the very name of Armenian hateful among all civilized people. He replied: "We are desperate; we shall do it." "But your people do not want Russian protection. They prefer Turkey,[12] bad as she is. There are hundreds of miles of conterminous territory into which emigration is easy at all times. It has been so for all the centuries of Moslem rule. If your people preferred the Russian Government, there would not now be an Armenian family in Turkey." "Yes," he replied, "and for such stupidity they will have to suffer." I have had conversations with others who avow the same things, but no one acknowledges that he is a member of the party. Falsehood is, of course, justifiable where murder and arson are. In Turkey the party aims to excite the Turks against Protestant missionaries and against Protestant Armenians. All the troubles at Marsovan originated in their movements. They are cunning, unprincipled, and cruel. They terrorize their own people by demanding contributions of money under threats of assassinations—a threat which has often been put into execution. I have made the mildest possible disclosure of only a few of the abominations of this Huntchaguist revolutionary party. It is of Russian origin; Russian gold and craft govern it. Let all missionaries, home and foreign, denounce it. Let all Protestant Armenians everywhere boldly denounce it. It is trying to enter every Sunday school and deceive and pervert the innocent and ignorant into supporters of this craft. We must, therefore, be careful that in befriending Armenians we do nothing that can be construed into an approval of this movement, which all should

abhor. While yet we recognize the probability that some Armenians in this country, ignorant of the real object and cruel designs of the Huntchaguists, are led by their patriotism to join with them, and while we sympathize with the sufferings of the Armenians at home, we must stand aloof from any such desperate attempts, which contemplate the destruction of Protestant missions, churches, schools, and Bible work, involving all in a common ruin that is diligently and craftily sought. Let all home and foreign missionaries beware of any alliance with, or countenance of, the Huntchaguists.[13]

This statement is significant. One does not really know whether Cyrus Hamlin was considered to be a prophet in the United States, but his prophetic faculties as far as the last Armenian revolt was concerned were not denied in the Ottoman Empire. They were simply marvelous; for, months before the occurrence of the Sassoun troubles, Hamlin had exactly and minutely shown what they would be.

In the British House of Commons during the debates held on March 3, 1896, Sir Ellis Ashmead-Bartlett, in response to a speech by Sir John Kennaway, said that he wished to protest against the language which had been used, to some extent in the House and to a greater extent in the country, with regard to the Sultan and the Ottoman government. He stated that the language of the most offensive character had been recklessly and without any real ground employed against the sovereign and the government of a friendly state, and that language was not only outrageous and unjustifiable, but it had had the most injurious effect on the cause which those who used such language espoused. Ashmead-Bartlett continued as follows. Kennaway and his friends seemed to think that they could revile the Turks and the Muslim religion to any extent without causing any resentment, but their abusive language was largely responsible for the terrible deeds which had lately occurred in Asia Minor. The so-called Sassoun atrocities were first heard in Britain fifteen months ago, and Kennaway and his friends denounced the Turks throughout Britain on the grounds of those atrocities, though they never dared to bring the question to an issue in the House of Commons. Now, when the question did come up, the sole basis of their charges was the atrocities which had occurred since October last. The House should note the disingenuosness of this conduct. The whole case against the Turks sent home with extravagant exaggeration by special correspondents had no reference to the events of the last four months, and the action of the Anglo-Armenian Committee was based entirely on the Sassoun massacres, which had practically no existence, at least in no proportion to the way in which they had been related in Britain. Column after column appeared in the London press of horrors unspeakable, which only existed in the imagination of the Armenian Committees on the Russian frontier. The Sassoun atrocities had been completely exploded by the Blue Books.[14] The statement that thirty thousand people had been massacred was reduced down to the fact that 265 people had lost their lives. The horrible stories of women and children being maltreated, as at the famous church at Galisau with its three hundred women, as the pits of death with their two hundred corpses, as the wives of Gyrgo and his comrades plunging themselves from a precipice, as the four children whose heads were described as cut off with one sweep of a Turkish scimitar—were one and all proved to be without foundation. The whole campaign founded on those sham atrocities was bogus atrocity-monger. It had gone on for ten months and had justly incensed the Turkish people against their maligners. Now, it should be noticed, the leaders of this campaign tried to mix up the series of events, and founded their charges on recent events only. The revolutionary conspiracies of the Armenian societies in the East, which were based on the fiendish designs of deliberately provoking these atrocities, were mainly responsible for the deplorable events of the last few months.[15]

Ashmead-Bartlett believed that Sir Philip Currie, the British ambassador to the Sublime Porte, had taken a part pris against the Ottoman Empire on this issue and had misled two governments to hopeless failure. The active and able Reuter's correspondent in the East, who was about the only correspondent who wrote the truth to Britain on the Armenian question, as long as March 1895 gave a most remarkable forecast of what since happened. Reuter's correspondent then wrote that the plan of the Armenian revolutionaries was to "provoke by the atrocities upon Mussulmans such cruelty, atrocity, outrage, and butchery that Christian humanity would rise in wrath. It will be the helpless women and children who will suffer most. The revolutionary leaders know that it will be so; in fact, they count upon it as the chief factor in their success." The same correspondent made the remarkable prediction seven months before the İstanbul riot of September 30, 1895, that the "chief attack will be made in the City of Constantinople itself, and that the brunt of the fighting will be borne by the Armenian residents therein." This wicked scheme was carried out at İstanbul, Bitlis, Diyarbekir, Trabzon, Harput, Karahisar, and other places with appalling results. There was plenty of evidence in the Blue Book to show that the Armenians were the first to provoke disturbance. The correspondent did not say the provocation justified the retaliation, but it must be remembered that all the cases of atrocities in Asia Minor during the last four months had been cases of mob violence. There had been no case proved in which Ottoman officers and officials had either helped or encouraged these atrocious events. He had seen statements that in certain places a portion of the soldiery took part in the plundering, but in many cases they found evidence given by the British consular authorities that the Ottoman Governors and Paşas and commanders did their best with such forces as they had to check mob violence. It must be remembered that in most places the forces at the disposal of the Ottoman authorities were very small.¹⁶

Ashmead-Bartlett said Kennaway denied there was any proof that the Armenian revolutionary societies had provoked outrages. The Blue Book teemed with proof. He asked: What happened at Trabzon before the massacre? And he gave the reply himself. The two Ottoman Paşas had been attacked and wounded seriously in the streets by Armenian conspirators. A private Ottoman citizen had been murdered by Armenians in the streets, and there was the additional statement that the rioting in Trabzon was actually begun by the firing of revolvers in the streets by excited Armenians. The conspirators, according to their usual methods, no doubt escaped punishment and left the bulk of the unfortunate, and, the Reuter's correspondent believed, perfectly harmless and helpless Armenian population to suffer for the revolutionary propaganda. On September 3, 1895, Ambassador Currie sent an extract from a private letter from Harput dated August 5, which Consul Robert Graves in Erzurum had received. In it it was stated:

> It appears that there are now in this place several Armenians belonging to the Hind-chagian Society, who are trying to organise revolutionary committees here and in the villages, and, as I understand, they have in a measure succeeded. They are inciting the people to violent action; since the liberation of political prisoners this party has become bolder, and they are making foolish demonstrations. They say they will attack the prison and liberate the six men still imprisoned, by force. Twice they went down to Mezré in procession in considerable numbers, and treated their Bishop very badly, when he advised them to disperse and not engage in so rash an undertaking. They were scattering papers here and there, threatening the lives of those whom they suspect of opposing them. Should they continue this reckless course, I am afraid of a serious result.

The serious result of this agitation was the deplorable massacre in which many people perished. On September 16, 1895, Consul H. Z. Longworth, at Trabzon, reported to Ambassador Currie that the procureur of Karahisar, his secretary, and his family, with two *zabtiyes* (gendarmes), were fired upon by a party of Armenians near Zara. One Turk was killed and a second wounded, and the party were robbed of £250. The Armenians then took the procureur off the road and sentenced him to death, and shot him there and then. Consul Graves added that "there is a band of well-armed Armenians around the city ready for business. The revolutionary Committee is making forced loans from wealthy Armenians, and the Armenian Archbishop has been obliged to pay £50 to save his head."¹⁷

There was also a deplorable *émeute* at Erzurum which caused the death of 280 Armenians. On September 15, 1895, Consul Graves, at Erzurum, telegraphed to Ambassador Currie that "Armenian revolutionary agents, belonging to the Hintchak and another society, are daily more active at Erzeroum, that they have threatened several Armenian notables with violence if they continue to sit on the Administrative Council, and have demanded money of them. These agents are mostly Russian Armenians, and they are now acting under orders emanating from a committee established in London." Armenian bankers and merchants were murdered by the Huntchak conspirators because they refused to be blackmailed; indeed, there was overwhelming evidence of the dangerous conspiracy on the part of Armenian revolutionary societies. Prince Lobanoff, the Russian high chancellor, had over and over again warned the British government that it was going mad upon this subject. Prince Lobanoff spoke with full knowledge of the subject and of the consequences: "This excitement, under which both Mohammedans and Armenians are labouring, is the net result of the uncompromising manner in which the Armenian Question has been taken up. England is chiefly responsible for this state of things, owing to the encouragement given to the Armenian Committees by so many of her leading men." And the British Chargé d'Affaires in St. Petersburg added: "Prince Lobanoff spoke very warmly on the subject." Sultan Abdülhamid II himself had warned the British government of the probable dangers of the course the agitators in Britain were pursuing.[18]

As to the provocation which the Ottomans received, Ashmead-Bartlett asked the House of Commons to remember what took place in İstanbul on September 30 to October 1, 1895. Two thousand Armenians assembled in İstanbul on September 30. They were mostly armed with revolvers. They made a violent march toward the Sublime Porte, and on their way they committed serious outrages against the Muslims they met. They were met by the police, the leader of whom most civilly asked them to disperse, and promised that if they would hand him their petition he would see the authorities received it. The police major was immediately shot dead by the Armenians, and there was considerable firing upon the Ottoman police. The police, of whom forty were killed and wounded, dispersed the party with only their swords and bayonets. Certain reprisals on the part of the Muslim *softas* (theological students) took place, and one hundred lives were lost. That was a deliberate attempt at civil war made by the Armenian revolutionary societies in the very heart of the Ottoman Empire. Ashmead-Bartlett wondered what would be the state of excitement in London if any sort of mob—Irish or German, for instance—were suddenly to rise and move to Whitehall, shooting down the chief of police and killing and wounding forty of his men? The report of the occurrence at İstanbul went like wildfire through Asia Minor, and reprisals were the result. The British ambassador at İstanbul did not attempt to deny the plots and evil deeds of the Armenian Huntchak Society. Yet in all his policy and his recommendations to the home government he acted as though no such body existed. Again, on October 2, 1895, Ambassador Currie addressed a very important dispatch to Marquess of Salisbury, the British foreign secretary, in which he stated:

> Unfortunately the demonstration had not the peaceful character attributed to it. The demonstrators were armed with pistols and arms of a uniform pattern. There is good reason to suppose that the object of the Hintchak was to cause disorder and bloodshed with a view of inducing the Powers of Europe to intervene. The first shot fire proceeded from the Armenians, and killed the major of the gendarmes. About thirty of the police, including four officers, were killed or wounded in the course of the day.[19]

Ashmead-Bartlett documents each of his analysis with extraordinary detail. He is as diligent in exploring the character of the men as he is in analyzing the movements, notably the rise of a virulent separatism based on atrocities.

An independent Armenian state was to be created in Cilicia, which was to coincide roughly with the one-time "kingdom of New Armenia." This plan became popular among the Armenian intelligentsia of İstanbul, who were encouraged by the results of the Zeytun rebellion of 1862 and by the liberal spirit of the early 1860s, reflected in the Armenian National Constitution. As early as 1851 Mekertitch Khirimian, later known as Khirimian Hairig, had been sent to Cilicia from İstanbul. Among other things, he was to organize a religious organization called Ser (Love), to be used as an instrument of furtherance of the proposed independence of Cilicia. Later, Nerses Varzhabedian, who became the Patriarch of İstanbul, also went to Cilicia to strengthen this organization. The Armenians of Diaspora also manifested much interest in Cilica. In 1865 Karapet Vardabet Shahnazarian, who lived in Egypt, bequeathed a large sum of money for the "intellectual, moral, and spiritual awakening of Cilicia [. . .] in preparation for the expected political rebirth" of the region. Educational improvement within the region was considered the groundwork for the anticipated political independence. Another step taken in preparation for the eventual independence of Cilicia was to encourage Armenian immigration into Cilicia. In 1863 Rafael Patkanian (Kamar Katiba) wrote an article in the journal *Hiusiss* (North), published in St. Petersburg, in which he advocated the movement of Iranian Armenians into the Zeytun area. An independent Zeytun might become the nucleus around which the rest of Cilicia could be eventually united. Mikael Nalbandian's secret list of code words and phrases indicates that he had an interest in Cilician immigration. He used the words "the cultivation of cotton" as the code expression for the phrase "to establish immigration to Cilicia."[20]

It may be useful to record at this point one interpretive issue which was as central to what had gone before as it was to what was to follow. A traveler, who reached Aleppo on March 15, 1912, from Zeytun and Maraş, furnished the British consul, Raphael Fontana, with the following information. Small bands of Armenian deserters from the Ottoman army had, for some time past, been making their way to Zeytun and the surrounding villages. Caravans passing through the area had been robbed by these bands, which might number all together from one hundred to two hundred. The *kaymakam* (lower district governor) of Zeytun proceeded, on or about February 20, 1912, with a detachment of fifty soldiers to a village four hours from Zeytun, on the road to Elbistan, where deserters were hiding, and a fight ensued in which the *kaymakam* was wounded and the Turks were repulsed. The *kaymakam* afterwards went to Maraş and reported that he would need a large force to cope with and capture the Armenian deserters. Troops were then drafted from Ayntab to Maraş, the authorities declaring their determination to capture the deserters at all costs. An Armenian Protestant pastor was sent from Maraş to Zeytun to treat with the Armenians there for the apprehension and delivery of the deserters in that area, but he was sent back with a message that the people of Zeytun could not take upon themselves to hunt down the deserters. On February 29, the deserters raided flocks from a certain Turkish village. The news of the Ottoman war vessels sunk by the Italians at Beyrout caused excitement at Zeytun, there was a call to arms, all the Armenians mustered, each man with a Martini, and a council of war was held. The Zeytun Armenians manufactured Martinis, including the barrel, and turned out very serviceable rifles. They, as well as the Armenians of the neighboring villages, were all armed with those weapons. It was thought that, in the event of serious trouble, from fifteen thousand to twenty thousand Armenians would rally at Zeytun.[21]

ARMENIANS IN ADANA

The Armenians who lived in Adana descended from followers of Prince Rupen, who migrated southward from eastern Anatolia during the eleventh century. Prince Rupen's followers at first dwelt only in the country surrounding the town of Sis, but later extended the frontier of their kingdom as far as the shores of the Mediterranean. They came under Ottoman rule after Sultan Selim I's defeat of the Mamelukes at the battles of Mercidabık and Rıdaniye in 1516. Adana thereafter remained a part of the Ottoman Empire.[22]

At the beginning of the twentieth century, the majority of the Armenians dwelling in the province of Adana had their original home in Diyarbekir, Sivas, and Mamuret-ul-Aziz. They migrated during the nineteenth century in the hope of seeking their fortune. The real Adana-born Armenians were to be found in the town of Hacin, on the northern border of the province, in a few villages in the neighborhood of Kozan, and in Dörtyol, on the shores of the Gulf of İskenderun, and some villages in its vicinity. The Turks and Armenians had previously lived together on the very best of terms, and there was no reason to anticipate any sort of strife between them. At the time of the disorders and massacres of 1894–1896, nothing at all had happened in the province of Adana, and Turks and Armenians had worked together to prevent the spread of disorder into the district. Their efforts had not been without success.[23] Hacin was a town of fewer than twenty thousand inhabitants, largely Armenian. The Turkish population consisted of some sixty families beside the officials and the standing army. This was unusual, for in only Hacin and Dörtyol in Cilicia was the population so preponderantly Armenian. The town was in the heart of the Taurus Mountains, about 150 kilometers north of İskenderun and nearly one hundred kilometers northwest from Maraş. It was four days distant from Adana. Hacin was built on a mountain thirty-five hundred feet above sea level and was closely hemmed in by mountains towering thousands of feet above the town. As the town was built around the mountain as well as on the top of it, the entire town could not be seen from any one point of view. Two roads along the valley, one from the southwest and the other from the northwest, entered the town, and the third came over mountains to the east. The narrow little valley was cultivated and little patches of gardens were seen on either side of the stream. The nearest cultivated plateaus were an hour or two distant, and some of the farms were nearly a day's journey away. Nearly all of the houses were small and had flat, ground roofs which were also used for yards. The houses were built one against the other and many had only openings in the walls for windows. As tier after tier of these houses were built up the mountainside, the roofs of the lower houses often formed the yard and entrance to the upper house and as the upper street was frequently level with the roof of the lower house, it was not an unusual sight to see men, women, and children, the babies in their cradles, chickens, dogs, cats, cows, and donkeys on the roof. Some of these steep streets had been repaired and so were much improved by having a stairway built in the road.[24]

After the hot months were past, streams of Armenians from Hacin were seen going to the Adana plain to spend the winter. Weavers, shoemakers, carpenters, blacksmiths, and men who followed all kinds of trades were scattered about in the villages on the plain while some of those who were unfortunate enough not to have a trade went to help cultivate the fields or to be the servants of the richer. Sometimes whole families moved to the plain for the winter while others left the women and children of the family in Hacin and bid them farewell until the following summer.[25]

Constellations of Armenian settlements extended in linked necklaces across Cilicia and intermingled with Turkish villages on the central Anatolian plain. Though the groups mixed in many aspects of social and political life, the Armenians retained certain cultural distinctions throughout the period of the empire. The lines separating them from their Turkish neighbors were, however, less starkly drawn among groups in Adana than in other parts of the country.[26]

Armenians in Adana differed from Armenians living in eastern Anatolia in at least three important respects. First, practically all of the Adana Armenians (Gregorians in belief making up the majority) spoke Turkish exclusively and had learned it as their mother tongue. It was the language they loved in, grieved in, joked in, fought in. In other words, Turkish was a language that belonged as much to the Armenians as it to anyone else. In the region, Turkish language had been practically the only one for centuries.[27] They were more Turkified than their kinsmen in the eastern provinces, whose mother tongue was Armenian. The Armenians in the region, under no compulsion and left free in all that concerns the internal affairs of their community, had adopted the language and habits of the Turks in place of their own ancient tongue and mode of living. They even wrote the Turkish language using their own alphabet. Armenian churches celebrated the liturgy in Turkish, not Armenian. The priesthood and various educational institutions widely used Turkish. For a considerable period they had become distinctly Turkish in manners and customs. The men wore the red fez, and the women veiled their faces. In the Armenian churches instructions and sermons were given in Turkish.[28]

The books, tracts, and newspapers printed were in Armeno-Turkish (Turkish printed in the Armenian character). The Scriptures in this language and character were at first published under the auspices of the American mission, but since 1858 this work had been under the care of the agents of the American and of the British and Foreign Bible Societies.[29] Adana Armenians, being more at ease with the Turkish language, could be taught more effectively in Turkish.[30]

Hrachik Simonyan asserts that the Armenians of the Cilician plains had in the late Middle Ages been made to speak Turkish only under the threat of "cutting off their tongues," and three or four generations later, they forgot their native tongue.[31] The truth of this statement cannot, of course, for a moment be admitted. It is clear that there is absolutely no archival evidence for that claim. Armenians, like all other non-Muslim peoples of the Ottoman Empire, had long enjoyed communal autonomy and lived as a legally protected distinct religious group. They have maintained their religious, cultural, linguistic, and national identity.[32]

A second distinguishing characteristic concerns the leading role played by missionaries in education. The Armenians of Cilicia and vicinity became the focus of attention for many Western Protestant missionaries, particularly those of the United States. Owing to the large network of schools, orphanages, and hospitals founded by them throughout the region, local Armenians steadily acquired a position of general ascendancy over their Muslim neighbors, who usually shunned these institutions through ignorance and suspicion born of their relative isolation from foreign influences. Because many Protestant Armenians received a Western-style missionary education, they were on average better educated than Gregorian Armenians; these individuals became a force for intellectual and technical progress for the population of Adana as a whole and for Adana Armenians in particular. Catholic Armenians were even fewer than the Protestants, but they too benefited from Catholic missionary influence.[33]

Third, whereas about 70 to 75 percent of the Ottoman Armenians lived in the countryside, especially in the eastern provinces, most Armenians in the province of Adana dwelt in cities and large towns.[34]

ARMENIANS' ROLE IN THE ECONOMIC AND SOCIAL LIFE OF ADANA

Adana was home to a large number of Armenians at the turn of the twentieth century. In Adana, as elsewhere, the Armenians occupied a separate quarter of the city, which compared favorably both as to the width and cleanliness of its streets and the architecture of its houses with the other quarters of the city, not excepting even that occupied by the so-called Franks, or Europeans. The Armenian quarter was the handsome, stone-built, and prosperous part of the city.[35]

Here, they played a vital role in economic and social life. Armenians owned shops, houses, vineyards, and vegetable gardens; they were small tradesmen in the bazaar, shopkeepers, drapers, exporters to foreign countries, middlemen, bankers, usurers, retailers, artisans, the progressive students of modern life and methods, the teachers, the scientists. They were especially busy in the manufacture of cloth, towels, handkerchiefs, bags, carpets, earthenware, and various silver adornments. They also labored in tanning of leather, dyeworks and painting, tinning, saddlery, and stone masonry. In humbler walks of life they were the capable and trusted servants, watchmen, and guardians of property, while such advance in agriculture as was made in Cilicia was largely due to their progressiveness and characteristic ambition.[36]

By 1891, Armenians had introduced new methods and machines for commercial agriculture, to which their landholdings were devoted. The activities of American missionaries also contributed to this development. They instructed Christian boys in modern agriculture and advised them how to profitably manage their farms. Furnished with improved knowledge of agricultural technique, the Armenian peasants became more successful than their Muslim neighbors and their villages were more prosperous than those of the Muslims.[37]

The most prosperous farmers and landowners, as well as the most successful, and clever peasants of the Adana plain, were the Armenians. They made the soil blossom. Their farmhouses were massive stone structures and their villages were substantial, trim, and dignified compared with those of Muslim population. When traveling over the country there were times when the broad harvests and flat prospect suggested well-cultivated American prairie farms.[38]

A total of 85 percent of the craftsmen in the region were Armenians, and 90 percent of all the business in the towns of Cilicia, and, indeed, all through Asia Minor, was in the hands of Armenians. As successful businessmen they far outnumbered Turks and were disproportionately represented in the professional classes. Most of the physicians, pharmacists, and dentists were Armenians.[39]

Damar Arıkoğlu describes the business center of Adana at the time as follows:

> There were two covered bazaars and two bedestens[40] in Adana. Large commodity shops and silk traders were concentrated in the bedestens. All the shop keepers, except four Muslim and Assyrian merchants, were Armenians. There were other Muslim shops in the covered bazaars, but their number could be counted on your fingers.[41]

Arıkoğlu was a native of Adana and a self-made man, and, albeit of little education, possessed considerable intelligence. He acquired much local influence, and, when the TGNA was instituted in 1920, was elected a member for Adana and served in that capacity until 1946. He was of liberal views, free from prejudices, generally anxious to see justice done, fairly upright, and during his membership of parliament for twenty-six years succeeded in winning the esteem and respect of all classes of the people.[42]

A poor correspondent and a very private person, Arıkoğlu left little written testimony of his personal life and intimate thoughts. So a biographer who sets out to reconstruct the life of this prominent figure of Adana would be daunted indeed.

Norman Naimark notes that the Armenians in the coastal Mediterranean cities of Cilicia increasingly took on the visage of a modern European middle class, heavily involved in the medical, engineering, and law professions, in textile manufacturing, and in agriculture.[43]

Armenians occupied with trade and artisanship actively participated in the public life of Adana. Considerable influence of Armenians in Adana could also be seen in Tarsus, Hacin, Kozan, and Cebelibereket. The Armenians of

Adana were mostly concentrated in the Hıdır İlyas neighborhood, around the Surp Asdvadzadzin church, and in the city center, where the community published the bilingual newspaper *Adana* in 1911 and developed several educational institutions. It is worth noting that in Hacin Armenian officials enjoyed predominant positions and high rank.[44]

The Gregorian, Protestant, and Catholic communities, not always on the best of terms with each other, were represented by their religious leaders in the provincial administrative council.[45] They were eminently active in the affairs of the city, playing parts which were way out of proportion to their numbers. Two or three Armenians were elected to the administrative council of Adana while the other administrative councils had one or two Armenian members. In the kazas of Yarpuz and Kozan there were generally two Armenian members. From three to six Armenians were elected to the municipality of Adana, while the other municipal councils had only one or two Armenian members. It is remarkable that the municipality of Hacin was almost entirely left in the hands of the Armenians.[46]

In the financial affairs, especially in Adana and Hacin, the Armenians took an important part. One to three were employed in the control of revenue and expenditure and in the taxation department, one or two in the Imperial Ottoman Bank, and between two and four in the branch of the Agricultural Bank, as well as in the Public Debt Administration[47] and in the Tobacco Régie or Monopoly.[48] Their service was considerable also in the Tobacco Monopoly where two or three of them were found. The tobacco departments were sometimes entirely run by Armenian officials.[49]

As to the judicature, the Armenians were included in the courts of first instance and of appeal at the headquarters. In each division of the courts (i.e., civil and criminal), there was at least one Armenian but in the criminal department of appeal there were often two Armenian judges. Their influence was strongest in the court of commerce where from three to five of them were to be found. They also worked as executive officials, members of trial councils, and as notaries. In the outlying kazas Armenians served the courts of first instance and of commerce, and the executive departments. In the courts of central sanjaks they participated in both offices of the judicial court, but in the courts of the outer kazas only in the department of first instance, which had no division into civil and criminal offices.[50]

In the technical field, Armenians filled the posts of chief and second engineers in the engineering department at Adana, and two or three of them were foremen as well. In the public works there were usually two, and in the post office at the section of foreign languages the directors and operators of the telegraphic service were frequently Armenian. There were Armenian technicians in printing. A compositor for Armenian is mentioned which implies that the press also had a section for Armenian printing. At the railway stations of Adana, Tarsus, and Mersin about twenty Armenians worked as station masters, mechanics, and locomotive drivers. Outside the center of the province, the technical activity of the Armenians was limited to the sphere of the postal and telegraphic service, and the public works. As to the secretariat Armenians often held the positions of clerk, accountant, and cashier in the various departments of the local government. They were principally employed in the departments of the chief secretariats, land registries, archives, customs, and control revenue. They were particularly many in the central sanjaks, but were fewer in the outlying kazas. In the latter Armenian clerks worked mainly in the offices of chief secretariat, land registry, and customs. It is worth noting that many province translators were Armenian, of whom one can record the names of Tiran and Avedis Efendis.[51]

Other fields of Armenian participation were agriculture, public health, education, and the police force. At Adana Armenian officials filled posts on the forestry board, agricultural inspectorate, and the board of trade, and in crafts and agriculture, there being about two or three in each. They were also employed in the other central sanjaks. In respect of education from two to four Armenians were included on the education council and committees, as cashiers or members, and a few taught in the preparatory, secondary, and girls' schools. The Ottoman Yearbook of 1901–1902 mentions a teacher of the Armenian language in the secondary school of Adana, which attests to the fact that Armenian was taught there. In the school of crafts as well, some Armenian masters taught shoe-making, tailoring, and cabinet-making. In the police force at the headquarters of the province, Armenians were sometimes employed as assistant superintendents of police, police sergeants, and policemen. In the public health service, at the centers of the sanjaks, Armenians held the position of doctor and chemist for the municipalities, and in Adana they were also employed in the infirmary and army medical corps.[52]

Armenians also figured frequently as *juges d'instruction*. Such delegation of authority attests to both a need and a willingness to rely on Armenian subjects. In kazas where there was European influence, Armenian participation in government appeared greater than elsewhere.[53]

Kirkor Bezdikyan and Sinyor Artin served as mayors of Adana respectively in 1877–1879 and 1879–1881.[54]

Hamparsum Boyacıyan, a native of Hacin, represented the sanjak of Kozan in the Chamber of Deputies following the elections of November–December 1908. Boyacıyan was a member of the Huntchak Party. He had been the instigator of the troubles against the Ottoman government in Sassoun in 1894. He had been a student for eight years at the Civil Medical College in İstanbul, and who afterwards had taken part in the affray of Kumkapı. He was wanted in consequence by the police of İstanbul. He, however, took flight to Athens, and from thence to Genoa, proceeding after a while to Talori (near Bitlis) under the assumed name of Murad, and in disguise, via Alexandria and Diyarbekir. He pretended to be a European, and he told the Asiatic Armenians that if they rose against the Ottoman government he knew as a fact that the foreign powers would support them, and, moreover, that he would get British soldiers to come from Britain to fight for them. He incited his hearers to kill every Muslim whom they might meet on the roads and to raid the city of Muş for the purpose of getting hold of the stores of arms and ammunition belonging to the *redif* (military reserve). He thus succeeded in raising the Armenian population of about ten villages, maltreating, by-the-by, those who did not care to join the rebellion. After supplying his followers with Berdan (Russian) rifles, old guns, flints, stillettos, and axes, he formed a few bands which attacked the tribe of Delikan at the end of July 1894. After having committed some murders and many robberies, they set upon the Yekran and Yedikan tribes, and perpetrated abominable outrages. The regular troops took the proper steps to put an end to such atrocious deeds. Boyacıyan and his confederates were arrested and delivered up to the governor of Muş to be dealt with by the criminal courts.[55]

Matyos Nalbantyan from Kozan and Agop Hırlakyan from Maraş, two wealthy Armenian proprietors, were deputies in 1914 to 1918. Nalbantyan stood well with the Sultans, and through their favor had accumulated considerable riches. Nevertheless, he served Armenians to the best of his opportunities. Hırlakyan was a notorious moneylender in the area.[56]

From the mid-1870s onward, the Christian ascendancy took an especially dangerous turn as the growing Armenian and Greek commercial class of Cilicia increasingly became creditors to Muslim petty tradesmen and cultivators. The Greek Orthodox came from Cyprus, the Islands of the Archipelago, and the provinces of Konya and Sivas. They settled in solid colonies in the west or around the towns of Tarsus and Mersin. They were bankers and usurers, and engaged in commerce.[57] Major Harold Armstrong, who had been a prisoner of war in the Ottoman Empire in the First World War and was later attached to the British High Commission at İstanbul as deputy military attaché, noted: "Adana had been the great centre of the Armenians before the war [First World War]. They had owned the town, shops, houses, gardens, and every Turk was in their power through loans and mortgages."[58] The Muslims naturally resented the economic power of the Christians during times of recession, drought, or Christian nationalistic agitation in the Balkans and Crete. Indeed, some immigrants among the Muslim debtors had already suffered impoverishment, violence, and dislocation in those very places.[59]

The manner of working the land favored usury. The peasants instead of laying aside capital for working purposes put everything into more land so that they had to be financed for at least three months every year. The government tried to do this through Caisse d'Agricole—later through Agricultural Bank—but did not succeed largely because of the red tape, guarantees, contracts, etc., which they demanded. The peasants would not sign their names, as they did not understand what it all meant. So they went to the usurer who in contrast to the banks acted the part of friend and neighbor, never asking any contract or guarantee of any sort. The oral promise was enough and was never broken. But the usurers asked 15 to 29 percent for three months and moreover the produce was valued at about 15 to 20 percent below the market price, so the total gain was about 40 percent—the banks asked only 9 percent. Furthermore, if the loan was not repaid the usurer had the right to take the piece of land which the produce had been earmarked for the loan and keep it until repayment. As he took good care that the peasant should never be out of his debt, they soon came to own the land even that of the great landed proprietors. Since most of the Turkish peasants were agriculturists, most of the great landowners were also Turks while the usurers, at least those around Adana city, were Armenian, great and increasing bitterness arose between the two peoples.[60]

Damar Arıkoğlu tells the relation between the Armenian merchants and Muslim peasants in Cilicia in the following manner:

> There was at least one Armenian moneylender in each Turkish village. They provided all the necessities for daily life, and they bought all the crops. The account was settled once every year, and the Armenians faithfully recorded the bills. But they never let the peasants rise up beyond the level of hunger-hunger and half-naked life.[61]

Following the 1870s the Armenians also began to acquire large landholdings in Cilicia. By 1875–1876, many Armenians and Greeks were already rich landed proprietors around Adana. Their lands likely belonged to Muslim Ottomans who became unable to pay their taxes and all their arrears. Seized by the state, such lands were sold to the highest bidder, usually a native Christian. Another reason for the transfer of property to Christians was the inability of their former Muslim proprietors to repay a debt to a Christian moneylender. From the late 1870s onward, this process resulted in foreclosure. Armenians and Greeks continued to acquire land into the 1880s. Stephan Astourian rightly points out that the long conscription of Muslim youth away from home—the Christian Ottomans were not conscripted until 1909—must have been largely conducive to this situation.[62]

Several Cilician Turkish memoirists and foreign travelers of this period have avowed that the Armenian merchants of Cilicia deliberately and systematically mired their Muslim clients in debts, both to hold them down and to lay claim to their lands. At any rate, the Armenians and Greeks of Cilicia steadily amassed agricultural property, often through an indivious process of foreclosure. In time the towns of the region gradually filled with an idle, volatile Muslim rabble ever mindful of the Armeno-Greek penchant for flaunting wealth.[63]

Cilicia was not specifically mentioned in Article 61 of the Berlin Treaty of July 13, 1878, which established European oversight of Ottoman internal affairs by stipulating that: "The Sublime Porte undertakes to carry out, without further delay, the amelioration and reforms demanded by local requirements in the provinces inhabited by the Armenians, and to guarantee their security against the Circassians and Kurds. It will periodically make known the steps taken to this effect to the Powers, who will superintend their application." Every European power that signed the Treaty had a right to inquire into, to investigate, and to supervise the reforms that were to be introduced by the Porte for the better government of the country.[64] That article was the starting point of the Armenian troubles. Turks saw foreign control as derogatory to national dignity. They resented any constraint or supervision from outside.[65]

In 1894–1896 order had not been disturbed at Adana, Tarsus, and Mersin. Tranquility prevailed in the province of Adana.[66] Therefore Oxford historian Eugene Rogan errs when he says "the roots of the pogrom [Adana affair of 1909] dated back to the 1870s."[67] Cilicia was also not included in the agreement signed between the Ottoman Empire and Russia (on behalf of the Europeans) on February 8, 1914, which recognized an autonomy almost amounting to quasi-independence to the provinces of Trabzon, Erzurum, Sivas, Van, Bitlis, Harput, and Diyarbekir.[68]

ARMENIAN SCHOOLING EFFORT

The Armenian populace certainly encountered European ideas and movements—not through military advisers and diplomats, but in schools established by Western missionaries and through travels to Paris, London, and other European capitals.[69] Men of the well-to-do class went abroad to study, and all over the province of Adana these men had gained a reputation in the various professions. But one influence which had had the most effect among the Armenians had been the presence of the American missions. They had established schools and colleges, where boys and girls had been trained and educated, and thus new ideas of life and better ways of living were carried back to the people and gradually all over the country. These Americans had made Protestant Armenians, while the old Armenians were Gregorians.[70]

American missionary activity in the Ottoman Empire dates from the 1830s. It is one of the most fascinating and astonishing as well as inspiring chapters in the entire history of American Protestantism. The principal endeavor was not to convert Muslims to Christianity, but rather to infuse life into the native Christian churches of the Ottoman east. Of the native Anatolian Christians, the Armenians proved most responsive. In time, an Ottoman Protestant church was created. This was not exactly the reinvigoration of native churches for which the more farsighted missionaries had hoped, but it represented a feasible solution in the face of the hostility of those churches toward the missionaries and their new converts. The Ottoman authorities eventually accorded these Protestants full status as a *millet* in the Empire's system. The Protestant *millet* never reached numbers great enough to rival the older forms of Christianity in the Empire, but what it lacked in size it tended to make up in its westernization and in what the missionaries themselves would refer to as old-fashioned Yankee "git up and git." Greek Protestants, Arabic-speaking Protestants, Bulgarian Protestants, and so on—all came into existence in response to the American movement, and all exist today. But the major response came from the Armenian people.[71]

The early missionaries arrived in a foreign world almost wholly unprepared, and they showed extraordinary speed and insight in adapting themselves to the strange realities they had to face. The more able of them realized from the first that exhortation and what might be only lip service conversion—that simply evangelization—were not what Ottoman Empire's Christian populations needed, but rather that education of native leadership was essential. Education entailed the translation and publication of the scriptures in the vernaculars, and this in turn meant no less than the development of local languages such as Armenian into modern literary language. Here, of course, the missionaries, knowingly or unknowingly, were pulling in harness with local nationalist agitators, for the cultivation of "national" languages was an essential element in the deliberate evocation of conscious nationalisms among the Ottoman peoples of the nineteenth century. In this matter the American Protestant missions registered sustained and productive activity, and no one who knows the facts is likely to try to minimize their role, although they were not of course the only or the leading forces at work.[72]

Much of American missionary activity in the Ottoman world was directed to the Armenians. One of its major results—perhaps one should instead say "major by-products," for it was certainly not an intentional result and it horrified those keen-sighted missionaries who understood the ultimate implications of what was going on—was to strengthen Armenian nationalist hopes, or to help transform young Armenians into potential revolutionaries against the Ottoman state. As the years went past, more and more of Anatolia's still large non-Muslim population thus became at least potential rebels while the impact of westernization and especially of Western nationalism worked relentlessly upon them. And it was the Anatolian Armenians who, beyond all others, came to be regarded as *the revolutionaries par excellence*. Only some of them merited this title, but events were moving too rapidly, and the region concerned was in every respect too backward, for careful distinctions of dispassionate judgment to be expected on the spot.[73]

Protestant missionary schools existed in some of the larger towns. In Adana and Hacin there were flourishing girls' schools conducted by American women. The language of the American Seminary for Girls in Adana was not Armenian. There were other nationalities in it. Armenian was taught to the Armenian children and Armenian history had its place in the program. In some towns there were also high schools for boys.[74]

At Tarsus there was a large college, St. Paul's Institute, opened in 1886, in which boys and young men from the province of Adana and from other parts of Asia Minor were trained under Thomas Davidson Christie who was sent by the ABCFM. In the spring of 1885, Colonel Elliott Shepard of New York City had a conference in Tarsus with the missionary of the ABCFM who at that time had charge of the work in the Cilician plain. The past glories of the town and its neighborhood, and the demand now made by the young churches of the province of Adana for higher education of their children, were set before the visitor; like his ancestors at Boston in 1630, he "began to think upon a College." The result was seen when, in March 1887, he got a bill passed through the legislature of the State of New York organizing "St. Paul's Institute at Tarsus." St. Paul's Institute ranked second to Robert College, named for Christopher Robert, a New York merchant and original donor, founded by Cyrus Hamlin in 1871 at İstanbul. St. Paul's Institute had a course of study covering eight or nine years, a faculty of twelve or fifteen teachers, and an average attendance of about 275. This school prepared men for entrance to the Theological Seminary at Maraş, the Medical Department of the Syrian Protestant College at Beirut, or teaching in the common and high schools of the country. The college graduated its first class in June 1893. Mrs. Christie at the same time started a little kindergarten among the very poorest Armenians in this town. The fact that St. Paul, one of the twelve apostles of Jesus Christ, was born in Tarsus probably had much to do with its being chosen as the site for the new institute rather than Adana, where there was already an American boarding school for girls, or Mersin.[75]

It is also important to recall that before 1914 Christian schools of some sort existed in all the larger towns and villages of Cilicia. These were taught by men and women who had studied in the Christian colleges or the high schools of the country. Among Catholics, Jesuits were famous as missionaries, intellectuals, and educators—and for often being stubbornly independent, skeptical, if also politically adept. In Adana there was a Jesuit College (Residence and College of St. Paul), with its six hundred pupils, in which the language of instruction was French, and also a Catholic school for girls (Notre Dame de Bethanie) under the management of twenty-five Sisters of St. Joseph of Lyons. At Mersin there was a Catholic school for boys and one for girls and at Tarsus a school. The French were intensely Roman Catholic and very anxious to have French influence expressed through the Church in Cilicia. The Catholic missions, through the creation of the various Uniate churches, were remarkably more successful in winning the hearts and minds of local Ottoman Christians, in terms of actual numbers, than were their Protestant competitors. Roman Catholic missionaries were attracting thousands of Cilician Christians to the Papal fold: Armenians who broke with the Gregorian communion became Armenian Catholics; Melchites who broke with the Greek Orthodox communion became Greek Catholics; Jacobites who broke with their traditional Monophysite communion became Syrian Catholics. The Catholic Armenians enjoyed the formal protection of France and Austria-Hungary.[76]

The government which had more schools and missionary societies than any other in the Ottoman Empire was France. After 1861, French Catholic missionaries flocked to Cilicia to set up schools, hospitals, orphanages, and asylums. Jesuits, Lazarists, the Sisters of St. Joseph, the Dames of Nazareth, the Daughters of Charity, and the Sisters of the Holy Family were some of the main orders which established charitable works in the region. The French government and private societies of French propaganda openly supported these groups. The French language long ago spread in the Ottoman realm and had even became the general language in important centers. It was the most spoken and written Western language in the country on the eve of the First World War and one all the other foreigners—British, Germans, and Italians—had themselves to speak. For this there were several reasons. (1) The Ottoman Empire received European civilization chiefly from France. (2) French was an international language. (3) The French had found many institutions of learning in the Ottoman Empire. (4) Catholic schools and missionaries were under the protection of France. The French schools in the Ottoman Empire in 1914 were eight colleges, nineteen high schools, and 892 elementary schools in all, with 33,487 pupils. France had twelve great missionary societies working in the Ottoman Empire.[77]

The Roman Catholic Church, which for centuries was engaged in proselyting activities among the Armenians, demonstrated the most vigorous opposition against Protestant missionary penetration onto Ottoman soil. The attitude of other Eastern churches was of deep concern, while the Armenian Patriarchate in İstanbul looked upon Protestantism as a sect with erroneous doctrines and a threat to its national strength, unity, and integrity. The ecclesiastics and other leaders among the Armenians, seeing that those brought under missionary influence began to forsake the confessional, neglected to pray to the saints, abandoned the use of pictures in worship, and appealed to the testimony of "the Word of God" on all questions of doctrine, set themselves to the work of opposing the missionaries.[78] As a result, the Armenian Patriarchate and magnates in İstanbul, who held ranking offices both in the Armenian church and in the Ottoman government, schemed to expel the missionaries from the Ottoman realm.[79] The Ottoman government, where no question of political disloyalty was involved, inclined to be tolerant and neutral.[80]

However, the Armenians in Anatolia saw the advantages they, as a community, would gain by giving their boys a thorough, general education, and so they not only patronized the schools the missionaries opened, and largely supported them, but schools under their own patronage and direction were established far and wide.[81]

The Gregorian Armenians had the Mushegian-Abkarian School and the Ashkhenian School with eight hundred pupils at Adana and schools of lower grade in many towns and villages. They had in all nearly two thousand pupils in various schools.[82] According to the national constitution, adopted by the Armenians of the Ottoman Empire in 1863, with the approbation of the Sublime Porte, the patriarchate's council of public instruction had the supervision of education in the Gregorian Armenian schools, the financial control of the schools being vested in communal councils. The course of study included religious and moral instruction, Armenian, Turkish, French, English, mathematics, geography, general and national history, notions of civic laws, manual training, gymnastics, singing, drawing, and calligraphy.

Adana was an important missionary center, and here as in many other places in the Ottoman Empire, American missionaries were doing extensive work. The city was a station of the ABCFM, with a working force of five missionaries and twenty-two native workers. It was an outstation of the synod of the Reformed Presbyterian church of North America and a Bible depot and sub-agency family Bible society. William Nesbitt Chambers and Mrs. Chambers, who were maintained by the First Congregational Church of Oak Park, a suburb of Chicago, were in this station from 1899 till 1922. Elizabeth Webb and Mary Webb, sisters, whose home was in Missouri, had been in Adana since 1886 and 1890, respectively. The American Mission building in Adana was situated at the edge of the Armenian quarter and was used as a girls' school under the direction of Elizabeth Webb. Chambers was also field secretary of the Young Men's Christian Association.[83]

So far as I know, no biography of William Nesbitt Chambers exists. This is unfortunate because he was one of the most interesting and significant American missionaries, and both his early career and his role in the Adana affair and the immediate post-1918 period merit close study.

In Mersin the American Reformed Presbyterian Church, connected with the Irish Church of the same denomination, had schools for boys and girls. The Capucin Convent, aided by sisters, had also schools for children belonging to the Latin community. In Tarsus there was one missionary family and one foreign family.[84] In 1910 there were four thousand Protestant Armenians in the town, meeting in three large churches, and 1,350 more in twelve outstations.

There was the Central Turkey Girls' College and the ABCFM supported the Maraş Theological Seminary to supply preachers for the churches of the mission.[85] The Roman Catholic Franciscan Fathers set up their mission in Maraş in the nineteenth century. Some Armenians were converted to that faith, and the Armenians had their own Catholic church in the city. Catholic life in the city was centered around the Latin Monastery. The ABCFM work began in 1854 in Maraş, but the resistance of the local authorities made their proselyting very difficult. As elsewhere, the American missionaries turned to the educating of the young people as their principal burden of occupation. In 1856, the Central Turkey Girls' College of Maraş had already been founded. Nine years later, a missionary school, originally opened in Ayntab in 1854, was transfered to Maraş. This institution first functioned as a high school, became a theological seminary in 1879, and finally, in 1888, assumed the character of a formal college. Nearly all the graduates from this institution were engaged in the work of teaching. The Marash Academia High School was opened by the ABCFM personnel in 1891. Most of the students at all these institutions were Armenians. On the eve of the First World War, there existed three large Armenian Protestant church structures in Maraş with a total of two thousand Armenian protestant worshipers. Equally impressive were the schools maintained by the Armenian Gregorian authorities of the city. Altogether, these many educational opportunities gave the city's Armenian community a high cultural level. The American and Armenian schooling efforts were also enhanced by the presence of a school kept by a small number of German missionaries attached to the local German orphanages and the German hospital. The Catholics too had their own places of instruction. Most personnel of the Franciscan fathers in the city were French. The Americans also maintained a hospital and orphanage in the city.[86]

NOTES

1. Alan Alfred Bartholomew, "Tarsus American School, 1888–1988: The Evolution of a Missionary Institution in Turkey," doctoral dissertation, Bryn Mawr College, 1989, p. 70.

2. George Bournoutian, *A Concise History of the Armenian People (From Ancient Times to the Present)* (Costa Mesa, CA: Mazda Publishers, Inc., 2006), p. 93. A Turkish translation exists.

3. Bedross Der Matossian, "From Bloodless Revolution to Bloody Counterrevolution: The Adana Massacres of 1909," *Genocide Studies and Prevention*, Vol. 6, No. 2 (August 2011), pp. 156 and 168fn30; Ali Münif Bey, Taha Toros, ed., *Ali Münif Bey'in Hatıraları* (Reminiscences of Ali Münif Bey) (İstanbul: İSİS Yayıncılık, 1996), pp. 46–48. Ali Münif Yeğena's memoirs is an indispensable source for those who want an unadulterated and firsthand account of a key moment of a problem in Cilicia.

4. Gaston Gaillard, *The Turks and Europe* (London: Thomas Murby and Co., 1921; French origin, 1920), p. 286. Also Erdal İlter, *Ermeni Kilisesi ve Terör* (The Armenian Church and Terror) (Ankara: Ankara Üniversitesi Osmanlı Tarihi Araştırma ve Uygulama Merkezi Yayınları, 1996), p. 55; Süleyman Kani İrtem, Osman Selim Kocahanoğlu, ed., *Ermeni Meselesinin İçyüzü Ermeni İsyanları Tarihi, Bomba Hadisesi, Adana Vakası, Meclisi Mebusan Zabıtları* (The True Nature of the Armenian Question: History of Armenian Revolts, Bomb Incident, Adana Event, Proceedings of the Chamber of Deputies) (İstanbul: Temel Yayınları, 2004), p. 148; Eyicil, "Maraş ve Zeytun Ermenileri," p. 322.

5. The term Young Turk is a European expression which was not used officially in the Ottoman Empire. Significantly, Young Turks themselves adopted this name only in the form of a French loan word, "Jön Türk." On this term, see Karal, *Osmanlı Tarihi*, Vol. 8, pp. 510–11. Sound scholarship on Young Turks includes Şükrü Hanioğlu's *The Young Turks in Opposition* (New York and Oxford: Oxford University Press, 1995) and *Preparation for a Revolution: the Young Turks, 1902–1908* (New York and Oxford: Oxford University Press, 2001). Since the publication of Hanioğlu's books a good deal of additional material has appeared in the Ottoman documents on the Young Turks, and revised editions are desirable. But the main lines and conclusions have in no sense been invalidated by later publications. The books are easily the best and most authoritative treatment of this important phase of Ottoman history. In regard to the subject, see also Ernest Edmondson Ramsaur, *The Young Turks: Prelude to the Revolution of 1908* (Princeton, NJ: Princeton University Press, 1957), and Naim Turfan, *Rise of the Young Turks: Politics, the Military and Ottoman Collapse* (London and New York: I.B. Tauris, 2000).

6. See Başbakanlık Osmanlı Arşivi (Prime Minister's Office Ottoman Archive), İstanbul (henceforth referred to as BOA), Dahiliye Nezareti Sicill-i Ahval İdare-i Umumiyesi (Ministry of the Interior General Administration of Status Registers), No. 99/177. Personal Records of Ali Münif Bey, February 17, 1874; *Türk Parlamento Tarihi* (History of the Turkish Parliament), Vol. 3: *Türkiye Büyük Millet Meclisi Üçüncü Dönem 1927–1931* (Turkish Grand National Assembly Third Term

1927–1931) (Ankara: Türkiye Büyük Millet Meclisi Basımevi Müdürlüğü, 1995), pp. 493–94, and Çankaya, *Mülkiye Tarihi ve Mülkiyeliler*, Vol. 3, pp. 317–18.

7. On the town of Zeytun, see Michel Paboudjian, "Zeytoun la Singulière," in Raymond Kévorkian, Mihran Minassian, Lévonian Nordiguian, Michel Paboudjian, and Vahé Tachjian, *Les Arméniens de Cilicie Habitat, mémoire et identité* (Beyrouth: Presses de Université Saint-Joseph, 2012), p. 115; F.D. Shepard, "Personal Experience in Turkish Massacres and Relief Work," *Journal of Race Development*, Vol. 1 (January 1910), p. 318.

8. Gaillard, *The Turks and Europe*, pp. 276 and 283; Lord Kinross, *The Ottoman Centuries: The Rise and Fall of the Turkish Empire* (New York: Morrow Quill, 1977), pp. 560–61. See also *Aspirations et Agissements Révolutionnaires des Comités Arméniens Avant et Aprés la Proclamation de la Constitution Ottomane*, pp. 64–65.

9. "Armenian Anarchist Society," *England and the Union*, October 12, 1895, p. 2.

10. Esat Uras, *Tarihte Ermeniler ve Ermeni Meselesi* (Armenians in History and the Armenian Question) (İstanbul: Belge Yayınları, second revised edition, expanded, 1987), pp. 432–37; Louise Nalbandian, *The Armenian Revolutionary Movement* (Berkeley and Los Angeles, CA: University of California Press, 1963), pp. 110–11.

11. See Cyrus Hamlin, *Among the Turks* (New York: Robert Carter and Brothers, 1878), and idem, *My Life and Times* (Boston, MA: Congregational Sunday School and Publishing Society, 1893). Also A. R. Thain, "Cyrus Hamlin D. D., LL. D. Missionary, Statesman, Inventor: A Life Sketch," *The Envelope Series*, Vol. 10, No. 2 (July 1907), and Marcia and Malcolm Stevens, *Against the Devil's Current: The Life and Times of Cyrus Hamlin* (Lanham, MD: University Press of America, 1988).

12. The Westerners (Europeans and Americans) routinely referred to Ottomans as "Turks" and the Ottoman polity as "Turkey." Nowhere throughout the present study outside of direct quotation Ottoman statesmen and officials are referred to as "Turks," the Ottoman world as "Turkish," or the Ottoman Empire as "Turkey." Some words of caution are necessary. These terms did not even exist in the early modern Ottoman mind. Western writers often denigrated the achievements of the Ottoman Empire, which they misnamed the Turkish Empire or Turkey. This confuses rather than enlightens.

13. "The Sassoun Massacre; Proof of the Assertion that Armenian Revolutionists Caused It; Testimony of Rev. Cyrus Hamlin," *The New York Times*, August 23, 1895, p. 3. The great daily newspapers of the United States included the important mass circulation dailies: *The New York Times*, *The Washington Post*, *Chicago Daily Tribune*, and *The Boston Daily Globe*. Their effect on the molding of public opinion was vast. These newspapers also acted as a guide for the rest of the American press on questions of foreign policy, which they covered through a network of foreign correspondents (a luxury which few other newspapers could afford), and on which they regularly took positions.

14. Two volumes of excerpts from British diplomatic records, known as Blue Books, were published on January 28, 1896. One contained consular reports, including the reports of Cecil Hallward and Charles Hampson, other diplomatic letters, and the report of the European Delegates to the Sassoun Commission. The other contained the *procès-verbaux* of the commission sittings. For the reports, see Enclosure in Philip

Currie to Marquess of Salisbury, Therapia, August 15, 1895, "Report of the Consular Delegates attached to the Commission Appointed to Inquire into Events in Sassoun," *Correspondence Relating to the Asiatic Provinces of Turkey: Turkey, No. 1 (1895), Part 1*, pp. 133–46 and annexes. This volume (part 1) and part 2 gives English translations of the French originals of the commission's sittings. See also FO 424/183, which contains the report, and FO 424/181 and 182.

15. House of Commons Debates, Vol. 38, cc 37–125, March 3, 1896.
16. Ibid.
17. Ibid.
18. Ibid.
19. Ibid.
20. Nalbandian, *The Armenian Revolutionary Movement*, pp. 74–77; Ali Münif Bey, *Ali Münif Bey'in Hatıraları*, p. 47; Cezmi Yurtsever, *Çukurova Tarihi* (The History of Cilicia) (Adana: Çukurovalı Yayınları, 2008), p. 60.
21. FO 195/135. Armenian Deserters from the Ottoman Army Collecting in Zeytun District. Raphael Fontana (Aleppo) to Sir Gerard Lowther (Istanbul), March 16, 1912.
22. Detailed accounts can be found in Yurtsever, *Çukurova Tarihi*, pp. 58–59; Mehmet Ersan, "Kilikya Ermeni Krallığı" (Armenian Kingdom of Cilicia) in Erman Artun and Sabri Koz, eds., *Efsaneden Tarihe, Tarihten Bugüne Adana: Köprü Başı* (From Legend to History, From History to Our Day Adana: Bridge Head) (İstanbul: Yapı Kredi Yayınları, 2000), pp. 326–43; Mehlika Aktok Kaşgarlı, *Kilikya Tabi Ermeni Baronluğu Tarihi* (History of the Cilician Vassal Armenian Barony) (Ankara: Köksav Yayınları, 1990); Mim Kemal Öke, "Hukuk-Tarih-Siyaset Üçgeninde Kilikya Ermeni Krallığı Polemiği" (Polemics of the Cilician Armenian Kingdom in the Triangle of Law-History-Politics), *Türk Dünyası Araştırmaları Dergisi*, No. 46 (February 1987); Razmik Panossian, *The Armenians: From Kings and Priests to Merchants and Commissars* (New York and London: Columbia University Press, 2006), pp. 63–66; Woods, *The Danger Zone of Europe*, p. 125; Béatrice Kasbarian-Bricout, *L'Arméno-Cilicie, royaume oublié* (Paris: Editions Astrid, 1982); Claude Mutafian et Catherine Otten-Froux, *Le royaume arménien de Cilicie: XIIe-XIVe siècle* (Paris: CNRS Editions, 1993).
23. Djemal Pasha, *Memories of a Turkish Statesman 1913–1919*, p. 257.
24. Mustafa Onar, *Hacın Dosyası* (The Hacin File) (Adana: Önder Matbaa, 1984), pp. 26–27; Rose Lambert, *Hadjin and the Armenian Massacres* (New York: Fleming H. Revell Co., 1911), pp. 24–25.
25. Lambert, *Hadjin and the Armenian Massacres*, p. 26.
26. Arıkoğlu, *Hatıralarım*, p. 42. See also Baskın Oran, ed., *"M.K." Adlı Çocuğun Tehcir Anıları 1915 ve Sonrası* (Relocation Reminiscences of a Child Called "M.K.": 1915 and Its Beyond) (İstanbul: İletişim Yayınları, 2005), pp. 13–16; Paren Kazanjian, ed., *The Cilician Ordeal* (Boston, MA: Hye Intentions, 1989).
27. Jennifer Manoukian, The Legacy of Turkish in the Armenian Diaspora, Repair, October 15, 2014. http://repairfuture.net/index.php/en/identity-standpoint-c; Garabed Çalyan, "Adana Vakası ve Mesulleri" (Adana Incident and Those Responsible For It), in Ari Şekeryan, ed., *1909 Adana Katliamı: Üç Rapor* (1909 Massacre of Adana:

Three Reports) (İstanbul: Aras Yayıncılık, 2015), p. 54; Taylan Esin and Zeliha Etöz, *1916 Ankara Yangını Felaketin Mantığı* (Ankara Fire of 1916: The Logic of the Disaster) (İstanbul: İletişim Yayınları, 2015), pp. 38–39fn51.

28. Arıkoğlu, *Hatıralarım*, p. 42; Ahmet Cevdet Çamurdan, *Kozan'ı Tanıyalım* (Let Us Know Kozan) (Adana: Önder Matbaa, 1973), p. 97; İrtem, *Ermeni Meselesinin İçyüzü*, pp. 148–50; Woods, *The Danger Zone of Europe*, p. 126; James Barton, *Daybreak in Turkey* (Boston, MA: The Pilgrim Press, second edition, 1908), p. 68. The last book appeared right after the restoration of constitutional government and went through several editions since then, a chapter being added after the fall of Sultan Abdülhamid II in 1909. It treats of all phases of the situation in the complex Ottoman Empire—the characteristics of the various peoples, their religious systems, and the different branches of missionary effort on their behalf. A great deal more research needs to be done to confirm and build on the findings of these works. Even so, the books mentioned here point us to some important themes for future research.

29. E. E. Strong, *Condensed Sketch of the Missions of the American Board in Asiatic Turkey* (Boston, MA: The American Board, 1908), p. 22.

30. Ephraim Jernazian, trans. Alice Haig, *Judgment Unto Truth: Witnessing the Armenian Genocide* (New Brunswick, NJ: Transaction Publishers, 1990), p. 28. The Armenian pastor Ephraim Jernazian was born in Maraş in 1890 and spent the first twenty-three years of his life in the area.

31. Simonyan, *The Destruction of Armenians in Cilicia, April 1909*, p. 31.

32. For a fuller discussion of this theme, see İlber Ortaylı, *Osmanlı Barışı* (Pax Ottomana) (İstanbul: Timaş Yayınları, 2007), pp. 135–57. Also E. Alexander Powell, *The Struggle for Power in Moslem Asia* (New York and London: The Century Company, 1923), pp. 118–19; Emil Lengyel, *Turkey* (New York: H. Wolff, 1941), p. 187; and Gorun Shrikian, "Armenians Under the Ottoman Empire and the American Mission's Influence on Their Intellectual and Social Renaissance," doctoral dissertation, Concordia Seminary in Exile (Seminex) in Cooperation with Lutheran School of Theology at Chicago, 1977, p. 45.

33. Astourian, "Testing World-System Theory, Cilicia (1830–1890)," p. 107. See also Karal, *Osmanlı Tarihi*, Vol. 8, pp. 128–29; and Robert Farrer Zeidner, "The Tricolor Over the Taurus: The French in Cilicia and Vicinity, 1918–1922," doctoral dissertation, University of Utah, 1991, p. 48.

34. Astourian, "Testing World-System Theory, Cilicia (1830–1890)," p. 108.

35. Lesley Blanche, *Pierre Loti: Portrait of an Escapist* (London: Collins, 1983), pp. 299–300.

36. Raymond Kévorkian, "Traductions d'Extraits du Livre Adanayı Hayots Badmoutiun, de Puzant Yeghiyayan, Antélias 1970," in Kévorkian, Minassian, Nordiguian, Paboudjian, Tachjian, *Les Arméniens de Cilicie*, p. 26; Arıkoğlu, *Hatıralarım*, pp. 125–26; Mesrob Krikorian, *Armenians in the Service of the Ottoman Empire, 1860–1908* (Boston, MA: Routledge and Kegan Paul, 1978), p. 65.

37. Astourian, "Testing World-System Theory, Cilicia (1830–1890)," pp. 552–54; Sahara, *What Happened in Adana in April 1909?* p. 85.

38. James Creelman, "The Red Terror on the Cilician Plain: How the Moslem Frenzy, Started by the Foolish Talk of a Christian Priest, Spread Far Beyond Adana,"

The New York Times, August 29, 1909, Part 6, p. 8. James Creelman was an American journalist and war correspondent whose work was known throughout the journalistic world for keenness of insight, fullness and accuracy of information, and balanced judgment. Creelman traveled widely, studied many lands and peoples, observed much, and weighed, compared, and reviewed his opinions. He was a trained and experienced investigator whom a leading journal sends on difficult or responsible tours of inquiry.

39. Arıkoğlu, *Hatıralarım*, pp. 42–43; Çamurdan, *Kozan'ı Tanıyalım*, p. 97; Simonyan, *The Destruction of Armenians in Cilicia, April 1909*, p. 23; Sarkis Atamian, *The Armenian Community: The Historical Development of a Social and Ideological Conflict* (New York: Philosophical Library, 1955), p. 230. See also Kamil Erdeha, *Milli Mücadelede Vilayetler ve Valiler* (Provinces and Governors During the National Struggle) (İstanbul: Remzi Kitabevi, 1975), p. 300. The book is a testament to the value of bringing individuals and anecdotes back into the history.

40. Vaulted and fireproof group of shops.

41. Arıkoğlu, *Hatıralarım*, p. 38.

42. A biographical sketch of Damar Arıkoğlu is in *Türk Parlamento Tarihi Milli Mücadele ve Türkiye Büyük Millet Meclisi Birinci Dönem 1919–1923* (History of the Turkish Parliament: The National Struggle and the First Term of the Grand National Assembly of Turkey 1919–1923), Vol. 3 (Ankara: Türkiye Büyük Millet Meclisi Basımevi Müdürlüğü, 1995), pp. 47–48.

43. Norman Naimark, *Fires of Hatred: Ethnic Cleansing in Twentieth-Century Europe* (Cambridge, MA: Harvard University Press, 2001), p. 20.

44. Osman Köker, ed., *Orlando Carlo Calumeno Koleksiyonundan Kartpostallarla 100 Yıl Önce Türkiye'de Ermeniler* (With Post Cards from the Orlando Carlo Calumeno Collection: Armenians in Turkey 100 Years Ago) (İstanbul: Birzamanlar Yayıncılık, 2005), p. 242; Uğur Ümit Üngör and Mehmet Polatel, *Confiscation and Destruction: The Young Turk Seizure of Armenian Property* (London and New York: Continuum, 2011), pp. 107–8; Raymond Kévorkian et Paul Paboudjian, *Les Arméniens dans l'Empire ottoman à la veille du génocide* (Paris: Editions d'Art et d'Histoire, 1992), p. 265; Krikorian, *Armenians in the Service of the Ottoman Empire 1860–1908*, p. 65.

45. The provincial administrative council was composed of the governor or his delegate as chairman and four ex officio members, namely the director of the provincial Nizamiye courts, the provincial financial director, the director of foreign affairs, and the governor's director of correspondence. In addition there were four public members, of whom two had to be elected by the Muslim subjects and two by the non-Muslims of the province.

46. BOA, Dahiliye Nezareti Emniyeti Umumiye Müdürlüğü (Ministry of the Interior Directorate General of Public Security), No. 39/249. Election of Christians to the Provincial Administrative Councils and the Presence of the Spiritual Leaders in the Commission Appropriations, March 17, 1914; Krikorian, *Armenians in the Service of the Ottoman Empire 1860–1908*, p. 65.

47. When in 1875 the Ottoman Empire defaulted on debts accumulated during the Crimean War of 1853–1856, the major European powers set up an autonomous tax agency, the Public Debt Administration, to levy directly taxes on produced goods.

This administration had monopolies over salt, silk, fisheries, stamps, and alcoholic spirits. See Jacques Thobie, "Les intérêts économiques, financiers, et politiques français dans la partie asiatique de L'Empire Ottoman, de 1895 à 1914," Thèse de doctorat d'état, Université de Paris, 1973.

48. The Régie Administration, or *Société de la Régie Cointeressé des Tabacs de l'Empire Ottoman*, was the monopoly which brought domestic Ottoman tobacco production and consumption under foreign control in 1884. See Donald Quataert, *Social Disintegration and Popular Resistance in the Ottoman Empire, 1881–1908: Reactions to European Penetration* (New York: New York University Press, 1983).

49. Krikorian, *Armenians in the Service of the Ottoman Empire 1860–1908*, pp. 65–66.

50. Ibid., p. 66.

51. Ibid.

52. Ibid., pp. 66–67.

53. Ibid.

54. Selma Aktan, *Dünkü ve Bugünkü Adana* (Adana of Yesterday and Today) (Adana: Güney Basımevi, 1967), pp. 16–17.

55. *Türk Parlamento Tarihi* (History of the Turkish Parliament), *Birinci ve İkinci Meşrutiyet* (First and Second Constitutionalism), Vol. 2 (Ankara: Türkiye Büyük Millet Meclisi Basımevi Müdürlüğü, 1998), p. 228; see also Vol. 1, p. 620. Cezmi Yurtsever, *Hacin Bir Yangının Külleri* (Hacin: Ashes of a Fire) (Adana: Çukurovalı Yayınları, 2010), pp. 77–84; idem, *Ermeni Terör Merkezi*, pp. 258–59; idem, *Çukurova Tarihi*, pp. 60–61; "The Sassoun Struggle," *Morning Advertiser*, November 24, 1894, p. 3.

56. Meclisi Mebusan Zabıt Ceridesi (Proceedings of the Chamber of Deputies), Session: 3, Meeting Year: 1 (1914), Vol. 1 (Ankara: Türkiye Büyük Millet Meclisi Basımevi, 1982), p. 2; Selahattin Adil Paşa, *Hayat Mücadeleleri* (Struggles for Life) (İstanbul: Zafer Matbaası, 1982), p. 331; Torkom İstepenyan, *Atatürk'ün Doğumunun 100. Yılında Türk-Ermeni İlişkileri* (Turkish-Armenian Relations at the Hundredth Birthday Anniversary of Atatürk) (İstanbul: Murat Ofset, 1984), p. 48; Cezmi Yurtsever, "Hamparsum Boyacıyan veya "Haçinli Murat'ın" Tarihi Yol Hikayesidir" (Hamparsum Boyacıyan or the Historical Road Story of "Murat of Haçin"), Hasan Celal Güzel, ed., *Yeni Türkiye Ermeni Meselesi Özel Sayısı*, Vol. 3 (Ankara: Yeni Türkiye Stratejik Araştırma Merkezi Yayınları, 2014), pp. 1969–83.

57. Billings, "The Causes of the Outbreak in Cilicia, Asia Minor, April, 1909," p. 22.

58. Harold Armstrong, *Turkey and Syria Reborn: Records of Two Years of Travel* (London: John Lane The Bodley Head Ltd., 1930), p. 138.

59. Zeidner, "The Tricolor Over the Taurus," p. 48.

60. Billings, "The Causes of the Outbreak in Cilicia, Asia Minor, April, 1909," pp. 24–25.

61. Arıkoğlu, *Hatıralarım*, p. 43.

62. Stephan Astourian, "The Silence of the Land: Agrarian Relations, Ethnicity, and Power," in Ronald Grigor Suny, Fatma Müge Göçek, and Norman Naimark, eds., *A Question of Genocide: Armenians and Turks at the End of the Ottoman Empire*

(New York: Oxford University Press, 2011), p. 77; Ronald Grigor Suny, *A History of the Armenian Genocide* (Princeton and Oxford: Princeton University Press, 2015), p. 54. See also Enver Ziya Karal, *Osmanlı Tarihi* (Ottoman History), Vol. 9: *İkinci Meşrutiyet ve Birinci Dünya Savaşı (1908–1918)* (The Second Constitutionalism and the First World War [1908–1918]) (Ankara: Türk Tarih Kurumu Basımevi, reprinted, 1996), p. 94; Yurtsever, *Çukurova Tarihi*, p. 60; İrtem, *Ermeni Meselesinin İçyüzü*, p. 147.

63. Zeidner, "The Tricolor Over the Taurus," pp. 48–49.

64. Nihat Erim, *Devletlerarası Hukuku ve Siyasi Tarih Metinleri* (Texts of International Law and Political History), Vol. 1: *Osmanlı İmparatorluğu Andlaşmaları* (Treaties of the Ottoman Empire) (Ankara: Türk Tarih Kurumu Basımevi, 1953), p. 423; J. C. Hurewitz, ed., *Diplomacy in the Near and Middle East: A Documentary Record*, Vol. 1: 1535–1914 (Princeton, NJ: D. Van Nostrand Company, Inc., 1956), p. 190. For the full text of the Treaty Between Great Britain, Germany, Austria, France, Italy, Russia, and Turkey for the Settlement of Affairs in the East of July 13, 1878, see Great Britain, *Parliamentary Papers, 1878*, Vol. 83, pp. 690–705.

65. Karal, *Osmanlı Tarihi*, Vol. 8, pp. 129–30 and 132–33; Ali Fuat Türkgeldi, *Mesaili Mühimmei Siyasiye* (The Important Political Questions) (Ankara: Türk Tarih Kurumu Basımevi, 1957), pp. 86–87; Cevdet Küçük, *Osmanlı Diplomasisinde Ermeni Meselesinin Ortaya Çıkışı 1878–1897* (The Emergence of the Armenian Question in the Ottoman Diplomacy 1878–1897) (İstanbul: Türk Dünyası Araştırmaları Vakfı, 1986).

66. Hayk Demoyan, "Foreword," in Ferriman, *The Young Turks and the Truth about the Holocaust at Adana in Asia Minor*, p. ix; Leon Arpee, "A Century of Armenian Protestantism," *Church History*, Vol. 5, No. 2 (June 1936), p. 165; Shepard, "Personal Experience in Turkish Massacres and Relief Work," p. 326.

67. Eugene Rogan, *The Fall of the Ottomans: The Great War in the Middle East, 1914–1920* (London: Allen Lane, 2015), p. 9.

68. Text of the Ottoman-Russian Agreement (also called the Yeniköy Agreement) of February 8, 1914, can be found in Yusuf Hikmet Bayur, *Türk İnkılabı Tarihi* (History of the Turkish Revolution), Vol. 2 (Sec.3) (Ankara: Türk Tarih Kurumu Basımevi, second edition, 1991), pp. 169–77.

69. Eric Weitz, *A Century of Genocide: Utopias of Race and Nation* (Princeton, NJ and Oxford: Princeton University Press, 2003), p. 3.

70. Archives de Ministère des Affaires Etrangères, Courneuve, Paris (henceforth referred to as MAE), NS Turquie, Vol. 84, pp. 79–83. Influences étrangères dans le vilayet d'Adana. Les Américains et les Anglais. M. Ronflard (Mersine) à Stéphane Pichon (Paris), 20 mai 1910.

71. Lewis Thomas and Richard Frye, *The United States and Turkey and Iran* (Cambridge, MA: Harvard University Press, 1951), p. 140; Roderic Davison, "Westernized Education in Ottoman Turkey," *The Middle East Journal*, Vol. 15, No. 3 (Summer 1961), p. 291.

72. Thomas and Frye, *The United States and Turkey and Iran*, pp. 140–41.

73. Ibid., p. 60.

74. Alan, *Osmanlı İmparatorluğunda Amerikan Protestan Okulları*.

75. United States National Archives and Records Administration, College Park, Maryland (henceforth referred to as USNA), Inquiry Documents: Special Reports and Studies, 1917–1919, Document 85, Report on the Vilayet of Adana, O. J. Campbell, p. 19; James Kay Sutherland, *The Adventures of an Armenian Boy: An Autobiography and Historical Narrative Encompassing the Last Thirty Years of the Ottoman Empire* (Ann Arbor, MI: Ann Arbor Press, 1964), p. 7; Armen Hovannisian, "The United States Inquiry and the Armenian Question, 1917–1919 The Archival Papers," *The Armenian Review*, Vol. 37, Vol. 1 (Spring 1984), p. 153. For more on St. Paul's Institute at Tarsus, see Bartholomew, "Tarsus American School, 1888–1988: The Evolution of a Missionary Institution in Turkey," and Kocabaşoğlu, *Kendi Belgeleriyle Anadolu'daki Amerika*, pp. 200–3.

76. USNA, Inquiry Documents: Special Reports and Studies, 1917–1919, Document 97, Turkish Survey, Adana, Thomas Davidson Christie, pp. 3–4; Redan, *La Cilicie et le problème ottoman*, p. 49; *The Adana Massacres and the Catholic Missionaries*, p. 21; Adnan Şişman, *Yirminci Yüzyıl Başlarında Osmanlı Devletinde Yabancı Devletlerin Kültürel ve Sosyal Müesseseleri* (Cultural and Social Institutions of the Foreign States in the Ottoman State at the Beginning of the Twentieth Century) (Ankara: Atatürk Araştırma Merkezi, 2006).

77. For more details on the subject, see in particular Jacques Thobie, "La France a-t-elle une politique culturelle dans l'Empire ottoman à la veille de la première guerre mondiale?" *Relations internationales*, Vol. 25 (1981), pp. 21–40.

78. Strong, *Condensed Sketch of the Missions of the American Board in Asiatic Turkey*, pp. 14–15.

79. Shrikian, "Armenians Under the Ottoman Empire and the American Mission's Influence on Their Intellectual and Social Renaissance," p. 130.

80. Albert Howe Lybyer, "America's Missionary Record in Turkey," *The Current History Magazine*, Vol. 19, No. 5 (February 1924), p. 805.

81. James Barton, "New Turkey and Modern Education The Influence of American Colleges and Schools," *The Delta Upsilon Quarterly*, Vol. 15 (September 15, 1909), p. 506.

82. William Nesbitt Chambers, "The Ambassador at Adana," *The Orient*, Vol. 5, No. 19 (May 13, 1914), p. 183. *The Orient* was a well-edited weekly record of the religious, educational, political, economic, and other interests of the Ottoman Empire and the Near East published between 1910 and 1923 in English at the American Bible House in İstanbul. *The Bosphorus News*, hitherto published for private circulation, appeared on April 20, 1910, under a new name, *The Orient*, and with the offical sanction of the Ottoman Press Bureau. It was hoped that this change in name would define more clearly the comprehensive and inclusive aim of the paper and that its official recognition by the Ottoman authorities would help to give it a free and wide circulation in the Empire and other countries. The primary aim of *The Orient* would be to keep English readers in touch with the new life in the Ottoman Empire and adjacent countries, and follow as closely as possible those currents which were making for the permanent civilization of the East. See *The Orient*, No. 1 (April 20, 1910), p. 1.

83. MAE, NS Turquie, Vol. 84, pp. 79–83. Influences étrangères dans le vilayet d'Adana. Les Américaines et les Anglais. M. Ronflard (Mersine) à Stéphane Pichon (Paris), 20 mai 1909.

84. Ibid; FO 424/169. On the Province of Adana. Thomas Jago (Aleppo) to the Marquis of Salisbury (FO), April 18, 1891.

85. MAE, NS Turquie, Vol. 84, pp. 79–83. Influences étrangères dans le vilayet d'Adana. Les Américaines et les Anglais. M. Ronflard (Mersine) à Stéphane Pichon (Paris), 20 mai 1909.

86. "The 22 Days of Marash: Papers on the Defense of the City Against Turkish Forces Jan.- Feb., 1920," Part I, *The Armenian Review*, Vol. 30, No. 4 (Winter 1977), pp. 384–85; Strong, *Condensed Sketch of the Missions of the American Board in Asiatic Turkey*, p. 25.

Chapter Three

Major Causes of the Outbreak, 1908–1909

One cannot understand the Adana affair without a consideration of developments and institutions in the Ottoman realm and polity from 1876 to 1909 in their proper context.

OTTOMAN *MILLET* SYSTEM

The policy adopted by the Ottoman Empire toward its Christian subjects was more liberal than that adopted by Russia toward the natives of central Asia. Except for the Turkoman militia, there was no military service whatever open to the natives of central Asia. There was little or no education and no civil employment for them. Hardly a single one was employed, and almost every appointment there, down to the lowest clerkship, was held by a Russian. This was the case not only with the administrative offices in central Asia, but the customs, postal, telegraph, railway, and every other sort of official was a Russian, and in Russian central Asia the native had practically no share in the administration of his country.[1]

Stanford Shaw, the late professor of Turkish and Judeo-Turkish history at the University of California at Los Angeles and professor of Turkish history at Bilkent University, Ankara, one of the most accomplished specialists in the arcane discipline of deciphering Ottoman scribal calligraphy, convincingly demonstrates that the Ottoman Empire constituted one of the most diverse societies the world has ever known. Added to the native Muslims, Jews, and Christians living in the lands conquered by the Ottomans were thousands of refugees who found sanctuary in the Empire: Jews fleeing from the Christian reconquest of Spain and Portugal and from oppression in Europe and Russia right up to and including the time of the Russian revolution and of Nazi persecutions in the twentieth century; Christians fleeing from revolutions in central Europe and Russia; and, most significant in numbers, hundreds of thousands of Turks and other Muslims fleeing from massacre and persecution in Russia and the independent states established in southeastern Europe during the nineteenth and early twentieth centuries. Whether in the great cities and towns, where they congregated in their own districts, or in separate villages, the non-Muslim peoples of the Ottoman Empire grouped themselves into autonomous communities usually called *millets*, in which they preserved their own languages, traditions, religious practices, and customs, while coming together in a manner that might well have produced the sort of conflicts that have characterized Middle Eastern society since the Ottoman Empire came to an end but did not. In considering Ottoman society, Shaw contends, the question one must ask above all others is why there were very few conflicts; why were all of these peoples able to live together for so long in relative peace and harmony?[2]

In the Ottoman Empire the term *millet* was used for the organized, recognized, religio-political communities enjoying certain rights of autonomy. The primary basis was religious rather than ethnic. The *millet*, with its own ecclesiastico-civil leader and internal administration, had complete charge of its own affairs. The religious hierarchy was responsible for the spiritual welfare of its particular *millet*, but it also had broad jurisdiction in legal matters affecting two or more parties in the same *millet*, and oversaw social and educational life. This meant that the non-Muslim communities could live under their own leaders in their own way and follow their own religions and customs as they had in the past. It was the beginning of a remarkable system of tolerance for minorities, perhaps best known for its welcome of tens of thousands of Spanish Jews to the Ottoman Empire in the days of the Inquisition.[3]

This mosaic pattern, in which a Muslim and a non-Muslim living side by side in the same state under the same sovereign were subject to different laws and different officials, had served the Ottoman Empire well for over four centuries.[4] Such a system may even be described as one of "shared sovereignty," with the non-Muslim communities as junior partners.[5]

Sir Charles Wilson, in his article "Armenia" in the *Encyclopaedia Britannica* (eleventh edition), 1911, says:

> This *imperium in imperio* secured the Armenians a recognised position before the law, the free enjoyment of their religion, the possession of their churches and monastries, and the right to educate their children and manage their municipal affairs. It also encouraged the growth of a community life, which eventually gave birth to an intense longing for national life. On the other hand it degraded

the priesthood. The priests became political leaders rather than spiritual guides, and sought promotion by bribery and intrigue. Education was neglected and discouraged, servility and treachery were developed, and in less than a century the people had become depraved and degraded to an almost incredible extent.

And Sir Charles Eliot (Odysseus) in his *Turkey in Europe* declares that until after the Ottoman-Russian war of 1877–1878:

> Turks and Armenians got on excellently together. The Armenians looked upon Russia as their enemy, and a large Armenian population from that country migrated into Kurdistan. The Russians restricted the Armenian Church, schools, and language; the Turks, on the contrary, were perfectly tolerant and liberal as to all such matters. . . . The balance of wealth certainly remained with the Christians. The Turks treated them with good-humoured confidence, and the phrase "millet-i-sadika" (the loyal community) was regularly applied to them.[6]

It is also to be reminded that the Ottoman conquest of Anatolia and the Balkans was a product of decay and degeneration which had taken place in the Byzantine Empire and its successor states before the Ottomans came on the scene. The Turks conquered an İstanbul which had long since been despoiled and depopulated by the Latin Crusaders as well as by centuries of internal strife and dissension. The Ottomans brought vitality and renewal to the area for many centuries before their Empire became subject to decline as well as to the inevitable results of nationalistic aspirations for independence on the part of all the subject peoples, including the Turks. Ottoman rule in Anatolia, far from being the "oppression"[7] characterized by Hrachik Simonyan, rather was characterized by tolerance of different ethnic, social, and religious communities to a considerably greater extent than any major state or empire in Europe.

Even under less enlightened rulers than the Young Turk government the Turks had been extraordinarily tolerant to other religions. During the five hundred years of Turkish rule of Jerusalem no religious shrine belonging to another people was molested. All sacred spots were open to visitors of the different faiths. And it may be noted in this connection that the inauguration of Allied control after the First World War precipitated an immediate squabble of nations and sects concerning the guardianship of the holy place. It is not likely, either, that any Western nation would have allowed to Muslim missionaries extraterritorial rights such as had been enjoyed by the Robert College in İstanbul.

What Christian state in Europe allowed those of other religions to live and worship freely and to prosper economically as did the Ottomans in the *millet* system? Ask the thousands of Jews who flocked into the Ottoman

Empire from persecution in Spain, central Europe, and Russia. The dark and systematic persecution, massacre, and expulsion of millions of Turks and other Muslims in the Balkan states which gained their independence from the Ottomans during the nineteenth century contrasted sharply with the toleration which they had experienced in Ottoman society. Simonyan and those who may still accept his viewpoint should consult the brilliant collection of articles published by Benjamin Braude and Bernard Lewis in *Christians and Jews in the Ottoman Empire: The Functioning of a Plural Society.*

Ronald Grigor Suny, Charles Tilly collegiate professor of history at the University of Michigan, points out that the *millet* system was extraordinarily important in distinguishing and preserving a sense of Armenianness. It provided considerable benefits and a degree of cultural and political autonomy. The church remained at the head of the nation; Armenians with commercial and industrial skills were able to climb to the very pinnacle of the Ottoman economic order. Suny says "without exagerrating the harmony of Turkish-Armenian relations between 1453 and 1878 or neglecting the considerable burdens imposed on non-Muslims, particularly Anatolian peasants, this long period can be seen as one of relatively benign symbiosis."[8]

RESTORATION OF THE CONSTITUTION, JULY 24, 1908

On the morning of July 24, 1908, Sultan Abdülhamid II issued an *iradé* (imperial decree), restoring the constitution[9] which had been suspended for thirty years, and ordering the election of a parliament.[10] The first clause of the decree stated: "Every individual subject, irrespective of ethnic origin or religion is entitled to personal freedom and to an equal share in the rights and obligations of the country"; most of the other clauses defined this freedom and these rights in greater detail. Civil liberty was to be the result of the substitution of legality for arbitrariness. Above all, legislative power was to be exercised in an orderly and legitimate manner. Henceforth things were to be done according to the book. By virtue of this decree, a circular telegram was dispatched by Said Paşa,[11] the grand vizier, to the provincial authorities. The following is the text of this document published by the Ottoman press: "An imperial iradé has been promulgated commanding the convocation of Parliament, in accordance with the provisions of the Constitution, which is the work of His Imperial Majesty the Sultan. This imperial decision has telegraphically been transmitted to all the Vilayets [provinces] and Mutasarrıflıks [subdistricts], urging them to proceed with the qualifications required by the Act of Constitution."[12] Thus a new era had begun.

July 24 may be characterized as an eventful and memorable day. An announced event of the greatest importance suddenly took place in İstanbul. This event was heralded as the end of absolutism and the inauguration of constitutional government in the Ottoman Empire, an almost bloodless revolution. The Young Turks called upon the world to see how in one day they could do what had taken Western peoples centuries to accomplish.[13]

This date marks the beginning of a period referred to in Ottoman historiography as that of "Second Constitutionalism 1908–1918" and the lifting of rigid censorship. Indeed, it is still remembered and celebrated by the Turkish press as the foundation of freedom of expression in publishing. Before July 24 no printed matter in book, magazine, or newspaper could be given to the public without official approval, and much that was altogether innocent and harmless was likely to fall under the ban. To edit a paper was about as hazardous a business as to manufacture gunpowder. Only the most circumspect survived. Opposition newspapers and periodicals were printed in Paris, London, or Geneva and smuggled into the country in private correspondence. Within a week after liberty of the press was decreed all editors in İstanbul were invited by the Muslim editors of a Muslim paper to meet and form a press association, which was done. Every facility of modern journalism could now be freely used for circulation of Christian literature.[14]

On July 25, the Ottoman newspapers called upon all the subjects of the sultan, regardless of origin or religion, to make the most of their newfound liberty for the common good of the Ottoman Empire, and gave expression to the joy felt by all classes at the commencement of a new era. The reality of the revival of the Constitution being evident from July 25's uncensored newspapers, the population of İstanbul gave expression to their joy by decorating the city and by enthusiastic demonstrations at the Ministry of Foreign Affairs and other public offices. Determination of all to combine in working for the good of the Empire and loyalty to the sultan formed the keynote of these demonstrations. The grand vizier, Said Paşa, was given a popular ovation the same date by several thousand Muslims, Christians, and Jews assembled at the Grand Vizierate, who insisted on him receiving and replying to an address. The crowd was animated with good humor, and it was remarkable to see the fraternization of Muslims and Christians, especially Armenians.

On July 26, a crowd of *mollas* (Muslim teachers or interpreters of the religious law) and *softas* passed from Yıldız Palace to fraternize with the Armenians, with the Greeks, and even with the Bulgarian Exarch. "Equality and fraternity; no distinction of men on account of their creed," was the note of all speeches delivered. On August 6, a new ministry was formed. The new minister of mines, Gabriel Noradounghian, was an Armenian.[15]

The *Serveti Fünun* commenced publishing every day. New journals under the names of *Cihan, Ceride, Nizam*, and *Selamet* appeared. The weekly newspaper *Mekteb* was converted into a daily one.

The next steps were abolishing the secret police and its prerogatives for searches, seizures, and suppression of the spies. A general amnesty for political prisoners was proclaimed, and this was extended to nonpolitical prisoners who had served more than two-thirds of their sentence. An official communiqué stated that all those who formed part of the bands in the Macedonian provinces and who surrendered their arms to the authorities would profit by a general amnesty. Those political offenders who were in Europe or imprisoned in provinces and who were pardoned would be employed in the government service. Policemen were urged to fulfill their duties in accordance with the law. The authorities of the provinces and *mutasarrıflıks* received an official communication of the imperial decree commanding that all correspondence should in the future be forwarded to the Sublime Porte, the Grand Vizierate being the center of public affairs. The Sublime Porte commenced the formalities for the return to their homes of the political offenders. Ali Kemal Bey[16] returned from Paris, profiting by the political amnesty. He was summoned to the imperial palace, where he was the object of sultan's kindness.[17]

A few days later, a more detailed imperial decree was published. The proclamation of the constitution was not brought about by direct foreign pressure upon the sultan, nor was it the work of a few statesmen ahead of their time like the promulgation of the constitution of December 23, 1876. It had been obtained by the joint pressure of the army and the Muslim subjects. The Young Turk revolution, or "Declaration of Freedom" as the Turks themselves called it, was singularly bloodless as compared with similar events in Christian lands. It took all Europe by surprise.[18]

The event raised great expectations among both natives and foreigners. An American missionary at Kayseri exclaimed, "This is nothing other than the birth of a genuine Ottoman nation. The Turks may surpass the Armenians in their appreciation of and devotion to the principles of real liberty and genuine civilization."[19] In the flood of sympathy for the Young Turks that swept over Europe the revolutionaries were pictured as a new version of the standard bearers of the French Revolution. The young staff officers from the boulevards of "Little Paris" (Salonika[20]) and the political exiles who had returned from the cafés and political clubs of Paris helped to establish this image. It seemed as if Pera (Beyoğlu) and Galata had entered a new era. The theaters put on patriotic plays, political and cultural clubs sprang up everywhere, educated Muslim women removed the veil, and newspapers and political pamphlets issued forth in an ever-growing stream from the printing presses.[21]

Foes became friends, nationality and creed forgotten, in the universal joy into which people were so unexpectedly plunged. "O country, O mother, be thou happy and joyful to-day," sang the large and mixed crowd, passing from under the windows of Halidé Edib's (Adıvar) house in Nuruosmaniye, an area close to the Sublime Porte in İstanbul. "No one who heard it sung in the ecstatic tones of the crowds could keep back his [or her] tears, so much did it express of sincerity and joy," she said. Halidé Edib was spurred to a life in letters by the events of 1908, which she witnessed firsthand.[22]

All—Turks, Armenians, Greeks, Jews, Albanians, Arabs, and the rest—would now constitute one people: Ottoman. Although no parliament met in İstanbul during the three decades, 1878–1908, the Sublime Porte annually published the constitution as the basic law of the Empire, thereby contributing unconsciously to the Young Turk agitation for the reestablishment of parliamentary government.[23]

Chastened by a bitter experience, the Turks became fully aware that they could only keep together what remained of the inheritance of Ottoman, their inheritance, through the contentment of the peoples they ruled. It was for this reason that the first care of the Young Turk party in its hour of triumph was to proclaim and emphasize what, *du reste*, constituted one of the fundamental principles of the resuscitated constitution of Grand Vizier Midhat Paşa, namely, the equality before the law, under the common name of Ottomans, of all the elements of the heterogeneous multitude which inhabited the empire. Many among the Turkish population cordially adhered to this notion of its leaders. Few incidents in history were more touching than the visit paid by a large assemblage of Turks to the Armenian cemetery in İstanbul in order to deposit floral tributes on the graves of the victims of the massacre of 1894 and to have prayers recited, by a priest of their own persuasion, over the dead.[24]

Similar ceremonies took place in the cemeteries of the Turks and Armenians in the capital and the suburbs. Many Young Turks took part in these ceremonies and spoke to proclaim the fraternity of the Turks and Armenians and their melting into one same Ottoman nationality under the aegis of the Constitution and the Liberty. In the Armenian church of Kadıköy, a vibrant patriotic speech was delivered at the end of the religious ceremony by a Young Turk.[25]

Many years since, the Macedonian provinces were a prey to bands of several nationalities. Everywhere, there were murders, fires, etc. That state of things had as its object the separation of the Ottoman Empire of three of its best provinces, known under the name of the three Macedonian provinces. The disturbers complained of the bad administration prevailing there. The government, notwithstanding all sacrifices, was unable to stifle the rebellion. The Macedonian question inspired the greatest anxiety to the Ottoman official circles. It even menaced the European equilibrium. It was the reason why the European governments intervened with pretensions. As soon as the constitution was reestablished, all those forming part of the various bands presented themselves to the local authorities, and assured them that they would never perpetrate any seditious acts.[26]

The change was a brilliant success and was brought about without bloodshed. The CUP acted with moderation and gave no sign of wishing to abandon that course. The experiment was of a most interesting kind and watched with keen interest. The CUP showed itself from the first keenly alive to the necessity of preserving order and of avoiding extremes. Its determination of purpose was constantly tempered by moderation. Its bloodless revolution was carried on with singular ability and dignity. It was kept well in hand. The approval of all Europe was gained by the astonishing moderation of the untried body of men, men absolutely without experience in government, who formed the CUP.[27]

The Times of London, dealing with the situation in the Ottoman Empire, said the only possible policy for the powers toward that state of things was to observe an attitude of nonintervention. All the European nations would join in congratulating the Young Turks, should they realize the transformation of the Ottoman Empire. The future of the Young Turks belonged, in large measure, to themselves, but they should still deserve the confidence of Europe.[28]

The French press comment was very favorable to the reestablishment of the constitution in the Ottoman Empire. This event met the general approval of the political and financial circles. The guarantee of a brilliant future for the country was seen in it.[29]

The German press saw in the reform movement in the Ottoman Empire an element of both useful and salutary for the country, and believed that from this new era would result an increase in the strength of the country, which would astonish the entire world. The newspapers added that German policy had always used its influence in the Sublime Porte against all that was capable of hindering the consolidation and development of the Ottoman Empire. All the German press and public opinion had, therefore, joyfully greeted the reform movement which took place in the country.[30]

The Italian newspapers welcomed with deep sympathy the declaration of the constitution. Agence Italiana stated that this was a great historical and political event which was preluded by the nomination of Said Paşa as grand vizier. It expressed its confidence in the new order of things which would certainly provide tranquility and prosperity to the Ottoman Empire.[31]

From the European newspaper articles, published up until the end of July 1908, it resulted that all hailed the new regime in a sympathetic manner, and expressed satisfaction at seeing a common joyfulness and a spirit of fraternity manifested between Muslims and non-Muslims in the Ottoman Empire. Several newspapers stated that the constitution was the only real guarantee of the stability of the Empire's future. Other journals laid stress on the necessity of reforming the finance, which would create an era of economic prosperity for the country.[32]

The European scholars and statesmen continued to express their confidence in the Young Turk revolution. For instance, celebrated Austrian Professor Herman Vambery published on August 9, 1908 in the *Pester Lloyd* an article headed, "The Constitutional Turkey." He said:

> Up to the present we have regarded the Young Turks as a political party of romanesque tendencies, and we did not consider simultaneously that all learned Ottoman was a Young Turk, and thus all the nation, except some old Conservatives, belonged to that party. Ten years ago, I knew Viziers and Ministers, who, in secretly, were Young Turks; and also male members of the Imperial family already belonged to that party, before Damad Mahmud Pasha and his sons commenced their action in Paris.

Vambery subsequently declared that the parliamentary regime was always appreciated and recommended by Islamism. The Koran states: Error is preferable to truth, if the former results from a consultative corps and the latter from an arbitrary one. Continuing, Vambery remarked: "The Turkish people, during these long years of oppression, have learned to appreciate the benefits of a Liberal regime, and the fact that in face of the new state of things, they observed an exemplary attitude, by avoiding excesses, proves than all other thing that they are ripe for the Constitutional life."[33]

E. J. Dillon, the foreign affairs editor of *The Contemporary Review*, wrote in September 1908:

> Meanwhile the highest praise is due to the Young Turkish Party, whose perspicacious leaders have given the world a precious lesson in political tactics and moderation. Whatever the upshot of their action they richly deserve success, and the warmest sympathies of the British nation will be with them until they have brought their patriotic work to a successful issue. They would do well, however, to bear well in mind the fact that in revolutionary movements it is much harder to keep than to win.[34]

In the French Chamber of Deputies on November 26, 1908, Paul Deschanel—a leading political figure who was later to become the president of republic—said the recent revolution changed the internal and external politics of the Ottoman Empire, where France must countenance the new regime. Ottoman government would work for the economic and pacific development of its prosperity. Deschanel subsequently spoke of French interests in the Ottoman land, where French companies possessed several railway lines, hospitals, and schools. The French were, therefore, interested to guarantee the territorial integrity and the independence of the Ottoman Empire, where welfare depended on the Young Turk regime which France supported. Stéphane Pichon, minister of foreign affairs, then read in the government's name a declaration concerning Eastern affairs, and said that from the outset of the Young Turk revolution, the French government congratulated the Ottoman government and expressed its confidence in the new regime.[35]

In the Italian Chamber of Deputies on December 4, 1909, Tommaso Tittoni, minister of foreign affairs, stated that the Ottoman Empire afforded to the world an admirable example of a profound revolution accomplished in a pacific fashion. Continuing, he said that Italy sympathetically hailed the new regime. Italy attached great importance to its relations with the Ottoman Empire. The minister then pointed out with pleasure that the new regime dissipated all misunderstandings and suspicions which existed between the Ottoman Empire and Italy. Never in the past was the intercourse between both govenments so fraught with such sincere and mutual confidence and sympathy.[36]

CONSTITUTION OF DECEMBER 23, 1876

The individual rights and civil liberties of Ottoman subjects were well stipulated in the constitution of 1876—individual freedom from arbitrary punishment, freedom of religion and of privileges accorded the *millets*, freedom of the press within the limits of law, freedom of commercial, industrial or agricultural association, the right of petition, security of property and domicile, and taxation according to law and the individual's means. Many of these principles had been stated before in the *Tanzimat*[37] pronouncements from 1839 on, but never all together nor so explicitly.[38]

Two documents of great value were issued by Sultan Abdülmecid (r. 1823–1861); one in 1839 known as the *Hattı Şerif* (Sacred Edict) of Gülhane,[39] and the other in 1856, known as the *Hattı Hümayun* (Reform Edict). The former did not touch the question of religious liberty, which was definitely taken up in the latter. The *Hattı Şerif*, the Magna Carta of the Ottoman Empire, treated in the main of three topics: the guarantees which would ensure the subjects perfect security for their lives, their honor, and their property; a regular method of recruiting and levying the army; and fixing the duration of the service. The main points of this rescript were there: (1) The cause of every accused party would be tried publicly, in conformity with the divine law; until a regular sentence was pronounced, no one could be put to death, secretly or publicly, by poison or any other form of punishment. (2) No one would be permitted to assail the honor of anyone, whosoever they might be. (3) Every person would enjoy the possession of their property, of every nature, and dispose of it with the most perfect liberty, without anyone being able to impede them. Thus, for example, the innocent heirs of a criminal would not be deprived of their legal rights, and the property of the criminal would not be confiscated. (4) These imperial concessions extended to all Ottoman subjects, whatever religion or sect they might belong to, and they would enjoy them without any exception. (5) Perfect security was therefore granted to the inhabitants of the Empire, with regard to their life, their honor, and their fortune, as the sacred text of the law demanded. (6) With reference to the other points, as they must be regulated by the concurrence of enlightened opinions, the Council of Justice, augmented by as many new members as might be deemed necessary, to whom would be adjoined, on certain days which should be appointed, the minister and the notables of the Empire, would meet for the purpose of establishing the fundamental laws on these points relating to the security of life and property and the imposition of the taxes. Every one in these assemblies would state their ideas freely and give their opinion. (7) The laws relating to the regulations of the military service would be discussed by the Military Council, holding its meeting at the palace of the *Serasker* (between minister of war and chief of the general staff). As soon as the law is decided upon, it would be presented to the sultan, and in order that it might be eternally valid and applicable, the sultan would confirm it by his sanction, written above by the Imperial hand. The *Hattı Şerif* took the first tentative steps toward granting civic equality for non-Muslims. It proposed a reform project to secularize the Ottoman courts and bring a greater degree of central control over the administration of the empire.[40]

The *Hattı Hümayun* of 1856 expressly confirmed the above and added clauses of confirming the privileges and spiritual immunities granted by former sultans to all Christian or other non-Muslim communities; it also contained this celebrated clause: "As all forms of religion are and shall be freely professed in my dominions, no subject of my Empire shall be hindered in the exercise of the religion that he professes, nor shall be compelled to change his religion." It also provided for the military service of non-Muslims, for equality of taxation, for the abolishing of everything that resembled torture, and of corporal punishment except in conformity with disciplinary regulations. This document was up to that time the most liberal that had ever been issued by any sultan. It affected everything from the military and bureaucracy to a secularization of education and the establishment of universities on French models. Perhaps most importantly, modernization at the War College resulted in Western ideas permeating the military. This edict was an attempt to transform the sociopolitical organization of the Ottoman Empire from the *millet* system to one of Ottoman citizens subject to the secular laws of the empire. These efforts led to the establishment of a constitution in 1876 in the hope of bringing the Ottoman Empire in line with the norms of the "Concert of Europe."[41]

Midhat Paşa, the grand vizier, proclaimed the new Ottoman Constitution before the Ministry of Foreign Affairs at the Sublime Porte on December 23, 1876, with blasts of trumpets. In the center of the building a box had been constructed, and here stood Midhat Paşa, who with various Greek, Armenian, and Jewish dignitaries awaited the sultan's firman, which, for the future, was to equalize Muslims and non-Muslims in the eyes of the Islamic law. The sultan's secretary rode up and presented Midhat Paşa with a richly decorated envelope, which the grand vizier at once kissed and pressed to his head in token of obedience, subsequently handing it to his subordinates to do likewise. He next read the terms of the constitution out to the assembled crowd. The guns finally boomed forth a salute, and the long promised constitution was an established fact.[42]

Midhat Paşa's constitution represented the capstone of *Tanzimat* liberal reform. He became the first grand vizier to honor the Greek and Armenian patriarchs by calling on them: they greeted him as "the resuscitator of the Ottoman Empire."

The first Ottoman Chamber of Deputies met on March 19, 1877, under the speakership of Ahmed Vefik Efendi, whom the sultan had chosen from the list of candidates submitted to him, in accordance of Article 77 of the constitution. This first speaker of the Ottoman Chamber of Deputies was a former pupil of the Lycée Saint-Louis at Paris. As noted in the Introduction, he was a devoted lover of literature. There were 115 deputies of which sixty-seven were Muslim, forty-four Christian, and four Jewish, comprising some fourteen different nationalities.

Both the religious and the secular institutions of the Ottoman Empire involved precedents for a parliament. Prophet Muhammed himself conferred with the wisest of his companions, and once spread his cloak to receive envoys of Christian tribes. The *ulema*[43] took counsel together on occasion up to the present time. The Islamic Law was fundamentally democratic and opposed in essence to absolutism. The habit of regarding it as fundamental law enabled even the most uneducated of Muslims to grasp the idea of a constitution. As mentioned previously, the non-Muslim nationalities of the Empire also had long governed their own affairs under special constitutive laws, which authorized national assemblies. Further, in the early Ottoman times the sultan gathered about him a *divan* (consultative council) of his chief servants, captains, judges, and secretaries. In the glorious period this assembly met regularly four days in the week for the transaction of business. Of late there had been at least a Council of State and a Council of Ministers. The Ottoman Parliament might therefore be regarded not as a complete innovation, but as an enlargement and improvement of familiar institutions. Midhat Paşa's attempt of thirty-two years before had prepared the way for it, both by providing a constitution and by leading to two parliamentary sessions.[44]

Article 8 of the constitution stated that all subjects of the Empire were, without distinction, called Ottomans, whatever religion they professed. The qualification of Ottoman could be acquired and lost according to the cases specified by law. According to Article 9, all Ottomans enjoyed individual liberty on condition that they did not interfere with the liberty of others. Article 10 stipulated that individual liberty was absolutely inviolable. None should, under any pretext, suffer any punishment whatever, except in cases determined by law, and following the forms that it prescribed. Article 11 said Islamism is the state religion. At the same time as guarding this principle, the state protected the free exercise of all forms of worship recognized in the Empire and maintained the religious privileges accorded to the various communities on condition that no breach of public order or good morals be committed. Article 17 declared all Ottomans were equal in the eyes of the law. Henceforth, there would be Muslims at the mosque, Christians at the church, and Jews at the synagogue, but all other times and all other places there would be, as far as the law was concerned, only Ottomans. They had the same rights and the same duties toward the country, without prejudice as to that which concerned the religion. This provision, later interpreted to require military service of non-Muslims, who had been exempt from conscription in return for the payment of a military exemption tax, was the source of a great deal of bitterness during the Young Turk revolution. Although the Christian populations of the Ottoman Empire were willing to accept equality in rights with Muslims, many of them objected strenuously to service in the Ottoman armies. Article 19 proclaimed that all Ottomans were admitted to public departments according to aptitude, their merit, and their capacity, subject only to the requirement that they know Turkish, which was declared to be the official language of the state.[45]

These provisions primarily benefited the Empire's non-Muslim peoples, but scattered throughout the constitution were guarantees of other individual rights which both Muslim and and non-Muslim could view with equal enthusiasm and which, collectively, comprised what might be termed an Ottoman Bill of Rights. These articles constituted perhaps the most radical innovation contained in the constitution, for never before had such extensive personal freedoms been decreed for the public at large.[46]

Probably the most beneficial aspect of the constitution was its emphasis on the equality of all Ottoman subjects—again an extension of the Ottomanism doctrine characteristic of the *Tanzimat* period. The enumeration of civil liberties was subject to no qualifications as to race or creed. It is obvious that almost the entire constitution was Western in inspiration. This was a big step in the direction in which Sultan Mahmud II (r. 1808–1839) had started Ottoman political development. There are many parallels to be found between the 1876 constitution and the Belgian Constitution of 1831.[47]

All of these developments laid the foundation for the creation of an equal Ottoman citizenry undifferentiated by religion. In their wake, inhabitants of the empire found themselves confronted with a new framework for understanding their world. This framework—often referred to as Ottomanism—was based on the assumption that all of the various religions and ethnic communities of the empire would unite in support of their homeland.[48]

The constitution of 1876 guaranteed new freedoms to the inhabitants of the Empire while simultaneously declaring that they should begin to consider themselves Ottomans regardless of faith or background. This move represented an innovation, since the term had originally referred to members of the ruling dynasty of the Empire and had for some time been reserved for an important class of Muslim officials employed by the state. Although attempts to create unity among the country's residents were not new, the constitution was arguably the clearest and most forceful articulation of this platform to date. It also led, within a year, to the opening of the first Ottoman Parliament, which drew delegates from the diverse regions and offered imperial citizens their first glimpse of representative government on an imperial scale.[49]

The constitution of 1876—the first written fundamental law adopted in a country outside the European tradition—firmly established the principle of secularization and Europeanization of the legal system. The whole adoption of European law codes in the period ahead was the logical culmination of that trend.

The suspension of the constitution in 1878 could not, however, conceal the fact that the Ottoman Empire had had its first parliament—a parliament which demonstrated a considerable amount of independence and held out high hopes that a future revival of representative government might rally round it a public opinion which no ruler would dare to defy. Although no parliament met in İstanbul during the three decades, 1878–1908, the Sublime Porte annually published the constitution of 1876 as the basic law of the Empire, thereby unconsciously led to the Young Turk agitation, for the reestablishment of parliamentary government.[50]

In fact, the thirty years of Hamidian rule had a curious educative effect. The autocratic nature of the government appeared to turn the minds of many thinking Ottomans toward the principles of the unused constitution. It alone seemed to promise the restoration of the nation to an honorable place before the world. In patience and silence the end of absolute government was awaited. When, on July 24, 1908, Sultan Abdülhamid II, forced by the army and the CUP, ordered the election of a new parliament and proclaimed his intention of governing under the constitution, the whole country responded with an outburst of joy and a unanimity of approval that seemed miraculous. So ready was the Ottoman Empire for the new regime, that in the twinkling of an eye, the nation transferred its obedience from the sultan to the power that had triumphed over him. The CUP, relying on the support of the army, accepted the sovereign control of the Ottoman realm, as a trust to be delivered over to parliament when it should assemble.[51]

The era of the *Tanzimat* was marked by an atmosphere of mutual trust between the Young Ottomans and the Armenian elites. Mustafa Reşid Paşa, Ali Paşa, Fuad Paşa, Midhat Paşa: they all had Armenian counsellors and employed competent Armenian secretaries and interpreters whose loyalty was beyond doubt. There were Armenians in the Ministry of Foreign Affairs and in the management of the Mint (the Bezciyan family).[52]

The Young Turk ideals summarized in Midhat Paşa's constitution aimed to build a society where all groups in the empire cooperated with one another in the spirit of brotherhood. The Young Turks wished to establish an Ottoman state in which all the subjects lived as equals. The different subject groups would meet together in a parliamentary structure, sending representatives to İstanbul to meet in regular sessions.[53]

Among those who worked with the veteran statesman Midhat Paşa at the establishment and working of the Ottoman Constitution, a large number were Armenian dignitaries. Krikor Odian, undersecretary of the Ministry of Public Works, particularly distinguished himself. Odian, trained as a lawyer, rose rapidly within the Ottoman civil service. One of the architects of the Armenian national constitution in 1863, he was the most illustrious of the collaborators of Midhat Paşa in his work of liberal reform. He was quiet and unassuming, but consecrated and capable, keenly observant and most diligent in duty.[54] A key adviser and member of the Ottoman State Council, Odian was given the highest rank in the Empire's civil service.[55]

The constitution was there; the sultan formally committed to it. This was, all elements of the situation considered, a remarkable achievement. A means for further development had been provided. The test would be how the opportunity was used.

The Young Turks pledged themselves to the principle of religious freedom and racial equality. They planned a state system of education for all elements. They undertook to develop the country's rich resources, to apply the standards of honesty and frugal piety that characterized the private life of the Ottoman nation to the corrupt administration of its public revenues, to pay a valiant army, and to recruit it from all elements. They told the Ottoman soldiers of the French Revolution; of the transformation of Japan, and that nation's successful stand against Russia; of the twenty thousand Russian Muslims who had a voice in the first Duma; of the unrest in India; the constitutional movement in Iran; the awakening of Asia. With the plea of reform they won the Ottoman army over to liberalism.[56]

Progressive reforms were inaugurated, far more religious toleration was declared and while the people celebrated their new liberty in unparalleled scenes of rejoicing, their leaders revealed a poise of judgment and an ability in reconstruction that promised well for the future. Now, said the Turkish reformers, as the Americans celebrate July 4, and the French July 14, so the Ottoman Empire would hereafter celebrate July 23 as the birthday of their liberty. Reformers said: "As Muslims, Christians and Jews we have our different religions, but we are all alike Ottomans. In national matters there is no distinction. According to our relative numbers, we will have the same share in the government and we will alike join the army in the defense of our common country." In James Reid's opinion, the Young Turks desired to create an Ottoman society where all within were Ottoman citizens who shared a common ideal.[57]

This attempt received official sanction from the Sheikh-ul-Islam, who, by a circular letter addressed to all the religious leaders of the Muslims, declared that, according to a correct interpretation of the Koran, the sacred law of Islam accords with the demands of a constitutional government and of modern civilization. This declaration was not in harmony with Muslim tradition or practice, but was most significant. The leading Turkish newspapers of İstanbul also labored to convince the Muslim population that the new movement harmonized with the teachings of the Koran. *Tanin* published this remarkable declaration: "We cannot survive as a nation without the sympathy of Europe, and we cannot get the sympathy of Europe unless we conform to European forms of government."

The proclamations which had been issued by the highest authority in the Islamic world, the Sheikh-ul-Islam, declaring that constitutional government was in accordance with the sacred law of Islam and that under a constitution the Christians and Muslims had equal rights, were most significant utterances and could not fail to have wide and permanent influence.[58]

In one important appointment, that of the Sheikh-ul-Islam, the Unionists made a radical departure from the precedent. Traditionally this powerful dignitary, the chief religious authority in the land through his mastery of Islamic theology and law, was appointed directly by the sultan and stood outside the parliamentary hierarchy. Hitherto he had been drawn from the strictest ranks of the *ulema*. As such he had, in his conservatism, recurrently served as a hindrance to liberal reform. Determined to rid themselves of this obstacle, the Unionists chose Sahib Molla and later Mustafa Hayri Efendi, those who no longer identified themselves with this religious elite, and who ceased to wear its symbol, the turban, as they came to play a more directly political role. They had become members of the Chamber of Deputies, serving on secular tribunals as ministers of religious endowments. The Unionists, thus using a traditional religious institution to further their plans for social and political modernization, now appointed Sheikh-ul-Islam. The appointments were accepted with favor not only by the *ulema* but by conservative elements in general.[59]

The Turks were changing. They were looking at Christianity and the Christian people with new eyes, with more wonder, interest, respect. A more liberal spirit of inquiry and of thought was apparent, and in many ways.[60] Like most other Englishmen in the Ottoman Empire at that time, Sir Edwin Pears came to the conclusion that the revolution gave a stimulus to the forces working for religious equality. It gave hope to the non-Muslim peoples and encouragement to those Muslims who, from various motives, wished to see the Ottoman Empire act justly to all subjects of the Empire.[61]

Among the most significant, which had largely disappeared in the sudden conversion of the Ottoman Empire, was the race prejudice and religious hostility. Turks and Armenians, Muslims and Gregorians, vied with each other in mutual consideration and testimonies of respect. Masses were said in Armenian churches for Muslims who had fallen in the cause of liberty. Islamic honors were paid at the graves of massacred Armenians as to martyrs who had died for their country. Oaths were sworn that all partisan differences of blood and of creed should be merged and forgotten in a brotherhood of a common freedom and one fatherland. Whatever backsliding there might be, whatsoever reaction might follow, the Ottoman Empire would never go back to where it was before July 24, 1908. Its liberties would never be wholly wrested from it again either by domestic tyrant or foreign invader. People who were capable of such self-control, of such abstinence from excesses and reprisals as they had shown themselves to be, must surely attain at length to stability in the freedom of which they had had so welcome a taste. A writer from the American Embassy in İstanbul said: "No one need to fear that any possibility exists of losing what has been secured so peaceably and admirably. The fraternity among the people and the unity of their aim for the preservation and progress of the country are a sure guarantee of ultimate success, whatever obstacles have to be met and overcome."[62]

RECEPTION OF THE RESTORATION OF THE CONSTITUTION

The restoration of the constitution was received throughout the Ottoman Empire with the liveliest demonstrations of joy. On July 24, crowds gathered in the public spaces of İstanbul and provincial towns and cities across the empire to celebrate the return to constitutional life. Over the following days, red and white banners emblazoned with flowers festooned the streets. Photographs of Niyazi, Enver Beys, and other freedom heroes were posted in town squares across the country. All classes and sects took part in these celebrations. Eloquent patriotic addresses were made, often at one meeting with in Turkish, Greek, Armenian, Arabic, Bulgarian, French, and other languages, by Muslims and Christians alike, and all wildly cheered by the assembly. Political activists gave public orations about the blessings of the constitution, sharing their hopes and aspirations with the general public. Members of the *ulema* fraternized with Greek and Armenian priests. The motto, "Liberty, Equality, Fraternity, Justice," appeared everywhere. Justice was in the oldest tradition of Islamic and Ottoman government. Equality and fraternity reflected the Ottomanism of the *Tanzimat* period of 1839–1876, a synthesis of Ottoman institutions and Western norms. It was the same in the province of Adana as elsewhere; again and again were the teachers of this and other schools called upon to give addresses to great gatherings of all sects in Adana, Tarsus, Mersin, Kozan, and Hacin. Cheers for the constitution, the parliament, the Army of Macedonia, for liberty, fraternity, equality, and justice resounded on every side.[63]

The consular dispatches are remarkably unanimous about these receptions. The Aleppo British consul H. Z. Longworth's account upon the progress of affairs in that province, which the British Embassy at İstanbul forwarded to the Foreign Office on August 20, 1908, was typical of what had occurred almost all over the country. The government telegram announcing the revival of the constitution was received with astonishment bordering on incredulity. Such a sudden break with the past was wholly unexpected, for none knew then of the revolt in Macedonia nor how perilously near dethronement was the sultan. It was only when detailed news of the movement and its progress poured in from Salonika, Edirne, and İstanbul that a burst of joy broke out in all directions. The staff officers of the garrison were the first to throw off the mask and give vent to their suppressed feelings. They boldly and publicly advocated the cause of liberty and justice, and they led the whole divisional army, from the commanding general to the last recruit, to swear on the Koran to defend the constitution with the "last drop of their blood." A local committee was speedily formed which placed itself in touch with the

Central Committee of the CUP. Self-constituted though it be, its members represented with fairness the public, the army, and the clergy, without distinction of race or creed. A strong body of men thus stepped forward, who with tact and zeal organized festive demonstrations, harangued the people on the true meaning of liberty, warned the reactionists from disturbing the peace, and exacted the dismissal of not a few corrupt officeholders. Most of them were amenable to reason and turned their efforts from hampering the authorities to assisting the governor in a manner strictly advisory. A cause of great rejoicing in many a home was no doubt the amnesty granted to all political prisoners and exiles. The Armenians so released numbered twenty-two at Aleppo and thirty-four at Maraş.[64]

The movement grew with marvelous rapidity. The CUP sent emissaries into Asia, where the movement spread as in the European provinces; to Paris, where it joined hands with the small band of exiles who had talked of Turkish revolution there for years, and also with Armenian revolutionary societies. It set itself, patiently and incessantly, to the task of winning over the various native Christian communities, its motto being "Equal rights for all Ottoman subjects irrespective of race or creed."

No opposition could be seen to the rule of the sovereign CUP, whose membership was judiciously enlarged until it contained, according to report, eighty thousand of the best of the Ottomans, of all nationalities and religious beliefs. Its inner circle, located at Salonika, acted in the formative days of the new regime with the perfect wisdom of the ideal enlightened ruler, effacing self utterly, smoothing away difficulties, recognizing the rights of all internal groups, gaining and preserving the good will of the Great Powers, passing between not one Scylla and one Charybdis, but safely and surely avoiding a hundred vortices of destruction. Thus was maintained for months a quiet unanimity of purpose in the Ottoman Empire, to which there were few parallels anywhere. Age-long difficulties and insoluble problems, fanatics, spies, and corruptionists dropped out of sight.[65]

The news announcing the reintroduction of the constitution in the Ottoman Empire was received with great enthusiasm by all the inhabitants of the Adana province. The sultan's decree to this effect was read publicly. With perfect harmony among the troops, Bahri Paşa, the governor, apparently yielded to *force majeure*. Tranquility prevailed in the city. A number of officers made their way into the *Konak* (government building) and administered an oath to the employees there that they would support the revolution proclaimed in favor of a constitution. All present, including the general in command of the garrison, took this oath, and the other officers and men were said to be favorably disposed to the movement. The *hojas* (Muslim clergymen) offered up prayers, the Armenian bishop and the representatives of the CUP made speeches, and an artillery salute was given. Official decorations and illuminations were organized. The members of the CUP and their friends wore red and white rosettes with the name of their society printed on the white ribbon. This distinctive mark of membership was to be seen worn by many others since, including minor officials at the *Konak*. Red ribbons stamped with the word "Liberty" were attached to school boys' sleeves, and scarlet bands bearing the words "Liberty, Equality, Fraternity, Justice" were displayed in the houses. The people manifested their joy by festivities and illuminations, where many speeches were delivered to the crowds by officers of the army, officials of the government, as well as by some civilians, all welcoming the new constitutional government. The people viewed the constitution as a new era of prosperity for trade, industry, and all commercial and financial enterprises.[66]

Bedross Der Matossian, assistant professor of history at the University of Nebraska, Lincoln, an Ottomanist, drawing on Armenian and Turkish sources, depicts the revolutionary festivities in Adana as follows. As soon as freedom was declared the people in Adana and Mersin began decorating all the streets and houses there. Masses were held in honor of the sultan and the Ottoman nation. Immediately the inhabitants began to visit each other. On August 2, 1908, a three hundred-person delegation of notables and dignitaries arrived from Adana at Mersin on a decorated train. It was received by a huge crowd hailing freedom and constitution. The crowd then moved to the government building, where they were received by the district governor and many public officers. The group was accompanied by live music. A reception held by the CUP in Mersin concluded the event. On their way back to Adana the group stopped in Tarsus, where they were received by a huge crowd shouting "Long live the sultan, Long live the freedom." The train was decorated with the Royal Coat of Arms and the Imperial Monogram. Upon its return to Adana, the delegation was received by more than four thousand people. Immediately afterwards, the crowd moved to the municipal garden where it was received by the governor and the provincial functionaries. İhsan Fikri, the leader of the local CUP, gave an enthusiastic speech about the new political order. On August 7, members of the Tarsus CUP paid a similar visit to Mersin to revive the covenant of brotherhood. A huge crowd and dignitaries greeted the train on its arrival at Mersin. Led by a band of musicians, the crowd of thousands moved toward the municipality, where speeches—many of them by military figures—were given in Turkish, Armenian, Arabic, and French.[67]

Mersin was illuminated on the occasion. A torchlight procession was organized. Speeches were delivered in front of the Government House and the municipality. Great enthusiasm prevailed among the population, incessantly acclaiming the name of the sovereign and the constitution. Tarsus was adorned by Ottoman flags. A great demonstration took place. Thousands of persons took part. Enthusiastic speeches were delivered.

The governor of Adana, in a dispatch dated July 28, to the ministry of the interior, announced that the seven political offenders incarcerated in that city were released. The latter called at the mosques and churches and offered up prayers for the long life of the sovereign.[68]

There was liberty of travel from one place to another which had been unknown for a generation. The words of liberty and equality were on everybody's lips. Muslims and Christians fraternized. It was not surprising that the mass of people believed that a good time had come and that a better was at hand. There would be freedom to speak and to act, justice in the law courts, the removal of restrictions upon trade, and a general improvement in all the relations of life.[69] Men whom it was before 1908 impossible to see, because it would get them into trouble, now readily associated with the foreigners and talked even in open places without fear. Schools and clubs were being rapidly built, even clubs of the Armenian revolutionary societies. Armenian village police guards had been appointed. On many roads one might drive without escort. Letters were delivered, even to agitators. Newspapers attacked the government.[70]

William Nesbitt Chambers, of the ABCFM in Adana, writing of a trip among some of the outstations in that mission, gave his observations of the changes which had come over the speech of the people, particularly the Muslims, as a result of new political conditions in the Ottoman Empire. Whatever the cause of this conduct might be, nothing, we consider, would be found more instructing and more edifying than the perusal of this remarkable letter:

> It was a marvelous thing to find people openly discussing the respective merits of candidates for Parliament; the probable work and influence of the Parliament; the probable action of the Sultan, as to whether he would be able to conform to the new program sufficiently to save himself from deposition; the necessary reforms in taxation; the probable changes in military service; the conditions on which Christians might serve in the army. These and such like subjects were freely discussed in public places with a freedom and confidence that indicated nothing of the horrid nightmare of repression that throttled all discussion a half year ago. I was impressed with this also, that I did not hear once the epithet *giavour* applied by a Moslem to a Christian. On inquiry the Christians testified that it was now seldom or never heard. That the whole Moslem community could in a day drop the use of an epithet that was the most common one in use by them as applied to Christians seemed a marked indication of their desire for good will. In talking over the situation with a Turkish official he declared that some of the Christians were agitating in a way that was hurtful to the new *régime* and

calculated to offend the Moslems; but he added, 'We Turks have decided that if they smite us on the one cheek we will turn the other and so do all in our power to preserve the new *régime*.' That a Moslem should quote Christ's words, to indicate their line of action towards Christians, was to me another indication of the good will of the Moslems.[71]

Chambers was treated with the highest courtesy by all Ottoman officials, all of whom vied with each other in showing special courtesies and honor. In every case opportunity was sought and obtained for meetings with local Armenian committees, some of which had been appointed by the government. Others were self-constituted. Repeated and very frank meetings were also held with the Turkish civil and military officials in every place visited.

Liberty meant a parliamentary check on autocracy, but it might mean more, and in some of the provincial cities especially it seemed to mean freedom from interference from outside powers. To the untutored, liberty sometimes meant license: for small kids to break windows, for their elders to refuse tax payments. The true meaning of the revolution of constitutionalism had yet to be revealed.[72]

At Adana, the governor on July 24, 1908, was Bahri Paşa. He had been occupying the post for the last ten years. He had served also in that capacity in İşkodra and Van provinces in August 1888 to January 1891 and January 1891 to July 1895, respectively. He lacked the College of Administrative Sciences education possessed by many of his colleagues. Sensitive to this fact, he nonetheless took it as a challenge. Bahri Paşa was a man of dubious principles or a man of no principles at all, lest these be personal power and the craven avoidance of removal from the office at any cost. Despite these glaring shortcomings, however, he enjoyed the one indispensable quality needed in absolutist government: the chief's current confidence. During his long career Bahri Paşa had been able to achieve what few other administrators had: he retained Sultan Abdülhamid II's confidence for decades. But being the trustee of such an autocrat remained a risky undertaking. In July 1908, his long run of luck ran out.[73]

The overthrow of autocracy took Bahri Paşa by surprise, who now began to take his instructions from the CUP at Salonika. The CUP laid hands on the telegraphic system and their numerous messages, calling for demonstrations and encouraging the populace with their new legal rights, and not brook the interference of officials attached to the old regime, went free to the chief centers and were then repeated to smaller places. Thus when Adana wired its complaint of the then unsympathetic attitude of the governor, Bahri Paşa, an answer by wire from Salonika to the effect that any governor or official who put obstacles in the way of the people manifesting their joy were enemies to the liberty of the people and lawless in their actions, and that such were not worthy of being kept in their positions. The regular authorities were unable to check the assumption of power by the local Young Turk faction in direct and independent communication with Salonika. The military were the heroes of the day, beyond question. Kept in comparative obscurity and deliberately ignored were the governor, the mayor, the chief of police, and other officials who still retained their functions although identified with the old style of rule. The junior officers, Young Turk in sympathy, were, together with their civilian associates in unmistakable control; the governor and the military commander were compelled to submit completely to their wishes. These Young Turk officers now made themselves responsible for order in Adana and set up a commission to investigate and recommend dismissal of officials. It was as a result of its activities that the governor, Bahri Paşa, was dismissed and sent to İstanbul under guard. He was later sent on retirement with a pension of 5,912 kuruş. Thereafter he disappeared from the pages of history. He died in İstanbul in 1917.[74]

The personality and stance of Bahri Paşa proved unequal to the task of administering Adana at a critical time. He could or would transact no business, and public affairs were at a standstill. He was spectator of all that took place. Further, he was known to have been appointed by the palace clique, and consequently he did not command the confidence of the Young Turks. At Adana the news of Bahri Paşa's dismissal caused universal satisfaction. His dismissal was rightly interpreted as a sign that the Ottoman Empire would now be more open to European civilization.

In those days, the amount of newspaper enterprise in İstanbul came as a surprise to many. The number of dailies was on the increase, and while many were ephemeral, a paper that gained a steady circulation of five thousand might be said to have financed itself. There were probably ten or a dozen dailies in the city with a circulation of from ten thousand to twenty thousand each. As for figures, there were about twelve dailies in the Turkish language; besides one, *Asia*, in what was known as Karamanlıca, or Turkish printed in Greek characters, for the Greeks of Karaman region who used Turkish; and one *Ceridei Şarkiye*, printed in Turkish with the Armenian characters, for Turkish-speaking Armenians. The *Azadamart*, an Armenian daily, had a column or two in Turkish also. The chief Turkish dailies were the *Tanin*, *İkdam*, *Tasviri Efkar*, *Sabah*, *Tanzimat*, *Yeni Gazete*, and *Alemdar*. They displayed able criticism and moderation. There were in Greek some seven dailies, chief of which were the *Tachydromos*, *Proodos*, *Ameroliptos*, and *Neologhos*. Of Armenian daily papers there were about the same number, those with the widest circulation being the *Puzantion*, *Azadamart*, and *Arevelk*. Besides these there were six dailies in foreign languages. *The Levant Herald*, originally titled the *Constantinople Messenger* when it was founded in 1873, was the only English newspaper in İstanbul, and it had appeared practically continuously between that date and 1913. It had two columns in English, and the rest were in French. The *Osmanischer Lloyd* was half German and half French. The others were all French, namely, *La Liberté, Jeune Turc, Stamboul*, and *Le Moniteur Oriental*. There were also printed in İstanbul some fifty to sixty weekly and monthly periodicals in Turkish, Greek, Armenian, Hebrew-Spanish, Albanian, Bulgarian, Serbian, and Arabic, besides English, French, and German. They represented the fields of religion, literature, science, law, medicine, commerce, politics, agriculture, and the army and navy. Each chamber of commerce had its monthly or quarterly, in its own language, that of the American Chamber of Commerce being the *Levant Trade Review*. This quarterly journal gave in each number valuable statistical tables regarding various branches of commerce, and suggestions as to the development of trade relations, besides articles about specific places or districts where certain lines of business might with profit be developed.[75]

During the revolutionary fervor of 1908–1909, the Young Turks proceeded to remove many of the ambiguities of the revived constitution and to establish beyond doubt the sovereign power of parliament. The most far-reaching revision was the one that denied the sultan any genuine powers, reducing him to little more than a figurehead who reigned but did not rule; the Chamber of Deputies was now the sole seat of Ottoman authority. Sultan Abdülhamid II was obliged to take an oath of fealty to the nation and to the constitution. The sultan's veto of legislation was sharply curtailed and was subject to being overriden by two-thirds veto of the Chamber of Deputies. Parliament was authorized to meet on the first of November of each year without formal convocation, and the calling of special sessions was authorized by petition of a majority of the members. Ministers were made individually and collectively responsible to the Chamber of Deputies, and the decision of a general election on any issue was declared to be definitive and final. As amended by the Young Turks, therefore, the constitution of 1876 became a liberal charter of parliamentary government.[76]

This question is of particular interest and demands discussion at some length. The Young Turks' general aim was to modernize the empire. This meant, in contemporary European terms, legal and economic reforms, greater bureaucratic efficiency, a well-armed professional army recruited by conscription, and patriotism (defined in terms of the Ottoman nation).[77] Edward Meade Earle fully concurs in this opinion. The Young Turks were liberals in their desire to introduce Western standards of administration into a tottering imperial rule, patriots in their desire to achieve reform before it was forced upon them.[78] This is an issue to which we will return a little further.

Following the revolution of 1908, Armenian societies—which, under the reign of Sultan Abdülhamid II, were perforce kept secret—openly proclaimed themselves and won the approval of the Young Turks, who declared that "the Armenian revolutionists were among the pioneers of Ottoman liberty." Their program was professedly socialistic and educational, aiming at the instruction of the people and their elevation to those ideals which the Young Turks themselves had espoused with such enthusiasm. When the test came, it was shown that how empty those programs really were.[79]

Lectures were given all over the country instructing the public on their changed citizenship and new rights, and so men were led on intelligently to the electing of members for the Chamber of Deputies which had to be formed. Several governors were dismissed and others appointed to fill their places. The Ministry of the Interior invited the provincial authorities to convoke the municipal councils, for the purpose of proceeding without delay with the formalities of the parliamentary elections.[80]

ELECTIONS AND THE INAUGURATION OF THE NEW PARLIAMENT, DECEMBER 17, 1908

At the turn of the twentieth century the Ottoman Empire was seriously conditioned by the actions and interactions of three sets of rival interests: the group of distinct nationalities within the country; the cluster of small but active neighboring states, formerly a part of the Ottoman Empire and not yet satisfied with the terms and bounds of separation; and the family of the distant great nations, seeking strenuously to apportion and regulate the world. In the presence of these numerous forces, the Ottoman Empire, once the strongest state in the Mediterranean sphere of civilization, had for some generations hung balanced on the verge of destruction. On July 23, 1908 a new spirit was breathed into it; a new life began. This new spirit and life strived to find a sure embodiment and an effective means of expression in and through the Ottoman Parliament.[81]

In the parliamentary elections, it was determined, all taxpaying males twenty-five years or older could vote for deputies who themselves were required to know Turkish. The parliament consisted of an elected Chamber of Deputies and an appointed Chamber of Notables. The members of the popular house were to be elected for four years on the basis of one to every fifty thousand males. They were to be apportioned by provinces, and each must be a resident of the province for which he was chosen. The deputies were, however, specifically stated to represent the entire nation. The Chamber of Notables consisted of members appointed for life by the sultan, to a number not exceeding one-third that of the deputies.[82]

The CUP was ready. It made no effort to stifle other parties from contesting the elections. It was the only well-organized party in the country and it was clear that even without the assistance of the government officials they would be able to secure a majority in the Chamber of Deputies. The CUP had restored the constitution and was preparing to revive parliamentary government, and therefore enjoyed a moral authority that disarmed its political rivals. In this climate, political aspirants had nothing to lose and much to gain by identifying with the CUP. Immediately after the revolution, it opened up provincial clubs and made contact with local groups, particularly in those parts of the empire where it had not been able to organize prior to the revolution.[83] The Greeks worked well under the leadership of the patriarchate. The Armenians did not appear to be able to unite on any settled program. There was much excitement in the Ottoman realm during the days of election.[84]

The Turks were novices at political combination, whereas the Greeks were skilled in electioneering trickery of every sort and were determined to obtain as large as an electioneering representation as possible in the Chamber of Deputies. The Greeks undoubtedly entertained the opinion that they should take a leading place in the administration of the country. Edward Frederick Knight was in İstanbul during the election operations, and very interesting and picturesque they were. At one manifestation which he saw here the Turk and Armenian electors joined forces, and there were to be seen in the combined procession Muslim *hojas* and Armenian priests in their full Muslim and Christian canonicals, walking hand in hand in amity.[85]

As in all electoral campaigns, a good deal of dissatisfaction was provoked and displayed during the struggle of the Ottoman parties. Religion, nationality, and politics divided the groups and united the individuals. In politics Conservatives coped with Liberals; in religion Muslims contended with Christians; and on racial or national lines Slav grappled with Turk, Greek joined issue with both, and Jew, Arab, Albanian, and Armenian supported each one of his nationality.[86]

On December 7, 1908, German Imperial Chancellor Prince Bernhard von Bülow delivered in the Reichtag an important speech on European policy. Speaking on the Ottoman Empire, he eulogized its liberal regime, which gained for it the sympathies of the civilized world. He rectified the numerous reports published in regard to Germany's role in the Ottoman Empire. Germany, he said, did not wish for any conquest in the Ottoman realm. It only demanded full liberty for each power, and, in the present dispute [the annexation of Bosnia-Herzegovina by Austria], it could but remain the friend of its ally, Austria, while doing all in its power to maintain the peace of the world.[87]

Elections were held in full swing throughout the country in late November and early December 1908, and the columns of the İstanbul press were filled daily with articles on the subject. The skill with which the elections were organized and carried out, despite serious difficulties, called for high praise.[88] The new parliament was duly inaugurated on December 17. The majority of the deputies who were elected belonged to the CUP. Some serving officers were elected, but the leading military revolutionaries, like Major Cemal Bey, did not stand.

The opening of the parliament was the occasion of a big parade, with a band leading the 115 carriages that carried the deputies and playing the Anthem of the Deputies, which made reference to heroes of liberty and revolution as Namık Kemal, Midhat Paşa, Enver, and Niyazi Beys. Crowds coming from the provinces to witness the opening filled the İstanbul hotels, forcing the late arriving deputies into the dormitories of the capital's schools.[89] The official entry into the parliament of the new representatives, in their simple black coats, side by side with the brilliant uniforms and the jeweled decorations of the Hamidian officials, marked the visible passage of the Ottoman Empire from the old regime to the new. As Halidé Edib watched the splendid procession with its streak of men in black, her heart cried out, "Behold the coming regime!"[90]

The inauguration of the new era of constitutional rule in the Ottoman Empire took place successfully in the opening of the new parliament by the sultan at the Ministry of Justice in İstanbul. Every detail of the program was carried out with great smoothness. An impressive array of troops were stationed along the streets of the vicinity, and their smart uniforms, together with the costumes of the thousands of people who waited to see the imperial cortège, made a lively scene. Before two o'clock the deputies took their places, and the Chamber of Notables marched in a body, most impressive in their uniforms and insignia. At a quarter to three o'clock, the Grand Vizier Kamil Paşa and the cabinet, with the Sheikh-ul-Islam Cemaleddin Efendi, filed into their ministerial bench. One of the surprises of the occasion was the composure with which the sultan drove through the streets of İstanbul, a thing which he did not do for many years, his usual custom having been to go by water. The people of İstanbul saw a unique sight when they witnessed the going of Sultan Abdülhamid II to the opening of the parliament. The streets were crowded, and the great dome of the Ayasofya Mosque was thick with people. The sultan drove to the parliament from Yıldız, by way of Beyoğlu, Galata bridge, and Eskisaray. Following him were the heir-presumptive, Prince Reşad Efendi, and the Imperial Princes Yusuf İzzettin and Vahdettin Efendis, with the high officials of the court. The speech from the throne was then read in a clear voice by the sultan's first secretary, Ali Cevat Bey, and was listened to in respectful silence by all the members standing. At its close, the *Nakib-ül-Eşraf*, or head of the lineal descendants of the Prophet

Muhammed, recited a prayer, and the sultan then saluted the assembly and left on his return to the palace. When the chamber was called to order, the temporary secretary read Article 46 of the constitution, concerning the swearing-in of new deputies to take oath of allegiance. The grand vizier then withdrew, and the senior deputy, Manyasizade Refik Bey of Salonika, took the chair. Elections followed for provisional officers. Manyasizade Refik Bey was elected temporary speaker. Until the permanent officers were selected, the four youngest members of the chamber acted as secretaries. The division of chamber into five sections for the transaction of business took place. These bureaux acted as committees on the various forms of business to come up before the chamber after they had considered each bill.[91]

The statement of Grand Vizier Kamil Paşa at the opening of the Chamber of Deputies was indicative of the determined policy of the new government. He said: "It is most necessary that we should strengthen among ourselves these feelings of brotherhood and patriotism by exhibiting in all relations of life the practical significance of equality of rights, by opening our schools of all grades for all non-Muslim citizens, we and they sharing together in the undertaking, and by arranging for the participation of non-Muslims in the military duties of our army."[92] Kamil Paşa's political program and his speech before the chamber reflected Unionist ideas.[93] Many people were impressed by the advantages of having at the head of the government a prudent old man, who was popularly believed, moreover, to carry a good deal of weight with European statesmen, especially in Britain.

Seventy-six-year-old Kamil Paşa was an experienced and high-minded patriarch. Born in Cyprus, he served first in the provincial government, and then as minister in İstanbul, becoming grand vizier for the first time in 1885. After a second term in 1895 he fell out of favor with Sultan Abdülhamid II. Returning to power in 1908, after the constitution had been reinstated, he soon fell out with the CUP, and achieved office for the fourth and last time when the CUP lost control on July 22, 1912. He was removed from office in the "raid on the Sublime Porte" on January 23, 1913, and retired to Cyprus. Known as a liberal and an Anglophile, Kamil Paşa was a foresightful statesman who did his best to safeguard the territorial integrity of the Ottoman Empire.[94]

Kamil Paşa was a figure of much controversy—lauded by some, pilloried by others, for being an old man from an old school. Chronologically, at seventy-six years of age in 1908 he was certainly the former, despite a level of energy envied by many much younger. But it is arguable how much of a traditionalist he was. Roughly put, the same can be said of Said Paşa, Kamil Paşa's predecessor from July to August 1908. Said Paşa was called to the Grand Vizierate in the troubled days before the Young Turk revolution, but remained in power for a few weeks only. He gave proof of much intelligence and soundness of judgment. He had all the old-world courtliness and serenity of the generation of Ottoman public men who preceded the Young Turks.[95]

Seats in the Chamber of Deputies had been assigned according to the population ratios of the different *millets* within the empire. The 147 Turkish representatives gave them a majority in the chamber, which also contained sixty Arabs, twenty-seven Albanians, twenty-six Greeks, fourteen Armenians, five Bulgars, four Jews, four Serbs, and one Vlach. About two-thirds of these had been the candidates of the CUP. Taken as a whole, the Chamber of Deputies seemed to represent well the best elements of the country: all varieties of opinion and of nationality, the Old Turk and the Young Turk, religion, law, leadership, and property.[96]

The number of thirty-nine was considered sufficient for membership of the Chamber of Notables, and the venerable and experienced Said Paşa was made president. Two Arabs, two Greeks, two Armenians, a Bulgarian, and a Vlachian were among those chosen. Four marshals, four ministers of state, two of the *ulema*, and a poet helped make the Chamber of Notables a dignified body of distinguished Ottomans, representing not so much vested interests, as eminent service to the state. It was expected to serve as a revising chamber and not have friction with the Chamber of Deputies.[97]

To show his good feeling, the sultan gave a banquet to the members of the parliament on New Year's Eve at the Hall of Ceremonies of the Şale Kiosk in Yıldız Palace, the first function of its kind ever celebrated in the Ottoman Empire. He sat between the presidents of the two chambers. The members of the press were also invited. A new era seemed to have dawned in which all the diverse communities of the empire would unite behind the principle of constitutional and representative government, under the banner of "the union of elements"—the common Ottoman citizenship that was to unite all the sultan's subjects, irrespective of race, creed, or language, in a single nationality and loyalty.[98]

The elections served both to legitimate the constitutional representative system and to promote political citizenship in the empire. They posited the Ottoman subjects as a people whose political activities were institutionally recognized as something that had to be taken note of. Electoral politics exercised a mobilizational effect that was not restricted to the polls. It also contributed to the expansion of the public sphere in the Ottoman Empire, as the proliferation of journalistic activity, petitions, rallies, and festivals accompanied the campaigns. Thus, elections expedited the process of social and political mobilization after 1908.[99]

Sir Gerard Lowther, the British ambassador in İstanbul between 1908 and 1913, happened to be at the Sublime Porte on November 23, 1908, when a deputation of Armenians arrived on their way to deposit the ballot box of the

Kumkapı district, an Armenian quarter of İstanbul, where the voting for the primary elections had taken place. Their object in coming to the Porte was to express their gratitude to the government for the fair and regular manner in which the election had taken place, and, according to Lowther, viewed in the light of the history of the Armenians during the past few years, it was a "truly remarkable scene." The British ambassador described the state of affairs as follows. An Armenian priest delivered a speech in excellent Turkish full of expressions of gratitude and appreciation and protestations of loyalty to the new regime. During the entire speech, intermingled with prayer, the Muslims present remained in a reverent attitude. The priest was followed by a Muslim *hoja*, who in a fine voice delivered a prayer admirably suited to the occasion, and concluded with cries in favor of the empire. The scene gave very evident satisfaction to the officials of the Porte. Lowther estimated that it yet furnished a remarkable evidence that the Armenians in İstanbul had decided to work with their Muslim countrymen, and he hoped that incidents of this kind would have a good effect in the provinces of eastern Anatolia, where good neighborly relations between the two elements were essential.[100]

Generally speaking, by whatever means the election of the members was brought about, the results might be described as distinctly satisfactory, as British consular officers spoke well of the persons elected, with very few exceptions. In the province of Erzurum, Hammond Smith Shipley reported the election of seven members, including two Armenians, which, he said, was generally agreed to be very fair treatment. Shipley pointed out that the entire change in the attitude of the Turks was well illustrated by their ready acceptance of these two men, one of whom was a member of the band which seized the Imperial Ottoman Bank in 1896, and the other a prominent member of the Dashnak (short for dashnaksutiun, or "federation" in Armenian) Society.[101]

Ever since parliament was opened in December 1908, Ahmed Rıza Bey had been the presiding officer of the Chamber of Deputies, having been re-elected each session with surprising unanimity until the beginning of 1912. He had been fearless and impartial in his treatment of deputies, and had upheld the traditions of parliamentary law and usage to a degree that most men in a similar position would have found impossible.[102]

Ahmed Rıza Bey, former director of state education in Bursa, was the ideologist of the positivist, centralistic, and nationalist tendency of the Young Turks. An intellectual and a man of great refinement, he was the archetype of a single individual within whom all these currents competed for attention. He developed his ideas in Paris where he first went to study farming and where he became chairman of the CUP local branch and published (from 1895) its organ *Meşveret* (Consultation), whose French edition attracted Western notice. His mother was a Bavarian woman, and he spoke both German and French. He might pass for a well-bred European if he did not wear a fez. Ahmed Rıza Bey was one of the most learned of Young Turk literati. Returning after the proclamation of the constitution in 1908, he was acclaimed as "the father of freedom" and elected speaker of the Chamber of Deputies. He advocated a strong central government with sweeping agricultural reform and massive economic redress within the empire to be the focus of any new government's responsibility. He was also passionately opposed to any form of foreign intervention or influence within the empire. His subsequent role in Ottoman politics was slight, as the iniative lay with domestic revolutionaries.[103]

The leading figures of all the national groups were chosen as deputies in the new parliament. The Ottoman Empire never had an assembly composed of so many daring and famous men; when they gathered together, the atmosphere thus created lacked harmony. Ideals and personalities clashed immediately and inevitably. All that was alive, vital, and energetic in the country had been hurled into the parliament. Though there was good will and simplicity in the power which sent them there, there was also ignorance about their conflicting properties. The Young Turks had every intention of creating a series of columns to hold the structure of the empire up, but the columns were so varied in size that they finally permitted the complete crumbling away of the imperial edifice they had sought to uphold.[104]

The Unionists hoped to use the expertise of better educated and more developed non-Muslim groups to further their own program of reform and progress. The non-Muslim deputies in the parliament were expected to play a vital role in the introduction and passage of legislation designed to bring about the modernization and economic revival of the empire. Many of the non-Muslim deputies were professionally qualified (engineers, agronomists, etc.) and were expected to provide expert opinion when matters related to their professions were discussed in the parliament.[105]

Under ordinary times the differences of language and creed might not develop other than usual parliamentary tactics, but in the critical times the nation was passing through each deputy was expected to remember, whatever his descent was, he was first an Ottoman and that his duty was to his country. For the ever-memorable work of July 24, 1908, the indebtedness was to the Turkish army and Turkish people, and both of these had since that had shown a disposition to cooperate with their non-Muslim fellow subjects that testified amply to their realization and appreciation of the duties and responsibilities of their position. Europe and the world would expect that such non-Muslim fellow subjects should do no less, should show that they know how to combine with their Muslim brothers for the welfare of the state.[106]

Despite the measure of sincerity that lay behind the promises of the Ottoman constitution, and although the Ottoman government continued to speak of "the union of elements," the spread of nationalism among the subject peoples of the empire ended the ideal of the free, equal, and peaceful association of peoples in a common loyalty to the country. Yorgi Boşo (Boussios), a Greek deputy from Serfice in the Balkans in the Chamber of Deputies, infuriated the Turks by his ironic remark "I am as Ottoman as the Ottoman Bank."[107]

Tarık Zafer Tunaya, the Turkish constitutional lawyer and historian, uses prodigious amounts of Ottoman sources to argue convincingly that the 1908 revolution was a crucial benchmark in the history of the Ottoman Empire and in the modern evolution of the Balkans and the Arab Middle East over which the empire ruled. It was the watershed between the old and new eras of Turkish history—the culmination of the political development of prerepublican Turkey and the beginning of the popular unrest that was to tear apart the fabric of the Ottoman state and society for the next decade. The Second Constitutional Period has long been regarded as a critical juncture in Turkish history, and Tunaya depicted these years as a sort of experimental phase preparing the way for the secular and national republic. A discussion of it must, therefore, look both backwards and forwards. From many perspectives, the revolution strengthened within Turkish-speaking populations and triggered non-Turkish counterforces that would come to demand either autonomy or separatism.[108]

Professor İlber Ortaylı of Galatasaray University and former director of the Topkapı Palace Museum in İstanbul—one of the most prolific and perspicacious historians of the Ottoman Empire—agrees with Tunaya and describes the 1908 revolution as a turning point in the political modernization of the Ottoman Empire and the Near East.[109]

The first ecstacy of joy passed away, and the people then found themselves face to face with the difficult problem of representative government among a conglomeration of races. A party of opposition began to form at once, under the name of the *Ahrar* or Liberal Union which favored administrative decentralization. But that the constitution itself had come to stay.

The Young Turk revolution of 1908 has an archetypal significance in subsequent Armenian politics, and its consequences and reverberations are, even today, far from being exhausted.

On July 23, 1910, in a dinner given in the Hotel Astor in New York by the members of the Armenian General Progressive Association in honor of the second anniversary of the reestablishment of constitutional government in the Ottoman Empire, the toast to Sultan Reşad (r. 1909–1918) was offered by the Armenian writer Vahan Cardashian. He referred to the obliteration of racial and religious controversies and antagonisms by the Young Turks. Cardashian stated:

> The august founder of the Ottoman Empire on his deathbed said to his successor: Be just, love goodness, show mercy, give equal protection to all subjects;

such are the duties of princes upon earth.¹¹⁰ The Ottoman State began its downward career from the time the judicious words of its great founder lost effect upon his successors. We know that the end and intent of the Constitution is to secure to the citizen the fullest enjoyment of life, which may be achieved only by the mutuality and reciprocity of sentiments and behavior of the individual citizen. The rights it confers upon its beneficiaries are supported only by the faithful observance of the duties it imposes. The Ottoman nation is to be congratulated upon having a sovereign who, since his happy accession to power, has given evidence of his sympathy with the spirit of constitutional government. The name of the incumbent of the august throne of Osman shall be inscribed among the greatest of the Ottoman history where we find the records of men whom by the valor and loftiness of their character command the admiration of the world.¹¹¹

No doubt he was substantially correct. In response, Ziya Paşa, Ottoman ambassador to the United States, said in part that nothing could aid more in bringing back the union of sentiment among all the Ottomans, a union without which all progress would remain illusory. He had nothing to add to the brilliant remarks of his compatriot, Cardashian, as to the eminently superior qualities of the great Ottoman sovereigns who made the greatness of the empire. Ziya Paşa remarked that the efforts of the government, in accord with the representatives of the people, were employed to place constitutional government upon a solid and broad base, and at the same time to preserve the prerogatives assured by the constitution of certain powers which represented national sovereignty as well as individual rights.¹¹²

But the honeymoon with the Young Turks was to be short-lived. It quickly became clear that the Armenian revolutionary societies were out to create an autonomous, or even an independent, homeland of their own. They were intent on seceding from the empire. They failed to live up to the ideals of the 1908 revolution. The call to a single Ottoman loyalty, greater centralization, and firmer discipline was the Young Turks' formula for regenerating the country; Armenians worked for the very opposite. The Armenian policies of nationalism and separatism disillusioned the Young Turks and dampened the optimism that had been created by the restoration of the constitution of 1876.¹¹³

Since the promulgation of the constitution, the Armenian people had been more or less under the domination of the Dashnak Party, which was simply a continuation of the revolutionary organization by that name. This party, while it contained some men of ability and principle, had, on the whole, had a pernicious influence in the country's affairs. Their strength had been due to thorough organization and remarkable zeal and activity. Their success had been due, to a large extent, to the fact that the great majority of Armenians, who were not in sympathy with their revolutionary doctrines, had been at a great disadvantage in having no thoroughly organized party to carry out plans for real reform, and, when necessary, to check their opponents.[114]

The 1908 revolution seemed to hold out to the Armenians, the hope for which they had waited so long, that of developing their own *millet* within the cadre of a progressive Ottoman Empire. Enough has been said to show the difficulties in the way of the peoples of the empire when it came to applying liberty, equality, fraternity, and justice, and especially of how the idea of liberty was misunderstood. Many enthusiastic Armenians wished to apply it politically in the form of an autonomous Armenia. Though the regular revolutionary Armenian societies worked for a time at least, with the Young Turks for a united Ottoman state, there is no doubt there was much talk among the Armenians of an Armenia independent or at least autonomous under the guidance of a European country, preferably Britain.[115]

The liberal Prince Sabahattin, a member of the Ottoman dynasty, lengthily wrote to *İkdam* on October 17, 1908, to combat the idea of the autonomy of the provinces, of which he was considered a partisan. The League for Personal Initiative and Decentralization of the prince was entirely in agreement with the policy to be followed by the CUP. During his exile in Europe, he had always written and spoken in praise of the political extension of the local powers in conformity with the constitutional regime. The aim of the directing circles must be education of the nation. But in order to make that education effective and establish the constitutional regime on solid bases by the union of all the elements of the Ottoman Empire, external and internal peace ought to be fully insured.[116]

The somewhat ponderous name of the League for Personal Iniative and Decentralization derives from the writings of Edmond Demolins, a French writer by whom Prince Sabahattin was profoundly influenced. Demolins's book *A Quoi tient la supériorité des Anglo-Saxons?* was published in 1897. It attracted a good deal of attention at the time, and in particular aroused the interest of Muslim reformers, liberals, and modernists looking for an explanation of the backwardness of their own societies. The prince's ideas were in fact foredoomed to failure. The Armenians and other Christian nationalities, whom he tried so hard to conciliate, found little to attract them in an Ottoman federation and preferred to seek the fulfillment of their political aspirations outside the empire altogether.[117]

Following the 1908 revolution in İstanbul there emerged in the city of Adana the political liberalization which could also be seen in the imperial capital: newspapers engaged more freely in criticism of the government, political clubs were formed, and previously unfelt anti-Turkish sentiment became clear.

IDENTITY OF OTTOMANISM AND THE CUP

By 1909, the appeal of Ottomanism began to wane. The official policy of Ottomanism encountered a major obstacle in the continued existence as separate legal entities of the Christian *millets* whose rights the Great Powers frequently supported, and whose members ultimately were more attracted to separatist nationalisms.[118] The Chamber of Deputies fractured on ethnic lines. The *millets* wanted both equality and the preservation, and if possible the extension, of their existing rights and privileges. The CUP believed that equality was sufficient.

The Ottoman Empire was peopled by nationalities and tribes, but there was no compactly organized body prompted by common principles or common interests that might be called a nation. Article 8 of the constitution of 1876 and Article 1 of the imperial decree of August 1, 1908, made an attempt to define the principle of what they called the Ottoman national citizenship. But this very theory met with the most passionate refutation. Eastern and Western nations clashed against one another. The Christian population inhabiting the scattered parts of the empire claimed autonomy. Still suffering from the terrible strain of warfare, still in peril of their lives, which every passing hour might carry away together with the constitution itself, the Young Turk reformers had to face the most anxious problem of contemporary history—the call of the newly awakened political conscience of the minor nations. One might, of course, conceive decentralization; indeed, the idea was not slow to impose itself by the formula: full autonomy to each nationality and formation of a vast unit by way of federalism. Was it, however, possible to form such small units and to combine the federal states under the supreme power of a central government? The student of the national problem as it presented itself in the Ottoman Empire felt inclined to deny the possibility. The various peoples were intermingled in the various parts of the empire, and so interspersed with Turks that there was practically no province where one of the nationalities would form a respectable majority as to allow of a geographical sub-division for the purpose of federalism. Precise statistics were not available. Such figures as were to be found in various books on the Ottoman Empire were mostly been prompted by the aim with which the book was written. Ottoman registrars did not mention nationality, which, indeed, was in most cases exceedingly hard, nay, impossible, to fix. They recorded the denomination of the newly born, viz., that to which the parents professed to belong.[119]

It will be useful to mention at this juncture that the CUP—nourished in the tradition of Western revolutionary liberalism—was a party of patriots, who were bent on saving the empire and on restoring the independence that it long ago forfeited. The Unionists meant to save every inch of territory and to place their country on a level with the Great Powers. This committee had gained the name in Europe of Young Turks. This was not surprising. Since the CUP had in its day fought the Hamidian regime, and had been founded with the object of starting in the Ottoman land an era of liberty, equality, and fraternity, it was but natural that the Europeans, as defenders of such enterprises, should appreciate and sympathize with their cause, and, to distinguish them from the men of the old regime, should give them the title of Young Turks. The CUP's leaders were indeed young Turks. They were mostly junior officers and low-ranking bureaucrats in their late twenties and thirties.[120]

It must be stressed that in its original incarnation the CUP was not constructed as an explicitly Turkish nationalist organization. The CUP began its history in 1889 as a group of disaffected intellectuals and highly placed administrators who had been exposed to Western ideas through the reformed Ottoman higher education system, and who were frustrated by the regime's inability or unwillingness to act on those ideas and to implement modernization on a systematic or thoroughgoing basis. Organizing themselves clandestinely within the Ottoman Empire and operating openly from exile in cities such as Paris and Geneva, the Young Turks regarded themselves as an intellectual elite whose mission it was to gain power within the Ottoman civilian and military bureaucracy and to use that power to apply the laws of science and the principles of reason to the problems of state and society.[121]

The CUP's original membership reflected the multiethnic composition of the Ottoman state's administrative elite. Before it came to power, its leading figures included Albanians and Arabs as well as the Turks. Graduates of the main educational institutions of İstanbul, they could all rally around the common struggle for the restoration of the constitution and the creation of a meritocratic government. This platform was so broad that there was even room on it for the radical Armenian nationalists of the Dashnak Party.[122]

It must further be borne in mind that the CUP was open to members of all non-Turkish elements, including Armenians and Jews, and here, too, they were treated as first-rate citizens. The Turkish members of the committee referred to them as brother. In other words, the Christian and Jewish Young Turks were equal to the Turkish. Prior to the First World War, both Bedros Hallaçyan and Emmanuel Carasso succeeded in being elected to the thirteen-member Central Committee of the CUP, the highest decision-making body of the empire.[123] Hallaçyan attended university in Paris and held a doctorate in jurisprudence and political and economic sciences from Sorbonne. After the restoration of the constitution, he was elected deputy for İstanbul in all the three elections of 1908, 1912, and 1914. He twice acted as minister of commerce and public works in the cabinets formed by Hüseyin Hilmi Paşa and

Hakkı Paşa, respectively, in 1909–1910 and 1911. He played an important role in the introduction and passage of legislation designed to bring about the modernization and economic revival of the empire. Hallaçyan rose in the councils of the party and gained influence in the higher echelons of the government.[124] Carasso was also a lawyer. He was elected deputy from Salonika in 1908 and 1912, and moved to İstanbul when Salonika was captured by Greece in October 1912. He represented the capital in the 1914 Assembly. Carasso joined the CUP before 1908 and was able to further its activities. He was part of the inner circle of the CUP, a confidant of Talat Paşa, and among the deputation consisting of two Muslims, an Armenian, and a Jew who came to present the Sultan-Caliph Abdülhamid II, "God's shadow on earth," with the *fetva* (Sheikh-ul-Islam's legal ruling) confirming his deposition.[125]

With *Becoming Ottomans*, Julia Phillips Cohen breaks new ground in her analysis of the Ottoman Jewry, and of the complex and changing forces that tested their allegiance to Ottomanism. She challenges the long-held master narrative that Ottomanism was an abstract ideology that managed to gain a foothold only among the Turkish elite. Surprisingly, this trope, which essentially suggests that Ottomanism was a failure, persists in Ottoman historiography to this day. Much-publicized Jewish adherence to Ottoman patriotism enabled Ottoman Jews to be counted and esteemed by the Muslim majority but often worsened their relations with other non-Muslim groups (mainly Armenians and Greeks). Jewish publicists and leaders advanced Ottomanism, thus taking advantage of the new possibilities offered to them by the project of imperial citizenship. By adopting Ottoman patriotism and by emphasizing allegiance to the Ottoman Empire as a token of gratitude to the Turks who received them in 1492, Jewish leaders wished to integrate to the broader society and gain its respect. It is plain that they were able to achieve such an acknowledgment.[126]

The CUP branch of Adana was founded immediately after the revolution. Like elsewhere, it was based mainly upon staff officers and educated officials. The branch was joined also by educated young men belonging to the families of Adana notables. Various elements rushed into the organization. Aside from Muslims, there were many Greek members. The Armenians also massively joined the party. The Armenian members were so active that their representative, Karabet Çallıyan, was appointed to be a member of the central committee of Adana branch. It shows that the CUP accepted everyone who declared to be supporters of the constitution and that neither ethnicity nor religion was of any significance.[127]

The CUP's first care had been to appoint, so far as possible, reliable and honest men to responsible posts. They caused the local branches of the CUP to supervise the action of the authorities without, however, interfering with their functions more than was inevitably necessary; they sent circular telegrams, which received a wide publicity in the press, to all the centers warning all patriots to abstain from interference with the authorities, from arbitrary action, and from proceedings which might disturb the public order. All complaints had to be addressed through the legal channels to the competent authorities, while complaints about high officials had to be addressed to the Central Committee of the CUP. They ended with an exhortation to be patient and moderate.[128]

The CUP, acting as a vigilance committee, did its work thoroughly, and its agents sprang, as it were, from the ground in every corner of the country. Corrupt governors and officials, and those on whom any suspicion rested, were dismissed or disappeared.[129]

Without a centralized or even nominal leadership, with no flourish of trumpets or public campaigning, with not so much as an office in İstanbul, the CUP had commanded support from the army, had compelled the sultan to revive the defunct constitution, had dominated in the election of a parliament, and had diffused through the empire at atmosphere congenial to constitutional government. Its vigilance and energy seemed to leave no point uncovered.[130]

As mentioned above, Ottomans of the party of reform or the Young Turks hoped for the creation of a new Ottoman Empire, with its present boundaries, filled with patriotism and nationality, financially solvent, and offering a united front against European aggression. The revolution of 1908 was followed by an effort in many directions toward reform and reorganization. The Ottoman reforms tried to establish equality of rights and responsibilities for all Ottoman subjects—Turks and non-Turks alike—in such areas as administration, military service, and taxes.[131]

Reuter's representative had an interesting interview with the Ottoman scholar Halil Halid who had returned to London at the beginning of November 1909, on the completion of a visit to Salonika and İstanbul, made for the purpose of studying the progress of the new regime under the Young Turks. He said:

> I have found a great change in public opinion since I was last in Turkey, at the time of the proclamation of the Constitution. Among the Mussulmans there is a general spirit of broad-mindedness in their relations with their non-Mussulman compatriots. As regards the Committee of Union and Progress, whose policy I have always upheld in the European Press in times of crisis, I think they have a great educational and social work to do through their branches and clubs in the provinces, but the time has come when the Committee should come forward boldly as a political party and not act merely as a power behind the Administration. The two members of the Committee at Constantinople, who are members of the Cabinet, are doing excellent work.[132]

Like all other Englishmen in the Ottoman Empire at that time, Edward Frederick Knight came to the conclusion that the Young Turks were quite sincere and that they were honestly desirous to have done with internal strife, to give equality to all the elements of the population, and to live in peace and friendship with all their non-Muslim fellow countrymen.[133] Marmaduke Pickthall's summary of Young Turk policy minces no words: "The Turks granted equal rights to all their subjects. Nationality was thenceforth to be everything, and no man's creed a subject for reproach. The program of reforms announced was radical and comprehensive."[134]

Directly after the proclamation of the constitution the problem of enrolling non-Muslims in the Ottoman army caused no little anxiety and gave occasion for sharp discussion, not only in Ottoman press but in that of foreign countries. This problem, however, difficult as it seemed, had been satisfactorily solved within the space of seven months.

The Young Turk attitude toward the non-Muslims, on the practical questions which at once arose, had been clearly laid down. In the army they were to serve side by side with Muslims. The official colleges and schools were to be thrown open to them.

The steady increase of the gendarmerie system, the enrollment in the army of twenty thousand Christian soldiers was a most effective and practical lesson in religious equality. Edwin Pears learned from the two great patriarchates—the Greek and the Armenian—that, all things considered, they were satisfied with the treatment the Christian soldiers received. Mahmud Şevket Paşa, the minister of war, paid several visits to the patriarchs and gave them satisfactory assurance that he would put an end to any misunderstanding whenever cases were brought to his knowledge. Pears believed that he was justified in saying that the heads of the Christian communities were persuaded that Mahmud Şevket Paşa and the ministers were determined to accord Christian soldiers all the protection that they could reasonably demand.[135]

Mahmud Şevket Paşa deserves special mention. After the War Academy, Mahmud Şevket Paşa was posted as an aide to the chief German instructor General Colmar Freiherr von Der Goltz and then sent for training in Germany. He was appointed governor of Kosova in 1905 where he won the trust of the CUP. He became commander of the Third Army in Salonika in 1908 and commanded the Movement Army which reestablished CUP rule in İstanbul the following year, when he became minister of war. Mahmud Şevket Paşa resigned, but was brought back by the CUP as grand vizier when it seized power on January 23, 1913.[136]

The Young Turks did not favor the policy of making Turkish the universal language of instruction. They wished to leave the existing schools alone, but to set up better equipped state schools, where the man who wanted the best training for his sons would prefer to send them. Among the most profound social changes brought about by the CUP were the establishment of subsidies for the education of women and a fundamental restructuring of the administration responsible for state-run primary schools.[137] The implementation of long-neglected legislation stipulating the use of Turkish in courts was not an attack on non-Turkish languages but an effort to establish uniform judicial procedures. Some disgruntled non-Turkish leaders invented the notion of a Turkification policy as a rhetorical weapon in their contest for influence with the CUP. Non-Turkish efforts to establish a decentralized imperial structure threatened the CUP's centralist policy.[138] As the Tufts professor Leila Tarazi Fawaz rightly points out in her work, *A Land of Aching Hearts*, research by many historians suggests that "the Young Turks did not impose Turkification on the populations and did not have a language policy that was substantially different from that of Sultan Abdülhamid II, but used centralization for purposes of integration as a safeguard against secessionist trends and planned for an Ottoman multinational imperial entity."[139]

Babanzade İsmail Hakkı, in a special article he contributed to the February 22, 1912, issue of *Tanin*, gave his opinion on the Ottomanist policy of the CUP. His sound reasoning ran as follows. What is the meaning of the word "Ottomanization" according to those who attribute this policy to the CUP? If Ottomanization signifies Turkification of Greeks, Armenians, Bulgars, Albanians, Arabs, Kurds, and others, this policy is really erroneous, dangerous, and fanciful. Even the children know that this is impossible. The Ottoman government did not resort to it and did not find it in conformity with its interests, even at the pinnacle of its power. The East and especially the Muslims of the East did not approve such a policy. To attribute a similar idea to the CUP is to admit a complete lack of logic in itself. If the aim of Ottomanization is to abolish the prerogatives of various communities, it is also a pure slander. Which privilege guaranteed by the constitution is adversely affected? The CUP looks at Ottomanization as the reinforcement of the sentiment of love for the country in the hearts of all citizens. According to the constitution, Turkish is the language of the state. Can one reprimand the CUP of having adopting this prescription? Besides nobody has demanded up to now that the Turkish should not be the official language. And once the Turkish is abolished as the official language, which element will accept the language of the other as such? Can anybody accuse France wishing to "Francize" everybody owing to the fact that one is obliged to learn its language, in order to be able to benefit from science? Ottoman government compels nobody to learn Turkish. It only does not wish to appoint officials who do not know this language.[140]

No Armenian writer has ever ventured to deny Babanzade İsmail Hakkı's courageous setting forth of the facts in his special article in *Tanin*, because they were established and attested beyond the shade of a question. For a man of around thirty-five years, Babanzade İsmail Hakkı had already attained an enviable position. He was a member of the General Council of the CUP and represented Baghdad in the Chamber of Deputies until his early death. His course in the Chamber of Deputies had marked him as a progressive patriot, broad-minded and wise, and constructive in his policy. He was for a short time minister of public instruction. Babanzade İsmail Hakkı died suddenly by a burst aneurysm as he was lecturing in the Law School of the İstanbul University on December 25, 1913.[141] On that date Cavid Bey made the following entry in his diary: "The unfortunate country had another very prominent victim and we personally lost a sincere friend, the CUP an intelligent scholarly member, the fatherland a son who loved it very much."[142]

The Young Turks promoted a new identity, Ottomanism, which sought to transcend the different linguistic and religious divides in Ottoman society. It was the conviction of the CUP's leading figures that the transformation of the empire into a modern, powerful state would entail the crystallization among the masses of an overarching sense of patriotism and identification with the institutions of government. The catchword associated with this notion was Ottomanism—a term denoting the cultivation of collective political identity based on civic equality among the peoples of the empire.[143] British journalist and historian Charles Woods reminded that when the Young Turks came into power, they proclaimed as their motto liberty, equality, and fraternity, and asserted that what they wished to bring about was a state of feeling by which the former differences between Turks, Greeks, Armenians, Bulgarians, Arabs, etc., should be obliterated—a state of feeling in which there would only be Ottomans.[144]

Ottomanism opened up new possibilities for thinking about citizenship, equality, and justice within a larger imperial setting.[145] As Ronald Grigor Suny noted: "The 1908 revolution proclaimed a new era for the empire, a progressive step into a European-style based on constitutionalism, equality, fraternity, and personal freedom. The Ottomanist program proposed a shared citizenship made up of diverse peoples united in their allegiance to the empire."[146] Therefore it is not surprising that the revolution of 1908 ushered in a period of growth in which Iraqi and Palestinian Arabs generally worked with the Young Turk policies rather than against them. Despite the rise of Arabism during this period, elites still tried to maintain their place in a reformed empire rather than rebel against it. Although Ottomanism, Turkism, and Arabism were fundamentally different ideologies, all shared a common conviction in upholding the integrity of the Ottoman Empire. This fact explains the overall Iraqi and Palestinian Arab loyalty to the empire during the First World War and the 1916–1918 revolt of Sherif Hüseyin.[147]

At the core of the Young Turk revolution is what Michelle Ursula Campos called "civic Ottomanism," a grassroots imperial citizenship project that promoted a unified sociopolitical identity of an Ottoman people struggling over the new rights and obligations of revolutionary political membership. Using her close reading of Ottoman language primary sources, she rightly points out that surprisingly, this active, dynamic process of making an Ottoman nation remains on the margins of the history of the modern Middle East as well as of the modern history of empires and nations broadly. Despite the fact that virtually every book on late Ottoman history mentions the nineteenth-century project of fostering imperial loyalty known as Ottomanism, this notion remains widely under-estimated, considered either an official state project alone or as the nucleus of an Islamist or Turkish ethnic nationalism. Campos is correct when she notes that several important studies on the overlapping Ottoman loyalties of outstanding Arab notables and intellectuals have addressed this gap to some extent, but the spread, content, and power of Ottomanism are still not well understood. There is much to like her contribution to the debate.[148]

The Young Turks affected profoundly the course of history among the peoples of the Middle East and the Balkans. Moreover they were the first group in the Ottoman state to approach the political, social, and cultural transformation of their society in the spirit of modern politics. Yet they remain the least studied and understood and the most distortedly portrayed power group in the history of the Middle East and the Balkans, which continue to be of constant and pressing importance in the contemporary world.[149]

ARMENIANS OF ADANA AFTER THE PROCLAMATION OF THE CONSTITUTION

From the very beginning it was recognized that the constitution of the Ottoman Empire was a very great experiment. It was not only a very great experiment, but it was a fine experiment, and an experiment that certainly deserved more sympathy and support than it got from the Armenians. Of course, there are many ways of looking at this experiment. The Adana Armenian way was to look at it from the point of view of their narrow communal interests. It was, however, expected that they did not desire separation and wished to remain Ottoman citizens doing their best to preserve the integrity of their country. There was no question of establishing autonomy in the province. The balance of population was such that anything like autonomy, even if the Ottoman government were to establish it, would be quite impossible.

As indicated earlier, the Young Turks' vision of the "unity of elements" did not materialize. After the initial burst of enthusiasm produced by the proclamation of the constitution, the various elements in the Ottoman body politic were anxious to further their own national aspirations. They established nationalist clubs to propagate their claims and entered the 1908 elections with their own "national programs." Armenians were very outspoken.[150]

After the promulgation of the constitution the Armenians of Adana founded local branches of the Dashnaks, Huntchaks, and Reformed Huntchaks in opposition to the Ottoman political committees which were being formed, or rather—to speak more accurately—they continued openly those activities of their organizations which they had hitherto carried on in secret. At this time the Armenian prelate in Adana was a young and ambitious priest named Musheg Seropian,[151] who was also leader of the Reformed Huntchaks. The Armenians could not say enough about the licentiousness of this man. Cemal Paşa remarked that if all the stories told about him by the Armenians were true, it might be stated without exaggeration that he was the incarnation of all the evil instincts.[152]

The Reformed Huntchak Party was a group that had splintered from the original Huntchak Party in 1898 in Alexandria, Egypt, due to internal ideological and tactical disagreements.[153] The organization was much smaller than the main stream of the Huntchaks and did not have much political significance. When the Young Turk revolution broke out, the organization split again. A part of them merged with the Ramkavars and named themselves as the Constitutional Ramkavar Party. Seropian became a member of this organization, most probably at the time of the merger. Whatever the doctrinal differences between the political parties, nationalism was their most significant characteristic.[154] Seropian was a most elusive and unassessable personality and seems always to have evoked the image of manipulator and opportunist.[155] By almost all accounts he was neither a man of principle nor one of great moral character. His energy and drive were fired principally by personal ambition. He talked in an aggressive, boastful, and threatening way, always trying to bluster his way out of difficult situations.[156] Scholars know surprisingly little about him.

This young, black-bearded Armenian bishop went about in his black robe making fiery speeches. He as a rollicking, wine-drinking, carousing fellow, who boasted that while other priests might show the way to heaven, his business was to lead the way to political progress and liberty. Again and again he publicly urged the Armenians to arm themselves. He declared that it was the duty of a true Armenian to sell the clothes from his back and buy arms, to eat less and buy arms, to stint his wife and children and buy arms, to sacrifice his home and buy arms.[157]

In Adana the great rejoicing of Armenians at the revival of the constitutional regime, and their increased communal activity upon the removal of the shackles of censorship and of the secret police, engendered a feeling of alarm among the Muslims. In the ferment that spread among them when they saw the Christians "raising their heads," the *hojas* and Muslim notables played a large part.[158]

At this time a considerable number of young Armenians—acolytes of Seropian—carried their effrontery so far as to proclaim publicly at various meetings that it would not be long before the Armenians were liberated from the Ottoman yoke. Cemal Paşa said to be fair, it should be added that the delegate of the Dashnak Party had no part in Seropian's excesses, and did not fail to draw the attention of the Dashnak deputies in İstanbul to the very evil results of his conduct.[159]

The tension between the Armenians and Muslims inhabiting the Adana and neighboring regions had been on the breaking point for several months since the reintroduction of the constitution, and that almost any incident might have precipitated a crisis. The Armenians benefited in many ways by the establishment of the constitutional government and busily imported arms and ammunition in an aggressive and self-assertive vein of enthusiasm, which led them to discourse on the great destinies of the Armenian nation and on the eventual setting up of an Armenian principality. The freedom allowed by the constitutional government in purchase and carriage of arms had led to several instances of crimes perpetrated by Armenians against Turks, and the hopelessness and incapacity of the government officials was made clear to everyone in their timid inaction and failure to arrest such criminals as were known to be at all popular. The strain and tension of the situation became unbearable; the sense of insecurity and nervousness all through the province of Adana reached such a pitch that only a spark was required to set alight the conflagration.[160]

ARMING AND BOASTING OF THE ARMENIANS IN ADANA

A large scale of importation of arms of all calibers—revolvers, pistols, rifles, or carabines of German, Austrian, and Belgian manufacture and ammunition had been underway since the summer of 1908.[161] As the ban on the imports and use of firearms was lifted, even the revolvers sent by post freely got through customs control. According to the official register, a total of 12,804 firearms were imported through the ports of Mersin and İskenderun from July 1908 to April 1909. No doubt, thousands of more arms were smuggled into the Adana province. Making use of the weakness of the government, smugglers freely carried arms by traditional routes via Aleppo and Beirut, and the number of firearms smuggled by way of Cyprus increased tremendously. The British vice consul at Mersin, Major Charles Doughty-Wylie, estimated that forty thousand guns, revolvers, and automatic pistols had been imported into the province since the restoration of the constitution. What was more serious was that these arms and ammunition were openly sold in the market along with other commodities for daily use. In Mersin and Adana baskets of revolvers were peddled in the streets. Shop windows were filled with arms and cartridges. In all the villages and on the farms the Armenians bought revolvers or guns. Damar Arıkoğlu recollects the scene as follows: "Various weapons were sold without any restriction, in markets, shops, and along the streets. The most popular was the Mauser gun with quick action cartridge. The weapon vendors even walked around shouting loudly, but no one stopped them. There was common understanding that 'liberty' meant no one interfered in any one's business." The dealers publicly sold revolvers and rifles, and they even frequented government offices. The arms dealers even encouraged people to buy more weapons by spreading the rumors that either Christians or Muslims would carry out massacre in the near future. Two months before the Adana events, twenty-five thousand kilograms of gunpowder was sent to Adana from İstanbul and many people rushed to purchase it.[162]

Some Armenian authors claim that it was the Muslims that profited from the process, but it is of no doubt that the Armenians also sold and purchased arms. Even Helen Davenport Gibbons, a strong sympathizer of Armenians, witnessed in her memoirs: "The Constitution has lifted the prohibition of owning firearms. We hear the Armenians have been buying them in large quantities."[163] The British vice consul at Mersin also describes the enthusiasm in which Armenians purchased firearms: "From the delightful novelty of the thing, many thousands of revolvers were purchased. Even schoolboys had them and flourished them about."[164] The practice was widespread and went beyond the border of the Adana province. The British consul general at Aleppo told an American admiral that there was no chance for an Armenian massacre to take place now in these regions, as every man was armed with a revolver.[165]

To get arms was not the thing that was connived, but recommended. Several Armenian leaders and priests, including Musheg Seropian, actually urged their congregations to buy arms. The Armenian newspapers justified the arming of the population and claimed it to be lawful, as it was necessary to defend their life, honor, and property. Tetsuya Sahara says it may be true that the Armenians had the right to purchase arms, but to possess the firearms and to use them are quite different things. Many Armenian youngsters not only purchased weapons, but also practiced them publicly.[166] It was a sign of things to come.

Not only did the Armenians arm themselves and openly display their weapons—a privilege never before assumed by Christians—but the two Armenian revolutionary societies, the Huntchak and the Troshag, became very active. Meetings were held, and orators exhorted the Armenians to remember their glorious past, when the country was ruled by Armenian kings. Rude portraits of the old Armenian kings were sold in the streets of Adana, Tarsus, Mersin, and other places, and the Armenians adorned their walls with them.[167]

The more Armenians armed, the more they talked, and the more they aroused the anxiety and alarm of the Turkish population. In the spring of 1909 the situation became one of extreme gravity. Certain members of the Huntchak Party had openly urged the people to fight the Turks.[168] Major Charles Doughty-Wylie, the British vice consul at Mersin, admitted that among the Armenians there was "much vain boasting and wordy provocation."[169] The Christians with all the assertiveness of the newly emancipated made equality seem to mean superiority. He described Armenians as "the most intelligent, the most educated, and by far the most talkative" section of the population, who imagined that the moment for demonstrating their superior ability had arrived, and that self-determination was virtually theirs for the asking; they chattered about it, in the *hans* (inns) and coffee shops, endlessly, and for men who knew the temper of the Turks, tactlessly.[170]

Such boasting had exasperated Turks at Adana. They expected the Armenians to claim their rights humbly.[171] Armenians in Adana and Mersin had taken to singing ancient Armenian war songs, and one braggart had stood up at a theatrical performance of *Julius Caesar*, shouting that while Caesar might refuse the proffered crown, the coming king of Armenia would not decline the crown that would be set on his head by loving patriots. The noisy Armenian bishop of Adana, Musheg Seropian, thereafter had himself photographed with a royal crown above his head, and it was said that he shipped rifles to Adana, making a personal profit on each weapon.[172] He gave every indication that he had made up his mind about his future course.

In their clubs the Armenian orators, drunk with their own verbosity, talked *ad nauseam*. They never seemed to have thought of the possible consequences of wild words. Natives of the country, they should have known its dangers, but with the word liberty they forgot them all. These were fatal errors.

Emil Lengyel noted:

After the first fraternal demonstrations of the revolution the Armenians adopted a manner toward their Muslim fellow-citizens provocative and unwise beyond belief. They had insulted and beaten Muslims in the streets of Adana. To the final influence of these follies were added the economic facts that Armenian landowners, already in possession of the richest areas of the Cilician plain, were rapidly increasing their holding; and that the Armenian population prospered and multiplied while the Muslim population declined. The Muslims of Cilicia, indeed, were gloomily brooding over Armenian affronts to their patriotism and economic Armenian encroachments on their position. These matters combined formed a mass of highly inflammable material.[173]

The clash of personal, national, and religious interests filled the air with electricity. An examination of the records suggests that Britain's diplomats were well informed about the developments in post-1908 Cilicia. Sir Gerard Lowther gave the following account of the situation in Adana in the first half of 1909. The picture fairly reflected the realities.

> Nearly no one in Adana was really satisfied. The Turks hated the idea that they were no longer masters. The Armenian wanted to rush into Home Rule. The Greek mistrusted the constitution because had not made it himself and because under it he seemed likely to lose certain facilities he had enjoyed under the old venal system. [. . .] Under the constitution all men might bear arms. From the delightful novelty of the thing, many thousands of revolvers were purchased. Even schoolboys had them and, boy-like, flourished them about. But worse followed. The swagger of the arm-bearing Armenian and his ready tongue irritated ignorant Turks. Threats and insults passed on both sides. Certain Armenian leaders, delegates from Constantinople, and priests (an Armenian priest is in his way an autocrat) urged their congregations to buy arms. It was done openly, indiscreetly, and, in some cases, it might be said wickedly. What can be thought of a preacher, a Russian Armenian,[174] who in a church in this city where there had never been a massacre, preached revenge for the martyrs of 1895? Constitution or none, it was all the same to him. "Revenge," he said, "murder for murder. Buy arms. A Turk for every Armenian of 1895." An American missionary who was present got up and left the church. Bishop, of Adana, toured his province preaching that he who had a coat should sell it and buy a gun.[175]

This expectation that a violent outbreak might arrive at any time was fueled by a genuine understanding of the situation in Cilicia. At the most basic level, this entailed a clear appreciation both of the state of the intercommunal rivalries and alignments and of the way in which they were beginning to harden in the face of a succession of crises. Reports conveyed from the British diplomatic and consular representatives contained detailed and up-to-date assessments on these matters. Hence, from the Foreign Office records, it is clear that Britain's diplomats were well aware of the Adana governorate's concern in local security.

In his memoirs, Cemal Paşa wrote as follows on Bishop Musheg Seropian and the provincial authorities in Adana in 1908:

> A young priest who passionately sought authority, named, Mushech, was at the time a member of the Adana Armenian Delegation, and was also one of

the leaders of the Hinchaks. Monsignor Mushech had begun to have rifles and revolvers brought from Europe to arm his men. He was publicly announcing that Armenians were now armed, that they would no longer fear incidents such as the 1894 massacres, and that should so much as a single hair on an Armenian's head be disturbed, ten Turks would be destroyed. It is here that the biggest responsibility of the Adana government begins. [. . .] To arrest and imprison His Excellency Mushech and his accomplices, to undertake legal investigation with regard to them, and even to declare a state of siege in the province was the best short cut. Unfortunately in Turkey [. . .] such a government did not exist in 1908. At that time, the province of Adana was administered by Governor Cevad Bey, who was a perfect example of a cultured gentleman. However, his lack of administrative talent could not be replaced by his culture. In short, he was not the man to serve as Governor of Adana at such a time.[176]

GOVERNOR CEVAD BEY'S WARNINGS AND EARLY DANGERS, OCTOBER 1908–APRIL 1909

The men who were responsible for running the provincial administration of the twentieth-century Ottoman Empire were sufficiently homogeneous in origin and outlook and sufficiently distinct from the rest of the population to be called an elite. Indeed, the public service remained a closely knit elite corps in which the traditional system of bonds of family and school still operated despite increasingly formal laws and regulations. Members of this elite had a shared social background and had similar career trajectories. They mostly came from the traditional bureaucratic families which dominated public life in the Ottoman Empire since the *Tanzimat* period in the mid-nineteenth century. They belonged to that section of the Turkish intelligentsia who usually attended the College of Administrative Sciences or the Faculty of Law in İstanbul during the last decades of the Ottoman Empire and formed their views in its spirit, tradition, and philosophy.[177]

The governor was the responsible head of the province and the representative, therefore, of each ministry. After 1908 he was appointed, on the nomination of the minister of the interior, by a decision of the Council of Ministers, confirmed by an imperial decree, and, legally, could only be dismissed by the same powers; all officials under him were only appointed after his consent had been obtained. He could dismiss all secondary officials on his own motion but "commissioned officers"—those appointed by an imperial decree confirming the minister of the interior's choice, as the *Defterdar* (treasurer general), *Mektubçu* (director of correspondence), etc.—could only be dismissed by the governor on his reporting to İstanbul; while if the Cabinet and Council of State failed to take action within one month, he might then remove the official himself, and he might even summarily dismiss any official who was actually a disturber of the peace. Thus he was seen to be a very powerful official, and far different from the figurehead lords lieutenant of English counties, or even from the French prefect.[178]

Although ultimate responsibility for making current policy rested with the Ministry of the Interior, in practice the provincial administrators frequently exercised real power not only in implementing but also in formulating policy. The political instability of the Second Ottoman Constitutional Period resulted in a rapid turnover of ministers, who were often either inexperienced when they assumed their ministerial responsibilities or only briefly in office. The provincial administrators, on the other hand, were professionals who tended to occupy positions of power within the Ministry of the Interior for long periods of time. They experienced the closing stages of the empire, a tumultuous and complicated time, and one that provided different challenges for the Ottoman officialdom. They had to deal with difficult situations. The prevailing circumstances were not of Cevad Bey's making, but they are essential background against which his career has to be studied.

The Turkish individual under a fair governor was often a quiet, industrious, and respectable citizen. Men of known judgment and ability, long resident in the Ottoman Empire, testified that all nationalities could live side by side peaceably, provided only the local governor was just and farsighted. A Muslim governor could, if he wished, protect his subjects from robbery and outrage and make life worth living.[179]

Cevad Bey was born in 1856 in Servi, a locality attached to the province of Edirne. After graduating from the Beşiktaş military secondary school, he attended the College of Administrative Sciences at İstanbul and completed his studies in 1885. Entering government service in the autumn of 1885 in the Translation Bureau of the Ministry of Foreign Affairs,[180] he was transferred to the Ministry of Finance in 1887. Cevad Bey was reassigned to the Translation Bureau a year later and in 1889 joined the Imperial Court as secretary.[181] Serving eleven years at the Yıldız Palace,[182] he was appointed governor in turn in Jerusalem, Ankara, Konya, and Adana in 1901, 1903, 1905, and 1908, respectively. Cevad Bey spoke French fluently and was a man of considerable culture and charm of manner. He was dismissed from his post in April 1909. Nothing is known about him after his dismissal. Apparently Cevad Bey did not keep copies of his own letters, and he retained no record of his communications with others. Giving an account of a man who left no diaries, no personal papers, and no autobiographical material is bound to encounter difficulties. Cevad Bey is therefore a figure whose personality and office can be approached only tentatively.[183]

For a governor, Adana was a promotion. The province of Adana was regarded in governmental estimation as of the first rank. The appointed governors saw Adana as a coveted reward and prize, no less important than one of the larger provinces of the empire. The reasons for Cevad Bey's appointment remain obscure, but it is reasonable to suppose that Adana was seen as a fitting capstone to his career and a mark of Sultan Abdülhamid II's appreciation of his services.[184]

The new governor of Adana, Cevad Bey, arrived at Mersin from İstanbul on October 15, 1908, by Khedivial main steamer and went straight away by a special train to the seat of the province. Without appearing worried, he was concerned about the current state of affairs of Adana. He was aware of Armenian intentions from the beginning and asked for a reinforcement of troops from Damascus, in anticipation of all eventuality.[185]

It was announced from Adana to the Armenian İstanbul daily *Arevelk* that the new governor succeeded in assuring the peace, his intervention against the intrigues of reactionaries resulted in restoring order and calming public opinion.[186]

Cevad Bey sent several reports to Minister of the Interior Hüseyin Hilmi Paşa[187] (notably on January 16, 1909) demanding Musheg Seropian be replaced because he was inciting the Armenians against the government and laws and gradually poisoning the minds of his fellow citizens. The governor also said that the Armenian bishop had donned the costume of a Cilician king and had himself photographed in it, that he had organized theatrical performances in which mythical kings of Armenia appeared on stage, and that he had encouraged the Christian population not to pay military and local taxes. The situation was dangerous in the extreme. The commander of the French fleet in the eastern Mediterranean, Rear-Admiral Pivet, corroborated the above. He said that at the instigation of their bishop, Musheg Seropian, the Armenians created insurrectional committees and circulated proclamations identifying the ministers and principal leaders of a future Armenian kingdom. What was more, he added, Armenians had armed themselves with up-to-date weapons and enjoyed showing them off to the Turks.[188] This vain, tricky, conniving prelate, a foul of ferment without morality but with a taste for intrigue, was scarcely the man to conduct communal affairs in the midst of the worst crisis in Adana in the past generations.

After the constitutional restoration, a large number of Armenians began to immigrate into the Adana province. Some of them were those who had fled from the province for political reasons, others were those who were attracted by the better working conditions of this fertile plain. But the local authorities were not well prepared to cope with this situation and were simply perplexed by the sudden influx of Armenians. Hence Cevad Bey reported that, within five or six months, a lot of families came in such an extent that it was not difficult to see several families living together in the same building.[189] These observations appeared to fall upon deaf ears. The Sublime Porte did not take the warnings seriously. It continued naively to suppose that the Muslims and Christians of the region would live in harmony.

It should also be noted that the above are far from a complete record of the warnings submitted by Cevad Bey. These passages, however, seem to be adequate to indicate the estimate of the governor as to the probability of an Armenian onslaught under certain given circumstances. This outburst might not have been difficult to avoid but Hüseyin Hilmi Paşa had done little to prevent it. He paid little attention to the governor's reports. He was not particularly impressed with Cevad Bey, who had a relatively weak position in the officialdom after the 1908 revolution. The minister of the interior's policy could be described as one of willful negligence. His lack of ardor was prompted by the Sublime Porte which was reluctant further to extend government commitments.

Armenian exiles returned from Europe and America and helped to work up the excitement. They harangued the people night and day. Why should Armenia not have the same rights as Bulgaria? The country was an Armenian kingdom before the Turks came. It was Armenian soil.[190]

To add to the intensity of the situation the Armenians gave a theatrical performance in Adana, in which a young woman in a black robe, with bound hands, and wearing a crown of thorns, represented Armenia. An angel appeared and announced that the cause of Armenia's troubles was the failure of Armenians to unite. Thereupon the black-robed figure had a vision in which the Armenian nation abandoned its dissensions and joined hands for the sake of liberty. Then the angel reappeared, unbound Armenia's hands, put a resplendent robe on her and replaced the crown of thorns with a golden crown.[191]

Cilicia became the hotbed of sedition and revolution. "At a banquet given by the Turkish mayor of the city [Adana] to emissaries of the reform party, Moslems and Christians sat together; it was a magnificent attempt to express brotherhood. The absence of the leading Gregorians was an unpleasant reminder of the tendency of the greater part of the Gregorian population to follow the minority wing of the Armenian revolutionary party." A native Protestant pastor, though perhaps prejudiced in favor of his own church, wrote: "The Moslem find it hard to confirm to Constitutional ways; the Catholic looks on the Constitution as being Protestant, the Gregorian Armenian fears it will endanger his Armenian nationality. Only the Evangelical (Protestant) falls into line." Still another wrote, "In this region [Cilicia] Armenian revolutionists proclaim a short sighted and zealous propaganda of separation from Turkey or at least decentralization."[192] This interpretation is difficult to deny.

Cemal Paşa wrote that at the beginning of 1909 a rumor was going round that the Armenians would rise and destroy the Turks in the immediate future.

They would use the opportunity to let the province be occupied by contingents from the fleets of European powers, and then proceed to form an Armenian state. The Turks were so convinced of the truth of these rumors that many reputable people took their families to place of safety.[193]

Six weeks before the first outbreak at Adana there was a powerful agitation among the Muslim masses all over the country. The constitution was bitterly criticized. The Christians were getting too pretentious. The Armenians were organizing a revolution. Islam was in danger. So the story ran from city to city, village to village, and farm to farm. The Mohammedan League spread exaggerated accounts of what the Christians were doing and intended to do. The air was full of suspicion.[194] The leading Muslim merchants and landowners in the province of Adana, jealous of the progress and prosperity of the Armenians, who owned the best shops and farms, lived better, dressed better, and, with the Christian Greeks, controlled the business of the country, fanned the flame of Muslim suspicion.[195]

Meanwhile the Armenian *Fedayee* (the one willing to sacrifice his life for his cause), under their leader and blond-haired fighting captain, continued to practice with their rifles in the vineyards; the Huntchak and Troshag societies continued to hold revolutionary meetings in various parts of the city of Adana; the Armenian bishop continued to go about exhorting his people to buy arms at any sacrifice; and the Armenians, generally ignorant of the deep passion of the Muslim masses, continued to display pictures of old Armenian kings in their houses.[196]

Within the Huntchak and Troshag societies was a secret military organization of about two hundred young men known as the *Fedayee*. These warriors were sworn to surrender their lives absolutely to the Armenian cause. They were thoroughly armed and drilled, and they practiced with rifles almost daily in the vineyards, even in the presence of Muslims. Their chief was a young Armenian named Zachariah Bezdikian, but their most redoubtable captain was Garabet Letchilian, a pale, slender youth with long blond hair falling about his thin shoulders. Their oath bound them to obey their officers' orders until death.[197]

In a dispatch, giving a general report for the first quarter of the year 1909, the British vice consul at Mersin said that the two provinces of Konya and Adana were apparently in a quite state, but that there were disturbing elements below the surface, such as the large importation of arms, and the dangerous weakness of the local authorities. The judicial authorities, for instance, refused to condemn guilty parties, however overwhelming the proofs of their guilt might be, for fear of incurring unpopularity, while the governor of Adana was being strongly attacked in the local press, which observed that he was a good clerk, but a bad governor; an honest man, but one who was incapable of action; and recommended him to return to İstanbul and resume his avocation there as a secretary. Charles Doughty-Wylie's account indicated a general spread of lawlessness, but he stated that there was "nothing that a small show of force would not at once put down and the force, though small, at the disposal of the authorities is sufficient, if they will only use it." It came, therefore, as an entire surprise that the British ambassador in İstanbul received on April 15, 1909, a telegram from Doughty-Wylie that he had proceeded from Mersin to Adana on the preceding day, having heard that the situation was very critical, and had found many people killed on the way, while a conflict was in progress in the city. The Armenian quarter was armed, and at the moment was safe, but the government was altogether incapable.[198]

For two days preceding the outbreak there had been a bitter feud between Muslims and Christians. In one vineyard shooting begun, and hatred was aroused on April 12, 1909. The cry of "Islam in danger" was readily listened to. The Muslim population was inflamed and ready to acquiesce in the suggestions of men who purposed to create disorder.[199] Tuesday (on this instance April 13) was market day in Adana, and many villagers would have heard of trouble coming, of *Fedayees*, of dynamite, and of armed revolution in which the Muslims were to be killed. Possibly they were told something of the fight for the Islamic law in İstanbul and to be ready to defend the faith.[200] There was a great Turkish mass meeting on the night of April 13 near the *Konak* under the direction of the Mohammedan League. An Armenian who ventured near the scene was caught by the crowd and clubbed to death. His friends carried the news about the Armenian quarter of the city, and the *Fedayee* got themselves in readiness.[201] Every kind of rumor was afloat as to the probability of a massacre. During that night, numerous patrols passed through the streets of Adana; no one thought of going to bed.[202]

The conduct of the chief of police in Adana during these last few days was of interest. He was a Turk of the best family in Adana named Tevfik Kadri (Ramazanoğlu)[203] and a good man. He had for long been asking for more help from the government and been bewailing the lack of official support. He now tried to warn the Armenians through the CUP club of which many of them were members. On April 10, he visited Zachariah Bezdikian. Tevfik Kadri talked of impending danger, but he did not say anything definite, probably because he did not know anything definite. Bezdikian thought that nothing would happen. On April 13, Tevfik Kadri tried again. He sent for Bezdikian to come to his house. Bezdikian went at the wrong hour and found the house full of Turkish notables. Tevfik Kadri, however, took him on one side and again warned him of danger, Bezdikian again thought that there was nothing particular in it. Some information which a Greek telegraphist gave Doughty-Wylie later throws light on the conduct of Tevfik Kadri. The Greek who was either crazed with terror or pretending to be crazed, came to the British vice consul one day to ask for asylum. He said that he would be hanged. On April 10, he had gone to Tevfik Kadri and asked for police protection. On being asked the reason of this, he had stated that he knew of seven hundred *Fedayees* among the Armenians who were going to burn the city and the *Konak*. Tevfik Kadri, after getting this news on April 10, went to warn Bezdikian.[204]

Although the situation had already been slipping out of Governor Cevad Bey's control, he could not realize its gravity. A Christian delegation, including the American missionary William Nesbitt Chambers, visited the governor's office on the night of April 13. They expressed serious concern about the conditions. They explained that the fever among the Muslim population had reached a dangerous point and warned that, if the government failed to take effective measures immediately, catastrophic consequences would follow. Cevad Bey, however, answered that he had taken necessary precautions and assured them that the people of the city were perfectly quiet and that there was no cause for fear. It was true that he tried to calm down the mob, but all he could do was to state that the rumor was groundless. It did not occur to him to use the regular units to dismiss the gathering. After the events, he claimed in his report to the Ministry of the Interior that he, together with the military commander, stayed at the office all night, energetically discussing the allocation of soldiers and other possible measures. The committee of investigation, however, concluded that the governor simply returned home that night as he failed to apprehend the urgency of the situation. Cevad Bey, though a well-meaning man, had evidently not the force of character to do anything but trim between the contending parties.[205]

According to an account by Abdurrahman (Paksoy), the son of Bağdadizade Abdülkadir, the governor sent for his father before the morning prayer on April 14 while it was still dark. The son went with his father, and said that the governor asked Bağdadizade's advice. In the night the governor had heard that the Turks were planning a massacre. Bağdadizade asked how the governor knew this thing and was answered that the *Konak* had been besieged by a crowd in the night, entreating the governor to give the order to kill. The governor had refused but was afraid that they might still kill in spite of him. Bağdadizade advised that at morning prayer they send to every mosque men to forbid the massacre. This was done, but the men returned saying that by some chance on that morning there were but very few worshippers and that so the prohibition would scarcely reach everybody's ears. Bağdadizade then advised that there was nothing to do but wait and say no word of massacre, lest the word should bring the thing. Thus his son acted accordingly.[206]

If the accelerating sense of crisis in early 1909 gave to Cevad Bey's office a somewhat heightened status, it also brought with it far more onerous and thorny responsibilities. All of this, the administrative impermanence, the relative inexperience, the mounting peril, made improbable any bold personal initiatives. If decisiveness and audacity were all it took to dispel ambivalence, Cevad Bey was not the man. Instead, he familiarized himself rather resolved the uncertainties over Adana; he familiarized his counterparts with the same arguments, on those occasions when order seemed to have figured prominently on the province's agenda.

NOTES

1. Earl Percy, *Highlands of Asiatic Turkey* (London: Edward Arnold, 1901), pp. 295–96fn1.
2. Stanford Shaw's review of Benjamin Braude and Bernard Lewis, eds., *Christians and Jews in the Ottoman Empire: The Functioning of a Plural Society*, Vol. 1: *The Central Lands* and Vol. 2: *The Arabic-Speaking Lands*, The American Historical Review, Vol. 94, No. 4 (October 1989), p. 1142. On the peoples of the Ottoman Empire, the *millet* system and the challenges of nationalism the only place to start for English-language speakers is this source. It is a splendid and enormously useful book.
3. For a general survey, see Halil İnalcık, *Osmanlı İmparatorluğunun Ekonomik ve Sosyal Tarihi (1300–1600)* (Economic and Social History of the Ottoman Empire [1300–1600]), Vol. 1 (İstanbul: Eren Yayınları, 2000), p. 54; Ali Güler, *Osmanlı'dan Cumhuriyete Azınlıklar* (Minorities from the Ottoman to the Republic) (Ankara: Tamga Yayıncılık, 2000), p. 12; Bilal Eryılmaz, *Osmanlı Devletinde Gayrimüslim Tebaanın Yönetimi* (The Governance of the Non-Muslim Subjects in the Ottoman State) (İstanbul: Risale Yayınları, 1996), p. 44; and Avedis Sanjian, *The Armenian Communities in Syria under Ottoman Dominion* (Cambridge, MA: Harvard University Press, 1965), pp. 30–31 and 40–43. A more extensive discussion of the theme can be found in Roderic Davison, "The *Millets* as Agents of Change in the Nineteenth-Century Ottoman Empire," in Braude and Lewis, *Christians and Jews in the Ottoman Empire*, Vol. 1, pp. 319–37.
4. Roderic Davison, "Turkish Attitudes Concerning Christian-Muslim Equality in the Nineteenth Century," *The American Historical Review*, Vol. 59, No. 4 (July 1954), p. 845.
5. Feroz Ahmad, *The Young Turks and the Ottoman Nationalities: Armenians, Greeks, Albanians, Jews, and Arabs, 1908–1918* (Salt Lake City, UT: University of Utah Press, 2014), p. 2. Feroz Ahmad is a leading expert on the Ottoman Second Constitutional Period, and his previous publications, such as *The Young Turks: The Committee of Union and Progress in Turkish Politics, 1908–1914* (Oxford: Clarendon Press, 1969), are highly influential works within the field and remain the first ports of call for students interested in studying this topic.
6. Sir Charles Eliot (Odysseus), *Turkey in Europe* (London: Edward Arnold,1900), pp. 438–39.
7. Simonyan, *The Destruction of Armenians in Cilicia, April 1909*, p. 5.

8. Suny, *A History of the Armenian Genocide*, pp. 44–45.

9. The Ottoman Constitution of December 23, 1876, and the vigorously experienced, but short-lived, constitutional politics of the Ottoman Empire in this period has been the subject of a study in English; see Robert Devereux, *The First Ottoman Constitutional Period: A Study of Midhat Constitution and Parliament* (Baltimore, MD: The Johns Hopkins Press, 1963).

10. For overviews, see Yusuf Hikmet Bayur, *Türk İnkılabi Tarihi* (History of the Turkish Revolution), Vol. 2, Sect. 1 (Ankara: Türk Tarih Kurumu Basımevi, second edition, 1964), pp. 59–61; Danişmend, *İzahlı Osmanlı Tarihi Kronolojisi*, Vol. 4, pp. 356–65; Süleyman Kani İrtem, Osman Selim Kocahanoğlu, ed., *Meşrutiyet Doğarken: 1908 Jön Türk İhtilali* (While the Constitutionalism Was Rising: Young Turk Revolution of 1908) (İstanbul: Temel Yayınları, 1999), pp. 60–65; İsmail Hakkı Uzunçarşılı, "1908 Yılında İkinci Meşrutiyetin Ne Suretle İlan Edildiğine Dair Vesikalar" (Documents on How the Second Constitutionalism Was Proclaimed in 1908), *Belleten*, Vol. 20, No. 77 (January 1956), pp. 103–74.

11. Grand Vizier Ferid Paşa was removed from office on July 22, 1908. He was replaced by the seventy-year-old Said Paşa, who had served six previous terms as grand vizier under Sultan Abdülhamid II. On Said Paşa, see İnal, *Osmanlı Devrinde Son Sadrazamlar*, Sects. 7–8, pp. 989–1263; *Türk Parlamento Tarihi, Birinci ve İkinci Meşrutiyet*, Vol. 2, pp. 692–95; Us, *Karikatür*, pp. 47–53 and 183–84; Ayşe Osmanoğlu, *Babam Sultan Abdülhamid* (My Father Sultan Abdülhamid) (İstanbul: Timaş Yayınları, third edition, 2015), pp. 44–46.

12. See, for instance, "Meclis'in İctimaı" (Convocation of the Parliament), *Tanin*, July 25, 1908, p. 1.

13. D. S. Margoliouth, "Constantinople at the Declaration of the Constitution," *The Fortnightly Review*, Vol. LXXXIV (July–December 1908), pp. 563–70; Viator, "The Turkish Revolution," *The Fortnightly Review*, Vol. LXXXIV (July–December 1908), pp. 353–68.

14. "A Nation's Sudden Conversion," *The Missionary Herald*, Vol. 54, No. 10 (October 1908), p. 457.

15. Edwin Pears, "The Turkish Revolution," *The Contemporary Review*, Vol. XCIV (July–December 1908), pp. 294 and 296. *The Contemporary Review*, a weekly journal published in London, was renowned for the important subjects it was dealing with. Since the restoration of the constitution in the Ottoman Empire, it contained many matters of high local interest.

16. On Ali Kemal Bey, see Yücel Güçlü, *Zeki Kuneralp and the Turkish Foreign Service* (Newcastle upon Tyne: Cambridge Scholars Publishing, 2015), pp. 30–63.

17. "Osmanlı Kanuni Esasisi" (The Ottoman Constitution), *Tanin*, July 27, 1908, p. 1.

18. Tarık Zafer Tunaya, *Türkiye'de Siyasi Partiler* (Political Parties in Turkey), Vol. 3: *İttihat ve Terakki, Bir Çağın, Bir Kuşağın, Bir Partinin Tarihi* (The Committee of Union and Progress, the History of an Age, a Generation, a Party) (İstanbul: İletişim Yayınları, third edition, 2000), pp. 52–55.

19. Arpee, "A Century of Armenian Protestantism," p. 165.

20. The city will be referred to throughout as Salonika, which, along with Salonica, represents the standard English language spelling used in the secondary literature. The city is called Selanik in Turkish.

21. FO 371/768/7053. Annual Report on Turkey for the Year 1908. Sir Gerard Lowther (Istanbul) to Sir Edward Grey (FO), February 17, 1909.

22. Halidé Edib, *Memoirs of Halidé Edib* (New York and London: The Century Co., 1926), pp. 271–72. Halidé Edib was a woman of strong personality, and her eventful life was full of stirring incidents. A prominent novelist, social activist, and journalist, she was one of Turkey's leading feminists in the Second Constitutional and Early Republican Period. She was the first Turkish graduate of the American College for Girls in İstanbul, the first Turkish woman to be invited to speak at the Williamstown Institute of Politics, a lecturer of marked ability, and a discriminating writer. Her first articles appeared in *Tanin*. She established a society to promote women's participation in social life and to some extent played a notable part in politics since 1908.

23. On the broad outlines of the political narrative of the year 1908 in the Ottoman Empire, see Nuri Akbayar, Raşit Çavaş, Yücel Demirel, Bahattin Öztuncay, Mete Tunçay, eds., *İkinci Meşrutiyetin İlk Yılı 23 Temmuz 1908–23 Temmuz 1909* (The First Year of the Second Constitutionalism: 23 July 1908–23 July 1909) (İstanbul: Yapı Kredi Yayınları, 2008). This great reference book should do much to stimulate further work in the field.

24. Alfred de Bilinski, "The Turkish Revolution," *The Nineteenth Century and After*, Vol. 114, No. CCCLXXVIII (August 1908), pp. 357–58. Alfred de Bilinski *alias* Ahmed Rüstem was the Ottoman ambassador in Washington before the First World War and well known in the diplomatic and social life of the American capital. He was given his passports by President Woodrow Wilson in 1913, having ventured to commit the diplomatic solecism of criticizing the United States for its lynchings in a very clever letter of defending the Ottoman government. He was a Pole by blood born a Christian, but embracing the Muslim faith as a young man. See James Harbord, "Mustapha Kemal Pasha and His Party," *The World's Work*, Vol. 15 (May–October 1920), p. 184; Syed Tanvir Wasti, "Ahmed Rüstem Bey and the End of an Era," *Middle Eastern Studies*, Vol. 48, No. 5 (September 2012), pp. 781–96.

25. "Turcs et Arméniens," *Le Moniteur Oriental*, 4 août 1908, p. 2.

26. "Rumeli Vilayati" (Rumelian Provinces), *İkdam*, July 27, 1908, p. 1.

27. Pears, "The Turkish Revolution," pp. 297 and 299–300.

28. *The Times*, July 27, 1908, p. 1.

29. "The Ottoman Constitution," Constantinople Agency, July 27, 1908.

30. Ibid.

31. Agence Italiana, July 27, 1908.

32. "La Constitution Ottomane," *Le Moniteur Oriental*, 31 juillet 1908, p. 3.

33. "The Ottoman Constitution," Constantinople Agency, August 10, 1908.

34. E. J. Dillon, "The Unforeseen Happens as Usual," *The Contemporary Review*, Vol. XCIV (July–December 1908), p. 384.

35. Constantinople Agency, November 27, 1908.
36. Constantinople Agency, December 5, 1908.
37. Tanzimat means "regulations," but when referring to the historical period of its name it is taken to mean "Reorganization."
38. Roderic Davison, *Reform in the Ottoman Empire 1856–1876* (Princeton, NJ: Princeton University Press, 1963), p. 387. Roderic Davison was long regarded as a senior specialist in *Tanzimat* studies.
39. Gülhane is the name of the gardens of the Sarayburnu (Seraglio Point), which were later opened as a park, and where, in olden days, stood the building in which the rose sweatments for the use of the court were prepared (*gül* meaning rose). Here the celebrated imperial edict was read in public.
40. For a detailed study of the *Hattı Şerif* and its consequences, see Enver Ziya Karal, *Osmanlı Tarihi Nizam-ı Cedit ve Tanzimat Devirleri (1789–1856)* (Ottoman History: Eras of New Order and Reorganization [1789–1856]), Vol. 5 (Ankara: Türk Tarih Kurumu, reprinted, 1988), pp. 169–95 and 248–52.
41. Enver Ziya Karal, *Osmanlı Tarihi İslahat Fermanı Devri (1856–1861)* (Ottoman History: Era of Reform Rescript [1856–1861]), Vol. 6 (Ankara: Türk Tarih Kurumu, reprinted, 1988), pp. 1–28.
42. İnal, *Osmanlı Devrinde Son Sadrazamlar*, Sects. 2–3, pp. 315–414; Ziya Şakir, *Sultan Abdülhamid* (İstanbul: Akıl Fikir Yayınları, reprint, 2010), pp. 119–25; "Proclaiming the New Constitution at Constantinople," *The Graphic*, January 6, 1877, p. 6.
43. *Ulema* were the scholars with expertise in the field of theology and religious law, often consulted as "masters of binding and unbinding" to resolve disputes and divisions of opinion about the best course for state policy, particularly in times of political crisis. As an advisory group their opinions were, however, nonbinding.
44. Alfred H. Lybyer, "The Turkish Parliament," *Proceedings of the American Political Science Association*, Vol. 7 (1910), p. 67. Alfred H. Lybyer was the founder of Ottoman historiography in the United States.
45. *Türk Parlamento Tarihi Meşrutiyete Geçiş Süreci: Birinci ve İkinci Meşrutiyet* (History of the Turkish Parliament Transitional Process to the Constitutionalism: First and Second Constitutionalism), Vol. 1 (Ankara: Türkiye Büyük Millet Meclisi Basımevi Müdürlüğü, 1997), p. 69; Devereux, *The First Ottoman Constitutional Period*, p. 74. Text of the Ottoman Constitution of December 23, 1876, is available in Turkish in Abdullah Şeref Gözübüyük and Suna Kili, *Türk Anayasa Metinleri Tanzimattan Bugüne Kadar* (Turkish Constitution Texts: From the *Tanzimat* to the Present) (Ankara: Ajans-Türk Matbaası, 1957), pp. 25–38; *Parliamentary Papers, House of Commons, 1877*, Vol. XCI, pp. 114–31, in French and English translations.
46. Devereux, *The First Ottoman Constitutional Period*, p. 75.
47. Davison, *Reform in the Ottoman Empire 1856–1876*, pp. 387–88. For an excellent analysis of the 1876 constitution see Karal, *Osmanlı Tarihi*, Vol. 8, pp. 227–30. Recai Galip Okandan makes similar points in his "Amme Hukukumuz Bakımından Tanzimat, Birinci ve İkinci Meşrutiyet Devirlerinin Önemi" (The Importance of the Periods of the *Tanzimat*, First and Second Constitutionalism Regarding Our Public Law), *İstanbul Üniversitesi Hukuk Fakültesi Mecmuası*, Vol. 15, No. 1 (1949), pp. 14–33.

48. Julia Phillips Cohen, *Becoming Ottomans: Sephardi Jews and Imperial Citizenship in the Modern Era* (New York: Oxford University Press, 2014), p. 10. Julia Phillips Cohen is an associate professor in the Program in Jewish Studies and the Department of History at Vanderbilt University. Her *Becoming Ottomans* won the 2014 National Jewish Award in the category of "Writing Based on Archival Material." She has published extensively on various aspects of the Ottoman world, especially Palestine, and is thus exceedingly well-qualified to author this work of synthesis mostly on primary literature.

49. Ibid., p. 20.

50. Earl, "The New Constitution of Turkey," p. 77.

51. Lybyer, "The Turkish Parliament," pp. 67–68.

52. Anahide Ter Minassian, "The Role of the Armenian Community in the Foundation and Development of the Socialist Movement in the Ottoman Empire and Turkey: 1876–1923," in Mete Tunçay and Eric Jan Zürcher, eds., *Socialism and Nationalism in the Ottoman Empire 1876–1923* (London: British Academic Press, 1994), p. 117.

53. Hayri Orhun, Celal Kasaroğlu, Mehmet Belek, Kazım Atakul, eds., *Meşhur Valiler* (The Famous Provincial Governors) (Ankara: İçişleri Bakanlığı Merkez Valileri Bürosu Yayınları, 1969), pp. 204–5. Ottoman provincial governors remained a comparatively faceless lot. The combined work of Hayri Orhun, Celal Kasaroğlu, Mehmet Belek, and Kazım Atakul goes some way toward changing this, although a revised edition is now needed. For an insightful discussion of the question of Muslim–Non-Muslim equality in the Second Constitutional Period, see İsmail Kara, "Müsavat Yahut Müslümanlara Eşitsizlik: Bir Kavramın Siyaseten/Dinen İnşası ve Dönüştürücü Gücü" (Equality or Unequality Toward Muslims: Political/Religious Construction of a Concept and Its Transformatory Force), in Azmi Özcan, ed., *Osmanlı Devletinde Din ve Vicdan Hürriyeti* (Freedom of Religion and Conscience in the Ottoman State) (İstanbul: Ensar Neşriyat, 2000), pp. 307–47.

54. Midhat Pasha, "The Past, Present, and Future of Turkey," *The Nineteenth Century*, January–June 1878, pp. 981–1000; Sommerville Story, ed., *The Memoirs of Ismail Kemal Bey* (London: Constable and Company Ltd, 1920), p. 254. On Krikor Odian's background and career, see Levon Panos Dabağyan, *Emperyalistler Kıskacında Ermeni Tehciri I (Türk Ermenileri)* (Armenian Relocation at the Pincer of the Imperialists I [Turkish Armenians]) (İstanbul: IQ Kültür Sanat Yayıncılık, 2007), p. 763.

55. Suny, *A History of the Armenian Genocide*, p. 62.

56. Kazım Karabekir, Faruk Özerergin, ed., *İttihat ve Terakki Cemiyeti* (The Committee of Union and Progress) (İstanbul: Emre Yayınları, reprint, 1993), pp. 465–67; idem, *Hayatım* (My Life) (İstanbul: Yapı Kredi Yayınları, reprint, 2011), pp. 210 and 215. Kazım Karabekir was the top graduate of the War Academy in İstanbul in 1905. He joined Enver Bey in founding the CUP branch in Manastır (Bitola). A prominent army officer, he fought in Gallipoli, Mesopotamia, and eastern Anatolia during the First World War. In 1920 he defeated Armenians and signed with them the Agreement of Gümrü assigning the province of Kars to Turkey. See also Nader Sohrabi, "Global Waves, Local Actors: What the Young Turks Knew About Other Revolu-

tions and Why It Mattered," *Comparative Studies in Society and History*, Vol. 44, No. 1 (January 2002), pp. 45–79.

57. James Reid, "The Armenian Massacres in Ottoman and Turkish Historiography," *The Armenian Review*, Vol. 37, No. 1–145 (Spring 1984), pp. 27 and 30.

58. James Barton, "New Turkey and Its Interpretation," *The Missionary Herald*, Vol. 55, No. 6 (June 1909), p. 255. *The Missionary Herald* was a monthly publication issued by members of the ABCFM for their colleagues at home and in the field, as well as their families and church members. The monthly issues of it included significant content about the work, experiences, and observations of the missionaries in the Ottoman Empire. They are useful as a historical source not just for missionary activities, but also for the circumstances in which attitudes and biases took shape.

59. Lord Kinross, *The Ottoman Centuries*, pp. 596–97. For Mustafa Hayri Efendi's diaries, see Ali Suat Ürgüplü, ed., *Şeyhülislam Ürgüplü Mustafa Hayri Efendi'nin Meşrutiyet, Büyük Harp ve Mütareke Günlükleri (1909–1922)* (Constitutional Period, Great War and Armistice Diaries of Sheikh-ul-Islam Mustafa Hayri Efendi of Ürgüp [1909–1922]) (İstanbul: Türkiye İş Bankası Kültür Yayınları, 2015).

60. William Strong, "Things That Remain in Turkey," *Envelope Series*, Vol. 19, No. 1 (April 1916), p. 24.

61. Edwin Pears, "The Situation in Turkey," *The Contemporary Review*, Vol. CI (June 1912), p. 768.

62. "A Nation's Sudden Conversion," pp. 457–58.

63. USNA, RG 84 Records of Foreign Service Posts, Diplomatic Posts Turkey, Vol. 126, From Consulates 1 January 1909–30 June 1909 American Embassy Istanbul. Gabriel Bie Ravndal (Beirut) to John Leishman (Istanbul), May 11, 1909. Enclosure: Letter of 6 May 1909 from Thomas Davidson Christie; Roderic Davison, *Turkey* (New York: Prentice-Hall, 1968), p. 105; Enver Ziya Karal, *Osmanlı Tarihi* (Ottoman History), Vol. 9: *İkinci Meşrutiyet ve Birinci Dünya Savaşı (1908–1918)* (The Second Constitutionalism and the First World War [1908–1918]) (Ankara: Türk Tarih Kurumu Basımevi, reprinted, 1996), pp. 40–42.

64. Kenneth Bourne and Donald Cameron Watt, eds., British Documents on Foreign Affairs: Reports and Papers from the Foreign Office Confidential Print, Part I: From the Mid-Nineteenth Century to the First World War, Series B The Near and Middle East 1856–1914, Vol.20: The Ottoman Empire Under the Young Turks 1908–1914 (Frederick, MD: University Publications of America, 1985), pp. 1–2.

65. Lybyer, "The Turkish Parliament," p. 70.

66. Arıkoğlu, *Hatıralarım*, pp. 43–44.

67. Bedross Der Matossian, "Ethnic Politics in Post-Revolutionary Ottoman Empire: Armenians, Arabs, and Jews during the Second Constitutional Period (1908–1909)," doctoral dissertation, Columbia University, 2008, pp. 74–75; idem, *Shattered Dreams of Revolution: From Liberty to Violence in the Late Ottoman Empire* (Stanford, CA: Stanford University Press, 2014), pp. 25–26.

68. *Tanin*, July 29, 1908, p. 1.

69. Edwin Pears, "Developments in Turkey," *The Contemporary Review*, Vol. XCVI (June 1910), p. 692.

70. Noel Buxton and Harold Buxton, *Travel and Politics in Armenia* (London: Smith, Elder and Co., 1914), pp. 109–10.

71. William Nesbitt Chambers, "Speaking with Other Tongues," *The Missionary Herald*, Vol. 55, No. 4 (April 1909), p. 167.
72. Davison, *Turkey*, p. 105.
73. On Bahri Paşa, see Ali Münif Bey, *Ali Münif Bey'in Hatıraları*, pp. 48–49; Aktan, *Dünkü ve Bugünkü Adana*, p. 9. Also Abdulhamit Kırmızı, *Avlonyalı Ferid Paşa Bir Ömür Devlet* (Ferid Paşa of Avlonya: State Service Throughout a Whole Life) (İstanbul: Klasik, 2014), p. 386. The author combines prodigious archival research with judicious analysis. The result is a work of astounding depth and objectivity that sets the standard for the field of historical biography.
74. "Valilerin Azli" (Dismissal of the Provincial Governors), *Tanin*, August 8, 1908, p. 1; *Tanin*, October 11, 1909, p. 2.
75. Orhan Koloğlu, *1908 Basın Patlaması* (Press Explosion of 1908) (İstanbul: Türkiye Gazeteciler Cemiyeti Yayınları, 2005); Kocabaşoğlu, *"Hürriyeti" Beklerken*, pp. 41–73; "Journalism in Constantinople," *The Orient*, Vol. 3, No. 45 (November 6, 1912), pp. 3–4.
76. Earle, "The New Constitution of Turkey," p. 79. The revised constitution of 1909 is available in English translation in Papers Relating to the Foreign Relations of the United States for the year 1909 (Washington, DC: U.S. Government Printing House, 1914), pp. 585–94.
77. John Grainger, *The Battle for Syria 1918–1920* (Woodbridge, Suffolk: The Boydell Press, 2013), p. 26.
78. Earle, "The New Constitution of Turkey," p. 73.
79. Tarık Zafer Tunaya, *Türkiye'de Siyasi Partiler* (Political Parties in Turkey), Vol. 1: *İkinci Meşrutiyet Dönemi* (The Period of Second Constitutionalism) (İstanbul: İletişim Yayınları, third edition, 2009), pp. 594–601. The book is rich in factual detail. This in itself makes it a valuable synthesis of existing scholarship and should make it a standard point of reference for scholars working on the subject.
80. BOA, Hariciye Nezareti Siyasi Kısım (Ministry of Foreign Affairs Political Department) (henceforth referred to as HR. SYS), No. 1851/2. Constitutionalism: Opening of the Chamber of Deputies, August 7, 1908.
81. Lybyer, "The Turkish Parliament," p. 65.
82. Aliyar Demirci, *Ayan Meclisi 1908–1912* (The Chamber of Notables 1908–1912) (İstanbul: İstanbul Bilgi Üniversitesi Yayınları, 2006).
83. Hasan Kayalı, "Elections and the Electoral Process in the Ottoman Empire, 1876–1919," *International Journal of Middle East Studies*, Vol. 27, No. 3 (August 1995), p. 271.
84. Ziya Şakir, *İttihat ve Terakki –II Nasıl Yaşadı?* (The Committee of Union and Progress–II How Did It Live?) (İstanbul: Akıl Fikir Yayınları, 2014), p. 77.
85. Edward Frederick Knight, *The Awakening of Turkey: A History of the Turkish Revolution* (Philadelphia, PA: J. B. Lippincot Co., 1909), pp. 276 and 299–301.
86. E. J. Dillon, "The First Pacific Struggle of Nationalities and Creeds," *The Contemporary Review*, Vol. XCV (January–June 1909), p. 126.
87. "L'Allemagne and La Turquie," *Le Moniteur Oriental*, 8 décembre 1908, p. 2.
88. E. J. Dillon, "The Opening of the Turkish Parliament," *The Contemporary Review*, Vol. XCV (January–June 1909), p. 125.

89. Kayalı, "Elections and the Electoral Process in the Ottoman Empire, 1876–1919," p. 272.
90. Halidé Edib, *Memoirs of Halidé Edib*, p. 273.
91. Şakir, *İttihat ve Terakki –II Nasıl Yaşadı?* pp. 79–82; "La Turquie Constitutionelle: Ouverture du Parlement Ottoman 1876–1908," *Le Petit Temps*, 18 décembre 1908, pp. 1–4.
92. "Kamil Paşa'nın Meclisi Mebusan'ın Küşadındaki Beyanı" (The Statement of Kamil Paşa at the Opening of the Chamber of Deputies), *Tanin*, December 18, 1908, p. 1.
93. Feroz Ahmad, "The Young Turk Revolution," *Journal of Contemporary History*, Vol. 3, No. 3 (July 1968), p. 24. Text of program in *Sabah*, August 16, 1908, p. 1.
94. On Kamil Paşa, see İnal, *Osmanlı Devrinde Son Sadrazamlar*, Sects. 9–10, pp. 1347–472; *Türk Parlamento Tarihi Birinci ve İkinci Meşrutiyet*, Vol. 2, pp. 683–85.
95. F. W. von Herbert, "Kamil Pasha and the Succession in Turkey," *The Fortnightly Review*, Vol. LXXXIV (July–December 1908), pp. 419–29.
96. Feroz Ahmad and Dankwart Rustow, "İkinci Meşrutiyet Döneminde Meclisler 1908–1918" (Chambers in the Period of Second Constitutionalism 1908–1918), *Güney-Doğu Avrupa Araştırmaları Dergisi*, Nos. 4–5 (1976), pp. 245–84; and Recep Karacakaya, "Meclis-i Mebusan Seçimleri ve Ermeniler 1908–1914" (Chamber of Deputies Elections and the Armenians 1908–1914), *Yakın Dönem Türkiye Araştırmaları*, No. 3 (2003), pp. 135–40.
97. Lybyer, "The Turkish Parliament," p. 71.
98. Ali Cevat, Faik Reşit Unat, ed., *İkinci Meşrutiyetin İlanı ve Otuzbir Mart Hadisesi* (The Proclamation of the Second Constitutionalism and the Incident of March 31) (Ankara: Türk Tarih Kurumu Basımevi, reprinted, 1991), pp. 31–32. Ali Cevat Bey joined the imperial court as eighth secretary on June 29, 1880, and following a successful and unbroken service of twenty-eight years, he was appointed first secretary on August 4, 1908. He relinquished the post on April 28, 1909, the day after Sultan Abdülhamid II was deposed.
99. Kayalı, "Elections and the Electoral Process in the Ottoman Empire, 1876–1909," p. 282.
100. Parliamentary Command Papers No. 4529, Correspondence Respecting the Constitutional Movement in Turkey 1908 (London: His Majesty's Stationery Office, 1909). Armenian Demonstration at the Sublime Porte to Express Gratitude for the Manner in Which the Elections Had Been Held, Sir Gerard Lowther (Istanbul) to Sir Edward Grey (FO), November 23, 1908.
101. Ibid. Conclusion of the Elections and the Armenians, Sir Gerard Lowther (Istanbul) to Sir Edward Grey (FO), December 15, 1908. Hammond Smith Shipley refers here to Karekin Pastırmacıyan and Vartkes Serengülyan, who were members of the Chamber of Deputies respectively in 1908–1914 and 1908–1915. See *Türk Parlamento Tarihi, Birinci ve İkinci Meşrutiyet*, Vol. 2, pp. 361 and 363.
102. "Ahmed Rıza Bey, Senator," *The Orient*, Vol. 3, No. 5 (January 31, 1912), p. 1.

103. BOA, Babıali Evrak Odası (Sublime Porte Records Office) (henceforth referred to as BEO), No. 3460/259495. Election of Ahmed Rıza Bey to the Speakership of the Chamber of Deputies, December 25, 1908; BOA, BEO, No. 3536/265181. On Ahmed Rıza Bey, April 17, 1909; Erdem Sönmez, *Ahmed Rıza Bir Jön Türk Liderinin Siyasi-Entelektüel Portresi* (Ahmed Rıza: Political-Intellectual Portrait of a Young Turk Leader) (İstanbul: Tarih Vakfı, 2012).

104. Halidé Edib, *Memoirs of Halidé Edib*, p. 271.

105. Feroz Ahmad, "Special Relationship: The Committee of Union and Progress and the Ottoman Jewish Political Elite, 1908–1918," in Avigdor Levy, ed., *Jews, Turks, Ottomans: A Shared History, Fifteenth Through the Twentieth Century* (New York: Syracuse University Press, 2002), pp. 215–16.

106. "Le Parlement Ottoman," *Le Moniteur Oriental*, 15 décembre 1908, p. 3; Fevzi Demir, "Bir Siyaset Okulu Olarak Meclis-i Mebusan" (The Chamber of Deputies as a School of Politics), in Ferdan Ergut, ed., *İkinci Meşrutiyeti Düşünmek* (Thinking About the Second Constitutionalism) (İstanbul: Tarih Vakfı Yurt Yayınları, 2010).

107. Talat Paşa, *Hatıralarım ve Müdafaam* (My Reminiscences and Defense) (İstanbul: Kaynak Yayınları, 2006), pp. 24–25; Kazım Nami Duru, *İttihat ve Terakki Hatıralarım* (My Recollections of the Committee of Union and Progress) (İstanbul: Sucuoğlu Matbaası, 1957), p. 3; Hüseyin Cahit Yalçın, Cemil Koçak, ed., *Tanıdıklarım* (My Acquaintances) (İstanbul: Yapı Kredi Yayınları, reprinted, 2001), p. 128.

108. Tunaya, *Türkiye'de Siyasi Partiler*, Vol. 1, pp. 42–43 and 46–47.

109. İlber Ortaylı, *Osmanlı İmparatorluğunda Alman Nüfuzu* (German Influence in the Ottoman Empire) (İstanbul: Timaş Yayınları, reprint, 2015), p. 194.

110. Following Osman's death in 1324, his son Orhan succeeded him.

111. "His Dignity Hurt; Quits Turks' Dinner," *The New York Times*, July 24, 1910, p. 3.

112. Ibid.

113. Hüseyin Cahid, "Ademi Merkeziyet" (Decentralization), *Tanin*, September 4, 1908, p. 1; "İttihad ve Terakki Cemiyetinin Siyasi Programı Altı İdarei Vilayat" (The Political Program of the Committee of Union and Progress Six Provincial Administration), *İttihad ve Terakki*, October 1, 1908, p. 1; Hüseyin Cahid, "Yeni İdare Memurları" (New Administrative Officials), *Tanin*, September 13, 1909, p. 1; Hüseyin Cahid, "Beyanname" (Declaration), *Tanin*, September 26, 1908, p. 1.

114. "Progress in Armenian National Affairs," *The Orient*, No. 33 (November 30, 1910), pp. 1–2.

115. Billings, "The Causes of the Outbreak in Cilicia, Asia Minor, April, 1909," p. 63.

116. "Sabahattin Bey'in Programı" (Program of Sabahattin Bey), *İkdam*, October 17, 1909, p. 1.

117. Bernard Lewis, *The Emergence of Modern Turkey* (London: Oxford University Press, second edition, 1968), pp. 203–4 and 231. More on Prince Sabahattin and his ideas, see Ahmed Bedevi Kuran, *Osmanlı İmparatorluğunda İnkılap Hareketleri ve Milli Mücadele* (Revolutionary Movements in the Ottoman Empire and the National Struggle) (İstanbul: Türkiye İş Bankası Kültür Yayınları, reprint, 2012); idem, *İnkılap Tarihimiz ve Jön Türkler* (Our History of Revolution and the Young Turks) (İstanbul:

Kaynak Yayınları, reprint, 2000); Ziya Şakir, *İttihat ve Terakki—I Nasıl Doğdu?* (The Committee of Union and Progress—I How Was It Born?) (İstanbul: Akıl Fikir Yayınları, reprint, 2014); Mehmet Alkan, ed., *Prens Sabahattin Gönüllü Sürgünden Zorunlu Sürgüne* (Prince Sabahattin: From Voluntary Exile to Forced Exile) (İstanbul: Yapı Kredi Yayınları, 2007); Muzaffer Budak, *Toplumbilimci Prens Sabahattin* (Sociologist Prince Sabahattin) (İstanbul: Kurtiş Matbaacılık, 1998); Prens Sabahattin, Ahmet Zeki İzgöer, ed., *İttihat ve Terakki'ye Açık Mektuplar, Türkiye Nasıl Kurtulabilir ve İzahlar* (Open Letters to the Committee of the Union and Progress, How Can Turkey Be Saved and the Explanations) (İstanbul: Dün Bugün Yarın Yayınları, 2013).

118. Davison, *Turkey*, pp. 80–81 and 111.

119. Ferdinand Leipnik, "The Future of the Ottoman Empire," *The Contemporary Review*, Vol. XCVI (March 1919), p. 292.

120. Key works on the CUP include (but are by no means limited to) Tunaya, *Türkiye'de Siyasi Partiler*, Vol. 3; Sina Akşin, *Jön Türkler ve İttihat ve Terakki* (The Young Turks and the Committee of Union and Progress) (Ankara: İmge Yayınevi, 2001); Tevfik Çavdar, *İttihat ve Terakki* (The Committee of Union and Progress) (İstanbul: İletişim Yayınları, 1991); Aykut Kansu, *Politics in Post-Revolutionary Turkey 1908–1913* (Leiden: E. J. Brill, 2000); Ahmad, *The Young Turks*; Kazım Karabekir, Faruk Özerergin, ed., *İttihat ve Terakki Cemiyeti 1896–1909* (The Committee of Union and Progress 1896–1909) (İstanbul: Emre Yayınları, reprint, 2000).

121. Aviel Roshwald, *Ethnic Nationalism and the Fall of Empires: Central Europe, Russia and the Middle East, 1914–1923* (London and New York: Routledge, 2001), p. 58. The book provides an invaluable and meticulously referenced synthesis of existing scholarship.

122. Ibid., p. 59.

123. Tunaya, *Türkiye'de Siyasi Partiler*, Vol. 1, p. 68; Hüseyin Kazım Kadri, İsmail Kara, ed., *Meşrutiyetten Cumhuriyete Anılarım* (My Reminiscences from the Constitutionalism to the Republic) (İstanbul: Dergah Yayınları, reprinted, 2000), p. 134; Şakir, *İttihat ve Terakki –I Nasıl Doğdu?* p. 579.

124. For Bedros Hallaçyan's biographical details, see *Türk Parlamento Tarihi, Birinci ve İkinci Meşrutiyet*, Vol. 2, p. 402; Çarkcıyan, *Türk Devlet Hizmetinde Ermeniler 1453–1953*, p. 151; Kevork Pamukcıyan, *Ermeni Kaynaklarından Tarihe Katkılar* (Contributions to the History from the Armenian Sources), Vol. 4: *Biyografileriyle Ermeniler* (Armenians With Their Biographies) (İstanbul: Aras Yayıncılık, 2003), p. 238; Dabağyan, *Emperyalistler Kıskacında Ermeni Tehciri I (Türk Ermenileri)*, pp. 775–76.

125. *Türk Parlamento Tarihi, Birinci ve İkinci Meşrutiyet*, Vol. 2, p. 514.

126. See Cohen, *Becoming Ottomans*. Also Karen Kern's, Yücel Güçlü's, and Alisa Meyuhas Ginio's reviews of this title in *International Journal of Middle East Studies*, Vol. 47, No. 1 (February 2015), pp. 196–98; *Middle East Policy*, Vol. 22, No. 4 (Winter 2015), pp. 155–58; and *International Journal of Turkish Studies*, Vol. 21, Nos. 1 and 2 (Fall 2015), pp. 193–94, respectively.

127. Arıkoğlu, *Hatıralarım*, p. 43; Sahara, *What Happened in Adana in April 1909?* p. 61.

128. Bourne and Watt, British Documents on Foreign Affairs, Part I, Series B, Vol. 20, p. 1.
129. MAE, NS Turquie, Vol. 83, p. 64. Nouvelles de la région. Barré de Lancy (Mersine) à Stéphane Pichon (Paris), 18 août 1908; Bourne and Watts, British Documents on Foreign Affairs, Part I, Series B, Vol. 20, p. 52.
130. "The Revolt at Constantinople," *The Missionary Herald*, Vol. 55, No. 6 (June 1909), p. 245.
131. Osman Selim Kocahanoğlu, "Önsöz" (Preface), in İrtem, *Meşrutiyet Doğarken*, p. xvi.
132. "The New Turkey: Interesting Interview with Halil Halid," *The Near East*, Vol. 2, No. 19 (November 5, 1909), p. 97.
133. Knight, *The Awakening of Turkey*, p. 89.
134. Marmaduke Pickthall, "The Black Crusade," *The New Age*, Vol. 12, No. 1 (November 7, 1912), p. 8.
135. Edwin Pears, "Developments in Turkey," *The Contemporary Review*, Vol. C (July 1911), p. 27.
136. For more, see İnal, *Osmanlı Devrinde Son Sadrazamlar*, Sect. 12, pp. 1869–92.
137. Hüseyin Cahid, "İttihat ve Terakki Politikasına Avdet" (Return to the Policy of the Committee of Union and Progress), *Tanin*, September 6, 1912, p. 1; Charles Roden Buxton, *Turkey in Revolution* (New York: Charles Scribner's Sons; London: T. Fisher Unwin, 1909), p. 140.
138. See Hasan Kayalı, *Arabs and Young Turks: Ottomanism, Arabism, and Islamism in the Ottoman Empire, 1908–1918* (Berkeley and Los Angeles, CA: University of California Press, 1997) for an excellent discussion of the theme. The number of sources cited in endnotes is impressive, and any interested scholar is certain to find useful directions to further reading here. Yücel Güçlü's review of this title is in *Perceptions*, Vol. 4, No. 4 (December 1999–February 2000), pp. 158–62. Consult also Zafer Toprak, "Bir Hayal Ürünü: İttihatçıların Türkleştirme Politikası" (A Figment of Imagination: The Turkification Policy of the Unionists), *Toplumsal Tarih*, No. 146 (February 2006), pp. 14–22.
139. Leila Tarazi Fawaz, *A Land of Aching Hearts: The Middle East in the Great War* (Cambridge, MA and London: Harvard University Press, 2014), p. 251.
140. Babanzade İsmail Hakkı, "Osmanlılaşma" (Ottomanization), *Tanin*, February 22, 1912, p. 1.
141. Çankaya, *Mülkiye ve Mülkiyeliler Tarihi*, Vol. 2, pp. 996–97.
142. Cavid Bey, *Meşrutiyet Ruznamesi*, Vol. 2, p. 418.
143. Hüseyin Cahid, "Anasır-ı Osmaniye" (The Ottoman Elements), *Tanin*, August 30, 1908, p. 1; idem, "Türklük, Müslümanlık, Osmanlılık" (Being Turk, Muslim, Ottoman), *Tanin*, September 29, 1909, p. 1; Orhan Koloğlu, "Mayıs-Eylül 1908 Belgelerine Göre İttihatçılarda Osmanlı Birliği Arayışı-I" (The Quest For Ottoman Unity By the Unionists According to the Documents of May–September 1908-I), *Toplumsal Tarih*, No. 55 (July 1998), p. 12; Roshwald, *Ethnic Nationalism and the Fall of Empires*, p. 59.

144. Charles Woods, *The Cradle of the War: The Near East and Pan-Germanism* (Boston, MA: Little, Brown, and Company, 1918), p. 14.

145. Orit Bashking, "Roundtable Jewish Identities in the Middle East, 1876–1956: The Middle Eastern Shift and Provincializing Zionism," *International Journal of Middle East Studies*, Vol. 46, No. 3 (August 2014), p. 579.

146. Suny, *A History of the Armenian Genocide*, pp. 157–58.

147. Yücel Güçlü, "The Role of the Ottoman-Trained Officers in Independent Iraq," *Oriente Moderno*, Vol. 21 (132), No. 2 (December 2002), pp. 123–38; Donna Robinson Divine, *Politics and Society in Ottoman Palestine: The Arab Struggle for Survival and Power* (Boulder, CO and London: Lynne Rienner Publishers, 1994); Kayalı, *Arabs and Young Turks*.

148. Michelle Ursula Campos, *Ottoman Brothers: Muslims, Christians, and Jews in Early Twentieth-Century Palestine* (Stanford, CA: Stanford University Press, 2010), pp. 3 and 256fn7. Michelle Ursula Campos is assistant professor of the history of the modern Middle East at the University of Florida. Campos has lived and done research in Israel, Turkey, Egypt, Jordan, and Lebanon. In her book she explores the development of Ottoman collective identity in the aftermath of the Young Turk revolution of 1908, tracing how Muslims, Christians, and Jews defined, practiced, and contested the contours of imperial citizenship and local belonging. A Turkish language translation entitled *Osmanlı Kardeşler* appeared in 2012.

149. Kemal Karpat, "The Memoirs of N. Batzaria: The Young Turks and Nationalism," *International Journal of Middle East Studies*, Vol. 6 (1975), p. 276.

150. Jacob Landau and Mim Kemal Öke, "Ottoman Perspectives on American Interests in the Holy Land," in Moshe Davis, ed., *With Eyes Toward Zion: Themes and Sources in the Archives of the United States, Great Britain, Turkey and Israel*, Vol. 2 (Westport, CT: Praeger Publishers, 1986), p. 273.

151. On Musheg Seropian, see Ali Münif Bey, *Ali Münif Bey'in Hatıraları*, pp. 48–49 and 51; Yurtsever, *Ermeni Terör Merkezi*, p. 258.

152. Djemal Pasha, *Memories of a Turkish Statesman 1913–1919*, pp. 257–58.

153. Hagop Tcholakian, "Armenian Settlements in the Antioch Region," in Richard Hovannisian, ed., *Armenian Communities of the Northeastern Mediterranean: Musa Dagh-Dörtyol-Kessab* (Costa Mesa, CA: Mazda Publishers, 2016), p. 108.

154. Panossian, *The Armenians from Kings and Priests to Merchants and Commissars*, pp. 204–5; Sahara, *What Happened in Adana in April 1909?* p. 30.

155. BOA, Dahiliye Mektubi Kalemi (Correspondence Division of the Ministry of the Interior) (henceforth referred to as DH. MKT), No. 2810/8. Circular to the Governors of Adana, Aleppo, Suriye, Aydın, and Beyrut and to the Mutasarrıfs of İzmid, Biga and Kudüs on the Arrest of Bishop Mushegh Seropian, May 12, 1909.

156. Mevlanzade Rıfat, Ahmet Nezih Galitekin, ed., *İttihat ve Terakki İktidarı ve Türkiye İnkılabının İçyüzü* (The Rule of the Committee of Union and Progress and the Inside Story of the Turkish Revolution) (İstanbul: Yedi İklim Yayınları, 1993), p. 150. Musheg Seropian in his memoirs quoted certain documents, but he selected his material subjectively with a view to justifying his own deeds. See Mousheg Seropian, *Les vêpres de Cilicie* (Alexandria: Della Rocca, 1909).

157. James Creelman, "Will Christendom Remain Silent?" *Pearson's Magazine*, Vol. 3, No. 3 (September 1909), p. 293. *Pearson's Magazine* (1899–1925), a monthly journal devoted to literature, politics, and the arts, was founded as a New York affiliate of the London periodical of the same name, part of which it reprinted.

158. David Farhi, "The Şeriat as a Political Slogan—or the 'Incident of the 31st Mart,'" *Middle Eastern Studies*, Vol. 7, No. 3 (October 1971), pp. 279–80.

159. Djemal Pasha, *Memories of a Turkish Statesman 1913–1919*, p. 258. Also *Aspirations et Agissements Révolutionnaires des Comités Armeniens Avant et Aprés la Proclamation de la Constitution Ottomane*, pp. 65–66.

160. FO 195/2363. Annual Report on Turkey for the Year 1909. Sir Gerard Lowther (Istanbul) to Sir Edward Grey (FO), February 7, 1910.

161. Brézol, *Les Turcs ont passé là*, p. 9.

162. Bayram Kodaman and Mehmet Ali Ünal, eds., *Son Vakanüvis Abdurrahman Şeref Efendi Tarihi: İkinci Meşrutiyet Olayları (1908–1909)* (History of the Last Chronicler Abdurrahman Şeref Efendi: Events of Second Constitutionalism [1908–1909]) (Ankara: Türk Tarih Kurumu Basımevi, 1996), p.110. The tome contains an exhaustive survey of the subject. On Abdurrahman Şeref Efendi as historian, see Necdet Öztürk and Murat Yıldız, *İmparatorluk Tarihinin Kalemli Muhafızları: Osmanlı Tarihçileri* (The Penned Guardians of the Imperial History: Ottoman Historians) (İstanbul: Bilge Kültür Sanat, 2013), pp. 210–11; and Mehmet Demiryürek, *Tanzimat'tan Cumhuriyet'e Bir Osmanlı Aydını: Abdurrahman Şeref Efendi (1853–1925)* (From the *Tanzimat* to the Republic: An Ottoman Intellectual Abdurrahman Şeref Efendi [1853–1925]) (Ankara: Phoenix Yayınevi, 2003); Salahi Sonyel, "Turco-Armenian 'Adana Incidents' in the Light of Secret British Documents (July 1909–December 1909)," *Belleten*, Vol. 51, No. 201 (December 1987), p. 1319; İrtem, *Ermeni Meselesinin İçyüzü*, pp. 167–68; Sahara, *What Happened in Adana in April 1909?* pp. 72–73; Creelman, "Will Christendom Remain Silent?" p. 292.

163. Helen Davenport Gibbons, *The Red Rugs of Tarsus: A Woman's Record of the Armenian Massacres of 1909* (New York: The Century Company, 1917), p. 11. The most valuable contribution of this work is the account of the author's experience as a witness. Her vivid descriptions of the conditions she and her colleagues endured is gripping.

164. FO 195/2037. Report on the Recent Events at Adana. Charles Doughty-Wylie (Adana) to Sir Gerard Lowther (Istanbul), July 24, 1909; Kamuran Gürün, *The Armenian File: The Myth of Innocence Exposed* (London, Nicosia, and Istanbul: K. Rustem and Weidenfeld and Nicolson, 1985), p. 131.

165. W. M. Ramsay, *The Revolution in Constantinople and Turkey: A Diary* (London: Hodder and Stoughton, 1909), pp. 137–38; Sahara, *What Happened in Adana in April 1909?* p. 73.

166. Sahara, *What Happened in Adana in April 1909?* p. 74.

167. Creelman, "Will Christendom Remain Silent?" p. 293.

168. For a larger discussion, see Kodaman and Ünal, *Son Vakanüvis Abdurrahman Şeref Efendi Tarihi*, pp. 71–81. See also Mehmet Asaf, İsmet Parmaksızoğlu, ed., *1909 Adana Ermeni Olayları ve Anılarım* (1909 Armenian Incidents of Adana and My Reminiscences) (Ankara: Türk Tarih Kurumu Basımevi, 1982); and Wil-

liam Nesbitt Chambers, *Yoljuluk: Random Thoughts on a Life in Imperial Turkey* (London: Simpkin Marshall Limited, 1928; republished, Paramus, NJ: Armenian Missionary Association of America, 1988), pp. 78–79. The scope of William Nesbitt Chambers's book is not exclusively missionary, but deals with the Ottoman Empire in broad outlines, giving a summary of historical development, and political, national, social, and religious conditions, with special attention to the progress of the empire in its last decades.

169. Akaby Nassibian, *Britain and the Armenian Question, 1915–1923* (London and Sydney: Croom Helm, 1984), pp. 21–22.

170. FO 195/2037. Report on the Recent Events at Adana. Charles Doughty-Wylie (Adana) to Sir Gerard Lowther (Istanbul), July 24, 1909; Christopher Walker, *Armenia: The Survival of a Nation* (New York: St. Martin's Press, revised second edition, 1980), p. 183.

171. Telford Waugh, *Turkey Yesterday, To-day and To-morrow* (London: Chapman and Hall's, 1930), p. 122.

172. James Creelman, "The Massacre of Adana Was Planned and Its Managers Have Gone Unpunished; Investigations That Suggest An International Protest," *The New York Times*, September 26, 1909, Part 6, p. 8. See also BOA, Hariciye Nezareti Mektubi ve Tahrirat Kalemi (Ministry of Foreign Affairs Division of Correspondence and Secretariat) (henceforth referred to as HR. MT), TDA-T-210-445. Armenian Troubles in Adana and Mersin. Babanzade Mustafa Zihni Paşa (Adana) to the Ministry of the Interior, June 3, 1909; Mehmet Asaf, *1909 Adana Ermeni Olayları ve Anılarım*, p. 7; Andrew Mango, *Atatürk: The Biography of the Founder of Modern Turkey* (London: John Murray,1999), p. 90.

173. Lengyel, *Turkey*, pp. 131–32.

174. The Russian Armenian in question is most probably Musheg Seropian.

175. FO 424/220/13. Situation in Adana. Sir Gerard Lowther (Istanbul) to Sir Edward Grey (FO), Therapia, July 6, 1909. Enclosure No. 44.

176. Cemal Paşa, Behcet Cemal, *Hatıralar*, pp. 345–46.

177. Abdulhamit Kırmızı, *Abdülhamid'in Valileri Osmanlı Vilayet İdaresi 1895–1908* (The Governors of Abdülhamid: Ottoman Provincial Administration 1895–1908) (İstanbul: Klasik, 2007); Syed Tanvir Wasti, "Süleyman Nazif—A Multi-Faceted Personality," *Middle Eastern Studies*, Vol. 50, No. 3 (May 2014), p. 493.

178. "Decentralisation in Turkey," *The Near East*, Vol. 6, No. 140 (January 9, 1914), p. 329.

179. Lucy Cavendish, "The Peril of Armenia," *The Contemporary Review*, Vol. CIII (January 1913), p. 37.

180. The Translation Bureau was created at the Ministry of Foreign Affairs by Sultan Mahmud II to take care of increased diplomatic correspondence in French and to train Turks in that language. The Translation Bureau became the nursery which produced many of the leading Ottoman statesmen of the nineteenth century. These men constituted a new elite developing within the bureaucracy—the elite of French-knowers, whose importance to Turkey into the twentieth century could hardly be exaggerated. For the importance of the Translation Bureau in the upbringing of the Turkish

officials, see İlber Ortaylı, *İmparatorluğun En Uzun Yüzyılı* (The Longest Century of the Ottoman Empire) (İstanbul: Timaş Yayınları, reprinted, 2013), pp. 272–73.

181. On the secretaries in the Imperial Court, see İsmail Müştak Mayakon, *Yıldız'da Neler Gördüm* (What I Saw in Yıldız) (İstanbul: Sertel Matbaası, 1940), pp. 142–49; Mehmet Tevfik Biren, Fatma Rezan Hürmen, ed., *II. Abdülhamid, Meşrutiyet ve Mütareke Devri Hatıraları* (Reminiscences of the Periods of Abdülhamid II, Constitutionalism and Armistice), Vol. 1 (İstanbul: Arma Yayınları, 1993), pp. 14–23.

182. On Yıldız Palace, see Halid Ziya Uşaklıgil, *Saray ve Ötesi* (The Palace and Beyond) (İstanbul: Hilmi Kitabevi, 1941), pp. 24–25.

183. For a brief biographical sketch of Cevad Bey, see Çankaya, *Mülkiye Tarihi ve Mülkiyeliler*, Vol. 3, pp. 189–90.

184. Ahmed Nezih Galitekin, ed., *Salname-i Nezaret-i Umur-ı Hariciyye* (Annual of the Ottoman Ministry of Foreign Affairs), Vol. 4 (İstanbul: İşaret Yayınları, 2003), p. 40.

185. BOA, DH. MKT, No. 1290/12. Appointment of Cevad Bey to the Provincial Governorship of Adana, September 7, 1908; BOA, BEO, No. 3395/254598. Appointment of Cevad Bey to the Provincial Governorship of Adana, September 14, 1908; BOA, DH. MKT, No. 2719/98. On Cevad Bey, January 25, 1909; MAE, NS Turquie, Vol. 83, pp. 84–85. Nouvelles de la région. Situation à Adana. Barré de Lancy (Mersine) à Stéphane Pichon (Paris), 23 octobre 1908.

186. "Le Vilayet d'Adana," *Le Moniteur Oriental*, 12 novembre 1908, p. 2.

187. Hüseyin Hilmi Paşa was the civil inspector general of Macedonia between 1902 and 1908, when he won the trust of the CUP. He had served as governor of Adana for three months in 1897. When the constitution was reinstated, he became, first, minister of the interior, and then grand vizier on February 14, 1909. Ousted in the mutiny of April 13, 1909, he was reappointed when the Movement Army entered İstanbul. For a brief biographical sketch of Hüseyin Hilmi Paşa, see *Türk Parlamento Tarihi Birinci ve İkinci Meşrutiyet*, Vol. 2, pp. 686–87. A lengthy discussion of his career can be found in İnal, *Osmanlı Devrinde Son Sadrazamlar*, Sect. 11, pp. 1654–703. On Hüseyin Hilmi Paşa's civil inspectorate general of Macedonia, consult Hasan Cemil Çambel, *Makaleler Hatıralar* (Articles Recollections) (Ankara: Türk Tarih Kurumu Basımevi, 2011), pp. 125–34.

188. Raymond Kévorkian, *The Armenian Genocide: A Complete History* (London and New York: I.B. Tauris, 2011), pp. 77–78. The French edition of the book was published in 2006 by Odile Jacob as *Le Génocide des Arméniens*. Also Ferriman, *The Young Turks and the Truth about the Holocaust at Adana*, p. 14.

189. Kodaman and Ünal, *Son Vakanüvis Abdurrahman Şeref Efendi Tarihi*, p. 80; Sahara, *What Happened in Adana in April 1909?* p. 92.

190. Creelman, "Will Christendom Remain Silent?" p. 294.

191. Ibid.

192. Billings, "The Causes of the Outbreak in Cilicia, Asia Minor, April, 1909," pp. 59–60.

193. Djemal Pasha, *Memories of a Turkish Statesman 1913–1919*, p. 259.

194. James Creelman, "The Slaughter of Christians in Asia Minor," *The New York Times*, August 22, 1909, Part 6, p. 8.
195. Creelman, "Will Christendom Remain Silent?" p. 293.
196. Ibid., p. 294.
197. Ibid., p. 293.
198. FO 424/219. The Situation in Adana. Sir Gerard Lowther (Istanbul) to Sir Edward Grey (FO), April 28, 1909.
199. Edwin Pears, *Turkey and Its People* (London: Methuen and Co. Ltd., 1911), p. 293.
200. FO 195/2037. Report on Recent Events at Adana. Charles Dougthy-Wylie (Adana) to Sir Gerard Lowther (Istanbul), July 24, 1909.
201. Creelman, "The Slaughter of Christians in Asia Minor," p. 8.
202. *The Adana Massacres and the Catholic Missionaries*, p. 23.
203. "Oğul" means "son" in Turkish and is used as a suffix to form family names either in the singular possessive "oğlu" or the plural possessive "oğulları."
204. FO 195/2037. Report on Recent Events at Adana. Charles Dougthy-Wylie (Adana) to Sir Gerard Lowther (Istanbul), July 24, 1909.
205. Kodaman and Ünal, *Son Vakanüvis Abdurrahman Şeref Efendi Tarihi*, pp. 82 and 102; İrtem, *Ermeni Meselesinin İçyüzü*, p. 178; Woods, *The Danger Zone of Europe*, p. 129; Sahara, *What Happened in Adana in April 1909?* p. 109.
206. FO 195/2037. Report on Events at Adana. Charles Dougthy-Wylie (Adana) to Sir Gerard Lowther (Istanbul), July 24, 1909.

Chapter Four

Dimensions of the Disorder, April 1909

On April 16, 1909, *The Times* of London carried a report from İstanbul, citing consular telegrams from Mersin, that fighting had broken out after the murder in Adana of a Muslim by an Armenian, and the failure to find the assassin.[1]

BEGINNING OF THE CLASHES IN ADANA

The dead Turk's body was carried through the streets, causing a great deal of ill-feeling between the Muslims and Christians. The whole of Adana was in a thrill of excitement. Events moved quickly in the city.[2]

There was a meeting of American missionaries in Adana in the morning of April 14, and William Nesbitt Chambers, head of the Adana mission, accompanied by his nephew, Lawson Chambers, called at the *Konak* to beg the governor to take steps to restore order and confidence. There they found the heads of the Gregorian, Armenian Catholic, and Armenian Protestant communities. Cevad Bey joined with several of the prominent Turks of the city in assurances that peace would be maintained.[3] He reassured the Armenians and asked them to calm their excited kinsmen. So as to still further tranquilize the crowd, the governor himself went down into the streets, accompanied by the officer in command of the troops. It took a long time to get the shops opened that morning.[4]

About noon on the same day gunfire erupted in the city. Ordinary Armenians withdrew from that spectacle. The oath-bound secret soldiers of the *Fedayee* gathered in the middle of the market place. Their young, boyish captain, with his long blond hair streaming from under a red-topped cap, stood among them, white-faced but resolute. He called upon them to show themselves to be true Armenians and true Christians. The Muslim mob pressed closer and closer. It howled and leaped in the air. Suddenly a few Armenian shops were smashed, the crashing of shutters was heard, and the mob began the work of looting. Instantly the *Fedayee* began firing their revolvers in the air. At this the mob surged forward and began a general pillage of the Armenian shops. Under the direction of their leader, the members of the *Fedayee* and their friends now fought a regular battle in defense of the Armenian quarter. They posted marksmen in the windows commanding strategic points. They threw up barricades in the streets. They poured volleys from the roofs. Scores of Muslims fell under this steady and careful fire. The mob wrecked many of the shops, but it could not penetrate in to the Armenian residential quarter. As the young Armenians picked off their enemies, the streets were red with Muslim blood.[5]

It was Armenian revolutionaries who first opened fire on Muslims. They were confident of European support that never came. The only way to achieve Armenian ends was by forcible foreign intervention—not the threat of it, but the intervention itself. Although the Armenians suffered the greater mortality, Armenian forces unquestionably started the shooting. The Muslims responded. The evidence is cumulative and overwhelming.

While the battle went on, some of the Muslims rushed to the *Konak* and called on the governor to give them arms to defend themselves against the Armenians. At this time the Muslims had gotten the worst of the fight and the trained Armenian marksmen were in command of the situation. The governor was in a white funk. His eyes rolled, and his hands trembled.[6]

Armenian men and boys continued to shoot the whole afternoon. Fires broke out in several neighborhoods, and gunshots were heard all night. This was interpreted in the Muslim quarters as an attack, and the word spread like wildfire that the Armenians were in revolt and must be quelled. Firing and fighting between Muslims and Armenians resulted in a number of casualties on both sides. Incendiaries were at work. The big bazaar was blazing. The wind fanned the flames and drove them house to house. Several districts of the city were covered by clouds of smoke, which rolled out far into the country, where vineyard and country houses also were burning. No soldiers or policemen had appeared nor had any pumps or apparatus for fighting fire had been brought out.[7] There was no government left; the city was given up to anarchy, save where the consecrated *Fedayee* kept the Armenian quarter from invasion and slew Muslims without ceasing.[8]

In time the Muslims mounted rooftops and climbed into the minarets of the mosques. They also took possession of a clock tower. From these high points they were able to fire on the Armenians with ease. The tide of the battle seemed to be changing. Then the long-haired captain of the *Fedayee* and a band of his most trusted comrades disguised themselves as Muslims by winding white turbans about their heads. They made their way to the nearest mosque, killed its keepers, and, mounting the minaret, opened fire on the men in other minarets and in the clock tower. For hours the battle in the air went on, and roars of anger went up from the mob as it saw Muslim after Muslim fall in the minarets. When his ammunition was exhausted, the Armenian captain withdrew his men from the minaret, rejoined his comrades, took the turban from his head, and, with his fair hair tangled about his face, resumed the battle in the streets. It was said that this one Armenian fighter killed thirty-seven Turks with his own hands in a single place on the second day of the struggle, and that at times his white, pinched face and blue eyes would light up as though he were inspired. Yet he was but a boy of twenty years, who had closed his shoemaker's shop to teach Christian children in the Gregorian school, and then had abandoned his books and pupils to strike for revolution.[9]

The military forces of the Adana province formed part of the Fifth Army, headquartered at Damascus. They comprised three battalions of infantry, two of which were stationed at Adana, and the other at Feke, in the Kozan area. The Adana battalions furnished small garrisons of twenty to thirty men each to Mersin, Tarsus, and Silifke.[10]

Cevad Bey called to their assistance the reservists of Payas and Karaisalı, but these, after receiving the arms and ammunition, refused to come into Adana, saying that their districts were also in a state of turmoil.[11] Shortly after daybreak on April 15 troops arrived from Misis (Mopsuestia), some five hours from Adana.[12] Up to that time no one had dared to go on the streets because of the shooting from one end by Muslims and the other by Armenians. The government gave assurances that it was doing its best to restore order at Adana and to protect foreigners. Martial law was proclaimed, and two additional battalions were sent in.[13]

The minister of the interior, Ferid Paşa,[14] gave formal instructions to the authorities in Adana for the repression of all attempts which would disturb public order in the province. The Ministry of War gave orders for sending new military reinforcements to Adana.[15]

BRITISH VICE CONSUL MAJOR CHARLES WYLIE-DAUGHTY'S ROLE IN THE CONTROL OF THE FIGHTING

On April 14, Charles Dougthy-Wylie received a letter from Constantine Tripani, the British dragoman[16] at Adana, saying that there was a very dangerous feeling in that city: threats had been freely offered, there were some murders, and the shops were all shut. He went to Adana by the next train, arriving about five o'clock in the afternoon. So little had he expected that any massacre was imminent, that he took his wife with him. From the train, about two stations from Adana they saw a dead body, and a little further several persons running toward the train. All the people from the second-class carriage got into the first, saying that there were men in the train to kill them. On going through the second-class carriage, he saw two armed Muslims threatening the Armenians running by the train. When they saw him they put away their pistols and were quiet. The nearer they got to Adana the more bodies there were, and while Doughty-Wylie was escorting his wife to Tripani's house which was near the station, two of the Ottoman guards, which had a little guard house about midway between Tripani's house and the station, stood by. He got into uniform, went to the guard, and sharply recalled to the officer his duty to prevent murder. He took four soldiers as escort, and Edwards, inspector of the Imperial Ottoman Bank, who asked protection, and walked through the city to the *Konak*, about two and a half kilometers. He saw several men killed on the way, and the town was full of a howling mob looting the shops. On arrival at the *Konak* he demanded more soldiers to go to the American mission and other places where there were British subjects. They gave him a few, very unwillingly, as they said they would take no responsibility for his life. They could not or would not give an officer, and there was no time to argue. He afterwards found out from American and British witnesses, Herbert Adams Gibbons of Tarsus and Lawson Chambers, missionaries of the ABCFM, that some little time before he got there two men had been killed in that very office, practically before the provincial governor's eyes—there was a grating between him and them—who was too frightened to protect them or punish the murderers.[17]

Dougthy-Wylie went in the dark to the American mission which was in the Armenian quarter. Around this place there was much firing. Finding all safe there, he left guards at the two schools. Days afterwards he found out that one of these guards did fairly well but the other melted away. He took Edwards to the Imperial Ottoman Bank, where he left more soldiers. He then made a search for Cokinakia and his wife—British subjects—at the other side of the city, and found them at last in a farm about one and a half kilometers from their factory, where they had taken refuge. The owner, called Dıblanoğlu, who was their friend swore to him that he could and would be answerable for them. He had then only four soldiers, and did not dare to take them through the mob in the city to Tripani's house, which was at least three kilometers away. However, two days after this he sent them an armed escort and brought them in as their position had become untenable. He then went back to the *Konak*; he found Governor Cevad Bey and military commander Mustafa Remzi Paşa had done absolutely nothing. He warned them that he should come again in the morning, and that he would require fifty men and a senior officer and a horse to ride round the city. He was then searching for an American and a Briton, who were missing from the mission; he found they had been safe in the *Konak* for several hours and had been eyewitnesses of the murders referred to. They were also witnesses of the beginning of the outbreak, when the military commander went out with the troops—at the first shot he had turned back to the *Konak*, and taken the troops with him. He then paid another visit to the American mission and returned through the city to Tripani's house. The city all this time was in undescribable tumult, with heavy fighting going on in the approaches to the Armenian quarter, and murder and fire everywhere. He had not force enough to do much to stop it. His four soldiers followed him faithfully through it all.[18]

When men claiming to be reservist soldiers received military rifles from the arsenal they at once joined the mob. The attack on the Armenians now became heavier as the government rifles were brought into play, but they stood their ground; in the midst of the battle, squads of the *Fedayee* were sent into the Turkish quarter to conduct Christian women and children to places of safety in the churches and schools.[19]

On the morning of April 15 Doughty-Wylie went again to the *Konak*, seeing on the way some soldiers joining in the murders—after some difficulty he obtained some fifty men from the *Konak*, and Commandant of Gendarmerie Alai Bey went with him. No officer superior to him would leave the *Konak*. They paraded through the city with bugles blowing. The military commander had lent him a horse, and he had three or four mounted men. Wherever they went, firing ceased. They cleared the streets, sometimes by charging with the bayonet, and sometimes by firing over the heads of the crowd. They went through the Armenian quarter. Both sides ceased firing when they recognized the British vice consul, with the exception of a few stray shots. He visited the Armenian and French schools. He had it cried everywhere that everyone was to go into their house, as he should fire down the streets. After he passed, fighting was freely resumed. He went back to the station and drove back a big crowd of villagers who were flocking into the city to loot and murder. When he arrived at the Armenian quarter, he found that two American missionaries were killed. They had been working for an hour to put out a fire which was threatening their school, and they were killed at the closest range by five Muslims who had previously promised to let them alone. The third missionary, Stephen van Trowbridge, who was with them, managed to escape. They told Doughty-Wylie in the school that the bodies were lying in the street and that nobody could approach. His party carried them in—they were both breathing. While carrying them in, fire was opened on them from a minaret within easy range. They went to clear it, but everybody ran away. Before this second visit to the Armenian quarter the British vice consul changed his infantry at the *Konak*, but Ali Bey, a gendarmerie captain, and the mounted men remained with him all day. They also visited the Turkish quarter and dispersed threatening crowds. The big bazaar was blazing, and Turks and Armenians were carrying on house-to-house fighting, which was extremely difficult, and in some places impossible, to stop.[20]

The entrance to the Armenian quarter was held by Armenians, well armed and secure in their storehouses, who without provocation shot at every one who approached. This did not, however, take away from the fearless sense of duty which led Dougthy-Wylie to pass through quarters where so much shooting was going on. Not only that he might protect the property and lives of foreigners but that he might arrange a truce between Muslims and Armenians and if possible prevent further shedding of innocent blood; although he had reason to hope he would not be shot at, he risked his life, for stray bullets (some of which came from houses and attacking parties) were always to be heard. Had his party been hit and the soldiers opened fire in reply, he had been in a trap. His bravery and devotion, as well as that of Mrs. Doughty-Wylie, who gave more than her whole strength to the wounded, and had times dressed wounds while shots were in the neighborhood, deserve particular mention and praise.[21]

Late in the afternoon Doughty-Wylie received an appeal for help from the Régie Tobacco Factory, inhabited by Abbott, a British subject—he went down there with the troops, and gave Abbott a guard. While there, they told him that certain wounded Ottoman soldiers were lying in houses among some burning ruins not far away. They went to look for them, and while searching a tiny garden where were eight or ten bodies of Turks and Armenians—men and women—an Armenian, from behind a window, fired at him very short range, and broke his arm.[22] Amazingly, Hrachik Simonyan claims that "The Turks wounded the consul [the British vice consul] and his horse."[23] This is not at all correct. According to many eyewitness accounts of the incident and the clear statement of Doughty-Wylie himself, it was Armenians who shot. For instance, F. G. Aflalo wrote: "It is said that to be a fact that one of them [Armenians], completely losing his head in the recent tragedy at Adana, fired point-blank at the gallant British vice-consul, Doughty-Wylie, who was doing everything in his power to stop the butchery, and broke his arm."[24] The attempt was apparently a direct effort on the part of the Armenians to get the British into a broil with the Ottoman government, in hopes that they, the Armenians, would profit thereby.

Being afraid that this unfortunate accident would be the signal for a general storm on the Armenian quarter, Doughty-Wylie sent Alai Bey to Cevad Bey and Mustafa Remzi Paşa to say that even now, if they would stop the massacre no indemnity or punishment would be demanded by him, but otherwise he had already telegraphed for a ship in the morning, and the responsibility lay with them. He told them that they should surround the Armenian quarter with regular troops and good officers, and should allow nobody in and out, that at the same time they should patrol the streets of the rest of the city, driving people into their houses and shooting freely if necessary. As regards the troops, the soldiers of his escort in the *Konak* and in some of the guards were regular units, and behaved with some exceptions fairly well wherever there were officers, especially when they began to get the matter in hand a little. The military commander had called up the reservists, who were armed from the barracks and turned loose without uniform into the streets. They came from outside villages and Tarsus, and did much harm. There were exceptions among them. The *hojas* were divided. The British vice consul found one to calm the crowd, others took a rifle and fought themselves. Dougthy-Wylie sent Lawson Chambers to the *Konak* overnight, and he told him that the governor and the military commander promised all that he wished, but that Chambers could get no officers to go with him to the Armenian quarter. The day was spent in continual telegrams and messages. Dougthy-Wylie was trying to save Germans at Bahçe, Englishmen at Osmaniye, and Americans at Hacin. The streets were nearly as the day before. The homeless began coming to Adana escorted by soldiers. The Germans from the German cotton factory in Adana took refuge in Tripani's house. Toward evening Cevad Bey sent him news that peace had been made, and the *hojas* and Armenian priests had kissed each other in the *Konak*.[25]

The consuls in this part of the world had not the same mainly commercial functions as consuls of the ordinary kind. They possessed the practical prerogatives of ambassadors, and they had always been treated practically as such in the interior of the sultan's dominions, where they had never confined themselves to questions of trade and to ordinary duties of consular representatives. In short, from the earliest times there had existed in the Ottoman Empire what Sir Edwin Pears had called a series of *imperia* in the *imperium* of the empire—a condition of things which did not exist in any European country.[26]

The British Levant Consular Service posts might be defined as those where the consul, beside the ordinary commercial duties of officers of the "General Service," had extraterritorial jurisdiction, and the political work due to the peculiar conditions arising under the capitulation regime. It was only natural that, closely associated with their work, they should be given the charge of relief operations when crises occurred. The utmost use was made of the consuls. The test of all was the actual saving of as much human life and preventing as much human misery as possible. Some of the members of the consular staff gained high honor in this connection.

The position of a British vice consul in Mersin and Adana gave the post a special authority. In importance it outranked many consulates.

It was Doughty-Wylie who stood out among the consuls. He was undoubtedly a strong man and an honest one, besides being intelligent, and the combination of those qualities ought to bring good results. He saw the events in Adana. He filed the initial report on the province. He maintained an objectivity, except perhaps on relief issues, that allowed him to convey under even the most confusing of times remarkably insightful reports. He took his assignments seriously and, for that or for personal reasons, recorded most of his experiences and impressions. He wrote straightforward analyses of events, without prejudices. Doughty-Wylie seemed to be one of the few foreign consuls who had any real grasp of the political situation in the province of Adana, or who took care to base his views of local matters on anything better than Adana city rumors and the tittle-tattle of the region. He notably paid attention to the Muslims, not only the Christians. His perspectives add color to our understanding of events in Adana in 1909. Cemal Bey, notwithstanding his suspicions of the British, had very good relations with him and sometimes sought his advice and help. Doughty-Wylie's intercourse was made simpler and less formal by the fact that Cemal Bey talked French.

Doughty-Wylie was made a Companion of the Order of St. Michael and St. George. The Ottoman authorities also decorated him for valor, awarding him the rare Order of Mecidiye—the traditional mark of military esteem.[27] The whole world heard the story of how Doughty-Wylie went to Adana on the first day of the fighting, forced the governor to give him a small body of soldiers, posted guards at the American mission and school, furnished protection to imperiled foreigners, and rode about the crazed city, entreating, threatening, and persuading the mob, until a bullet broke his arm on the second day.[28] Messages of thanks and congratulations came to him from all over the world, including the governments whose nationals had been saved by his action.[29] He highly deserved them. He lost his life at the Dardanelles in 1915 and gained the Victoria Cross fighting the Turks whom, in the words of Aubrey Herbert, "he understood and admired."[30]

The first fifteen years of Doughty-Wylie's military service involved him in one military campaign after another: the Hazara expedition (1891), Chitral (1895), Crete (1896), the Sudan (1898–1899), South Africa (1900), Tientsin (1900), and Somaliland (1903–1904). His military service was not only intense but also varied, involving service on the northwest frontier of India, east and south Africa, the Mediterranean, and the Far East. His posting to the British garrison on Crete during the tumultuous period of civil unrest that resulted in the removal of the Turkish presence on the island (November 1898) brought him into contact for the first time with the Ottoman Empire, an involvement destined to become a central part of his career. In September 1906 he became British military vice consul at Mersin and Konya. This appointment brought him international acclaim. Doughty-Wylie's achievements at Adana were rewarded by promotion to consul general at Addis Ababa. He served there for three years, until 1912, when he became chief director of the Red Cross on the Turkish side in the First Balkan War, a role in which he won the considerable respect and affection of the Turks. The trust that Doughty-Wylie had established with the Turkish authorities made him an excellent choice as chairman of the commission that arbitrated the Greek-Albanian frontier in the wake of the Second Balkan War.[31]

It is worth remembering that the sympathy between the British and the Turks, and especially the Turkish soldiers, lasted ever since the old days they fought together in the Crimean War of 1853–1856. Many British officers served in the Ottoman army during that war. No greater compliment could be paid by the soldiers of one nation to the soldiers of another that what was said by Turkish soldiers at that time. That was the feeling of respect of one brave man for another. All British officers acknowledged what grand fighters the Turkish soldiers were, and respect was mutual. Strong friendship between the two nations still existed.[32]

In 1909 Dougthy-Wylie was the only British official at Adana legally capable of performing a consular act even of a routine nature. Yet the work of the British vice consulate, both political and ordinary, was much more extensive and important, and was likely to remain so than that of any other foreign consulate at Adana. The reasons were the great preponderance of British trade and the growing number of British subjects.

END OF THE CLASHES IN ADANA, APRIL 16, 1909

On the evening of April 15 the Armenians, who were by this time running short of ammunition, decided to try to communicate with the government and thus to ask for protection. The formal request, addressed to the governor, was taken to the *Konak* the following morning by a friendly Turkish *hoja*, who happened to reside in the Armenian quarter. In answer to this letter, a large company of soldiers, led by this *hoja* and under the command of a colonel, were sent to patrol the streets and to restore order in the city. As this motley possession passed through the Armenian quarter, it was joined by some of the leading members of that community. During the time occupied by the march of these peacemakers William Nesbitt Chambers ascended to the flat roof of his house, from which he could command the attention of both Turks and Armenians, and while waving a white pocket-handkerchief ordered both parties to cease fire. He could speak both in Turkish and Armenian. Chambers shouted in Turkish repeatedly, "Cease firing!" Turkish riflemen on another roof answered. "Let the Armenians surrender." The missionary waved his white pocket-hankerchief again and cried, "They are ready to surrender to the government. Cease firing!" Then he shouted to the Armenians everywhere to put up white flags. Meanwhile one of the Jesuit priests at the French school asked a Turkish bugler to go to the roof of his building and sound, "Cease firing!" The bugler refused to move. Seizing the man by the throat, the priest actually forced him to the roof and compelled him to blow the signal. Then the firing slackened. A truce was finally concluded at the *Konak* provided that the heads of the Armenian revolutionary societies agreed certain conditions, the most important of which was a kind of disarmament. It was thus on April 16 that the first outbreak, which practically amounted to a drawn battle, was concluded in Adana. Peace had been made, and the *hojas* and Armenian priests had kissed each other in the *Konak*. It was estimated that between five hundred and six hundred Muslims and about seven hundred Armenians perished in the three days. During the ensuing night three or four large fires broke out in the city, while the inhabitants of Adana could discern others in the neighboring villages and vineyards. The magnitude of the disaster was even then too obvious to everybody.[33]

Then the members of the *Fedayee* and their captain promptly fled from Adana. The general leader, Zachariah Bezdikian, and one of his accomplices were sheltered by the British vice consul in the house of his dragoman. The fury of the Muslims grew as they counted their losses and realized that the *Fedayee* had escaped. The work of the *Fedayee* was an unbearable challenge to Muslim pride.[34]

In Adana there was a large Greek population, but neither there nor elsewhere had the Greeks been molested. Special care had also been taken to avoid injury to the subjects of foreign nations, with the idea of avoiding foreign complications and the payment of indemnities.

The French consular agent at Adana assessed the number of deaths in this city to be more than sixteen hundred. There was no French national among the victims, but the covenants of Jesuits and sisters of Saint Joseph in Adana were destroyed by fire.[35]

Henry Rickards, a French citizen employed in Adana, in a letter he sent to his family in Egypt, wrote the following on the destruction in the city. The shops, the bazaars, three factories, a caravanserai, and fifteen hundred people were burned down and pillaged. German engineers working on the Baghdad railway construction lost all their plans, maps, instruments, in a word, all their possessions in Bahçe. The work of a whole year was thus wiped out.[36]

EVENTS IN THE VICINITY OF ADANA AND THE PROVINCE OF ALEPPO, APRIL 16–24, 1909

Regarding the broad outline of events in the provinces of Adana and Aleppo, it must suffice here to summarize. On April 16 the situation in Adana was better but the movement began to spread to the surrounding districts. At Tarsus, half an hour from Adana, a train load of some two hundred toughs came from Adana and were joined by some of the native Turks and two hundred Afghans of the town, destroyed many houses and shops. It was said that the mob spread with kerosene and fired the great historic Armenian church. They demolished marble statues and shattered important historic tablets. Everything portable was carried away, but the church itself resisted their attempts to burn it. Missions, which gave shelter to three thousand people, were well protected. Martial law was declared and the situation showed improvement. Five hundred houses were burned in the Armenian quarter of the town. Many were made homeless but few were killed. According to Thomas Davidson Christie, there were only approximately fifty Armenians killed in Tarsus. This, he thought, was particularly owing to energetic orders from Esad Rauf Bey, the *mutasarrıf* of Mersin, and perhaps more to the timely arrival of the guard from Adana.[37]

By April 16 the likelihood of the disturbance at Adana spreading to Mersin increased. Panic seized the inhabitants of the town. Hundreds of Armenians and others took refuge in the American consulate and in the American mission in Mersin. The consuls and the prominent people of the district appealed to Esad Rauf Bey to save the town and prevent the people from the country about from entering the town to plunder and kill. The *mutasarrıf* bravely did his duty and stationed troops at the entrance to Mersin, and no one was allowed to enter the town unless disarmed and known to have business therein. This prompt and decisive action saved the town.[38]

Esad Rauf Bey was a conscientious and dedicated administrator who saved Mersin from danger and rendered unforgettable services after the incidents.[39] Many praised and admired him for his conduct.[40] During his two years' tenure of office, he distinguished himself for his activity, intelligence, and honesty. Esad Rauf Bey was no doubt a man of courage. At his time justice was carried out and public security established to an extent unknown before for years.[41] Though a hot-tempered man, his feelings were never allowed to overcome for long his sense of right. He left no personal records of his deeds for posterity. Yet Esad Rauf Bey's career is in many respects worthy of study. His son, Selim Rauf Sarper, a foreign service officer, became Turkey's ambassador to the Soviet Union in 1944–1946 and to Italy in 1946–1947. Having served as permanent representative in the United Nations from 1947 to 1957 and in the

North Atlantic Treaty Organization from 1957 to 1960, he became minister of foreign affairs between 1960 and 1962.[42]

Asaf (Belge) Bey was rather a weak *mutasarrıf* at Cebeli Bereket without power to cope with hostile conditions. He was under the influence of notables and former officials. He distributed Martini rifles and ammunition to the Muslim population from the store in Erzin. If the Armenians could be given the assurance of adequate protection, they would quickly recover from the shock and become self-supporting and more. Without this assurance, they were hopeless.[43]

Grave alarm was felt at İskenderun. Several Armenian farms in the neighborhood of this town were destroyed. İskenderun, being a seaport with a considerable foreign population and Western consuls, suffered less than the towns of the interior where there were no such restraining influences. At Belen and nearby villages of Kanlı Dere, Kışla Deresi, Soğuk Oluk, Atik, and Nergizli, the people escaped to the mountains and were brought in by the relieving force from Aleppo, who had with them the French consul. On April 18 the situation of Payas and Dörtyol, where bands of Circassian settlers and mountaineers were said to be gathering, was extremely serious. The following day the prison at Payas was broken open and its four hundred inmates went off to join the attack on Dörtyol. From there the mob went to Antakya where there were violent disturbances on April 16, 17, 18. On April 19, the massacre broke out. At Antakya were some Greeks, but they were almost untouched. The panic at Aleppo was great: the population sought refuge in the foreign consulates, the churches, the warehouses on the shore, and even on boats. There were only four hundred Ottoman soldiers in the city. Business was at a standstill. The locality was full of Bedouin Arabs, Kurds, and Circassians.[44]

On April 22, serious alarms reached the people of Kessab, a town of about six thousand inhabitants, almost all Armenians, of whom some twenty-five hundred were Protestants. The locality is situated on the landward slope of Mount Cassius (Arabic, Jebel Akra; Turkish, Keldağ) which stands out prominently upon the Mediterranean seacoast halfway between İskenderun and Lazkiye (Latakia). It was known that a massacre of the Armenians had taken place in Antakya, about sixty kilometers to the north, and that attacks were being planned on the Christian villages of the mountains. A parley was arranged with the *müdür* (magistrate) of Ordu (Yayladağ), the nearest seat of government. And a telegram asking for military protection was dispatched to the governor of Aleppo. The *Müdür* met the Kessab delegation halfway down the mountainside and assured them that he had already scattered the mobs that had gathered with evil intention. But on that evening the Kessab scouts brought word into the town that great crowds of Muslims had gathered in the nearest village. Before daylight, the following morning, rifle shots told of their advance. Armenians resolved to hold out as many hours as possible, so as to furnish time for the women and children to escape into the clefts and caves of the mountains to the south. For five hours the fusillade continued with fierce determination. Toward evening the men had been compelled to give up the defense. They fell back without any panic or noise. And the Muslims rushed into the streets of the town and the plunderers fought with one another over the stores of raw silk, the chief produce of Kessab. The houses were set on fire. The loss of life was not great. On the evening of April 23, it occurred to the Armenian Dr. Soghomon Apelian that if he could reach the seaport Lazkiye, seventy kilometers to the south, he could telegraph for assistance by sea. With a trusty guide he set out that same evening for the house of a Muslim chief in the mountains. This Turk agreed to ride with him to Lazkiye and thus give him protection along the way. Without this escort the doctor could never have made this trip. Even as it was he took his life in his hands. They arrived at Lazkiye at two o'clock at night, called the British and French consuls to Dr. James Balph's home, sent telegrams to İskenderun and Aleppo, and at dawn notified the *mutasarrıf*, Mehmet Ali Ayni, of the attack on Kessab. Ottoman soldiers were dispatched at once, and a Messageries steamer started to the rescue from İskenderun. Meanwhile all day on April 24 the sacking and burning went on. The large village of Kaladouran (Karaduran) was devastated.[45]

The Messageries steamer took aboard about four thousand Armenians and brought them to Lazkiye, where they were divided among several churches and schools. On April 26, a French cruiser brought four thousand more. The *mutasarrıf* of Lazkiye, Mehmet Ali Ayni, had from the start done everything in his power to protect and provide for these fugitives. He himself patrolled the streets at night, and with the few soldiers at his command dispersed the angry Muslim mobs which repeatedly made attempts at disorder. He furnished a ration of flour for all, and expressed his sympathy with those who were in sorrow. When he saw the rapid increase of sickness he advised that they should all return to Kessab, and to give the people assurance of safety on the road he went with them in person. The courageous and kind-hearted action of this Turk saved Lazkiye, and the thousands of Kessab people sheltered there, from the dreadful event of a massacre.[46]

The *mutasarrıf* of Lazkiye, in his memoirs, as a whole confirms the above accounts.[47] Mehmet Ali Ayni—a striking personality with his white hair, slim figure, and old-fashioned courtly demeanour—distinguished himself by his self-sacrificing conduct and the commanders of the French warships were on several occasions able to appreciate the intelligence, courage, and the good will of this Ottoman official.[48] He was awarded the Saint Gregorious Knighthood

Order of Third Rank for his eminent services to the humanity by Pope Pius X on March 22, 1910.⁴⁹

Mehmet Ali Ayni was born in 1869 in Serfice, a town in the province of Manastır. Upon graduating from the Gülhane military secondary school, he attended the College of Administrative Sciences at İstanbul and completed his studies in 1888. Entering government service on July 14, 1889, in the Ministry of Education, he taught general history, Ottoman language, and economics at high schools in Edirne, Dedeağaç, Aleppo, and Diyarbekir up to 1895. Mehmet Ali Ayni served two years as chief secretary of the Department of Statistics in the Ministry of Education and in 1897 joined the Ministry of the Interior. After serving sixteen years at Kosova, Kastamonu, Sinop, Taiz, Basra, Balıkesir, Lazkiye, Mamuretülaziz, Bitlis, Yanya, and Trabzon successively as provincial secretary, *mutasarrıf*, and governor, he retired from public administration and began to concentrate on teaching and scholarly work until his decease in 1945.⁵⁰

The crowds were also getting ready in the morning of April 22 to attack the Armenian villages in Musadağ but the aggression was prevented thanks to the efforts of Halid Efendi, *müdür* of the locality of Süveydiye (Samandağ). He gave very severe orders to arrest and to hand over to the authorities all those who came from outside with the aim of stirring troubles. The instructions of the *müdür* were carried out and no unfortunate incident took place. The inhabitants also joined their efforts with the zeal of the *müdür* and contributed to the appeasement of the spirits. They saved both their lives and property. Halid Efendi stood firm and endeavored on his part to protect the Armenian villagers.⁵¹

On April 22 M. Roque-Ferrier, the French consul in Aleppo, cabled that the Ottoman authorities were taking all possible measures to bring back tranquility to the region. Soldiers were sent from İskenderun to Dörtyol to release several thousands of Armenians besieged by Kurds and Circassians. Two battalions hastily found their way to Ekbez where French Lazarists took in their establishments a large number of Armenians whose existence was in danger. M. Roque-Ferrier in Aleppo was allowed to accompany this expedition. Ekbez was a town of three thousand inhabitants, situated in the mountains about forty-five kilometers northeast of the Gulf of İskenderun and the battlefield of Issus. It was the trade center for all the Muslim and Christian villages in the surrounding area, and the site of two Roman Catholic monasteries, one Lazarist, the other Trappist.⁵²

At Kozan the district governor armed the Armenians (a thing unheard of before) and told them to protect themselves.⁵³ At Misis, a village thirty kilometers from Adana, the cry was aroused "The Circassians are coming" and the Turkish major of the regular troops stationed went out to meet them.

They showed him personally the greatest respect, but could not understand why he, a Muslim, should try to protect Armenians. At one time the mob got out of control, but order was soon restored. The major, however, was sent to Hacin to the relief of the people there and then the mob pillaged and burned. Hacin, situated far off in the mountains, had a largely Armenian population, though the village population was Muslim. As rumors of trouble came, the Armenians took possession of the town and closed all the gates. Both the district governor and military commander was absent and only a few regular soldiers were in the barracks. These shut themselves up away from the armed Armenians. Miss Rose Lambert, who had charge of an American orphan asylum containing three hundred children, telegraphed for help. On April 25 a Turkish major arrived—the same one who had saved the people of Misis with three hundred regular troops—but Armenians distrusted him and would not let him inside the walls, though he offered to come alone. At last on April 26 the Turkish major came alone into the town; he and the Armenian prelate paraded the streets together as a sign of amity and all was quiet.[54]

Many Armenians took refuge in the houses of their Turkish neighbors in Karsı Bazaar. Among Muslims of this town, several saved Armenians and, in case of need, even fought against the attackers. Musa Efendi, Veli Efendi, and Lieutenant Hüsnü Efendi led the defense with sixty soldiers under their command. Poyrazoğlu Köse, Harabanoğlu Mehmed Bey, and Gharman Soumbas accommodated and looked after three hundred Armenians for twenty-six days. Arif Ağa, son of the mufti of Karsı Bazar, saved six hundred Armenians.[55]

For many weeks there had been great uneasiness at Maraş. The district governor was a weak man and had done little. This was, however, known at İstanbul, and a new governor had been sent. During the days of trouble, the mob pillaged some, but the Sheikh-ul-Islam at İstanbul sent word to the *ulema* at Maraş, and the Muslims of İstanbul did the same to those of Maraş that no blood was to be shed. So the Armenians and Muslims of Maraş held meetings every day until finally the CUP at İstanbul sent word that they had regained leadership. The government in Maraş stood firm, and the son of the most influential Turk chiefly instrumental in stirring up trouble had been arrested.[56]

From April 18–24 Göksun, a town situated in the midst of a fertile plain about eighty kilometers northwest of Maraş, was surrounded by the mobs. The government, especially the *kaymakam*, did their best but the soldiers were few. If the chief men from two neighboring Circassian villages had not come and saved the Armenians, they should all have perished. For six days these men with their Martini rifles stood between the Armenians and the mob. Armenians could never forget such goodness. On April 24, soldiers came from Elbistan and officers from Zeytun. The part the Circassians played in saving Göksun had gratified the American missionaries exceedingly, as one especially of the two villages was one where they had often stopped at night when journeying, one whose people had sometimes sent presents of fresh cheese or other delicacies, and one for whose children lady missionaries once took pleasure in making up a package of dolls and other American toys. Had these friends taken to pillage and murder, it would sadly had shaken the faith of the American missionaries.[57]

A representative from Dörtyol explained the Armenian predicament to the commander of a British naval vessel docked in the harbor of İskenderun. On April 30, the two British commanders, vice consul Joseph Catoni, missionary Samuel H. Kennedy, some Armenian leaders, the mufti of İskenderun, and several Ottoman officials boarded a ship and sailed off to open waters off Dörtyol for negotiations. According to Armenian sources, in the early stages of the discussions, the Ottoman side offered the following terms: (1) the Armenians must surrender their weapons and barracks, and (2) the outsiders fighting in Dörtyol must leave immediately. The Armenians offered counter terms: (1) they would keep their weapons but pledged that they would not open fire on nonhostile Turks; and (2) they had built the barracks with their own resources and would surrender the building only to the regular army. On May 1, Italian, French, and German battleships arrived in the harbor of İskenderun. The admiral of the Italian warship *Filomen* reportedly called on the militay commander of İskenderun and asked for measures to ensure the withdrawal of the armed Muslim groups at Dörtyol, indicating that he might otherwise be constrained to bombard the surrounding Muslim villages. The presence of a European naval force near İskenderun had a calming effect on subsequent developments.[58]

The government in İstanbul instructed the army to dispatch two battalions to Dörtyol to diffuse the situation and ordered a full investigation of the disorder. The Ottoman Chamber of Deputies, too, addressed the provincial governor in Adana to take the necessary steps to restore peace. Hence, a military officer from Adana, Kiliades Efendi, was sent together with an infantry unit to the conflict zone. Meeting with the local Armenian notables on May 1, Kiliades Efendi urged them not to involve the British in Ottoman affairs but rather to trust the CUP. He outlined the following concessions: (1) Dörtyol would remain the center of the kaza with a Greek *kaymakam* instead of a Turk serving as the provincial governor's deputy; (2) the district's military barracks would be expanded and the number of personnel increased in order to safeguard the area; (3) the telegraphic office on the first floor of the government building would be expanded to include postal services; (4) the main street in Dörtyol connecting the crossroads leading to Toprakkale, Payas, and İskenderun would be widened, and a railroad station near that intersection would be constructed by European companies; and (5) the small landing at Dörtyol would be upgraded to facilitate the export of millions of oranges annually. In addition, the governor of Adana offered to grant various community and cultural rights. Certain philanthropic, religious, and educational institutions such as the Red Crescent Hospital and the Kelekian Orphanage would be allowed to operate freely; the clergy would be permitted sermons in the Armenian language on various holidays such as the New Year, Christmas, Candlemass/Presentation of Christ in the Temple, Easter, and the Feast of the Holy Mother of God; and bonfires and gunshots into the air would be allowed during weddings and other celebrations under the direct supervision of the barracks commandant.[59]

The governor of Adana also promised fair trials in cases dealing with land taxation and usurpation and to take heed of the interests of the various communities. In return, the Armenians were to pledge loyalty to the Ottoman government and to hand over their weapons to district commander Nedim Bey. The people of Dörtyol accepted these terms. After 1909, the town of Dörtyol and surrounding Armenian villages witnessed a swift revival in many fields until the outbreak of the First World War in 1914. According to Armenian sources, the boom in orange exports to İstanbul, Odessa, and Manchester was paralleled by the flourishing of the educational efforts.[60]

Ayntab had a population predominantly Muslim though with a large Armenian element which was decidedly revolutionary. Some months before April 1909 there had been a real mutiny in the American college, coming mostly from the Armenian revolutionary students. This had been put down by the Americans, official Turks, and conservative Armenians all working together in perfect harmony. Therefore, the people and the district governor had a certain assurance that the Armenian elements were loyal. Nevertheless, when rumors began in April, the district governor had difficulty in calming the people, but with the help of the American doctor who was loved by all, and a certain rich Turk, he succeeded, though the lives of all three were seriously threatened.[61]

The kaza of İslahiye, close to Ayntab, had escaped massacre through the exertions of one man, Hacı Mehmet Ağa, a wealthy Turk who had for years been a sergeant of gendarmerie; he was known as Hacı Çavuş. İslahiye was a small place on the plain that had only a few Armenian traders among its inhabitants. Among its many villages there were three whose people were mostly Armenians. The Armenians in the outside villages of Keller and İntilli had been harried, their houses burned, many of the men killed, and those who had escaped had found refuge in İslahiye when it was determined to kill them there. The mob was advancing to attack the escapees who had sought asylum in the government house and the mosque, when, Martini in hand, old

Hacı Çavuş confronted them. He told them in vigorous Turkish, no language better adopted to the purpose, what he thought of them and then called for any friends of his to stand by him. Then he said, "You off-scourings who call yourselves Muslims but neither respect the law nor fear God, do you clamor for blood? You shall have it. We will fire upon you as soon as we can load our guns." He threw a cartridge into his Martini, and knowing him of old, they scattered like a covey of partridges.[62]

There were about four hundred escapees in İslahiye. Hacı Çavuş had eighty women and children in his house. One of the Armenian girls in the house of Hacı Çavuş, who was teacher of the girls' school at Hasanbeyli (a town halfway between Maraş and Dörtyol), an Ayntab girl of a good family, had been carried off by a Kurd; a Circassian had forcibly taken her from the Kurd; and then the son of Hacı Çavuş with his retainees had rescued her.[63]

The Armenians from the outlying districts were pouring into Adana from their burned villages, and the problem of their food and shelter devolved on the leaders of various communities. A large boys' school belonging to the Gregorian Armenians was filled with people as were practically all the churches and schools of all denominations.[64] Thousands of Armenians, mostly women and children, took refuge in the American mission school, in the house and factory of the British dragoman, in a German factory, and in the schools of the French Jesuits and nuns and the churches of Notre Dame and Saint Etienne.[65]

GOVERNOR CEVAD BEY'S DISPATCHES TO THE MINISTRY OF THE INTERIOR AND THE DEBATE IN THE CHAMBER OF DEPUTIES, APRIL–MAY 1909

On April 16, 1909, the governor of Adana, Cevad Bey, sent the below dispatch to the Ministry of the Interior stating that he and the military commander worked day and night to restore order:

> The disordery which broke out on the 1st (14th) April, at the chief town of this vilayet, between Armenians and Moslems lasted three days. The commander and myself worked day and night, and, in spite of the smallness of the military force and of other difficulties, order was re-established and lasted until yesterday afternoon, when reports of arms from the Armenian quarter were heard. The Moslem population became greatly excited and rushed the Government building. Soldiers were turned out and the quarter from which the reports came were put under guard and then it was conclusively shown that the incident had been caused by some Armenian "fedais" (i.e., men ready to sacrifice their lives). At night fire broke out in two places, and although efforts to extinguish

them were made, complete success was impossible, owing to the disorder and to inadequacy of the fire appliances. Yesterday morning a few regular battalions arrived and were split up into guards. Every possible military measure was taken, order has been restored, and foreign residents' quarters, institutions, and property have been placed under protection. Disorder continues in some parts of the district and in Hajin, but the Sis Battalion of Redifs was sent by forced marches to Hajin, and an Advisory Committee was dispatched, so it is expected that order will be restored there in a day or two. A battalion of regulars has been sent to Deurtyol, in the Sanjak of Jebel Bereket, to quell the disturbance there. It is clear that this force will serve to tranquilize both that district and those of Khassa and Islahie, and strict instructions on this point have also been sent wherever necessary. In carrying out measures, great difficulties have been caused by the excitement and violence with which the regrettable affair began, by the fact that at first there was only one regular battalion of about 300 men, because the few battalions of Redifs who have been put under arms were local men without order and without uniforms (clothes). The quieting in three days of the population of 50,000 or 60,000 engaged in civil war, by such measures as instructing the soldiers to use their weapons in case of resistance from any quarter and by sending an Advisory Committee, is due to nothing but the adoption of military measures. Hence it is evident that had the military force which had been repeatedly asked for been present at the beginning of the incident quite could have been restored yet more quickly.[66]

Adil Bey, the undersecretary of state in the Ministry of the Interior, in a speech he made during the debate in the Chamber of Deputies on the Adana events on May 3, 1909, stated as follows. On April 14 a telegram was received from the province of Adana announcing the breaking out of disorder and the appearance of plunderers. The necesary instructions were at once sent to the province, their purpose being "(T)urn out soldiers, gendarmes, police, whatever force you have, even the guards; give necessary instructions to both parties; restore absolute order. We will, moreover, write to the Ministry of War and the necessary military force will be sent. Until that time you must take all possible steps." At the same time a dispatch was sent to the Ministry of War asking that sufficient soldiers should be provided from the nearest point. On the two succeeding days the matter was followed up and instructions were continued. The next day when Edhem Paşa, the minister of war, was asked during a Cabinet meeting whether the military force on the spot was sufficient, he gave a negative answer. It was said that men would be sent from the Second Army Corps area. As the news from the province stated that two battalions would not be enough, it was demanded that the Silifke Regiment should be sent also. It was replied that in that case there would be no need to send two batallions as well, but it was said that both the two batallions and the Silifke Regiment should be sent. Unfortunately, for reasons such as the lack of steamers, the military arrived somewhat late, and the outbreak could not be prevented. A telegram was sent from the province to the Ministry of Police. It stated that the police were insufficient and asked that an adequate police force should be sent. A conflict was going on between Muslims and non-Muslims. Foreigners were impartial in such matters, so any attack on them would cause foreign intervention and political complications. The telegram did not easily lend itself to misinterpretation, but unfortunately it had been misconstrued. In correspondence with the military commander orders were given that guards composed of soldiers and gendarmes should be formed, that looting should be absolutely prevented, that the various classes of the population should not interfere with each other, and that special care should be taken of the consulates and of property. This was natural and merely the government's duty. The government had no cause for regret.[67]

Adil Bey then went on thus. On the second day of the events the matter was discussed at a Cabinet meeting. It was asked what gave rise to the incident, and it was replied that that would appear from the investigations of a Special Committee to be sent, and this idea was accepted. A special court martial would be formed and sent, and offenders, whoever they might be, would be punished. The work of the committee of investigaton would result in the punishment of the criminals, whoever they might be. A few days previously some members of the Armenian National Assembly came and questioned the grand vizier. Telegrams from the governorate of Adana was read, but they replied that the incident was not caused by the Armenians, there being very few Armenians there as compared with Muslims. It was said that the information given was founded on information received from the spot. There was no need to discuss the question on the basis of race. The real culprits must be sought out. A telegram had been sent authorizing the expenditure of the sum necessary to feed and house the sufferers. If the future necessitates the expenditure of more it would be spent. News was received from the scene of the occurrence that at the commencement a state of siege was proclaimed. As to the number of deaths, the truth would transpire after local inquiries.[68]

The Sublime Porte never denied that serious disturbances had taken place at the province of Adana. What it denied, as was the case in the Sassoun incidents of 1894, was the accusation that there was a premeditated massacre, and yet this was the basis upon which was built the whole Armenian agitation, both in Europe and America. The mere idea that the sultan would order a massacre of his Christian subjects, Armenians or no Armenians, was senseless in itself, and denoted a credulous belief in the falsehoods and calumnies propagated by the Armenian revolutionary committees. People could not understand in the Ottoman Empire how serious some American newspapers could accept and print in their columns assertions made with the object of throwing odium on the legitimate authority of a friendly power. Mere affirmations ought not to be considered as sufficient. Proofs ought to be asked above everything else. If such were the case, the most extreme claims about the Ottoman government would never appear in some of the American daily press. What, however, surprised some people most was to see the boldness and fanaticism of not a few American clergymen, who tried to impart a religious and fanatical tendency to a question that was, and ought to remain, a political one.[69]

The Ottoman Chargé d'Affaires in London gave the following account of the disorders:

> An Armenian of Adana having, in consequence of a quarrel about a woman, wounded two Muslims, one of whom died of his wounds, disorders have occurred in that town, and riots took place between Muslims and Armenians. There have been wounded and killed on both sides. The authorities have taken the necessary measures with a view to the re-establishment of order. Military forces have been sent from Beirut and Dédéaghatch. A thorough inquiry has been opened for the punishment of guilty officials, in case there are any.[70]

Hüseyin Kazım Bey, the Ottoman ambassador to the United States, on April 18 received official dispatches from İstanbul confirming press reports of the disturbance at Adana. The whole incident was provoked, the dispatches stated, by a question of women. An Armenian shot two Muslims, one being killed, after which a battle occurred between Muslims and Armenians, and in consequence a number were killed and injured on both sides. At the same time fire broke out in the city and, most of the buildings being frame structures, could not be easily controlled. Steps to establish the security of citizens had been taken, military having being sent from Beirut. The government was making a thorough inquiry to find out who were the real instigators of trouble, and if any functionaries were found to have been involved assurance was given that they would be severely punished.[71]

At the April 18 sitting of the Chamber of Deputies, Ali Münif of Adana, Arif Hikmet of Mersin, Hamparsun Boyacıyan of Kozan, Ali Cenani of Aleppo, Abdülhamid Zehravi of Hama, Nazaret Dagavaryan of Sivas, Ohannes Vartges of Erzurum, and Bedros Hallaçyan of İstanbul demanded that immediate measures be taken to restore order in the province of Adana and to punish ringleaders of the massacre. The following motion to this effect was adopted unanimously: "The Chamber of Deputies recommends that the government send 20,000 gold liras to Adana and Aleppo provinces to assist the people who have suffered damages; punish high-and low-level officials who caused the incidents; and immediately dispatch a court martial."[72]

AMERICAN MISSIONARY STEPHEN VAN TROWBRIDGE'S ACCOUNT OF EVENTS AND BISHOP MUSHEG SEROPIAN

Young and energetic Stephen van Trowbridge was one of the most vocal of the American missionaries. Stationed at Ayntab, he was in Adana on the day of the fiercest fighting. His letters to the ABCFM in Boston tell us much about events in this city. He was the only American or European who was an actual eyewitness of the killing of Daniel Miners Rogers and Henry Maurer, fellow missionaries at Adana. At the time of the outbreak of the first disturbances in the locality there were a number of Americans having come from Maraş, Tarsus, Hacin, and other Turkish mission centers to attend the fiftieth annual convention of the Central Turkey Mission of the American Congregational Board, which had been called for on April 14, 1909. Among them were Maurer, connected with the Mennonite Mission at Hacin and Rogers, from the mission at Tarsus. Trowbridge supplied the following account of the occurrence in richest detail, dated Adana, April 19, to representatives of the grand vizier, and he wrote it out also for the Mission Board at home:

> Firing and fighting began April 14 between Moslems and Armenians, which resulted in a number of casualties on both sides. By nightfall it was clear that incendiaries were at work, for several districts of the city were covered by clouds of smoke, which rolled out far into the country, where vineyards and country houses also were burning. All night long reports of firearms rang out from all sides. The roofs and parapets of houses, minarets, windows with shutters, and other ambuscades were used. The most persistent and dangerous fusillade came from one of the minarets on the border of the Armenian quarter. The next morning, April 15, the conflagrations had spread to such an extent that we were obliged to watch closely the environs of the building of the girls' school and the residence of William N. Chambers. All streets were deserted, and the firing from the ambuscades was kept up all the morning. A fresh outburst of smoke near the girls' school showed that we were threatened by fire. The wind fanned the flames and drove them from house to house in our direction. Mr. Rogers was guarding the home of Miss Wallace[73] and the dispensary across the street from the school. It was clear that the large school, a building of brick and wood, was in danger. We spent the morning in ripping off projecting woodwork and the porch posts. It soon became evident that direct efforts to put out the flames must be undertaken. Up to that time no one had dared to go on the streets because of the shooting from one end by Moslems and the other by Armenians. Moslem pillagers, armed and in desperate mood, were looting the houses opposite the buildings on fire. Mr. Maurer and I took a crowbar and an axe and crossed the street to destroy the wooden porches, shutters, and stair-ways of the houses between the fires and the girls' school. We carried pails of water, which we threw wherever we saw flames breaking out.

All this time there had been no sign of any effort on the part of the Government authorities to stop the rioting, pillaging, and burning. No soldiers or policemen had appeared, nor had any pumps or apparatus for fighting fire been brought out. The only news we had of the soldiers was the galling rifle fire from the minarets. This shooting apparently was directed at the houses where the Armenians were resisting by a return fire. When I first climbed to the roofs near the flames armed Moslems appeared on three sides within close rangs. When they understood that I was not firing on them, but had come to work against the flames, they lowered their rifles and assured me with many pledges that I might go on unmolested. Then three Turks appeared at the windows of a house just across the street, and after assuring me of my safety dropped back again to their work of plunder. Back of that house, in a well-protected position, was a turbaned Moslem covering these looters with his rifle and firing frequently to protect them. Two other Moslems appeared suddenly on my left, but perceiving my purpose they bade me feel no concern. In the meanwhile Mr. Maurer, who had been carrying water in pails from the yard of the girls' school, came up to me and made use of a crowbar in throwing down a wall, one side of which was burning fiercely. We worked with pails of water, the crowbar, and the axe for over an hour. It seemed that we must have help. We repeatedly begged some Armenian young men who were lurking around the street corners shielded from the Moslem fire to put away their arms and come and save the school building. The real danger that pressed upon our minds was not the possible loss of the building, but the perilous situation in which our American friends, the hundreds of Christian refugees, and the eighty school girls would find themselves in case the building burned. In every direction there were rioting and shooting. There was no refuge except possibly in the Protestant church some distance away, and even this was threatened from three sides by the conflagration. So we came back to the school and asked for volunteers. Mr. Rogers came at once. He had been in Miss Wallace's house and did not know how close the fire had come. He carried water back and forth three times. Mr. Maurer was using the crowbar against a wall, and I, higher up on the roof, was pouring water on places just catching fire. We had thus worked a considerable time without being harmed by the Moslems when the Armenians at the other end of the street commenced firing on the houses where the looters were at work. Suddenly two shots rang out not more than eight yards from where we were working. Mr. Rogers, who was in the street bringing water, was mortally wounded. He called to me by name and then fell in the middle of the street. The other bullet hit Mr. Maurer in the left lung near the heart, a wound that caused him to suffer great pain. The crowbar fell from his hands. He then climbed down the ladder and collapsed at the side of Mr. Rogers. Immediately after these two shots several other bullets from the Moslems, who had fired them, whizzed past me. I dropped almost flat on the roof and made my way to the edge, whence I could see Mr. Maurer climbing down the ladder with the greatest difficulty. I could also hear Mr. Rogers groaning. My first thought was to help my two comrades home to have their wounds treated. Consequently, without concealing my intention, I stepped to the lower roof and climbed down the same ladder Mr.

Maurer had used. It was clear that both men would have to be carried in. I went on rapidly to the school to tell Dr. Thomas D. Christie and Mr. Frederick W. Macallum[74]. Just then the British Vice Consul at Mersina, Major Doughty-Wylie, arrived with twenty Turkish soldiers on a tour of the city. They rode up and found Mr. Rogers and Mr. Maurer lying wounded in the street. The entire neighborhood was deserted. The soldiers were ordered to the roofs to fire in several directions, but by this time the murderers had disappeared. Mr. Maurer died a few minutes later in the school building, and Mr. Rogers lived only a few minutes longer than Mr. Maurer. He did not regain consciousness.[75]

The Ottoman Ministry of Foreign Affairs, replying to an inquiry made by the United States ambassador John Leishman regarding the killing at Adana of American missionaries Henry Maurer and Daniel Miners Rogers on April 15, 1909, said it appeared that two men came to their death at the hands of Armenians, who were firing from their dwellings near where the missionaries were helping to put out a fire in the house of an aged Turkish woman. The Ministry of Foreign Affairs laid the blame for the killing of the missionaries on the Armenians.[76]

In another letter sent on April 20, Trowbridge said:

We do not know the exact origin of the struggle. I say struggle because this has not been a massacre in the sense that the Armenians died unresisting. On Monday, the 12th, an Armenian in the city in angry passion shot one of his opponents dead and wounded two others. This Armenian escaped to Mersin and took passage by sea.[77]

According to Trowbridge, it was no doubt true that agents of the Armenian revolutionary societies had been at work in the province of Adana for months past and had aggravated the already strained relations between Turks and Armenians. Bishop Musheg Seropian had made a tour through this region not long before and had advocated the arming of Armenian young men to be ready in the event of a crisis. This leader had left Adana for Egypt before the outbreak of events, and despite efforts to return, he had been prevented from reaching Cilicia. The Turks had been gratified at the prevention of his return, and in Trowbridge's view, it was clearly in the interests of peace and order to keep such men away.[78]

Charles Doughty-Wylie reported the following on April 21, 1909, to his superiors:

The Armenian bishop of Adana (Gregorian) was announced to be returning on 21 April, by the Khedivial steamer. Many Turks have spoken to me of this man, as one of the prime causes of the trouble. On 20 April, certain notable Armenians asked me to prevent his return if possible as they feared he would again stir up strife. I took upon myself to telegraphing to the Mutasarrif of Mersina to prevent him from coming to Mersina, if he could, in spite of me, succeed in landing. He appealed to the captain of the *Swiftsure* who backed me up.[79]

Musheg Seropian stormed and threatened, but the captain of the *Swiftsure* compelled him to return to his ship. It was an order from a British man-of-war that kept the Episcopal agitator from increasing the danger of the situation in Adana by his presence. The steps taken to keep him out of the country were heartily approved by the Armenians generally, who were anxious to avoid further trouble.[80]

In Seropian's guilt, the French military occupation forces at Adana in the early 1920s agreed with Stephen van Trowbridge and Charles Doughty-Wylie. The Permanent War Council of the French First Armed Division of the Levant sitting in this city on April 23, 1920, found the Armenian prelate culpable of "criminal conspiracy, fabrication and possession of lethal explosive devices, possession of arms and ammunition of war and complicity of manslaughter." Consequently, he was sentenced in absentia to the penalty of ten years of forced labor and twenty years of ban on residence.[81]

Tetsuya Sahara concludes that the Armenians in Adana were not the helpless people that were decimated one-sidedly by their Muslim assailants. They were well prepared and fought effectively. In his opinion, the rapid deployment of the *Fedai* units and their disciplined behavior presuppose the existence of military organizations established long before the events. The massive armament and military training of the Armenians must have something to do with the underground revolutionary organizations, most probably Huntchaks.[82]

RESUMPTION OF THE CLASHES, APRIL 25, 1909

Unfortunately, the truce was only too brief. After barely ten days' peace, it was on April 25 that the fresh outbreak began in Adana. In the morning everything seemed quiet. Medical supplies which had just arrived had been distributed. Suddenly, toward the close of the afternoon service at the Protestant church, the sound of a few shots were the signal for an almost universal panic. The exact origin of these shots is still uncertain. One of the first incidents in the outbreak was the firing on the tents of the troops who had just reached Adana from Salonika. These men were camped on the drill ground close to the right bank of the river Seyhan. A report was immediately spread that the Armenians had opened fire from a church tower in the city. There was another claim that a party of local Turks, dressed up as Armenians, fired at the Salonikan soldiers in order to incite them to think that a second Armenian insurrection had begun. Whatever might have provoked their action, it was certain that these units not only opened fire on the Armenians, but that they joined in attacking the Christian quarter of the city. Thereafter events proceeded at a bewildering pace. It was estimated that at least two thousand men, women, and children perished, either by the shootings or in the flames. The Armenians suffered the most of the losses.[83]

The warships of Christian nations smoked on the seacoast. On April 25 the British cruiser *Triumph* came to anchor in Mersin, and the next day, the French battleships *Jules Ferry* and *Jules Michelet*, and two armored cruisers, the French *La Vérité* and Italian *Francesco Ferruccio*, arrived.[84] The commanders of these vessels were instructed to lend their assistance to their consuls to give, in case of necessity, refuge to their nationals and, in a general manner, to foreigners as well as to natives, Christian or otherwise, whose lives would be in peril. They found their citizens working at their usual avocations and undisturbed by acts of molestation on the part of the Ottoman government or by its subjects. The interrogation of their citizens by the officers of the ships developed the fact that nothing had occurred to disturb them in their occupations and that they had not interfered with in any way.[85]

Damar Arıkoğlu remarks: "It is beyond doubt that the second riot was brought about by Armenian political figures for the purpose of creating a pretext for foreign intervention."[86] It is instructive that Gerard Lowther, the British ambassador at İstanbul, in his annual report on the Ottoman Empire for the year 1910 concurs and notes that the outbreak of the second massacre in Adana gave rise at the time to ugly stories of the complicity of the Roumelian troops (i.e., units of the Third Army from Salonika). There was no truth in these reports; it was in reality started by some Huntchak revolutionaries, who, in the wild hope of provoking foreign interference, attacked and killed fifteen Roumelian soldiers newly arrived and picketed in the Armenian quarter. It was chiefly owing to the soldiers' ignorance of the topography of the city that the irregulars and other riotous elements were able to descend under cover of night and continue the interrupted work of plunder, murder, and arson.[87]

Remarkably, the British ambassador was able to come to an accurate analysis. He could do this by giving some credence to Ottoman reports, evaluating them as he did the evidence that he received from missionaries and Armenians. He understood the aims of the Armenian revolutionaries.

Philip Graves, who spent a good deal of his professional life reporting from İstanbul for his highly prestigious British paper *The Times* and who later served as a member of the Arab Bureau at Cairo which engaged in extensive intelligence activities in the Asiatic portion of the Ottoman Empire during the First World War, agrees with both the Turkish politician and the British ambassador: "On April 24–25 troops from European Turkey arrived at Adana, where shooting and burning had ceased for the best part of a week. On the evening of the 25th the local Hintchakists, hoping to bring about foreign intervention, attacked and killed fifteen of the new-comers and thus provoked a fresh outbreak in which half Adana was burned and many more Armenians were killed. The troops took no part in this second attack which was the work of armed mobs."[88] The opinions of Arıkoğlu, Lowther, and Graves suggest that the subject is one worth exploring further.

The destruction was rendered the easier owing to the manner in which the houses had been constructed. Nearly all the dwellings and shops had wooden planks built longways into the walls, so that as the fire got hold of each successive building these layers of timbers became ignited. The burning of these beam-like wooden layers caused the walls to fall in on their occupants. Moreover, where the outer shell of a house still remained standing after the fire, the walls were practically useless for reconstruction purposes, owing to the charred and rotten state of the timbers of which they were partly constructed.[89]

In the burned quarters, the collapsed houses completely prevented traffic. According to the results of the inquiry made by the municipal council of Adana, the total number of the buildings destroyed by fire was 1,072: three mosques, fifty-two schools, five churches, two hotels, five inns, three presses, 369 stores, and 680 residential houses. The number of wounded presently under treatment in the hospitals of the city was around five hundred, of which two hundred and thirty were Muslims and two hundred and fifty Armenians. All the wounded Armenians were treated in the hospitals while the Muslims, which were many, were looked after in their families.[90]

INCAPABILITY OF GOVERNOR CEVAD BEY AND THE MILITARY COMMANDER MUSTAFA REMZI PAŞA

Governor Cevad Bey contended that the Adana affair was a quarrel among Muslims and Armenians. Both sides misunderstood the meaning of the constitution. There was much foolish talk about liberty and equality. Speeches were made and feelings were hurt. The whole thing had been greatly exaggerated. It did not concern outside countries.[91]

There is no doubt that both Cevad Bey and Mustafa Remzi Paşa, the military commander at Adana, if not the actual cause of the outbreak in Cilicia, were by their cowardly conduct entirely responsible for the proportions which it assumed. From the moment when Cevad Bey assured that no disturbance would occur until the second outbreak was over, neither the governor nor the military commander took any adequate measures to restore public order. Whether it was an Armenian insurrection against the government or not, and whoever and whatever was the cause of the outbreak, it must have been the duty of the local officials who represented the government either to reestablish tranquility or to risk losing their lives while attempting to perform those obligations with which they were entrusted. Mustafa Remzi Paşa, who ventured into the streets during the early hours of April 14, turned away from wherever he heard firing and finally bolted to the *Konak* as soon as any real danger became apparent. This soldier, together with the governor, did not again leave the government building until the first outbreak was over. During the first outbreak, and while Cevad Bey and Mustafa Remzi Paşa were cowering upstairs, the yard which surrounded the government offices was crowded with soldiers, but no orders were given to the men that they should patrol the streets or take adequate measures to protect the population.[92]

The regular troops had made little attempt to preserve order and put down the mob, and both Cevad Bey and Mustafa Remzi Paşa appear to have failed to call on the troops to do their duty.[93] The two officials were paralyzed with fright, and they retired to the shelter of the *Konak*, making no effort to call out the soldiers, who could easily have quelled the mob or calmed the storm.[94] At the *Konak* all was in disorder. Cevad Bey and Mustafa Remzi Paşa were both in the telegraph office in a state of panic. Two men had been killed in that very office, practically before Cevad Bey's eyes—who was too frightened to protect them or punish the murderers.[95]

Herbert Adams Gibbons saw these two prominent Armenians, who had come to arrange how the disturbance might be quelled, killed in the presence of Cevad Bey, he being frightened to interfere. As further showing the inefficiency of the governor, he noted "that troops stationed near the bridge over the Sarus (river) were firing to prevent any more country people from entering the town. This was however not kept up long. It was the only effort that we saw made to keep out the country people from entering Adana. As there was no other entrance to Adana from the east except by this bridge, it would have been practicable to have shut out from the city a large part of the country rabble." These country people on entering the city joined with the other irregulars that did most of the work of plunder and destruction. The governor stated that Adana was under martial law, but Gibbons was sure that Charles Doughty-Wylie's guard was the only body of troops patrolling the city on the morning of April 15. Without the British vice consul's guard the lives of all foreign residents would have been jeopardized.[96] Cevad Bey did not even interfere to stop the tins of petroleum stored in the government depots from being taken out to set on fire the Armenian quarter.[97]

Elizabeth Webb heard, though it seemed quite possible, that because of the disturbance in İstanbul, officials in Adana did not know which side to join, so they simply let things take their course and permitted the Turks and

Armenians to fight it out.⁹⁸ It is no disparagement of other zealous missionaries to say that Elizabeth Webb was the outstanding lady missionary figure in Adana. Her knowledge of Turkish, Armenian, and German, all of which she spoke with fluency, her fine education at Drury College, Springfield, Montana, of which she was a graduate, and her forceful character combined to make her one of the strong influences in this province and had enabled her to play a part in the stirring events of April 1909.

Herbert Adams Gibbons, who in company of the Armenian clergy and others was sent with Mustafa Remzi Paşa to the marketplace at the beginning of the disturbance, said:

> A great and angry crowd was congregated in the market place. We urged upon the military commander to go ahead with his soldiers and clear the market of everybody, Moslems and Christians alike, ordering a volley to be fired if necessary. He stipulated that the Armenian Bishop should go ten yards or so ahead. This the bishop did not do. While they were arguing the point volley after volley of shots rang out. We could see this shooting plainly. It was done by young Armenians in the center of the market. They shot in the air with revolvers. We could see the extended arms and the revolvers pointed upwards. This was enough for the *Ferik* [Major General]. The military commander was by my side when the firing commenced. He had not the courage to endeavor to disperse the mob; he returned to his residence and did not venture to go out for two days. Throughout the whole troubles he remained in a pitiful state of funk. We made representations to the governor. This official said he could do nothing. He was afraid of his own life, and he made no attempt to protect us. We managed to get to the interior of the *Konak*, where we remained at the side of the government officials for forty-eight hours. That afternoon the situation grew distinctly worse. The Armenians withdrew to their quarter of Adana, which is situated on a hill, and converted the houses that held advantageous positions into fortresses. Here the fighting went on for two days, during which the Armenians succeeded in beating off their Turkish assailants.⁹⁹

This statement by an eyewitness is of value as showing that the Armenians at the beginning took an active part in the disturbances and that the disturbances might have been checked at the beginning if the officials had been firmer in the discharge of their duty. They could easily have suppressed the riots at their inception. A few volleys over the heads of the rioters, fired by the soldiers of the garrison, would have sufficed to quell the disturbance and subsequent arrests and trials of both Muslim and Armenian troublemakers would have bridged over the difficulty.¹⁰⁰

Mustafa Remzi Paşa often complained of the lack of discipline in the army, especially since Sultan Abdülhamid II came to the throne in 1876. To what extent the military commander himself was responsible for the lack of discipline among the *redifs* of the Adana province is debatable. But having proved the unsuitability of arming the villager-*redifs*, having heard of the excesses committed by them, and having promised to disband them as soon as regular troops arrived, he did not only make no attempts to regain the arms from the *redifs* who deserted, but he kept one battalion of irregulars under arms.[101]

Cevad Bey was feeble and negligent.[102] Gibbons and another American missionary, Lawson Chambers, who were with Cevad Bey for the first two days in the *Konak*, were witnesses that he made no effort to stop the affair.[103] According to Gibbons, the governor made absolutely no effort to stop the killing. Indeed, he displayed great cowardice, and cried, "They will kill us!" Gibbons supposed he was afraid for his own life, because he had not given the crowds arms upon their first demand. By the advice of the mufti Gibbons had taken to a corner, so as not to be seen out of the window. When shooting was feared the governor came up beside Gibbons and tried to get behind him. Gibbons demanded roughly, "What are you doing? You can stop this miserable business. Do you not know that you will be held responsible?" The governor had paid no attention to Gibbons, other than to judge his form as ample shelter (he was a little man); then he cried again, "Where is the Ferik? Where are the soldiers?" and, turning to an officer, he commanded, "Go to the window and call the soldiers." The man responded, "Call them yourself."[104]

Trowbridge related how he had reached the governor by a dash across the city, carrying an Ottoman flag and accompanied by two *zabtiyes* (gendarmes):

> There was a scene of greatest confusion. The governor was running about in dismay, and he could scarcely give a coherent answer to my questions and demands. I told him of the murder of Henry Maurer and Daniel Miners Rogers, American missionaries. He turned pale at my statement, although he must already have heard of the killings. His answer was: "We cannot be responsible." To this I replied: "You must be responsible; we have no other force to rely upon except the governorate. You have completely abandoned us throughout this crisis." The governor was so confused that it was clear that he had no mastery of the situation. Prisoners and soldiers, common Turks, were running in and out of the governor's audience chamber.[105]

This was not all. Trowbridge continued:

> One man is responsible for the disorders here. This is the *vali* [Governor] himself. He had the power to suppress lawlessness and massacre, but deliberately refrained from doing so. The better class of Turks in Adana, the members of the CUP, are deeply grieved at these dreadful events. Some of them are ready to join us in relief work for the Armenians. One *bey* also has opened his house to the refugees.[106] It is probable that the best elements of Adana will demand the execution of the *vali*.[107]

Cevad Bey may certainly be regarded as a model of uprightness, but, unfortunately, he was also a model of administrative incapacity. He was in no way equal to the demands made upon a governor of Adana. Mustafa Remzi Paşa in his youth had come to the front through his energy, and he always maintained the traditions of honorable patriotism. But it cannot be said that this officer, who was both old (he was of seventy-five years of age) and without any police powers, possessed the qualifications required by the military commander of Adana.[108]

NOBILITY OF THE TURKS OF ADANA

The Boston Daily Globe, in its edition on April 20, 1909, indicated that the Young Turk movement found its strongest adherents among the nobility of the Turks of Adana. The Young Turk committee of Adana had always been considered as the wealthiest branch of the order, having once as much as 450,000 dollars at its disposal. The majority of Turks in Adana were not favorable to fanaticism. It was generally the other Muslim elements who were looking for plunder. The same source draws attention to the fact that Sultan Abdülhamid II around 1897 brought in some fifteen thousand Circassians to the Adana province who were exiled from Caucasia by the Russian government. About 1,500,000 Circassians were bundled out of their homeland by the Russians in the 1860s. About a third or fourth died or were killed on the way, losing everything, and they were settled throughout the Ottoman Empire. These fierce men for years had been wandering through the length and breadth of the Adana plain, living exclusively by pillage and brigandage.[109] The ordinary course of Armenians in the Adana province deteriorated with the arrival of the Circassian refugees. These brought into the region both competition for space and resources and a considerable residue of bitterness about the treatment they had received at the hands of Russians—bitterness that they often took out on the indigenous Christians. The Circassians had been subjected to a program of forced expulsion, deportation, and massacre by the czarist authorities.[110]

Dorothea Chambers Blaisdell agrees with Trowbridge on the subject of some Turks opening their houses to the Armenians and notes that "Subhi Pasha and other Turks had filled their homes as well with frightened people and guarded them from the fanatical crowd."[111]

In the region were many Turks who were on friendly terms with the Armenians. These Turks, at no slight risk to themselves, when the clashes went on, received Armenians into their households and had hidden them there.[112] Some of their houses were vast and contained spacious courtyards. They were in fact fortresses which could be defended by a dozen armed men against a mob almost indefinitely. Hagop Sarkissian, a man of magisterial character and intellect who was an eyewitness to the events in Kilis in 1909, remarked: "A pure blooded Turk is a fair-minded man who can be a true friend and risk his life for you if you are a true friend to him."[113]

Hüseyin Daim, the former commander of the gendarmerie, had from the first worked to help Armenians.[114] More than a thousand found sanctuary in his premises. His conduct was above all praise.[115] He saved many lives to the personal knowledge of British vice consul Charles Doughty-Wylie, and nearly all the houses in his quarter. Hüseyin Daim did this, Dougthy-Wylie believed, by telling the headman of the quarter that the British vice consul would shoot him if anything occurred. After the massacres Doughty-Wylie employed him in the relief camps, and he was finally placed by the government in charge of the Yeni Mahalle camps, and was later in charge of the tents which were still in use. He was also a member of the International Relief Committee and had proved himself an extremely useful and intelligent man. He had been officially thanked by the late M. Roqueferrier, the French consul general at Aleppo, and by the Italian officers.[116]

Tevfik Kadri was in the thick of these events and did his best to warn the Armenians; he repeatedly begged for support for the police, and he was nearly killed on the first day while trying to arrest a Turk who had fired revolver shots in the Armenian quarter. He and his brother Subhi Paşa's house was burned during the massacres, the cry against them being that they were sympathizers with the Christians.[117] In an unnamed village, an ancient gendarme, a Turk, placed himself with his rifle before a large building full of Armenians and defied the mob, which earlier had overpowered the district governor. There he defended the Armenians day and night until relief came. Then he organized a company among the better Turkish elements and sent companies into the mountains to bring in the fugitives from there. He saved six hundred.[118]

This was not the case with the Greeks who had refused to give Armenians shelter. Instead, they sat quietly at home watching what was going on outside and thanking God that they had not been born Armenian. Indeed, there were instances that they handed those Armenians who had tried to find shelter with them over to the mob.[119]

Of all the non-Muslim communities in the region the Armenians alone had openly shown a spirit of opposition to the government. The Greeks and others were law-abiding and contented; they had not the slightest sympathy with the riots, nor had the authorities subjected them to any inconvenience. Many of the influential Christians did not countenance the disturbances, and they expressed their strong disapproval of the action of their coreligionists.

Brothers Subhi and Tevfik Kadri were of the principal family of Adana, which had for long been at enmity with Bağdadizade and İhsan Fikri of *İtidal*. After the massacres Tevfik Kadri was made president of the municipality, as an enlightened, kind-hearted man in whom everybody had confidence. In this capacity he showed great energy and public spirit. Meanwhile his brother was chosen by the Armenians as their president on the Ottoman Commission of Relief. He was highly spoken of for integrity and administrative ability.[120]

Subhi Paşa garnered considerable recognition during his lifetime. He was awarded with the order of Mecidiye in 1910 and became member of the Ottoman Chamber of Deputies for Adana in 1914–1918. A witty and charming man, outgoing and enthusiastic, he was an engaging sort of person. He had private means. He and his brother Tevfik Kadri were men of undoubted patriotism and of marked ability.[121] To date scholars have given little sustained analysis to their roles and activities. They are two under-studied figures in recent Turkish history and both await their biographers.[122]

Trowbridge gave his view of Tekelizade Osman's efforts as follows:

> We conferred with the commandant, who dispatched a captain with orders for Osman Bey and military officers to hasten to the American school with one hundred and fifty troops. After the relief troops had been ordered, I hastened back with the two *zabtiehs* through an armed Turkish mob of from four to five thousand. As we hastened along I called out that my errand was to make peace, and the mob opened up a passage. When we reached the school once more the troops had already arrived and Osman Bey and the colonel were in command of the situation.[123]

Tekelizade Osman was a kindly notable of Adana. His appearance was that of an easy-going elderly gentleman, but he was very alert. He lived in the Armenian quarter of the city. A broad-minded man, he worked honestly and sincerely to stop the massacre. Being indefatigable, upright, and just, he had the respect of all to a remarkable degree. After 1909, Tekelizade Osman remained on the periphery of events.[124]

ARRIVAL OF THE FOREIGN WARSHIPS IN MERSIN

Throughout the clashes, railroad, postal, and telegraphic communications were cut off in the district. It was not until April 17, the fourth day, that one could send or receive news. All these facts show the utter weakness of the provincial government.[125]

On April 18, 1909, the first French warship arrived in Ottoman waters on its way to Mersin, followed by British, Russian, German, American,

Austrian, and Italian vessels. Each cruiser on arrival was saluted in the usual manner, and ceremonial visits were exchanged with the Ottoman officials and the rest of the foreign ships. Aware of the irritation their presence caused among the local population and the authorities, they prudently limited their intervention to the landing of observation missions, to courtesy calls to local officials, and to humanitarian assistance through religious institutions.[126]

As we have seen in the Introduction, the Capitulations granted to European powers did not at all imply protection over the native Christian communities. Nor for that matter were there any direct historical precedents. This is a fact well worth bearing in mind.

Charles Doughty-Wylie had urged that as soon as a man-of-war reached Mersin, a guard, a doctor, and food should be sent to him. The Ottoman minister of foreign affairs, however, earnestly begged that no guard might be sent, as it would irritate the population and be the signal for further disturbances, and the local authorities were ready to guarantee the absolute safety of the British consulate and subjects. He further offered to place a detachment of Ottoman troops at the disposal of the consul if the latter desired it. The British battleship *Swiftsure* landed provisions and medicines intended for Adana.[127]

On April 21, a Muslim commission called on the British vice consul, begging him to prevent the landing of officers and men from the war vessels, as it would have a bad effect on the populace.[128]

In the British House of Commons during the debates held on April 22, 1909, Sir Edward Grey, the foreign secretary, in response to a question by Major Anstruther-Gray as to whether he could make any statement with regard to the present state of affairs in the Ottoman Empire and as to what steps were being taken to protect British life and property in the present crisis, said that he was unable to state what the final settlement at İstanbul would be, but no disturbances had occurred in the last day or two, and a proclamation issued by the investing army expressed that neutral persons would be protected and that foreign embassies and subjects would be unmolested. With regard to other parts of Ottoman territory where disturbances might occur, the Lords Commissioners of the Admiralty had given permission to the British ambassador at İstanbul to arrange directly with the commander-in-chief of the Mediterranean station for the dispatch of ships to any point at which danger to foreigners might be anticipated. Grey continued and indicated that disturbances had occurred at Adana, Mersin, Tarsus, Antakya, and, it was rumored, at Birecik; however, according to their latest intelligence, things appeared to be quiet at all these places now. The only places on the coast at which troubles were anticipated were Mersin, İskenderun, and Beyrout, though order had been maintained at the two latter towns. One of British ships had been sent to each of these three places, and fifty sailors had been landed at İskenderun.[129]

Sir Edward Grey occupied a unique position at the time both in Britain and in the councils of Europe. He had an influence second to none among foreign ministers, and therefore a statement made by him was one which would not fall upon deaf ears. It is, however, to be noted that the British foreign secretary errs in the second point of the last sentence in the preceding paragraph, for the Ottoman government did not allow any British or any other foreign ship to land troops at İskenderun, or, for that matter, at any other Ottoman port during the crisis.[130]

Major Anstruther-Gray asked Sir Edward Grey on April 27, 1909, whether he could make any further statement with regard to the present state of Ottoman affairs in Europe and Asia, and whether British life and property were adequately safeguarded. The foreign secretary replied that he was still unable to say what was likely to happen in the Ottoman Empire, but it was satisfactory to note that foreigners were efficiently protected during the recent fighting in İstanbul. With regard to the provinces, the situation still showed signs of unrest, but it was to be hoped that the authority which had gained full control in İstanbul might have a pacifying influence elsewhere. The disposition of the British ships in Ottoman waters was, in the main, as described in his answer to Anstruther-Gray's question of April 22. The British ship *Triumph* had proceeded from İskenderun to the Antakya coast, to be as near as possible to Antakya, where disturbances had occurred.[131]

The commanders of the foreign warships at the port of İskenderun had under consideration the landing of a force to relieve the besieged town of Dörtyol, but they finally decided that this was wholly impracticable, as they had no right to interfere in a purely internal affair, and the *kaymakam* declined to give his permission to the landing of an armed force. If relieving forces were sent out in opposition to the *kaymakam*'s wishes it was recognized that such an expedition would be equivalent to a declaration of war, and, in addition, the largest commands that the warships could muster would stand in great danger of being overwhelmed if they attempted to force their way against the immense odds which they must meet once beyond the protection of their ships.[132]

On April 24, 1909, Charles Dougthy-Wylie reported to Sir Gerard Lowther, the British ambassador at İstanbul, that Captain C. F. Thursby of the *Swiftsure* accepted his proposal to announce that the Consular Guard was held in readiness to have if required, and only to assist Ottoman authorities. The British vice consul accordingly wrote to the governor of Adana stating that as he had asked him not to land a guard, and as they were extremely unwilling to do anything which could be thought to hinder instead of help the return of tranquility, and as he had every confidence in the Ottoman soldiers whom he had placed at his disposal, he would ask that the guard be not sent to Adana, but that the right to disembark for consular protection was reserved in case of necessity. He suggested to Captain Thursby that an official visit from the captain to the governor of Adana would have a calming effect on the city. Captain Thursby much improved on this by asking the captains of the French and German ships to accompany him, and to make a formal visit together. Captain Thursby, with the captains of the French and German ships, together with French vice consul and American consul, were to arrive to pay official visits. The program was arranged as follows: visits to the governor, military commander, American mission house, the Jesuit Fathers, the French nuns, and the German factory. Two other visits, to the French dragoman's house and the Armenian Catholic bishop, were suggested by the French dragoman. Doughty-Wylie felt bound to oppose both, unless the French captain and vice consul particularly wished for them, as a joint official visit to the Armenians would certainly have been misunderstood, and if the captains visited one dragoman, they would have been expected to visit all, for which there was no time.[133]

By the morning train of May 1 arrived Captain Thursby and the captains of the German and Italian warships, to pay their official visit to the new governor, Babanzade Mustafa Zihni Paşa.[134] The three captains said to the governor that they congratulated him upon his appointment, but that he had arrived at a very difficult time, and they hoped by his efforts tranquility would be restored. They stated that the various interests in the country were solely those of humanity and commerce, but they wished to aid in every possible way the Ottoman government by helping to feed the wounded and hungry, and by endeavoring to restore a little confidence among the homeless persons. They also spoke of several cases which had occurred this last few days of assaults of soldiers, and hoped that stern discipline would be enforced. Babanzade Mustafa Zihni Paşa replied that he would do his very best to help and thanked all friends willing to assist him, and the soldiers in fault would be severely punished. Later on that morning, he also said that in two days' time he hoped to be able to house the greatest part of the people, that those whose houses had been burned would be placed in huts which had already been ordered. Colonel Mehmet Ali Bey, the new military commander, was to organize, assisted by the military police, that no soldiers without passes and not on duty had to be allowed in the city. Both Babanzade Mustafa Zihni Paşa and Mehmet Ali Bey believed implicitly in the existence of an Armenian riot to set up an independent community. They said that they could now prove that the Huntchak Committee had plans (1) to assassinate all the Ottoman officers, (2) to kill the soldiers, (3) to kill as many Muslims as they could, and (4) to make themselves an independent community, under the protection of some foreign power. They stated that Gregorian Bishop Musheg Seropian and Garabet Gökdereliyan were the chiefs, and that there were thirty-four members of the committee, among whom were the three men now in refuge in the British dragoman's house.[135]

The presence of the foreign warships and their hundreds of marines on board had a somewhat quieting effect on the overwrought nerves of the populace, as all came to realize that they were here not merely for the protection of foreigners but to assist the civil authorities, should any need arise, in preserving order in the district.

THE GOVERNMENT'S FIRST STEPS TO RESTORE ORDER

The Ottoman government was emphatic in assurances of its purpose and ability to restore order in the affected localities: new governors were appointed in many of the districts, and troops were sent to the scene of recent or apprehended disorders. The Imperial Ottoman Embassy in London informed Reuter's Agency that eight battalions of reservists left Konya, three battalions of troops of the line belonging to the Second Army Corps, and two battalions from İzmir proceeded by ship and rail to the province of Adana. All the available troops of the Fifth Army Corps were also dispatched to the scene of the disorders.[136]

Until the calm was entirely restored, many Armenians who had remained shut up in houses and stores were lodged in the edifices of the civil and military authorities. Those individuals and families who were deprived of means of support were cared for in some Turkish houses, receiving bread and whatever was necessary to them. When order was finally entirely restored, the offenders and the accused were handed over to be tried by court martial, while the others regained their own fire sides. The Armenians who had sought protection at the foreign consulates—at the moment of the riots—were envoyed under escort to their homes, and for the purpose of protecting from all attack the foreign consulates and the schools and other religious establishments as well as the residences of foreigners—those were while the troubles lasted—guarded by the regular troops and the *zabtiyes*. Certain Armenian families were lodged for protection in the houses of prominent Turks, and wherever the troops and *zabtiyes* failed, it was the Turkish leading men who took their places.

George Gooch asked Sir Edward Grey in the House of Commons on May 18, 1909, what steps were being taken by the Ottoman government and the representatives of the Great Powers to relieve the distress resulting from the massacre of Armenians in Adana and to prevent their recurrence.

The foreign secretary replied that the two battleships of the Mediterranean fleet had visited Mersin and had done what was possible to relieve distress by landing stores and by lending medical assistance. German, Italian, and French warships had also visited the port, and two United States cruisers were proceeding thither. On the first outbreak of disorders the Ottoman government dispatched military tents and provisions to Adana, Grey said, and the Ottoman parliament had voted a sum of twenty thousand Turkish liras for relief work, which, it was believed, was to be regarded as a first installment only. Troops from other towns had been drafted to Adana to prevent the recurrence of disorder, and the governor of the province had been replaced. A court martial had been sent from İstanbul to inquire into the origins of the disturbances and to punish the instigators.[137]

A direct result of the disturbances was the commercial paralysis of Adana and the surrounding areas. What promised to be a wonderfully prosperous year was suddenly turned into one of dismal failure. The large crops of wheat and barley were ready to be harvested, but with the Armenians either killed or too intimitated to work, and the Muslims too gorged with plunder to stoop to labor, it would be difficult to secure the necessary laborers. The destruction of numerous harvesting machines, many of which were new, increased the difficulties of the harvest. All outstanding orders abroad for importations were immediately canceled—orders valued at hundreds of thousands of dollars. Credit abroad ceased. Land values which had been determined in the past decade suddenly fell. All works or improvement ceased. The Baghdad railway construction had been halted. The country in general had received a setback which it would take some time to retrieve.[138]

NOTES

1. "Attack on Armenians," *The Times*, April 16, 1909, p. 3. *The Times* published considerably on Adana, but much of what was printed did not reflect the realities of the period in question.
2. These events are well detailed in İrtem, *Ermeni Meselesinin İçyüzü*, p. 172.
3. Creelman, "Will Christendom Remain Silent?" p. 294.
4. *The Adana Massacres and the Catholic Missionaries*, p. 23.
5. Creelman, "The Slaughter of Christians in Asia Minor," p. 8.
6. Creelman, "Will Christendom Remain Silent?" p. 295.
7. BOA, BEO, No. 3536/265166/1-5. Shooting of the British Vice Consul by the Armenians and Order in Adana, April 18, 1909; Hüseyin Cahid, "Adana Vakası Üzerine" (On Adana Incident), *Tanin*, May 11, 1909, p. 1. See also Stephen van Trowbridge, "Letters from the Scene of the Massacre, Adana, Asia Minor," *The Missionary Review of the World*, Vol. 22 (January–December 1909), p. 599.
8. Creelman, "The Slaughter of Christians in Asia Minor," p. 8.

9. Ibid.

10. FO 424/169. On the Province of Adana. Thomas Jago (Aleppo) to the Marquis of Salisbury (FO), April 18, 1891.

11. Ferriman, *The Young Turks and the Truth about the Holocaust at Adana*, p. 20.

12. MAE, NS Turquie, Vol. 83, p. 116. Note Pour le Ministre au Sujet des Troubles d'Asie Mineure, 12 mai 1909.

13. Trowbridge, "Letters from the Scene of the Massacre, Adana, Asia Minor," p. 599.

14. Ferid Paşa was known as Avlonyalı, after the town in Albania where his family originated. Being grand vizier at the time of the Young Turk revolution in 1908, he resigned on its eve, unable, and perhaps unwilling, to control his Albanian kinsmen who were inveigled into the constitutional movement. He held cabinet positions until 1913 when the CUP achieved a monopoly of power, and then spent the last year of his life in Egypt. For a comprehensive biography of Ferid Paşa, see Kırmızı, *Avlonyalı Ferid Paşa*. Also İnal, *Osmanlı Devrinde Son Sadrazamlar*, Sects. 10 and 11, pp. 1587–653.

15. "Adana'daki Vaziyet" (The Situation in Adana), *Tanin*, May 11, 1909, p. 1.

16. Dragomans in the Ottoman Empire became pivotal in the conduct of embassy and consular affairs in view of their skills in translating and interpreting. They negotiated with Ottoman and European officials, gathered intelligence for their employers, helped to administer consular business, and drafted reports on legal, commercial, and diplomatic matters. Drawn principally from Italian, French, Greek, and Armenian families with longstanding ties to the Levant, and familiar with the intricacies of Ottoman society and institutions, dragomans supposedly had proficiency in the languages of eastern Mediterranean trade and diplomacy—Turkish, Arabic, Italian, French, Greek, and Armenian. See Prousis, *British Consular Reports From the Ottoman Levant in an Age of Upheaval, 1815–1830*, p. 17. Also D. C. M. Platt, *The Cinderella Service: British consuls since 1825* (Hamden, CT: Archon Books, 1971); Lucia Patrizio Gunning, *The British Consular Service in the Aegean and the Collection of Antiquities for the British Museum* (Farnham, Surrey: Ashgate Publishing Limited, 2009), pp. 22 and 25; G. L. Iseminger, "The Old Turkish Hands: The British Levantine Consuls, 1856–76," *The Middle East Journal*, Vol. 22, No. 3 (Summer 1968), pp. 297–316.

17. USNA, RG 84 Records of Foreign Service Posts, Diplomatic Posts Turkey, Vol. 216, From Consulates 1 January 1909–30 June 1909 American Embassy Istanbul. Copy of the Report of the British Vice Consul Charles Doughty-Wylie from Adana, April 21, 1909.

18. Ibid.

19. Creelman, "The Slaughter of Christians in Asia Minor," p. 8.

20. Ibid., pp. 3–4.

21. USNA, RG 84 Records of Foreign Service Posts, Diplomatic Posts Turkey, Vol. 216, From Consulates 1 January 1909–30 June 1909 American Embassy Istanbul. Disturbances in Adana, Tarsus and Vicinity. Edward Nathan (Mersin) to John Leishman (Istanbul), May 11, 1909.

22. Creelman, "The Slaughter of Christians in Asia Minor," p. 5. See also BOA, BEO, No. 3536/265166/1-5. Shooting of the British Vice Consul by the Armenians and Order in Adana, April 18, 1909.

23. Simonyan, *The Destruction of Armenians in Cilicia, April 1909*, p. 47.
24. A. F. Aflalo, *Regilding Crescent* (London: G. Bell, 1911), p. 42.
25. USNA, RG 84 Records of Foreign Service Posts, Diplomatic Posts Turkey, Vol. 216, From Consulates 1 January 1909–30 June 1909 American Embassy Istanbul. Copy of the Report of the British Vice Consul Charles Doughty-Wylie from Adana, April 21, 1909.
26. Charles Woods, " Capitulations and Christian Privileges in Turkey," *The Contemporary Review*, Vol. CXXI (December 1922), p. 699. This subject is discussed in more detail in the Introduction.
27. Georgina Howell, *Daughter of the Desert: The Remarkable Life of Gertrude Bell* (London: Macmillan, 2006), p. 240.
28. Creelman, "Will Christendom Remain Silent?" p. 296.
29. H. V. F. Winstone, *Gertrude Bell: A Biography* (London: Barzan Publishing, second revised edition, 2004), p. 185.
30. Aubrey Herbert, Desmond MacCarthy, ed., *Ben Kendim: A Record of Eastern Travels* (London: Hutchinson and Company, 1924), p. xiv.
31. H. C. G. Matthew and Brian Harrison, eds., *Oxford Dictionary of National Biography*, Vol. 60 (Oxford: Oxford University Press, 2004), pp. 645–46.
32. Colonel Yate's remarks in House of Commons Debate, Vol. 32, cc 43–165, November 27, 1911.
33. Woods, *The Danger Zone of Europe*, pp. 133–34; Creelman, "Will Christendom Remain Silent?" p. 296.
34. Creelman, "Will Christendom Remain Silent?" pp. 296 and 298.
35. MAE, NS Turquie, Vol. 83, p. 114. Note Pour le Ministre au Sujet des Troubles d'Asie Mineure, 12 mai 1909.
36. "Détails rétrospectifs à Adana," *Le Moniteur Oriental*, 14 mai 1909, p. 1.
37. BOA, DH. MKT, No. 2826/108. Situation at Adana and in Adjacent Districts. Cevad Bey (Adana) to the Ministry of the Interior, April 17, 1909; USNA, RG 84 Records of Foreign Service Posts, Diplomatic Posts Turkey, Vol. 216, From Consulates 1 January 1909–30 June 1909 American Embassy Istanbul. Copy of the Report of the British Vice Consul Charles Doughty-Wylie from Adana, April 24, 1909.
38. USNA, RG 84 Records of Foreign Service Posts, Diplomatic Posts Turkey, Vol. 216, From Consulates 1 January 1909–30 June 1909 American Embassy Istanbul. Disturbances in Adana, Tarsus and Vicinity. Edward Nathan (Mersin) to John Leishman (Istanbul), May 11, 1909.
39. Terzian, *Cilicia 1909*, p. 139.
40. See, for instance, Ferriman, *The Young Turks and the Truth about the Holocaust at Adana*, p. 33; and Brézol, *Les Turcs ont passé là*, p. 335.
41. MAE, NS Turquie, Vol. 85, p. 192. Nouveau Mutasarrıf de Mersine. M. Grapin (Mersine) à Raymond Poincaré (Paris), 11 juillet 1912; MAE, NS Turquie, Vol. 85, p. 209. Changement du Vali. M. Grapin (Mersine) à Raymond Poincaré (Paris), 20 septembre 1912.
42. On Selim Rauf Sarper, see Hamid Aral, ed., *Dışişleri Bakanlığı 1967 Yıllığı* (1967 Annual of the Ministry of Foreign Affairs) (Ankara: Ankara Basım ve Ciltevi,

1968), pp. 159–60; Güçlü, *Zeki Kuneralp and the Turkish Foreign Service*, pp. 263–64.

43. On more Asaf Bey, see chapter 6.

44. BOA, DH. MKT, No. 2826/95. Situation at İskenderun. Asaf Bey (Cebelibereket) to the Ministry of the Interior, April 16, 1909; BOA, DH. MKT, No. 2826/108. Situation at Adana and in Adjacent Districts. Cevad Bey (Adana) to the Ministry of the Interior, April 17, 1909; BOA, DH. MKT, No. 2826/140. Situation at Adana and in Adjacent Districts. Ministry of the Interior to the Ministry of War, April 19, 1909.

45. ABCFM Papers, Houghton Library, Harvard University. Unit 5 (ABC 16.9.5) Reel 660. Vol. 15 Central Turkey Mission 1900–1909 Documents Minutes Reports Tabular Views ABC 16: The Near East 1817–1919. Stephen van Trowbridge, The Sack of Kessab, June 21, 1909.

46. Ibid.; MAE, NS Turquie, Vol. 83, p. 162. A.s. de Mehmed Ali Aini. Maurice Bompard (Istanbul) à Stéphane Pichon (Paris), 11 août 1909; Brézol, *Les Turcs ont passé là*, p. 78.

47. Mehmet Ali Ayni, İsmail Dervişoğlu, ed., *Hatıralar* (Memoirs) (İstanbul: Yeditepe Yayınevi, reprinted, 2009), pp. 96–100. Last of the author's many books, these memoirs contain some information not to be found elsewhere.

48. "Adana Hadisatı" (Adana Events), *Tanin*, May 19, 1909, p. 1.

49. Nezih Neyzi, *Osmanlılıktan Cumhuriyet'e Kızıltoprak Anıları* (From the Ottomanness to the Republic: Recollections of Kızıltoprak) (İstanbul: Türkiye İş Bankası Kültür Yayınları, second revised and expanded edition, 2016), p. 126.

50. For Mehmet Ali Ayni's life and career, see Çankaya, *Mülkiye Tarihi ve Mülkiyeliler*, Vol. 3, pp. 294–300; Orhun, Kasaroğlu, Belek, Atakul, *Meşhur Valiler*, pp. 293–307; Ali Kemali Aksüt, *Profesör Mehmet Ali Ayni: Hayatı ve Eserleri* (Professor Mehmet Ali Ayni: His Life and Works) (İstanbul: Ahmet Sait Matbaası, 1944); Neyzi, *Osmanlılıktan Cumhuriyet'e*, pp. 124–29; Ali Neyzi, *Meyzi ile Neyzi* (Meyzi With Neyzi) (İstanbul: Karacan Yayınları, 1983); Öztürk and Yıldız, *İmparatorluk Tarihinin Kalemli Muhafızları*, pp. 293–94.

51. Brézol, *Les Turcs sont passé là*, pp. 48 and 78.

52. MAE, NS Turquie, Vol. 83, p. 116. Note Pour le Ministre au Sujet des Troubles d'Asie Mineure, 12 mai 1909.

53. Çalyan, "Adana Vakası ve Mesulleri," p. 82.

54. Billings, "The Causes of the Outbreak in Cilicia, Asia Minor, April, 1909," pp. 13–16.

55. Brézol, *Les Turcs ont passé là*, p. 64.

56. Billings, "The Causes of the Outbreak in Cilicia, Asia Minor, April, 1909," p. 16.

57. ABCFM Papers, Unit 5 (ABC 16.9.5) Reel 660. Vol. 15 Central Turkey Mission 1900–1909 Documents Minutes Reports Tabular Views ABC 16: The Near East 1917–1919. Letter From Maraş, May 13, 1909.

58. Minas Kojayan, "The Chork-Marzban/Dörtyol Armenians: Three Episodes of Self-Defense," in Hovannisian, *Armenian Communities of the Northeastern Mediterranean*, pp. 339–40.

59. Ibid., pp. 340–41.

60. Ibid., pp. 341–42.

61. Billings, "The Causes of the Outbreak in Cilicia, Asia Minor, April 1909," p. 16.

62. Shepard, "Personal Experience in Turkish Massacres and Relief Work," pp. 329–30.

63. Ibid., p. 330.

64. Dorothea Chambers Blaisdell, *Missionary Daughter: Witness to the End of the Ottoman Empire* (La Vergne, TN: 1st Book Library, 2002), p. 67. This dramatic personal narrative is a notable contribution to understand past events in Adana. These recollections of the daughter of the American missionary William Nesbitt Chambers reveal little known aspects of some events in Cilicia in the early twentieth century, give valuable insights to their background, and describe inter-relationships with the Western world. Those perceptions are woven into the story of the author's protracted experiences.

65. MAE, NS Turquie, Vol. 83, p. 114, Note Pour le Ministre au Sujet des Troubles d'Asie Mineure, 12 mai 1909; MAE, NS Turquie, Vol. 84, p. 48. Distinctions accordées à l'occasion des évènements de Cilicie. Maurice Bompard (Istanbul) à Stéphane Pichon (Paris), 28 avril 1910; Creelman, "The Slaughter of Christians in Asia Minor," p. 8.

66. FO 424/219. Summary of the Debate in the Chamber of Deputies on the Adana Massacres, Sir Gerard Lowther (Istanbul) to Sir Edward Grey (FO), May 4, 1909. Enclosure in No. 341.

67. Ibid; *Meclisi Mebusan Zabıt Ceridesi* (Proceedings of the Chamber of Deputies), Vol. 3 (Ankara: Türkiye Büyük Millet Meclisi Basımevi, 1982), pp. 108–9.

68. FO 424/219. Summary of the Debate in the Chamber of Deputies on the Adana Massacres, Sir Gerard Lowther (Istanbul) to Sir Edward Grey (FO), May 4, 1909. Enclosure in No. 341; *Meclisi Mebusan Zabıt Ceridesi*, Vol. 3, pp. 109–19, 127, 131, and 135.

69. A Correspondent, *The Armenian Troubles and Where the Responsibility Lies* (New York: J. J. Little and Co., 1895), p. 6.

70. "The Outbreaks in Asia Minor," *The Times*, April 20, 1909, p. 5.

71. "Thousands Dead, Hub Asked to Aid," *The Boston Daily Globe*, April 19, 1909, p. 3.

72. *Meclisi Mebusan Zabıt Ceridesi*, Vol. 3, pp. 69–71.

73. Miss Wallace was a British nurse connected with American mission work in the Ottoman Empire.

74. Frederick W. Macallum was sent to the Ottoman Empire by the ABCFM.

75. ABCFM Papers, Library of Congress Manuscript Division 87/257 Unit 5 (ABC 16.9.5), Reel 665, Letter from Stephen van Trowbridge to "Dear Friends," Boston, April 19, 1909, Adana.

76. "Blames Armenians; Turkish Foreign Office Lays Entire Blame on Them for Killing of American Missionaries," *The Boston Daily Globe*, April 20, 1909, p. 6.

77. ABCFM Papers, Library of Congress Manuscript Division 87/257 Unit 5 (ABC 16.9.5), Reel 665, Letter from Stephen van Trowbridge to William Peet, Bible House, Istanbul, April 20, 1909, Adana.

78. ABCFM Papers, Library of Congress Manuscript Division 87/257 Unit 5 (ABC 16.9.5), Reel 665, Letter from Stephen van Trowbridge to William Peet, Bible House, Istanbul, April 23, 1909, Adana.

79. USNA, RG 84 Records of Foreign Service Posts, Diplomatic Posts Turkey, Vol. 216, From Consulates 1 January–30 June 1909 American Embassy Istanbul. Copy of the Report of the British Vice Consul Charles Doughty-Wylie from Adana, April 21, 1909.

80. Creelman, "The Red Terror on the Cilician Plain," p. 8.

81. Centre des Archives Diplomatiques de Nantes (CADN), 1 SL/IV/154. Verdict de la justice militaire française condamnant l'archevêque Moushegh Séropian, 23 avril 1920.

82. Sahara, *What Happened in Adana in April 1909?* pp. 116–17.

83. Kodaman and Ünal, *Son Vakanüvis Abdurrahman Şeref Efendi Tarihi*, pp. 84–85; Woods, *The Danger Zone of Europe*, pp. 135–36.

84. Simonyan, *The Destruction of Armenians in Cilicia, April 1909*, p. 64.

85. MAE, NS Turquie, Vol. 83, p. 115. Note Pour le Ministre au Sujet des Troubles d'Asie Mineure, 12 mai 1909.

86. Arıkoğlu, *Hatıralarım*, p. 54.

87. See Bourne and Watt, British Documents on Foreign Affairs, Part I, Series B, Vol. 20, p. 145.

88. Phillip Graves, *Briton and Turk* (London: Hutchinson and Company, 1941), p. 135.

89. Woods, *The Danger Zone of Europe*, p. 138.

90. "Adana Hadisatı" (Adana Events), *Tanin*, May 26, 1909, p. 1.

91. Creelman, "The Red Terror on the Cilician Plain," p. 8.

92. An intelligible summary of all this is in Arıkoğlu, *Hatıralarım*, pp. 48–49; Kodaman and Ünal, *Son Vakanüvis Abdurrahman Şeref Efendi Tarihi*, pp. 83–84 and 112–13; Woods, *The Danger Zone of Europe*, pp. 138–39.

93. Kodaman and Ünal, *Son Vakanüvis Abdurrahman Şeref Efendi Tarihi*, pp. 119–20.

94. FO 195/2363. Annual Report on Turkey for the Year 1909. Sir Gerard Lowther (Istanbul) to Sir Edward Grey (FO), February 7, 1910.

95. USNA, RG 84 Records of Foreign Service Posts, Diplomatic Posts Turkey, Vol. 216, From Consulates 1 January 1909–30 June 1909 American Embassy Istanbul. Copy of the Report of the British Vice Consul Charles Doughty-Wylie from Adana, April 21, 1909.

96. USNA, RG 84 Records of Foreign Service Posts, Diplomatic Posts Turkey, Vol. 216, From Consulates 1 January 1909–30 June 1909 American Embassy Istanbul. Disturbances in Adana, Tarsus and Vicinity. Edward Nathan (Mersin) to John Leishman (Istanbul), May 11, 1909.

97. Edwin Pears, "Turkey: Developments and Forecasts," *The Contemporary Review*, Vol. XCV, No. 6 (June 1909), p. 708.

98. "Woman Describes Riot at Adana," *The New York Times*, May 3, 1909, p. 5; "Missionary at Adana Tells of Fearful Scenes; Woman Vividly Describes Turkish Massacres; Incendiary Fires Add to Horror of Revolution," *Los Angeles Herald*, May 3, 1909, p. 1.

99. "Adana Massacre Still Unchecked," *The Chicago Daily Tribune*, April 28, 1909, p. 4; "Days of Horror Described; American Missionary an Eyewitness of Murder and Rapine," *The New York Times*, April 28, 1909, p. 3.

100. USNA, RG 84 Records of Foreign Service Posts, Diplomatic Posts Turkey, Vol. 216, From Consulates 1 January 1909–30 June 1909 American Embassy Istanbul. Edward Nathan (Mersin) to John Leishman (Istanbul), May 9, 1909.

101. Ibid., May 11, 1909.

102. Arıkoğlu, *Hatıralarım*, pp. 47–49.

103. "Tales of Adana," *The Literary Digest*, Vol. 39, No. 5 (July 31, 1909), pp. 166–67.

104. USNA, RG 84 Records of Foreign Service Posts, Diplomatic Posts Turkey, Vol. 216, From Consulates 1 January 1909–30 June 1909 American Embassy Istanbul. Disturbances in Adana, Tarsus and Vicinity. Edward Nathan (Mersin) to John Leishman (Istanbul), May 11, 1909.

105. "Killed 23,000 Armenians; Turks in Adana Province Had Heavy Losses; Struggle for Supremacy Is Vividly Described," *The Boston Globe*, May 6, 1909, p. 9.

106. The use of the word "refugee" is incorrect as no Armenians were moved outside the boundaries of the Ottoman Empire, but were left homeless or resettled within them.

107. "Stephen Trowbridge Blames the Vali Chiefly," *The Boston Daily Globe*, April 27, 1909, p. 7; "Pestilence Adds to Asia Minor Horrors," *The Philadelphia Inquirer*, April 30, 1909, p. 6.

108. Djemal Pasha, *Memories of a Turkish Statesman 1913–1919*, p. 259.

109. Adana A Large Province, pp. 1 and 6.

110. Donald Bloxham, "The Armenian Genocide of 1915–1916: Cumulative Radicalization and the Development of a Destruction Policy," *Past and Present*, No. 181 (November 2003), p. 148.

111. Blaisdell, *Missionary Daughter*, p. 64.

112. Terzian, *Cilicia 1909*, p. vii; Ferriman, *The Young Turks and the Truth about the Holocaust at Adana*, p. 23.

113. Sutherland, *The Adventures of an Armenian Boy*, p. xi.

114. MAE, NS Turquie, Vol. 83, p. 164. Sujet du Vali d'Adana. Barré de Lancy (Mersine) à Stéphane Pichon (Paris), 30 août 1909; Çalyan, "Adana Vakası ve Mesulleri," p. 82.

115. "Aprés la Tragédie d'Adana," *Le Moniteur Oriental*, 15 juillet 1909, p. 2.

116. FO 195/2037. Hüseyin Daim's Effort. Charles Doughty-Wylie (Adana) to Sir Gerard Lowther (Istanbul), August 10, 1909.

117. Ibid.

118. Billings, "The Causes of the Outbreak in Cilicia, Asia Minor, April, 1909," pp. 13–14.
119. Simonyan, *The Destruction of Armenians in Cilicia, April 1909*, p. 47; Brézol, *Les Turcs sont passé là*, p. 22.
120. FO 195/2037. Hüseyin Daim's Effort. Charles Dougthy-Wylie (Adana) to Sir Gerard Lowther (Istanbul), August 10, 1909; Kasım Ener, *Çukurova Kurtuluş Savaşında Adana Cephesi* (Adana Front in the War of Liberation of Çukurova) (Adana: Türkiye Kuvayı Milliye Mücahit ve Gazileri Cemiyeti Yayınları, 1970), p. 286; Mahmut Yüksel Canbaz and İbrahim Kılıç, eds., *Kuvayı Milliye Komutanı Tekelioğlu Sinan Bey'in Günlüğü* (Diary of the Commander of the National Forces Tekelioğlu Sinan Bey) (Ankara: Genelkurmay Personel Başkanlığı Askeri Tarih ve Stratejik Etüt Dairesi Başkanlığı Yayınları, 2012), p. 125n72.
121. BOA, BEO, No. 3709/278153. Awarding of Mecidiye Order to Subhi Paşa, February 27, 1910; BOA, Dosya Usulu İradeler Tasnifi (File Method Imperial Decisions Classification) (henceforth referred to as DUİT), No. 62/20. Awarding of Mecidiye Order to Subhi Paşa, October 21, 1917; BOA, DH. Kalem-i Mahsus (Private Cabinet of the Minister), No. 45/57. Awarding of Mecidiye Order to Subhi Paşa, October 28, 1917; "Adanalıların Bir Feryadı Muhikki" (A Justified Cry of the People of Adana), *Hadisat*, December 13, 1918, p. 1.
122. Oral history can make a contribution in the reconstruction of the lives of Subhi Paşa and Tevfik Kadri Bey. Admittedly there are problems with interviews, particularly when these are gathered several decades later, when the memory of those interviewed has been affected by consequent events and experiences. Nevertheless interviews can be checked against other evidence and other interviews for corroboration.
123. Trowbridge, "Letters from the Scene of the Massacre, Adana, Asia Minor," p. 602.
124. Brézol, *Les Turcs ont passé là*, p. 20.
125. Trowbridge, "Letters from the Scene of the Massacre, Adana, Asia Minor," p. 602.
126. Raymond Kévorkian, "The Cilician Massacres, 1909," in Richard Hovannisian and Simon Payaslian, eds., *Armenian Cilicia* (Costa Mesa, CA: Mazda Publishers, 2008), p. 347.
127. FO 424/219. The Situation at Adana. Sir Gerard Lowther (Istanbul) to Sir Edward Grey (FO), April 28, 1909.
128. *The Adana Massacres and the Catholic Missionaries*, p. 52.
129. House of Commons Debates, Vol. 3, cc 1653-4, April 22, 1909.
130. BOA, DH. MKT, No. 2808/48. Information Supplied to the British Commander-in-Chief of the Mediterranean Station and to the British Vice Consul at Mersin by the Governor of Adana. Mustafa Zihni Paşa (Adana) to the Ministry of the Interior, May 11, 1909.
131. House of Commons Debates, Vol. 4, cc 168–9, April 27, 1909.
132. "Cannot Send Help to Besieged Town; Turks Refuse Foreign Warships Permission to Land Force to Save Starving Thousands," *The New York Times*, April 27, 1909, p. 2.

133. USNA, RG 84 Records of Foreign Service Posts, Diplomatic Posts Turkey, Vol. 216, From Consulates 1 January 1909–30 June 1909 American Embassy Istanbul. Copy of the Report of the British Vice Consul Charles Doughty-Wylie from Adana, April 24, 1909.

134. For Babanzade Mustafa Zihni Paşa, see İbrahim Alaettin Gövsa, *Türk Meşhurları Ansiklopedisi* (Encyclopedia of Famous Turks) (İstanbul: Yedigün Yayınları, 1946), p. 57; and Sinan Kuneralp, *Son Dönem Osmanlı Erkan ve Ricali Prosopografik Rehber (1839–1922)* (The Late Period Ottoman Statesmen and Officialdom [1839–1922]) (İstanbul: İSİS, 1999), pp. 10 and 102.

135. USNA, RG 84 Records of Foreign Service Posts, Diplomatic Posts Turkey, Vol. 216, From Consulates 1 January 1909–30 June 1909 American Embassy Istanbul. Copy of the Report of the British Vice Consul Charles Dougthy-Wylie from Adana, May 1, 1909.

136. Reuter's Agency, April 22, 1909.

137. House of Commons Debates, Vol. 5, c 382W, May 18, 1909.

138. USNA, RG 84 Records of Foreign Service Posts, Diplomatic Posts Turkey, Vol.216, From Consulates 1 January 1909–30 June 1909 American Embassy Istanbul. Disturbances in Adana, Tarsus and Vicinity. Edward Nathan (Mersin) to John Leishman (Istanbul), May 11, 1909.

Cemal Bey, Governor of Adana, 1909–1911

Cemal Bey, Governor of Adana, 1909–1911

Cemal Bey, Governor of Adana, 1909–1911

Cemal Bey, Governor of Adana, 1909–1911

Cemal Bey, Governor of Baghdad, 1911–1912

Cemal Bey, Governor of Baghdad, 1911–1912

Cemal Paşa, Minister of Marine Inspecting the Naval College in Heybeliada/İstanbul, 1914

Cemal Paşa, Minister of Marine Visiting the French Fleet at Toulon, 1914

Cemal Paşa with His Aides-de-Camp in Kabil, 1922

Cemal Paşa with Turkish Officers at His Command in Kabil, 1922

Cemal Paşa's Funeral Ceremony in Kabil, July 1922

Cemal Paşa's Wife Seniha Cemal with Family Members

Hüseyin Hilmi Paşa, Minister of the Interior and Grand Vizier, 1908–1909

Ferid Paşa, Minister of the Interior, 1909

Mahmud Şevket Paşa, Minister of War
and Grand Vizier, 1909 and 1912–1913

Talat Bey, Vice President of the Chamber of Deputies, 1908–1909

Talat Bey, Minister of the Interior, 1909–1911 and 1913–1918

Talat Paşa, Grand Vizier, 1917–1918

Sultan Reşad, 1909–1918

Chapter Five

Responsibility for the Outrages

Very salient differences emerge on the question of the responsibility for the outrages. Much of the responsibility rested on the Armenian committees and revolutionary societies established notably in Europe and the United States. The steps they took were fraught with trouble and danger to the very people they wanted to help. Agents from abroad returned to Asia Minor and went from village to village stirring up the people to rebellion, distributing arms or the materials for making them, and urging the villagers to rise and sacrifice themselves for the causes of Christianity and Armenian nation, and thus to force the hand of Europe to intervene on their behalf. The result was that the committees in Geneva, London, or New York were able to point to further horrors and excesses on the part of the Muslims, and adduce additional reasons for the Armenians to be protected, but that was but consolation to the suffering people in the Ottoman Empire where homes were destroyed and where people were left destitute, sullen, and only vaguely thankful at having escaped death.[1]

Rıza Tevfik (Bölükbaşı),[2] deputy for Edirne, declared in a conversation that the responsibility for the Adana events was also equally incumbent upon the Armenians. He added that Krikor Zohrab, deputy for İstanbul, had already admitted this truth. The leader of the older reform section of the CUP, Rıza Tevfik was a well-known writer of political history and philosophy. Zohrab, replying in *Azadamard*, said that he considered Rıza Tevfik as the first—and not the last—liberal among the Muslim deputies; he held Rıza Tevfik as an intellectual and a scholar. It was him who, during the first session of the Chamber of Deputies, had dared to state that religion was a matter of conscience. Zohrab still heard the cries of protest and insults that Rıza Tevfik's word had aroused, but he thought that it was his duty to correct what his Turkish colleague uttered on the Armenian question. Zohrab argued as follows. From the law and conscience point of view the whole responsibility for the Adana massacres fell on the Muslim population. No one could question it. The Armenians had seen the proclamation of the Ottoman Constitution as the proclamation of an effective equality. In that, they were mistaken. He believed Islam did not accept political equality between Muslims and Christians. If the centuries-old social state of affairs were added to this, one would then very easily understand that the Muslims—despite all their good will—could not renounce immediately the idea of being the dominant element over the non-Muslim peoples. Only time could imperceptibly change this state of affairs. Upon the proclamation of the constitution the Armenians of Adana believed that they began to enjoy absolute equality. Their words and their acts inspired by this idea provoked the amazement and fury of all the Muslims without exception. Muslims wrongly maintained that they were under the domination of Armenians due to the sole reason that the Armenians were considered equal to Muslims.[3]

This is questionable. Zohrab's statement was a mass of inaccuracies, and it was a feeble effort on his part to prove his kinsmen guiltless of their separatist activities. He was a short story writer, novelist, editor, attorney, and member of the Armenian National Assembly. Being a member of the Ottoman Chamber of Deputies from 1908 to 1915, he was very active in political affairs.

BISHOP MUSHEG SEROPIAN'S UNRULY AGITATION

Cemal Paşa, who was appointed governor of Adana at the beginning of August 1909, three and a half months after the occurrences, deftly reveals in his memoirs that after the promulgation of the constitution Bishop Musheg Seropian regarded himself as the religious and political head of Adana, took advantage of the weakness of the governorate, adopted a most insulting attitude toward Cevad Bey at a meeting of the Administrative Council, and left the assembly in a furious rage after threatening to box the ears of the gendarmie colonel for the province. But the bishop was not content with all this. He sent to Europe for rifles and revolvers with which to arm the Armenians.[4]

Cemal Paşa effectively illustrates that it is at this point that the heavy responsibility of the governorate of Adana began. When Seropian's unruly agitation began to have its evil influence on the local population the safest conduct would have been at once to arrest him and his adherents, and also any Turks who seemed likely to promote disorder, hold a legal investigation without delay, and, if necessary, threaten the province with martial law. Cemal Paşa's personal opinion is that Seropian was the real culprit, but his responsibility was almost shared by Cevad Bey, who must have realized what a danger this man represented and yet did not take the necessary steps to avert it.[5]

In his journey among the destroyed villages in Cilicia James Creelman asked many Turks to explain how it came about that in a single day the people of a prosperous farming country could change into "wild beasts." The answer was invariably that the Armenians intended to rise in arms and establish an independent kingdom, and that it was only fair that loyal Turks should defend themselves. Here and there a Muslim spoke of photographs representing Armenians dressed as kings, princes, or armed warriors.[6]

OPINION OF SOME ARMENIAN HISTORIANS ON THE EVENTS

Sarkis Atamian maintains that the exact occurrences and their causes in Adana in 1909 have always remained intensely controversial. According to him, there is voluminous evidence of the massacres in which both sides of the story are exaggerated. It was his conviction that the Muslim mobs, who saw some of their prerogatives curtailed by the new regime, probably grew apprehensive over the loss of their former status of superiority over the Armenians. The Armenians, on the other hand, probably threw their former caution to the winds in their newfound freedom.[7]

Hagop Sarkissian advances that in 1909 the Armenian revolutionary committees were especially active in the Armenian schools trying to make the boys "freedom conscious." They had so many revolutionary activities in the Central Turkey College in Ayntab that an American missionary by the name of William Goodell forbade the Armenian boys at the college, who constituted 100 percent of the students, to read revolutionary books. This situation resulted in the revolt of the student body, who attacked and beat some of the teachers whom they considered informers and traitors. Consequently, the college was ordered closed by its president and all of the students were sent home. Before they left the school the students broke all the windows and damaged the college building to a great extent. Sarkissian draws attention to the fact that this incident happened a short time before the outbreak of events in Adana and he concludes there may be a strong relationship between the revolutionary movement of the Armenian secret committees and the massacre which followed.[8]

Aram Arkun argues that the return of Armenian exiles to Cilicia after the constitutional restoration, the influx of seasonal Armenian agricultural laborers, the settlement of embittered Muslim refugees from the Balkans, and the exacerbation of famine conditions in 1908–1909 had already created tensions between Armenians and Muslims. Rumors began to spread that Armenians intended to create their own kingdom.[9]

Bedross Der Matossian shows that Adana was an economic hub to which migrant workers flowed from the towns of eastern provinces, complicating the ethnic makeup of the city. A microcosm of the Ottoman industrial and agricultural economy, Adana housed thousands of Muslim migrant laborers, half as many Armenian migrants, in a world dominated at the top by foreign and Christian (Greek and Armenian) textile plants.[10] Every spring about thirty thousand to forty thousand migratory workers would come to Adana from Aleppo, Harput, Sivas, Diyarbekir, Erzurum, Hacin, Bitlis, and Bayburt to work in factories or as farmers, tilling, reaping, and cultivating in the cotton fields.[11]

According to Avedis Sanjian, it is certain that the relative prosperity of the Armenians of Cilicia, the activities of the revolutionaries in the region, and the general jubilation of the Armenian population over the establishment of the new Ottoman constitutional regime had incited the hostilities of the local Turks, whether Hamidian or Young Turk, against the growing spirit of Armenian nationalism.[12]

Hrachik Simonyan indicates that some Cilician Armenians adorned the walls of their homes with pictures of national heroes of ancient centuries painted with vivid romanticism. Some Armenian figures did not properly weigh what they were saying and writing. According to Simonyan, the ostentatious course, arrogant statements, and boastful advertising agent behavior of Armenian political groups left a disagreeable impression upon their Muslim neighbors.[13]

Several contemporary sources offer compatible views on the causes of the violence. A few examples will suffice.

İSMAİL SAFA ÖZLER SETS THE RECORD STRAIGHT, APRIL 20, 1909

İsmail Safa (Özler),[14] deputy editor-in-chief of the Adana daily *İtidal* and an active and energetic officer in the provincial government, followed the local events with insight and observation. He was educated in European manners and customs. After the proclamation of the constitution, he began to take part in public life. He was far-sighted and perfectly understood the troubles which were agitating Cilicia in his day. Özler gave one the impression of possessing a strong character and considerable intellectual force, with ideas well in advance of those of his colleagues in other parts of the country. The depth of his convictions gave him a moral self-confidence that served to enhance his character. He was tall and slender, and his appearance suggested that of a college professor.

The April 20, 1909, issue of the *İtidal* presented some very strong articles on vital themes, and it deserved careful and wide reading. Özler set the record straight in this issue and laid the responsibility for the incidents that had taken place on the Armenians, accusing them of having revolted against the lawful authorities. He wrote:

> How sad that the upsurge of anger and the [desire] for independence that had stirred and then put down roots in the depths of the Armenians' heart should have led to the ruin of the region . . . ! Let us have a look at this insurrection that has condemned the inhabitants of Adana to dire poverty. Like the Turks, the Armenians were, during the thirty-three years of a tyrannical rule, crushed under tyranny's hellish burden; they raised their voices in protest. When the Ottomans entered a magnificent period of happiness and peace, the Armenians ceased to protest [literally: they shut their mouths] and cry out for revenge and, as equals with us, applauded our sacred revolution. But that was soon over, and they began preparing their own project. Sometimes, they created tensions by putting on dissatisfied expressions and making it understood that they could not possibly live alongside Muslims. [. . .] Our demand for unity and mutual understanding was not enough to stem their dangerous inclinations and this led to a difference in the Turks' and the Armenians' ways of looking at things. [. . .] The Armenians worked virtually without pause to acquire what they lacked, and devoted a great deal of effort to arming themselves. At market and or in the public squares, the Armenians even outdid each other in purchasing Martinis, Mausers and other weapons of battle. After they had stockpiled such weapons, they lost their traditional restraint. [. . .] They brazenly made threats of this sort: "one of these days, we shall massacre the Turks; we are no longer afraid; the old wounds are still bleeding." Thus they provoked the Turks as a way of casting off their own responsibility. The Turks, however, accepting and obeying the advice of their great men, who preached appeasement, sought to avoid incidents of all kinds. The Armenians, observing the unbearable silence and patience displayed by the Muslims planned to commit various crimes in defiance of the law. [. . .] The fact that the state was not sufficiently powerful engendered fear and alarm among the Turks; among the Armenians, it was a source of strength and courage.[15]

There was much truth in this barbed comment. Özler's instincts, and his reading of Armenian intentions, were sound. A number of newspapers appeared in Adana after the 1908 revolution, many of which were short-lived and of limited significance. Among those which were politically important, it is possible to mention *İtidal*, *Rehberi İtidal*, *Teceddüt*, and *Anadolu*. They dealt with a variety of subjects but paid particular attention to political affairs.

These newspapers had an audience among the educated classes. They served as a forum for the discussion of current issues and had considerable influence on the opinions of their readers.¹⁶

AMERICAN CONSUL EDWARD NATHAN'S REPORT, MAY 9, 1909

Edward Nathan, the perspicacious and broad-minded American consul at Mersin, reported to John Leishman, ambassador at İstanbul, that the cause of the disturbances was given as the killing of a Turk by an Armenian, but that disturbances of this magnitude had deeper-lying causes. It appeared that since the proclamation of the constitution, the prohibition against the sale of deadly weapons had been disregarded, and Armenians had purchased large quantities of arms. Nathan wrote that many Armenians had begun to boast that they were no longer afraid of Turks, and to talk of autonomy and independence. The Gregorian Armenian bishop of Adana was said to have openly preached armed resistance. Various secret societies—chiefly Huntchaks, a branch of which existed in the United States—furthered this movement of agitation. In Nathan's opinion, it could be affirmed that the Armenians had provoked Turkish hostility; the charge of any complicity of the local Ottoman authorities was not proved, but it was certain that they had been woefully negligent in not suppressing the movement at its inception and preventing it from attaining its magnitude.¹⁷

AMERICAN CONSUL GENERAL GABRIEL BIE RAVNDAL'S DISPATCHES, MAY 10–11, 1909

In a dispatch dated May 10, 1909, Gabriel Bie Ravndal, the American consul general in Beirut, informed his superiors that the aspirations of revolutionary Armenians had waxed rapidly since the proclamation of the constitution. He noted fresh activity by Huntchak and Troshag committees, and that the Central Turkey College at Ayntab recently had been closed by the faculty to regain control of the institution, which had become a hotbed of Armenian revolutionary propaganda. At Kessab, Adana, and other places, Armenian revolutionaries had gradually become irritatingly overbearing and arrogant. At Adana, they could be heard at night singing their national war songs and "foolishly shouting threats and exultation at their ancient enemies." Their bishop, described by Ravndal as a fiery young man, openly called upon his spiritual children throughout his diocese to provide themselves with arms and to prepare "for self-defense." The Armenians, he said, were sure to be attacked sooner or later. Last time they were slaughtered like sheep. Now it must and should be different.[18]

Ravndal maintained that the idea of a greater Armenia appeared to have been abandoned, and the program of the revolutionaries reduced to the restoration of the Rupenian kingdom. As an independent state, which had also included Cilicia and Cappadocia, the kingdom had prospered between approximately 1100 and 1374 A.D., long after the fall and disintegration of Armenia Major. The Rupenian kings took a prominent part in the Crusades. The American consul general believed that the activities of the Armenian committees had aroused the Ottomans and created mounting tension. According to his report, Turks presumably thought that consummation of the revolutionaries' plans would mean the expulsion, if not annihilation, of the Turks and confiscation of their property. To the Ottoman officials, the movement may have seemed a real danger to the empire. Ravndal noted that when numerous Armenians persistently and vociferously demanded admission into the army, in accordance with the constitution, the Ottomans became suspicious and perceived indications of Armenian treachery, inferring that the Armenians wanted the guns and military training solely for their own purposes of secession and national independence. Significant also, he added, was the fact that the present disturbances were confined to the territories of the ancient Rupenian kingdom, believed to be the focal point of the revolutionaries' program.[19]

On May 11, 1909, Ravndal reported that he had received a verbal communication from the chairman of the Beirut branch of the CUP regarding the bloody events at Adana. Münir Bey, the said chairman (presiding judge of the Mixed Commercial Court in this city), informed him that, after much inquiry, he was satisfied that the Adana riots were the result of machinations (1) on the part of the Armenian revolutionaries on the one hand, desirous of bringing about foreign intervention; and (2) on the part of Sultan Abdülhamid II on the other hand, operating through the governor at Adana and the local Muslim clergy with a view to embarrassing and discrediting the Young Turk administration and paving the way for the restoration of the old regime. As Judge Münir Bey was a gentleman of discrimination and high character, Ravndal was gratified to know that his views did not differ widely from his own. The American consul general went on as follows. As regards the connection between the Adana riots of April 14 and the political upheaval at İstanbul on April 13, it might be observed that telegrams were dispatched from the capital reaching the provinces in the evening of April 13 giving the names of the principal members of the new ministry and stating in effect that henceforth the Muslim sacred law would govern all legislation, taking precedence of the constitution. The sultan was referred to as the Caliph. Other telegrams ordered the arrest of the members of the CUP, by force if necessary. It was obvious that the Young Turks had been badly defeated, and that the reactionary forces were in the saddle, and that this startling change had been brought about by an appeal to Muslim religious sentiment. At Adana, where conditions were ripe for an outbreak, this exciting news might have precipated the crisis.[20]

The impression of Ravndal was that the military commander was equally guilty with the governor in failing to suppress the riots at its inception. Both of them, Ravndal contended, should be unmercifully punished as also some of the Armenian revolutionary leaders, including the Gregorian bishop of Adana. According to the United States diplomat, a precedent was found in the punishment of the chief criminals responsible for the Mount Lebanon massacres of 1860, a considerable number of whom, including Ahmet Paşa, the governor, were shot in Damascus, thus ensuring peace in Syria for forty years.[21]

Ravndal was a journalist who served many years in the American consular service including in Beirut (1898–1910) and İstanbul (1910–1917). Few Americans had such a long and varied experience in the Ottoman Empire as Ravndal, and his treatment of the growth of Ottoman patriotism and the movement for reform deserves careful attention. The American official, frank, outspoken, and critical, does not mince words in discussing the Ottoman scene.[22]

AMERICAN MISSIONARY THOMAS DAVIDSON CHRISTIE'S CONFIRMATION, MAY 6, 1909

Thomas Davidson Christie, president of St. Paul's College at Tarsus, largely confirmed the accounts of Nathan, Özler, Ravndal, and Sarkissian in a letter of May 6, 1909. He emphasized that it was a cause of great regret that many religious and secular leaders among the Armenians of the Gregorian church pursued a policy in contradistinction to the new constitutional movement. They refused to cooperate with the Ottomans of the party of reform. They preached in their secret societies, and often from their pulpits, their dreams of political independence and the necessity of arming themselves to secure it.[23]

Christie also noted in his aforesaid letter of May 6, 1909, that the hot-headed bishop of Adana went all over his diocese proclaiming the doctrine of political independence and the necessity of arming themselves to secure it; another who was very active was Garabet Gökdereliyan of Adana, who had been in prison for twelve years.[24] The president of St. Paul's College said:

In our talks with these men and their followers we tried to show them that an unsuccessful revolution is a crime; and that with ten Moslems to one Armenian in this region and with the army and the Government against them, an Armenian revolt must be a failure. All sensible Christians agreed with us; but there were enough of the other sort to greatly irritate the Turks with their vain boastings and preparations. These few men sewed the wind, and alas! Thousands of innocent men, women and children have had to reap the whirlwind.

It was sound advice. But Seropian, Gökdereliyan, and the like were having none of it. They were such men. If Gökdereliyan and his cohorts had concentrated their minds and wills on the defense of Armenian community's interests the history of the Armenians and of the Ottoman Empire might have turned out differently.

Christie also underlined another danger posed by the purchase of arms and ammunition (which had been prohibited under the former regime): even in missionary schools, he pointed out, one had difficulty in keeping revolvers, daggers, and the like out of the hands of Armenian students.[25]

HALİDÉ EDİB'S BELIEF, 1926

Halidé Edib believes the Adana events of 1909 were set in motion by a mutual feeling of distrust and fear, and that events transpired in some such way as this. In the Turkish quarters a rumor had been circulating that the Armenians were going to use their bombs and kill the Turks, who, as a rule, were without arms in those days. Hearing of bombs in the hands of the Armenian revolutionaries undoubtedly would have made them nervous. The same rumor went around in Armenian quarters, and the potential fear and hatred, already exacerbated by the politicians, exploded, the leaders disappeared, and the people proceeded to throttle each other. Thus the discovery of arms in the Armenian quarters and a personal quarrel between the two individuals started the Adana events.[26]

SULTAN ABDÜLHAMİD II'S ALLEGED ROLE IN THE EVENTS

Why a series of incidents should burst out in Adana just at the moment the Ottoman Empire had restored its constitution had been a question puzzling many observers. It was averred in some quarters that Sultan Abdülhamid II instigated such outbreaks of reaction in order to discredit the reformers, the

Young Turk party, and cause the interposition of the powers, as they interposed to halt Russia in the Crimean War.

From the very first days of the incidents, the conviction emerged in the public consciousness that what had happened was one of the last crimes of the Hamidian clique, that the main actors were the Adana Governor, the commander of the local troops, and other Armenian-hating Hamidian forces of the province. The fact that the Adana incidents took place concurrently to the military rebellion in İstanbul[27] convinced many people that Sultan Abdülhamid II's supporters had carried out the massacres on orders from the Yıldız Palace. This view was first put forward by the Armenian Revolutionary Federation, which had since the end of 1907 been connected by ties of friendship with the CUP. The position of the Armenian Revolutionary Federation was that the Adana calamity was Sultan Abdülhamid II's last attempt to restore his former unlimited power, a chance "misunderstanding" and a deed committed by individuals. Yet the official investigation conducted in Adana did not corroborate the former sultan's guilt. The court martial published a statement in which it absolved the former sultan of responsibility for the Adana incidents.[28]

Abdülhamid II, the thirty-fourth sultan of the empire and (following the conquest of the Holy Places in 1517) twenty-sixth Ottoman caliph of the Islamic faithful, continues to remain a prime subject for historical reexamination. He is one of the rare late nineteenth-century figures in Ottoman history who is still remembered and whose policies go on to be discussed and debated. That discussion, however, has generally been far from dispassionate, despite the high number of scholars who have engaged in the debates.[29]

There is little consensus regarding the character or the nature of conduct of Sultan Abdülhamid II. In fact, his name has elicited reactions that range from harsh scorn to profound gratitude. On the one hand he has been praised as a clear-headed, far-sighted statesman, with an unbounded capacity for hard work and a strong interest in what he held to be the true welfare of his subjects. Under his rule the Ottoman Empire was arguably in a stronger strategic position than it had been in decades. Railways, telegraphs, and paved all-weather roads were beginning to unite the empire, improving communications with provincial authorities while giving a solid spur to internal trade. By the turn of the twentieth century, over eight hundred kilometers of new roads were being laid every year, and another four hundred and fifty kilometers repaired. While the empire still ran a large trade deficit with Europe in manufactured goods, Ottoman exports of foodstuffs, cotton, silk, carpets, tiles, and glass, along with coal and certain increasingly strategic metals like chrome, borax, and manganese, were booming in turn. He was quietly supporting the expansion of European-style education in the empire. Eighteen new professional colleges were established during his reign, teaching subjects like French, composition, geography, statistics, economics, and commercial, civil, and international law. Hundreds of new state schools were being built across the empire, along with new public libraries serving an increasingly literate urban population. The number of students attending secondary schools with a secular curriculum doubled in the last three decades of the nineteenth century. Sultan Abdülhamid II's life was one of incessant labor. He devoted himself most assiduously to the work of his great office. He was absolute master of his ministers and of his state. His fez and Western coat testified to his ambition to modernize his empire. His idea of the modern was order, stability, and centralized power. He loved opera and carpentry, making much of his furniture in the Yıldız Palace. On the other hand, he has been denounced in unmeasured terms as a loathsome, cowardly tyrant, with his hands dipped in the blood of his subjects, lacking in all moral sense and working with a sort of low cunning merely to maintain himself on the throne regardless of the impending ruin of his empire. Western politicians, publicists, and cartoonists, under strong impressions of the massacre of Armenians in the 1890s, have seen him not only as a despot but as the "red sultan." From the testimony of all who came in contact with him, Sultan Abdülhamid II appeared reserved, polite, always affable, with a lively intellect and a certain charm of personality which fascinated everyone who approached him. Rather timid by nature, he was a man of extreme tenacity of purpose and determination of will.[30]

In a conversation held with James Creelman in May 1909 Mahmud Şevket Paşa, the minister of war, said that there would be no more massacres of Christians in the Ottoman Empire. That sort of work had come to an end. According to this powerful Ottoman general, in whose hands the real control of the empire rested and who declined to become grand vizier in order not to give the appearance of a military dictatorship, the former Sultan Abdülhamid II was the sole cause of the murders. They were ordered by him. He wished to keep his people divided and so weak that he might rule as a despot, without any law other than his own will. "You say that the old Sultan ordered the massacres in Asia Minor—is that merely your opinion, or is there evidence to support such a charge?" inquired Creelman. Mahmud Şevket Paşa's answer was:

> I say Abdul Hamid caused the massacres, that he alone caused them. I say that after careful investigation of the evidence. You may assure the whole Christian world that the motive which inspired the attacks on the Armenians was not a religious one, although religion was used as a pretence to serve the Sultan's purpose. There is nothing in the Moslem faith to promote the murder of Christians. Hereafter the army and the government will protect Christians, Moslems and Jews alike. With the end of Abdul Hamid's reign[31] we have seen the last of

massacres in this country, I believe. From this time on we shall have Christians in the army. They shall bear arms like Moslems. In the taking of Constantinople and the establishment of constitutional government Christians, Jews and Moslems marched side by side under the Ottoman flag. They were brothers in arms for the sake of liberty and they shall remain brothers in arms. The whole army understands this, and our Moslem soldiers will welcome Christians into their ranks. About one-fourth of the Turkish army will be Christian. I need not tell you that there will never again be a general massacre of Christians. In the future murderers will not have Abdul Hamid as an excuse for their crimes. I have never met Abdul Hamid. He regarded those of us who worked for freedom and progress as absolute beasts. But I know the new Sultan and have talked much with him. He is a good and kind man and you may be sure that he will never allow any of his subjects to be persecuted for religious or other reasons. Is the army to be depended upon? Yes; to a man. It will be loyal to the new régime. There is not the remotest chance of a return to the old order of things. Abdul Hamid will never regain power.[32]

That there had been bad blood between Turks and Armenians in the Adana region for weeks, stirred up by Armenians who were arming themselves and speaking abusively of Muslims, that finally this bitterness broke out into mob violence which was soon organized into a desperate warfare of extermination against Christians, and that the Adana governor did not dare to interfere—that is one explanation. That the Muslims in Adana took their cue from the reactionary movement at İstanbul, and that the governor of the province, not being able to foresee the final outcome at the capital, feared to take sides, and so allowed the work of race hatred and extermination to run its course—that is another explanation. That the central government was cognizant of this movement in the interior, if it did not arrange it; that soldiers were allowed to share in the rioting, if not ordered to do so; that for this reason the Adana governor was able to say, "We are not responsible"; that this explains the definite and desperate purpose of the mob, the great extent of the territory which they covered in their work, and its thoroughness; that men did these things in the name of the religion—these were gleanings from reports. The matter could not be unraveled easily.[33]

Among the newspapers directly under the control of the CUP, *Tanin* was probably the most widely read. Its editor, Hüseyin Cahid, was both a brilliant journalist and a man of action. His every article became an event in the newspaper world of İstanbul. People read and reread them, quoted them, waxed enthusiastic over their pungency, simplicity, and directness. Hence little wonder that Phillip Graves could state that "Hüseyin Cahid was a first-class combative journalist, an excellent translator, and a man of honour and courage."[34] Hüseyin Cahid had some very sensible remarks in *Tanin* on the subject of the Adana affair, which had formed the basis of editorials in other papers as well. He is worth quoting in length:

> The province of Adana has been the scene of terribly tragic events. Men, women and children were massacred mercilessly with savage fury. Nearly 20,000 of our citizens have perished. Whole families have disappeared. The orphans are many. The humanity in its entirety has trembled with horror before this plight. Adana tragedy, the last spasm of Absolutism[35], stretches as far as İstanbul. But the cries which arose over the piled up dead bodies in the middle of the heap of blood shed shows the satanic work of annihilation carried on by the ancien regime. All Ottomans who hope that the constitutional government will dispense justice by unveiling the truth wait impatiently the result of the inquiry undertaken on the scene of massacres. One would ask only a thing from the government: the truth and the justice! For us, the Adana affair was neither a Muslim question nor an Armenian one and it could not have possibly be. No religion tolerates murder, nor excuses them. No religion can be criminal *en masse*. It is therefore necessary that in the massacres of Adana the government prove just and adopt a frank and sincere attitude; for the absence of any official information allows most diverse rumors. These noises, even without ulterior motive, sowing discord among elements, become more and more terrifying passing from mouth to mouth. In this way two currents of opinion are formed. According to one, the Armenians of Adana have provoked the Muslims and have obliged them to defend themselves. According to the other, the Muslims have attacked Armenians and have savagely massacred them. How could it be possible that in a locality where Muslims and Armenians lived side by side for so long as brothers, in full confidence and with entire sincerity, they would all of a sudden become enemies cutting each other's throats? Each element can have its criminals; this is not a motive of reprobation and accusation for the whole people; unless one takes the side of the guilty. From the beginning, therefore, we have said: "According to us, there are neither Armenians nor Turks in this affair, there are victims and executioners wherever they may belong." We have never had the idea of incriminating one element to prove that the other is innocent. We want first the truth and then the justice. The magistrates, superintendents, deputies went to Adana. We are still waiting for the result. We can still understand nothing. How can one forget the deep impression that this crime has created in our hearts when nothing occurred to enlighten and dissipate it! Thus day after day becoming more impatient, we expect the government to enlighten the public opinion, to calm down the souls, to restore confidence and security in hearts. Nervousness increases. The most contradictory rumors circulate, overexciting our spirits. We suffer before the civilized world as if our forehead is branded by red iron in disgrace. What have we done? What is the number of victims? Who are the responsibles and instigators? How would the local government fulfill its task? The government can only answer these questions with an obstinate silence. Agop Babikian was sent to Adana by the Chamber of Deputies, he returned, talked and nothing is known of

what he said. Is it possible not to shiver before such an attitude? We understand the silence of Abdülhamid in front of the evils he himself perpetrated, but we can not interpret the silence of the government on the result of the inquiry. One can only say that it must be unfinished. If the affair can not be enlightened now, it will never be. So why does the government act in this way? It is said that an Armenian, before being hanged, has accused a priest of pushing him to act, telling: "In such and such places the Armenians are cleared of, start here, you also" and a telegram proved the thing. Where is the truth? Cruel riddle. But it must be known well that regarding the Adana tragedy the new regime must take the Ottoman nation and the humanity into account. It is a question of honor for us. The new regime can only wash this stain by following the path of justice and truth. Justice, from our first steps, in the work of reorganization, can not remain hidden in blood. We, therefore, once more turn ourselves towards the government asking it: "What has happened? We want the truth!"[36]

British journalists had been most indulgent to Young Turkey in 1909. Sir Edwin Pears noted that a well-informed "occasional correspondent" of *The Times* whose letter appeared in the *Mail* of August 20, 1909, and who, from internal evidence was evidently a man with exceptional local knowledge, said that "all through the Asiatic provinces it is believed that he (Abdülhamid II) instructed the high officials to destroy the Christians. The report varies in detail but is always the same in substance. It is to the effect that a telegram was received from Constantinople by the Vali, the commandant or the Mutesarif directing them to create disturbances." He further claimed in detail how dates had been fixed for massacres in several big provincial towns and communicated to the country population. According to the same source, the sultan hoped for a *Jehad*, or religious war, against the Christians and against the CUP as consisting of unfaithful Muslims, Jews, and Freethinkers.[37]

Pears said the movement planned by the party of reaction throughout Anatolia came off only in Cilicia and its neighborhood and principally in Adana. He contended:

> It was a terrible success there (in Adana) and was contemporaneous with that in the capital. Elsewhere the reactionaries waited to see which side in Constantinople would win; and when, in less than a fortnight, the result showed the powerlessness of the Sultan, no further attempt at reaction took place. Amid some problems which are still unsolved, it cannot be doubted that there was a deliberate attempt to raise Anatolia against the new regime.[38]

The same British author maintained that in Adana exceptional circumstances favored the party of reaction, among them being the foolish conduct of a section of the Armenian population. He continued on following lines. Some Armenians, flushed with the wonderful changes brought about by the revolution, gave vent to their newly raised hopes, and declared that Christians and Muslims were now equal. A few were foolish enough to talk of Armenian independence. The cry of "Islam in danger" was readily listened to. The Muslim population was inflamed and ready to acquiesce in the suggestions of men who purposed to create disorder.[39]

Sir Edwin Pears was the veteran correspondent of the London paper *Daily News*, equally distinguished as the leader of the Consular Bar at İstanbul, and an author who had thrown new light on the history of the Ottoman Empire. He was a highly respected advocate, whose knowledge of the Levant almost reached to encyclopedic proportions. He knew İstanbul intimately for nearly forty years, and his personal knowledge of the empire extended far beyond the capital. Moreover, his personal relationship with travelers in Asia Minor and his exhaustive knowledge of the literature of travel within the empire enabled him to supplement with full critical judgment his personal evidence with that of witnesses scarcely less weighty. But he certainly labored under one disadvantage. He was writing so near to his material that perspective became a difficult matter.[40]

James Creelman claims that there could be no reasonable doubt that Sultan Abdülhamid II secretly ordered the massacre of Armenians in Asia Minor from his palace in İstanbul. According to the American journalist, Sultan's agents, often disguised as religious teachers, went about among the most debased Muslim elements of the provinces of Adana and Aleppo calling their attention to the fact that the Armenians were arming themselves for a revolution. They persuaded the people that the Armenians intended to extinguish their religion. Creelman believed that it was not a religious movement at all, but a political plot hatched out in the Yıldız Palace. There were hundreds of men in the lower orders of Islam—who wore the turban badge of a religious vocation—engaged in the conspiracy, but there was abundant evidence to show that the real leaders of the Muslim faith had nothing to do with it and were honestly opposed to the attacks upon either Christians or Jews.[41] That fully explains, Creelman asserts, the indifference or complicity of the public authorities of Adana. The fact that massacres began in Adana, Hamidiye, and Osmaniye simultaneously on the very day that the garrison of İstanbul murdered its officers and seized the parliament building shows an exact concert between the despot and his agents in Asia Minor.[42]

Some thought to the contrary. Charles Woods writes that almost immediately after the outbreak a report was spread, and forthwith accepted by Europe, that Sultan Abdülhamid II was himself responsible for the incidents.

Woods says he had often been informed that the slaughter was ordered from the Yıldız Palace. He had even seen in print the translation of a telegram describing the zeal with which Christians were to be killed. This telegram was supposed to have been addressed by Sultan Abdülhamid II to the then governor of Adana. However, as the British author indicates, there is no proof that such a telegram was ever sent to Adana from the capital, and if it were transmitted, no evidence has been produced that its dispatch was authorized by Sultan Abdülhamid II.[43]

Woods, after reminding that the first outbreak in Adana occurred on April 14 but a few hours following the party of reaction had gained the upper hand in İstanbul, advances that even if Sultan Abdülhamid II or his malefactors had at once secured control of the telegraph offices at the capital, which he believed that they had not, then no order could have reached Adana until the situation in that city had already become most acute. He then continues to argue as follows. Besides, when the outbreak began, nothing was known by the ordinary man in Adana of the events in İstanbul on April 13. If even, therefore, a telegram dispatched from the capital on April 13 had reached the governor of Adana during the night of April 13–14, it is difficult to see how it would have been possible for him, as a result of this order, to have arranged for an onslaught to begin early in the morning. Again, although it may be put forward that the order was dispatched from İstanbul prior to April 13, it is difficult to agree with this theory because, notwithstanding the fact that the power of Sultan Abdülhamid II was not entirely swept away by the revolution of 1908 yet, it was impossible for those intimately acquainted with the condition of affairs in the Ottoman Empire between July 1908 and April 1909 to believe that during the closing months of his reign Sultan Abdülhamid II was actually in a position to send any direct or secret orders to the governmental authorities in the provinces.[44]

Charles Woods was born and raised in the Ottoman Empire. He was in İstanbul at the time of the Adana disorders of 1909.

A writer in the German daily *Frankfurter Zeitung* denied that either the intrigues of Sultan Abdülhamid II or a volcanic eruption of Muslim extremism led to the bloodshed. It was purely political. He tells us that Adana was full of inflammable materials as a powder magazine. The population numbered forty-five thousand souls, twenty-seven thousand of whom were Muslims and three-fourths of the balance were Armenians, the rest Greeks. The Armenians were the great traders, and rich men of the city, living in a separate quarter. Of the political causes that led to Muslim acts of violence this writer, Wendland, says:

> The Armenian agitators, who had made many pecuniary sacrifices to aid in the bringing in of the new Constitution, expected to exercise a vital political influ-

ence through its operation, and their elated bearing was such as to exasperate the Mohammedans. The leaders of this agitation were generally foreign members of the Armenian committee or certain stirrers up of race hatred in Adana. While these leaders took care to secure safety for themselves they proved the ruin of their poorer fellow countrymen, who were sacrificed by thousands for no fault of their own.[45]

The Armenians also incensed the Turks by reviving in pictures and plays the patriotic reverence of their fellow countrymen for the old heroes and historic events of Christian Armenia. They actually contemplated the revival of Armenia as an independent state. To quote the words of Wendland:

> It may easily be imagined that this new awakening of national Chauvinism was soon perceived by the Mohammedans and while the Armenians were giving too free a rein to their tongue and their enthusiasm, the Mohammedan authorities were kept fully informed by Turkish spies. It is therefore a gross error to declare that religious fanaticism was responsible for the late massacres.[46]

Fred Douglas Shepard, medical missionary of the ABCFM at Ayntab, believed that the Adana massacre was not arranged and ordered by the central government at İstanbul. It seemed to him to have been a spontaneous local outbreak, and its only connection with Sultan Abdülhamid II was that, when the reactionaries got the welcome news that he was again in the saddle, they thought that by a "massacre of Armenians they could feed fat their ancient grudge, enrich themselves, and at the same time ingratiate themselves with the Sultan." Shepard observed that the Armenians, intoxicated with the new wine of liberty, often gave offense by wild talk or arrogant behavior. The bishop of Adana openly advised his people to arm themselves, and many of the young men purchased arms and ostentatiously carried them. The Muslim population only too readily believed the exaggerated reports that were circulated about the treasonable designs of the Armenians; and so all things were ready when the news came that Sultan Abdülhamid II had seized the reins and was again in full power.[47]

Herbert Underwood, medical missionary of the ABCFM at Erzurum, could hardly venture an opinion as to whether Sultan Abdülhamid II was responsible for the incidents at Adana and elsewhere, in the sense that he originated the idea, ordered its execution and supported it. Underwood said:

> It seems to me the origin was in the independent and injudicious action of the Armenians themselves, who, until after the triumph of the constitutional party last year, were not allowed to carry arms. Being given this liberty for the first time, they did it very indiscreetly and even audaciously. This created suspicion and jealousy among the Turks (Moslems), and both sides were disturbed, and

a feeling of uncertainty as to what the government was doing or would do, ripened into a feeling of hostility. All these things tended to augment the feeling of unrest, although there were no overt acts, Armenians and Turks fraternizing, and no rumors of trouble were heard anywhere. But the feelings of jealousy and animosity were growing between Turks and Armenians in the Adana district.[48]

The American missionary's reading of the subject was remarkably insightful.

Agop Babikyan, deputy for Tekirdağ, who was one of the Armenian members of the Parliamentary Commission sent to investigate the events of Adana, agrees with Woods and Underwood: "I have not been able to secure a single document in evidence of Abdul Hamid having any finger in the whole affair of Adana. . . . On the other hand," claimed Babikyan, "the local government has been an accomplice in the massacres, and even the central government is guilty of carelessness and prompt action."[49]

Sir Gerard Lowther, the British ambassador at İstanbul, in his annual report on the Ottoman Empire for the year 1910 said to lay the responsibility for the Adana massacres at the door of the ex-sultan, as was at first done, was now impossible; no evidence of any sort had been produced to incriminate his majesty, though there could be no doubt that a number of *hodjas* and reactionaries had done all they could to fan the flame of Muslim fanaticism. Nor was there any ground to assume that the Armenians were planning an insurrection, or that the Muslims had been preparing a carefully premeditated massacre. Lowther considered the causes of the massacre were rather to be found in the vainglorious talk of equality on the part of the young Armenians who were all in theory revolutionaries and advocates of home rule, in the fear which their attitude inspired among the Muslims of some definite act of aggression, a fear which was somewhat justified by the constant stream of arms which flowed into the country for the use of the non-Muslim population, in the extravagance of the orators on both sides, and in the lamentable weakness of the government authority.[50]

SUPPORT OF THE YOUNG TURK MOVEMENT TO THE EVENTS?

Another question in regard to the April events in Adana was, "Had the movement the support of the CUP or not?" There was hardly any question which in the Ottoman capital at the time had been more fully discussed. Sir Edwin Pears arrives at the conclusion that the Central Committee of the CUP which practically held power in the Ottoman Empire strongly disapproved the outbreak.[51] Charles Woods believes it is inconceivable that the Young Turks as a body were any party to the outbreak. There was no evidence which justified the assumption that the Central Committee or the principal members of the CUP were really in any way implicated in the incidents. According to him, it was obvious that a massacre must have been so detrimental to the cause of successful reform, that, leaving all arguments of good intent out of consideration, it was incomprehensible that the leaders of the New Regime, who had so cleverly brought about an almost bloodless revolution, could possibly have connived at such a horrible crime.[52]

Edward Alexander Powell, an American consular official in Syria and Egypt in 1906–1909, held that, though the origins of the Adana massacre remained obscure, there could be no doubt that some form of official prompting lay behind them. According to him, the only question was whether the instigation came from the adherents of Sultan Abdülhamid II in an attempt to discredit the Young Turk movement, or from the Young Turks themselves. Powell believed that certain it was, however, that the diabolical scheme was encouraged, if not actually abetted, by the German military party, which saw in the energetic and ambitious Armenians, already highly successful in industry and finance, a menace to the scheme for bringing the whole of the Ottoman Empire under German economic domination. The Young Turks, in the opinion of Powell, were hand in glove with the militarists of Berlin, whose emissaries, in the guise of military advisers, instructors, consuls, traders, and the like, were working indefatigably throughout the sultan's dominions laying the foundations for the meditated *Drang nach Osten*. But, he concluded, it must not be assumed that the Armenians themselves were without blame for the Adana massacre.[53]

Shortly after the Adana massacres a proposal for the colonization of Cilicia by Jewish immigrants was muted in Judeo-Turkish circles. This scheme, which might have entailed considerable hardship on the many Armenian widows and orphans who had lost their title deeds, was finally abandoned, partly owing to the fear of Armenian opposition, partly, it was believed, to the unofficially expressed disappropriation of a foreign embassy or of members of that embassy. The said embassy since that date became a mark for the attacks of certain Jewish journalists both in the Ottoman realm and abroad.[54]

In June 1909 Grand Vizier Hüseyin Hilmi Paşa, while visiting the British embassy, purposely or accidentally disclosed that his government had been approached by a strong Jewish organization which proposed the settlement of large numbers of Jews in Cilicia, northern Syria, and Iraq. The settlers in Cilicia and northern Syria were apparently to occupy lands and properties left vacant by slain or fugitive Armenians. The grand vizier intimated that the scheme had the support of certain Salonikan circles, but that he did not like the look of it. The embassy did not like it, either; it was unjust to the

Armenians and was likely to cause trouble with the Arabs. Hüseyin Hilmi Paşa appeared to have told the CUP that the proposal was likely to encounter British opposition and it was eventually dropped. The Jewish influence on the CUP was strong; many Jewish and Turkish members of that body made a grievance of the Adana affair.[55]

The Parisian daily *Le Temps* of October 14, 1909, devoted a leader article to the Adana events with a lengthy comment. It brought out the responsibility of the Turkish side, but added that the interest of the Armenians was not to accuse the Young Turk party of responsibilities that had their roots in the past. The Armenians, it said, must have faith in the 1908 revolution. The Young Turks could not do everything all at once. They needed time and more confidence. The two parties must endure the bitterness, the leader ended.[56]

In France, the relations between the Ministry of Foreign Affairs and the press were unique at the time. The Quai d'Orsay often had direct links with leading papers such as *Le Temps*, which was, on foreign affairs at least, a semiofficial organ. It was the most noted and famous French newspaper, with influence rivaling *The Times* of London. *Le Temps* also often acted as a guide for the rest of the French press, especially on the question of international diplomacy. *Le Temps*, *Le Figaro*, and *Le Journal des Débats* were the "quality" press. They served as a basic source of information for the political and economic elites, whose ideas on contemporary issues they influenced to a great extent. Because of their prestige, their influence among important social strata, and their authoritativeness on questions of policy, the "quality" newspapers wielded considerable political power, which they employed to affect politics in the Chamber of Deputies and decision making in government.

The CUP refuted the claims by the Armenian daily *Puzantion* to the effect that it had prior knowledge of the massacres which took place in Adana and that its members had not acted effectively to prevent them. The CUP retorted that it had only one aim and that was of reconciliation between the Ottoman elements. It rejected the slander.[57]

Marmaduke Pickthall was the son and grandson of Anglican ministers. He was a novelist and reporter and spent considerable time in the Ottoman Empire before the outbreak of the First World War. Pickthall, in several essays published in *The New Age* (a scholarly and literary journal of significance in London), urged caution in interpreting news reports alleging massacres of Armenians. In his letter of December 16, 1915, to the journal, Pickthall said he probably knew more about the CUP than either Arnold Toynbee and Lord Bryce or their informants, and could tell a good deal in reply to the accusations in their *Armenian Atrocities: The Murder of a Nation*. For instance, the massacres at Adana in 1909 were ascribed to the Young Turks by Toynbee, as if there were doubt about the matter. Pickthall was in Syria at the time, and fanatical emissaries landed at Tripoli, Beyrout, and Jaffa with the same purpose with which they landed in Mersin, of preaching massacre of Christians. But they were arrested by the local CUP and deported, which did not look as if the Young Turks were the instigators. It was true that members of the local committee at Adana took part in the massacres, but that committee had been captured by disguised reactionaries.[58] Pickthall's talents as a linguist and as an authority on Syria, Palestine, and Egypt would have been used by the British army during the First World War but his reputation as "a rabid Turcophile" prevented him from being offered a job with the Arab Bureau in Cairo, a job that went instead to Thomas Edward Lawrence.[59]

Ronald Grigor Suny maintains that neither Sultan Abdülhamid II nor the central government played a direct role. According to him, local officials, intellectuals, and clerics inflamed the inchoate fears of the Muslims who, participating in some action by the Armenians, preemptively launched brutal attacks on them. Even though the Young Turks in İstanbul were not involved, influential adherents of the CUP in Adana incited people to riot and soldiers affiliated with the CUP participated in the massacres. The Michigan professor concludes that Adana was more like an urban riot that degenerated into a pogrom rather than a state-initiated mass killing.[60]

SEVERAL CONTEMPORARY OBSERVATIONS

Arthur Tremaine Chester, in his article which is noteworthy for its fairness and impartiality, blows away the fog of obfuscation and denials. He relates that he was in the Adana district two weeks before the protests incited by the Armenian killing of a Turk. The British consular agent, a man[61] who had spent his life in that section and knew the country and its people perfectly, told him that despite the efforts of the Ottoman government to amalgamate all racial factions in order to build up a united country, the Armenians were openly arming. The British official added that should any reports of a massacre there emerge, they should not be believed, for such an affair would be a contest between two armed forces. It is possible that the Armenian revolutionary leaders wanted their followers to be armed to ensure that a "massacre" occurred at the appointed time. Be that as it may, the plotters had the advantage once the Armenians were armed for conflict: they needed only for the Muslims to perceive that their lives were in danger for a single overt act by an Armenian to touch off disaster.[62]

Rear Admiral Colby Mitchel Chester, who had been interested in Turkish affairs for over twenty years, had returned in July 1922 from İstanbul, where he had gone to ascertain whether conditions would be suitable in the near future for renewing work on the Chester project. Rear Admiral Chester, studying all the texts in regard to the affairs in Asia Minor, wrote a far-reaching article in the *Current History*, as he boldly exposed the part played by the Armenian element in the Turco-Asian conflicts. He believes that the Adana affair was in no sense a massacre, as the term is interpreted by international law, because Armenians, fully armed, arose in their might and drove the Muslims from Adana, killing more of them than they lost by their own casualties. This fact was certified to before the director of the ABCFM in Boston, in the presence of the rear admiral, by a woman missionary whose son had been accidentally killed in the fighting.[63]

Major Harold Armstrong maintains that he has sufficient evidence to assert that the Armenians in 1909 mounted a coup d'état, assisted by Russian advice and money, with the goal of establishing a separate Armenian state based in Adana. For some ten days, Armstrong contends, they held absolute control of Adana and its area, and were defeated only after the Ottomans sent a large number of troops.[64] He further claims that after the seizure of Adana, Armenians declared a republic.[65] It is relevant to note here that, according to Gaston Gaillard, Russia at the time strove hard to spread orthodoxy in the districts around Adana, Maraş, and İskenderun, in order to enlarge its zone of influence on this side and thus get an outlet to the Mediterranean.[66] Adana was of great significance as a strategic point for a Russian push from Caucasia into the Mediterranean. Since the defeat at the hands of the Japanese in the Far East in 1905, and the closing of that military option, the importance of the region for driving southward to the warm waters was magnified. Adana was attributed added crucialness by a prominent Huntchak presence and a sizeable Armenian population, one with established connections with the Russian consulate in Mersin.

No one could visit Adana at the time that W. J. Childs, formerly of the British Naval Intelligence, did without hearing much about the great incidents. He wrote that three thousand to four thousand citizens could not be killed in street fighting, or burned alive in buildings, or otherwise butchered in racial or religious hatred, without leaving deep effects. There were, indeed, memories and physical evidence enough of the tragedy for any one who went about Adana a few years later. Many buildings had been destroyed by fire, and gaunt walls remained looking down upon heaps of debris. Many influences went to the making of the massacre, Childs recounts, some more or less obscure, as the part taken in planning it by the Turkish Jews of Salonika, and others belonging to the deeper causes of faith and race which ever underlie these horrible affairs. But some also were local and exhibited the inconceivable unwisdom which Armenians so often displayed in their larger dealings with Muslims.[67]

It is true that the anti-Jewish sentiment here was masking political and economic rivalry on the part of Ottoman Armenians.[68] Anti-Semitic conspiracy theories were new to the Ottoman Empire. As Elie Kedourie, Bernard Lewis, and Feroz Ahmad have shown, at the beginning of the twentieh century, British diplomats articulated anti-Semitic conspiracy theories centering on the Jewish and the *Dönme* (Jewish convert) to explain away the events surrounding the 1908 revolution.[69] Sir Gerard Lowther repeatedly alleged a crypto-Jewish-Judeo-Masonic conspiracy and called the ruling CUP "the Jew Committee of Union and Progress." Minister of Finance Cavid Bey was a "secret Jew, an official manifestation of the Cabinet who really count, and the apex of Freemasonry in the empire," Lowther claimed.[70] Originating "in a line of clerical and nationalist thought familiar on the Continent," the notion of a Jewish-Masonic plot "was taken up in some British circles, and a few years later seized upon by Allied propagandists as a means of discrediting their Turkish enemies," Bernard Lewis asserts.[71] Feroz Ahmad also locates anti-Semitic conspiracy theories in "British Foreign Office reports and the dispatches of the Istanbul correspondent of *The Times* (London)."[72]

Sober Armenians of Cilicia told Childs that these proceedings were folly, the work of revolutionary societies and hotheads, and that the mass of the Armenian population held aloof. But the former British intelligence official believed there could be no doubt that the movement had been approved and supported by many, and intended to involve the whole people, and that it had, in fact, got beyond the control both of those who desired to go more slowly, and those who disapproved of it altogether. According to him, the Armenians in Cilicia had greater hopes of independence than did their brethren in eastern Anatolia, which was under the shadow of Russia. Cilicia lay beyond the sphere of Russian aspirations; it also touched the sea and was therefore accessible to friendly Western powers. Furthermore, and as no slight consideration, it was by nature a rich district, which eastern Anatolia was not. Armenians long had felt that if an independent Armenia could be reestablished anywhere with prospects of permanence, it would be here. Childs states that these hopes, and the expression of them, had much to do with the Adana affair.[73]

Childs asserts that the Armenians in Cilicia were themselves an invading people who had pushed down from the northern mountains during the twelfth and thirteenth centuries. They had made their capital at Sis, in the northeastern extremity of the Cilician plain, and for nearly three hundred years had maintained a difficult independence. Along the coast, their territory sometimes ran from Silifke to Antakya; it was bounded on the northwest by the Taurus and in the northeast it extended to the nearer highlands of the Anti-Taurus, where lived their most warlike population.[74]

Childs also touches on several points mentioned by sources of his day. Cilicia was a district closely connected with Armenian history and independence, and here, in the sudden period of liberty that followed the downfall of absolutism in 1908, Armenians gave unrestrained vent to their aspirations. Their clubs and meeting places were loud with boastings of what was soon to follow. Postcards showing a map of the future Armenian kingdom of Cilicia were printed and circulated through the Ottoman post. Armenian nationalists marched in procession in the streets, bearing flags purported to be that of Lesser Armenia come to life again. The name of the future king was bandied about: not some aloof, nebulous personage, but a well-known Armenian landowner from the Cilician plain, held in disfavor by Muslims.[75] Giving fuller meaning to these matters was the steady assertion that an Armenian army gathering in the mountains by Hacin and Zeytun would presently march upon Adana and reestablish an Armenian kingdom.[76]

Dr. Herbert Underwood observed in 1909: "The origin of the massacres lay with the independent and injudicious actions of the Armenians themselves who, when given the right to carry arms after 1908 did it very indiscreetly and even audaciously. This created suspicions and jealousy among the Turks [. . .] although there were no overt acts."[77] W. M. Ramsay stressed also in 1909: "It is quite certain that there was a good deal of fighting in the city of Adana and many Turks were killed. One Armenian butcher, being accustomed to use a weapon, is said to have killed six Turks with his own hand. Whether all this was purely in self-defence, or whether quarrels began, with faults on both sides, one cannot say with certainty."[78] F. G. Aflalo, writing in 1911, agreed with Ramsay: "I think it is only fair to add that these people [Armenians] are not always the inoffensive victims."[79] In 1911 Sir Edwin Pears mentioned the foolish conduct of a section of the Armenian population. A few talked of Armenian independence. Many Armenians had bought arms, and the quantity purchased, greatly exaggerated by the fears of the Muslims, contributed, together with incendiary speeches, to drive Muslims into a panic.[80]

Even such an author as Christopher Walker, who is a strong proponent of the Armenian genocide claims, fully concurs on this opinion:

> The Armenians of Adana were not the innocent passive sufferers that they have sometimes been pictured. They were insufferably and tactlessly loquacious, and their archbishop, Mousheg, was a foolish firebrand who had urged his people to buy arms at any price during the months preceding the violence. (It later transpired that he had a commercial interest in the sale of arms.)[81]

Latterly the truth began to filter through into European and American public opinion. A private letter received in Paris from an officer on board the

French armored cruiser *Victor Hugo*, at Mersin, dated April 24, 1909, while fully confirming the horror of the recent incidents, said that the previous attitude of the Armenian population was undoubtedly provocative. The writer declared that after the proclamation of the Ottoman constitution in July of last year, the Armenians became insolent and quarrelsome. They boasted openly of their separatist intentions and of their purpose of reestablishing the Armenian kingdom. At Armenian theaters plays were produced flouting the Turks, the authors of these pieces going back to the days of Tamerlane to find subjects with which to inflame the hatred against Muslim "oppression."[82]

Robert Farrer Zeidner agrees and points out that continuing Armenian revolutionary activity remained evident in boisterous parades, the frequent flying of Armenian national flags, the stocking of weapons, and much boasting of the coming independence of all "Armenia." Added to the two Armenian uprisings at Zeytun, this was sufficient to instill deep suspicion of all Armenians among Muslim elements.[83]

To sum up, Eric Weitz, dean of humanities and arts and professor of history at The City College of New York, author of several books on the Holocaust and genocides, writes that the Adana events of 1909 seem not to have been organized from the center of power in İstanbul, either by the sultan or the CUP. These incidents took place alongside an attempted counterrevolution by more conservative, religious forces in the Ottoman Empire. The activists opposed the liberal proclamations issued by the Young Turks, which seemed to herald the end of Muslim predominance in the empire. Rumors circulated that Armenians had slaughtered Muslims and had desecrated Adana's major mosque. According to Weitz, underlying all this were longstanding prejudices against Christians, the increasing wealth and stature of some Armenians over the course of the nineteenth and into the twentieth century, and the strong current of suspicion that Armenians were always allied with the European powers, now an even more incendiary sentiment in the wake of the territorial losses of 1908. In this way, too, international and domestic factors played off against one another.[84]

NOTES

1. Arthur FritzHenry Townshend, *A Military Consul in Turkey: The Experiences and Impressions of a British Representative in Asia Minor* (London: Seeley and Co. Limited, 1910), pp. 191–92.

2. Rıza Tevfik acted as minister of education in November 1918–January 1919. He was member of the Chamber of Notables in March 1919 and head of the Council of State in May–August 1919 and August–October 1920. See Kuneralp, *Son Dönem*

Osmanlı Erkan ve Ricali (1839–1922), p. 118; and Rıza Tevfik, Abdullah Uçman, ed., *Biraz da Ben Konuşayım* (Let Me Also Talk a Bit) (İstanbul: İletişim Yayınları, second revised edition, 2008).

3. BOA, DH. MKT, No. 2817/85. Articles in the Armenian Press on the Adana Incidents. Ministry of the Interior to the Grand Vizierate, May 19, 1909.

4. Djemal Pasha, *Memories of a Turkish Statesman 1913–1919*, p. 258. Records taken in the Administrative Council of Adana in this period is not available. Consequently, one is dependent on contemporary utterances, private and public, and subsequently on post-1919 testimonies and published memoirs. The result, often, is a series of accounts which are different wholly or in part.

5. Ibid., pp. 259–61.

6. Creelman, "The Slaughter of Christians in Asia Minor," p. 8.

7. Atamian, *The Armenian Community*, p. 174.

8. Sutherland, *The Adventures of an Armenian Boy*, pp. 31–32.

9. Aram Arkun, "Into the Modern Age, 1800–1913," in Edmund Herzig and Marina Kurkchiyan, eds., *The Armenians Past and Present in the Making of National Identity* (London and New York: Routledge Curzon, 2005), pp. 86–87.

10. Suny, *A History of the Armenian Genocide*, p. 167.

11. Matossian, "Ethnic Politics in Post-Revolutionary Ottoman Empire," pp. 447–48.

12. Sanjian, *The Armenian Communities in Syria under Ottoman Dominion*, p. 279.

13. Simonyan, *The Destruction of Armenians in Cilicia, April 1909*, p. 28.

14. İsmail Safa Özler became member of the TGNA for Mersin and Adana between 1920 and 1927 and for Seyhan in 1939 until his death in 1940. He acted as the first minister of education of the Republic of Turkey from November 6, 1922, to March 8, 1924. Özler's administration of the Ministry of Education showed decision, energy, and no little wisdom. His biographical sketch can be found in *Türk Parlamento Tarihi Milli Mücadele ve Türkiye Büyük Millet Meclisi Birinci Dönem 1919–1923*, Vol. 3, pp. 782–83, and Çankaya, *Mülkiye Tarihi ve Mülkiyeliler*, Vol. 3, pp. 1180–82. Seventy-eight years have passed since the death of Özler, and still there is no biography that presents his complex figure in every facet. Despite the passage of several decades—with the opening of archives, expansion of scholarship, and exploration of new hypotheses—he remains largely invisible.

15. İsmail Safa, "Müdhiş Bir İsyan" (An Awful Uprising), *İtidal*, April 20, 1909, pp. 1–2, cited in Kévorkian, *The Armenian Genocide*, pp. 87–88.

16. For a succinct discussion of this issue, see İsmail Hakkı Tevfik Okday, *Adana Vilayeti Matbuatı* (The Press of the Province of Adana) (Ankara: Hariciye Vekaleti, 1932), pp. 3–5, 17, 24, 27, 33, and 42–43.

17. USNA, RG 84 Records of Foreign Service Posts, Diplomatic Posts Turkey, Vol. 216, From Consulates 1 January 1909–30 June 1909 American Embassy Istanbul. Edward Nathan (Mersin) to John Leishman (Istanbul), May 9, 1909.

18. USNA, RG 84 Records of Foreign Service Posts, Diplomatic Posts Turkey, Vol. 216, From Consulates 1 January 1909–30 June 1909 American Embassy Istanbul. Gabriel Bie Ravndal (Beirut) to John Leishman (Istanbul), May 10, 1909.

19. Ibid.

20. USNA, RG 84 Records of Foreign Service Posts, Diplomatic Posts Turkey, Vol. 216, From Consulates 1 January 1909–30 June 1909 American Embassy Istanbul. Gabriel Bie Ravndal (Beirut) to Assistant Secretary of State (Washington, DC), May 11, 1909.

21. Ibid.

22. See Gabriel Bie Ravndal, *Turkey: A Commercial and Industrial Handbook* (Washington, DC: Government Printing House, 1925). This concise book published by the United States Department of Commerce gives the reader an excellent idea of the geography, natural resources, and the commerce of Turkey at the time.

23. USNA, RG 84 Records of Foreign Service Posts, Diplomatic Posts Turkey, Vol. 216, From Consulates 1 January 1909–30 June 1909 American Embassy Istanbul. Gabriel Bie Ravndal (Beirut) to John Leishman (Istanbul), May 11, 1909. Enclosure: Letter of May 6, 1909, from Thomas Davidson Christie.

24. On Garabet Gökdereliyan, see Ali Münif Bey, *Ali Münif Bey'in Hatıraları*, p. 49; Arıkoğlu, *Hatıralarım*, pp. 49–50fn1; Yurtsever, *Çukurova Tarihi*, pp. 66–68; İrtem, *Ermeni Meselesinin İçyüzü*, p. 152.

25. USNA, RG 84 Records of Foreign Service Posts, Diplomatic Posts Turkey, Vol. 126, From Consulates 1 January 1909–30 June 1909 American Embassy Istanbul. Gabriel Bie Ravndal (Beirut) to John Leishman (Istanbul), May 11, 1909. Enclosure: Letter of May 6, 1909, from Thomas Davidson Christie.

26. Halidé Edib, *Memoirs of Halidé Edib*, p. 284.

27. The military rebellion was the events of April 13–27, 1909, which began by a mutiny of troops at İstanbul, demanding the restoration of the sacred law, and ended with the deposition of Sultan Abdülhamid II, enforced by Young Turk officers in control of the Third Army in Macedonia, who marched on the capital from Salonika. It was one of the most important moments in Ottoman history in the twentieth century. April 13 was March 31 according to the old style calender then in use in the Ottoman Empire. In Turkish literature the episode is known as March 31 Incident. To this date it arouses controversy and—around the date of its anniversary—finds an echo in the Turkish press, where its interpretation is shaped by the prevailing political climate. See İsmail Hami Danişmend, *Sadrazam Tevfik Paşa'nın Dosyasındaki Resmi ve Hususi Vesikalara Göre 31 Mart Vakası* (The March 31 Incident According to Official and Private Documents in the File of Grand Vizier Tevfik Paşa) (İstanbul: İstanbul Kitabevi, 1961); Sina Akşin, *31 Mart Olayı* (The March 31 Incident) (Ankara: Ankara Üniversitesi Siyasal Bilgiler Fakültesi Yayınları, 1970); Cavid Bey, *Meşrutiyet Ruznâmesi*, pp. 35–39. Also Francis McCullagh, "The Constantinople Mutiny of April 13th," *The Fortnightly Review*, Vol. LXXXVI (July–December 1909), pp. 49–69; Paul Farkas, trans. Kenneth Kronenberg, *Palace Revolution and Counterrevolution in Turkey (March–April 1909)* (İstanbul: The Isis Press, 2005); David Farhi, "The Şeriat as a Political Slogan—or the Incident of the 31st March," *Middle Eastern Studies*, Vol. 7, No. 3 (October 1971), pp. 275–99; Victor Swenson, "The Military Rising in Istanbul 1909," *Journal of Contemporary History*, Vol. 5, No. 4 (October 1970), pp. 171–84; Feroz Ahmad, "The Young Turk Revolution," *Journal of Contemporary History*, Vol. 3, No. 3 (July 1968), pp. 19–36.

28. Simonyan, *The Destruction of Armenians in Cilicia, April 1909*, pp. 163–64.

29. Şükrü Hanioğlu's review of Selim Deringil's *The Well-Protected Domains: Ideology and the Legitimation of Power in the Ottoman Empire, 1876-1909*, The American Historical Review, Vol. 105, No. 1 (February 2000), p. 319. For recent Turkish press accounts of Sultan Abdülhamid II, see among others Doğu Perinçek, "Abdülhamit'in Sonunu Paylaşırsınız" (You Will Share the End of Abdülhamit), *Aydınlık*, September 20, 2016, pp. 1 and 8; Emin Çölaşan, "Bir Zavallı Adam: Abdülhamit" (A Poor Man: Abdülhamit), *Sözcü*, September 20, 2016, p. 5; Erhan Afyoncu, "II. Abdülhamid'in Devleti Ayakta Tutma Siyaseti" (Abdülhamid II's Policy of Survival of the State), Tarihin Pusulası (Compass of History), *Sabah*, September 25, 2016, p. 22.

30. A considerable body of literature exists on this subject. See, for example, Tahsin Paşa, *Abdülhamid ve Yıldız Hatıraları* (Abdülhamid and Yıldız Recollections) (İstanbul: Muallim Ahmet Halit Kitaphanesi, 1931); Osmanoğlu, *Babam Sultan Abdülhamid* ; Ömer Faruk Yılmaz, *Belgelerle Sultan İkinci Abdülhamid Han* (Sultan Abdülhamid Han II With Documents) (İstanbul: Osmanlı Yayınevi, 1999); Metin Hülagü, *Sultan II. Abdülhamid'in Sürgün Günleri (1909-1918): Hususi Doktoru Atıf Hüseyin Bey'in Hatıratı* (Days of Exile of Sultan Abdülhamid II [1909-1918]: Recollections of His Private Physician Atıf Hüseyin Bey) (İstanbul: Pan Yayıncılık, 2003), pp. 5-40; Vahdettin Engin, *Sultan Abdülhamid ve İstanbul'u* (Sultan Abdülhamid and His İstanbul) (İstanbul: Simurg Yayınları, 2001), pp. 22-28; Mehmet Tosun, ed., *Osmanoğulları ve Aydınların Anlatımıyla İmparatorluğun Yüzük Taşı II. Abdülhamid* (The Ring Stone of the Empire Abdülhamid II As Narrated By the Royal Ottoman Family and the Intellectuals) (İstanbul: Yeditepe Yayınevi, 2009); Coşkun Yılmaz, ed., *II. Abdülhamid Modernleşme Sürecinde İstanbul* (Abdülhamid II: İstanbul in the Process of Modernization) (İstanbul: İstanbul 2010 Avrupa Kültür Başkenti, 2010); Edward Creasy, Archibald Cary Coolidge and Harold Claflin, *The History of Nations*, Vol. 14: *Turkey The Balkan States* (New York: P. F. Collier and Son Company Publishers, 1928), p. 489; François Georgeon, *Abdulhamid II Le sultan calife (1876-1909)* (Paris: Librairie Arthème Fayard, 2003); Suny, *A History of the Armenian Genocide*, p. 99; Stanford Shaw and Ezel Kural Shaw, *History of the Ottoman Empire and Modern Turkey*, Vol. 2: *Reform, Revolution, and Republic: The Rise of Modern Turkey 1808-1975* (Cambridge: Cambridge University Press, second edition, 1977), pp. 112-13, 230-35, and 249-53.

31. Sultan Abdülhamid II was dethroned on April 27, 1909. It was a *fetva* of the *ulemas*, drawn up and delivered by the Sheikh-ul-Islam, that deposed Sultan Abdülhamid II from his office as successor of the prophet and made it legal for the parliament to dethrone him. See Abdurrahman Şeref, *Sultan Abdülhamid-i Sani: Suret-i Hali* (Sultan Abdülhamid II: His Dethronement) (İstanbul: Hilal Matbaası, 1918). Although published a century ago, this outstanding work is perhaps the best single study in the historiography of the subject.

32. Creelman, "The Moslem Answer to Christendom," pp. 168-69.

33. "The Conflict in the Provinces," *The Missionary Herald*, Vol. 105, No. 6 (June 1909), pp. 247-48.

34. Graves, *Briton and Turk*, p. 162.

35. By Absolutism is meant the autocratic rule of Sultan Abdülhamid II between 1878 and 1908.

36. Hüseyin Cahid, "Hakikati İstiyoruz" (We Want the Truth), *Tanin*, July 11, 1909, p. 1.
37. Pears, *Turkey and Its People*, p. 291.
38. Ibid., pp. 292–93.
39. Ibid., p. 293.
40. "Sir Edwin Pears on Turkey," *The Contemporary Review*, Vol. C (November 1911), p. 738.
41. Creelman, "The Moslem Answer to Christendom," p. 174.
42. Creelman, "The Slaughter of Christians in Asia Minor," p. 8.
43. Woods, *The Danger Zone of Europe*, p. 172.
44. Ibid., p. 173.
45. "Motive of the Adana Massacres," *The Literary Digest*, Vol. 39, No. 1 (July 3, 1909), p. 13.
46. Ibid.
47. Shepard, "Personal Experience in Turkish Massacres and Relief Work," p. 327.
48. "Bright Future for Turkey; Dr H.L. Underwood is Optimistic; Returns from Erzurum With Faith in Young Turks; Thinks Armenians Started Massacres," *The Boston Globe*, May 5, 1909, p. 7.
49. " The Massacres of Cilicia and the Young Turks," *The Armenian Herald*, No. February 1918, p. 55. *The Armenian Herald* was the monthly periodical of The Armenian National Union of America.
50. Bourne and Watt, British Documents on Foreign Affairs, Part I, Series B, Vol. 20, p. 145.
51. Edwin Pears, *Forty Years in Constantinople: The Recollections of Sir Edwin Pears 1873–1915* (London: Herbert Jenkins Limited, 1916), p. 298.
52. Woods, *The Danger Zone of Europe*, pp. 174–75.
53. Powell, *The Struggle for Power in Moslem Asia*, pp. 130–32.
54. "Jews and the Situation in Albania," Letter to the Editor, Your Constantinople Correspondent, *The Times*, August 9, 1911, p. 3.
55. Graves, *Briton and Turk*, p. 136.
56. "Les massacres d'Adana," Editorial, *Le Temps*, 14 octobre 1909, p. 1.
57. "Cerh" (A Refutation), *Tanin*, October 15, 1909, p. 1.
58. Marmaduke Pickthall, "Armenian Atrocities," *The New Age*, Vol. 18, No. 7 (December 16, 1915), p. 153.
59. Peter Clark, *Marmaduke Pickthall: British Muslim* (London: Quartet Books, 1986).
60. Suny, *A History of the Armenian Genocide*, pp. 172–73.
61. Here it is referred to Constantine Tripani, the British dragoman in Adana. The knowledge of foreign languages and having commercial and social standing were adduced by British consuls to justify appointments of candidates they proposed for these positions. Thus, Tripani, who was engaged as dragoman in Adana in 1909, was considered the best man for the job because he knew English and was a large cotton factory owner. His palatial red plaster home and English governesses put the seal of wealth and importance on him.
62. Arthur Tremaine Chester, "History's Verdict on New Turkey's Rise to Power," *Current History*, Vol. 19, No. 1 (October 1923), p. 81. Arthur Tremaine

Chester was the son of Rear Admiral Colby Mitchel Chester. He resided in İstanbul for fifteen years and knew Turkey well.

63. Colby Mitchel Chester, "Turkey Reinterpreted," *Current History*, Vol. 16, No. 6 (September 1922), p. 941.

64. Harold Armstrong, "Turkey," *Royal Central Asian Society Journal*, Vol. 15, Part 4 (1928), p. 428.

65. Armstrong, *Turkey and Syria Reborn*, p. 138.

66. Gaillard, *The Turks and Europe*, p. 286.

67. W. J. Childs, *Across Asia Minor on Foot* (Edinburgh and London: William Blackwood and Sons, 1918), pp. 349–50.

68. See Stanford Shaw, "Christian Anti-Semitism in the Ottoman Empire," *Belleten*, Vol. 54, No. 68 (1991), pp. 1073–149.

69. Marc David Baer, "An Enemy Old and New: The Dönme, Anti-Semitism, and Conspiracy Theories in the Ottoman Empire and Turkish Republic," *The Jewish Quarterly Review*, Vol. 103, No. 4 (Fall 2013), p. 530.

70. Elie Kedourie, "Young Turks, Freemasons and Jews," *Middle Eastern Studies*, Vol. 7, No. 1 (January 1971), p. 92.

71. Lewis, *The Emergence of Modern Turkey*, p. 211fn4.

72. Feroz Ahmad, *From Empire to Republic: Essays on the Late Ottoman Empire and Modern Turkey*, Vol. 1 (İstanbul: İstanbul Bilgi Üniversitesi Yayınları, 2008), pp. 133–34.

73. Childs, *Across Asia Minor on Foot*, pp. 347 and 350–51.

74. Ibid., pp. 347–48.

75. W. J. Childs's reference here is to Garabet Gökdereliyan of Kozan. See Çalyan, "Adana Vakası ve Mesulleri," p. 70.

76. Childs, *Across Asia Minor on Foot*, p. 350.

77. *Boston Morning Globe*, May 5, 1909, p. 7; *Boston Evening Transcript*, May 12, 1909, p. 3.

78. Ramsay, *The Revolution in Constantinople and Turkey*, p. 64.

79. Aflalo, *Regilding the Crescent*, p. 42.

80. Pears, *Turkey and Its People*, p. 293.

81. Walker, *Armenia*, p. 187.

82. "Provocation by Armenians; Report They Were Insolent, Quarrelsome and Boastful of Plans to Set Up a Separate Nation," *The Boston Globe*, May 7, 1909, p. 5; and "Armenians Blamed for Trouble," *The Chicago Daily Tribune*, May 8, 1909, p. 5.

83. Zeidner, "The Tricolor Over the Taurus," p. 49.

84. Eric Weitz, "Germany and the Ottoman Borderlands," in Omer Bartov and Eric Weitz, eds., *Shatterzone of Empires: Coexistence and Violence in the German, Habsburg, Russian, and Ottoman Borderlands* (Bloomington and Indianapolis, IN: Indiana University Press, 2013), p. 159.

Chapter Six

Reestablishing Order, May–August 1909

MEASURES TAKEN BY THE GOVERNMENT

In his address to the Chamber of Deputies on May 20, 1909, Sultan Reşad denounced the massacres in Adana as "contrary to the precepts of religion, the sentiments of humanity and the brotherhood of compatriots"; declared that the guilty would be punished; and promised that such horrors should never again occur. The applause that came from Muslims, Christians, and Jews alike seemed to stir him and there came into his face a smile, succeeded by a look of fatherly kindness. One of the sultan's most trusted advisers told James Creelman that His Majesty shed tears when he heard the real story of the butcheries in Adana.[1] An international relief committee was formed under the patronage of the sultan to collect and distribute relief in Adana and the districts of Syria where there was suffering. The president of the Committee was Said Paşa, the former grand vizier.[2]

Sultan Reşad received personally at his palace the Armenian patriarch Mateos İzmirliyan in great state and expressed his sorrow at the past sad events and spoke of the assurances of peace and quiet for all citizens of the empire under the constitution.[3]

Sultan Reşad was a most kindly and liberal sponsor. Few foreigners knew that during the thirty years of his confinement to his palace and garden prior to his accession to the throne, this unassuming old gentleman had gathered much knowledge and wisdom and showed much greater independence of judgment than was generally assumed.[4] The sovereign was an amiable man, beloved by his entourage, and he had produced a favorable impression on such foreigners as had been received by him.[5] His one and sole desire was to be at peace with other countries and to ensure the prosperity of his own country and the welfare of his people. A constitutional sovereign in the true sense of the term, Sultan Reşad followed the political situation closely, but left an entirely free hand to his ministers.[6] He was the perfect constitutional monarch, fulfilling his prerogatives.[7]

The *ulema* denounced the outrages and joined with the Armenian Church leaders to show their sympathy with the victims. Orders were issued to the local authorities to check disturbances at all costs, and the Sheikh-ul-Islam and the Armenian patriarch issued strict injunctions to the muftis and clergy to abstain from provocative language.[8] The *ulema* articulated the public interest much in the spirit of civil society, which existed in latent form in the late Ottoman Empire and had great historical legacy.

Since the sources of Islamic law—mainly revelation and the recorded practice of the prophet—were beyond the competence of temporal rulers, the *ulema* enjoyed extensive autonomy. Nevertheless they remained clearly subordinate to secular authority.

In May 1909 James Creelman saw Sheikh-ul-Islam Sahib Molla[9] and heard from his lips the true Muslim view of the persecution and murder of Christians. "Why do Moslems persecute Christians in Turkey?" Creelman asked. "What's there in the Koran to justify it?" The Sheikh-ul-Islam laid his right hand palm down on his desk and leaned forward, looking Creelman straight in the eyes. "The thing can be put in a few words from the standpoint of the law," he said. "In the Ottoman Empire the Moslems go to the mosque, the Christians go to the church and the Jews go to the synagogue. There is no other difference, absolutely none." "But," Creelman said, "the suspicion of the world generally and the opinion of Americans is that Moslem law or Moslem policy calls for bitter opposition to Christians and that to a large extent the massacres of Armenians are due to the open or secret influence of the teachers of the Moslem faith." The venerable Sheikh-ul-Islam raised his splendid turbaned head high and lifted both hands. The color came into his face and his great brown eyes shone with a sudden intensity. "Such an idea is utterly false," he said in a deep voice. "There is nothing in the law, nothing in the Koran, nothing in Moslem policy or intention that sanctions hatred or strife between subjects of the empire, be they Moslems, Christians or Jews. The truth is that our sacred law makes it the absolute religious duty of a Moslem to live on terms of peace and equality with non-Moslems. It is his duty, not only not to molest, but to protect, his fellow subjects, regardless of race or religion. I say this officially and without any reserve." "But is it not the duty of a good Moslem to kill all who reject the faith?" "Never, never." "Is not 'Islam or the sword' the real motto of the followers of the Prophet?" "Never. We have no such policy. It is false." "Do you repudiate it officially as Sheik-ul-Islam?" "I do. I repudiate it altogether. There is no such Moslem idea. It is contrary to our sacred law."[10]

The Sheikh-ul-Islam drew his soft mantle close about him, moistened his lips with his tongue, and put his fingertips together in an Ottoman gesture. "In the old days," he said, "we were permitted to offer our faith to other peoples. If those to whom we came yielded their allegiance to the Moslem government they might reject our religion and keep their own. When they became Moslem subjects it was the religious duty of all Moslems to protect them, no matter how they worshipped God." "But that was all in the old days of conquest," he added. "We do not speak, we do not think of conquest now. We wish to live at peace with the world." "Do you oppose the teaching of the Christian religion in Turkey?" "If we did not believe in Jesus Christ and His gospels we would not be Moslems. We accept Christ as a prophet of God and we accept His teachings. But which are the gospels of Christ? Those which exist? Those which are offered by Christians? We doubt it; indeed we doubt it very strongly." He half rose from his seat and shook his head slowly as he spoke. "Will you name any one of the teachings of Christ which you accept? Do you accept, for instance, the sermon on the Mont?" A flush came into the noble face. He raised his hands in protest. His brows were drawn together. "That is a delicate question," he replied. "I would not, as Sheikh-ul-Islam, undertake to indicate any particular teaching of Christ which we accept. We believe in Him as a prophet and we believe in anything taught by Him that does not conflict with the Koran. As an example, but not as an exact parallel, it is a fact that you have laws in the United States and that the people are obliged to obey these laws. You have methods of changing the laws, and everyone must obey the new laws—as against the old laws. But there are often provisions of the old laws which do not conflict with the new laws; and in such cases the provisions of the old laws continue in full force. So it is with the teachings of Christ and the law as given by God through the Prophet Mohammed."[11]

"It seems strange to hear what you say," Creelman said, "for there are many millions of good men and women who believe that 'Islam or the sword' are still the alternatives offered by Moslems when they are strong enough to have their way. A large part of the world believes that the ulemas and other leaders of the Moslem faith, while pretending to deplore the massacres of the Armenians, secretly rejoice and gloat over the destruction of so many Christians." The Sheikh-ul-Islam threw his hands up and a look of angry astonishment shone in his eyes. "We look on the massacres with horror," he exclaimed in a voice that, for the first time, shook with emotion. "The ulemas were the first to weep over them. Ah"—his great breast heaved and his lips trembled—"we all wept over those dreadful crimes." "How does it happen that the Moslems in Adana attack their Christian neighbors?" "The events there have been greatly exaggerated. Besides, at the bottom of all was deep ignorance and the desire for personal gain. The government is doing all in its power to prevent any repetition of the massacres. It is absolutely sincere in its attitude. The ulemas will also do their whole duty and teach the people that such acts are contrary to their religion. Nothing will be left undone from this time forward. We are determined to have no more massacres." "But can you succeed?" "God willing"—with outstretched hands and uplifted eyes—"God willing. We are in his hands. I believe we shall succeed."[12]

"Is it not a fact that you are opposed to the work of the Christian missionaries in Turkey?" "You mean foreigners?" "I mean American missionaries." "Well, unofficially, I must say I am opposed to them, not because they are Christians, but because they are foreigners. We only permit their work as a compliment to the American nation." The Sheikh-ul-Islam touched the most sensitive spot in the problem, for in the Ottoman Empire, there was no religion separate from the government and there was no government separate from the religion. The empire was a theocracy. "But," Creelman urged, "the Armenians, who are all Christians, declare that the restrictions in Turkey are so great that it is impossible for them to develop educated preachers or to get sufficient education for their children. Therefore they send to America and the presence of American missionaries in Asia Minor is an answer to earnest appeals for instruction." Sahib Molla smiled and stroked his white beard as he nodded his head. "If that is so, we should remember a saying of the Prophet: 'We must take science wherever we find it, even if it be in China.'" At this point the Sheikh-ul-Islam stood up and folded his arms, raising himself to his full height. "Religion is not at the bottom of these troubles," he said, "but poverty, ignorance and greed. Believe me when I say this. What we need is capital from England, America, Germany and other countries to develop railways, telephones, telegraphs, factories and mines. When the people are prosperous they will soon forget their differences." "It has been charged that the American missionaries in Turkey stir up a spirit of sedition and rebellion. Have you found it so?" A beautiful look came into the fine old face. "I will say nothing against them. We are all travellers and our journey is soon done. All we can hope in this life is to do a little good and leave it behind us. I do not propose to stir up any unkind feelings, whatever I may think."[13]

Creelman left the Sheikh-ul-Islam, the ecclesiastical head of the empire and the final interpreter of the Koran to the entire orthodox Muslim world, with the feeling that an honester man did not breathe. All through their talk Sahib Molla conveyed the impression that he held the fallen Sultan principally responsible for the massacres of Christians, although, out of some sense of official propriety, he did not name him.[14]

The American journalist Herman Bernstein during an interview he had with the Sheikh-ul-Islam Sahib Molla at the end of July 1909 asked how

Islam looked upon people of other faiths and nonbelievers. His answer came slowly, in measured tone:

> There is no difference between Mohammedan, Jew, or Christian in the eyes of a true Moslem. All are equal. The only place where our ways part is at prayer— we go to the mosque, while they go to a synagogue or church. In fact, as far as we are concerned, our ways need not part even then, for we Moslems are at liberty to pray anywhere. We do not make the slightest discrimination against those who do not believe as we do. We look upon their goods as our good, and upon their life as our life, and we try to protect them in every way. The Moslem who does not believe in Moses, the founder of Judaism, and Christ, the founder of Christianity, as prophets, is not a true Moslem. Of course, Mohammed, who came later than Moses and Christ, and who found the world in a state of dreadful demoralisation, has improved upon their teachings. Otherwise all the prophets are equal. As for the unbelievers, we feel sorry for them, we pity them, but we do not persecute them. Our sympathies are naturally with believers, we are not angry at agnostics. Their conscience is their own affair.[15]

It was a fact that faithful and law-abiding Armenians were not only protected, but also employed in very high official positions, one of them even being, at the present moment, minister of trade and public works. The fact was, also, that the Armenians in the Ottoman Empire had their own schools, that their language and literature were preserved, that their nationality was respected, that their leading men were promoted in the scale of high honors and positions, while Christian Europe and America had no care for the Jews, and while Catholic Spain had not allowed a single Muslim family to remain on its European territory, and had centuries ago expelled them all. The reason of this colossal difference lay in the fact that Islam was indeed a religion essentially and radically tolerant.[16]

Ferid Paşa, minister of the interior, as soon as he learned what had happened in the provinces of Adana and Aleppo, took energetic measures to stop the outrages and sent a military commission at once to report, with authority to take what steps they thought best to prevent recurrence, and to deal out exemplary punishment to the wrong-doers.[17] This commission left on May 8, 1909, by steamer via Mersin and expected to reach Adana on May 13. It was composed of Kenan Paşa as president and seven other army officers. The men were selected by Mahmud Şevket Paşa, commander of the Third Army, with extreme care, and they had been instructed to try under martial law those inciting the Muslims to riot. They would also determine whether the provincial governor and commander of the troops were negligent. The phrase so often used by Mahmud Şevket Paşa, "order is the foundation of liberty," might be regarded as the principle guiding the commission.[18]

The grand vizier and Ferid Paşa received a deputation of the Armenian clergy and laity on May 8. The delegation was headed by Arscharani, the provisional representative of the patriarchate, who was assured that the government would inquire thoroughly into the Adana massacres and severely punish those guilty of instigating them. The ministers said the investigation would be conducted by a military court. Ferid Paşa told the delegation that eight physicians had been sent from İzmir to Adana and that several also had gone there from İstanbul. The physicians, he added, carried with them large quantities of medical supplies. A number of notable Armenians met in İstanbul on May 9 and submitted to the government the following requests: First, that the murderers of Christians be punished; second, that stolen property be returned and indemnities be paid for property destroyed; third, that the women and girls who were abducted be returned, and also that men and women who were compelled forcibly to adopt Mohammedanism be allowed to resume their original faith; fourth, that the investigation conducted under the chairmanship of the governor be suspended and that a new investigation of the disorders from their commencement be made by a militay commission; fifth, that Christians be permitted to participate in the local police establishment; and sixth, that Armenians be allowed to participate in defraying the cost of erecting a monument to those who fell in the army of liberty.[19]

Ferid Paşa informed a representative of *Tanin* at the end of May 1909 that several of the soldiers who took part in the massacres in Cilicia were arrested. Nine persons were already condemned to death by the court martial. With regard to the responsibility for the outbreak, the minister said that, while he could not definitely ascribe it to official promptings, certain officials had failed to do their duty, among them the *mutasarrıf* of Cebelibereket, who had been imprisoned pending an inquiry into his conduct. The reactionaries had certainly played a part in fomenting the outbreak, but other elements—which the minister did not specify—had contributed thereto. The government had made up its mind to discover the criminals and to inflict on them the most severe punishment. There would be no attempt to conceal the truth.[20]

The Ottoman cabinet took up the consideration of the situation in Adana and neighboring districts. The problem of searching out the persons responsible for the events, inflicting punishment and settling the district was the first which faced the government on its reconstitution after the troubles of April. On the morning of April 23, 1909, the cruiser *Mecidiye* left for the Cilician coast. The commander of a British warship applied to the *kaymakam* of İskenderun for permission to land a relief party, but his application was refused.[21]

The new governor, Babanzade Mustafa Zihni Paşa, appointed immediately after the events, arrived at Adana on April 30. He was instructed to take the most energetic measures to reestablish order and relieve the sufferers.[22] Colonel Mehmet Ali Bey was dispatched at the same time from Beirut to act as the military commander. Muslihittin Adil Bey, undersecretary of state in the Ministry of the Interior, on the same date said the government would make a searching investigation in the cause of the disorders and punish the instigators. Reports received at the ministry of the interior indicated that quiet now prevailed everywhere. The undersecretary said that the government recognized the necessity of providing food, medicine, and shelter for the sufferers and had taken steps to provide these and inaugurate other measures of relief. Fresh troops were dispatched from the Third Army in Salonika, and the local authorities began to face the grave and pressing problem of relief and shelter for the homeless and orphaned ones.[23]

By May 3, Colonel Mehmet Ali Bey had twenty-one battalions under his command and he told British vice consul Charles Dougthy-Wylie among other things that he was going to remove the *sarık* or the white hat band round the fez that all Muslims put on for the massacre and were still wearing. He also related that he was sending a battalion of troops out the following day to cut some of the harvest. This was highly necessary work and Dougthy-Wylie was very glad Colonel Mehmet Ali Bey was taking it in hand. When certain matters of discipline among his troops had been brought to his notice, he said he was most anxious to discover the perpetrators of such crimes and to punish them severely. Dougthy-Wylie judged him to be an honest, capable, and hardworking officer.[24]

Forty-eight hours had been given for looted property to be returned. At the end of this time anybody found in possession of stolen goods would be dealt with under martial law. Colonel Mehmet Ali Bey said that he would not hesitate to shoot or hang a few men for the tranquility of the country.[25]

Dougthy-Wylie heard on May 8 that the Greek patriarchate had demanded the dismissal of the *mutasarrıf* of Mersin, Esad Rauf Bey. If this was correct it was due to the local intrigues that the man had saved Mersin from massacre and was an excellent official. The local enmity against him arose from the fact that he was the first Ottoman official there to refuse bribes and to refuse to be entirely ruled by the Greek clique in Mersin headed by a certain Mavromati, who was the Russian consul. Personally, Dougthy-Wylie would have liked to see this official made governor of Adana. Nothing could be expected from the present governor.[26]

The correspondents of the *Berliner Tageblatt* and the *New York Herald* visited Governor Mustafa Zihni Paşa on May 21. The governor declared that thirty thousand Turkish liras voted by the Chamber of Deputies as relief aid were placed in the hands of the three committees: one, to restore stolen cattle; two, to restore stolen goods; and three, to feed those in want and to reestablish them in their trades. The truth of the matter was that some stolen cattle and stolen goods were restored at practically no cost to the government, and that they sent food to Adana sufficient for about three thousand people, as well as furnished some tents and a few buckets for wells. In outlying parts of the province, the homeless were given enough food to keep them alive, but Dougthy-Wylie did not believe that this was due to anybody except energetic local officials.[27]

An imperial decree issued on July 13 ordered the trial by court martial of Cevad Bey, former governor of Adana; Mustafa Remzi Paşa, the military commander at Adana; and Asaf Bey, *mutasarrıf* of Cebelibereket. They were implicated with the Armenian massacres. Cevad Bey, who failed to make any effort to quell the disorders, was placed under detention. His defense was that he simply carried out the orders which he received from İstanbul, and he was therefore not responsible for anything that happened. For some time prior to April 1909 he had been keeping his superiors in the Sublime Porte informed about the possibility that existing tensions in the province of Adana might easily spill into violence at any time. Cevad Bey was attentive to detail and focused on practical matters, yet he was not always the best judge of events and men.[28] The *mutasarrıf* of Cebelibereket and the *kaymakam* of Erzin were arrested and sent under a strong escort to Adana under clouds of suspicion, accusation, and complaint.[29]

REPORT OF THE GOVERNOR CEVAD BEY ON THE EVENTS TO THE SUBLIME PORTE, MAY 25, 1909

The report on the events given to the Sublime Porte on May 25, 1909, by Cevad Bey can be summarized as follows. During the last two weeks in March, two Muslims, İsfendiyar and Rahimi, were wounded by an Armenian with a firearm. It was understood afterwards to be a question of a woman, between Ohannes (the Armenian) and the former. İsfendiyar died of his wounds. The murderer, not being discovered and arrested, it was rumored, was saved by Garabet Gökdereliyan and hidden by the Armenians. The authorities did all they could to find the criminal and took no notice of current rumors. Then came Easter. As for some time there was a cool feeling between the Turks and the Armenians, it would have been wiser not to fire revolver shots on this occasion (it was a custom with the Christians to fire into the air on Easter days, by way of rejoicing), but far from obeying orders, several shots were fired, disturbing the Muslims. The authorities then stationed patrols round the churches to avoid disagreeable incidents. On April 13 it was rumored that a Turkish woman and a few men had been killed by Armenians in the vineyards. This news spread like lightning, the Turkish populace, already set against the Armenians, gathered in quarters and in cafés round the *Konak*, and made demonstrations. Thereupon the governorate got the police to make inquiries, and having stated that the rumors were without foundation the order to restore calm was given, by spreading the truth. In the night the governor went out himself on a tour, accompanied by the military commander; they gave good council, and the governor tried hard to be understood by telling people everywhere that the news was erroneous, and that they must not believe hearsay. In the same vein, they tried to discover the inventors of these stories and they ordered patrols to go round the city. They learned the same night, at about 10:30, that an Armenian, Mason Loutfik, had been killed near the *Konak* by some Muslims who were gathered there. An inquest was held, and a police inquiry was opened to investigate the cause and the manner of this assassination. The whole night was spent with the military commander organizing patrols and to take such measures as the situation demanded.[30]

Early in the morning of April 14 the notables and the *ulema* were invited to the *Konak* to renew the good advice, having heard that the Armenians were closing their shops and that the Muslims were following their example; the Armenian notables were also invited to come to the *Konak* and ordered to go and give good advice to their comrades in order that the situation might not farther be embittered. At this very moment it was learned that the troubles had recommenced: they went to the town, where the shops and markets were, to disperse the crowd, which was blocking the streets. Being the season just before spring, ten thousand to fifteen thousand agricultural laborers had come from outside and had invaded the inns, augmenting the population of the city, so that those moved on in one street went to crowd in another, and the patrol followed them. On their returning to the *Konak* the first gunshots were heard. An inquiry was opened on the troubles. This report was signed by the chief inquirer of the province, the police commander, the police commissary, the commander of the regular troops, and the central police commissary. This document contained much detail. It was said there that during the disorders a carriage was passing in the market place carrying two Armenians armed with rifles and ammunition, which had been sequestered and given to the military authorities. At that moment, an Armenian on horseback galloped toward the bridge, swearing at the Muslim religion; it was said that it was he who fired the first shot. Almost at the same time, a shot was fired from the house of Avedis Sisliyan, a former director of correspondence of the province, killing a Çerkez Mehmed: thus the troubles commenced on different spots at the same time. As the troubles spread, the working population joined the mob and began to pillage and ransack, and the fires broke out in the night.[31]

Directly after the beginning of these events, conferring with the military commander, the governorate decided to declare a state of siege and the Sublime Porte was informed of this. However, it was impossible to maintain public order with four hundred soldiers, when from ten thousand to fifteen thousand outsiders set themselves against the forty thousand to fifty thousand inhabitants of the city, to check the mob, full of hatred and ill-feeling, given to pillage; the governorate was unable to decide on the state of siege, and the events lasted three days. In the meantime the governorate took all possible measures, with the military commander, to put an end to the troubles, but for reasons already mentioned they were unable to stop them. They sent for two battalions of reservists of Tarsus and Karaisalı, and they managed to arm them, but as they were irregulars and without uniform, being natives, they dispersed, under pretext of going to their villages to protect them, thus the battalions could not profit by their services. They appealed then to the reservist batallion of Misis, which was later sent to Hacin, where they were successful in restoring peace. The British vice consul who was coming from Mersin to Adana on the first day of the events wanted to go round the streets, braving all danger. The governorate put at his disposal policemen and regular soldiers; he went visiting several quarters. The second day he was shot at from an Armenian house and a sergeant fell. The vice consul raised his arm as a signal of peace; a ball touched his arm and wounded it. After the troubles, other events took place in the suburbs. The governorate sent soldiers and took all measures to thwart the progress of the mob, but without avail.[32]

During the events and the following days, immediate military measures were taken. Every day the governorate sent, here and there, notables and *ulemas* to preach peace and secure tranquility. A commission was formed to tend the wounded and to feed them. Measures were taken to discover and return to their owners articles and animals that had been stolen, pillaged, and carried away to the suburbs or neighboring villages. The authorities, through the same commission, returned to their owners merchant goods and other articles found in the villages. But on account of the insufficiency of soldiers, it was not possible to make serious searches of the pillaged goods until April 25. As soon as the troubles commenced the governorate seriously telegraphed for military reinforcements. It was only on April 24 that eight hundred and fifty regular soldiers at last arrived. The next day the governorate held a council, and it was decided to send clerks and soldiers to search out the pillaged goods. In the meantime, at about 4:30, the troubles commenced, and the frightened people ran in all directions. The number of the watch houses was augmented, and the watch became very strict. These troubles were renewed, because at 4:30, in the Salcılar quarter of the watch, the Armenians had killed a soldier, at Kalekapısı, another Armenian had shot at another soldier of the Station Corps de Garde. The next day peace and order were ordered.[33]

Enormous bombs and explosives had exploded in the burned houses of the Armenians; in others were discovered armorial badges, flags of Armenia, engravings representing men armed with guns, dynamite caps, and unused bombs. Also found in an Armenian village were two cannons made out of water pipes, covered with wood and kept together with iron rings, which were used during the troubles. They were handed to the military authorities. A detailed report on the situation of Cebelibereket was sent directly to the minister of the interior. It appeared that the troubles at Hamidiye took place on April 15. According to an eyewitness, a French subject and inspector of the Régie, M. Pens, an Armenian priest fired three shots at Arslan Bey of the Régie, who was sitting at the café, opposite the *Konak*, the latter replied and the priest was wounded, both died of their wounds. The truth was acquired that the troubles were an outcome of this fact. At Sis, the chief town of the Kozan district, people were excited, from the environs, a group of Circassians, Afşar, and Çeçen cavaliers, after an encounter with the reservists and the police, and after having left on the ground only a few of their men, were dispersed so that nothing surprising happened in the town. In spite of that, later on the governorate sent two battalions of soldiers. In the Hacin town the Armenians, barricading themselves in their houses, fired into the street. They stopped the traffic and did not even let the reinforcements sent by Feke to restore order enter the town. The Circassians and the tribes of Aziziye (Pınarbaşı) and of other villages gathered near the town and began to threaten Hacin. The central authorities sent a commission to advise obedience and calm, but this commission was not successful; it was not received, and returned empty handed. In the meantime, the Misis battalion, composed of four hundred soldiers, was sent; its commander succeeded in penetrating the town and the invading mob dispersed. During the troubles at Tarsus, conflagrations, killing, and losses occurred, but thanks to the measures adopted, this did not last long. At Mersin, too, the emotion was great, but again, thanks to the measures taken, nothing happened; the same might be said of the İçili district.[34]

The chief cause of the events was the ignorance of the Christians and Muslims, the result of the tyrannical epoch, the want of fusion of various elements, as well as of the insufficiency of sentiments toward the union. As everywhere else, also in Adana, since the proclamation of the constitution, everybody, even the children, armed themselves with firearms and discharged right and left, without anyone being able to prevent it. The world was under the influence of a deep emotion, provoked by the publication of papers which said that the Muslims were about to attack the Christians. The lower-class Armenian excited the people by such phrases as this: "Since the constitution, the importance of the Muslims is diminished, we are going to pass your turbans round your necks and drag you about." This provoked anger. It was true that people of this kind were arrested and put into the hands of justice, and that, on the other hand, good advice was given to the people, through the men of influence and standing, Turk or Christian; but the Armenian papers of İstanbul, such as *Arevelk*, and many other publications of this kind, overexcited the Muslims and deadened the effect of their refutations. On the other hand, Bishop Musheg Seropian advised the Armenians to trespass the laws of the government and poisoned their minds. The governorate had asked the Ministry of the Interior on January 29 and March 2, 1909, to replace him with another. His words incited the Armenians against the Muslims and the government itself.[35]

The police forces and the number of police agents were very small, compared to the extent of province. The need demanded their reinforcement. How many times did the governorate not appeal to the minister of the interior, as well as to the ministers of war and police. On November 11, 1908, the instructions were to do whatever was necessary. On January 21, 1909, it was suggested to organize and augment the police force by one hundred fifty men in order to keep tranquility in the province; by the governorate's requests on February 28 and March 2, 1909, it was said that if the projected organizations were not carried out, there might happen disagreeable events. In the governorate's request of March 5, 1909, it was written that people were discharging arms in the city; the authors were handed over to the police, but the punishments imposed were ridiculous, they ought to have been much more severe, and the number of police increased. In the governorate's letter of March 11, 1909, the Sublime Porte was warned that on account of the season, ten thousand to fifteen thousand cultivators arrived in Adana from various provinces, and that a little later, in and outside the city, there would be fifty thousand to sixty thousand nomadic people, thinking differently, and that for this reason it would be necessary to increase the police force. Apart from all these warnings to diverse ministers before and after the events, for keeping order and peace at Mersin, and for guarding the Payas prisoners, the governorate asked for soldiers to replace the one hundred soldiers then sent on Dörtyol, during the siege.[36]

MUTASARRIF ASAF BEY'S EXONERATION

Asaf Bey, the *mutasarrıf* of Cebelibereket, was anxious to have the accusations brought against him thoroughly investigated. His purity of purpose and rectitude of conduct, he hoped, would exonerate him from all blame and enable him to gain once more the confidence of the Sublime Porte.[37] Although one does not expect memoirs to be wholly objective, his memoirs are still valuable to the historian. Asaf Bey was interested primarily in demonstrating the correctness of his actions and the soundness of his attitude in 1908–1909. Many people of prominence accepted his explanations; the Sublime Porte put him back into office again as *mutasarrıf* in 1915.[38] He was an ambitious man and what he wanted was to be promoted to the provincial governorship. Although Asaf Bey would show himself to be a man of certain talents, he scarcely seemed the sort of figure destined to shine in administration. A laconic, sarcastic man with no flair for public speaking, he seemed to be made by nature for the role of an ordinary bureaucrat. He hoped to arrive at the rank of governor some day by dint of seniority. Asaf Bey, who did not get on well with his superiors, never rose above the rank of *mutasarrıf* in the Ministry of the Interior.

Asaf Bey was born in 1870 in İstanbul. After graduating from the College of Administrative Sciences in 1893, he entered the Ministry of the Interior at the beginning of 1895. After serving eleven years as *kaymakam* in Tercan, Tortum, Hamidiye, Vadiülacem, Selimiye, Benisaab, Birüssebi, and Yafa, he was promoted and appointed *mutasarrıf* in Cebelibereket on September 14, 1908. Cevad Bey and Asaf Bey had a similar background in that they were all born in Ottoman Europe to families of officials, received training in the same profession, and in the same College of Administrative Sciences, whose curriculum at the time included the teaching of international law, statistics and methodology, political economy, administrative law, penal law, commercial law, economics, geography, history, accounting, cosmography, and international treaties. Asaf Bey had the opportunity to observe many of eastern Cilicia's seminal events of the years between 1908 and 1910 and became familiar with the region's important individuals. He was dismissed from his post on July 6, 1910. He was later able to pursue his career in the civil service for a short time. He then went into practice of private law until his death in 1950. Asaf Bey adopted the surname Belge in 1934.[39]

Asaf Bey served as *mutasarrıf* of Çankırı from May 15 to July 28, 1915. This posting was his final appointment. For reasons that remain unclear, he was finally removed from all posts and sent into forced retirement. Grigoris Balakian, a Gregorian Armenian priest who was relocated from İstanbul to Çankırı on April 24, 1915, saw Asaf Bey a righteous Turk and spoke well of him. Balakian showed him kind and thoughtful.[40]

ECONOMIC LOSSES INFLICTED BY THE EVENTS

According to the annual report of the British embassy in İstanbul on the Ottoman Empire for the year 1910, of the economic losses inflicted by the actual events in April there were no statistics, but it was estimated that the revenues of the district which usually amounted to 2,000,000 Turkish liras would be reduced to less than 500,000 Turkish liras. The losses inflicted on foreign subjects during the period of the events were considerable; the French, German, American, and Italian governments approached the Ottoman government with a view to obtaining compensation for the damage done to the property of their subjects, but the Ottoman government repudiated all responsibility on the plea of *force majeure*, and recommended that individuals who suffered such losses should take their legal remedy through the law courts. The foreign powers considered further action, either by united representations or by submission of the question to arbitration. The British government took no steps to recover compensation for the injury done to British interests, amounting to many thousands of pounds in value, in consideration of the failure of other powers to obtain any such compensation. Of course, appeal could be made to the courts. The Armenian patriarch, after vain appeals to the central government, supported the Armenians in bringing cases into the law courts against the insurance companies, the majority of which were British institutions.[41]

In reply to the queries of the two European ambassadors with regard to the claims of their nationals in connection with the events of Adana in April 1909, the grand vizier replied that, while not disapproving in principle of the idea of submitting the question of the liability of the Ottoman government to The Hague Tribunal, it was quite impossible for him at present to lay such a suggestion before parliament here. He evidently dreaded making a suggestion which would arouse the feelings which had recently been showing themselves in that assembly, and which, he feared, might have repercussions throughout the country.[42]

Levant Herald of İstanbul reported on October 12, 1909, that the German embassy had recently presented to the Porte a claim on account of the losses sustained by German subjects during the late massacres at Adana. The French and Italian embassies likewise had claims. The Italian claim exceeded 100,000 French francs.[43] *Tanin* and *Tasviri Efkar* had learned from the Ministry of Foreign Affairs that the Porte, basing itself on the principle that no indemnities were due for losses sustained during an insurrection, refused to recognize the claims presented by the embassies.[44] The London daily *The Daily Telegraph* wrote the following day that the powers requested the Porte to compensate foreign subjects for losses sustained in the Adana massacres, and the Ottoman authorities had replied that these troubles constituted a case of *force majeure* and that consequently no compensation could be forwarded. The powers had pressed their claims, and the Porte was preparing a further note of refusal.[45]

The Western Insurance Company at London, in a statement to the Foreign Office on February 28, 1912, suggested that the following be at once brought officially before the Ottoman government with a view to recover the sum paid by their company as the result of a compromise arrived at to settle three insurance claims under the policies in regard to which a final sentence was pronounced by the Mixed Commercial Court in İstanbul. The claims in question were brought by a certain Aristakes Gasparian, an Armenian and Ottoman subject, who was an advocate. He had effected two insurance policies on his own properties in Adana, and was acting at the same time for a certain Aprahamian, the holder of another policy. All three properties were completely destroyed in the riots and disturbances at Adana on April 14, 1909. On the same day the three houses insured were burned, hundreds of other houses were also burned to the ground. No salvage was recovered or was recoverable. Thereupon the assured brought an action in the Mixed Commercial Court in İstanbul. The Western Insurance Company pleaded that it was not liable because the case came under one of the articles of the "Conditions" endorsed on its policy. Almost the only argument before the court turned on the question whether the article in question exempted the Western Insurance Company from payment. It was not denied that the property had been destroyed. Nor was it claimed that it had been overinsured. The article relied on was the following: "En cas de guerre, d'invasion, d'émeute, de complot, dans tous les cas où les bâtiments assurées sont occupés, en tout ou en partie, par des troupes nationales ou étrangères, armées ou non armées, belligérentes ou non belligérentes, la Compagnie n'est responsable de l'incendie que si l'assuré prouve qu'il ne provient ni directement, ni indirectement, des causes ci-dessus." This may be translated as follows: "The Company is only responsible for loss by fire if the assured proves that the fire did not happen either directly or indirectly from any of the following causes, namely, in case of war, invasion, riot, conspiracy, in cases where the buildings insured are occupied either wholly or in part by national or foreign troops, whether armed or not, belligerents or non-belligerents."[46]

The fire occurred beyond a doubt during a terrible riot in which thousands of Armenians were killed. The company claimed that the word "émeute" signified riot. Various dictionaries were quoted to show that "émeute" was equivalent to "riot" and "general disorder." The plaintiff asserted that the fire did not happen during an "émeute," and that there was no "émeute" during the Adana troubles. The court, presided over by an Armenian, decided that the word signified "a seditious movement of the people against the constituted authority," and that there was no seditious movement at the time. Thereupon it gave a formal judgment to that effect and condemned the company to pay the full amount of the policies with interest and cost.[47]

In view of the adverse judgment of the Mixed Commercial Court, the Western Insurance Company asked that the British government should claim compensation from the Sublime Porte on their behalf on the ground of the injustice of that decision. It did not appear to Sir Edward Grey, the foreign secretary, to be possible to put forward a claim on this ground. "Denial of justice" was a well-recognized basis for diplomatic intervention, and for claiming compensation on behalf of the party injured thereby, but the term meant something more than a feeling on the part of the authorities of the claiming government that, had they been members of the tribunal which dealt with the case, their conclusion would have differed from that arrived at by the court. In Grey's view the term "denial of justice" which, so far as he was aware had never been exhaustively defined, necessarily entailed this idea: that the tribunal with all the facts before it could not honestly have arrived at the decision which it gave. Judged by this test the decision complained of did not appear to amount to a denial of justice, for whatever confidence might be felt in London that the decision was erroneous, it was impossible to maintain that the point of law was not one about which there was reasonable doubt. The grounds on which this claim was based seemed therefore inadequate to justify its presentation to the Ottoman government.[48]

THE DEBATE IN THE CHAMBER OF DEPUTIES, MAY 1, 5, AND 7, 1909

At the May 1 sitting of the Chamber of Deputies, Arif Hikmet first took the floor and declared that Governor Cevad Bey's telegrams had distorted the truth about the painful and deplorable disaster in Adana. He suggested sending a parliamentary commission to Cilicia to assess the situation, submit recommendations to the parliament, and punish those responsible for the events. After Arif Hikmet, Ohannes Vartges took the floor. He recommended that martial law be introduced in Adana, that investigative commissions set up by the parliament and the army in Salonika be sent to Cilicia, that looted belongings be returned to their owners, and, since the former sultan had had a hand in this black endeavor, that some of his earnings be allocated to the people who had suffered losses. Similar statements and suggestions were made by Nazaret Dagavaryan and Hamparsum Boyacıyan. After a debate, a statement jointly signed by deputies Arif Hikmet, Ohannes Vartges, Hamparsum Boyacıyan, Kegam Der Garabedyan, Ali Cenani, Vahan Papazyan, Agop Babikyan, and Nazaret Dagavaryan was considered. It recommended that Adana Governor Cevad Bey, the undersecretary of state in the Ministry of the Interior, Adil Bey, and other felonious officials, whose professional negligence had brought about the massacres or who had directly participated in the events, be tried before a military tribunal. The signatories also recommended declaring a state of siege in the Aleppo province, in Antakya, Zeytun, and other areas affected by the disaster; sending a court martial to Cilicia, not from Salonika but from İstanbul; sending a cable demanding an immediate raising of the siege of Dörtyol; and rendering aid to the starving and homeless people without delay.[49]

The Chamber of Deputies on the same day adopted a resolution that a parliamentary commission be dispatched to Adana to investigate the massacres and to organize a military court to court martial the guilty persons. The resolution also included the following steps: the recent events being the result of the neglect of Governor Cevad Bey and of undersecretary of state in the Ministry of the Interior Adil Bey to perform their duty, and of the actual participation of certain officials, these persons should be tried by court martial; places like Antakya and Zeytun in the province of Aleppo, where there had been signs of disturbance, should also be placed under martial law, and to ensure the impartiality of the court martial it should be appointed from İstanbul; to insure the safety of Dörtyol, which was now besieged and in danger, the necessary steps should be taken by telegraph; to save the unhappy sufferers from famine, and to provide them with shelter and food, the necessary sums should be granted, and the collection of funds locally being difficult, money should be sent at once from the capital; mixed and impartial commissions should be formed in each town to restore the plundered goods to their owners, to assess the number and value of the buildings burned, to find out the number and the names of the dead, and to present a return to the government. A total of 100,000 dollars was appropriated to relieve the distress in the district. Armenians raised funds, to which Sultan Reşad subscribed.[50]

The governor of Adana, Babanzade Mustafa Zihni Paşa, informed Grand Vizier Hüseyin Hilmi Paşa on May 2 that order and tranquility were totally reestablished in the city. According to police and gendarmerie reports no incident occurred until this date.[51] In an interview with James Creelman in that month Babanzade Mustafa Zihni Paşa said that the tragedy in Adana was a quarrel among themselves (Muslims and Armenians). "Both sides misunderstood the meaning of the Constitution. There was much foolish talk about liberty and equality. Speeches were made and feelings were hurt. The whole thing has been greatly exaggerated. It does not concern outside countries." "The American missionaries? Oh, they do much good in enlightening a part of the population. I recognize that, of course. But their teachers are altogether Christian. That is bad. No Turk will send his children to them, for they would be taught to make the sign of cross. The teachers in the American schools should be half Moslem and half Christian. That would be a good arrangement, a very good arrangement. Then the benefits would not be confined to the Armenians."[52]

The Adana branch of the Agricultural Bank demanded 50,000 liras and fifty combine harvesters to put at the disposal of the farmers, for during the recent events all agricultural implements were destroyed. Stéphan Pichon, the French minister of foreign affairs, sent an aid of 4,000 francs.[53]

The Chamber of Deputies on May 5 adopted unanimously the suggestion of the cabinet that the sum of 150,000 dollars be appropriated for the relief of the sufferers in the Adana province.[54] It was a ray of light that the government had ordered a searching investigation and had voted 150,000 dollars in relief of the sufferers, but would it reach those who were in need, for whom the aid was intended, and would it be enough? The government took hold of the relief work in the district with vigor. It was announced on May 9 that 150,000 dollars had been sent there. This amount was distributed by a committee under the presidency of the governor of Adana. The Agricultural Bank arranged to loan 75,000 dollars without interest to the farmers of Adana province, to aid them in planting new crops.[55] Effective measures were taken to punish the perpetrators of the atrocities in Adana and to prevent the occurrence of such outrages in the future. A total of one hundred and thirty Muslims and ninety-five non-Muslims had been arrested for participation in the deviltries that were committed.[56]

On May 7, the Armenian National Assembly held a session in İstanbul presided by Stepan Karayan. The majority of speakers criticized the government for its sluggishness in providing help to Cilicia. In his statement, Krikor Zohrab, member of the Ottoman Chamber of Deputies for İstanbul, disagreed with those delegates who believed that the government was not interested in helping Armenians and other Christians subjected to the massacres. "I would like to ask," he said, "that we have faith in the goodwill of that supreme body [the Parliament]." Archbishop Hmayag Timaksiyan interrupted Zohrab saying, "That's wrong, it is false, I don't believe it." Zohrab continued, noting that criticizing the actions of the Ottoman Parliament was beyond the scope of the Armenian National Assembly and was insulting to "our Turkish compatriots." He reminded the assembly that the parliament had unanimously adopted a proposal to send financial aid to Adana and added, "I don't find this unnecessary attack on that well-disposed attitude to be correct, and it also contradicts our policy." He thought it necessary "not to become desperate, but holding sorrow and grief in our hearts, to adhere to the Ottoman constitution, which has become stronger now." He then proposed setting up a trustworthy mixed commission and dispatching it to Cilicia to justly distribute the donated 30,000 gold liras.[57]

The prompt vote of parliament, appropriating from the public treasury 150,000 dollars for the relief of the wounded and helpless homeless in the province of Adana, knowing that the most of these were Armenians, was suggestive of Christian rights, and should materially help to establish among Western nations' confidence in the new government. The appointment of a court martial to look into the cause of the massacres, with orders to punish the guilty parties, should prove a deterrent to a repetition of such an act of violence.[58]

RESTORATION OF ORDER IN DÖRTYOL AND BELEN

The Forty-eighth Regiment of the Second Army Corps was stationed at Dörtyol, under the command of Colonel Rıza Bey. Efforts were being made to capture the elements of the neighborhood who incited massacre. Several scouting parties were scouring the vicinity, meeting with considerable success, and as fast as the marauders were captured they were being sent to Adana for trial by court martial. The military officials who lately arrived from Salonika made a favorable impression by their good behavior, courtesy, and energetic attitude, which was strengthened by the reports of the Armenian inhabitants of Dörtyol. The people were gradually assuming their former occupations as a sense of security slowly made itself felt. Seventeen Muslims who had been recently arrested for the killing of seven Armenians and the burning of their houses in the village of Nergizli had a preliminary hearing in the minor criminal court of İskenderun on May 22, 1909. A certain mufti testified that these men, all personally known to him, had endeavored to induce him and his followers, consisting of about fifty families, to join them in their work, which he refused to do. The prisoners were bound over to await trial in the higher court. At Belen twenty-nine Muslims were in prison awaiting trial for the massacre of the Armenians of Atik, near the formerly mentioned place. The steps taken by the authorities toward bringing to justice the perpetrators of the recent outrages in that community had a noticeable salutary effect and tended greatly to reestablish something of the former state of security for Armenians and Christians in general.[59]

The news reaching İstanbul on May 18, 1909, indicated that the *kaymakam* of Belen who saved the kaza from attacks by Kurdish and Circassian bands was mentioned with praise.[60]

COMMISSION OF INQUIRY TO INVESTIGATE THE EVENTS

On May 24, 1909, Grand Vizier Hüseyin Hilmi Paşa discussed the Adana affair in the Chamber of Deputies. He presented a list of measures taken such as the declaration of the state of emergency in Cilicia and the establishment of courts martial in Adana, Maraş, and Ayntab. He announced also that the military had restored order and that goods stolen during the events were being returned to their owners. Finally, he added that in order to determine the number of the victims and the responsibility of the local authorities, he had set up a commission of inquiry composed of two deputies and two magistrates, whose findings would help in identifying and punishing the culprits.[61]

Sir Gerard Lowther, in his annual report on the Ottoman Empire for the year 1909, assessed Hüseyin Hilmi Paşa and his role in the Adana episode as follows:

> Hüseyin Hilmi Pasha was Minister of the Interior when the Adana trouble was brewing, and no light has ever been thrown on his action when the vali [Cevad Bey] reported to him the seriousness of the situation and requested that measures should be taken to prevent an outbreak. He was Grand Vizier on the 13th April, and must be held responsible to a certain extent for the events of that day. He never enjoyed the confidence of the Committee of the Union and Progress, against whom he sent reports to the Palace when he was inspector-general in Macedonia. His appointment as Grand Vizier after the events of the 13th April has never been satisfactorily explained, and some hint that he knew more than was convenient and that it was safer to have him in office than in opposition. [62]

A mixed Turkish-Armenian commission left İstanbul on May 15 for Adana to direct the work of relief in the interests of the sufferers from the uprisings and to supervise the civil authority's investigation into the whole affair. It intended to learn the motives of the regrettable events in the province, to study their origins, as well as examining the means so that no similar thing would happen in the future. The commission which represented the government was composed of Faik Bey, chief of Court of First Instance at the Council of State; Artin Müzeciyan, inspector of courts at Manastır; Yusuf Kemal (Tengirşek), deputy for Kastamonu; and Agop Babikyan, deputy for Tekirdağ.[63] Esad Rauf Bey, *mutasarrıf* of Mersin, also joined them.[64]

Herbert Adam, the commanding officer of the British warship *Barham*, on his arrival to Mersin on July 8, 1909, received the following written report by telegram from Charles Doughty-Wylie, the British vice consul in Adana: (1) The commission at Adana was reconstituted by the arrival of deputies from İstanbul, and the military commander at İzmir was to be the new president of the same. (2) The Armenian refugees numbering five, who were taken refuge at the British consulate ever since the Adana massacre, voluntarily surrendered themselves to be tried by the commission. This gave great satisfaction to the Ottoman authorities, whom Doughty-Wylie considered would treat them leniently. (3) Relief work was much lighter, and the Ottoman Committee took over charge of the refugee camp. (4) The Ottoman authorities selected a new site for the refugee camp, and the camp appeared to be well organized. (5) The Ottoman authorities issued money relief to the refugees. (6) There appeared to be every effort made on the part of the Ottoman authorities to bring about a reconciliation with the Armenians.[65]

The investigation commission visited Dörtyol, Hamidiye, Osmaniye, Hasanbeyli, Bahçe, and other places and collected eyewitness accounts and conducted hearings. However, it did not publish an official statement or report.

Yusuf Kemal told Doughty-Wylie that the Muslims of Adana were annoyed with Agop Babikyan because in his inquiries he made no effort to understand their side of the case, but talked only to Armenians, especially Armenian priests. Probably the Armenians would accuse Yusuf Kemal of being prejudiced against them in a similar fashion. He declared that *hojas* were still persuaded that there was an Armenian revolution, that he was prepared to dissuade them of this in a public speech, but that the accusatory speeches of Armenians rendered this impossible.[66]

İhsan Fihri, editor-in-chief of *İtidal*, addressed to Babikyan the following open letter on July 25, 1909, which was perhaps one of the most arresting and incisive documents that ever emanated from his pen:

> I have read in *İttihad* the declaration you have made in İzmir to one of its editors on the subject of Adana events. In your formal statement you mainly aimed against the governor, the military commander, Bağdadizade Abdülkadir, Boşnak Salih and me, as having directly taking part in the massacres. The news of the arrival of two deputies led us to suppose that the city would return to calmness; we thought that the mission you were vested would have salutary effects and the city would achieve in a short time the same flourishing state of affairs as in the past. However, after your arrival you have forgotten that you were the representative of 32 million citizens and, by only thinking of your community, you have began to attack against the Muslims. I do not enter into details. The government was charged of unveiling with whom and what deliberations you have had during your stay and the aim you followed. I have one single proposition to make to you off-handedly. I request you either to deny the talks you have had with the correspondent of the said newspaper or to prove my guilt clearly by evidence. If you refrain from accepting one or other of my propositions I will accuse you before the public as a liar and as a cowardly slanderer. At the same time I let you know that I will go to the court.[67]

Agop Babikyan did not respond.

The government ordered the Sheikh-ul-Islam to prepare a circular showing by quotations from the Koran and references to the Sacred Law that it is the duty of all true believers to look upon Christians as equals, entitled to the same treatment as Muslims. This proclamation was to be broadcast in every Muslim congregation over the empire, by the muftis, cadis, and *hojas* of various towns and villages. Further, the most enlightened of the *ulemas* were instructed to take the equality of the Christians as their text in the sermons which they were to preach during the month of Ramazan.⁶⁸

The Sheikh-ul-Islam declared that the Koran commanded the friendship toward Christians, and that there was no justification in it for calling the Christians "unbelievers." A prominent Muslim preacher in İstanbul declared in a sermon, which was widely spread through the empire, that the Christian population constituted a trust given to the Muslims by God, and that Muslims should guard the rights of Christians more jealously than their own.⁶⁹

At the request of John Leishment, American ambassador, Grand Vizier Hüseyin Hilmi Paşa received James Creelman at the Sublime Porte on July 30, 1909. The grand vizier was a tall, thin, hooked-nosed man in a frock coat, seated at a modern desk, with an elaborate telephone on a table by his side, dictating to a stenographer. "There could be no greater mistake than the idea that the massacres in Adana were prompted by religious hatred of Christians," said Hüseyin Hilmi Paşa. "You must remember that the Christians in the empire have numbered little more than 5,000,000 in a population of 30,000,000. If Moslem faith or policy required or encouraged attacks upon Christians because of their religion, there would not be one Christian alive in Turkey to-day. For 500 or 600 years Moslems and Christians have got on well together under Ottoman rule. The truth is that there is no people in the world so tolerant of other religions as the Moslems of this empire." "Then how do you explain the wholesale killing of Christians in Turkey?" Creelman asked. "It is a political, not a religious question," said Hüseyin Hilmi Paşa. "Before the Armenian political committees began to organize in Asia Minor there was peace. I leave you to judge the cause of the bloodshed." "Well," Creelman said, "I have been told that the Sultan Abdul Hamid actually ordered the extermination of the Armenians." The grand vizier stated that he had been one of Sultan Abdülhamid II's most trusted officers and was inspector general of Macedonia when Europe intervened after the massacres of Christians in that region. "Is it not so?" American journalist insisted. "I cannot say that the Sultan was not guilty," the Ottoman statesman answered gravely. "But the whole truth will be known when the present official investigations, which are being made by a commission of Moslems and Christians, are completed. No guilty man will be spared." "What is the future to be?" "I hope there will be no more massacres." "But you are a statesman, at the head of the Turkish Empire. Can you only express hope?" "No. I can say sincerely that it seems certain that in the future Moslems and non-Moslems will live together as brothers and that there will never be another massacre." "What do you say as Grand Vizier regarding the maintenance of Christian worship and Christian teaching in the empire? Do they conflict with Moslem law or Moslem policy?" "Certainly not. We are bound to protect Christians and Jews as well as Moslems. Loyalty to the State is all that is required. I cannot say too strongly that Christians, Jews, and Moslems are absolutely equal before the law, and the Government will see that this equally is maintained from this time on. The constitutional régime is firmly established, and there will be no going backward."[70]

From the Sublime Porte Creelman went to the Ottoman parliament, where Ahmed Rıza Bey, president of the Chamber of Deputies, a tall, bearded Turk of noble bearing, told him that the world might rest content as to the future of Christians in the Ottoman Empire. "We Moslems have no desire to harm non-Moslems," Ahmed Rıza Bey said. "The constitutional Government is strongly founded, and there will be no return to the murderous methods of Abdul Hamid. The Chamber of Deputies has sent word to all parts of the empire that Christians, Jews, and Moslems are equal under our flag, and that, at any cost, this equality will be enforced. There are forty-three Christians and four Jews in our Parliament. That fact ought to be enough to show the real situation. We are all pledged to the policy of equal rights and religious liberty, and we are ready, if need be, to die in defense of the new order."[71]

Creelman accurately reported events that he saw himself. The future safety and liberty of Christians in the Ottoman Empire were guaranteed as much by devout, educated, and conscientious leaders of the Mohammedan faith, working upon the Muslim masses through means so long suppressed by the old sultan, as by the army which was now devoted to the defense of the constitution and the principle of universal equality without distinction of race or religion. Based on a detailed investigation of all the facts, and supported by the testimony of many contemporaries, Creelman felt no hesitation in saying that the Muslim religion and its teachers were not to be blamed for the massacres in Asia Minor, and that it was reasonably certain that Christians were safe at last. The sultan said it, the Sheikh-ul-Islam and the *ulema* said it, the parliament said it, and the army said it. Nobody but a blind bigot could be in the Ottoman Empire today without realizing that a new day had dawned here for Christian and Jew alike.[72]

TOTAL CASUALTIES DURING THE MASSACRES

No definite figures had been produced of the total casualties during the massacres. On this question there was and is much controversy. The numbers vary greatly.[73] In Adana alone twenty-two hundred bodies, of whom six hundred were stated to be Muslims, were buried, and many more were thrown into the river. The Ottoman government subsequently issued an official estimate of fifty-four hundred casualties for the whole district,[74] but this was underestimated, and the figure probably be somewhere between fifteen thousand to twenty thousand.[75] Dikran Mesrob Kaligian considers that between ten thousand and twenty thousand Armenians were killed.[76] According to other Armenian sources, the number of Armenian victims in Cilicia ranges between twenty thousand and thirty thousand, and the number of other Christian victims is between fifteen hundred and twenty-five hundred. Hagop Terzian claimed 22,512 Armenian deads, which is undoubtedly an overestimate.[77] Simbad Gabriel, president of the Armenian General Progressive Association, the leading Armenian organization in the United States, went further and said the Young Turks massacred thirty thousand Armenians in Cilicia in 1909.[78] But he produced no detailed information on the subject, nor did he inform of the sources from which he had derived his information. Most other Armenian estimates were in this range. This claim is certainly a gross exaggeration.[79]

I would suggest that as a general proposition one should take such opulent figures with much reserve. The need for this would be clear when we remember that the original figure of sixty thousand which was given as the number of Bulgarian Christians slaughtered in 1876 was proved to have been thirty-five hundred souls. In 1877 Sir Henry Layard, the British ambassador in İstanbul, wrote to Lord Derby, foreign secretary, as follows:

> A great portion of the English public are still probably originally founded true—the 60,000 Christians outraged and massacred; the cartloads of human heads; the crowds of women burnt in a barn; and other similar horrors. There are persons, and amongst them, I grieve to say, Englishmen, who boast that they invented these stories with the object of "writing down" Turkey, to which they were impelled by a well-known hand. People in England will scarcely believe that the most accurate and complete inquiries into the events of last year in Bulgaria now reduce the number of deaths to about 3,500 souls, including the Turks, who were, in the first instance, slain by the Christians. No impartial man can now deny that a rising of the Christians, which was intended by its authors to lead to a general massacre of the Mohammedans was in contemplation, and that it was directed by Russia and pan-Slavist agents.[80]

Similarly in the case of the "massacres of Sassoun" of 1894, the total number of Armenians killed was at first stated to be eight thousand, and afterwards reduced in the final report of the Commission of Enquiry to nine hundred. With such appalling fabrications before us, it is small wonder that the 1909 campaign of Armenian atrocities should have fallen so completely flat.

All of the figures provided in various publications are approximate and do not give an exact picture of the casualties in Adana. Such figures have to be used with caution. It is difficult to determine the real number of the human losses, for no fact sheet containing a precise number of fatalities in the course of massacres was compiled.[81] Cemal Paşa estimates that seventeen thousand Armenians and 1,850 Muslims were killed in April events in Adana. Fifty-five Turks and Armenians were condemned to death for murder and incitement to riot, forty-seven of these sentences were carried out.[82]

REPORT OF THE COURT MARTIAL, JULY 20, 1909

The court martial in Adana had been investigating the responsibility for the outbreak. It was composed of able men. They were instructed to try all civilian and military personnel who were responsible, including the provincial governor and the commander of the troops. The commissioners were warned against being influenced by local feelings and were assured that their authority would be backed by ten battalions from constitutional forces.[83] Their method of investigation was prompt and thorough. They were keenly interested in the question as to how far any of the Armenians had given provocation or had shown disloyalty. The court martial asked for definite evidence which would aid in convicting either Turks and Armenians who were guilty of having caused disturbance, conflagration, or massacre.[84]

The report of the court martial was presented on July 20, 1909, and its contents might be summarized as follows. The causes and the motives of the Adana events must be searched for in the past. Bahri Paşa, the former governor of that province, never ceased the persecutions and the squireen of the country, generally ignorant people, not only never protested against the behavior of this little tyrant, but on the contrary found their opportunity to enrich themselves. The Armenians submitted, willingly or unwillingly, under the old regime to all the fancies and fads of their old tyrants. A certain number of Armenians who cherished separatist ideas had however facilitated the settlement of a great number of their coreligionists in this city, which offered conditions proper to facilitate their aims, inasmuch as Adana might be considered almost as a maritime or naval town. The quantity of arms introduced by the Armenians after the proclamation of liberty was extraordinary, the city of Beirut, had the aspect of a great depot of arms which they were continually sending them to Adana and the environs. The separatist Armenians had experienced a little disappointment in seeing the improved relations of the Turks and the British. Although the Muslims had begun, after July 1908, to fraternize with the non-Muslims, they despised the committees of Huntchak and Dashnak. They thought these committees were pursuing a special end, by creating clubs in all the towns of the province. But one of the chief causes of the troubles was, without contradiction, the weakness of the authorities.

After the first lights of liberty, the Armenian Committees in Europe began to awaken in the minds of the Armenians the idea of an autonomy and with this idea, they spread anecdotes, pictures, and coats of arms, referring to the Armenian history. The chief instigator of all this was Bishop Musheg Seropian. Thus the tension between Armenians and Muslims was accentuated and incidents occurred now and again, which were to end in the painful events of Adana.[85]

İhsan Fikri, exiled to Diyarbekir under the old regime, later transferred to the fortress of Payas and finally settled in Adana, where he got married, had worked by every means to become a government functionary, and in the end succeeded in being appointed the director of the Arts and Crafts School. Some time later on, being dismissed, İhsan Fikri devoted himself entirely to the execution of all sorts of machinations against those who had not served his interests, at the same time to shake the position of the Governor Cevad Bey, who at the time received him rather coolly. İhsan Fikri even got bills posted, accusing the governor of incapacity. He undertook to organize a meeting to protest against the local government's conduct. But an opposition party was organized with the intention of baffling İhsan Fikri's and his acolytes' plan. This counterparty was composed of Bekçibaşı Mehmed, Halid Çavuş, etc. Later on, two parties, fearing grave results, abandoned the idea of meetings. In all these affairs and above all in the affair of revolver and rifle shots, the authorities showed an extraordinary and unpardonable weakness. Yet the Armenians, arrested for having fired in the air (on the occasion of Easter festivities) were soon liberated, while the Turks, arrested for the same reason, were imprisoned. In the meantime, Armenian merchants, in their personal interests, related to the Armenians and to Muslims separately that they were going to be massacred. Without counting those arms smuggled, there were twelve thousand guns introduced into Adana by the ports of Mersin and İskenderun.[86]

In the meantime a Muslim was killed by an Armenian who was hidden by his coreligionists. The government demanded the criminal, but the Armenians refused, saying that they could not give up the Armenian without a Muslim being given to them who previously had killed an Armenian. On the evening of April 13, a certain Mahmud fired a revolver at Tepebağ quarter. The military patrol wanted to arrest him, but they were prevented by a crowd of five hundred Muslims, who rushed at the patrol, asking why they did not arrest also the Armenians. The next day other Muslim prisoners were set at liberty by the mob and by the chief of the police. After these incidents, the armed Muslims began to circulate about the city and organized anti-governorate manifestations; a Muslim was then killed by an Armenian. During all this effervescence, the Armenians who were already excited by the demonstrations, also armed, came out into the streets. The governorate had called out the reservists under arms and, as the soldiers coming out of the military depots, for want of uniform, still wore their civil costumes, thereupon the population as a whole, believing that the government had officially authorized the massacre of Armenians, made a rush on the depots, got hold of the arms and ammunition, and executed atrocities which made the martial court shudder and weep. The authorities, during that time, had only sought to save their own lives and all had disappeared: they imprisoned a crowd of Armenians as being disturbers. This was then the governorate's attitude; as for the court martial, it judged and condemned fifteen persons, Muslim and non-Muslim, whose culpability had been established, and they had been executed. There were still seven hundred to eight hundred people who were as criminal as those who were hanged. So, if the court martial must punish all those who made themselves guilty of violences and all sorts of ordinary crimes, they must judge yet ten thousand to fifteen thousand people, and if all the crimes were to be punished, the whole population of the province must be punished.[87]

The court martial conducted inquiries in the areas of the Aleppo province where massacres took place. In Maraş, around five hundred persons were arrested. This number comprised most part of the officials, notables, and the well-to-do of the town. Searches were made in the Armenian church where it was believed that dynamite and ammunition were stored. Three individuals accused of having cut the hands and ears of a woman for taking away her bracelets and golden earrings were sentenced to death. The arrest of a big landowner enjoying great influence over the population was announced in Antakya. He was accused of having distributed ammunition at the gate of a mosque exciting those who massacred the Armenians.[88]

PUNISHMENT OF THE OFFICIALS AND NOTABLES

Cevad Bey, the former governor of Adana, was debarred from service in any official position for a period of six to seven years. Mustafa Remzi Paşa, the ex-commander of Adana, was sentenced to three months detention in Mersin. The mildness of these sentences was explained in many quarters by the statement, which had obtained general credence that the governor did warn the Hüseyin Hilmi Paşa Cabinet of the gravity of the situation, but that no attention was paid at the time to his reports. Cevad Bey was held blameless in intention but was punished without severity for his incapacity: that he had telegraphed to İstanbul for help and found none, neither there nor from the old and equally incapable Mustafa Remzi Paşa, nor from the rest of the feeble functionaries. İhsan Fikri, the owner of *İtidal*, was sentenced to two years of exile. On June 11, 1909, his newspaper was closed by an order from the Ministry of the Interior. Bağdadizade Abdülkadir, one of the leading notables of Adana and who had served as the mayor of the city in 1883 and 1884, was condemned to exile in Hejaz for two years. İsmail Safa, deputy editor-in-chief of *İtidal*, was sentenced to one month's imprisonment. The decision of his guilt seemed to have hung on his use in print of the word "truce," which was found to imply a projected continuation of the massacres.[89]

İhsan Fikri was one of the many Old Turks who joined the CUP in the Asiatic provinces and, for a time perhaps, deceived their liberal associates. After the establishment of court martial at Adana, İhsan Fihri was condemned to two years' exile, but, owing presumably to the fact that he was a member of the Adana branch of the CUP and was strongly supported by a number of local notables, he was allowed to choose his place of residence. He went to Egypt and there published a statement in the press that the inflammatory articles in the *İtidal* were not written by him, but given him by the governor of Adana's director of correspondence, and that the real responsibility for the massacres lay with "the authorities at Constantinople, as Hilmi Pasha knew." İhsan Fikri subsequently came to İstanbul, but after a private interview with Talat Bey, the minister of the interior, left the same day for Konya, where he lived in enforced retirement.[90]

The Bağdadizades were the wealthy Muslim family that had been influential in local politics. Although the family was relatively a newcomer to the province, they succeeded in constructing big estates and consolidating their power among the Muslim notables. Bağdadizade Abdülkadir died quite suddenly on the morning of November 29, 1911. He had only lately returned from his two years' exile. Not surprisingly, his close association with, and participation in, the armed clashes made him vulnerable to a starkly negative portrayal.[91]

ARMENIAN DESIRE FOR THE ESTABLISHMENT OF A SEPARATE KINGDOM

A strong tendency among the Armenians to exaggerate their troubles and get sympathy and help from foreign powers was visible. The Armenian riots apparently aimed at the establishment of a separate kingdom or principality with foreign assistance. Armenian instigators hoped the incidents would compel outside interference. They considered that Europe could not stand idly by while thousands of Christian men, women, and children lost their lives. Whatever the cost, the powers ought to intervene. Warships of seven countries—Britain, France, Germany, Austria, Italy, Russia, and the United

States—did in fact anchor in the Mersin roadstead, two hours from Adana, in April 1909. British and French cruisers also laid anchor at the mouth of the river Asi around Samandağ, which is in close proximity to Adana. All vessels carried large forces that could set foot on the shore at any moment. European diplomats were aware of the potential for this crisis to get out of hand and took steps to limit its impact. A few British marines went to Adana to assist the work of relief, but no armed force was landed. One can surmise that the Europeans knew well that the Armenians provoked massacres that would lead to intervention in Cilicia. There is, then, plenty for the historian to deliberate upon. The Armenians, it appears, have only themselves to blame for all their woes.[92]

Because the European nations feared the political effect of intervention and were opposed to the ascendancy in the Ottoman Empire of one or the other, they held back from landing detachments on Cilician soil. European statesmen might also imagine that to interfere at Adana would precipitate a large-scale war costing many more lives than had fallen. One need not therefore be surprised that while Europe stood aghast at the scenes enacted at Adana, it cautiously refrained from interfering. If the powers were to intervene, immediately all the jealousies and rivalries would burst out anew and the eternal Macedonian question be reopened with more threatening and perilous results than ever before. Europeans thought that it was up to the Ottoman government to act.[93]

The Ottoman Empire in southern Anatolia affected European powers very directly. If the Mediterranean littoral passed into the hands of other nations with fleets, their position there would be precarious. The whole position of Egypt with an efficient European power armed on a wide scale in Adana would be different. Egypt would have to have an army which Egyptian finance could not support, and there would end all British dreams of the prosperity of the country. British capital would probably be hampered from sharing and participating in the Adana plain, one of the last great pockets of material which were open for development in the twentieth century. Moreover, the occupation of Adana must add to British difficulties and British diplomatic relations with Russia and Germany. Russia would naturally have to have its share in the region, and British diplomatic relations with it would consequently be more difficult than in the past. Britain did not disturb the integrity of Ottoman rule in the province for fear the Russians, who pressed upon its Indian frontier by land, should get a naval base in the Mediterranean, and so, in case of war, cut off the troops it might send to India by sea. Germany would have to have its share, and any shadow of ill-feeling which might exist at present would certainly be accentuated. Supposing both those powers had territory in Adana, which they undoubtedly would have if the region was occupied, Britain would be obliged to deny them access to the Gulf of İskenderun, and that denial would naturally bring about friction and trouble and through the years another Eastern question.

Officially, the French rejected the idea of a European intervention to address the consequences of the Adana events. British Foreign Secretary Sir Edward Grey considered a limited diplomatic intervention to be useless and provocative since the Armenians might be encouraged to take actions that would incite Muslims to stage massacres on a massive scale and necessitate a full-scale military intervention by the powers.[94]

In the French Chamber of Deputies, Denis Cochin, developing his interpellation on Armenian massacres in Adana, denounced the complicity of the Turkish troops, but said he did not accuse the Young Turk government which stood the test of the great difficulties to save its country. Cochin wished Turkish diplomacy to take a more clear attitude in favor of "the civilization." The speaker advocated energetic French intervention, going, in case of need, up to protecting Armenians. But a landing, he remarked, would overexcite the spirits. Cochin ended in stating: "One has to know that we are resolved to protect the Christians." The French minister of foreign affairs, Stéphan Pichon, in response, deplored the Adana massacres during which perhaps two thousand unfortunates were killed. Continuing, he stated:

> All the Powers having warships there [Mersin] are agreed to protect the threatened lives. I have considered useful to avoid landing, which could be interpreted as excitement. The French government has intervened energetically in Constantinople. It is a question of protecting the traditional influence of France. The government will not fail in its task. We are not anymore in the presence of a Turkish government which is in complicity with the massacres of Armenians. We must have confidence in the Young Turk regime and through that give it the force to repress the massacres which are a shame for the civilization. This will be the best sign of friendship we can give it.[95]

An editorial of the Swiss *Journal de Genève*, according to Davide Rodogno, put forward the below on the events of Adana and the nonintervention of the European powers. Anchoring warships off the Cilician coast was a very ineffective act. Even if marines had landed, they could have protected only the port and some coastal areas. Such a landing might have triggered further massacres inland. Hence, the only sensible intervention would have been to land a big army in Asia Minor. Which European power would have agreed to undertake such a military operation to save the lives of strangers? Such an operation would have been a long-lasting military operation, indistinguishable from a war of conquest. Only one power seemed to have the military capacity (and geographical proximity) to undertake it: Russia. The other powers,

Journal de Genève wrote, would have never accepted such a plan. The only thing that one could do to reduce the suffering of these Christian populations (who, the editorial noted, belonged to the same "race" as the Europeans) was to send them money, clothing, and food, and to support humanitarian relief actions. This was what the mighty European powers could do on behalf of fellow Christians.[96]

Little wonder, therefore, that the representatives of the Christians of Cilicia and the city of Adana presented on June 30, 1909, to the various departments of the government the declaration, whose content ran as follows. The Christians desired to express their deep regret concerning the great misfortune which had befallen them and the false imputation raised against them. They wanted to make declaration as to their real position. They had been faithful to the constitution from the time of its proclamation, and they earnestly wished its continuance and success. As true Ottoman subjects their desire and effort had been to protect the constitution and to be found on the side of those who loved and served it. They emphatically protested against all imputations of rebellion made against them. They had never rebelled and the idea of rebellion had never entered their minds. They, although loyal subjects, had suffered and been persecuted, and they had been sacrificed to the envy and malevolence of bigoted and evil-minded persons. They were the victims of machinations and schemes which had caused Heaven and earth to weep and wonder. Their loyalty to the government was proved by the fact that in the very beginning of the troubles they had appealed for government protection, and later, on the first possible opportunity, they renewed their appeal. They again declared their loyalty to the constitution. They were ready and eager to make any sacrifice for the true welfare of their beloved land; they declared also that they cherished no spirit of revenge notwithstanding the suffering which they had endured. Their earnest plea to their Muslim fellow countrymen was that they should work in harmony with the various other communities which composed the Ottoman Empire. May the goodwill and fellowship which appeared at the time of the proclamation of the constitution appear again. With malice toward none and charity and justice toward all, and with the hope of healing the grievous wounds in the vitals of their country, let them unite in securing the present and future prosperity of their land. In other words, let unity, fraternity, equality, and justice prevail. As sincere Ottoman subjects they desired the welfare and prosperity of their beloved native land. They would express their affection for the sultan, who had devoted himself to the realization of this desire, and also for their brethren, the members of the CUP, the noble victorious army, and all true Ottoman subjects who were loyal to the constitutional government, and they declared themselves to be in sympathy and harmony with all such.[97]

On July 23, 1909, the people of Adana celebrated for the second time the revival of the Ottoman Constitution. July 23 was a gala day in Adana, as in the other cities of the country. Extensive preparations had been made to make the day a memorable one. The streets of the city, public buildings, stores, and residences were gay with red and green flags. Banners of every hue and shape, bearing all kinds of patriotic mottoes, were being sold at every corner together with a variety of fireworks. The military review, with its infantry, artillery, and cavalry, took place as per program in the morning, before a large crowd, and was followed by a reception at the *Konak*. In the evening there were grand fireworks, enjoyed by the whole city. School processions, theatrical performances, and other celebrations were the order of the day. A sense of relief and satisfaction pervaded the general public. *Tanin* and *İkdam* in İstanbul gave their readers news from their local correspondents, which was read with interest and profit.[98]

YOUNG TURK–DASHNAK COOPERATION

Talat Bey, minister of the interior, relied on Armenians to march hand-in-hand with the Turks in the effort to strengthen and perfect the constitutional government. The CUP was true to its name: it worked for the union of all the elements of the nation, and the moral and material progress of all. Such considerations were paramount, but they had to be met within the existing context of events. Compromise was imperative.

Consequently, despite the events of Adana in 1909, both the CUP and the Armenian Revolutionary Federation agreed to continue to cooperate and on September 6, 1909, they signed a four-point declaration. In order to strengthen permanently the implementation of the constitution and public improvements in the country, they would work and struggle with combined forces, sparing no sacrifice: (1) They would cooperate with total mutual support and unified direction, using all options as permitted by law, to counter the likely reactionary movements. (2) As preserving the sacred Ottoman fatherland from partition and division was a reason for the joint cooperation of the two organizations, they would work practically to dispel the false impression in public opinion inherited from the despotic regime that the Armenians strived for independence. (3) The two parties also wished to announce that they were in agreement on the subject of expanding provincial rights, which would guarantee further development and progress for the Ottoman fatherland as a whole. And (4) the CUP and the Armenian Revolutionary Federation, accepting the events of March 31 and the grievous Adana massacres as a warning of possible atrocities to come, decided to work hand-in-hand to realize the goals listed above.[99]

The Turkish-Armenian relationship improved soon thereafter. There came about an agreement between the Unionists and the Dashnaks, by which the latter pledged themselves to support the CUP at the parliamentary elections of 1912.[100]

During the next few years, Baron Max von Oppenheim, the Arabist archaeologist-explorer and head of the German Information Service for the Orient, had seen many Armenian soldiers and gendarmes in Syria and Mesopotamia, who were treated like brothers by their Muslim comrades. According to the German official, the exceptionally accommodating attitude of the Turks exceeded beyond the Balkan Wars despite the bad experiences they had at that time with the Christian soldiers and particularly the Armenians. Even in the early years of the First World War, individual Armenian soldiers were in command of parts of the Muslim troops on the Suez Canal front and had received the medal for bravery. It was only during a later phase in the war that Armenian soldiers were disarmed and assigned to labor battalions.[101]

MAX VON OPPENHEIM'S REPORT, AUGUST 29, 1915

In his report drafted in Damascus on August 29, 1915, Max von Oppenheim went on as follows. Nonetheless, already at the beginning of the present war, the Armenians basically took sides everywhere with the enemies of the Ottoman Empire and Germany. Both before and after the Ottoman declaration of war, large numbers of Armenians joined the Russian, British, and French flags as volunteers. The Armenians played a major role in the conspiracy instigated by Şerif Paşa in Paris in the interests of the Triple Entente. They did their best in the Caucasus to support the Russians: entire villages sided with the enemy, and some individuals served in leader positions, etc. In the area around the province of Van and in other parts of eastern Anatolia, it soon became clear that this was an operation that had been planned together with the enemy long in advance to throw off Ottoman rule. The events in Van were known. Numerous Ottoman officials, officers, and private people had reported to von Oppenheim about the bloody, repulsive atrocities that the Armenians carried out against the Muslims in Van and the surrounding area. Russian and Armenian soldiers and officers trained the Ottoman Armenians. In many parts of their territory, the Turks had to fight their Armenian subjects, who, under Russian supreme command, had become real troops. In Diyarbekir and other Anatolian towns, the threads of a militarily organized conspiracy were discovered: the most respected Armenians were designated as captains, colonels, etc. Russian weapons and bombs were found in the cellars of notables and even bishops (Mardin), as well as pieces of uniforms that were to distinguish the Armenians as fighters for separation and Russia. The announcement of the events in Van, like the machinations in Zeytun, and on the Gulf of İskenderun, in a Lausanne newspaper (of which Cemal Paşa spoke to von Oppenheim) even before all of this had happened was typical.[102]

The connection between the western Armenians in the area of Adana, Zeytun, etc., with those in eastern Anatolia followed from various circumstantial evidence. In Zeytun, a gang organized itself in the spring of 1915. It was reinforced by deserting Armenian soldiers at the end of March, and even extended the audacity of its attacks to an ammunition transport accompanied by gendarmes, which was on its way from Maraş to Zeytun. Four battalions had to be sent out to turn out the rebels, who had entrenched themselves in a convent near the town. At the same time, the chronically terrible state of affairs caused by the gangs in the Cilician mountains became more vividly noticeable. On several occasions, gendarmes and soldiers on the military road from Osmaniye to Racu were ambushed and murdered. All sorts of suspicious signs were observed, especially among the Armenian coastal population on the Gulf of İskenderun. Undoubtedly, secret service and other means of assistance were carried out during the temporary enemy landing, which had led to the destruction of the railway line outside İskenderun. An Armenian spy, furnished with extensive funds, had crossed over from Cyprus on the British cruiser *Doris*, was caught in Dörtyol, and in addition, several boxes of ammunition of Italian origin were found hidden in the same area. The accumulation of these and other individual cases had to arouse the fears of the responsible Ottoman offices that in the case of an enemy landing here, in the west, the Armenians would join the enemy in a joint uprising, and it was just at this point, here on the Gulf of İskenderun and near Mersin, that such a landing was first expected. The consequences in connection with a large Armenian revolt could have been immeasurable: once having taken hold of the crossings over the rivers Seyhan and Ceyhan and the Cilician mountains, the enemy would have separated Asia Minor and the European part of the Ottoman Empire from the entire southern and southeastern half of the empire; consequently, the Egyptian campaign would not have been possible before the intruders had been driven out again.[103]

Cemal Paşa and his officers repeatedly assured von Oppenheim that this must be prevented at all costs, and that this could only then take effect in a really far-reaching manner if the dangerous majorities of Armenians were transformed everywhere to harmless minorities and if, in general, they were removed from the strategic danger zone in particular. To this end, the basic decision to relocate the Armenians had been made in İstanbul. The Armenian inhabitants of the villages (not the large towns) along the coast, within the sphere of the Fourth Army, should be relocated in smaller groups of at least twenty-five to thirty families far into the interior in such a manner that any kind of reunification would be impossible. Cemal Paşa gave such orders from the beginning to avoid any unnecessary harshness against the Armenians.[104]

The Germans von Oppenheim spoke to in the province of Adana, especially senior engineer Winckler, as well as senior engineer Föllner in Aleppo at a later date, were of the same opinion as him, namely, that the Ottomans in these areas were forced to take measures against the Armenians for reasons of self-preservation. The Ottomans, on their part, were now fighting for their existence. Those who led the Armenians to join the enemies of the Ottoman Empire were the ones primarily responsible for the misfortunes of the Armenians. Therefore, it would have been an unforgivable carelessness on the part of the Ottoman rulers if, after their experiences in Van, they had not prevented even the remote possibility of a similar, much more disastrous, treason in the west with all the means available to them while there was still time.[105]

In the Ottoman Empire revolt of Christians was not due to any oppression on the part of the government, but to the liberality which the government observed in matter of religion and nationality. The Turks had never interfered in affairs, religious or national, of their subjects. Christian schools had never been subject to Turkish control in any way. The idea of fomenting trouble at all costs, with a view to making Europe intervene, had never left the mind of the Christians in the Ottoman Empire. Those who had worked to bring about revolts experienced as much difficulties in presenting the Turks as assassins of Christians as they had in causing the revolts.[106]

ARMENIAN DESCRIPTION OF ADANA EVENTS AS GENOCIDE

"The massacres there [in Adana] were another major step in the devaluation of this minority culture, and a step forward on the road to genocide."[107] The Armenian writer Peter Balakian concludes his chapter on Adana in 1909 by these remarks. "In the memory of Armenians, the 1909 massacre in Cilicia has always been perceived as the first stage of the 1915 Genocide," adds Hrachik Simonyan.[108] But that was not the case. There has been to date no work of synthetic history that satisfactorily finds the connections between 1909 and 1915. Also genocide is not a word that should be tossed around lightly. It is neither a fact nor a historical summation of events. It is a legal term of art. It is a word invented in 1944 by a lawyer, Raphael Lemkin (a Holocaust survivor), to describe a crime. It was his wish that it be treated as a legal term. It is the worst crime that international law has ever defined.

Investigating, analyzing, and interpreting history is a matter for historians. Historians establish facts; lawyers must judge whether these facts amount to a breach of international law.

In legal practice, the meaning of genocide is undisputed. It has only one meaning, that given to it by the United Nations General Assembly in the United Nations Convention on the Prevention and Punishment of the Crime of Genocide of December 9, 1948 (UNCG). Genocide is a specific crime defined by international law. The UNCG tells us what genocide is and how it can be ascertained. Only a competent local or international tribunal can determine whether an event is genocide, and such a tribunal has not been held on this matter. Such a court decision exists for the Holocaust and for Rwanda but not for the Armenian suffering.

Governments have had numerous opportunities to amend the original definition of the genocide to address any shortcomings or new developments—but never have done so. As late as in 1998, on the fiftieth anniversary of the UNCG, states decided to use the original definition word by word when drafting the treaty establishing the new International Criminal Court.[109]

It should be remembered that although the UNCG does not give rise to state or individual liability for events which occurred prior to January 12, 1951, the term genocide as defined in the convention cannot be used to describe the Armenian events of 1909. There was no indication of any premeditated attack upon Armenians in the disturbed districts. There appeared no preconcerted plan for the massacre of the Armenians. No documentation has ever been found to prove that a policy to exterminate Armenians existed.

The term "genocide" has increasingly been recruited to serve controversial political and cultural aims and contexts, usually falling beyond the legal scope of the term itself. References to unwarranted instances of violence and destruction as equivalent to the crime of genocide tend to distort the concept and weaken its applicability. What determines genocide is not necessarily the number of casualties or the cruelty of the persecution but the "intent to destroy" a group. Historically the "intent to destroy a race" has emerged only as the culmination of racism, as in the case of anti-Semitism and the Shoah. Turks have never harbored any anti-Armenianism. Any judgments on whether genocide has occurred should be a mattter for the international judicial system rather than governments or other nonjudicial bodies. The UNCG and the subsequent legal history of the prosecution of genocide by international tribunals should form the backbone of our contemporary understanding of the term. The recognition of genocides should be a matter of international courts. It should be a legal, rather than political, determination, decided by international judges after consideration of all the evidence available in the context of a credible international judicial process.

By contrast Armenians look at "genocide" only as a matter of history. This view is also exploited by other anti-Turkish groups who have variously accused Turkey of a "Pontic Genocide," a "Smyrna Holocaust," a "Kurdish Genocide," "Assyrian Genocide," and others. The accusers rely on a historical analysis, not a legal one. History is far more vulnerable than law to bias and hyperbole. Another weakness inherent in purely historical analyses is the ability to establish a conclusion and then search for historical events that support it. The process, of course, disregards information which does not support the conclusion, no matter how historically or legally valid.

According to Ronald Grigor Suny, the word "holocaust" was used in Adana for the first time in the twentieth century to describe "the mass killing of a defenseless population."[110] Vahakn Dadrian describes Armenian suffering in Adana in 1909 as the "Holocaust."[111] He offers no direct evidence to support his argument and makes no reference whatsoever of central importance to the Ottoman and foreign material in this period. Michael Reynolds, associate professor of Near Eastern Studies at Princeton University, notes that Dadrian's misrepresentation of sources attracts criticism even from among those who agree with the genocide thesis.[112]

THE REALITY IN ADANA

The reality in Adana was very different. As Steven Katz, professor of Jewish history and religion and director of the Elie Wiesel Center for Judaic Studies at Boston University, shows no case of massacre was such an instance as the Holocaust. The Holocaust has been intended as an exclusive term to point to the sufferings and destruction of European Jewry. At no time in the history of humanity has there been a counterpart to such a phenomenon. The Armenian experience in the late Ottoman Empire and the Jewish experience in Nazi Germany are in no way comparable and should not be connected. The Holocaust and the Armenian events of 1909 were totally dissimilar. There is no meaningful analogy between the Jews and the Armenians or between the Nazis and the Ottoman Turks. To suggest otherwise is to obliterate the essence of the Holocaust and to reduce it to the status of innumerable other bloody and mournful events in human history. The Holocaust in human experience cannot be compared to past events. It is plain that the Nazi Germany genocide policies were unparalleled in the history of man and should not be diluted by the spurious claims of other ethnic groups or countries. The Holocaust was clearly unique in any number of historical particulars.[113]

The record of the Nazi slaughter is unambigous. Others should not be permitted to take advantage of the sympathy and understanding felt for the victims of the Holocaust. Equating that genocide with events of 1909, whose characterization is a matter of serious dispute, dilutes the moral force that recollection of the Holocaust should generate for us all. Furthermore, it would be an irony to place the Turkish people, who have provided sanctuary to the persecuted, including Jews fleeing from the Spanish Inquisition in the fifteenth century and the many fleeing from Adolf Hitler in the twentieth century, in the same category with the Nazis.

The policy of the World Jewish Congress has been that the Holocaust was a unique event in the size of its tragedy, and that it bore no comparison to other mass deaths, however tragic they were. They mourned the events surrounding the Cambodians, the Ibos, the Indians in Argentina, but they had clearly stated to the United States government that the Jewish Holocaust was the one overriding consideration. The Armenians could lobby for their cause, as they were numerous in the United States, and the World Jewish Congress could not be able to do anything about this, but they certainly did not support merging the two events.[114]

Yad Vashem's chairman, Avner Shalev, felt that the use of terms and images related to the Holocaust as part of political, ideological, or social battles was unacceptable. He wished that politicians and historians did not use it as a support for their opinions. Anything which used the Holocaust to stigmatize an entire segment of the population, or contained racist elements or trivialized the Holocaust itself, should be banned, he thought. Shalev was uncertain that legislation was the ideal way to handle this and would prefer educational means, while the international director of the Yad Vashem Holocaust Museum, Yosef Burg, favored the law.[115] It is to be noted further that the United States Holocaust Memorial Museum in Washington, DC, an entity of the United States government established by Congress for the purpose of documenting, studying, and educating about the Holocaust and its lessons, absolutely nowhere in its records refers to the Adana troubles of 1909 as holocaust. Accordingly, directors of the museum have never made any public statement reflecting Dadrian's unfounded claim. In much of Europe and the United States, governments, human rights groups, and Jewish organizations have struggled to keep tight reins on powerful words like "genocide" and "holocaust." And they have largely succeeded. For invoking such words means something serious.[116]

Bernard Lewis, dean of foreign historians of modern Turkey, neatly summarized the case in 1998:

> I am not a Turk nor an Armenian and I have no allegiance to any of these groups. I am a historian and my loyalties are to truth. The concept of genocide

was defined legally. It is a term that the UN used and the Nuremberg trials made use of it [as well]. I side with words, which have accurate meaning. In my view a loose and ambiguous use of words is bad. The meaning of genocide is the planned destruction of a religious and ethnic group, as far as it is known to me, there is no evidence for that in the case of the Armenians. [. . .] I do not say that the Armenians did not suffer terribly. But I find enough cause for me to contain their attempts to use the Armenian massacres to diminish the worth of the Jewish Holocaust and to relate it instead as an ethnic dispute.[117]

NOTES

1. Creelman, "The Moslem Answer to Christendom," p. 163.
2. "Sultan Determined to Stop Massacres; Mehmed V, in a Speech from the Throne, Deplores Those That Have Occurred; Relief Committee Formed," *The New York Times*, May 21, 1909, p. 4.
3. On Mateos İzmirliyan, see Kuneralp, *Son Dönem Osmanlı Erkan ve Ricali (1839–1922)*, p. 90.
4. Liman von Sanders, trans. Carl Reichman, *Five Years in Turkey* (Annapolis, MD: US Naval Institute, 1927; republished Nashville, TN: The Battery Press, 2000), p. 4.
5. Knight, *The Awakening of Turkey*, p. 352.
6. "The Sultan's Desire for Peace," *The Near East*, Vol. 5, No. 123 (September 12, 1913), p. 535.
7. Ali Fuad Türkgeldi, *Görüp İşittiklerim* (What I Saw and Heard) (Ankara: Türk Tarih Kurumu Basımevi, reprint, 2010), pp. 265, 267–70, 272, and 274–75; Uşaklıgil, *Saray ve Ötesi*, pp. 67–70 and 78–81; Lütfi Simavi, *Osmanlı Sarayının Son Günleri* (The Last Days of the Ottoman Palace) (İstanbul: Hürriyet Yayınları, 1970), pp. 317–27.
8. "The Outbreaks in Asia Minor," *The Times*, April 22, 1909, p. 5.
9. On Sahib Molla, see Kuneralp, *Son Dönem Osmanlı Erkan ve Ricali (1839–1922)*, pp. 10 and 102.
10. Creelman, "The Moslem Answer to Christendom," pp. 163–65.
11. Ibid., p. 167.
12. Ibid.
13. Ibid., pp. 167–68.
14. Ibid., p. 168.
15. Herman Bernstein, "The Sheikh-ul-Islam Chief of All the Moslems Defines Religion of Turkey," *The New York Times*, July 25, 1909, Part 5, p. 3.
16. A Correspondent, *The Armenian Troubles and Where the Responsibility Lies*, p. 31.
17. BOA, DH. Muhaberatı Umumiye (General Correspondence), No. 2-3/49. Establishment of the Courts Martial, October 24, 1909; Pears, "Turkey," p. 708.

18. "Unearth 22,500,000 dollars of Abdul's Fortune; Adana Commission Starts; Court-Martial Appointed by Chefket Pasha Will Have Support of 6,000 Young Turk Troops," *The New York Times*, May 9, 1909, p. 9.

19. "Will Gird Sword on Sultan Today; Turkish Government Sends Relief to Adana; Armenians Ask for Punishment of Rioters," *The New York Times*, May 10, 1909, p. 3.

20. "Turkey; The Adana Massacre," *The Times*, May 31, 1909, p. 5.

21. For decisions taken by the Ottoman government, see BOA, Meclisi Vükela (Minutes of the Council of Ministers) (henceforth referred to as MV), No. 126/61, April 18, 1909; BOA, MV, No. 126/58, April 19, 1909.

22. BOA, HR. MT, TDA-T-210-460. Reestablishing of Order. Ministry of the Interior to Babanzade Mustafa Zihni Paşa (Adana), May 29, 1909.

23. *Meclisi Mebusan Zabıt Ceridesi*, Vol. 3, pp. 119–36; Arıkoğlu, *Hatıralarım*, pp. 54–55; "Hadjin Now Safe from Butchery," *The Chicago Daily Tribune*, April 30, 1909, p. 7.

24. FO 195/2306. Conversation with Colonel Mehmet Ali Bey. Charles Dougthy-Wylie (Adana) to Sir Gerard Lowther (Istanbul), May 3, 1909.

25. FO 195/2306. Colonel Mehmet Ali Bey's Statement. Charles Dougthy-Wylie (Adana) to Sir Gerard Lowther (Istanbul), May 8, 1909.

26. FO 195/2306. Mutasarrıf of Mersin. Charles Dougthy-Wylie (Adana) to Sir Gerard Lowther (Istanbul), May 8, 1909.

27. FO 195/2306. Government Relief. Charles Dougthy-Wylie (Adana) to Sir Gerard Lowther (Istanbul), May 21, 1909.

28. BOA, DH. MKT, No. 2872/7. Cevad Bey Under Custody, July 11, 1909; BOA, BEO, No. 3597/269716. Detention of Cevad Bey and Some Other Persons, July 13, 1909.

29. BOA, DH. MKT, No. 2854/6. Preliminary Investigations on Cevad Bey, Asaf Bey and Other Persons, June 23, 1909; BOA, BEO, No. 3597/269747. Detention of Asaf Bey and Some Other Persons, July 14, 1909.

30. Ferriman, *The Young Turks and the Truth about the Holocaust at Adana*, p. 79.

31. Ibid., pp. 79–80.

32. Ibid., pp. 80–81.

33. Ibid., p. 81.

34. Ibid., pp. 81–82.

35. Ibid., pp. 82–83.

36. Ibid., pp. 83–84.

37. BOA, DH. MKT, No. 2843/48. Accusations Brought Against Asaf Bey. Grand Vizierate to the Ministry of the Interior, June 14, 1909; BOA, DH. MKT, No. 2849/10. Petition Presented By Asaf Bey to the Grand Vizierate. Ministry of the Interior to the Investigation Committee (Adana), June 19, 1909; BOA, DH. MKT, No. 2862/85. Discussion of Asaf Bey's Case in the Council of State. Ministry of the Interior to Babanzade Mustafa Zihni Paşa (Adana), July 2, 1909.

38. Mehmet Asaf, *1909 Ermeni Olayları ve Anılarım*, pp. 62–80.
39. Çankaya, *Mülkiye Tarihi ve Mülkiyeliler*, Vol. 3, p. 515; Aytaç Yıldız, *Üç Dönem Bir Aydın: Burhan Asaf Belge (1899–1967)* (Three Periods One Intellectual: Burhan Asaf Belge [1899–1967]) (İstanbul: İletişim Yayıncılık, 2011), pp. 30–31.
40. Grigoris Balakian, trans. Peter Balakian with Aris Sevas, *Armenian Golgotha: A Memoir of the Armenian Genocide, 1915–1918* (New York: Alfred Knopf, 2009), pp. xiv, xviii, 80–82, 98, and 441–42.
41. Bourne and Watt, British Documents on Foreign Affairs, Part I, Series B, Vol. 20, p. 146.
42. FO 371/998. Adana Claims. Sir Gerard Lowther (Istanbul) to Sir Edward Grey (FO), February 8, 1910.
43. "The Adana Massacres," *The Levant Herald*, October 12, 1909, p. 1.
44. "Babıali Tazminatı Reddediyor" (The Sublime Porte Refuses Indemnities), *Tanin*, October 11, 1909, p. 1; "Adana Hadisatı" (The Adana Events), *Tasviri Efkar*, October 11, 1909, p. 1.
45. "Adana Massacres Compensation Refused," *The Daily Telegraph*, October 13, 1909, p. 3.
46. FO 195/1701-1702. Western Insurance Company's Claims. Sir Edward Grey (FO) to Sir Gerard Lowther (Istanbul), March 27, 1912.
47. Ibid.
48. Ibid.
49. BOA, BEO, No. 3540/265467/1-4. Debates of the Adana Incidents in the Chamber of Deputies, May 3, 1909; Simonyan, *The Destruction of Armenians in Cilicia, April 1909*, pp. 181–86; "Court Martial for Turkish Officials," *The Philadelphia Inquirer*, May 2, 1909, p. 2.
50. Ibid. MAE, NS Turquie, Vol. 83, p. 116. Note Pour le Ministre au Sujet des Troubles d'Asie Mineure, 12 mai 1909.
51. "Adana'daki Vaziyet" (The Situation in Adana), *Tanin*, May 3, 1909, p. 1.
52. Creelman, "Will Christendom Remain Silent?" p. 300.
53. "Adana Hakkında" (On Adana), *Tanin*, May 14, 1909, p. 1.
54. BOA, MV, No. 127/55. Decision of the Council of Ministers on Sending 150,000 Dollars for the Relief of Sufferers, May 2, 1909.
55. *Meclisi Mebusan Zabıt Ceridesi*, Vol. 3, pp. 458 and 468–70; "Meclisi Mebusan Müzakereleri" (Debates in the Chamber of Deputies), *Tanin*, May 6,1909, p. 1; and "Meclisi Mebusan Müzakereleri" (Debates in the Chamber of Deputies), *Tanin*, May 10, 1909, p. 1.
56. BOA, HR. MT, TDA-210-382. Arrests. Babanzade Mustafa Zihni Paşa (Adana) to the Ministry of the Interior, May 25, 1909.
57. Simonyan, *The Destruction of Armenians in Cilicia, April 1909*, p. 147.
58. Barton, "New Turkey and Its Interpretation," p. 255.
59. USNA, RG 84 Records of Foreign Service Posts, Diplomatic Posts Turkey, Vol. 216, From Consulates 1 January 1909–30 June 1909, American Embassy Istanbul. Jesse Jackson (Aleppo) to John Leishman (Istanbul), May 31, 1909.

60. "Adana Hadisatı" (Adana Events), *Tanin*, May 19, 1908, p. 1.

61. For setting up a parliamentary commission of inquiry to look into the Adana affair, see BOA, DH. MKT, No. 2804/36. Communication from the Correspondence Division of the Ministry of the Interior to the Ministry of Justice, May 6, 1909; *Meclisi Mebusan Zabıt Ceridesi*, Vol. 3, p. 264; Kévorkian, "The Cilician Massacres, April 1909," p. 347.

62. FO 195/2363. Annual Report on Turkey for the Year 1909. Prominent Men in 1909. Sir Gerard Lowther (Istanbul) to Sir Edward Grey (FO), February 7, 1910.

63. BOA, DH. MKT, No. 2814/69. Assignment of a Mixed Turkish-Armenian Commission to Investigate the Adana Affair. Ministry of the Interior to Artin Müzeciyan at Manastır, May 17, 1909; *Meclisi Mebusan Zabıt Ceridesi*, Vol. 3, pp. 397–405; Yusuf Kemal Tengirşek, *Vatan Hizmetinde* (In the Service of the Fatherland) (Ankara: Kültür Bakanlığı Yayınları, reprinted, 1981), p. 120. See also Arıkoğlu, *Hatıralarım*, pp. 55–58; and "Armenians on Commission; To Investigate Adana Riots Recently; Mixed Board Will Supervise Civil Trial; It Will Also Direct Work of Relief," *The Boston Globe*, May 14, 1909, p. 16.

64. BOA, DH. MKT, No. 2810/40. Assignment of a Mixed Turkish-Armenian Commission to Investigate the Adana Affair. Ministry of the Interior to the Grand Vizierate, May 13, 1909.

65. FO 371/780. Letter of Proceedings from H. M. Ship Barham. Admiralty to FO, August 25, 1909.

66. FO 195/2037. Agop Babikyan's Attitude Toward Turks. Charles Doughty-Wylie (Adana) to Sir Gerard Lowther (Istanbul), July 12, 1909.

67. "Adana Hadisatı" (The Events of Adana), *Tanin*, July 25, 1909, p. 1.

68. G. F. Abbott, *Turkey in Transition* (London: Edward Arnold, 1909), p. 306; *İkdam*, April 18, 1909, p. 1.

69. *İkdam*, April 18, 1909, p. 1.

70. James Creelman, "The Vizier at Close Range; Hilmi Pasha Sees Politics, Not Religion in the Massacres," *The New York Times*, August 1, 1909, p. 3.

71. Ibid.

72. Ibid.

73. BOA, DH. MKT, No. 2863/68. Total Casualties During the Incidents. Ministry of Foreign Affairs to the Ministry of the Interior, July 3, 1909; BOA, DH. MKT, No. 2864/56. Total Casualties During the Incidents. Ministry of the Interior to Babanzade Mustafa Zihni Paşa (Adana), July 3, 1909.

74. BOA, DH. MKT, No. 2807/40. Total Casualties During the Incidents. Babanzade Mustafa Zihni Paşa (Adana) to the Ministry of the Interior, May 9, 1909.

75. Bourne and Watt, British Documents on Foreign Affairs, Part I, Series B, Vol. 20, p. 145.

76. Dikran Mesrob Kaligian, *Armenian Organization and Ideology Under Ottoman Rule 1908–1914* (New Brunswick, NJ, and London: Transactions Publishers, 2009), p. 36.

77. Terzian, *Cilicia 1909*, p. 144.

78. "Says Extinction Menaces Armenia," *The New York Times*, September 25, 1915, p. 3.

79. BOA, DH. MKT, No. 2809/80. Exaggerated Armenian Estimates of the Casualties. Ministry of the Interior to the Grand Vizierate, May 12, 1909; BOA, DH. MKT, No. 2810/95. Unfounded Armenian Claims on the Casualties. Ministry of the Interior to Babanzade Mustafa Zihni Paşa (Adana), May 13, 1909.

80. Sir Henry Layard Papers, British Library; Yuluğ Tekin Kurat, *Henry Layard'ın İstanbul Elçiliği, 1877–1880* (Istanbul Ambassadorship of Henry Layard, 1877–1880) (Ankara: Ankara Üniversitesi Basımevi, 1968).

81. Simonyan, *The Destruction of Armenians in Cilicia, April 1909*, pp. 154–55.

82. Djemal Pasha, *Memories of a Turkish Statesman 1913–1919*, pp. 261–62.

83. *Boston Evening Transcript*, May 8, 1909, p. 2.

84. Trowbridge, "Letters from the Scene of the Massacre, Adana, Asia Minor," p. 607.

85. Ferriman, *The Young Turks and the Truth about the Holocaust at Adana*, pp. 104–5. See also BOA, BEO, No. 3621/271523/1-3. The Report Prepared by the Court Martial on Adana Incidents, July 20, 1909; Kodaman and Ünal, *Son Vakanüvis Abdurrahman Şeref Efendi Tarihi*, pp. 104–16; Kévorkian, *The Armenian Genocide*, pp. 80–81.

86. Ferriman, *The Young Turks and the Truth about the Holocaust at Adana*, p. 105.

87. Ibid., pp. 105–6.

88. " Divanı Harbin Halep'teki Tahkikatı" (The Inquiries of the Court Martial in Aleppo), *Tanin*, July 15, 1909, p. 1.

89. BOA, BEO, No. 3630/272217. Punishment of Cevad Bey, September 8, 1909; BOA, BEO, No. 3632/272358. Punishment of Cevad Bey and Others, September 10, 1909; BOA, DH. Muhaberat-ı Umumiye, No. 37–2, 6. Punishment of the Accused, January 8, 1910.

90. "Ihsan Fikri," *The Times*, April 30, 1910, p. 13.

91. BOA, DH. MKT, No. 2881/51. On Bağdadizade Abdülkadir. Ministry of the Interior to Babanzade Mustafa Zihni Paşa (Adana), July 20, 1909; Ener, *Tarih Boyunca Adana Ovasına (Çukurova'ya) Bir Bakış*, p. 225; Çallıyan, *Adana Vakası ve Mesulleri*, p. 3; "Provinces," *The Orient*, Vol. 2, No. 35 (December 13, 1911), p. 6.

92. BOA, HR. MT, TDA-T-210-219. Establishment of an Armenian Principality. Mehmed Lütfi (Mufti of Adana) to Ahmed Rıza (President of the Chamber of Deputies), May 8, 1909; Talat Paşa, *Hatıralarım ve Müdafaam*, pp. 25–26. See also Arıkoğlu, *Hatıralarım*, p. 47; Selahattin Sert, *Haçlıların Son Kurbanı Ermeniler* (The Last Victim of the Crusaders: Armenians), Vol. 1 (İstanbul: Kum Saatı Yayınları, 2005), pp. 122–38; Clair Price, *The Rebirth of Turkey* (New York: Thomas Seltzer, 1923), pp. 83–84; Gibbons, *The Red Rugs of Tarsus*, pp. 164–66; Abbott, *Turkey in Transition*, p. 306; "The New Rule in Turkey," *The Literary Digest*, Vol. 38, No. 19 (May 8, 1909), pp. 782–84.

93. Şevket Süreyya Aydemir, *Makedonya'dan Ortaasya'ya Enver Paşa* (Enver Paşa: From Macedonia to Central Asia), Vol. 2: 1908–1914 (İstanbul: Remzi Kitabevi, reprint, 2010), p. 155; "Who Will End the Armenian Killing?" *The Literary Digest*, Vol. 38, No. 23 (June 5, 1909), pp. 957–58.

94. Davide Rodogno, *Against Massacre: Humanitarian Interventions in the Ottoman Empire 1815–1914* (Princeton, NJ: Princeton University Press, 2012), p. 204; Arman Kirakossian, *British Diplomacy and the Armenian Question, from the 1830s to 1914* (Princeton, NJ: Gomidas Institute Books, 2003), p. 304.

95. "L'interpellation au Parlement français sur les massacres arméniens," Agence Constantinople, 18 mai 1909.

96. Rodogno, *Against Massacre*, pp. 204–5.

97. "Adana Hıristiyanlarının Beyannamesi" (The Declaration of the Christians of Adana), *Tanin*, July 1, 1909, p. 1.

98. MAE, NS Turquie, Vol. 83, p. 159. Nouvelles du Vilayet. Barré de Lancy (Mersine) à Stéphane Pichon (Paris), 27 juillet 1909; "Kanuni Esasımızın İkinci Senei Devriyesi" (The Second Anniversary of Our Constitution), *Tanin*, July 24, 1909, p. 1; *İkdam*, July 24, 1909, p. 1.

99. Dikran Mesrob Kaligian, "The Armenian Revolutionary Federation in Constantinople, 1908–1914," in Richard Hovannisian and Simon Payaslian, eds., *Armenian Constantinople* (Costa Mesa, CA: Mazda Publishers, 2010), p. 375; idem, "A Prelude to Genocide: CUP Population Policies and Provincial Insecurity, 1908–1914," *Journal of Genocide Research*, Vol. 10, No. 1 (March 2008), p. 78. Text of the CUP-Armenian Revolutionary Federation declaration was published in *Tanin* of September 19, 1909.

100. "Parliamentary Elections," *The Orient*, Vol. 3, No. 10 (March 6, 1912), p. 4.

101. PA-AA; R 14087; A 27584. Head of the German Information Service for the Orient, Baron Max von Oppenheim, to the Imperial Chancellor (Bethmann Hollweg), August 29, 1915, cited in Wolfgang Gust, ed., *The Armenian Genocide Evidence from the German Foreign Office Archives, 1915–1916* (New York and Oxford: Berghahn Books, 2014; German origin, 2005), p. 333. On the life and career of Max von Oppenheim, see Tilman Lüdke, *Jihad Made in Germany Ottoman and German Propaganda and Intelligence Operations in the First World War* (Münster: Lit Verlag, 2005), pp. 70–75.

102. Gust, *The Armenian Genocide*, pp. 333–34.

103. Ibid., p. 334.

104. Ibid., pp. 334–35.

105. Ibid., p. 336.

106. "Armenian Massacre," *Muslim Outlook*, No. 24 (April 1, 1920), p. 13.

107. Peter Balakian, *The Burning Tigris: The Armenian Genocide and America's Response* (New York: HarperCollins, 2004), p. 157.

108. Simonyan, *The Destruction of Armenians in Cilicia, April 1909*, p. 261.

109. Martin Mennecke, "The Crime of Genocide and International Law," in Barbara Boender and Wichert ten Have, eds., *The Holocaust and Other Genocides: An Introduction* (Amsterdam: Amsterdam University Press, 2012), p. 149.

110. Suny, *A History of the Armenian Genocide*, p. 170.

111. Vahakn Dadrian, "The Circumstances Surrounding the 1909 Adana Holocaust," *The Armenian Review*, Vol. 41, No. 4 (Winter 1988), pp. 1–16; idem, *The History of the Armenian Genocide: Ethnic Conflict from the Balkans to Anatolia to the Caucasus* (Providence, RI and Oxford: Berghahn Books, second revised edition,

1997), p. 386; and idem, "The Armenian Genocide: Review of Its Historical, Political, and Legal Aspects," *University of St. Thomas Journal of Law and Public Policy*, Vol. 5 (April 2011), pp. 151–52.

112. Margaret Lavinia Anderson, Michael Reynolds, Hans-Lukas Kieser, Peter Balakian, A. Dirk Moses, and Taner Akçam, "Taner Akçam, The Young Turks' Crime Against Humanity: The Armenian Genocide and Ethnic Cleansing in the Ottoman Empire (Princeton, NJ: Princeton University Press, 2012)," *Journal of Genocide Research*, Vol. 15, No. 4 (December 2013), p. 474.

113. For the uniqueness of the Holocaust see, among many others, Steven Katz, *The Holocaust in Historical Context*, Vol. 1: *The Holocaust and Mass Death before the Modern Age* (New York and Oxford: Oxford University Press, 1994). This volume is the first of four intended to demonstrate that the Holocaust is the only instance of true genocide. It promises to be an unusually massive work. Volumes 2 to 4 of this project are now in preparation and will be forthcoming from the Oxford University Press. Idem, "The Uniqueness of the Holocaust: The Historical Dimension," in Alan Rosenbaum, ed., *Is the Holocaust Unique? Perspectives on Comparative Genocide* (Boulder, CO: Westview Press, 1996); idem, *Historicism, the Holocaust and Zionism: Critical Studies in Modern Jewish Thought and History* (New York and London: New York University Press, 1992); idem, *Post-Holocaust Dialogues: Critical Studies in Modern Jewish Thought* (New York and London: New York University Press, 1983); idem, "The Unique Intentionality of the Holocaust," *Modern Judaism*, Vol. 1, No. 2 (September 1981).

114. Letter from Israel Singer of the World Jewish Congress to Raya Jaglom, President of the Women's International Zionist Organization, New York, July 22, 1988.

115. Nadav Shragai, "Attempting to Legislate the Meaning of the Holocaust," *Haaretz*, January 14, 1998, pp. 1–2.

116. Benjamin Smith, "Groups Try to Put a Definition on Genocide," Political Notebook, *The Wall Street Journal Europe*, May 22, 2001, p. 13.

117. Dalia Karpel, "There Was No Genocide: Interview with Professor Bernard Lewis," *Haaretz Weekly*, January 23, 1998, p. 3.

Chapter Seven

Cemal Paşa's Governorship in Adana, August 1909–June 1911

THE 2009 CENTENARY OF THE ADANA AFFAIR

The 2009 centenary of the Adana affair in 1909 saw a number of symposia, conferences, round tables, and publications refocusing historical interest on that episode and its principal protagonists. The occasion provided an opportunity to reexamine the causes and the dimensions of the incidents, the responsibility of the outrages, and the reestablishment of the order. Here it should also be mentioned that these were not prepared with purely scholarly objectives in mind.

Catholicos Aram I of the Holy See of Cilicia in Antelias, Beirut, demanded on October 29, 2009, reparations for the Adana events of 1909 during a symposium to mark the one hundredth anniversary of the occasion. "In Adana we lost 30,000 lives, the massacres left us with widows, orphans, destroyed churches, homes, schools, farms, mills and everything else that touched the people's livelihood," Aram I said in his opening remarks. "Hence, today on behalf of all Armenians we demand compensation from Turkey for those losses inflicted upon our people. As Armenians we should set aside our differences and unite in our just claims for reparation for the Adana tragedy. The demand for justice is not constrained by time. We must ensure that the consequences of the genocides are recognized and remedied."[1]

In 1909, however, as far as international law is concerned, there was no restriction whatever upon a state to abstain from maltreating to any extent its own citizens. In 1920, Lassa Francis Lawrence Oppenheim wrote in his preeminent textbook of international law:

> Several writers maintain that the Law of Nations guarantees to every individual at home and abroad the so-called rights of mankind. [. . .] Such rights are said

to comprise the right to existence, the right to protection of honour, life, health, liberty, and property, the right of practicing any religion one likes, the right of emigration, and the like. But such rights do not in fact enjoy any guarantee whatever from the Law of Nations, and they cannot enjoy such guarantee, since the Law of Nations is a law between States, and since individuals cannot be subjects of this law [. . .] a guarantee of the so-called rights of mankind cannot be found in all these and other facts. Nor do the actual conditions of life to which certain classes of subjects are forcibly submitted within certain States show that the Law of Nations really comprises such guarantee.[2]

Given the fact that more than 109 years have passed since the alleged events occurred, the question arises whether any obligation to make reparation, if there ever was one, has run the statute of limitations. The chances of success of any Armenian reparation claim before the International Court of Justice, the United Nations Treaty Bodies, or the European Court of Human Rights do not exist under international law. Turkey can not be held responsible for any material or moral injury resulting from the events of 1909 as the conduct of the Ottoman Empire did not violate any obligations under the rules of customary international law applicable at the time.

Sabancı University in İstanbul on November 6–7, 2009, hosted an international workshop titled, "Adana 1909: History, Memory, and Identity from a Hundred Year Perspective." Scholars from the United States, Canada, Britain, France, Italy, and Turkey participated in the workshop, which was cosponsored by the Gomidas Institute (London), Sabancı University, the International Hrant Dink Foundation, and the history departments of İstanbul Bilgi University and Boğaziçi University. Each session was chaired by a senior scholar and was followed by a discussion. The workshop also benefited from the presence of additional senior scholars, such as Selim Deringil, Cağlar Keyder, Mete Tunçay, and Hülya Adak.

Abdulhamit Kırmızı of Şehir University in İstanbul examined the presence of righteous Turkish officials who saved Armenians in 1909. The role played by such Turks was actually acknowledged by the Ottoman government after 1909. The speaker's focus was Major Hacı Mehmed Efendi and his men who defended Sis, the seat of the Armenian Catholicosate of Cilicia, from attacks by neighboring tribes and villages. Kırmızı used Ottoman documentation to discuss these individuals, many of whom were decorated by the Ottoman government. Looking at factors that may have led to the massacres, Sinan Dinçer of Ruhr University in Bochum identified the presence of tens of thousands of impoverished migrant workers who could not find work in Adana in 1909. Ara Sarafian and Zakarya Mildanoğlu discussed Armenian sources related to the events of 1909. The role of American missionaries as witnesses was examined by Lou Ann Matossian of Cafesjian Family Foundation and

Barbara Merguerian of Armenian International Women's Association, with papers regarding the clashs in Adana and Tarsus. Marc Nichanian of Sabancı University and Rita Soulahian of McGill University dwelled on the literary response to the Adana events, with particular reference to Arshagouhi Teotig, Taniel Varoujan, and Zabel Yessayan.[3]

Scholars look forward to reading and studying the published versions of the papers presented at this workshop complete with questions, answers, and comments.

Regretfully, most of the Sabancı University workshop participants selectively used limited Ottoman official sources. These sources were used only when they concurred with the participants' views. The same is true about much of the secondary material used by them. A balanced analysis would have shed light on a difficult period and would have helped the public and the academia attain a better understanding of an important subject.

The cataclysmic events of April 1909 continue—109 years later—to fascinate historians and the public alike. There are reminders that much remains unknown.

Over the decades scant attention has been paid to the provision of humanitarian relief and reconstruction in the region following the summer of 1909 and the role that Cemal Paşa played in that regard during his governorship in Adana. He was about thirty-seven years old at that time, and a man of extraordinary promise. It is here, arguably, where there is greatest potential and greatest need for further study.[4]

CEMAL PAŞA'S PERSONAL AND PROFESSIONAL LIFE

Cemal Bey was born on May 6, 1872, in Midilli (Mytilene), an island in the Aegean Sea near the coast of Anatolia, where his parents then resided. Turks and Greeks made up the population here. The Turks were employed by the state, which they served as soldiers or civilian officials; some were also landowners and peasants. The Greeks provided almost all the merchants, tradesmen, and craftsmen, as well as making part of the peasant population. Because of their religious affinity with western Europe, Greeks took to new learning long before their Muslim neighbors. Nevertheless, with its profusion of minarets and domes Midilli was Muslim in aspect. Mosques, almshouses, dervish monasteries, shrines, Turkish baths, and fountains graced the island. The multinational Ottoman Empire into which Cemal Bey was born was creaking, but it was still functioning.

It was customary among Turks to give a newborn baby a name when the umbilical cord was cut. This was known as the "belly name," and it was chosen among the honorific titles applied to the Prophet Muhammad or other names having a pious connotation. Later the child might be given a second or even a third name, by which he or she would become known. The use of two given names was a mark of social distinction. Cemal Bey started life as Ahmed Cemal.

Ahmed Cemal's birth was not entered in the population register in Midilli but in İstanbul. He was the second child of a family of six children. The names of his two brothers and three sisters in seniority were: Şadiye, Saffet, Fehime, Naciye, and Kemal. His father, Mehmed Nesib Bey, was not the aloof and distant authority often regarded as typical of that generation of Turks but, rather, an active if strict parent who took considerable interest in the upbringing and activities of Cemal and his siblings. He was a pharmacist in the Ottoman army, a relatively privileged position. This allowed Cemal the opportunity to be educated by a series of French tutors, followed by admission to the prestigious Kuleli military secondary school in the capital on the Asian shore of the Bosphorus. In 1890 he became a cadet at the War College in İstanbul. The college buildings, now used as a military museum, were set on a hill overlooking the Bosphorus, in a new part of the city developed in the nineteenth century. Cemal Bey worked hard during his three years in the War College. He was ranked second in his class, and after two years completed his staff studies at the War Academy. The Ottoman War Academy used a German curriculum which stressed the operations of higher-level formations, as well as foreign languages and international law. Many of its graduates, the highly trained staff officer corps, were proficient administrators and planners. At the War Academy Cemal Bey was exposed to military instructors considered to be the army's best, and this institution was perhaps one of the strongest influences in his later life. He learned there not only respect for military virtues but also the trust for Western education, which were to mark his later thought. Cemal Bey was sent to Germany for training tours. In addition to being a staff officer, he was an ardent advocate of modernization.[5]

We should not be surprised at this. Ottoman military training was, by the last decade of the nineteenth century, dominated by German instruction and the tradition of the Prussian General Staff. Germans taught at the War College and War Academy in İstanbul, and approximately 90 percent of the Ottoman teachers at these schools had been trained in Germany. While in the War College, they learned French and attended classes by German instructors on the history of war, weapons, military organization, strategy, tactics, and military literature. As army cadets, they were impressed with the technical and military education they received, by the general staff system that instilled order and respect for efficiency, and with the elevation of the methods of war to the level of science, once again creating the possibility of Muslim ascendance.

The central focus of this teaching was the German military model, which was applied not only to military matters but to state and society as well. The influence of Carl von Clausewitz, with his idealization of the strong state which would educate its people as soldiers, and Otto von Bismarck, with his paternalism, *realpolitik*, and above all, his strategy for the unification of Germany, was powerful and appealing. Reading the chief German instructor General Colmar Freiherr von Der Goltz's *The Nation in Arms*, they were impressed by his thoughts on the role of the army and education in society. The Prussian military tradition, with its emphasis on the state and obedience to it, and on discipline, instilled in its students a strong sense of statecraft and a proclivity toward a centralizing govenment.[6] Cemal Bey's early education and military training set his character and determined his course as a public figure.

Cemal Bey (as he was called prior to January 3, 1914)[7] was aware of the European issues of the day. He was a careful observer of the Occident and had obtained knowledge of European cities and Western civilization from visits which he had made to Paris, Budapest, and other foreign capitals. He understood and spoke French moderately well and read widely. Cemal Bey was considered as having an up-to-date understanding of modern war. He was the author of the book *Plevne Müdafaası* (Defense of Plevna) published in 1900 by the Ahu Asaduryan Press Company in İstanbul, and the manuscript of another work by him *Kırım Harbi Tarihi* (History of the Crimean War) was lost in the press of *Tanin* newspaper, the office of which was ransacked and set on fire during the counterrevolution in April 1909. Given the Ottoman Empire's grave circumstance, they were buoyant studies.

Cemal Bey rose to the rank of a staff captain in 1895. He was employed in the construction section in Kırkkilise (Kırklareli) within the body of the Second Army until 1898. Afterwards, he was appointed to Salonika as the chief of staff of the Third Reserve Division under the command of the Third Army. In October 1905 he was promoted to the rank of major. In October 1906 he became a member of the Ottoman Freedom Society, a grouping in Salonika inspired by the CUP's ideas that was established a month previously. Thence he joined the CUP. In this city he was assigned as the military inspector of railroad construction. By means of this post, Cemal Bey could easily travel in Macedonia and make a significant contribution to the organization of the Ottoman Freedom Society there. His efforts to spread the influence of the society in Macedonia made him one of the most prominent figures in the group. He also worked with Ali Fethi (Okyar) and Mustafa Kemal (Atatürk) on the staff of the Third Army.[8]

It should particularly be mentioned here that Salonika was the feverish center of the Macedonian question in all its entanglements. Macedonia was the area north of the Aegean Sea which included the Ottoman provinces of

Salonika, Manastır, and Kosova, and contained a mixed population of Turks, Albanians, Greeks, Bulgarians, Serbs, Jews, and Vlachs. The neighboring Balkan states were in open conflict for the possession of Macedonia. Encouraged by various great powers, their "protectors," certain native groups were not only involved in political intrigue in the area, but were engaged in actual fighting by organized bands. At the same time, Salonika was the city where the underground revolutionary movement of the Ottoman Empire's regeneration and democratization made headquarters.

As a member of the Central Committee of the CUP, Cemal Bey was sent to Adana to restore order. But his influence in the committee was unimpaired. The appointment was a judicious one.[9] The Ottoman government could not have made a better choice for this important office. It was a hard and delicate task.[10] Attached to the ideas of the union of elements, fraternity, and Ottomanism, and not being a "remnant of the ancient regime," his nomination was mainly due to the complaints of the Armenian patriarchate, criticisms in the press, debates in the parliament, and the desire of the CUP to appease the public opinion and to prevent the quarrels that would put the regime in danger.[11] Cemal Bey was undoubtedly the best man for the position. His appointment as governor of Adana was most favorably received by the people of that city and province.[12] Tarık Zafer Tunaya aptly portrayed him as "a man of difficult times."[13]

Cemal Bey had from the first been a prominent figure in the Young Turk administration. Soon after the climbdown of Sultan Abdülhamid II on July 23, 1908, he was among a Committee of Seven dispatched by the CUP to İstanbul to negotiate with the palace. Quitely, the Committee of Seven exercised pressure on Abdülhamid to reform the government and ensure that the parliamentary elections would be freely conducted. He participated energetically in the suppression of the March 31 incident and later earned a great reputation as *mutasarrıf* of the Üsküdar district. This was a relatively unusual position for a staff officer, but Cemal Bey welcomed the opportunity to develop a public administrative dimension to his career. He knew that his promotion would be a temporary arrangement. But he must have made the sensible calculation that, in the long term, it would provide more permanent progress. Not having any other occupation than the army until then, he was all of a sudden and unexpectedly improvised a *mutasarrıf*. He had no previous experience of this new office. But intelligence, aptitude, patriotism, and love of duty soon made up for the inexperience. Shortly after his assumption of office, the situation in Üsküdar changed drastically. He turned out the corrupt officials of the old regime and put men of ability in their places. The presence of a firm hand was immediately felt in the district.[14] According to Talha Çiçek, in this post, he stood out with his policies, which could be interpreted as steps in the direction of the "Westernization" and "control" of society. He applied strict measures to give order to public life.[15] Cemal Bey began as a soldier, a role for which his upbringing and his talents had prepared him well, and he developed into an administrator.

In 1912 Cemal Bey took command of the Konya reserve division and, in the First Balkan War, fought Bulgarians at Vize, was defeated at Pınarhisar, and later served as supply inspector and army administrative chief of the Çatalca front. After the assumption of power by the CUP on January 23, 1913, he became military governor of İstanbul and showed great skill in organizing the police forces and directing their work for the safety of the government.[16] As the executive agent of the CUP this suave gentleman proved himself extraordinarily useful. He took a firm grasp before the opponents of the Unionists really knew what was happening.[17] Cemal Bey showed nervousness for and watchfulness over the security of the government. In İstanbul he remained master of the situation. The calm was maintained by the exercise of disciplinary measures, in which he had demonstrated himself a past master from the day of January 23, 1913. He told to a correspondent of *Tanin*:

> Since my appointment, I have had my eyes fixed on the suspect individuals who could disturb public order. First of all, there were in İstanbul a number of officers without official duties who were occupied with matters other than their military business. These officers have been assigned to various posts in the country and ordered to join them. Some has obeyed. The others have shown indiscipline and fled abroad.[18]

Upon the assassination of Grand Vizier Mahmud Şevket Paşa on June 11, 1913, Cemal Bey acted quickly and resolutely. He banished a number of persons identified with opposition to the regime from İstanbul to Sinop. A list of principal exiles was published in the press. The banished persons were provided with means of immediate livelihood and openings for continued subsistence. He strongly supported the Unionists' plans for recapturing Edirne in the Second Balkan War. As military governor of the capital city, he was nominated by the Sublime Porte as one of its military representatives to carry on the negotiations with the Bulgarian delegates after the Balkan Wars. At forty-two he was as much a diplomat as a soldier. The other military representative was İsmet (İnönü) Bey, of the General Staff.[19] Cemal Bey had the reputation of being very strict in discipline. He would certainly not hesitate to resort to the severest measures when the general good order or the reformation of the nation required it. He was respected in the army and the CUP.[20]

Having an inquiring mind, the extent of the influence exerted on Ottoman affairs by the German military reform mission to İstanbul in December 1913 deeply worried Cemal Bey, who feared Teutonic encroachment on Ottoman sovereignty, yet the need for the mission was undisputed. As its performance in the Balkan Wars had just shown, the Ottoman army was desperately in need of an overhaul, and given the Germans' performance in their three wars of unification, no one questioned the idea of the Turks emulating a winner.[21] Interestingly, Cemal Bey was widely regarded by Otto Liman von Sanders, head of the German military reform mission and field commander in the Ottoman army from 1913 to 1918, as "unquestionably combining great intelligence with a determined attitude."[22]

Cemal Bey's personal and professional life was one of rectitude. He was rigorous with himself about financial matters. His life was molded by military virtues—valor, obedience and self-discipline, careful training, and self-sacrifice. In this regard, it is noteworthy that among his distinguished acquaintances in the Ottoman Empire, Wyndham Deedes had "always counted him [Cemal Bey] the most agreeable."[23] Deeds had been a captain with the Ottoman gendarmerie in North Africa and the Ministry of the Interior at İstanbul, before moving to the Turkish Section of Military Intelligence, London in 1914.[24]

Cemal Paşa also served as provincial governor of Baghdad, commanded the First Army Corps with responsibility for the security of İstanbul and the Straits, and acted as minister of public works and minister of marine and commander of the Fourth Army in Syria and Palestine between 1911 and 1918. Lieutenant Colonel Percival George Elgood, the British commander and director of the Military Intelligence Office at Port Said during the First World War, notes that in his post in Syria and Palestine "Jemal Pasha acted with vigor and discretion. He chose subordinates according to their capacity and not from motives of favouritism, and treated the civilian population with tenderness. Kress von Kressenstein and other German officers who served in this theater habitually spoke well of Jemal Pasha's energy and moderation."[25]

As minister of marine, Cemal Paşa devoted himself to the reorganization of the navy. The whole French press, without any exception, was unanimous in cordially saluting him during his official visit to France on July 3–18, 1914. *Le Temps* of July 4—recalling his value, energy, and the patriotic devotion—editorialized as follows. Cemal Paşa was, in all respects, a distinguished statesman to greet. The last clouds over the Ottoman-French relations had dispersed and the traditional friendship between the two countries would be resumed. The political relations between the Ottoman Empire and France under Francis I were struck by a naval alliance. All the same, the Ottoman minister of marine would find direct and intimate contacts in his dealings with the French government. *Le Temps* also referred to the peaceful efforts exerted by the CUP government and said that these young and intelligent men tried to reform their country and secure it stability.[26]

Cemal Paşa's efforts, during his trip to Paris, to bring about a closer understanding between the Ottoman Empire and France bore no fruit and he later supported, somewhat reluctantly, Enver Paşa's policy of alliance with Germany. Enver Paşa was undoubtedly the supreme power behind the Ottoman First World War effort. He had an almost entirely free hand in military affairs. In addition to his portfolio as minister of war, Enver Paşa further consolidated his hold over the army by retaining the title of acting commander-in-chief and chief of the general staff as well. Holding these three offices concurrently enabled him to establish primacy over strategic direction and policy, supervise and direct the general staff, and command the Ottoman army operationally. It was a staggering consolidation of power in the hands of a single person, and no other individual in any country had similar authority. Enver Paşa's influence was far superior to the sultan's, and his power not even the Sheikh-ul-Islam, that supreme authority of the Muslim world, cared to challenge.[27]

Cemal Paşa was usually considered to be Francophile in tendencies. But those who gave him this reputation grossly mistook him. In fact, like the other CUP members, he was first and foremost an Ottoman patriot and as such entirely ready to be completely realistic and pragmatic in taking care of what he regarded to be his country's vital interests. Though his knowledge of the French language brought him into closer touch with the French than any other European nation, he considered his best political friends to be those who were most prepared to aid the Ottoman Empire. Cemal Paşa's appreciation of France's cultural richness and financial strength did not detract him from admiration of German military might and of Britain's cunning use of power. He was less a friend of the French than is often imagined. It was he, for example, who, together with Enver Paşa, led the Ottoman Empire to enter the First World War against the Entente powers. Other evidence indicates that if he seemed pro-French, it was because of his apprehension of the Russians. One would say that he was greatly influenced by the conviction that French friendship was and always would be essential to the Ottoman Empire as a makeweight against Russia. His essential objective had been to protect the Ottoman Empire's national interests—a goal which he carried out with full government approval. It was an injustice to Cemal Paşa to suspect him of less than wholehearted devotion to the Ottoman-German Treaty of August 2, 1914. He had declared on several occasions that the treaty of alliance existed and must be implemented if Germany wished. Subsequent events amply justified him.[28]

Cemal Paşa played a great role in the government of the Young Turks; he was one of the four leading figures, sharing responsibility with Talat and Enver Paşas, and Cavid Bey, the financial expert. Cavid Bey was an intellectual of deep culture with a powerful brain; he was characterized by an alertness and incisiveness of mind. Well educated and blessed with the gift of oratory, he made devoted friends and bitter enemies. He possessed a far more liberal and flexible intelligence than most of his colleagues in the CUP, a single-minded, upright man who carried great weight. He spoke fluently, eloquently, with a remarkable command of language and developed his ideas in conversation with an orderliness, precision, and felicity that were very striking. Through his efforts, he essentially determined the boundaries of the financial ties between the Ottoman Empire and Germany. He was thirty-four when he was appointed minister of finance in 1909, the first CUP member to serve at cabinet rank. Despite his CUP affiliation, he was careful to become neither too closely identified with nor beholden to the Young Turk leadership, particularly by keeping Enver Paşa at arm's length. Cavid Bey's assertion of his independence proved to be important, for it enabled him to ensure his continued place at the heart of the empire's financial administration, providing an unprecedented measure of stability to the administration of the Ottoman treasury by standing apart from the factionalism by which the government was soon riven. Cavid Bey's particular talent lay in his ability to secure loans for the Sublime Porte in the years prior to the First World War. In doing so, he served as something of a counterweight to Enver Paşa, repeatedly tapping the Germans for fresh infusions of cash while shunting aside their demands for further economic concessions. Colleagues in the same cabinet, they were associated with quite different currents of opinion. As a result, they could not help but further the sense of ambivalence which for so long had characterized the policies of successive Unionist governments.[29] It is, however, to be remarked that Cavid Bey, who is an almost inescapable presence to the student of early twentieth-century Ottoman history, remains undeservedly unfamiliar to the nonspecialist.[30]

CEMAL BEY'S ARRIVAL IN ADANA, AUGUST 19, 1909

The Turkish press of August 13, 1909, cited a circular telegram addressed by the Sublime Porte to the governors of all the provinces and sanjaks of the empire on the Adana affair. It was the inertia and bad administration of the Adana province which had been the principal cause of the massacres.[31]

Before the new governor's arrival in Adana, the Armenian-language İstanbul daily *Azamard* published an interview with him that ran partly as follows:

> As a sincere Ottoman, I deplore the regretful events which were the nefarious consequences of the absolutist regime. I sincerely like Armenians who seek their happiness in the prosperity of the Ottoman Empire. My first will be search the proper means to consolidate the union of various elements. To that effect, I intend to open international clubs and schools. I will spare no effort for return-

ing to the flourishing state of affairs in a relatively short period of time. Having consulted the minister of public works, I will also give great impulsion to public utility works. In short, I will do everything in my power to achieve the task facing the Turkish front. I will go to Adana either to reorganize or die.[32]

Armenians generally expressed gratification over Cemal Bey's appointment.[33] Cemal Bey was a man of his world, and his promise once given was secure. His chief virtues were punctuality, industry, and devotion to his official duties.[34]

The inhabitants of Adana were anxiously awaiting Cemal Bey's arrival, hoping that he would be able to improve the state of affairs in the province. The ambitious governor set off for his post immediately. It was not long before it became apparent that he was a man of very different character to his predecessor.[35]

This young soldier-governor surprised everyone. He did not allow religious prejudices to interfere with the impartial manner in which he endeavored to perform his duty toward Muslim and Christian without favor or affection. Not only had he endeavored to introduce reforms throughout his province, but by the personal interest which he had taken in all that was going on around him, as well as by the unceasing energy with which he had occupied himself with the affairs of state, Cemal Bey had begun to reestablish confidence among the inhabitants of his province—a confidence which was so conspicuous by its absence when he took over the reins of governorate from Babanzade Mustafa Zihni Paşa on August 19, 1909. The personality of the latter had unfortunately proved quite unequal to the task of governing Adana at a critical time.[36]

Babanzade Mustafa Zihni Paşa was not the man who would be required in the present circumstances, and Barré de Lancy, the French vice consul in Mersin and Adana, doubted that he promoted many things. Babanzade Mustafa Zihni Paşa was an honest man but he was not an administrator capable of reorganizing and reconstructing a region.[37] His greatest merit besides his honesty was being the father of a young influential deputy from Baghdad, Babanzade İsmail Hakkı, a contributor to *Tanin* and a member of the delegation recently sent to Paris and London by the Ottoman parliament.[38] The French vice consul does not tell everything, but what he does tell is truthful and enlightening. Charles Woods concurs and says: "Everyone recognized the honesty, fairness, and impartiality of Mustafa Zihni Pasha, who, whilst a thorough old Turk, appeared to be a man of the highest class. Largely owing to the influence of his son—Babanzade Ismail Hakkı—Mustafa Zihni Pasha was supported by the Central Committee of the Committee of Union and Progress."[39] Mustafa Zihni Paşa later served as governor of the Hejaz province from January to September 1912. He died in 1929.

The distress occasioned by the tragedies in Adana, and beyond that province as far as Aleppo, was regrettable. Two international relief commissions were founded in İstanbul to come to the aid of the victims of Adana.[40] The first commission, in charge of gathering offerings, was composed of the following: M. M. Huguenin, director general of the Anatolian railways, chairman; Talat Bey (to be called Talat Paşa after 1917), vice president of the Chamber of Deputies, deputy chairman; Ernest Giraud; Hüseyin Cahid Bey, deputy for İstanbul; Said Halim Paşa, member of the Council of Notables; Jost; Edwin Pears; A. Aslanyan; Isaac Fernandez; Mıgırdıç Manukyan; Simon Kayserliyan; Hrand Han Şamdancıyan; Emmanuel Carasso; Joseph Back; N. H. Margaritis, director-owner of *Le Moniteur Oriental* and *Tachydromos*; Taranto; Minas Ceraz; Zare Pekmez; R. Couteaux; Dr. Eizen; Ardaşez Hürmüz; Aram Hallaçyan; Mihran, director-owner of *Sabah*; Krikor Agopyan; Etiénne Eugénidès; Abud Efendi; Sidérides; Régis Delbeuf, director-owner of *Stamboul*; Vahan Esayan; Ahmed Nesimi Bey; Lorens Binus; İsmail Hakkı Bey; Henry Stock; Aram Köçeoğlu; Emile Baudouny; Maksud Şahbaz; T. Geseryan; Dr. Rıza Tevfik; and Remzi Bey, members. The second commission, in charge of sharing out and distribution of the relief, comprised the following: M. M. Pitt, chairman; Zare Dilber, deputy chairman; Stepan Karayan; Arşak Şımavonyan; M. Şirinyan; Vitali Kamhi; Yusuf Kemal Bey, deputy for Kastamonu; James William Withall; A. Fındıklıyan; A. Topalyan; Puzant Keçiyan, director of *Puzantion*; M. Gazarosyan; Professor Cediciyzan; K. Feradyan; H. Esayan; Von Mach; M. Voutiras; Leonidas Zarifi; B. Şerbetçiyan; Dr Grunwald; D. Gümüşgerdan; H. Sinanyan; A. Kasparyan; Nogara; and H. Hagopyan, members.[41]

The International Relief Commission published the statement three months after the events in question that the number of victims who required relief was nearly eighty thousand of whom five thousand were orphans.[42] In Edwin Pears's opinion, it was, of course, unreasonable to think that Hüseyin Hilmi Paşa, Talat Bey, or any other of the ministers approved the massacres. Pears was convinced that they regarded them as purely mischievous, and as endangering their course.[43] The British author further considered Talat Bey impressed those he met in England a few years ago with the openness of his mind and good judgment. He had done nothing to discredit this impression.[44] Leadership of the Unionists was collegiate and remained so to the end of their existence. But some leaders were more prominent than others.

TALAT BEY'S PERSONALITY AND STRENGTH

Talat Bey was an extraordinary personality, and he was clearly capable of giving strong direction to policy during his tenure of office.[45] Of the other Ottoman leaders, it is no exaggeration to say, he stood out among all. No one could escape the charm of his sympathetic and attractive personality.[46] He was, in fact, the one strong personality that the Ottoman Empire had since Sultan Abdülhamid II was overthrown by the Young Turk party in 1908. Being famous for his spotless integrity, he was undoubtedly the most important man in the Ottoman Empire at the present time.[47] His advice was heeded everywhere, and he virtually directed the public affairs of the country. Talat Bey, tall and erect, with a keen face and alert eyes, had probably the most notable, statesmanlike intellect in the Ottoman realm of that time. He was thoroughly rational, facing facts with cool deliberation, and a practical politician. He was all strength, exuberance, and vivacity.[48] Talat Bey was a man of virility and gusto, powerful in frame, humorous in talk, warm and genial in manner, with a frank simplicity which masked a swift supple mind and a realistic outlook. Forceful in action, he was a patriot wedded to his country's interests, who had come, through his moderation, to be known as the Danton of the Constitutional Revolution.[49] These phrases suggest his character.

Talat Bey was always at the center of things. He was clever, strong-willed, and comfortable in his dealings with foreign diplomats.[50] The British ambassador at İstanbul, Sir Louis Mallet, in his annual report on the Ottoman Empire for 1913, described Talat Bey as one of the most striking personalities of the CUP. According to Mallet, he played an important part in the revolution of 1908, and his influence whether as minister or as one of the members of the Central Committee of the CUP, which dictated the policy of the government, had since that time been all-powerful. In appearance he was a contrast to Grand Vizier Said Halim Paşa, being tall and heavily built, with a look and gait which recalled descriptions of Mirabeau, Danton, or Dr. Johnson. He was a man of high capacity and great energy, and absolutely fearless. He was intensely patriotic, and the main object of his ambition, which could hardly be called personal, since with many opportunities he had not enriched himself, was the regeneration of his country.[51]

One can go further. In November 1915, Alfred Nossing of the Berlin daily *Lokal Anzeiger* referred to Talat Bey's unusual energy, statesmanlike qualities, calmness, and composure of mind, and said he might be called the Turkish Bismarck.[52] He was highly respected by Kaiser Wilhelm II, who in 1917 conferred on him the Prussian Order of the Black Eagle, one of the highest German decorations seldom conferred on non-Germans.[53]

Talat Bey was born in Kırcaali, a kaza of Edirne, in 1874. After getting his primary instruction, he taught Turkish in Alliance Israélite—the Paris-based Jewish educational society, which maintained secular schools mainly for Jews in the Ottoman Empire. Before the proclamation of the constitution, he had taken two years in the Salonika Law School. The first official position he held was that of second clerk in the office of posts and telegraphs in Edirne.

Like many young men making the transition from late adolescence to adulthood, Talat Bey found himself drawn to radical politics. It was an attraction that caused him to run afoul of Ottoman authorities, who arrested him in 1893 on a charge of subversive political activity. On his release two years later, he was appointed to a government post. A skilled telegraphist, Talat Bey was named secretary of the postal service in Salonika, supervising both the post offices and the telegraph service there. Rising through the bureaucracy, by 1908 he was running the whole of the postal services in the province. But 1908 saw his career with the post office come to an end, as Talat Bey was dismissed when it was discovered that he had become a member of the CUP. It proved to be only a temporary setback, as in December he was elected a deputy to the new Ottoman Parliament for his home province of Edirne. His colleagues quickly recognized his talents, and in 1909, he was elected vice president of the Chamber of Deputies, and later he was appointed minister of the interior and afterwards minister of posts and telegraphs. In the cabinet of Said Halim Paşa, he held the portfolio of the interior. On the resignation of Said Halim Paşa in 1917, he assumed the position of grand vizier.[54]

Talat Paşa was of humble and indistinct origin. He began his career as a telegraph clerk but rose to the rank of Paşa and grand vizier. "When I became minister," he once remarked, "everyone began nursing the same ambition."[55] Talat Paşa honestly believed that there were other men, by hundreds, far better fitted than himself to fill high offices of state. And so he was forever hanging back from opportunities which most men would have pounced on. He was the true spirit of the CUP which regarded personal ambition as a poor delusion.[56]

It should also be added that as minister of the interior, Talat Bey shared many traits with other leaders of the twentieth century who rose from humble backgrounds. His natural charisma, intelligence, and single-mindedness combined to give birth to a strong political pragmatist. Always careful to make strategic moves that enhanced his power, he cooperated with his Central Committee members while never relinquishing power.[57]

Talat Paşa was assassinated while walking from his home to a cigarette kiosk in Berlin. An Armenian, Soghomon Tehlirian, approached him on March 15, 1921, and shot him dead. His corpse arrived at İstanbul in the morning of February 25, 1943, and was buried at the Hill of Eternal Liberty. The funeral, which took place in great state, was attended by the representatives of the president of the Republic, İsmet İnönü, and the prime minister, Şükrü Saraçoğlu, the local leading civil and military officials, former ambassadors, deputies and the German consul general. German ambassador Franz von Papen addressed a telegram to Madame Hayriye, the wife of the late grand vizier, expressing sympathy and his satisfaction at the burial in Turkey of "this great statesman who was a dear friend of Germany."[58]

It was the prime minister, Saraçoğlu, who had taken the principal part in getting Talat Paşa's remains back to Turkey. He could not, of course, had done so without the approval of the president, and it might be reasonable to state that the purpose of the Turkish government was to link up more definitely with the past. It was a desire to back up the Republican revolution with the pride of the nation and of history. It was not only the more pro-Axis newspapers which had welcomed the event. Hüseyin Cahit Yalçın wrote a glowing article,[59] the semiofficial *Ulus* published a series of articles on Talat Paşa's life, and newspapers of all shades of opinion produced laudatory comment. The reburial was attended by representatives of the president of the Republic and the prime minister—and also, though much to the annoyance of the Turks, by a representative of von Papen.[60]

Yunus Nadi Abalıoğlu's article provided some of the real reasons for this event. The theme was that Talat Paşa, the symbol of the CUP, was a revolutionary in the epoch of history in which he worked. Because historical conditions were then different he might appear to have no connection with the Kemalist revolution. In fact, however, the CUP was the essential precursor of that revolution, and İsmet İnönü had recognized this. The government of which Talat Paşa was a leading member was largely responsible for the Ottoman Empire's entry into the First World War on the side of Germany, but was Talat Paşa wrong in this? Abalıoğlu quoted the late President Kemal Atatürk as saying that, in principle, Talat Paşa's policy in this connection was justified. Abalıoğlu tried to show that the internal struggle against the sultanate, and the external struggle against a hostile world, followed logically from Talat Paşa's policy, and that from these struggles followed, in its turn, the new Turkey. The Turkish nation was therefore grateful to its president and to the Saraçoğlu government for taking the initiative in bringing about the return of Talat Paşa's remains, which would now rest forever on the Hill of Eternal Liberty, in Talat Paşa's own country, where his own ideals had now been realized.[61]

Abalıoğlu's analysis received solid confirmation. Ahmet Emin Yalman wrote in *Vatan*: "The honors rendered to Talat Paşa are the first manifestation of Turkish gratefulness to this great patriot and an amend for the oblivion into which the great man had fallen."[62] Many Turkish streets are now named after Talat Paşa, including one of the main boulevards in Ankara.

CEMAL BEY'S APPEARENCE ON THE SCENE

The following extract from a letter of William Nesbitt Chambers, written at Adana, on August 23, 1909, was given to the newpapers shortly after it was received by the ABCFM. Its exceptional news value was promptly recognized, and wide circulation had been given to it through the secular press. This is noteworthy here for reading and for future reference:

> The hopelessly desperate element in the situation has been the supineness of the Turkish government. From the first the local government did virtually nothing to reassure the people and develop confidence. Parliament voted 30,000 Turkish liras (13,000 dollars) for feeding the destitute. About half of this has been definitely accounted for; of the rest, much was sent to the villages and the treasury is now emptied, with the people hungry as before and depending upon the government dole.[63]

At this point Cemal Bey appeared on the scene, and the whole situation began to change. It should, however, be noted that the evidence of the Ottoman documents here leaves no doubt that the subject of Adana events was under active consideration before Cemal Bey's departure from İstanbul on August 13, 1909.[64]

The new governor arrived in Adana on August 19, his predecessor leaving overland for İstanbul the following morning. Cemal Bey did not wear any medals nor ribbons on his uniform. He spoke calmly, with assurance, thinking over each word he said. He gave the impression of a clever, careful, determined, and agreeable man. All the notables and the officials were at the railway station to welcome him. One thousand soldiers standing in the corner paid him honors and different pieces were played by the military music, recently arrived from İstanbul.[65]

R. E. W. Chafy, the acting British vice consul in Adana, paid an official call on him the next day. Cemal Bey dressed like an English gentleman—a contrast to his collarless and slippered predecessor—possessed a most courteous presence, and a pretty wit. He made an exceedingly good impression on others. Chafy judged that he possessed an untiring energy and a determination brooking no interference. He evidently faced the situation in an attitude radically different from that of the old-fashioned type of provincial governor. He had the chance of making a fine reputation for himself and the prestige of the army and Young Turks to vindicate before the eyes of Europe. In conversation Cemal Bey expressed disgust at the deplorable events in Adana, and the supine incompetency of justice as well as dissatisfaction with the delay in the work of the local authorities to deal with them. He touched among other subjects on that of the whole change of officers and officials, and the good results expected from a radical reform of police and gendarmerie, which was apparently to take early effect in Adana. He told Chafy he intended to make separate harangues to public meetings of Muslims and Armenians. He seemed anxious to establish at once a *modus vivendi* between the two elements, and asked the acting British vice consul if he could help him in identifying certain persons whom he apparently suspected of putting deliberate obstacles in the way of reconciliation. He was dead set against idling and battening on temporary relief doles, and meant to drive the loafers from tavern and bazaar to lend a hand in the work of reconstruction. He made Chafy the medium of his thanks for British help during the disturbances.[66]

The acting British vice consul believed that if Cemal Bey would be given a free hand with full support from İstanbul, and would be able to steer clear of the obstacles which local jealousies and petty cabals might strive to put in his path, excellent results might be expected from his efforts. The principal danger to his career would perhaps be his rather headlong nature, judging from its beginning. He would probably make a camp of enemies in a week, and he told Chafy himself that the first attempt to hamper his designs would be sufficient to produce his resignation. It was a lucky coincidence that he professed a longstanding friendship with the military commander Colonel Mehmet Ali Bey: this should serve to avert all friction between them. Cemal Bey was evidently determined to strike at once at the roots of the relief problem, and to this end contemplated to in a week's time making a personal tour of inspection of the affected districts. Such an undertaking should have the very best effects, as serving the double objects of establishing a complete and comprehensive relief organization, and of pacifying and inspiring confidence throughout the country. It was to be hoped that this project might be duly realized.[67]

THE NEW GOVERNOR'S ENERGY

The new governor's energy seemed to be undoubted. Although he arrived on Thursday evening, Friday morning found him, after seeing off his predecessor at the station, personally inspecting the camp of the homeless people outside the city and questioning its inmates. The following day he convened a joint meeting in the *Konak* of the International and Ottoman Relief Committees, over which he presided for four consecutive hours in the full heat of the afternoon. The work in hand being still uncompleted, further meetings took place on the two following days.[68]

At the public reading of his appointment decree on August 23 Cemal Bey took occasion to address the assembled crowd. Emphatically he called down a thousand curses on the authors and perpetrators of the massacres, referred to the necessity for the union of all classes in the work of reconstruction, and declared his intention of suppressing all idling with a strong hand. In this speech he announced the possibility of the beginning in a month's time of work on the Baghdad railway both from the Eregli and Adana extremeties. The crowd roared its support. Cemal Bey was a person of iron character; he had come to Adana with the firm intention of putting back the city on its course and arousing its spirits. He frankly explained in his admirable speech before the most part of the population:

> Forget the past, gentlemen, it is stained. Let us now try to recover ourselves and show that we are capable of whatsoever waits for us. All eyes are fixed on Adana. We have to be worth of this attention. I want that everybody work. I want that all runaway victims get under shelter here in a month. We all will work, without any distinction, to rebuild Adana to give it its former look. I promise, on my part, that I will give all my support, and I will do my utmost to help you in this task; and for our duty to be accomplished as it should be, I only tell you this: gentlemen, be united! I do not want to hear Armenian, Greek, Arab, Israelite. You are all brothers, you must help each other.

This speech left a very great impression on the public.[69]

At the initial meeting of the Relief Commission, which the acting British vice consul attended in his capacity of member of the International Committee, the governor called on the twenty members present to forget for the time being their separate callings, official positions, and nationalities, and to unite in the common work of humanity. He aptly compared the various bodies formed for relief to the different doctors, anaesthetists, and assistants cooperating in a surgical operation. The healing of the patient was the principal object to be attained. As a result of these three meetings it was decided that the International Committee was to maintain its separate identity, and to continue for the present the useful work of repairing damaged houses and fitting out artisans with tools and capital which it already had in hand. Of one of the sums of 100,000 Turkish liras voted by the Chamber of Deputies, 15,000 liras were to be devoted to the actual feeding of the hungry in Adana and in the districts for the next three months, by which time it was hoped that building construction, the now ripening cotton crop, and work on the Baghdad railway would have largely reduced the distress.[70]

During an interval of the meeting he was pleased to talk to Père Joure, superior of the French Jesuit Mission at Adana, and M. Grabowski, director of the Adana branch of the Imperial Ottoman Bank, both of them members of the International Relief Committee, and he said that he had every confidence in both of them which, according to French vice consul, Maurice Bompard, the French ambassador at İstanbul would much like to witness. The new governor spoke to Père Joure and Grabowski on various plans, among others that of soon going all over those areas of the province which had been particularly afflicted by the disasters.[71]

Grabowski was a Pole and a French subject, and, possessing as he did a sound business capacity united with a tactful address and a sincere desire to forward the interests of the relief organization, was, in the opinion of acting British vice consul R. E. W. Chafy, a most suitable person to act as counterpoise against possible abuses coming from Turkish quarters. As a matter of fact Chafy fancied that in the present case he would prove useful rather as financial adviser to than as a check on Cemal Bey, who, though fired with a genuine reforming zeal, had not much more than the average Turk's share of business instinct.[72]

Cemal Bey was sociable and easy to access. Polite in his manners, with an assured air of authority, he was cool in his intelligence. He talked very easily and fluently. His arguments were orderly and logical. His personality comfortably dominated the participants of the gatherings.[73]

The following separate committees had been formed or were in process of formation: (A) In Adana City. (1) A committee for the finding of work for the unemployed, and for the distribution of the 15,000 Turkish liras voted for feeding the hungry, to embrace the whole province; (2) a committee to draw up a plan for the reconstruction of the ruined quarter of the city, and for estimating the cost of rebuilding Christian churches and schools; (3) the subcommittee of the International Committee formed for repairing damaged houses in and near Adana was to be reinforced by three members appointed by the government. Their work was also to include the erection of houses for former householders now homeless; (4) a committee to draw up a plan for the foundation of orphanages; (5) a committee to prepare an exhaustive report as to the needs of agricultural relief; and (6) a general advisory financial committee, to consist of the governor, the director of the Ottoman Bank, the representative of the British consulate, and possibly a government commissioner. (B) In the Districts. Separate committees for the distribution of relief and for rebuilding were to be formed in the following kazas, which included all the affected districts, namely, Bahçe, Hacin, Erzin, and Kozan.[74]

The governor seemed to appreciate the urgent necessity of beginning the work of reconstruction at once, and there were talks of employing all the available local architects and engineers, as well as of accepting the services of the engineers employed on the Baghdad railway. The following official notice had on August 25, 1909, been posted up in the city: "Notice is hereby given that as the reconstruction of burned and ruined houses will be begun in three or four days, individual petitions to the Government and formal expenses are superfluous." Timber for construction was to be supplied from the government forests at the sole cost of carriage. Cemal Bey in the presence of the assembled committees gave explicit orders on this head to the inspector of forests, and forcibly overruled various objections advanced by that functionary. The committee for the kaza of Bahçe was telegraphically formed as the result of the first meeting. It was to include Fredrick Douglas Shepard of the Azariah Smith Memorial Hospital at Ayntab, who already had the situation there well in hand. Cemal Bey appeared anxious for an explanation as to the expenditure of the first 30,000 Turkish liras voted by the Chamber of Deputies, and the *Defterdar* (chief treasury officer), brought to book on this head, was obliged to confess to the lack of the "Defter" in question. Possibly satisfactory accounts would be concocted later.[75]

Upon hearing of his appointment, Shepard immediately went to Adana, arriving on August 21. To his surprise he found that he had been made chairman of the Government Commission of Relief and Rebuilding for the three kazas of Bahçe, İslahiye, and Hassa; there was, however, no work to be done in Hassa. Bahçe in a long narrow valley on the seaward side of the Amanus Mountains was a settlement of about two hundred and fifty houses. The valley leads up to the lowest pass over the range, and so was chosen as the route of the Baghdad railway. The kaza had about sixty-five hundred or seven thousand Muslims and fifty-five hundred Christians. The Muslims were agriculturists and officials; the Christians comprised all the artisans and traders and a good many of them were also agriculturists.[76]

William Nesbitt Chambers introduced Shepard to Cemal Bey, who was cordial and gave him the privilege of meeting the Relief Commission the next day and presented at length the needs of their (Shepard's) district. The commission at once voted them 10,000 Turkish liras, with which to begin the work of rebuilding, and 1,800 Turkish liras for food. Shepard's commission consisted of four members besides himself, viz., Lieutenant Şakir Efendi, of the regular army, detailed for this special service; Ziya Efendi, an official from the civil service; and two Armenians, Garabed Ağa Parsekyan of Hasanbeyli and Avedis Efendi of Bahçe. Şakir Efendi and Shepard saw the 11,800 Turkish liras placed to their credit in the Imperial Ottoman Bank, and taking part of it with them, started for Bahçe the next day. They immediately made contracts with timber cutters and set them at work, and began the difficult task of apportioning the money to the owners of the burned houses, the principle being to make such a grant in aid to each individual as would enable him to get a roof over his head before winter. They also had the widows and orphans to feed. With funds received from the International Committee, Shepard was trying to see that each farmer had a yoke of oxen, each weaver a loom, each muleteer a mule, etc.[77]

The work was greatly increased because the villages were scattered over a large area and connected by difficult bridle paths over precipitous mountains. Shepard pointed out that Şakir Efendi proved to be an efficient and honorable gentleman, with whom it was a pleasure to work. He was a fit man for the place. The other members of the commission also proved good workers, and before the winter came Shepard and his collaborators had the satisfaction of seeing every one sheltered, having assisted in the rebuilding of over nine hundred houses, and leaving in the hands of a responsible committee 1,600 Turkish liras for the rebuilding of churches and schools, which they were unable to attempt in the time at their disposal. These, however, were built in the next spring.[78]

Cemal Bey also wished to give all his care and attention to the reorganization of the gendarmerie; the Italian officer who was nominated for this service at the province of Adana had arrived a few days previous and taken up his duties. The governor showed great activity, standing out by his energetic attitude that would hopefully bring back full confidence among the Christian populations. To that regard most recently one hundred and fifty Armenians arrived from Cyprus and returned to their homelands in Adana. The state of health was satisfactory at Adana, contrary to what was published in the Syrian press that also gave wrong news on the subject of the reconstruction work undertaken by the International Relief Committee. More than one hundred houses were already repaired.[79]

The new governor exerted an ordor to reconstruct the city of Adana that drew the admiration of all the populations. He did not remain a minute idle and even took time in the evenings that he lacked during the day to deal with many questions he studied all by himself. Thus in a recent evening he met with the spiritual chiefs of all the Christian communities, including the superior of the Jesuits, and he talked to them about the desiderata of the population. And this discussion lasted for four hours from eight o'clock in the afternoon until midnight. Cemal Bey listened with an attentive ear to the stories of the events. He was painfully upset when he was told about the role of the Roumelian soldiers, who instead of protecting the people had been the most ardent perpetrator of pillage and arson of the Armenian quarter.[80] He spoke tactfully but frankly on matters concerning the Christian communities and succeeded in leaving a happy impression on all his hearers. This invaluable knack of inspiring confidence and good temper in all classes should prove an important means to the success of Cemal Bey's reforming efforts.[81]

The governor announced his intention of suppressing as soon as possible the various officious and unofficial Armenian sources of rumor and so-called reports in Adana. This was a most welcome measure, as absurdly inaccurate reports and newspaper paragraphs emanated apparently from Adana and had the most harmful results.[82]

CEMAL BEY AND THE RELIEF COMMITTEES

In its meeting on August 28, 1909, the International Relief Commission at İstanbul decided to set up a committee which would appeal to Europe to request help for the Adana victims. It was also decided to ask the 30,000 francs, the amount of the receipts of the theater performance given for *Turquie Nouvelle*. According to the report of the commission, the amount received till then reached to 9,172 liras. A total of 7,048 liras were sent to Adana and the rest were in the bank.[83]

Cemal Bey adopted as principle the unification of the two committees, that of the government and the International Committee, in order to move forward with all the work to be done and to concentrate their efforts and resources on the same places. Moreover, he turned to all the people who by their position or their abilities could help him with their advice, and this without any distinction of religion or nationality. The governor also appealed to M. Zarzecki, a French engineer in Adana, who had been employed for irrigation services and entrusted him to make studies on the land routes. The Frenchmen and Frenchwomen of Adana vied with each other to help the new governor in the reconstruction work which he had undertaken and which he led with so much energy and perseverance. The activity of the governor was not only conducted in the aid of the city of Adana but also stretched upon the whole province, and Cemal Bey cared to visit himself the places that had suffered and imposed by his energetic attitude the most urgent reforms to be made. Barré de Lancy, the French vice consul at Adana and Mersin, could only admire the efforts of the new governor and wished that they were crowned with success.[84]

Anyone who saw Cemal Bey in action could not help being impressed by his prodigious industry and knowledge. His personality, too, captured the hearts of many of those who served under him. All of them stressed his personal charm. William Nesbitt Chambers was warm in his praise of Cemal Bey's work. He believed that Cemal Bey was a man of broad outlook, high aims, sympathetic temper, and patriotism. Within twenty-four hours of his arrival the new governor had government relief work reorganized on radical lines, and after a few days he had inaugurated the only effective reconstruction movement set in motion since the month of April. He fairly trampled on a few strong prejudices. He organized a relief committee of twenty-one persons, only three of whom, besides himself, were Muslim, and nine of whom were foreigners. With this committee he made arrangements for the administration of over 800,000 dollars, which all realized to be entirely inadequate to the needs of the situation, and he secured the honest and effective handling of these funds by making the Imperial Ottoman Bank the custodian of the money, with a financial committee composed of himself and two foreigners.[85]

The Adana Government Relief Committee, under the presidency of Cemal Bey and consisting of the persons mentioned below, was formed for the spending in a proper and expeditious manner of the 100,000 Turkish liras voted for the special uses of the province of Adana. The objects to which this sum was to be devoted were the repair and reconstruction of dwellings and other edifices burned during the events of Adana, and the adoption of measures for the amelioration of the social conditions throughout the province. The list of members included Cemal Bey; M. Grabowski, director of the Adana branch of the Imperial Ottoman Bank; William Nesbitt Chambers; Edward Nathan, American consul in Mersin; R. E. W. Chafy, acting British vice consul in Adana; Herr Stoeckel (German subject), General Bewollmaechtiger, *Deutsche Levantinische Baumwoll Gesellschaft*, Adana; Père Joure, superior of the French Jesuit Mission in Adana; Subhi Paşa, Turkish notable of Adana; Boghos Efendi, representative of the Catholic Armenian Patriarchate; Dr. Salibian, physician attached to Miss Wallis's English Mission Pharmacy (Ottoman subject); Garabet Efendi, an İstanbul lawyer acting as patriarchal delegate in Adana; Artin Efendi, Catholic Armenian bishop; İstepan Efendi, representative of the Chaldean Patriarchate; İstepan Bezdikian Efendi (Ottoman subject); Charles Chartier (French subject), engineer employed for public works by the Adana municipality; Rıza Bey, Turkish engineer; Stanislas Kozlovski, engineer employed on the Baghdad railway; Hamparsum Efendi, Armenian Protestant pastor; İbrahim Sadık Efendi, local notable; and Kalust Geulbenkian Bey.[86]

The gendarmerie in Adana was undergoing a process of reorganization under Cemal Bey's personal supervision. Several new gendarmerie officers had arrived, apart from Lutfi Bey who was appointed commander some time ago and seemed to be capable and intelligent officer. Signor Lodi, an Italian, had taken up his duties as inspector of gendarmerie. The rank and file of the force were being individually overhauled and those pronounced physically or mentally unfit eliminated. A gendarmerie school was to be opened in Adana on the Macedonian model. A new director of police had arrived from Macedonia. The organization of these forces should have the best effects in restoring law and order throughout the province, and their establishment on an efficient footing would no doubt hasten the removal of martial law. Orders had arrived in Adana to enroll Christians liable for military service. Several changes had recently been effected in the personnel of the *Konak*. Hüseyin Bey, the new translator of the province, a former Young Turk exile, was an intelligent and agreeable official of enlightened views. The freshly appointed *Mektubçu* was a gentlemanly and cultivated young man of about twenty-five years of age who contributed to some modern newspapers. The governor himself and Mehmet Ali Bey, the military commander, honored acting British vice consul R. E. W. Chafy with their personal friendship, and made him the medium for the expression of their pronounced pro-British sympathies. The latter read Rudyard Kipling. The great advantage to British of appointments of this kind was that they rendered possible the efficient discharge of business arising between the consulate and the *Konak* through a medium of personal friendships without recourse to the old-fashioned and wearing methods of "bluff" and tiresome official formalities. The governor was displaying a military deliberateness in disposing his own picked men in subordinate positions throughout the province. Cemal Bey was also aware of the danger of defective sanitary conditions in the city at the break up of summer, and was charging the municipal sanitary inspector with the preparation of a report of the conditions and needs under this head.[87]

All the homeless who passed the summer under canvas in the big camp had now been housed in the dwellings repaired by the International Relief Committee. Plans for the building of a new quarter outside the city were in preparation, and a fine site had already been provisionally chosen for the purpose. An orphanage to contain one thousand children of both sexes was to be built in Adana and to be placed under strictly Ottoman direction. This scheme would probably not be realized without friction with the representatives of the Armenian churches, though so far the patriarchal delegates in Adana appeared to be in harmony with the idea. Zabel Yessayan, an Armenian lady working under the auspices of the patriarchate, proposed to open an industrial institute in Adana to provide work for one hundred widows—always provided the necessary funds were forthcoming from some source other than Armenian.[88]

The governor recognized the great difficulties implied by the word "reconciliation," but there was no doubt that his determined and broad-minded attitude and personal tact and charm of manner were in the right way toward restoring some degree of confidence and sense of hope and security among the Christian population. The preacher in a Greek church emphasized to his congregation the harmfulness of useless retrospect and the importance of looking with hope to the dawning of a brighter era in the future. Words of this nature uttered by a Christian priest were clearly traceable to the new governor's influence. The acting British vice consul had not yet been able to detect anything in Cemal Bey's attitude likely to offend Muslim susceptibilities to a dangerous degree, but this was a ground of extreme difficulty of penetration, and time alone could show the full effects of this experiment in Young Turk military provincial administration.[89]

The acting British vice consul thought in the relief work any open abuse was out of the question. The governor was obviously sincere, but he had no particular experience in financial matters, and, being new to local conditions, was naturally very much under the influence of the Imperial Ottoman Bank director who was well versed in those conditions and as a matter of fact had a very large share in the disposition of the 100,000 Turkish liras loan money. If Cemal Bey's efforts failed it would not be for want of energy. Twice in the week the Financial Commission remained in session from 9:30 p.m. until 2:30 a.m. The work was being steadily pushed forward. In view of the approaching seed time and the importance to the province of its agricultural resources, the farmers were to be the first to receive advances from the 100,000 liras voted for that purpose. The needs of tradesmen and artisans, the other two classes to benefit under this head, were considered to be less pressing. Plans and drawings of the projected Adana orphanage, executed by the French engineer Charles Chartier, were examined and approved on September 21, 1909, by the Financial Commission. This orphanage, as at present projected, was to house five hundred children. The cost of its erection was estimated at 6,000 Turkish liras. Newspapers stated to the effect that local Muslims were also to contribute to this scheme. The expense was to be met partly from existing relief funds, and partly, it was hoped from large gifts of the Tobacco Régie, Baghdad railway, and other big concerns. Cemal Bey hoped to squeeze perhaps 500 liras from Muslim residents.[90]

According to William Nesbitt Chambers, all of this was like a cooling, life-giving breeze from the sea to thirsty souls on the scorching sands. On the part of the Christians hope revived, confidence grew apace, and a quick response was made by them. For the last few days one heard much less of the sufferings from the massacre and the seeming supineness of the court martial, and much of plans for finding occupation for the people and the reconstruction of the city and province. Cemal Bey steadily refused to have any one suspected of participation in the massacre as a member of any his commissions. He was the first Turkish official Chambers had met in thirty years of his service in the Ottoman Empire with whom he found it a real pleasure to work. Taking him as a representative of the Macedonian Young Turk, Chambers could easily conceive how the revolution of a year ago became possible. The American missionary noted that, on a previous day, the governor entered his office at 7 o'clock in the morning and left it at 7:30 in the evening. Chambers's amazement was quite genuine.[91]

Alert, frank eyes, and pleasing manners made Cemal Bey a delightful conversationalist. Henry Morgenthau, the American ambassador to the Ottoman Empire in 1913–1916, described his physical strength thus: "As soon as he began to move [. . .] it was evident that his body was full of energy. Whenever he shook your hand, gripping you with a vise-like grip and looking at you with those roving, penetrating eyes, the man's personal force became impressive."[92] Cemal Bey possessed a personal magnetism.[93]

Cemal Bey put all his energy and idealism into the task ahead of him, that of rebuilding a once thriving city, which was now in ruins, and reassuring the

Armenian population of a good faith which had been badly shaken. More immediate was the case of homeless groups and wounded and sick people. The cooperation of missionary and military foreigners was soon at his service. He found both William Nesbitt Chambers and Major Charles Doughty-Wylie a type of person who was only too glad to work with him. The governor had the perspicacity to avail himself of this willing cooperation. The Emergency Committee which Doughty-Wylie and Chambers had formed was enlarged and continued by Cemal Bey, and he asked Chambers to be chairman of the Industrial Relief Commission. When an inadvertent remark of his showed Cemal Bey that Chambers was contemplating a trip through the villages, he begged him not to go just then. "I desire your help and advice. Perhaps we shall make the trip together." And they did. Twin pictures of Cemal Bey and Chambers on horseback in front of the fountain at Şar (the ruins of Comana), a village in Hacin, are interesting reminders of this intelligent, sympathetic cooperation of Muslim governor with American missionary.[94]

Cemal Paşa's memoirs show that when he was appointed to the governorship of Adana the Sublime Porte placed a sum of 200,000 Turkish liras at his disposal. Divided into two equal parts, the first 100,000 liras was a present from the country and was utilized to give immediate relief to the sufferers, to supply shelter for the homeless, to establish a reserve fund to be devoted to setting up, not only tradesmen but also smaller farmers in their former occupations, and to allot special sums with which to provide work for the destitute. The other half was to be lent, on easy terms, to the Armenian traders, artisans, and farmers to enable them to resume business. The loans were not to be paid back for ten years. A building committee was established in Adana and Cemal Bey took the chairmanship himself. The committee consisted of several foreigners, such as William Nesbitt Chambers, and a large number of natives, the majority being Armenians. Thanks to the steps Cemal Bey took, four months after his arrival all the Armenian houses in the province had been built and in the city of Adana itself there was not a single small family house which had not been finished. In brief, within five or six months the Armenians had freely resumed their trade, agriculture, and industry.[95]

CEMAL BEY'S SUCCESS IN RECONSTRUCTION AND RESTORATION OF ORDER

Cemal Bey writes tellingly that the Armenians themselves fully recognized all the efforts he made on their behalf and the restoration of their property while he was governor of Adana. Many foreigners—Americans, British, French, and Russians—who came to the city were witnesses of his work and congratulated him upon it. The great orphanage he had built for the reception and bringing up of the children orphaned in the Adana affair was still in existence.[96]

All agreed that most of the commendation for the improvement in conditions was due to Cemal Bey, whose "untiring efforts and energy" inspired confidence in the population. A man of medium height, and manifestly of great strength and activity, he might be legitimately styled as Cemal Bey the indefatigable, for he seemed to be unceasingly at work. Early in the morning he was to be seen in his office and on Fridays, the Muslim Sunday, as well. The impression that a visitor got, after talking some time with him, was one of his immense vigor, his intense eagerness for the peace and welfare of his country, and his wish to have positions judged by facts, which he was willing to lay before the impartial inquirer.[97] It is instructive on this point that Raymond Kévorkian, associate professor at the Institut Français de Géopolitique of the Université de Paris VIII and director of the Nubarian Library in Paris, concurs that Cemal Bey was "known to be energetic and liberal."[98]

Cemal Bey's qualities, combined with firm principles, made him a formidable provincial governor in Adana. Andrew Ryan, who served at the British embassy in İstanbul in various consular and diplomatic positions from 1897 to 1922 and who dealt with the Sublime Porte in all day-to-day matters, expressed with confidence: "It is fair to say that Jemal Bey gained much credit in that post."[99] Ryan further commented: "He did well as governor at Adana."[100] Though well down the embassy pecking order, Ryan's reputation, both in his own lifetime and subsequently, cast a much more longer shadow than those of the ambassadors he served. The British official was an excellent Turkish scholar; his talents were acknowledged even by his enemies. But he had made himself exceedingly obnoxious to the Young Turk party by intriguing against them.

British and American cruisers were coming and going at Mersin, and each train day a contingent would come up to Adana and call upon Cemal Bey with due and proper formality. Suddenly the Adana affair, fraught with political importance, and centering the eyes of Europe on the capacity of the Young Turk party to reconstruct and keep faith, brought the region right into the limelight. A new touch with the outside world was made under dramatic circumstances.[101]

Commander Herbert Adam of the British warship *Barham*, after a visit to Adana in October 1909, spoke highly of Cemal Bey as to the manner he dealt with matters and praised his power of discretion. Adam reported to the Admiralty in London:

> The new Vali, Dhjemal Bey, has a very good reputation, and His Britannic Majesty's Acting Vice Consul has a high opinion of him. He is young, active, and is

doing all in his power with the relief work. The Relief Camp has been abolished, and the Armenians have been housed in various parts of the town. The financial relief is in the hands of an International Committee, with Vali as President, and appears to be working well. They are advancing money for Armenians to open shops and start work generally; and a new plan of the ruined portion of the town is being made and will be completed in a month; and after that re-construction of houses will be commenced by the Turkish Government, and when they are built, it is proposed to let Armenian families live in them for two years free.[102]

Rumors of fresh troubles in Adana were persistently circulating—or circulated—during the last few days of September 1909. The shattered nervous system of the Christians of Adana was now ripe for wholesale panic. The merest accident could suffice to produce it. On September 28, the dragomans of the German, Austrian, and Russian consulates called on acting British vice consul R. E. W. Chafy collectively to ask his advice on the situation. The Christians were being frightened by the usual stories. Here an old and trusted servant was dismissed by his Muslim employer who refused to be responsible for his safety should events occur; there an Armenian woman overheard *hojas* talking massacre in the street; the girls at the American Mission School were terrified by the alarming talk of a man from Hamidiye, etc. Chafy endeavored to allay the fears of the dragomans and dissuaded them from making formal representations to the *Konak*, especially urging against their trying to defer the departure of the governor on September 29 on his tour in the districts. He was convinced that the babblings of a collection of frightened dragomans would do more harm than good, and certainly not cause Cemal Bey to alter his plans. Chafy had a friendly talk with the governor himself on the afternoon of September 28 and hinted at the advisability of taking steps to restore the public peace of mind. The rumor had not been excluded from the *Konak*. It was extremely difficult to probe the origin of panics of this kind and to judge impartially the diametrically opposed views of the different elements. Having in this case considered both the Christian and Turkish views on the situation, Chafy adhered to his final conviction that there was no danger at all. He was not able to obtain one single piece of reliable proof of danger; apart from all other considerations, there were too many Young Turkish officers in Adana with fine reputations to prevent the repetition of the events which took place under such widely different circumstances last April. It would be best to judge the probability of this panic being deliberately engineered by some party or other anxious to advance their own interests. Possibly the Armenian patriarch, for one, would not regard as unwelcome a justification of his attitude in the shape of apparently renewed audacity on the part of the savages of the Adana massacre. Meanwhile Adana was still outwardly the quietest and best behaved of provincial cities.[103]

Cemal Bey's orphanage scheme was meeting with opposition. His ill-wishers were making it an opportunity for attack. The help of Hüseyin Cahid and *Tanin* were enlisted in its favor. In view of the many inaccurate press reports which abounded on this and kindred subjects, the governor was authorizing one or two reliable correspondents in Adana to print firsthand accounts of his aims. Stanislas Kozlovski, a Polish Austrian subject employed as an engineer on the Baghdad railway and a member of the Relief Committee, sent on September 29 to *La Turquie* and *Stamboul* an interview with Cemal Bey. The *Mektubçu* of the Province Hakkı Behiç (Bayiç) was to be his mouthpiece in the Ottoman press.[104]

The fears of the Christian population of Adana continued in October 1909. Chafy believed these fears quite groundless and merely the natural outcome of the shattered nervous system of the Christian population. Cemal Bey, who was fully aware of the situation, informed him that he had replied in a similar sense to a query on this subject from the minister of the interior. He made the earliest rumors of danger the subject of careful investigation and called a meeting of Christian notables and did his best to reassure them. He declared his intention of addressing the Muslims in the mosque. No proof of genuine danger had so far been forthcoming, and the Christians were ironically accused of this time themselves arranging to compass their own destruction. Chafy suspected that extra police precautions would be taken during the next few days, and military commander Colonel Mehmet Ali Bey told him that he had still seven battalions of troops under his command in the province. Ample force was at hand to repress the slightest outbreak of disorder.[105]

The fact was unique in history. The way in which Cemal Bey, a young regimental officer with no experience of work of this nature and no precedents or compatriots to guide him, having to contend with a mountain of apathy on the Turkish, and a thorny hedge of suspicion and discontent on the Armenian side, had risen to the occasion, had the good sense to apply to foreigners for advice and cooperation, grasped the main principles of relief work, and got his machinery going was surely worthy of the best ideals of the Young Turks.[106]

With the impending advance of the Baghdad railway the growing German influence in the province of Adana was visible. An important share in the laying out of the new quarter of Adana had been assigned to an Austrian subject employed as an agent of the Baghdad railway, while the projected loan of 30,000 Turkish liras, for the erection of a new quarter of this city near the proposed site of the railway station, had been advanced by the Deutsche Bank.[107]

Chafy made on November 1909 a tour of inspection of a magnificent farm of nearly a million Turkish acres near Hamidiye. This immense farm was crown property and was allowed to run waste under a military estate agent appointed by Sultan Abdülhamid II. Chafy was informed by an agricultural specialist that the possibilities of this almost virgin corn land situated on the banks of the river Ceyhan were practically unlimited. Cemal Bey was alive to them, had abolished the Military Estate Agency, and was anxious to turn the whole concern with all possible dispatch into money for the construction of roads throughout the province. The Germans were already planning to secure a footing there. It seemed a pity to Chafy that British capitalists could not be interested in this matter.[108]

In the early morning of December 11, 1909, twenty-five men, nearly all Muslims, some of them men of wealth and high rank, were hanged. The nooses were set about their necks and the stools were kicked from under their feet. They died easily. The placards were placed on their breasts declaring their names, crimes, and the sentence of the court martial. They had been adjudged guilty, by the military court martial, of killing Christians, and this judicial execution was ordered, not by pressure from Britain or Germany or from any power outside, but by Turks themselves and under direction of the Ottoman governor. In Adana and vicinity the purpose to deal justly and the power to carry out the laws were evidenced by the execution of these men and others to the number of nearly fifty. It certainly was a new day for the Ottoman Empire. There was no little apprehension felt that this unprecedented course of visiting punishment upon the Muslims for the killing of Christians might arouse a storm of wrath that would result in rioting, but no such disturbance occurred.[109]

The three Muslims sentenced to capital punishment by the court martial of Adana were already executed on the bridge of Adana in the early morning of August 3, 1909. These were a gendarmerie brigadier from Adana, an inhabitant of the village of Namrun around Tarsus, and the headman of the village of Ayas. After the executions an official statement was distributed in all quarters of Adana, Tarsus, and Mersin.[110]

The hanging of Muslims in Adana had an effect on the population which was surprising. William Nesbitt Chambers could not forget that morning as he walked through the city and watched the people—the cowed aspect of the Muslim crowd. It was that show of determined authority that wrought the change, and so greatly facilitated later reconstruction efforts. One could not expect anything of a similar nature.[111]

Fred Douglas Shepard said the following about the work of the court martial which tried the perpetrators of the massacres in Cilicia. The investigating committee, which sat in Bahçe while taking evidence in regard to the massacre in Bahçe and Hasanbeyli, was impartial; the central work, which sat in Erzin, pronounced judgment in accordance with the evidence, and seven of the leaders (including the Mufti İsmail Hakkı Efendi, a very influential man) were hanged. The investigating committee, also sitting at Bahçe, which investigated the Haruniye massacre, was prejudiced from the start and whitewashed the whole thing. Nevertheless the central court at Erzin condemned Hacı Halil Bey, the real leader, to perpetual banishment with his whole family, upon evidence coming to its knowledge from other sources. The court martial sitting in Antakya found eighty-five sentences of varying severity.[112]

On January 24, 1910, Charles Doughty-Wylie, the British vice consul at Mersin, reported that there existed, unfortunately, a new feeling of panic among the Christians in Adana. According to him, it arose from the rearrest of certain Armenians, such as the notorious Garabet Gökdereliyan, from the prevalence of burglary, and from the direct threat of renewed massacre circulated among their Armenian neighbors by Turkish women. Personally, Doughty-Wylie did not think there was any chance of any further massacre. There might be a few murders, but organized killing would be at once stopped by Cemal Bey by all means in his power, and Mehmet Ali Bey, the military commander, who had four battalions in Adana at present, must know that his reputation and advancement depended on the maintenance of order. The situation arose, said the British vice consul, from the intrigues of the many enemies of the governor. His reforming zeal, his constant solicitude for Christians, and the execution of the twenty-five Turks had offended the great majority of Muslims. There was a further sore caused by the appointment of the new mufti. Instead of election by the *softas*, the election of the mufti on this occasion appeared to have been, by the governor's orders, in the hands of the municipality. The result was the nomination of a clever but unpopular *hoja*, who was freely accused of corruption. Doughty-Wylie was assured that this supposed infraction of their privileges had set the religious more against Cemal Bey than anything else, even the executions.[113]

There was another story going around which, in the opinion of Doughty-Wylie, had probably some substratum of truth. Colonel Mehmet Ali Bey, the governor's senior officer under martial law, still held a great amount of power. The sitting court martial was under his influence. He himself was certainly more susceptible than the governor to the influence of *hojas*. He had probably felt a personal grievance at serving under his junior, and now, when the time was approaching to lay down his power (for the end of martial law was announced for the end of February), he might feel a little reluctant to revert to an ordinary staff officer. Those who wished to weaken and discredit Cemal Bey lost no opportunity of pulling them apart, and even the story of a difference and its supposed consequence, the resignation of the governor, spread panic among the Christians. Neither the governor nor Mehmet Ali Bey in their frequent conversations with Doughty-Wylie let fall the slightest sign of any tension between them, but it would have to be very acute before they allowed a foreigner to find it out from their own lips. Cemal Bey's difficulties were those that beset any reformer, and it was not, the British vice consul believed, likely that he would succumb to them as long as he was backed by, as he was at present, the government in İstanbul.[114]

It must be noted that although Cemal Bey was a soldier, as the governor he was answerable to the Ministry of the Interior and the civilian government. Mehmet Ali Bey answered only to the Ministry of War, a separate chain of command that sidestepped civilian control. He claimed a free hand in all military matters, whereas Cemal Bey was disposed to think otherwise. It was stated that they telegraphed to İstanbul on the subject. How stark were the differences between the two men was never reliably confirmed.

Meanwhile much material progress had been made with relief and rebuilding. The money voted by the Chamber of Deputies had, on the whole, been wisely expended. There was much work to do, and it would still take years for the province to recover. But the corner was turned. The bad economic effect of the present panic would, it was to be hoped, be only temporary. As regards trade activities, the Germans, already well to the fore with the well-managed *Deutsche Levantinische Baumvoll Gesellschaft*, were using, as was natural, the advent of the Baghdad railway to make a few steps further. They seemed to be trying to buy land and farms. Capital was of course wanted. Cemal Bey's idea as a patriotic Young Turk was to have Ottoman companies, but so far as Doughty-Wylie knew nothing had yet resulted, foreign control in some shape being demanded as the price of foreign capital. Doughty-Wylie had heard of no schemes for the working of similar undertakings by Englishmen, but he saw no reason whatever to think that Germans would be unduly favored. Any trader able to accept the new Ottoman conditions would be encouraged to work.[115]

In the district the Armenian population was being gradually housed, thanks to the efforts of Cemal Bey, and a better feeling was reported to be manifesting itself among the leaders of the Christian and Muslim communities. Owing to Armenian opposition the proposal to settle Jewish immigration on "vacant" lands in Cilicia was abandoned.[116]

Not everyone in Adana was content with this way forward.[117] According to the annual report of the British embassy in İstanbul on the Ottoman Empire for 1910, the beginning of the year found Adana in a rather disturbed state. The population had hardly calmed down after the events of the preceding year. The Christians were apprehensive, owing to the fear of another movement against them, in consequence of the executions of Muslims for their participation in the recent massacres, while among the Muslims there was much hostile feeling against the "Giaour" (unbeliever) governor, Cemal Bey, who was held responsible by them for the executions. In fact, early in the year, the governor had to bow to the strong *hoja* influence and remove his nominee for the muftiship of the city. High hopes were, however, entertained as to the governor's administration. His attitude was energetic and highly commendable, and though but few of the richer Armenians who had fled from the country during the summer of 1909 returned, the economical situation of the province, backed by German influence, was distinctly improving. The governor's policy, however, showed little attempt at using the velvet glove and he spoke of teaching the old by force and the young by education, while his friendly attitude toward the Christians isolated him from the influential Muslims in the town, so that already in February his position was not an easy one. In February he undertook a tour of inspection in his province, in order to examine the poorer villages, but in spite of his excellent intentions there had not been much to show in the way of improvements for the considerable sums put at his disposal for relief work.[118]

The general condition of the city of Adana and the surrounding districts as it appeared to G. C. Donaldson Rawlins, the acting British vice consul at Adana, on February 10, 1910, was as follows. Rawlins's remarks were based upon his own personal observations and interviews which he had with the provincial governor, the American missionaries, several well-known merchants, and various other notable and influential inhabitants. It appeared to be admitted upon all sides that the city of Adana, as in the whole province, was in a perfectly tranquil state, and no fears were expressed that this satisfactory state of affairs would not continue. Muslims, Christians, and the foreign residents all agreed that the greater part of the credit for such a happy condition was due to the Governor Cemal Bey, who, by his untiring efforts and energy, was inspiring confidence in all classes of the population. The day before Rawlins's arrival in Adana, the governor had given a large banquet with the object of bringing about a reconciliation of Muslims and Christians, and although—as was natural—nothing very definite had, as yet, came of it, it had, nevertheless, been the means of laying a good foundation for a better understanding in the future. Among the guests were the consuls of the foreign powers, the mufti of the city and other Muslim notables, the Armenian catholicos, and the heads of various Christian communities. On the right and left of Cemal Bey sat the mufti and catholicos, respectively. Many speeches were made, and, with the exception of one by an Armenian pastor, they appeared all to have been in good taste and conciliatory in tone, while Rawlins had heard that the speech of the catholicos was most dignified and to the point. Naturally there was still a good deal of mutual distrust between Christians and Muslims, but "Rome was not built in a day," and it was evident that things were daily getting better in this respect.[119]

CEMAL BEY'S RECONCILIATION EFFORT BETWEEN THE ELEMENTS AND THE CREATION OF A MIXED CORPS OF GENDARMERIE

The reconciliation dinner given by Cemal Bey to all the Ottoman elements of various races and religions in the presence of the representatives of the foreign powers took place on February 5, 1910. This event gives an idea of the efforts exerted by Cemal Bey whose extraordinary activity and savoir faire would soon expel the sorrowful remembrances that the word Adana conjured. For the first time a big banquet of three hundred seats was held in the city.[120]

Each attendee was seated at the tables without difficulty and a true organization governed the choice of places. Firstly, the governor read a long speech in a scholarly language. He spoke of the fraternity that was created in Adana for everybody and he devoted a page to the Colonel Mehmet Ali Bey whom he praised pompously and whose pacifying role he recalled. After him a Muslim from Tarsus read a speech which was a long panegyric of the governor. Then it was the turn of the Armenian catholicos, whose speech was sensible. He developed the idea that the Muslims and the non-Muslims could live together without harming each other and that this dinner was the symbol of the peaceful coexistence of all the nationalities in the Ottoman Empire. Afterwards a Muslim clergyman from Adana read a level-headed speech extolling the virtues of especially the governor. After him a Greek from Adana spoke. Finally, an Armenian Protestant, preacher at the American mission in Adana, read with an excessively strong and clear voice the most characteristic as well as the boldest speech one could imagine of the evening. He started by saying that they tried several times to reconcile the Christians with the Muslims. He reminded the audience of the efforts of Deputy Yusuf Kemal who had been responsible for the parliamentary inquiry after the events, then those of the Governor Babanzade Mustafa Zihni Paşa; but, he said, in order to realize the reconciliation plan one had to wait for the arrival of Cemal Bey.[121] Eugen Büge, the German consul in Adana, who was present at the dinner reported that this Armenian clergyman exclaimed, "It is true that during the days of this massacre we Armenians lost many things: our men, our women, our children and our possessions. But you Muslims lost more. You lost your honor."[122] There appears to be no record of this remark in the Ottoman archives, and Cemal Bey himself neglected to mention this allegedly pivotal meeting in his memoirs.

The banquet was an almost complete success. As regards the general condition of the Christian inhabitants of the city, Rawlins was happy to be able to report that good progress had been made, and although much misery and poverty still existed, nearly everybody now had a roof over their head and food to eat. The acting British vice consul had been through the burned and ruined quarter of the city and found the work of rebuilding being pushed on apace, and there only seemed to be few houses which remained absolutely ruined and untouched and upon which no start had been made. Such houses belonged to people who had fled to Cyprus, İzmir, and other places, and had not yet returned. Rawlins had not been able to get any accurate information of the number of people (Christians) who left the city after the massacres and had not yet returned, but from information which he had been able to obtain, he thought it could be said that, of the twelve thousand to fifteen thousand who left, about eight thousand to ten thousand had already returned. A short while previously labor was very difficult to procure in the city and prices were exceedingly high, but at the present time the rate of daily wages had decreased somewhat, a fact which tended to show that the workman and artisan class were becoming more numerous, that to say, that many who left were returning. The general rate of foodstuffs of all kinds had gone up, it was said, almost one-third, which made living dear to every class in the city.[123]

The International Relief Committee was almost at the end of its labors, and no more money or free food was now being distributed. Deserving persons were, however, being helped by being granted loans at a small rate of interest, while the government was also granting money, as a loan, to the various traders. The government grant for the rebuilding of houses—30 Turkish liras for a family of five persons, over five persons 45 liras, and 60 liras for a family of over ten—was certainly a not too munificent one, but it was always something, and as the poorer people were building their houses very cheaply, and using old material and the debris of their former dwellings, besides doing the work themselves for the most part, a sum of even 30 liras provided substantial help. In the villages, and at Hacin and Osmaniye, Rawlins heard that things were not so forward, and that the population was more wretched and in harder straits, but even there great strides had been made in the last two or three months.[124]

Rawlins visited the American hospital in Adana, where about twenty-six patients, male and female, were being catered for, and he only wished that this good work could be put upon a surer basis. There were at present no beds in the wards, and the patients laid upon mattresses on the floor, while the hospital itself was in rather a precarious condition as regards funds. That such a hospital was a necessity here was open to no doubt, and the acting British vice consul felt that it was of the utmost importance that this institution, so urgent at the moment and so essential for the future, should be aided and helped in every way, so as to become a permanent agent for good and a lasting memorial of the disasters which had overwhelmed this district. Among the patients at present being cared for were some who were badly crushed by the newly built houses falling down upon them during the recent floods, and it would be a hard struggle for these people to start for the second time rebuilding their ruined homes.[125]

The last batch of prisoners condemned in connection with the massacres, numbering about ninety Muslims and half a dozen Christians, were entrained in Adana for Mersin, whence they would be dispatched to the prisons at Bodrum in southwestern Anatolia. The sentences ranged from one to fifteen years. A great crowd of people were at the station when they left, and what with the hysterical sobbing and shrieks of the women, the sight was not a pleasant one. There was a strong guard of soldiers, and although some of the women were shouting out curses, the crowd was perfectly orderly, and nothing untoward occurred. Of new projects there were galore. Cemal Bey had informed the acting British vice consul that he was hard at work upon the subject of road repairing—the roads were at present in a very bad condition—while he also talked of instituting electric lighting for the city and a telephone system. While Rawlins was at Mersin, the *mutasarrıf* Rauf Esad Bey told him that a telegraph line was being arranged—to be opened in summer—from Mersin to Gözne, the mountain resort, five hours distant from the town, and it appeared that some sort of telegraph station was really being built up at the latter place. As regards the Baghdad railway, it appeared to be likely that, within a month, work was to be begun at making the permanent way both toward Eregli and toward Hamidiye. It was also said that twenty thousand men would be employed for this purpose, and that small sections of ten miles or so would be let out on contract, thus providing work for the maximum quantity of villagers. Rawlins stated from what he had heard from many quarters, trade was in general recovering, and the dangerous condition of the Adana province might happily be considered a thing of the past. There was much more upon which he could write, such as, for instance, the government orphanage, which had been established under the auspices of Cemal Bey, but he felt that he required more time in order to be able to get accurate and useful information, after which he would be able to report fully upon all and sundry points of interest.[126]

Rawlins summed up: (1) the general condition of the city of Adana and its inhabitants was satisfactory, and promised well for the future; (2) general security was good; (3) local trade was reviving, and things were on the upgrade; (4) the ruined houses were gradually being built; and (5) Cemal Bey was taking everything in hand in a most energetic way, and was the object of commendation from all classes of the population.[127]

On the anniversary of the accession of Sultan Reşad on April 27, 1910, about one hundred prisoners were released in the province of Adana. These persons had been condemned for various terms of imprisonment in connection with the disorders of April 1909. About eighteen Armenians were among the released men and there were no Armenian prisoners left in the province, at least none of those condemned on account of the abovementioned disorders. There were, however, still some Armenian and Muslim prisoners in the jail of Bodrum, who were condemned at the same time but who had not been released nor included in the recent pardon. It was expected that these persons would be released in July on the anniversary of the granting of the constitution.[128]

Sir Louis Mallet, the British ambassador at İstanbul in 1913–1914, had also been favorably impressed by Cemal Bey. His term as governor of Adana had given him experience in provincial administration, and he seemed to be "thoroughly honest and self-sacrificing, possessed of exceptional determination and wanting in breadth of view in dealing with the non-Turkish elements."[129]

In December 1909 William Nesbitt Chambers sent from Adana the following items of interest which serve to keep freshly in mind the critical situation of that afflicted region:

> The governor is still "going strong." He announced to me yesterday that he had "bagged" the brigand that robbed Dr. Shepard two or three weeks ago. The brigand was tracked to the Diarbekir region and is on his way back here to stand trial with good prospect of the gallows. A present of fifty pounds is to be given to the officer who effected the capture, with two pounds each to the soldiers who were with him, as reward. The brigand's accomplices are being hunted down. Ramazan[130] overtook the work of the court-martial and the execution of sentences is delayed. Only three Armenian prisoners remain of the crowd that was arrested in Adana. Some others have been condemned and sent away. A large number of Moslems remain in prison. It is said that a goodly number have been condemned to death, amongst whom are five Armenians from Hadjin. This Ramazan has afforded time for the Moslems to agitate, and they have taken advantage of the religious fast to press their claims to Constantinople and their friends outside have been working to arouse sympathy. Any sinister remark on the part of the Moslems is sufficient to throw the Christians into doubt and fear. However, the men in command at this time give every indication of serious purpose and determined action. As long as the army remains loyal to them the city is safe, and there is no definite ground for suspicion that any part of the army is disaffected. At the same time one cannot help but feel that the Western Powers had made a mistake in withdrawing their ships, thus showing that they had no definite thought of intervention to stop atrocities. The Moslem population is persuaded of this. However, if they were present and had demonstrated at the first outcrop of disturbance, the effect would be most salutary. This situation has a depressing effect. The outcome of the court-martial has given no confidence. This makes it all the more difficult for the governor to reassure the people of his honest

intentions. However, in spite of very great difficulties he is pushing his work along lines laid down at the beginning. He has just today issued a proclamation that all plunder has to be returned during the ensuing month. Any one found with plunder in his possession will be liable to fifteen years' imprisonment. He proposes to make a tour of the villages starting tomorrow.[131]

Cemal Bey became the commander of the Composite Forces in Adana on January 25, 1910. Some eight thousand to ten thousand of the twelve thousand to fifteen thousand Christians who left Adana after the incidents had returned by February 1910.[132] Cemal Bey tried to keep the Ministry of the Interior supplied with fuller information by more travel in the province. He left on February 17 for Hacin and would be absent about two weeks, inspecting the condition of the inhabitants of Hacin and the neighboring villages. He had heard much of the poverty and distress in those parts, and was determined to go there himself and do his best for the people. It was generally known in Adana, also, that the governor left the city in a rather hurried way because of the friction between himself and certain important and influential Muslims who were not in sympathy with him in his continual endeavors to help the lot of the Christians, and looked askant at his energetic efforts in the cause of law and order. It was, however, to be hoped that the governor would receive sufficient backing in high quarters in order that he might be left to continue his labors uninterruptedly. He was naturally very much tired out, as he felt—and probably rightly—that there was no one upon whom he could depend to help him in his work, and that he must, therefore, give every matter his own personal attention.[133]

The trip was made partly by carriage and partly on horseback. The roads proved to be passable. His route took him through the heart of the district affected during the late events. The governor visited the little villages in places along his route and met the people. He returned from his tour of inspection satisfied, where his presence calmed down the anxieties of the Armenians and stimulated the vigilance of the officials. The majority of Armenians went off in the winter to the villages, where they pursued trades, or as pedlars, or to Adana to seek employment, and so earn an amount sufficient to keep them going through the summer, which they spent at Hacin.[134]

After completing his tour of the province in April 1910, Cemal Bey sent a telegram to İstanbul saying: "In my tour, I did not meet a single needy in Hacin to give assistance; that is why 1,000 Turkish liras (23,000 French francs) that I have taken with me for distributing to the poor, has been used upon my orders for the repair of the sewage of the town."[135]

Thomas Davidson Christie said one could never forget the impression made by a first view of Hacin:

You approach the city from the north over mountain heights seven or eight thousand feet above the sea-level. The road winds around one of the peaks and all at once you see the narrow, almost circular valley, lofty mountains surrounding it on all sides: as Mr. Perry used to say, it looks just like an immense mill-hopper. Two-thirds down the steep slope over which you are looking, a narrow nose of rock runs out towards the south, and terminates in a precipice at the centre of the valley. This rock is covered with houses,--its steep side, its top, every part occupied, houses above houses, four or five tiers or stories, propped up where necessary with tall posts, scarcely anything you can call a street in the whole city,--just a hive of human beings, 20,000 of them swarming on that narrow rock. Indeed, from where you first see it, the town resembles nothing so much as a huge honeycomb torn off so as to show many irregular series of cells. You could almost toss a biscuit down upon the flat roofs of the tiers of houses, a thousand feet below.[136]

A disastrous fire in the summer of 1883 had left six thousand people homeless, and the effects of this below were felt for many years. The whole town was so discouraged by this that it had never fully recovered. The bare rocks and steep slopes of this valley seemed to the young men to offer scant prospects for the future, and many had migrated from its inhospitable recesses. Add to this the destruction of 1909, and it was not strange that much relief had been needed in Hacin of late.

Latterly the Government Industrial Commission has enlarged its weaving equipment here, and put the management of this in the hands of the American missionaries. The Gregorians have started a stocking factory; and the Oriental Carpet Manufacturing Company have laid the foundation for quite a rug industry in Hadjin.[137]

The new governor had in so many practical ways put in operation plans for a better administration of justice and for the relief of the distressed that the old Turks were looking on and rubbing their eyes with surprise. He also undertook the plan of settling nomad tribes in various parts of the province. He believed that their wandering habits were due to traditional customs, rather than necessity, and that they would settle down if they were given favorable places in which to cultivate the soil. He had been successful in completing his plans for the agricultural development of his province and in arranging for the construction of certain public works.[138]

The governor, anxious to restore security in his province and to inspire confidence in the Armenians, formed a plan for the creation of a mixed corps of gendarmerie, whose recruitment would be purely local and would be comprised two-thirds of Muslim subjects and one-third of Christians. For the technical training of this new police, a school run by an army captain, assisted by four other instructor officers, from İstanbul was opened in Tarsus. It taught with the newest methods. The total number of students would, in principle, be three hundred, out of which one hundred would be Christian. But the non-Muslim population did not respond eagerly to the appeal of the governor, and it was with great pain that only sixty young men of the Christian families of Adana could be recruited. Be that as it may, the experience tempted to appear fairly successful. The running of the school seemed good. No serious clash took place between the recruits of the two religions and at the first graduation ceremony attended by Cemal Bey the Tarsus school could supply 270 gendarmes whose level of instruction was higher than that of the old *zabtiyes*. Out of this contingent, thirty men were dispatched to Beirut to serve as instructors there and the rest was distributed between the various localities of the province. These new police officers had a good standard: their clothing was solid and confortable, their weaponry serious. As to the professional value of these men, it was quite difficult to make an exact estimate. At present, the situation was most calm and these gendarmes did hardly anything more than going for a walk, in pairs, around the railway stations, marketplaces, and ports, but one had the liberty to ask themselves what would be their attitude in the event of new conflicts between the Armenians and the Muslims. Among the Christians, some had hope in these troops; they were considered a possible guarantee for the day of danger. Others feared that in case of troubles the non-Muslim soldiers would either be removed or disarmed. The actual size of the Tarsus school was much reduced: one hundred and fifty students only, and all Muslims. The Christians in fact were not able to make their mind on supplying a new contingent. Moreover, two instructor officers went to Damascus and to Aleppo, with unclear intentions. Perhaps it was a matter of recruiting young men in these two cities to be trained in Tarsus for sending back afterwards to their regions and to work there toward the maintenance of law and order.[139]

It seemed to acting British vice consul G. C. Donaldson Rawlins at Adana that this school, in which Muslims and Christians were banded together, was a great success, and that the Christian students were all fairly treated and got on well with their Muslim comrades.[140]

Cemal Bey organized festivities in the province of Adana in view of the reconciliation of the Muslim and non-Muslim elements.[141] Dikran Mesrob Kaligian acknowledges that "his generally fair treatment of the Armenian population had allowed them the freedom to restore much of their prior prosperity."[142]

There was some unrest among the Armenian population of Adana at the beginning of May 1910 and for the following reason. It appeared that a Muslim, riding on horseback near the village of Şeyh Murad (about three hours distant from Adana), addressed a villager who was working in the fields and asked him whether he had not heard the news, namely that massacring was going on in the Dörtyol area and the Christians would soon be massacred in other places also. It was supposed that the villager on hearing this—he was an Armenian—became frightened and spread the report that another massacre was beginning. The report reached Adana soon and a good many villagers came into the city in a great state of terror, while many Armenians flocked to the Gregorian church for refuge. There could not be said to have been a general panic, but it could not be denied that there was a great feeling of uneasiness among a large portion of the poorer Armenian population. At the time, however, all was quiet again and there was no reason to suppose that a similar "scare" would crop up. Nobody seemed to know who the Muslim was who spoke to the villager but it was to be hoped that, in the future, such cases might be severely dealt with, as, though seemingly unimportant, they might be the cause of untoward events.[143]

In mid-January 1911 a *molla* from the top of a minaret in Adana proclaimed death to the unbelievers, which he said comprised this time such Turks, who by their ideas of reform in the Ottoman Empire abandoned the old conservative spirit prescribed by the Koran. As a result the *molla* was imprisoned and the following day was let free on the plea of drunkenness the previous evening. This proclamation, coupled with the fact that firearms (mainly revolvers) and ammunition were been sold freely to Turks for some time past, considerably frightened the Christian population. Several Armenians interviewed Cemal Bey on the matter, who comforted them with the declaration that they should have no fears whatsoever. That same afternoon the governor drove in Adana in an open carriage as a double manifesto of restoring confidence to the one and of warning the other that the authorities were wide awake to their duty of keeping order. On January 20 it was noticed, in the neighborhood of the American Mission in Adana, on several doors of Armenian houses a red paint mark in the shape of a cross. This greatly impressed a great many Armenians, who applied for refuge to the Jesuits in Adana, but the latter did not deem it necessary to afford same. Subsequent to that, the head of the Jesuit Mission came to Mersin and interviewed the French consul, who left for Adana the following afternoon. The situation in Adana was one of uneasiness as the result of the foregoing. The authorities seemed at present ready to repress any sign of disturbance. According to the acting British vice consul, the prevalent idea of the causes on the unrest created were the personal unpopularity of the governor among a large class of Turks in Adana and the feeling of the waning influence of the CUP.[144]

Following the incidents related above, Cemal Bey, under his signature, published an article in the local press *Anadolu*, qualifying these advents the puerile doings of irresponsible parties, exhorting everybody to quiet and peace and declaring that the breakers of good order in the city would be severely dealt with. At the same time he expressed his astonishment that people among the "thinking class" should have displayed such lack of "thinking capacity" in this instance by giving these last incidents any other significance than the childish nature they purport. Rawlins believed this comment to be a hit at the French, German, American, and Russian consuls who had gone up to Adana to inquire into the matter. Adana was perfectly quiet at present, the uneasiness of the population was gradually wearing out, and Rawlins heard from persons who had lately returned from the interior of the province that thorough good fellowship reigned everywhere.[145]

Among the works undertaken by Cemal Bey at Adana itself was the embankment to stave off the floods coming from the Seyhan river. An enormous amount of labor was expended on it, and the traces of it remained to all times as a monument of him.

Major General James Harbord, who led a fact-finding mission to Turkey and Trans-Caucasia in September–October 1919, notes that American testimony in Adana was that while governor there Cemal Bey saved many Armenians from death, erected the orphanage which now housed hundreds of orphans, and built a dike to protect the city from the annual river flood, as well as other good works.[146]

The International Relief Committee at a meeting in mid-November 1909, in view of the urgent appeals sent from the local distributing centers in Cilicia, representing that a continuance of its work through the winter would be absolutely necessary, decided to make a final appeal to the benevolence of the world on behalf of the victims of the late events in Cilicia. The press of the world had already given in full detail the story of the horrible deeds which had thrown the survivors upon the mercy and which had filled the most fruitful provinces of the Ottoman Empire with want and sadness. Governor Cemal Bey, in an appeal to the public for the afflicted children in his province, used the following words:

> The recent tragedy enacted in Adana, which has already met with a sympathetic response in all parts of the world, has entirely destroyed a great part of the city of Adana and its suburbs, leaving many families without shelter and even without the necessaries of life. The country around is also ruined and the condition of the victims is so lamentable, the destruction of families is so painfully sad, that no one being acquainted with the facts of the case can refrain from shedding tears.[147]

The above testimony from the governor of the province, who had lately been an eyewitness of the results of the events referred to, shows that the task of rehabilitating the people was much larger than was at first supposed. The International Relief Committee had until mid-November 1909 received the amount of 9,512.35 Turkish liras of which the sum of 8,887.91 had been distributed to the needy, leaving a cash balance in hand of 824.44. In addition to the receipts mentioned above there had been sent, mainly through the foreign consuls, directly to the stricken district a further sum of approximately 17,000 Turkish liras, all of which had been expended.[148]

A late letter from Fred Douglas Shepard contained the following: "About one house in three among the 900 houses burned in the Baghche district is absolutely without a single quill or bed covering for the whole family. Many large families have but a single bed and clothing is scarce in proportion." Samuel H. Kennedy of the International Relief Committee of İskenderun wrote: "As far as I can judge the Government is greatly hampered for want of money. Of the sum voted by Parliament only a very small portion has thus far been sent down here, perhaps more will be given later. A matter of great importance is the supply of plough oxen and seed corn. At least 6,000 pounds Turkish will be needed to resupply this district. Scarcely any one has plough oxen left. One large land-owner had 120 oxen, but has recovered only 8. There are 336 orphans and widows in my district and 1,106 persons who are in extreme need." The large agricultural region about Harput was outside the devastated district, but information showed that over one thousand laborers, from more than forty villages in this region, who went to Cilicia to find work in the harvest fields, there lost their lives, killed generally "with sickle or mattock in hand." Their death meant great want and suffering for this region. Dr. Barnum of Harput wrote: "You telegraphed the other day that you could give us L.T. 30. Let me say that a great deal more will be needed. The Adana massacre destroyed more lives on our plain and in the Palu region than did that of '95. From a single village (Haboosi), for example, as many as 63 men were murdered in Adana, all wage earners. Through all this region an unusual number of men were in the Adana plain, seeking work, when they were mercilessly butchered. We are receiving urgent appeals for help to meet the needs of the surviving families. So please send us what one can rightfully give."[149]

From Ayntab the International Relief Committee had the following: "These days have revealed a distressing state of poverty. I cannot say how we can get through this winter. I am sure there will be actual starvation before spring. The political disturbances have reacted badly on trade. The grasshoppers [locusts] and harts have destroyed much of the wheat, and the other crops, including the olives, were hurt by frost, so that prices are very high. There are large numbers of unemployed people who cannot possibly get their food. Today there are being fed in part or wholly by the churches of this city (including 120 Jews) 1,930 people. The Moslem population is in a worse condition even than the Christian. This is the situation at the close of the harvest, the easiest month of the year. What must we see before spring comes!"

From Tarsus: "The rainy season has begun but many of the people are still living under tents. We have waited anxiously six months for the rebuilding which has not begun." From Hacin: "Disease like typhoid are increasing. In a short time the winter season will be here when work will cease. A careful estimate shows that LT. 600 at least will be needed to take the people through the winter." From Maraş: "In the city of Marash our people are feeding 300 people, mostly widows and children, but they are entirely destitute. No government aid is given here for food. In twenty surrounding villages there are also needy people to the extent of 1,619, or 2,119 in all, needing help in this district. This will require 3,920 pounds Turkish for food. A further sum of 230 pounds Turkish should be provided for seed to sow the fields or we shall have a shortage of food next year."[150]

A careful estimate of the number of victims still requiring aid and help to regain that position of self support which they formerly held showed that at least eighty thousand would need to receive assistance of some sort to enable them to pass the coming winter while many of this number were wholly dependent upon outside aid for the daily food needful to sustain life. Indeed actual starvation faced many of the individuals mentioned above.[151]

The material losses attending the massacres in Cilicia were enormous. To a large extent two prosperous provinces had been despoiled, leaving poverty in the place of former abundance. The amount representing these material losses had been variously estimated. In no case had they been estimated at less than 1,000,000 Turkish liras, while some careful observers thought that a much larger sum would more correctly represent the real losses sustained by the survivors. It followed that although the Ottoman government had undertaken to distribute help toward relief of the sufferers and the rebuilding of their ruined houses, the funds supplied from this source could not meet, except in a certain measure, the requirements of the situation. Upon the International Relief Committee therefore fell the task of supplying food and shelter, as might be required, to supplement the grants made by the government; furnishing the houses with beds, bedding, and domestic utensils; clothing the people; as well as providing all other necessaries for restarting their lives. This disaster had been so great and the calls at this season of the year so urgent as to make it impossible for the International Relief Committee to lay down its work now. In the face of the appeals which the International Relief Committee were daily receiving they could not do otherwise than to lay the situation again before the benevolence of the world, trusting that the response might be in some degree commensurate with the existing need.[152]

Meanwhile William Nesbitt Chambers confessed that Cemal Bey made a deep impression on him. He asked the question: Are we catching at a bubble? He then replied: I think not. It was true that Cemal Bey was only one man, and one of the heaviest burdens in the country had been placed on his shoulders. But he was gathering about himself men of serious mind, both Muslims and Christians of the various sects, and uniting them in a common cause. The American missionary writes that soon after the Turkish-Armenian communal fighting of 1909 at Adana, Cemal Bey organized commissions of relief and reconstruction on which the various communities were represented, both Muslim and Christian. The governor obtained 1,300,000 dollars from the central government which were economically and efficiently administered for the relief of the Armenians. He made grants for food and rebuilding of burned houses. He made loans at low interest and long, easy terms to enable large numbers to begin business again and for villagers to reconstruct their farm work. This was a very great boon to the Armenians. The relief was confined to the Christians who had suffered. But his most spectacular and radical undertaking, Chambers goes on, was the organization of courts—mail for the trial and punishment of those guilty of massacre.[153]

ESTABLISHMENT OF AN ORPHANAGE AND A COMMISSION OF INDUSTRIAL RELIEF FOR WOMEN AND GIRLS

Chambers acknowledged that in the prosecution of relief work there were two enterprises that Cemal Bey organized and put forth every endeavor to establish on a permanent basis. One was an orphanage. To care for the many children left orphans by the massacres at Adana was among the most urgent demands of the situation in that stricken city. Cemal Bey had organized a committee to provide for this need. Its first meeting was held in Chambers's house. After the governor had laid his plan for an orphanage before the committee, Chambers had a private interview with him, in which the objections and difficulties in the way of it were frankly discussed, and the governor outlined his plan to the missionary somewhat as follows:

> One of the great difficulties blocking progress in this land has been the large number of divisions, both racial and religious. There has been very strong race antipathy to make impossible the harmonious working together of the various races. Religious fanaticism, hatred, and hostility amongst the various religious communities have been the bane of healthy progress and enlightment in the land. The foreign missionaries, Catholic and Protestant, with the best of intentions, only added to the number of these divisions instead of diminishing them. Division is weakness; union is strength. It is the aim of the Young Turk to develop and promote unity. The only basis on which all these warring divisions may arrive at peace and unite is that of Ottoman nationality. We must no longer

look on the people as Turks, Kurds, Armenians, or Greeks; they must all become Ottomans and be treated as such. The people must be educated. Every autocratic sovereign in all history has been opposed to education, for in the ignorance and narrow-mindedness of the people lay his strength. Education must break that power and set the people free. This religious intolerance must be removed and broad tolerance in religious matters substituted, in so far as these do not interfere with the best interests of the state. In the matter of orphans, an awful calamity has left hundreds of widows and orphans homeless and helpless. These orphans have lost their natural protectors and the state is responsible for them and must perform its duty in feeding, clothing, and educating them. They are the ward of the nation. This can be done only along lines on which all can unite, that of Ottoman citizenship. Time will be necessary, but it is the duty of the present generation to do its work conscientiously and well and pass the work on to their children to carry on to completion. The orphanage must be established by the government. The children must be received, not as the children of this or that community, but as Ottomans. Religious divisions must be eliminated; neither Moslem *hoja* nor Christian priest can be admitted as such. The children may repair to their respective places of worship and receive any religious instruction that may be thought necessary—the Moslem to the mosque on Friday, and the Christian to the church on Sunday, but they must receive a high moral training in the orphanage.[154]

For the project Cemal Bey raised, largely by voluntary subscription, 30,000–40,000 dollars. It was to be open for all the communities. However, it was filled with Armenian orphans left so by the fightings, about two hundred of them. The government financed it and it was entirely in the hands of Armenians appointed by the government. Orphan boys from the age of twelve to seventeen were to be trained here in lessons and in trades.[155]

The other enterprise was industrial relief for women and girls for which a commission was appointed composed of a Turk, a Syrian, three Armenians, and an American missionary. It was to provide a means of livelihood for poor girls and women of every sect and faith. To accomplish this end the commission aimed to revive and develop the arts of Oriental embroidery, lace work, and handweaving, and to find a market for the finished articles. For the carrying out of this commendable purpose Cemal Bey had framed a constitution which provided for the organization of a central commission and branch commissions at several points in the province, with 18,000 dollars of government money assigned as capital for the enterprise.[156]

The constitution of the Commission of Industries was formed for the purpose of providing work for needy women and for reviving the oriental handweaves and needlework. The commission was constituted under the presidency of William Nesbitt Chambers; it was composed of the said president, together with a treasurer, a secretary, and four honorary members which would be elected by a board of election, said board consisting of the provincial council, the municipal council, and the commercial court. The provincial governor and the president of the Commission of Industries would appoint the treasurer and secretary and decide their salaries. The half of these four honorary members would be elected every two years. The time of election would be announced by the president and the provincial governor fifteen days before the time of election. This would hold regular meetings every fifteen days, or more frequently at the call of the president, and would consider and decide concerning the propositions presented by the president in reference to (1) the instruction of the women in oriental needlework and handweaves, (2) the construction of home for this work, (3) the arranging of places for the work, (4) the provision of sufficient teachers, (5) the sale of the manufactured articles, and (6) any other question that might be presented. The president and treasurer would present a report of expenditure and income once a month which after examination and endorsement by the commission would be placed in the files of the commission, and a copy would be presented to the local government. The looms, teachers, the work of the women, the sale of the manufactured goods, the collection of the materials, the expenses of the commission, and the execution of the decisions of the commission would be under the supervision of the president. The correspondence would be carried on by the president and the secretary, the financial transactions conducted by the president and treasurer, and the president, treasurer, and secretary together would be responsible for all the work of the commission. At the close of the year a careful financial report with statistics concerning (1) the number of women working, (2) the quantity and kinds of goods manufactured, and (3) the entire work of the commission would be prepared and after endorsement by the commission would be presented to the board of election through the provincial governor. The members of the commission would all be responsible for all the irregularities both in the administration of funds and other transactions.[157]

There would be formed a mixed commission under the temporary presidency of Mrs. Shepard (the wife of the well-known American missionary doctor) for the purpose of selecting the women that might be adapted for this work and of encouraging them. This commission would decide upon the kind of work that would find favor among the people, and so report to the central commission and otherwise assist it. In the case of Mrs. Shepard's resignation the provincial governor and president of the central commission would appoint her successor. In suitable places in the adjoining districts branch commissions would be organized on the same plan with the central commission. The presidents, treasurers, and secretaries of these branch commissions would be appointed by the provincial governor and the president of the central commission of industries. The other four members would be appointed by local boards by election formed on the plan prescibed in the above paragraph. The monthly and yearly accounts and reports of these branch commissions, properly endorsed, would be presented to the central commission, and the central commission, combining these accounts and reports with its own accounts and reports, would dispose of them accordingly. In the case of the resignation of the president for any reason whatever, three names of persons proper to succeed them would be presented to the board of election, and one of them would be elected by this board by secret ballot; the treasurer and secretary of the commission of industries would be present at the election of the president and would have the right to vote. A sum of 4,000 Turkish liras would be assigned by the government as capital for this industrial work, and appropriate portions of this sum would be sent for use to the branch commissions by the decisions of the central commission with the consent of the provincial governor. The central commission with the branch commissions were to transference the capital in an unobjectionable way, but only with the knowledge of the government. Of the net income of the commission 50 percent would be added to the capital, 20 percent would be given as royalty to the workers, and 30 percent would be appropriated for the Ottoman orphanage established in Adana. On the representation and request of the president, the board of election, the president himself being present and voting, might revise any change of the constitution, when the capital assigned to this commission by the government became double, nevertheless the capital assigned to the purposes as above put forth might not be diverted from those purposes, nor might the industries be closed.[158]

In urging Chambers to accept the presidency of the central commission, Cemal Bey pointed out that the purpose of this work was in line with Chambers's purpose in the uplifting of this stricken people. He added that he felt assured, in entrusting this undertaking to Chambers's direction, that it would be administered with perfect integrity, and with the fullest intention to make it beneficial to all communities of all faiths. This tribute showed that the untiring and efficient efforts of Chambers for the betterment of conditions in Adana had not passed unnoticed. It was also due to Chambers's work and direction that a hospital had been established with its door open to all. For an Ottoman governor so to have recognized a foreigner and a Christian missionary, and to have given this large sum of money entirely into his control, was an act without precedent and of great moment.[159]

Despite his Young Turk fervor, Cemal Bey held the missionaries in fairly high esteem, recognizing them as agents of European civilization. He sought their aid without fear of being misled or betrayed. His trust of the missionaries went hand in hand with a general taste for Europeans. From his standpoint, the missionaries were ideally suited for the task ahead. The most senior had been in the province of Adana for more than three decades, most understood the terrain, and many spoke Turkish and Armenian. They had nurtured personal friendships with various local inhabitants, bonds that might now be beneficial. The missionaries on their part were eager to play a wider role in the district.

Cemal Bey, Chambers maintains, showed his confidence in the American missionaries and his sympathy for their ideals in that he made the head of Adana station of the ABCFM president of the commission and so placed in his hands a sum of about 17,000 dollars (4,000 Turkish gold liras) to be expended in the work.[160] Colonel Mehmet Ali Bey, the head of the military force of Adana, in speaking to Chambers as the leader of the American Mission, expressed appreciation of his work in the interests of humanity, remarking, as he did so, "that service for humanity is the only thing of permanent value in human life." This remark was most significant coming from a Muslim.[161]

With the object of further assisting the women of the Adana region Mrs. Shepard, who some eighteen years ago had so successfully founded an embroidery industry at Ayntab, was invited by Cemal Bey to establish a branch of her work in Adana. The splendid exhibit of activities accomplished was due very largely to the devoted labor of Mrs. Shepard, who without any salary had come and given weeks of service to starting the enterprise. She had been ably assisted by a committee of Muslim and Christian ladies, including Mrs. Chambers and the wives of Cemal Bey and the Iranian consul. Owing to the initiative of the governor a liberal allowance was made by the Government Relief Committee in order to allow this industry to be started on a satisfactory basis.[162]

COME-BACK FROM THE MASSACRE PERIOD

According to the report Cemal Bey sent to the Committee on Building and Relief the following disbursements had been made up to the end of December 1909: (1) Out of the sum of 15,000 Turkish liras, 188,354 piasters was paid for the rental of churches, school buildings, and orphanages; 1,353,018 piasters for the relief of the destitute, and 3,550 piasters for the salaries of clerks and other officials. (2) The committee had agreed that those families in which there was no able-bodied person, and mothers with several small children, should receive instead of money, food and wheat. In accordance with this arrangement 8,092 such persons were fed at a cost of 1,316,174 piasters. (3) A sum of 4,000 Turkish liras to be used in providing employment for widows was given to the American missionary William Nesbitt Chambers. (4) A total of 20,000 Turkish liras given for rebuilding the houses was distributed in the following way: 30 liras was given to families consisting of five members for the building of one room, 45 liras to families of ten members for the building of two rooms, and 60 liras to families of more than ten members for the building of three rooms. (5) A total of 37,246 Turkish liras were given to the building committees in Bahçe, İslâhiye, Osmaniye, Erzin, Dörtyol, Kozan, Hacin, Tarsus, Adana, Hamidiye, and Karaisalı. And 5,000 liras was given for the building of orphanages. The government had expanded 81,397 Turkish liras in the above ways and had set aside 6,796 liras for two months' rations for the destitute in Hacin; 1,048 liras for expenses up to February 28, 1910, of the government orphanages opened in Adana, Mersin, Dörtyol, and Hacin; 1,000 liras to the building committee in Dörtyol; 120 liras for the Tlan farm; 250 liras to the monastery of Kozan; and 200 liras for the monastery at Hacin.[163]

Ahmet Şerif, the roving correspondent of *Tanin*, who as a young journalist in the 1910s had been attracting much attention by his candid views and impartial statement of facts, wrote from Adana in an optimistic vein in regard to the relations now existing between the Christians and Muslims. He attributed this favorable state of affairs to the fidelity and the impartiality of the new government. He said that the Armenians were satisfied with Governor Cemal Bey as a man zealous in the cause of justice, and they wished that in Anatolia there might be at least ten governors like him. The Turks, however, were extremely dissatisfied with Cemal Bey, even "the most enlightened Muslims" criticized him.[164]

Chambers remarked:

> I have just returned from Hadjin, after an absence of two weeks. The country is quite. Indications of the massacre are few. Business is brisk, and the promise of a large harvest is extremely good. It was a pleasure to ride through miles of fields of heavy grain, wheat and barley. The sad, sad indications of the awful massacre are the widows and orphans. The energy of the Vali, Djemal Bey, has accomplished wonders, but there are wonders still to be performed.[165]

This was certainly true. Cemal Bey was an extraordinary governor in comparison with others. He was not the sort of person who merely received instructions and sent reports. He acted in accordance with his own discretion, understanding, and abilities. Within his limits, he tried to shape and steer the provincial policy, in relation both to the local circumstances and the Sublime Porte.

Thanks to Cemal Bey's wise administration, the come-back from the massacre period had been remarkable. The ruins of the downtown section were all cleared away, and houses rebuilt. People no longer picked their way to the bazaars over debris and past charred walls. The French chain store of the Near East, Orosdiback, had established quite a good sized department store.[166]

One thing more. In recording his impressions of the reconstruction of Adana Cavid Bey, the minister of public works, wrote in his diary entry of April 24–29, 1912: "Every civil work in the city is done by Cemal Bey. Orphanage, Agricultural College, Teachers Training College, the Seyhan Embankment. Foreigners also say in general that if he had stayed here a few years longer Adana would have been transformed into a prosperous city."[167] Nevertheless, this province, rich in historical association, scenic beauty, fertile soil, plantations, orchards, forests, and mines, would once more become a veritable treasure house to the Ottoman Empire.

ECONOMIC RECOVERY OF ADANA

The incidents of 1909 disrupted life in the province of Adana for about a year after which the economic recovery was remarkable. Since April 1909, the population of Adana had greatly increased, owing to the newly opening work to be found there. The new Baghdad railway enterprise distributed a great deal of money and added impulse to trade. Aiming to expand the agriculture Cemal Bey decided to set up an agricultural school in Adana. The site was chosen in a very convenient location, with the support of the Ministry of Agriculture, Mines, and Forestry; as soon as the formalities of buying and transfer of land to be completed the construction of the school would start.[168]

Adana was having a boom in the summer of 1910. The opening of work on the Baghdad railway had filled the city with Germans. The number of Europeans in Adana at the time was estimated at one thousand. The city was rapidly being rebuilt with wider streets and in many cases better houses. There was talk of a dike to insure against flood, of irrigation and a water supply for the city, of electric lights and a street railway.[169]

In mid-February 1910, the Ottoman Council of State finished the examination of the contract drawn up by the Ministry of Commerce and Public Works concerning the cleaning out of the rivers Seyhan, Ceyhan, and Tarsus Çay, and the irrigation and drying out of marshes in the province of Adana. These works consisted of the repairing of the Misis route of the Adana railway, and of the site between Ceyhan, Misis, and the Mediterranean. The method of "Colmatch" was to be applied in the sphere of drying out. Dikes were built between the rivers. In some locations dikes were to be extended up to the sea, from one part to the other up to the Adana plain. The necessary measures were to be taken to prevent a possible swelling of the water. Thus the Adana plain was to be wholly irrigated. The Yumurtalık harbor, which filled in with sands that the current carried daily, was to be cleaned out in order to facilitate navigation; bridges of fifty meters in length and nine meters in width were to be constructed. Topographical maps on the scale of 1:10,000 were to be drawn up for the carrying out of the works. The report on these works, drafted by the Ministry of Commerce and Public Works was submitted to the Grand Vizierate.[170]

The German colony, few in number until recent years, increased day by day; chambers of commerce were opened; engineers, enterpreneurs, machine operators flowed. In combination with their Ottoman counterparts, these people enabled the expansion effort. Deutsche Orient Bank opened a branch in Mersin. At the beginning of 1910, a career diplomat with the grade of consul, Eugen Büge, was appointed to Adana; this official, whose way of acting was firm, secured his nationals an effective protection. He instructed his vice consul in Mersin to appear, especially then, strict on the enforcement of the capitulations and to maintain the whole of the privileges conceded to his nationals. Büge was the most active representative of his colony, and, if the latter took their tone from him, they must cherish big ambitions. He looked upon his work as of real importance for the future, and thought his compatriots in Adana were to him but the pioneers in the eventual absorption of the province by Germany. At the same time, there was nothing sensational in all this activity. The Germans were obviously prepared to bide their time, make themselves agreeable to the local population, by whom apparently their presence was far from being resented, and built up their interests on a solid foundation.[171]

The most important German society in Adana was naturally the Baghdad Company with Herr Winkler as local director and his large staff. These gentlemen were most exclusive, held together, and seemed to be unwilling to mix in any foreign society whatever. The acting British vice consul, G. C. Donaldson Rawlins, remarked that although he himself had several conversations with Winkler in his office, he had never come to the British vice consulate either for social or official purposes. As evidence of what Rawlins called this exclusiveness he mentioned the following incident. A short while previous, Willim Nesbitt Chambers attempted to approach people with a view to obtaining subscriptions and forming an international committee for the hospital in Adana. There was great need for such an institution and the present building was quite inadequate. Chambers approached Rawlins and told him that his idea was that the hospital should be as international as possible, and that sufferers of every nationality and creed would be admitted. Rawlins immediately saw the benefits of such an institution and promised him his support. The Imperial Ottoman Bank was also approached and most willingly agreed to help with subscriptions. The Deutsche Orient Bank also lent an ear to the proposal but did not give any definite answer. When, however, the same matter was brought to Winkler's notice, as head of the Baghdad

Construction, it met with a most cool reception, and a few days later—after a meeting between the German consul and the heads of the German colony—Chambers was given to understand that the Baghdad company was unwilling to contribute; the *Deutsche Levantinische Baumvoll Gesellschaft* took the same course and the Deutsche Orient Bank followed suit. This meant that no money would be given by any of the Germans for this purpose. On the contrary, they had decided to build at once a hospital themselves, which would be a thoroughly German institution, and to which only Germans and employees of the Baghdad line would be admitted. The railway company had also a cooperative store at Mersin which was only to be used by employees of the company, and it was said that a German club might also be formed to which none but Germans would be admitted.[172]

The local influence of the Baghdad company was great, and also evident. Besides, the company made a great "show," a fact which went a long way toward producing an impression on the Ottoman mind. For instance, the company's offices were imposing and they were the best decorated in the city on the occasion of the sultan's birthday. Minor details such as the residence of the director—one of the most expensive houses in Adana—and his smart German carriages all went to impress still further the native mind. Then there was the Adana-Mersin railway with Herr Endricks as director. The latter was a young and extremely capable man, formerly an officer in a German dragoon regiment. He ran the railway on the sternest Prussian discipline lines and had the reputation of being a pronounced Anglophobe. He was hand in glove with the Baghdad company and the two railways might be counted as one. The Deutsche Orient Bank had branches at Adana and Mersin, and the former branch carried on business in a lavish and advertising way. A large German flag and a Turkish one were flown daily at this branch. The director, a Herr Mordtmann, was most energetic but seemingly rather tactless in his conversation, unless he believed in open speaking. When speaking with Rawlins lately, he went so far as to say that "whether the *Vali*, or even the Turkish Government, liked it or not, the whole of the district was pratically in Germany's hands and would be so *ipso facto* very shortly." Rawlins heard that he often talked in this strain and did not mind who heard him. He was also, so it was said, going to introduce a German company to compete with British traction, engines, threshers, and machinery in general, and if any future good luck attended his efforts, one of Britain's sole important markets in Adana would be crippled.[173]

On March 10, 1910, the French vice consul in Adana and Mersin, Barré de Lancy, paid a visit to the new military commander of the province of Adana, Nasır Paşa, the son of Nusret Paşa who had been the commander of the Sixth Army Corps in Baghdad, and got the impression that this officer would be of great help for the governor in the maintenance of public tranquility. Nasır Paşa had served three years in a German regiment, and he had brought back from his stay in Europe very liberal views.[174]

By March 1910, about 10,000 Turkish liras were distributed to the sufferers in the villages of Kessab for rebuilding their burned houses. The *kaymakam* of Jissr, together with the engineer of the province of Aleppo, was sent to Kessab by Governor Fahri Paşa to distribute the money and to put the work in hand. The money was fairly and honestly dealt out, and the British consul at Aleppo Raphael Fontana learned from Miss Chambers, the American missionary there, that all that possible was done in the way of reconstruction, so that no Armenians lacked a roof to cover them through the worst of the winter.[175]

In April 1910, the situation in Kessab was very much improved. Few of the people were in need and while they did not have as much as they would like, on the whole the people had enough to eat and all had work. As soon as the silk crop was disposed of the inhabitants could face the coming winter in comparative comfort. In a letter dated April 17, 1910, Esther Kundakçıyan, the wife of the local Protestant Armenian pastor, said that the government gave 150 liras toward the rebuilding, and with this money the foundation of the new church was laid on November 29, 1909. It was a great and happy day for all Armenians.[176]

Cemal Bey was planning a voyage to Europe in the summer of 1910, and he would take with him about sixty notables of Adana, both Christian and Muslim. His idea was that a journey of this sort would broaden the minds of the people he took with him, and that they would thus come back inspired by new ideas, whereby the whole province would gradually benefit. The taking of Christians and Muslims together was naturally a continuance of the governor's avowed policy of trying to promote better feeling between the two religions. Definite arrangements as to this journey were not yet made, but it was understood that the tour would be made in July, and last about two months. After leaving İstanbul, the party would visit Hungary, Austria, Germany, and France, while Cemal Bey expressed his intention of crossing over to Britain alone. As to why he was not going to take his party of notables with him to Britain, the governor did not give any definite reason, but only mentioned that they would have seen enough upon arriving in Paris. The plan appeared, in the opinion of acting British vice consul G. C. Donaldson Rawlins, to merit considerable interest, and it seemed a pity that the journey should not be extended to Britain.[177]

The aim of this trip would be, according to the governor, to show to the local notables various aspects of the civilization and the progress made in agriculture and industry; in a word, to give to the Ottomans, recently promoted to the status of citizenship, the taste of the European life and the desire of sending their children abroad for education, and then coming back to the country to contribute to the social and economic development. For the organization of this trip, Cemal Bey convened a committee in Adana which included, besides the locals, a certain number of Europeans. The governor exerted intensive effort for the realization of this plan: he talked about it to all and sundry, took an interest in it as it was a thing of his own, and devoted himself to gather participants all over the province. However, the result of these endeavors was not very satisfactory. The Muslims hesitated to put their names down.[178]

On April 29, a committee meeting at the *Konak* was convened for the purpose of discussing ways and means with regard to this tour. British and German consuls were invited to this meeting and there were present the directors of the Imperial Ottoman Bank, Régie, and Adana-Tarsus-Mersin Railway Company, the mufti of Mersin, the president of the Adana municipality, and several other influential Muslims and Christians. Cemal Bey explained the objects and scope of the proposed tour through Europe. He said that they were making this tour for the purpose of gaining a better insight into European life, commercially and domestically, and that they would be able to return here with new ideas the best of which he hoped they would put into practice. The governor went on to say that the object of the journey was a commercial and not a political one. They were a band of persons who were intent on seeing how their country could be bettered agriculturally and commercially. The governor made a special point of the fact that they did not want to be received in a specially official way but asked for the aid of the British and German consuls in the matter of getting them to see the most interesting places and industries in Britain and Germany, and for helping in the way of getting special reductions in railway fares and hotels.[179]

The details of the tour as arranged at the time and discussed at the meeting were as follows. (1) Those taking part in the tour with the governor of Adana would number about eighty, and they would include notable Christian and Muslim merchants, landowners, officials, etc., from Adana, Tarsus, and Mersin. (2) The party would leave Mersin on July 28 whence they would go to Salonika, arriving there on July 31. Thence they would go to İstanbul (two days), Rumania-Hungary (Budapest three days), Vienna (two days), Berlin (three days), Brussels, Britain (five days), Paris (seven days), Switzerland, and Italy, and return direct to Mersin for Adana. (3) It was estimated that the cost of the whole journey—if facilities were granted in all these countries—should not amount to more than 2,000 French francs per head. The party intended to leave Ostend for Britain on August 26, but as no completely accurate timetable could be made beforehand, it could be said that the party with Cemal Bey would be visiting Britain between August 20 and 30. The governor intimated that he hoped that the acting British vice consul could suggest that some sort of reception committee should be formed in Britain to whom the governor could telegraph upon leaving Ostend and who would receive the party in London and draw up a plan for places, industries, etc., they should visit during their five days in Britain.[180]

Rawlins suggested to his superiors in İstanbul and London that it would be a most excellent thing if this large party was well received and well shown round so that they would all come back to Adana deeply impressed with the commercial as well as political strength of Britain: the more so as the other countries were sure to do their best for the visitors and the German consul assured them that in Germany, during their three-day stay, they could count on being well received and their railway and sundry excursion fees would all be paid for. How the German consul was able to take the responsibility of such a remark, Rawlins did not know, but it naturally evoked loud applause and he trusted that he might as soon as possible be empowered to assure the governor that a committee was formed for their reception in Britain and that special reductions would be made in all their railway fares, free carriages provided on excursions, and arrangements for hotels and dinners made. The German consul also informed the meeting that he himself would be going on leave at that time and would probably be with them in Berlin and act as their guide. This also made Rawlins think that whoever was charged to act as interpreter to the party in Britain should not only know French but also Turkish, if possible, as many of the travelers had no knowledge of any European language.[181]

Rawlins, therefore, begged to request that steps might be taken, if possible, for a committee of reception to be formed in Britain and a program of how the five days should be spent, and what reductions in fares, etc., could be made and the details sent in as soon as possible to himself in order that he might be able to inform the governor and his committee as to what could be done for them to make their visit interesting and agreeable. Lastly, he only begged to urge once more the importance of this journey which might tend greatly toward an increase of commercial relations between Britain and this important and flourishing province, and, if the tour in Britain was well planned and carried out it could not but leave a good impression and have an effect on local politics. The governor expressed the hope that the acting British vice consul should be able to inform him whether any arrangements for their reception in Britain would be possible or not, within a month.[182]

Cemal Bey left Adana for İstanbul on June 3, 1910, to be absent about three weeks. To the general public in Adana this journey came as a surprise and was much commented on, but the governor told Rawlins that he had for some time past been writing for permission to make this journey as there were many local matters which were hanging fire and which he felt could be more easily settled if he were to have the opportunity of conferring with certain high government officials personally. The governor seemed anxious to assure Rawlins that his sudden departure for İstanbul had no ulterior purposes whatever and stated that he had various local matters on hand which he wanted to settle satisfactorily. Popular rumor was rife on the subject of the governor's visit to İstanbul, many people saying that he was going to a secret meeting of the CUP, at which the Cretan question would be discussed and also questions of internal policy. Some of Cemal Bey's enemies were also trying to spread the report that he was at loggerheads with the central government and had been called to give an account of himself. Needless to say, not too much credence should be attached to these rumors; it was probable that the governor had other business on hand as well as purely matters of local interest.[183]

Cemal Bey arrived in Adana in the evening of July 7 from his journey to İstanbul. He was received at the railway station by all the higher officials of the city and a guard of honor, composed of soldiers, gendarmes, and police with a military band, was drawn up on the platform. After the first greetings he mounted onto an extempore stage, decked with flowers, and made a speech to the assembled crowd. He stated that his efforts on behalf of this province had been successful and that a bright future was in store for the people of this district. On the morning of July 9 the acting British vice consul paid the governor a visit and congratulated him on his return to Adana. Cemal Bey appeared in excellent health and spirits and informed the British official that he was much pleased with the result of his journey to İstanbul and said that he had been able to obtain a considerable amount of money for municipal and public purposes, such as street repairing and building.[184]

The proposed tour of Cemal Bey, together with a number of notables of Adana, to Europe was later abandoned. It appeared that the governor, while in İstanbul, was given to understand that his absence from his post for a period of three months would not be possible and he, therefore, had to give up his intention of accompanying the notables of Adana on their journey. The latter, also, when they saw that the governor was no longer going to take part in the tour, decided not to go on with the scheme and the whole matter was indefinitely postponed.[185]

This proposition was the embodiment of an idea without precedent in the Ottoman Empire. It represented an unusual approach to the pressing moral and social problems of the country, and recognized the potential importance of the European civilization.

Just how seriously one ought to take this vision is certainly open to question. It is fair to say, however, that the increasingly desperate notion of constructing a unified nationality is not only a reflection of the Ottoman concern for the Armenian problem but also of the pivotal role which they attributed to the European civilization.

In the Cilician plain, five hundred thousand hectares (1,237,970 acres) of land awaited the German irrigation engineers. The country around Adana was to be made another Egypt. Already it was producing considerable quantities of cotton for export beside supporting a local cotton manufacturing industry which was rapidly expanding.[186] Although the wheat crop in Adana had been poor the cotton crop had proved unusually good. In 1909 the crop amounted to between fifty thousand and fifty-five thousand bales; in 1910 there were fifteen thousand bales more than the previous year.[187] The general production of cotton in the province of Adana in 1911 surpassed all previous years by 25–30 percent and reached the amount of ninety thousand to one hundred thousand bales. This increase was due to the greater yielding of the soil through better cultivation by machines and to the increased amount of planting caused by the higher ruling of prices these last years. The yielding of the soil was greater in 1911 than that of the preceding years.[188] There had been an increase of about 30 percent in the acreage devoted to cotton cultivation. The cotton spinning mills of Adana and Tarsus required about thirty-five thousand bales as a large mill, in addition to the three already existing, had begun operations in Tarsus. Two new cotton seed oil mills in Mersin were also working and used a large part of the local cotton seed which was produced in 1911. Decorticating machines, similar to those used in Russian Turkestan to separate the cotton from the boll, had already been introduced and were expected to gradually replace hand labor.[189]

In 1910 export rates again reached the high levels attained in the period between 1900 and 1905 and even surpassed them. The exports of cotton from Mersin in 1911 were valued at 1,875,870 dollars, divided principally as follows: Austria, 1,252,002; France, 83,722; Germany, 115,324; Italy, 180,042; and Spain, 209,238. The cotton seed crop amounted to thirty thousand tons, of which fifteen thousand tons were used locally for cattle feeding and six thousand tons for the Mersin oil mill. The remainder was exported to Britain. The cotton seed to the value of 28,466 dollars, the first ever made in Mersin, was exported to Britain also. Until 1915, there was no ethnoreligious tension indicating serious changes in the economic situation in the region.[190]

In mid-March 1910, it was communicated from Ceyhan to the Armenian patriarchate in İstanbul that the buildings burned during the recent events in the province of Adana were reconstructed. The good harmony between the various elements was augmenting more and more. The efforts exerted by Cemal Bey to bring out a complete union were above all praise.[191]

Sarkis Souine, who was sent by the Armenian Orphan Committee and the patriarchate to investigate the condition of the widows and orphans in Cilicia sent a detailed report from Adana. A few of the items were as follows. In Adana the 20,017 liras given by the government for the rebuilding of houses were used for 515 families, of which four hundred were Armenian. The loan of 50,000 liras for the farms in the province was at 6 percent for five years. A loan of 50,000 liras had been provided on the same terms for those merchants who owned immovable property. In Adana alone four hundred marriages took place among the Armenians from September 1909 to February 1910. The four Armenian schools of the city included twelve hundred pupils. The number attending the American, Jesuit, and Protestant Armenian schools was 450. In Adana there were 798 Armenian widows. Of these 350 became so at the time of the massacre. The remaining 448, however, having lost their relatives in the massacre, were equally in need of aid. These might be classified again as follows, 478 were absolutely dependent on aid, of whom 334 were able to work, if work was provided, and 144 were helpless. The most prevalent disease was affection of the eyes. The remaining 320, though in need at the time, would be able ultimately to support themselves. The number of widows in Catholic, Protestant, Syrian, and Chaldean circles was 342. The kinds of industries recommended by Souine as employment for these widows were stocking knitting, *yazma* making (muslin kerchiefs used for head coverings and turbans), and tailoring.[192]

The special commission of the Chamber of Deputies sent a request to the Armenian patriarchate asking for what object or objects the 10,000 Turkish liras voted in 1910 for the benefit of the widows and orphans in Adana province had been expended. The answer of the Kumkapı patriarchate was to the effect that this sum had been spent in establishing shops or factories where these widows might work. Several such factories had been opened at several points. Seventy-five knitting machines for knitting stockings had been secured from Britain, each giving employment to five women; of these about one-quarter had been sent to Tarsus and the rest to Hacin. A factory was also to be started in Adana city to teach these widows to sew.[193]

Toward the end of June 1910 there was a certain feeling of unrest throughout the province of Adana, as the Christian—and more especially the Greek—population became very nervous and imagined that rioting, or even massacre, might begin at any moment. This was due in great part to the rumors that were being spread abroad as to the strained relations between the Ottoman Empire and Greece on account of the Cretan difficulty. Meetings of protest against Crete, Greece, and the action of the powers were held throughout the Empire and they had a disturbing effect. Lately Mersin was thrown into a great state of alarm owing to the report that a secret meeting, under the auspices of the CUP, was held and a decision arrived at to make an attack on the Christians and foreigners in general, and more particularly Greeks. This plot was supposed to have been betrayed by two certain persons, and it was heard that some of the Mersin consuls and consular agents had telegraphed to their respective embassies and asked for the protection of some warships. In Adana there could not be said to be any open danger at the moment. The German consul at the city remarked that so long as the central government had made up its mind to keep things quite in the provinces, no disorder would ever take place at Adana or anywhere else; on the other hand, if the central government, either purposely, or through weakness, let it be shown that it was not going to take up any definite stand in the matter either one way or the other, then trouble might break out at any moment. All this was true, and the question as to the relative importance and meaning of the present state of alarm in Adana depended upon the policy of İstanbul, and also on the policy of the CUP.[194]

The presence of an officer of Cemal Bey's standing and experience was considered a pledge for the maintenance of authority and the protection of the lives not only of Christians but of the Muslims. At the beginning of July 1910, the correspondent of *Tanin* wrote from Adana in an optimistic vein in regard to the relations now existing between the Christians and Muslims. He attributed this favorable state of affairs to the fidelity and the impartiality of the new government.[195]

On July 23, 1910, the third anniversary of the establishment of constitutional government in the Ottoman Empire was celebrated. The world looked back to July 23, 1908, with astonishment and admiration for the way in which a nation secured for themselves a constitution and a representative government, without shedding blood. Constitution Day was celebrated in Adana with great signs of rejoicing. There was a great show of flags, and main streets were spanned by triumphal arches. The celebrations opened with a military review held on a large open space by the horse market. Besides the review, there was the singing of the Ottoman national anthem and the parade of the guilds. Cemal Bey had at the review made a long patriotic oration.[196]

On January 30, 1911, the vicar of the Armenian patriarchate called at the Sublime Porte to see Talat Bey, minister of the interior, but was obliged to go to the Chamber of Deputies before he succeeded in finding him. Disquieting word had been received at the patriarchate, as also in the Bible House, to the effect that a few days before, an intoxicated man had mounted to the gallery of a minaret in Adana and given the call to prayer, when it was not the prayer hour; this had terrified the Armenians, who were certain this must be a preconcerted signal. Certain red chalk marks were also found on the houses of some Armenians, and this added to the panic. When the vicar spoke of this to Talat Bey, the latter said that he had already inquired by telegraph of Cemal Bey, the governor of Adana, as to the situation: Cemal Bey had wired confirming the reports, saying that the guilty parties had been arrested and several punished, and that quiet was established. Talat Bey paid tribute to the noble ideals and the administrative ability of the governor of Adana, and assured the vicar that every precaution would be taken to avoid all trouble. He begged him to send someone to the Sublime Porte the next day to get all the information that might come from Adana. Later in the day, Talat Bey sent another telegram to the governor instructing him to complete the information by fuller inquiry and enjoined him to redouble his efforts to maintain order and to punish severely any one attempting to raise the least disturbance.[197]

The following letter from Thomas Davidson Christie gives the facts as seen at close quarters. On January 24, 1911, he wrote from Tarsus to William Peet, editor of *The Orient* and treasurer of the ABCFM in İstanbul, on the recent situation in Adana. The communication is worth quoting in length:

> About ten days ago some things took place in Adana that frightened the people there and here. A number of Christian houses and places of worship were marked in the night with red crosses, and threats were uttered. In consequence, several Christian families went down to Mersin. Mr. Chambers and the Consuls, among them Mr. Nathan the American Consul, went to see the *Vali*, who assured them that tranquillity would be maintained. He also remarked that the attack was really directed against him, rather than against the Christians—which was no doubt true, as he has many enemies. He has been as good as his word. Several men have been arrested and are now in prison. In order to discover them, it is said that the *Vali* went around by night disguised (as Haroun al Rashid used to do), and was successful. He also called together some suspicious characters of rank and reputation, and warned them in the most outspoken way of what the consequences would be to them in case of an outbreak. Yesterday he marched over a thousand soldiers through the principal streets, with trumpets and a full band of music, he and his officers at their head. This is said to have made a deep and wholesome impression. So the scared families are now coming back from Mersin. And all of us have more confidence than ever in our Governor-General, the most energetic and capable ruler that we have seen in these regions. It would be simply a terrible thing, if all that he has done in this Providence during the past year and a half for the restoration of confidence, peace, and prosperity, should now be overthrown.[198]

A lone and unauthenticated dispatch from Athens, which appeared in the public press in March 1911 to the effect that Adana and its region were on the verge of another outbreak of massacres, was sufficiently punctured by a paragraph from a letter sent by William Nesbitt Chambers, in which he described a fresh tour over the Cilician plain:

> A word in reference to the governmental administration of the district. We were impressed with the fact that travel was quite unrestricted and the district was in

perfect tranquillity. There were no reports of robbers or robbery. At one *gendarme* post I found a young Armenian *gendarme* in command of the post, with Moslem *gendarmes* serving under him; and this in the midst of villages almost entirely Moslem. He said that he had encountered no difficulty from Moslems in the discharge of his duty. This does not introduce the millenium in Turkey, but it is an interesting fact.[199]

The letter was written at and sent from Adana, where impartial and correct information was accessible. The author had only one wish in view, and that was to impart to his readers a true and thorough knowledge of the present Armenian troubles. He believed that the whole atmosphere on this subject had been polluted with falsehoods and exaggerations, and trusted that his letter would help in bringing some light on a question so often misrepresented.

After all, there was a disturbance at Adana, although, as was reported in the previous issue of *The Missionary Herald*, the implication that the city and region were on the eve of a wide outbreak of massacres was entirely unfounded. It seemed that when an intoxicated man mounted to the gallery of a minaret in Adana and gave the call to prayer at an hour not appointed, the Armenians, easily terrified after what they had endured, guessed it was a preconcerted signal. As a number of Christian houses and places of worship had been marked in the night with red crosses, and some threats had been uttered, a panic was quickly started; some families fled from the city. But Chambers and the consuls went at once to the governor, who promptly assured them that order would be maintained, and declared that the attack was really against him for having protected the Christians in their rights. At once he took steps to arrest and imprison the leading offenders; other suspicious characters were warned that he would hold them accountable for any outbreak. Soldiers were marched through the principal streets, with their officers and the governor at their head, to demonstrate the forces behind the law. Immediately order was restored, and the people who had been scared into flight returned to their homes. The total effect of the disturbance was to furnish new testimony to the capacity, zeal, and fairness of Cemal Bey. Chambers's statement concerning the good order in the district stood undisputed.[200]

Under the date of August 4, 1910, Chambers wrote from Adana to William Peet as follows:

> The day in Adana was a great success. I telegraphed the Governor of Adana from Smyrna asking him to receive the company. His aide de camp, with his carriage, was at the station to meet us. We all proceeded to the *konak* and enjoyed a half to three quarters of an hour call on His Excellency Djemal Bey. General Beaver and Dr. D.N. Beach made addresses, translated to Turkish by Pastor Ashgian. The *Vali* was not to be outdone and he made a very neat speech in reply which I put into English. At the close the Governor handed me the

decoration issued for Dr. Shepard for his most excellent work in relief work in the Baghche region. This I passed over to Mr. Nathan the American Consul for transmission to Dr. Shepard.[201]

For the special service rendered by Fred Douglas Shepard in the reconstruction work, he was awarded a decoration by Sultan Reşad. The following congratulatory letter of February 1, 1911, was from Cemal Bey:

> Your most honored favor, dated October 29, 1910, on hand. It was a great pleasure to me to hear from one of our sincere friends. The Young Turks, who are struggling for the welfare of their beloved country, know well how to appreciate the services even of those generous persons though of foreign birth. The decoration bestowed upon you by our Ottoman government is nothing compared with your most admiring sympathy shown to the suffering humanity. America is happy in having given birth to devoted sons like you, whose motto is to serve mankind. It was my humble duty to reach to the help of my wretched country; and I thank you for the sentiment which you will arouse toward the Ottoman Empire in America. We are grateful to our most true and humanitarian friends, who sympathetize with us at such a critical time as this. I wish to see you decorated with higher honors than this, and will feel myself always happy to hear from you and your good health.[202]

The American hospital at Adana was a direct outgrowth of the massacre of 1909; it was also a symbol of the better time that seemed to have dawned in the region, an era of growing confidence, recovery, and good will. The second year's work in the hospital showed that more than three hundred patients had been in the wards, representatives of ten different races and religions; seventy-seven hundred attended the daily clinics; and twelve hundred medical visits were made. In all, there were about twenty-six thousand treatments. Among the patients there were found many nationalities: Turks, Armenians, Greeks, and others living together, getting to know each other and often helping each other. Surely there could be no better way than this of breaking down prejudice and native hatred.[203]

In 1914 the hospital had room for from thirty to thirty-five beds. The men's ward was full, mostly of surgical cases. The record from 1913 reported three hundred inpatients, eight thousand clinic patients, and one hundred thousand treatments.

CEMAL BEY'S VIEWS ON LOCAL AND GENERAL POLITICS AND HIS DEPARTURE FROM ADANA

G. C. Donaldson Rawlins, the acting British vice consul at Adana, had the opportunity of taking a ride with Cemal Bey one day in August 1910, when the latter was passing a few days in the mountains above Mersin. On this occasion Cemal Bey spoke very openly and Rawlins had thought, therefore, that his thus freely expressed views upon local and general politics might not be without interest. The British official noticed firstly that the governor, when touching on national subjects, continually used the expression "we," and gave him the impression that this meant "the CUP." Touching on the general conditions of the country, Cemal Bey said that the present time was most critical as "they" had many enemies, but that, if the present line of policy could be continued for five years more, all opposition would be done away with and the country saved. To this end, went on the governor, a general disarmament must be carried out. Then branching of into more general politics Cemal Bey said that he, for his part, did not see the Ottoman Empire entering into any alliance whatsoever at present; the country was far too weak and poor and would, therefore, be certainly given the worst of the bargain. With regard to Greece the governor could hardly veil his dislike and indignation; he even said that the colors of that country ought not to be flaunted in the Ottoman Empire and that he had given orders that all Ottoman Greek subjects who had printed their houses white and blue, in this district, should repaint them a different color. Ending his somewhat heated remarks on this subject, the governor said that now that they had bought two battleships from Germany, the Ottoman government would be more easily able to hold its ground. The governor expressed his regrets at the battleships not being new, but added with a smile, that "half a loaf is better than no bread."[204]

Cemal Bey did not mince words in his protests. The governor told Rawlins that he was much grieved to see some articles in *The Times* which he thought were unnecessarily hostile to the present Ottoman policy, while the German press was unanimously favorable. To this the acting British vice consul replied that he had not read the articles in question and so was not competent to make any remarks on the subject; for his part, however, he said that it had pained him also to see several articles in Ottoman newspapers which had made use of rather harsh language when touching on Britain's attitude. Here Cemal Bey immediately said that he knew that there were many irresponsible writers but that he was sure that the general public opinion in the Ottoman Empire had not changed from its sympathetic attitude toward Britain; he had read, he said, lately a most favorable article in *Tanin* on the subject. The governor expressed great annoyance at the recent telegrams that some of the consuls at Mersin had sent—during his absence at İstanbul—reporting great unrest at that port and asking for warships. Cemal Bey appeared to have learned the exact contents of some of these consular dispatches and told Rawlins that what had annoyed him most was a dispatch to the Russian embassy in which the government at Adana was characterized as "weak and incapable"; this, said the governor, was a base insinuation, adding "the government of Adana is strong and fears nobody." From this last part of the governor's conversation it was easy for Rawlins to understand how deeply Cemal Bey resented foreign interference and criticism, and how awkward it would be for any consul in this district if any criticisms or written remarks of his were ever to come to the governor's knowledge.[205]

Charles Woods of the weekly *London Graphic*, after visiting Adana in 1911, noted that if the majority of local governors in the Ottoman dominions were as fair and liberal-minded as Cemal Bey, the reforms promised by the Young Turks would now be at least on the way to realization. One of the most liberal and up-to-date ideas possessed by Cemal Bey was his desire to found a permanent Ottoman orphanage at Adana for boys and girls left destitute by the intercommunal fightings. Woods indicated that the instruction in the school, which it was hoped might eventually contain five hundred children, was to be purely secular. Notwithstanding the fact that the Muslim and Christian children were to be allowed to go to their places of worship on Fridays and Sundays, respectively, no priest, Muslim or Christian, was to be allowed to enter the establishment. In order to be eligible for the orphanage, children had to be between the ages of six and eleven and have neither father nor mother.[206]

A letter from William Nesbitt Chambers, dated November 18, 1911, discusses a new educational life in that section of the Ottoman Empire: "The situation here in educational work is very interesting. The *Vali* has an efficient group of young men in the education department. At the present moment compulsory education is the most prominent thought; children between the ages of seven and fourteen are to be in school, and delinquents are to be fined. The consequence is that the schools are more than full."[207]

It is to be remembered that during the First World War years cordial interest in the American College in Beirut was evinced by Cemal Paşa. He paid a visit to the institution on April 3, 1915, during which he was accompanied by the governor of the city, Bekir Sami (Kunduh) Bey; Dr. Ali Galib Bey, the surgeon general of the Fourth Army; Ali Fuad (Erden) Bey; and several others of his staff. He was met at the steps of West Hall by the president and the professors. Cemal Paşa greeted Dr. Ward as an old friend and stated that he was warmly indebted to the American Red Cross Medical Mission (of which Dr. Ward was the director) for the excellent services which it had rendered to the sick and wounded soldiers. He said that he had already informed his colleagues in the cabinet at İstanbul of his satisfaction with this work. As the party entered the building, the spacious common room, which was appropriately decorated with the Ottoman and American flags and with the Red Crescent and Red Cross flags hanging side by side, presented an attractive appearance in the afternoon light.[208]

When diplomatic relations were broken off between the Ottoman Empire and the United States for two weeks from April 22 to May 7, 1917, the institution was closed, or rather its active work was suspended, except in the School of Nurses.[209] But doubtless owing to the influence of Cemal Paşa, the college was reopened and never closed again. Moreover, wheat and other supplies were obtained from the government at army rates at a time when the market price had become prohibitive.[210] The institution was the recipient of many favors from the commander of the Fourth Army.[211]

Zeeneb Charlton says as governor of Adana, Cemal Bey secured the confidence of all classes of the Armenian and Muslim population, as well as the regard of the foreign officials with him he came into contact; and his transference to Baghdad, in the capacity of governor, was deeply regretted.[212]

NOTES

1. "Catholicos Aram I Demands Reparations for Adana Massacres," *Asbarez*, October 30, 2009, p. 1.
2. Lassa Francis Lawrence Oppenheim, ed. Ronald Roxburgh, *International Law: A Treatise*, Vol. 1: *Peace* (London: Longmans, Green and Company, third edition, 1920), pp. 461–63. The same passage can be found in the first edition of the work published in 1905, ibid., pp. 346–47.
3. Roland Mnatsakanyan, "Adana Massacres Focus of Istanbul Workshop," *The Armenian Weekly*, November 13, 2009, p. 1. On Zabel Yessayan, see her (trans. Kayuş Çalıkman Gavrilof from the original Armenian edition published in 1911), *Yıkıntılar Arasında Tanıklık* (Among the Ruins: Testimony) (İstanbul: Aras Yayıncılık, 2014).
4. For a notable exception see, for example, Nejla Günay, "1909 Adana Olaylarından Sonra Yapılan Yardım Çalışmaları" (Relief Work Done After the Adana Events of 1909), *Akademik Bakış*, Vol. 2, No. 4 (Summer 2009).
5. On Cemal Paşa's life and career, see Nevzat Artuç, *Cemal Paşa: Askeri ve Siyasi Hayatı* (Cemal Paşa: His Military and Political Life) (Ankara: Türk Tarih Kurumu Basımevi, 2008) and Hikmet Özdemir, *Cemal Paşa ve Ermeni Göçmenler: 4. Ordu'nun İnsani Yardımları* (Cemal Paşa and the Armenian Emigrants: Humanitarian Assistance of the Fourth Army) (İstanbul: Remzi Kitabevi, 2009). Abridged English translations of both works are to be hoped for. Also consult Friedrich Freiherr Kress von Kressenstein, "Ahmed Djemal Pascha als Soldat," *Mitteilungen des Bundes des Asienkampfers*, Vol. 4, No. 9 (1922), pp. 1–5; Günter Herlt, "Aus Zeitschriften und Zeitungen," *Der Neue Orient*, Vol. 5, No. 1 (October 1918), p. 218; Willy Meyer, "Djemal Pascha," *Germania*, No. 49 (February 1923).
6. Yücel Güçlü, "The Role of the Ottoman-Trained Officers in Independent Iraq," *Oriente Moderno*, Vol. 82, No. 2 (2002), pp. 442–43.

7. Colonel Cemal Bey being promoted to the rank of Brigadier General on January 3, 1914, was thenceforth called Cemal Paşa. See BOA, Harbiye İradeleri (Imperial Decrees of the Ministry of War), January 3, 1914.

8. Yalçın, *Tanıdıklarım*, p. 53; Cemal Paşa, *Hatıralar*, p. 14; Çiçek, *War and State Formation in Syria*, pp. 3–4.

9. Cemal Bey was appointed to provincial governorship of Adana on August 1, 1909, and his term of duty terminated on June 14, 1911. See BOA, Dahiliye İradeleri (Imperial Decrees of the Ministry of the Interior), August 1, 1909 and June 14, 1911.

10. Kodaman and Ünal, *Son Vakanüvis Abdurrahman Şeref Efendi Tarihi*, p. 129.

11. Nazan Maksudyan, "Cemal Bey'in Adana Valiliği ve Osmanlıcılık İdeali" (The Adana Governorship of Cemal Bey and His Ideal of Ottomanism), *Toplumsal Tarih*, No. 176 (August 2008), pp. 22–23.

12. "Adana Valisi Cemal Bey" (The Governor of Adana Cemal Bey), *İttihad*, August 5, 1909, p. 1.

13. Tunaya, *Türkiye'de Siyasi Partiler*, Vol. 3, p. 277.

14. MAE, NS Turquie, Vol. 83, p. 162. Le Lt. Colonel Djemal, Vali d'Adana. Maurice Bompard (Istanbul) à Stéphane Pichon (Paris), 11 août 1909; Yalçın, *Tanıdıklarım*, p. 53.

15. Çiçek, *War and State Formation in Syria*, p. 4.

16. Murat Bardakçı, ed., *Mahmud Şevket Paşa'nın Sadaret Günlüğü* (The Grand Vizierial Diary of Mahmud Şevket Paşa) (İstanbul: Türkiye İş Bankası Kültür Yayınları, 2014), pp. 242, 256, 277, 279, and 297.

17. Dagobert von Mikusch, trans. John Linton, *Mustapha Kemal: Between Europe and Asia* (London: William Heinemann Ltd, 1931), p. 124.

18. "İstanbul Muhafızı Cemal Beyefendi İle Mühim Bir Mülakat" (An Important Interview With the Military Governor of İstanbul Cemal Beyefendi), *Tanin*, June 23, 1913, p. 1.

19. İhsan Nuri Sır, "Cemal Paşa İstanbul Muhafızlığından Nasıl İstifa Etmişti?" (How Had Cemal Paşa Resigned From the Office of İstanbul Military Governor?), *Tarih Konuşuyor*, Vol. 2, No. 17 (December 1950), p. 719.

20. Ahmad, *The Young Turks and the Ottoman Nationalities*, p. 15.

21. Daniel Allen Butler, *Shadow of the Sultan's Realm: The Destruction of the Ottoman Empire and the Creation of the Modern Middle East* (Washington, DC: Potomac Books, 2011), p. 52.

22. Sanders, *Five Years in Turkey*, p. 5.

23. Frank Chambers, *The War Behind the War 1914–1918: A History of the Political and Civilian Fronts* (London: Faber and Faber Limited, 1939), p. 541fn22.

24. On Sir Wyndham Deeds, see John Presland (pseud. for Gladys Skelton), *Deeds Bey. A Study of Sir Wyndham Deeds, 1883–1923* (London: Macmillan, 1942).

25. Percival George Elgood, *Egypt and the Army* (London: Oxford University Press, 1924), p. 104.

26. *Le Temps*, Editorial, 4 juillet 1914, p. 1.

27. Yücel Güçlü, *Historical Archives and the Historians' Commission to Investigate the Armenian Events of 1915* (Lanham, MD: University Press of America,

2015), p. 103; Edward Erickson, *Ottomans and Armenians: A Study in Counterinsurgency* (New York: Palgrave Macmillan, 2013), p. 113; Aydemir, *Makedonya'dan Ortaasya'ya Enver Paşa*, Vol. 3: 1914–1922, pp. 15–25. For details of Enver Paşa's military career, see Hülya Toker and Nurcan Aslan, eds., *Birinci Dünya Savaşına Katılan Alay ve Daha Üst Kademedeki Komutanların Biyografileri* (Biographies of the Regiment and More Senior Level Commanders Who Participated in the First World War), Vol. 3 (Ankara: Genelkurmay Basımevi, 2009), pp. 8–10.

28. Karl Klinghardt, *Denkwürdigkeiten des Marshalls Izzet Pascha. Ein kritischer Beitrag zur Kriegsshuldfrage* (Leipzig: K. F. Koehler, 1927); Theodor Werner, *Die Türken unter des britischen Faust 1918–1923* (Berlin: Deutsche Informationsstelle, 1940). Text of the Secret Treaty of Alliance Between the Ottoman Empire and Germany of 2 August 1914 in Carl Mühlman, *Deutschland und die Türkei, 1913–1914* (Berlin-Gruneland: Walther Rothschild, 1929), pp. 94–95.

29. See Nazmi Eroğlu, *İttihatçıların Ünlü Maliye Nazırı Cavid Bey* (Cavid Bey: The Famous Minister of Finance of the Unionists) (İstanbul: Ötüken Neşriyat, 2008); Yalçın, *Tanıdıklarım*, p. 25; Murat Bardakçı, *Enver* (İstanbul: Türkiye İş Bankası Kültür Yayınları, 2015), p. 114; Us, *Karikatür*, pp. 31–34 and 182; Butler, *Shadow of the Sultan's Realm*, pp. 62–63.

30. Polat Tunçer, *İttihatçı Cavit Bey* (The Unionist Cavit Bey) (İstanbul: Yeditepe Yayınevi, 2010), p. 3.

31. See, among others, the front pages of *Tanin* and *İkdam* of August 13, 1909.

32. "Les projets du vali d'Adana," *Le Moniteur Oriental*, 7 août 1909, p. 2.

33. "Young Vali of Adana; Armenians Are Pleased with Appointmet of Djemal Bey," *The New York Times*, August 3, 1909, p. 3.

34. Margaret McGilvray, *The Dawn of a New Era in Syria* (New York: Fleming H. Revell Company, 1920), pp. 142 and 146–47. This is an ordinary survey written with a pronounced bias and without any attempt to put the Armenian question into a larger setting. Margaret McGilvray was the secretary of the Beirut Chapter of the American National Red Cross in 1914–1917.

35. BOA, DH. MKT, No. 2896/86. Appointment of Cemal Bey as Provincial Governor of Adana, August 11, 1909; MAE, NS Turquie, Vol. 83, p. 163. Nouvelles d'Adana et de Mersine. Barré de Lancy (Mersine) à Stéphane Pichon (Paris), 16 août 1909.

36. BOA, DH. MKT, No. 2888/15. Dismissal of Mustafa Zihni Paşa, July 31, 1909; BOA, DH. MKT, No. 2892/34. Change in the Governorship of the Province of Adana, August 4, 1909; BOA, BEO, No. 3610/270712. Dismissal of Mustafa Zihni Paşa, August 4, 1909; Woods, *The Danger Zone of Europe*, pp. 194–95.

37. MAE, NS Turquie, Vol. 83, p. 162. Nouvelles de la région. Barré de Lancy (Mersine) à Stéphane Pichon (Paris), 10 août 1909.

38. MAE, NS Turquie, Vol. 83, p. 161. Nouvelles d'Adana. Barré de Lancy (Mersine) à Stéphane Pichon (Paris), 3 août 1909.

39. Charles Woods, "The Internal Situation in Turkey and the Effect of the War Upon It," *The Fortnightly Review*, Vol. XCI (January–June 1912), p. 336.

40. BOA, MV, No. 130/68. Decision of the Council of Ministers on the Formation of the International and Ottoman Relief Committees, August 15, 1909.

41. "Adana Hadisatı" (Adana Events), *Tanin*, May 26, 1909, p. 1.

42. Pears, *Turkey and Its People*, pp. 293–94.

43. Edwin Pears, "Developments in Turkey," *The Contemporary Review*, Vol. XCVII, No. 6 (June 1910), p. 695.

44. Edwin Pears, "Turkey and the War," *The Contemporary Review*, Vol. CVI, No. 5 (November 1914), p. 585. An eighteen-member Ottoman parliamentary delegation, led by Talat Bey, visited London and other British cities on July 17 to August 1, 1909. They visited the Foreign Office and the House of Commons and held talks with officials and politicians. At the Buckingham Palace they were received by the king. See "Turkey in England: The Visit of the Delegates from Constantinople," *The Near East*, Vol. 2, No. 16 (July–August 1909), pp. 25–30.

45. Hüseyin Cahid Yalçın, *Talat Paşa* (İstanbul: Yedigün Neşriyatı, 1943), pp. 45–49; Ali Haydar Mithat, *Hatıralarım 1872–1946* (My Reminiscences 1872–1946), pp. 299–300; Biren, *II. Abdülhamid, Meşrutiyet ve Mütareke Devri Hatıraları*, Vol. 2, pp. 79, 101–102, and 110; Howard Sachar, *The Emergence of the Middle East 1914–1924* (New York: Alfred Knopf, 1969), p. 104.

46. Sanders, *Five Years in Turkey*, p. 4.

47. Aubrey Herbert, Desmond MacCarthy, ed., *Ben Kendim: A Record of Eastern Travel* (London: Hutchinson and Co., 1924), p. 307.

48. See Dagobert von Mikusch, trans. John Linton, *Mustafa Kemal: Between Europe and Asia* (London: William Heinemann Ltd, 1931), pp. 132–33.

49. Lord Kinross, *The Ottoman Centuries*, p. 596.

50. Eric Bogosian, *Operation Nemesis: The Assassination Plot That Avenged the Armenian Genocide* (New York: Little, Brown and Company, 2015), p. 63.

51. Bourne and Watt, British Documents on Foreign Affairs, Part II, Series B: Turkey, Iran, and the Middle East, Vol. 1: The End of the War, 1918–1920, p. 446.

52. "Empire News," *The Orient*, Vol. 6, No. 48 (December 1, 1915), p. 7.

53. Bogosian, *Operation Nemesis*, p. 64.

54. A lengthy discussion of Talat Paşa's career can be found in İnal, *Osmanlı Devrinde Son Sadrazamlar*, Sect. 13, pp. 1933–72.

55. Ibid., p. 1962.

56. Yalçın, *Tanıdıklarım*, pp. 41–42.

57. Bogosian, *Operation Nemesis*, p. 64.

58. Anatolian News Agency, February 25, 1943.

59. Hüseyin Cahid Yalçın, "Sirkeci Garında" (In the Railway Station of Sirkeci), *Tanin*, February 25, 1943, p. 1.

60. "Talat Paşa'nın Naşı" (Remains of Talat Paşa), *Ulus*, February 26, 1943, p. 1.

61. Yunus Nadi Abalıoğlu, "Talat Pacha," *La République*, 26 février 1943, p. 1.

62. Ahmet Emin Yalman, Editorial, February 26, 1943, p. 1.

63. "A Man to the Rescue," *The Missionary Herald*, Vol. 105, No. 11 (November 1909), p. 484. For the voting of the Ottoman Chamber of Deputies of 30,000 Turkish liras for feeding the destitute see, *Meclisi Mebusan Zabıt Ceridesi*, Vol. 3, p. 210.

64. BOA, DH. MKT No. 2899/23. Departure of Cemal Bey from İstanbul. Ministry of the Interior to the Acting Governor of Adana, August 13, 1909; BOA, DH. MKT No. 2914-1-2. The First Practices of the New Governor of Adana Cemal Bey, August 28, 1909.

65. "Cemal Bey'in Adana'ya Vusulu" (Cemal Bey's Arrival in Adana), *Tanin*, August 20, 1909, p. 1.
66. FO 195/2307. Arrival of the New Governor in Adana. R. E. W. Chafy (Adana) to Sir Gerard Lowther (Istanbul), August 25, 1909.
67. Ibid.
68. Ibid; MAE, NS Turquie, Vol. 83, p. 164. Arrivée du Vali d'Adana, Djemal Bey. Barré de Lancy (Mersine) à Stéphane Pichon (Paris), 20 août 1909.
69. "Lettre d'Adana," *Le Moniteur Oriental*, 10 septembre 1909, p. 2.
70. FO 195/2307. Arrival of the New Governor in Adana. R. E. W. Chafy (Adana) to Sir Gerard Lowther (Istanbul), August 25, 1909; MAE, NS Turquie, Vol. 83, p. 164. Arrivée du Vali d'Adana, Djemal Bey. Barré de Lancy (Mersine) à Stéphane Pichon (Paris), 20 août 1909.
71. MAE, NS Turquie, Vol. 83, p. 164. Arrivée du Vali d'Adana, Djemal Bey. Barré de Lancy (Mersine) à Stéphane Pichon (Paris), 20 août 1909.
72. FO 195/2307. Cemal Bey's Meeting With the Heads of Christian Communities. R. E. W. Chafy (Adana) to Sir Gerard Lowther (Istanbul), September 1, 1909.
73. Frederick Bliss, "Djemal Pasha: A Portrait," *The Nineteenth Century and After*, Vol. DXIV (December 1919), p. 1151.
74. BOA, MV, No. 130/86. Formation of Relief Committees, August 15, 1909; FO 195/2307. Arrival of the New Governor in Adana. R. E. W. Chafy (Adana) to Sir Gerard Lowther (Istanbul), August 25, 1909; MAE, NS Turquie, Vol. 83, p. 164. Arrivée du Vali d'Adana, Djemal Bey. Barré de Lancy (Mersine) à Stéphane Pichon (Paris), 20 août 1909.
75. Ibid.
76. Shepard, "Personal Experience in Turkish Massacres and Relief Work," pp. 331 and 337.
77. Ibid., p. 337.
78. Ibid., p. 338.
79. MAE, NS Turquie, Vol. 83, p. 164. Arrivée du Vali d'Adana, Djemal Bey. Barré de Lancy (Mersine) à Stéphane Pichon (Paris), 20 août 1909.
80. MAE, NS Turquie, Vol. 83, p. 164. Sujet du Vali d'Adana. Barré de Lancy (Mersine) à Stéphane Pichon (Paris), 30 août 1909.
81. FO 195/2307. Cemal Bey's Meeting With the Heads of Christian Communities. R. E. W. Chafy (Adana) to Sir Gerard Lowther (Istanbul), September 1, 1909.
82. Ibid.
83. "Adana Hakkında" (On Adana), *Tanin*, August 30, 1909, p. 1.
84. MAE, NS Turquie, Vol. 83, p. 164. Sujet du Vali d'Adana. Barré de Lancy (Mersine) à Stéphane Pichon (Paris), 30 août 1909.
85. "The Conflict in the Provinces," p. 484.
86. BOA, BEO, No. 3622/271581. Entrustment of the Presidency of the Adana Government Relief Committee to Cemal Bey, August 19, 1909; BOA, DH. MKT, No. 2907/35. Adana Government Relief Committee, August 22, 1909; FO 195/2307. First Report of the Adana Government Relief Committee. R. E. W. Chafy (Adana) to Sir Gerard Lowther (Istanbul), September 22, 1909.

87. FO 195/2037. Changes in the Province of Adana and the Progress of the New Governor's Reforms and Relief Measures. R. E. W. Chafy (Adana) to Sir Gerard Lowther (Istanbul), September 15, 1909.

88. Ibid.

89. Ibid.

90. BOA, BEO, No. 3622/271581. Entrustment of the Presidency of the Adana Government Relief Committee to Cemal Bey, August 19, 1909; BOA, DH. MKT, No. 2907/35. Adana Government Relief Committee, August 22, 1909; FO 195/2307. First Report of the Adana Government Relief Committee. R. E. W. Chafy (Adana) to Sir Gerard Lowther (Istanbul), September 22, 1909.

91. "A Man to the Rescue," pp. 484–85.

92. Patricia Goldstone, *Aaronsohn's Maps: The Untold Story of the Man Who Might Have Created Peace in the Middle East* (Orlando, FL: Harcourt, Inc., 2007), p. 9.

93. McGilvray, *The Dawn of a New Era in Syria*, p. 142.

94. Blaisdell, *Missionary Daughter*, p. 76.

95. Djemal Pasha, *Memories of a Turkish Statesman 1913–1919*, pp. 261–62. Also BOA, DH. MUİ, No. 1-4/23, Enclosure No. 2. Sum of 200,000 Turkish liras Placed at the Disposal of Cemal Bey, November 9, 1909.

96. Djemal Pasha, *Memories of a Turkish Statesman 1913–1919*, p. 262.

97. Arıkoğlu, *Hatıralarım*, pp. 58–61; Artuç, *Cemal Paşa*, pp. 71–79.

98. Kévorkian, "The Cilician Massacres, 1909," pp. 364–65.

99. Andrew Ryan, *The Last of the Dragomans* (London: Geoffrey Bles, 1951), p. 66.

100. Ibid., p. 85.

101. Blaisdell, *Missionary Daughter*, pp. 77–78.

102. FO 371/780. Affairs in the Levant: Report from H.M.S. "Barham." Herbert Adam, Commander to Admiralty, October 13, 1909.

103. FO 195/2307. Rumors of Fresh Troubles in Adana. R. E. W. Chafy (Adana) to Sir Gerard Lowther (Istanbul), September 29, 1909.

104. Ibid.

105. FO 195/2307. Panic Among Christian Population of Adana at Approach of Bairam. R. E. W. Chafy (Adana) to Sir Gerard Lowther (Istanbul), October 13, 1909.

106. FO 195/2307. Comments on Second Report of Adana Government Relief Committee. Growing German Influence in the Adana Province. R. E. W. Chafy (Adana) to Sir Gerard Lowther (Istanbul), November 10, 1909.

107. Ibid.

108. Ibid.

109. MAE, NS Turquie, Vol. 83, pp. 182–83. Exécutions à Adana. Barré de Lancy (Mersine) à Stéphane Pichon (Paris), 14 décembre 1909; MAE, NS Turquie, Vol. 83, p. 184. Nouvelles exécutions dans le vilayet d'Adana. Barré de Lancy (Mersine) à Stéphane Pichon (Paris), 23 décembre 1909. For a lucid analysis of the theme, see Cezmi Yurtsever, *Müftüyü İdam Ettiler* (They Executed the Mufti) (Adana: Çukurovalı Yayınları, 2013); and "Fifty Moslems Hanged," *The Missionary Herald*, Vol. 106, No. 1 (January 1910), p. 126.

110. MAE, NS Turquie, Vol. 83, p. 162. Nouvelles d'Adana et de Mersine, Barré de Lancy (Mersine) à Stéphane Pichon (Paris), 6 août 1909.

111. ABCFM Papers, Houghton Library, Harvard University. Unit (5) Reel 669. Vol. 23 Central Turkey Mission 1910–1919 Letters A-CHA ABC 16: The Near East 1817–1919. Letter from William Nesbitt Chambers (Geneva) to James Barton (Boston), March 22, 1918.

112. Shepard, "Personal Experience in Turkish Massacres and Relief Work," p. 338.

113. FO 371/2337. The Situation at Adana. Charles Doughty-Wylie (Adana) to Sir Gerard Lowther (FO), January 24, 1910.

114. Ibid.

115. Ibid.

116. "The Asiatic Provinces of Turkey," *The Times*, February 16, 1910, p. 5.

117. For this point I am in debt to Cezmi Yurtsever.

118. Bourne and Watt, British Documents on Foreign Affairs, Part I, Series B, Vol. 20, p. 198. On the hostile feeling against Cemal Bey among the Muslims, see also MAE, NS Turquie, Vol. 84, p. 26. Voyage à Adana. M. Ronflard (Mersine) à Stéphane Pichon (Paris), 14 avril 1910.

119. FO 195/2337. The General Condition of the City of Adana and the Surrounding Districts. G. C. Donaldson Rawlins (Adana) to Sir Gerard Lowther (Istanbul), February 14, 1910.

120. "La Fraternisation à Adana," *Le Moniteur Oriental*, 7 février 1910, p. 1.

121. MAE, NS Turquie, Vol. 83, pp. 238–39. Sujet de réconciliation à Adana. Barré de Lancy (Mersine) à Stéphane Pichon (Paris), 9 février 1910.

122. Gust, *The Armenian Genocide*, p. 635.

123. FO 195/2337. The General Condition of the City of Adana and the Surrounding Districts. D. C. Donaldson Rawlins (Adana) to Sir Gerard Lowther (Istanbul), February 14, 1910.

124. Ibid.

125. Ibid.

126. Ibid.

127. Ibid.

128. FO 195/2337. Release of Prisoners on the Anniversary of Sultan's Accession. D.C. Donaldson Rawlins (Adana) to H. C. A. Eyres (Istanbul), April 29, 1910.

129. Joseph Heller, *British Policy towards the Ottoman Empire 1908–1914* (London: Frank Cass, 1983), pp. 104–5.

130. Ramazan is the ninth month of the Muslim year, when Muslims fast during the hours of daylight.

131. "The Latest from Adana," *The Missionary Herald*, Vol. 105, No. 12 (December 1909), p. 551.

132. FO 195/2337. The General Condition of the City of Adana and the Surrounding Districts. D. C. Donaldson Rawlins (Adana) to Sir Gerard Lowther (Istanbul), February 14, 1910.

133. FO 195/2337. Governor's Visit to Hadjin. G. C. Donaldson Rawlins (Adana) to Sir Gerard Lowther (Istanbul), February 18, 1910.

134. MAE, NS Turquie, Vol. 84, pp. 6–7. Nouvelles d'Adana. Barré de Lancy (Mersine) à Stéphane Pichon (Paris), 10 mars 1910.

135. Brézol, *Les Turcs ont passé là*, p. 137.

136. "The Hadjin Problem," *The Orient*, Vol. 3, No. 34 (August 21, 1912), pp. 5–6.

137. Ibid., p. 6.

138. Harold Gardner, "A High Commission of Embroidery," *The Missionary Herald*, Vol. 106, No. 3 (March 1909), p. 109; "The Provinces," *The Orient*, No. 10 (June 22, 1910), p. 6; "The Provinces," *The Orient*, No. 21 (September 7, 1910), p. 4.

139. MAE, NS Turquie, Vol. 84, pp. 45–46. L'organisation de la police du Vilayet. Le Gendarmerie du Vilayet. M. Ronflard (Mersine) à Stéphane Pichon (Paris), 25 avril 1910.

140. FO 195/2337. The New Gendarmerie School. D. C. Donaldson Rawlins (Adana) to Gerard Lowther (Istanbul), March 29, 1910.

141. "News Items," *The Levant Herald*, February 2, 1910, p. 1.

142. Kaligian, *Armenian Organization and Ideology Under Ottoman Rule 1908–1914*, p. 71.

143. FO 195/2337. Unrest Among the Population of Adana. D. C. Donaldson Rawlins (Adana) to H. C. A. Eyres (Istanbul), May 9, 1910.

144. FO 195/2366. Nervousness at Adana. D. C. Donaldson Rawlins (Adana) to H. A. C. Eyres (Istanbul), January 21, 1911.

145. FO 195/2366. Nervousness at Adana Subsiding; Governor's Article in the Local Press. D. C. Donaldson Rawlins (Adana) to H. A. C. Eyres (Istanbul), January 28, 1911; MAE, NS Turquie, Vol. 85, p. 22. Nouvelles d'Adana. Barré de Lancy (Mersine) à Stéphane Pichon (Paris), 26 janvier 1911.

146. James Harbord, "Investigating Turkey and Trans-Caucasia," *The World's Work*, Vol. 15 (May–October 1920), p. 41. James Harbord had commanded American troops at Soissons and Château-Thierry in France, and served as chief of staff under General John Pershing in 1917–1918.

147. ABCFM Papers, Houghton Library, Harvard University. Unit 5 (ABC 16.9.5) Reel 664 Vol. 19 Central Turkey Mission 1900–1909 Letters M-R ABC: The Near East 1817–1919. The International Relief Committee For the Sufferers in the Vilayets of Adana and Aleppo.

148. Ibid.

149. Ibid.

150. Ibid.

151. Ibid.

152. Ibid.

153. Chambers, *Yoljuluk*, pp. 91–93.

154. "An Ottoman Ideal," *The Missionary Herald*, Vol. 105, No. 12 (December 1909), pp. 544–45.

155. BOA, BEO, No. 272207. Orphanage of Adana. Ministry of the Interior to Cemal Bey (Adana), September 3, 1909; MAE, NS Turquie, Vol. 84, p. 53. Prêtre Français recueille orphelins d'Adana. M. Ronflard (Mersine) à Stéphane Pichon (Paris), 7 mai 1910. For a discussion of renewed scholarly interest in the Cilician orphans of

1909, see Cezmi Yurtsever, *Çukurova Tarihi Valiler, Derebeyler, Eşkiyaların Bitmeyen Kavgaları* (The History of Cilicia: Unending Fights of Provincial Governors, Feudal Lords and Brigands) (Adana: Çukurovalı Yayınları, reprinted, 2011), p. 254; idem, *1915 Sahibini Arayan Belgeler* (1915: Documents Looking for Their Owner) (Adana: Çukurovalı Yayınları, 2009), p. 49; idem, *Atatürk ve Çukurova Kahramanları* (Atatürk and the Heroes of Cilicia) (Adana: Çukurovalı Yayınları, 2010), pp. 79–80. The books are valuable for the information they contain and for the author's judgments. They merit more attention than they deserve.

156. Gardner, "A High Commission of Embroidery," pp. 109–10.

157. ABCFM Papers, Houghton Library, Harvard University. Unit 5 (ABC 16.9.5) Reel 662. Vol. 17 Central Turkey Mission 1900–1909 Letters B-C ABC16: The Near East 1817–1919. The Constitution of the Commission of Industries, December 27, 1909.

158. Ibid.

159. Gardner, "A High Commission of Embroidery," pp. 109–10.

160. Chambers, *Yoljuluk*, p. 94.

161. Gardner, "A High Commission of Embroidery," p. 109.

162. Ibid., pp. 110–11; Woods, *The Danger Zone of Europe*, p. 142; Alice Shepard Riggs, *Shepard of Aintab* (New York: Interchurch Press, 1920), pp. 123–24.

163. BOA, BEO, No. 275112. Report to the Committee on Building and Relief. Cemal Paşa (Adana) to the Ministry of the Interior, October 15, 1910; "The Government Relief in Adana," *The Orient*, Vol. 1, No. 1 (April 20, 1910), p. 3.

164. Ahmet Şerif, "Adana," *Tanin*, April 21, 1910, p. 1. Ahmet Şerif, Çetin Börekçi, ed., *Anadolu'da Tanin* (Tanin in Anatolia) (Ankara: Türk Tarih Kurumu Basımevi, 1999), p. 191. This book provides exceptionally good information on the general situation of the bureaucracy and the demands of the newly rising local elites in Anatolian and Syrian towns. It is interesting to note that this was the first instance in the history of the Turkish press that a correspondent visited the countryside reporting with the purpose of establishing channels of communication with the towns in order to learn what the countryside people expected from the government and to disseminate there the ideas of the Young Turk revolution. This was in fact the first major occasion in which a modern pattern of communication between the government and the citizens at large was established. See Karpat, "The Memoirs of N.Batzaria," p. 279fn1. Also "A Turkish Correspondent's Views," *The Orient*, Vol. 1, No. 2 (April 27, 1910), p. 2; "The Provinces," *The Orient*, No. 12 (July 6, 1910), p. 3; and Yesayan, *Yıkıntılar Arasında*, p. 244.

165. "Notes," *The Orient*, Vol. 1, No. 3 (May 4, 1910), p. 4.

166. MAE, NS Turquie, Vol. 84, pp. 6–7. Nouvelles d'Adana. Barré de Lancy (Mersine) à Stéphane Pichon (Paris), 10 mars 1910; Blaisdell, *Missionary Daughter*, p. 102.

167. Cavid Bey, *Meşrutiyet Ruznamesi*, Vol. 1, p. 316.

168. Ali Rıza Bey, "Adana ve Havalisi Hakkında İktisadi Tedkikat" (Economic Studies on Adana and Its Vicinity), *Ayın Tarihi*, Vols. 10–11, Nos. 29–34 (September 1926–1927), p. 1563; MAE, NS Turquie, Vol. 83, pp. 243–244. Nouvelles de la région. Barré de Lancy (Mersine) à Stéphane Pichon (Paris), 19 février 1910.

169. MAE, NS Turquie, Vol. 84, pp. 6–7. Nouvelles d'Adana. Barré de Lancy (Mersine) à Stéphane Pichon (Paris), 10 mars 1910; Elizabeth Webb, "Report of Adana Seminary 1909–1910," *The Orient*, No. 14 (July 18, 1910), p. 2.

170. "Les Travaux Publics à Adana," *Le Moniteur Oriental*, 15 février 1910, p. 2.

171. MAE, NS Turquie, Vol. 84, pp. 71–74. Les Puissances étrangères dans le Vilayet d'Adana. Les Allemands. M. Ronflard (Mersine) à Stéphane Pichon (Paris), 17 mai 1910.

172. FO 195/2337. German Enterprise and Activity in Adana. D. C. Donaldson Rawlins (Adana) to H. C. A. Eyres (Istanbul), July 6, 1910.

173. Ibid.

174. MAE, NS Turquie, Vol. 84, pp. 6–7. Nouvelles d'Adana. Barré de Lancy (Mersine) à Stéphane Pichon (Paris), 10 mars 1910.

175. FO 195/2337. Government Reconstruction in Kessab. Raphael Fontana (Aleppo) to Sir Gerard Lowther (FO), March 5, 1910.

176. "Notes," *The Orient*, Vol. 1, No. 4 (May 11, 1910), pp. 3–4.

177. FO 195/2337. Planned Voyage to Europe by Djemal Bey. D. C. Donaldson Rawlins (Adana) to Sir Gerard Lowther (Istanbul), March 18, 1910.

178. MAE, NS Turquie, Vol. 84, pp. 56–59.Voyage en Europe du Vali et la groupe d'habitants d'Adana. M. Ronflard (Mersine) à Stéphane Pichon (Paris), 8 mai 1910.

179. FO 195/2337. Planned Voyage to Europe of Djemal Bey. D. C. Donaldson Rawlins (Adana) to H. C. A. Eyres (Istanbul), April 29, 1910.

180. Ibid.

181. Ibid.

182. Ibid.

183. FO 195/2337. Departure of Djemal Bey for Istanbul. D. C. Donaldson Rawlins (Adana) to H. C. A. Eyres (Istanbul), June 2, 1910.

184. FO 195/2337. Arrival of Djemal Bey in Adana. D. C. Donaldson Rawlins (Adana) to H. C. A. Eyres (Istanbul), July 9, 1910.

185. FO 195/2337. Governor's European Tour Abandoned. D. C. Donaldson Rawlins (Adana) to H. C. A. Eyres (Istanbul), July 10, 1910.

186. "Irrigation in Anatolia," *Levant Trade Review*, Vol. 1, No. 1 (June 1911), p. 60.

187. "The Provinces," *The Orient*, Vol. 1, No. 31 (November 16, 1910), p. 6.

188. Demosthenes Lydiardopoulos, "News from Mersine," *Levant Trade Review*, Vol. 1, No. 3 (December 1911), p. 336.

189. "Irrigation in Anatolia," pp. 111–12.

190. Toksöz, *Nomads, Migrants and Cotton in the Eastern Mediterranean*, pp. 197–98; idem, "Adana Ermenileri ve 1909 İğtişaşı" (Armenians of Adana and the Revolt of 1909), in Fahri Aral, ed., *İmparatorluğun Çöküş Döneminde Osmanlı Ermenileri: Bilimsel Sorumluluk ve Demokrasi Sorunları* (Ottoman Armenians in the Decline Period of the Empire: Scholarly Responsibility and the Questions of Democracy) (İstanbul: Bilgi Üniversitesi Yayınları, 2011), p. 154; Edward Nathan, *Levant Trade Review*, Vol. 2, No. 2 (September 1912), p. 126; Redan, *La Cilicie et le problème ottoman*, p. 116.

191. "A Adana," *Le Moniteur Oriental*, 16 mars 1910, p. 1.

192. "The Provinces," *The Orient*, Vol. 1, No. 11 (June 29, 1910), p. 7.

193. "Adana Widows and Orphans," *The Orient*, Vol. 2, No. 41 (January 25, 1911), p. 5.

194. FO 371/2337. Uneasiness Among Christian Population. G. C. Donaldson Rawlins (Adana) to H. C. A. Eyres (Istanbul), June 23, 1910.

195. *Tanin*, July 1, 1910, p. 3.

196. "Kanuni Esasimizin Üçüncü Senei Devriyesi" (The Third Anniversary of Our Constitution), *Tanin*, July 24, 1910, p. 1; *İkdam*, July 24, 1910, p. 1.

197. "Situation at Adana," *The Orient*, Vol. 3, No. 43 (February 8, 1911), p. 4.

198. Ibid.

199. "An Interesting Fact," *The Missionary Herald*, Vol. 57, No. 3 (March 1911), p. 103.

200. "Disturbance at Adana," *The Missionary Herald*, Vol. 57, No. 4 (April 1911), pp. 153–54.

201. "The Athena Party in Adana," *The Orient*, Vol. 1, No. 19 (August 24, 1910), p. 5.

202. Riggs, *Shepard of Aintab*, pp. 124–25.

203. "A Busy Hospital," *The Missionary Herald*, Vol. 57, No. 9 (September 1911), pp. 407–8.

204. FO 195/2337. Summary of a Conversation With H. E. The Vali of Adana. G. C. Donaldson Rawlins (Adana) to Sir Gerard Lowther (Istanbul), August 27, 1910.

205. Ibid.

206. Woods, *The Danger Zone of Europe*, p. 195. On the orphanage at Adana and Cemal Bey, see also "Le patriarche arménien et le vali d'Adana," *The Levant Herald*, June 27, 1910, p. 2.

207. "Where Turk and Christian Cooperate," *The Missionary Herald*, Vol. 107, No. 2 (February 1911), p. 82.

208. "Editorial," *The Orient*, Vol. 6, No. 19 (May 12, 1915), p. 5.

209. The United States never declared war on the Ottoman Empire, though it withdrew all its consular officials from Ottoman domains upon entering the war against Germany.

210. Daniel Bliss, *The Reminiscences of Daniel Bliss* (New York and London: Fleming Revell Company, 1920), pp. 225–26.

211. McGilvray, *The Dawn of a New Era in Syria*, p. 141.

212. Zeeneb Charlton, "Six Ottoman Patriots," *The Nineteenth Century and After*, Vol. 124, No. CCCCXLII (December 1913), p. 1227.

Chapter Eight

Post–1911 Adana and Cemal Paşa

CEMAL BEY'S GOVERNORSHIP IN BAGHDAD

The arrival of the new governor, Cemal Bey, formerly governor of Adana, was eagerly awaited at Baghdad. The reports about him were mostly favorable.[1]

"To the lover, Baghdad is not far off." "A false account will come back even from Baghdad." By these and such like proverbs the Turk of İstanbul, more than a century ago, confessed the remoteness of the sun-baked lands of Euphrates and Tigris. Thanks to its ancient fame, its strategic position, and present scale, Baghdad had always had easy primacy over the two other renowned cities of Iraq, Mosul, and Basra; and even at the turn of the twentieth century, after Mosul had emerged finally as a province in 1879 and Basra in 1884, the governor of Baghdad was by every standard the senior of the three governors. Iraq's place in the Ottoman Empire was determined by various factors. Its remoteness and its fierce climate were among considerations which made service in it the dread of most Ottoman officials.[2]

John Gordon Lorimer, the British resident and consul general at Baghdad between 1909 and 1913, wrote in his political diary for the month of March 1910 that the universal Ottoman system of administration was in almost every respect unsuitable to Iraq. He continued as follows. The Ottomans themselves must recognize that it was a failure here, but probably few of them appreciated the cause, though that was sufficiently obvious. Iraq, in the opinion of Lorimer, was not an integral part of the Ottoman Empire, but a "foreign dependency," very much in the rough; its government by sedentary officials according to minute regulations, framed at İstanbul for Anatolia, could never be satisfactory. The British resident and consul general had no idea before coming to Baghdad of the extent to which the Ottoman Empire was a country of red tape and blind and deaf officialdom, nor of the degree in which the

Ottoman position in Iraq was unsupported by physical force. One could not but admire, however, the dogged and uncomplaining resolution with which the Ottoman civil bureaucracy and skeleton army persisted in their impossible tasks, the former in that of governing according to code and paragraph, the latter in that of maintaining a semblance of order. This description might be taken as indicating the position of affairs in the province of Baghdad when Cemal Bey assumed his governorship on August 30, 1911.[3]

However, this interpretation calls for two comments. First, the province of Baghdad benefited from the restoration of the Ottoman Constitution in 1908. As the new government in İstanbul did its best to disseminate the idea of constitutionalism throughout the empire, it sent emissaries to the provinces of Baghdad, Basra, and Mosul and elsewhere to educate the population in the benefits of the constitution. Each of the provinces returned three members to the Chamber of Deputies in İstanbul and so acquired what experience of parliamentary government and constitutional rule could be obtained in ten years as an outlying part of a loosely knit empire. The new administration not only seated that parliament but also organized elections in 1908, 1912, and 1914.[4] Second, as Hasan Kayalı explains, Ottoman elections, despite their shortcomings, provided precedents and standards that have yet to be equaled in the Arab Middle East and many other parts of the world. They introduced the Middle Easterners to fundamental norms of political participation and mobilization, and defined main contours of political contestation that have endured long after the empire. These elections served both to legitimate the constitutional representative system and to promote political citizenship in the state.[5]

The Arabs were brethren in faith with the Turks but had a number of grievances against the Ottoman administration. In Baghdad, the poets Maruf al-Rusafi and Jamil Sidqi al-Zahawi criticized absolute rule's injustices while remaining loyal Ottoman subjects. When the Young Turk revolt occurred, therefore, Iraqis saw the new regime as one of reform. The Young Turks, following their revolution, made a gesture of good will toward the Arabs. The policy of Ottomanism was adopted with a view of assuring common loyalty to the Empire on the basis of equality. Iraq never was a Turkish colony; it was part of the Ottoman Empire which had been independent for more than six centuries. Neither was the state Turkish, but Ottoman. This meant that it gathered under its banner different peoples. The Iraqis were not under the yoke of Turkish rule. They shared, rather, government together with the Turks and the other peoples, in all departments of the state: there was no discrimination in rights and duties between the Turks and the Iraqis; they shared offices, high positions, and the good and the bad equally. The Iraqis had exercised government, justice, administration, and politics for succeeding centuries, not only in Iraq, but in all parts of the Ottoman Empire, which extended to Europe, Asia, and Africa.[6]

It is important to keep in mind the fact that the main source of the constitution of the Ottoman Empire was the Holy Book, from which both the Turk and the Arab derived their religion, spirituality, law, and culture. Ottoman rule did not affect, in any way, Arab authority in the country. Arab lands indeed continued to be ruled by Arab chiefs whose authority was recognized as legitimate by the Ottoman sovereign. Thus the effective rulers of Baghdad went on to be the Gaylanis, of Mosul the Umaris, of Süleymaniye the Babans, and so on. The Turks had only a governor in Baghdad who represented the central government there. Otherwise the Arab chiefs enjoyed autonomy in their respective zones. After the introduction of the new Ottoman system of public administration by the *Hattı Hümayun* of 1856 the Arab continued to keep his status, as the equal of the Turk. Careers were open to talent. From Iraq many Arabs held high position in the Ottoman state hierarchy. Many ministries were occupied by Arabs and many a general, governor, and ambassador were Arabs. Arab officers and officials were not distinguished from their Turkish colleagues. They received the same pay and exercised the same authority as their equals of Turkish mother tongue. Therefore it was plain that the Arab was coruler with and not a subordinate to the Turk, and they enjoyed full share of power and representation in the Ottoman Empire.[7]

There is one point which one must always bear in mind, and that is that British interests in the Baghdad province were of far longer standing to those of any other country. The British resident was of far older standing and had a far superior position to the consul generals of the other powers. British interests, and especially British Indian interests, comprised not only the ancient trade between India and Mesopotamia, but there was also all the pilgrim trade traffic between India and the Holy Places at Kerbela and Nejef to be considered, as well as the large trade with Iran through Baghdad.[8] The British resident and consul general at Baghdad presided over a far more considerable establishment than other foreign representatives. With their own residency surgeon and dispensary, the river steamer the *Comet* of the Royal Indian Marine, their guards of sepoys, and their extraterritorial Indian post offices, successive residents had been forced by the jealous disfavor of the Ottoman governors to fight hard for their privileges.[9]

The retention of the title "resident" was questioned by the Young Turks, to whom it suggested the status of a native state in India. This resemblance was confirmed in Turkish eyes by the fact that the post was always given to a member of the Indian Political Service, supported by a guard of thirty-odd sepoys and by a small vessel of the Royal Indian Marine. The Ottoman government recognized the official only as consul general, but in the India Office

List he was shown as "Resident in Turkish Arabia" until the outbreak of the First World War.[10]

The first dragoman of the British Consulate General visited Cemal Bey, shook hands with him, and congratulated him on behalf of John Gordon Lorimer on the very first morning of his arrival at Baghdad. Some foreign consuls were accustomed to send dragomans to meet the governor at distance from the city and might have done so on the present occasion but such had not been the British practice. Lorimer was the first consul to call personally on the governor and, by way of doing him honor, he took with him the whole European staff of the residency, namely the commander of the Royal Indian Marine steamship *Comet*, Lieutenant C. O. Campbell; the residency surgeon, Captain Norman Scott; and the commercial assistant, J. C. Gaskin. On Cemal Bey's returning Lorimer's call, the British consul general invited him to dinner but he declined on account of *Ramazan*. Lorimer said he neglected no means of showing consideration for the governor and could only regret that contrary impression had been conveyed to İstanbul. In conveying it to the governor, in the opinion of Lorimer, might have had some political end in view, for example, to make the British consul general appear to his government as hostile and prejudiced against him from the beginning.[11]

New conditions always involve new duties. The abstract of the appointment decree of Cemal Bey to the province of Baghdad is given in the following. (1) The governor was to turn the rivers of Mesopotamia, to use the conventional though somewhat inaccurate designation, to account by means of navigation and irrigation. (2) At least 40,000 liras would be granted annually by the Ministry of Public Works for Baghdad purposes. (3) The governor was empowered to appoint and dismiss all civil officers, except those of the ordinary Judicial and Shar'i Departments. (4) The governor was to reorganize the police and open a police school if possible. (5) The gendarmerie were to be entirely under the governor's orders, and all gendarmerie correspondence with İstanbul would be conducted through him in future. (6) The governor was to formulate a scheme, with the least possible delay, for the settlement of the nomad tribes upon the land. (8) Two regular regiments at Baghdad and one at Basra were to be at the governor's disposal; if at any time he thought it necessary that the reservists should be called out he might, without previous reference to İstanbul, request the inspector general of the Fourth Inspectorate to summon them.[12]

After the public reading of his decree of appointment at the government house on August 30, 1911, the new governor delivered the following speech whose outlines ran as follows. Cemal Bey was conscious of three feelings in regard to Iraq: the first was a feeling of respect and admiration for its former state; the second was a feeling of grief and sorrow for its present state; and the third was a feeling with regard to its future—to its bright future, which was inseparable from the constant progress and elevation of the Ottoman nation—and to its honor. It was impossible that any one reading the history of the past of this fortunate region should not pause long in admiration. In the distant past ages also, before the illumination of the whole world by the light of Muhammadanism, very great services were rendered to the civilization of mankind by the human being whose brain was developed by the heat of the sun here; as regards the civilization which the land of Iraq attained after the appearance of Islam, it reached a degree of elevation not vouchsafed to any spot in the regions of the earth, and when the whole human world was crushed under a heavy nightmare of ignorance, the land of Iraq presented to the view a heavenly world bathed in the beautiful rays of the sciences and branches of knowledge, and all the regions of the earth directed their glances of observation and admiration, relevant to the time, toward this point. The Muhammadan scholars of Baghdad who composed and put into literary form the invention of the clock—that orderer of the time of man—the proof of the roundness of the world, the determination of the meridian and, finally, countless and innumerable eternal monuments including medicine, philosophy, literature, mathematical sciences and astronomy, breathed the air of this very land, were warmed by this very sun, slaked their thirst with the water of this very land, and lived on the natural products afforded by this very land for the use of humanity. But, alas, the successors who came after them did not make the necessary effort to follow the traces of their glorious ways; the bright sun of learning and knowledge which had been revealed in this land of Iraq became gradually dim; and naturally, in this manner, wealth and affluence disappearing, they were left in a state of ignorance, nomadism, dispersion, and weakness.[13]

Some attributed the present ruined state of the region to the thirty-three-year-long Hamidian regime, but this view was not correct; the period of decline of the land of Iraq had begun five hundred or six hundred years ago, and the Hamidian regime had only been the cause of its reaching an extreme point. Because of the national rights having been restored after the 1908 revolution, because of a constitutional and legal government having been established, because of the land of Iraq being still the same land, the air being the same air, the sun being the same sun, the Tigris and Euphrates—each of which was a spout flowing with gold and silver—being the same Tigris and Euphrates, and because of its inhabitants also having been fostered in exactly the same environment and under the same influences, Cemal Bey was absolutely sure of the future, of the brilliant future, of this happy region. As long as he remained among the inhabitants of Baghdad he would work for this future to the utmost of his power. And the new governor hoped that he would have all his fellow countrymen with him in the conversion from an idea into a reality of this difficult duty entrusted to him, for the strength and sole support of constitutional government was nothing else than the organization of individuals in a group. Therefore the government and the nation must be one and must help and support one another in undertakings for making the region flourish. It was necessary to unite in the form of a single group against the assailants of the nation in order that the acquisition of life and power might be rendered possible. Only Cemal Bey was determined to break the power of the traitors and dissidents who made bold to stretch out the hand of injury toward this honored and united group.[14]

There was no difference in the eyes of the government or of the law between poor and rich, between great and small, or between any of the individuals of the Ottoman body which was composed of the individuals forming the nation. All of them were equal. The rights of everyone were and would be protected. The officials of government, in consequence of their being appointed to secure the maintenance of good relations among individuals, and in consequence of their receiving their salaries also from the individuals of the nation, were the servants of the nation. Accordingly everyone should know that the door of the government was open to everybody, and that, for the purpose of a reference to government, there was not the slightest need for the intervention of Zeyd or Ömer (the equivalents in Islamic law of the English John Doe and Richard Roe).[15]

This well-publicized speech was not mere rhetoric. In private, too, Cemal Bey expressed himself in similar tones. The speech foreshadowed the direction that governor's policy would take. The development of undertakings in which Cemal Bey was interested included river navigation and construction of irrigation works. He wrote several reports on the economic potential of this remote province on the eastern marches of the Ottoman Empire. The problem was that it was easy to list goals but difficult to lay down how to attain them. The governor meant business, but the task would not prove easy. The main obstacle to carrying out works of improvement on a large scale was the problem of finding sufficient funds to meet the initial outlay.

In the nineteenth century some measures of reform were effected in the land. The territory was reorganized into three administrative provinces. The bureaucracy and the financial arrangements were improved. During the governorship of Midhat Paşa in 1869–1872, an enlightened reformer, land tenure reform was initiated, a more effective police system introduced, and an attempt at town planning and at enforcement of modern laws was made. In addition, some secular schools were established, and the tribes were brought under much closer discipline.[16]

Midhat Paşa discerned that if nomad tribes were to be reduced to anything like permanent order, a radical change had to be brought about in their general status, and especially the conditions of land tenure in the region. The Arab cultivator, for the most part, held their lands from the state on the condition of giving three-fourths of the produce to the state, retaining one-fourth for themselves. Such a system naturally discouraged agriculture and rendered all improvements in cultivation impossible. The consequence was that, for the most part, the Arab shunned the soil, preferring predatory to industrial modes of gaining their living. Midhat Paşa determined to attach the Arab to the soil by giving them rights of proprietorship, and divided large tracts of land into plots, which were offered for sale on easy and advantageous terms, special provision being made against accumulation of plots into single hands. The success of this policy was remarkable, and whereas the revenues of the state increased, the turbulence of the tribesmen, and the risings which had become chronic, greatly diminished.[17]

The agricultural prosperity that resulted from these measures stimulated other branches of industry and rendered it necessary to provide outlets for the newly created surplus of the region. The first step in this direction was to render nagivable the Euphrates and Tigris, the great arteries of the land, and to improve or create the means of communication between their two banks, and between the different towns situated along their course. The only service of the kind that existed consisted of the boats of a British company plying between Baghdad and Basra. Midhat Paşa decided to start a service of Ottoman boats to supply adequately the needs now felt, in the same way that he had formerly done on the Danube when he was governor of Tuna province. He ordered the existing vessels to be repaired, new vessels of a larger tonnage to be constructed, and coal depots to be formed at Muscat, Aden, Bender Abbas, and Bushire; now, for the first time in history, steamers under the Ottoman flag were to be seen periodically in the Suez Canal, on their way to İstanbul.[18]

Drainage works on a large scale, with a view of reclaiming marsh lands and of curing the insalubrity, were also undertaken. Irrigation works were likewise started, and much attention was devoted to this subject by Midhat Paşa. A tramway, too, between Baghdad and Kazimiye was constructed, and its entire length, eleven kilometers, completed within a year. A textile manufactory, too, was started, and an engine of seventy horsepower ordered in France, the dispatch of which was only delayed by the breaking out of the Franco-German War (1870).[19]

While energetically pursuing these material improvements, Midhat Paşa was far from neglecting the moral side of the problem of reform. Schools were opened in every district; hospitals, refuges for old age, and loan banks everywhere rose; a printing press was established where the newspaper *Zora* was published; and municipal institutions for lighting and watering and other local purposes were instituted in all the principal centers. A petroleum spring discovered in the province of Baghdad was immediately utilized for public purposes. It was not too much to hope that a decade of such enlightened government would have repaired the neglect of centuries and restored their ancient prosperity to the rich valleys of the Euphrates and Tigris.[20]

In 1911 the province of Baghdad was no longer the isolated backwater of a hundred years previously. Although the way of life of most of its people had scarcely changed, the region was supporting an increasing population and improvements in living standards, especially in the cities, were discernible.[21]

The province of Baghdad had vast potential riches in material resources—oil, water, and underdeveloped land—and the expectation of important future development. At the beginning of the twentieth century not only foreign travelers and diplomats but Ottoman statesmen in the Sublime Porte and incoming governors eager for progress spoke of railways, canal schemes, minerals, extended river navigation, bridges, and town planning. The territory had held for many years its place in world trade, with its interest for steamship lines and market seekers reorientated by the opening of the Suez Canal in 1869. It was valued by strategists then as now the only land approach to the Persian Gulf and, more generally, as the traditional land bridge of East and West.[22]

It is to be mentioned that it was the desire of the Ottoman government not only to ameliorate the province of Baghdad and to increase and develop its wealth and trade, but also to reorganize and improve the Thirteenth Army Corps. The province of Baghdad was also important in regard to foreign policy. The political situation of Iran and the delimitations of the zones of influence in this country were the factors that had prompted the Sublime Porte to choose a strong governor. Cemal Bey was known to be zealous and trustworthy, and he possessed a wide knowledge of civil and military affairs. The new and ambitious governor set to work to consolidate his reputation as soon as he arrived in Baghdad and took matters in hand almost immediately. He investigated the condition of the staff of the Army Corps, that of the military officers and the civil officials. He dismissed at once those who were incapable among them and substituted others. And he saw to it that the technical requirements in connection with these measures were fulfilled without delay by the various departments concerned.[23]

Public interest at Baghdad chiefly centered in Cemal Bey, the new governor. Political circles of all descriptions were much occupied by him. He made a striking impression. He was a very effective speaker. When he made his long, unprepared, rambling speeches, he paused at the appropriate points to permit the chanting and cheering of the crowds.

On September 7, 1911, Major General Ali Rıza Paşa, the commander of the Thirteenth Army Corps, entertained the governor at dinner at the Military Club and after dinner made a speech in which he said that the good relations existing between the military and civil elements were a happy augury for the future of the country, and especially for that of Iraq. Cemal Bey replied, and an eloquent speech was made by the *kaymakam* of Najaf, who was also present. On the next day, which was Friday, the governor visited Muadhdham, a few kilometers from Baghdad, where the tomb of the great Sunni theologian Abu Hanifah was situated, and where the government now proposed to establish a famous college on the model of those which existed at Baghdad in the days of the Caliphate. The same evening, at a dinner given at the club of the CUP, the governor spoke strongly in favor of the CUP and said that he was sorry that they had only one school at Baghdad. At an ordinary meeting of the Union and Progress Club, about three weeks later, speeches were delivered and subscriptions collected on behalf of the CUP's existing school. The contributions amounted to 170 liras, of which 20 was given by the governor. A current story illustrated the undecided attitude, as yet, of the people toward their new ruler. According to this story a man in the bazaar criticized the governor for having done nothing since his arrival. "What would you have?" said the person addressed. "Has he not come to Baghdad?" The first desideratum in a governor of Baghdad was, no doubt, that he should come to Baghdad. The former Governor Nazım Paşa's arrival here was awaited for six months, and that of the new governor during about three. In each case the delay seemed to have been due to protracted bargaining between the governor and the Sublime Porte in regard to the terms of his appointment.[24]

On September 17, Cemal Bey gave a dinner at his residence to all the editors of newspapers in Baghdad. At this dinner he was reported to have said that the contract given to the Germans for the construction of the Baghdad railway would ruin the Ottoman Empire. The fault was that of Sultan Abdülhamid II, who originally gave the contract. The former monarch had made the mistake of giving "too much face" to foreigners in general, with the result that the said foreigners now considered themselves the rulers of the country. Even foreign travelers conducted themselves in the Ottoman Empire as if they were governors. The present Ottoman constitutional government should not give way to foreigners any longer. The interests of Ottoman subjects should be considered before those of foreigners; at present they came in the second place. He advised the editors to impress these ideas on those whom they met. The governor seemed also to have promised that the Baghdad official newspaper or gazette, the *Zaura*, should again appear in Arabic as well as Turkish, as was the custom before Nazım Paşa's time, and that its scope should be increased. A few days later the governor, when dining with the *Naqib* (the head representative of the notables) of Baghdad at the latter's house near the shrine of Abdul Qadir, was said to have inculcated the same views on his host as he had done on the journalists, and to have asked him to give them currency in the Arab world. According to the British consul general's information he added, on this occasion, that the Arabs, though they might be offered cheap rifles and ammunition for purchase imported from abroad, should not imagine that the Ottoman government was too weak to put an end to the illegal traffic.[25]

At both the Military Club and Union and Progress Club dinners Cemal Bey was reported to have said that the Ottoman Empire was in a position to defy any single great power with impunity, because the other great powers would immediately intervene to prevent unfortunate consequences. At the Military Club he was said to have added "Europeans are accustomed to think that the Turks are afraid of them. This is no longer the case, and Europeans ought to know it." It was impossible for the British consul general to be certain that the above speeches had been reported with perfect correctness, but, according to him, due allowance being made for exaggeration, enough remained to show that Cemal Bey was making it a habit to talk more or less publicly in a strain unbecoming to any official, and especially to one a large part of whose functions was (or should be) to maintain friendly relations with the representatives of foreign powers. Russia, Britain, Austria, and Italy had all been attacked by him by name, and even Germany had not been spared. So far as the Arabs were concerned his language was likely to fall on deaf ears, but it was calculated to encourage junior officers of the army, petty officials, *et hoc genus omne*, to provocative conduct toward Europeans.[26]

The governor as the representative of the sultan dealt with the heads of local communities, foreign consuls, and the greater tribal chiefs. The general and nondepartmental administration was in his hands. He directed the municipalities, settled tribal disputes, heard multifarious grievances, and through the *Defterdar* influenced or controlled the all-important field of land revenue.[27]

Cemal Bey's right-hand man appeared to be Sevian Efendi, the Armenian sent from İstanbul as director of the Ottoman Government Line of Steamers. He was a remarkable linguist. He talked English idiomatically and with a perfect accent, though he had never lived in any English-speaking country. He had traveled in India, however. Though strongly prejudiced in this gentleman's favor by the opinions of European friends who had known him before at Baghdad, the British consul general formed a very unfavorable impression of his attitude at one of their first interviews, and John Gordon Lorimer was not surprised afterwards to hear a European remark: "Sevian Effendi s'est vendu aux Turcs." The British consul general was convinced that F. W. Parry (the representative of Stephen Lynch and of the Euphrates and Tigris Steam Navigation Company) and Whitley (Sir John Jackson and Company Limited's representative) would be very imprudent if they relied on the good will and offices of this individual, as they at present seemed disposed to do.

In the opinion of the British consul general, in some respects Cemal Bey was more intelligent than Nazım Paşa, but he seemed to command less respect. His invitation of the Baghdad journalists to dinner was a good move, and one that would never have been taken by Nazım Paşa, who regarded all pressmen as vermin. Lorimer took Cemal Bey for an honest and public-spirited but tactless and wrongheaded man. Kudret Bey, the new governor's political secretary, was a Turk of good family, about thirty years of age. He was brought up partly in Beirut and spoke Arabic as well as Turkish, which was a great recommendation and one not possessed by his predecessor Eram Bey, though the latter was born at Baghdad.[28]

Sevian Efendi held an important position. Cemal Bey must have appreciated the devotion, discretion, and reliability of the man. He was the model of an Ottoman gentleman, a man of *haute culture* as well as *bon vivant*. The Armenians were useful to the Turks. They supplemented each other's qualities, and they worked well together.

On October 5, a meeting was held at the Union and Progress Club, at which the most influential Muslims of Baghdad was present. Patriotic speeches were delivered, and resolutions were passed in favor of enrolling volunteers and collecting subscriptions for the war with Italy over Tripolitania.[29] The members of the meeting attended by a large crowd, then adjourned to the *Konak*. Here they were received by Cemal Bey, who made a speech complimenting them on their patriotism and saying that they had verified his description of Iraq as an "iron door" of the Ottoman Empire, but counseling calmness and attention to the instructions of government. He remarked that the Italians at Baghdad were few in number, and that the relations of the Ottoman Empire with all powers except Italy were friendly. The governor was followed by Jamil Effendi, brother of the Mufti of Baghdad, who spoke in Arabic and urged the people to join a Committee of National Defense. This committee was said to have been founded by Cemal Bey. On October 11, a mass meeting of Jews was held in one of the Baghdad synagogues, at which the grand rabbi spoke. He urged that the Jews should support the Turks who had treated them well when the rest of Europe persecuted them, as part of it did still. A Jewish Branch Committee of National Defense was thereafter formed.[30]

There were four Italian subjects with their families at Baghdad: Dr. Lanzoni, quarantine inspector under the Board of Health, İstanbul; de Kirico, an official of the Régie; Enriquez, a merchant; and one of the teachers in the school of the Alliance Israélite Universelle. None of these had been treated in a manner in which he could fairly complain. Dr. Lanzoni and de Kirico had been suspended, but they had no right to expect different treatment. Enriquez was at first ordered to discontinue his business, but he had since been allowed to carry it on. Dr. Lanzoni was sent for in the beginning by Cemal

Bey, three or four gendarmes came to his house to fetch him, which made him fear that he would be imprisoned. He accordingly called at the German consulate (which was in charge of Italian interests at Baghdad) on the way and asked that, if he did not return in two hours, inquiries might be made about him; his interview with Cemal Bey was, however, of an ordinary character. The attitude of the Ottoman authorities here had been, the British consul general said, correct and praiseworthy. They did their best to arouse patriotic feelings without exciting fanaticism; when it appeared that the volunteering movement might get out of hand, they quietly and promptly checked it. Everywhere officials had set a good example by subscribing very liberally to the war fund, some of them perhaps beyond their means.[31]

At the beginning of November 1911, the governor of Baghdad advertised for a dragoman with a knowledge of English and Turkish. It was stated that Cemal Bey was desirous of understanding the views of the Indian newspapers on political questions. This dragoman would also attend to the province's correspondence with manufacturers in Europe and America.[32]

Positive changes took place in the city and province of Baghdad since the arrival of Cemal Bey. He desired to supervise personally the slightest details of the administration. The governor visited the schools personally again and again, and he worked tirelessly to secure permanent and practical results. He was absolutely impartial toward all creeds and races. Matters did improve over time. With the exception of Friday, the *Konak* was a veritable beehive for seven hours in the day in spite of the terrible heat. The governor's successful efforts to regulate the price of bread brought him the blessings of women and children as he passed through the streets. Another fact worth recording was that, since the coming of Cemal Bey, robbery and petty thieving had entirely ceased. Things did move, especially where he had anything to do with them.[33]

The force of civil police in Baghdad was increased from seventy to two hunded men, and four public-spirited citizens undertook the cost of building four new police stations in the city. These satisfactory developments were attributed to the representations and influence of Cemal Bey.[34] He was also anxious to form a police camel corps, and the idea seemed a good and practical one.[35]

In the days of Cemal Bey there was security of life and property in the province. People usually left their houses unguarded and shots did not ring out at night over Baghdad as a matter of ordinary occurrence. Respectable men moved about outside the city and the desert roads were peaceful. People longed for peace and permanent security which the new governor's strength was able to supply. The inhabitants of Baghdad witnessed the progress, material and moral, under an efficient administration. The development of the city in the matter of roads, bridges, lighting, water, telegraphs, etc., turned the minds of all classes in a practical direction, and all were anxious to share in the improvements introduced.[36]

Financially the budget of the province of Baghdad had until 1911 presented a deficit which had been converted into a small surplus as the result of financial readjustments and increased taxation. How complicated the existing financial arrangements were may be judged by the fact that no less than five departments of government, apart from the General Revenue, were independently collecting monies and remitting them to İstanbul. These departments were firstly the Régie, a foreign concession; secondly, the *Wakf* (religious endowments); thirdly, the *Sanniyah* (crown lands); fourthly, the Ottoman Debt, to the service which some twenty odd petty taxes were allocated besides 3 percent on customs; and fifthly, the International Board of Health which collected so-called quarantine fees impartially from the dead and from the living. The net result of these five excrescences was that the normal life of the people was interfered with at almost every step and that no unification of system or taxation was possible. References to İstanbul on petty details of administration were incessant, and the hope of local autonomy which had come to birth in the Arabic-speaking provinces of the Ottoman Empire after the 1908 revolution could not, even if it received official approval, had taken place.[37]

Nothing had made for public contentment more than that the voice the people had been allowed in their own affairs. This applied particularly to the municipalities. Municipal bodies existed before 1908, but they lacked organization and guidance and were never allowed adequate power. Cemal Bey cared for all these things and succeeded to supply a certain driving power essential to Arabs. The affairs of the Baghdad Municipality were a source of great difficulty, Nazım Paşa having left that body bankrupt without the means of carry on even its ordinary duties. The municipality was almost entirely without funds even for necessary purposes. The normal requirements of municipalities, cleaning, lighting, organization of markets, and the like had been met out of municipal funds as directed by municipal councils under the guidance of the new governor.[38]

The ruins of the old dams and canals that once turned the Euphrates and Tigris to useful ends were still visible. The water was there; the soil was exceptionally rich, for the floods carried down a greater percentage of fertilizing silt than the Nile; and nothing was needed to bring back the prosperity of the land but good government, enterprise skillfully directed, and an outlay which, compared with the prospective return, was a mere trifle.[39]

Such occurrences and conditions are not to be explained as due solely to Ottoman "misrule" nor can they be entirely accounted for through the Ottoman Empire's "neglect" to provide any proper system of administration for the peoples within its domain. In part, at least, the conditions in Baghdad and the adjacent provinces were the result of the kind of diplomatic policy followed by the Great Powers concerned for their own interests and actuated by motives of rivalry, or fear of a predominating influence of one power over a portion or the whole of Mesopotamia.[40]

The governor of Baghdad made a flying tour in January 1912 to the Khalis, an irrigated tract lying a short distance to the north of Baghdad. Cemal Bey creditably distinguished himself among Baghdad governors by his activity in making himself personally acquainted with different parts of his province.[41] He was also busy with schemes for the improvement of Baghdad and was referring for guidance to town planning experts in France. Another scheme of the governor was one for preventing floods at Baghdad by embanking the Tigris above the city.[42]

Cemal Bey did his best to free the administration from corruption and abuses and increase its efficiency. Measures were studied to introduce agricultural credit, assist irrigation, correct the injustices or inequalities of taxation, and farm fees. A liberal and progressive policy was pursued. Both townsmen and tribesmen were freely consulted on their own problems, and they were given unrestricted access to the office of the governor.[43]

Like in Adana, Cemal Bey was not swayed by motives of self-interest nor proved lax in the execution of his duties. He was strictly scrupulous in matters of finance. When he left office he could boast, as was the case with Vespasian before he was emperor of Rome, that he was poorer man than when he was appointed.[44] In mid-September 1911, he indignantly refuted the accusation brought against him by the İstanbul daily *Alemdar* that he acquired vast property in Adana. Cemal Bey telegraphed his lawyer in the capital, Abdurrahman Adil, asking him to start legal proceedings against *Alemdar* for libel. It is extremely unlikely that there was anything in the nature of conspiracy, but Cemal Bey was genuinely upset and indignant. The affair highlighted the importance which he attached to his career, and his self-image as a patriotic servant of his sovereign and country. It left him depressed and embittered.[45]

The details regarding the alleged malpractices of Cemal Bey, during the tenure of his post in Adana, provided by acting British vice consul Lieutenant Ian Smith in that city in his report of October 30, 1911, ran as follows. Since the departure of the present governor of Baghdad from Adana there was a good deal of persistent talk both in Muslim and Christian circles about certain contracts which he made and transactions which took place during his governorship, in which he was said to be associated with several Europeans holding prominent positions in the city. So far nobody in Adana came forward to make public allegations of malpractices against the late governor himself, and owing to the wholesome respect which Cemal Bey's authority still inspired among the people in the province and to the knowledge that he was closely connected with the leaders of the CUP, it was unlikely that any individual would venture to do so. Still the fact remained that there was a very general feeling among the people in Adana that the late governor was not above using his position for the furtherance of his personal interests. There was no proof of such being the case, and even were a thorough and impartial investigation made of the transactions which were the subject of suspicion, it would appear that they were conducted in such a secret manner that nothing would result. However, no steps were taken by the central government in the way of appointing a committee of investigation.[46]

In the course of one or two conversations Smith had with the present Governor Muammer Bey, the subject of the allegations against Cemal Bey came to the front. The former admitted that everything was not right and that malpractices took place in several instances. He was personally quite sure that Cemal Bey served no personal interests in what he did, but he blamed him for making contracts for public works in which several foreigners intrigued to fill their own pockets at the expense of the state. He mentioned the names of M. Rosetti, the late municipal engineer, and M. Grabowsky, the late manager of the Imperial Ottoman Bank, recently transferred to Baghdad. The fact that he followed the governor to Baghdad gave point to the allegations made by people in Adana. Stanislav Kozlovski, general agent to the construction of the second section of the Baghdad railway, was also mentioned.[47]

Smith was personally very loath to believe that there was any truth in these stories about Cemal Bey. He was a man with a great belief in himself, he had little experience of the financial side of business or administration, he had large ideas for the improvement of Adana, and seeing only the end in views, he was impatient of the details leading up to it. Taking into account that one part of the inhabitants in Adana were always ready to charge an official with malpractices for the reason that he was a Turk, and the other part because they were accustomed to dishonesty on the part of their former governors, the allegations made against Cemal Bey might very likely be void of foundation and there was more reason to believe that the malpractices which took place were carried out by those who knew how to take advantage of his belief in his own powers and his comparative ignorance of financial and business matters.[48]

The matters which formed the subject of allegations were as follows. (1) The distribution of the amounts sent from İstanbul for rebuilding in the province after the massacres of 1909. It was said in Adana, particularly among the Armenians, that there was very little result to show for the expenditure of the large sum allotted by the parliament for this purpose; that though the accounts of the committee presided over by Cemal Bey were published, they proved little; that subcommittees drew amounts in cash from the Imperial Ottoman Bank and made all payments in cash; and that the names of individuals shown as having received grants in the accounts of these subcommittees were in many instances fictitious, and that other individuals received unduly large sums. It was impossible to say whether there was any basis for these allegations, but the opinion was widespread. Grabowsky and Kozlovski gave much assistance to Cemal Bey in the affairs of the committee. (2) The contract for the construction of an embankment from the city to the new Baghdad railway station at Adana. This contract was awarded by the governor to the construction company of the Baghdad railways for 40,000 Turkish liras. In the opinion of everybody, the present governor included, this was a very excessive price to pay for the work carried out. Moreover, lower tenders were submitted but the contract was obtained by Kozlovski for the company. This embankment was made with the object of protecting the city from the destructive spring floods but it was equally necessary to protect the new railway station buildings, and it would appear reasonable that the company should bear part of the cost. (3) The contract for the building of the agricultural college. Grabowsky was said to have been instrumental in getting this award as it was. In the first instance there were several tenders at about 8,000 liras submitted. Subsequently the *cahier des charges* was altered and several small additions made to the plan, and the contract was awarded suddenly to Rosetti at a price of 12,000 liras. He sublet the contract to a French contractor, de la Fouconnerie, who in its turn sublet it to other small contractors. No deposit or security was required from the successful tenderer, and it appeared irregular that Rosetti who was charged with the inspection and approval of work done should be given the work, or even allowed to tender. After the late governor and Grabowsky had left Adana there was a good deal of discussion about this contract in the local Ottoman press, and charges were brought against Grabowsky and Rosetti but no action was taken to refute them. Since the arrival of Muammer Bey, inspection showed that the work was not in accordance with the *cahier des charges*, and that an inferior material was employed. Smith was not aware whether it was contemplated to do anything further in the matter, as the contractor, Rosetti, left the country. The late governor had arranged that he was to join him at Baghdad, but the Ottoman-Italian War over the province of Tripolitania prevented their plan being carried out. (4) Sale of government lands in the *mutasarrıflık* of Hamidiye. Several Armenians and Turks, including one Avedis Goulbenkian, who was much consulted by the late governor, bought government lands in the Hamidiye district, and appeared to have robbed the treasury in the following manner. A piece of land of fifty *deunums* (acres) was bought, say, for 50 liras and registered in the government office at Hamidiye. On the actual ground, however, the boundaries were laid out so as to include an area of five hundred or five thousand *deunums* and, by collusion with the official responsable for registration, the books and documents were altered so as to show the larger area. Several sales were made in this manner, the total being between thirty thousand and forty thousand *deunums*. This land question had been the subject of investigation during several months by a committee under a president from İstanbul by the Ministry of Finance, and Smith heard that as a result of their report, criminal proceedings were being taken against the officials and landowners implicated, of whom there were about fifteen, chiefly Armenians. There was no obvious reason why the name of Cemal Bey should be connected with this matter, but the fact remained that local opinion in Adana did not hold him blameless.[49]

During the January–February 1912 elections to the Chamber of Deputies, Cemal Bey treated the adherents of the opposition Party of Liberty and Entente sternly. Baghdadis wrote numerous petitions and complaints forcing him to defend his policies to İstanbul. This he did by instigating a progovernment petition campaign and publicizing a statement that he elicited from the province's electoral committee that denied any gubernatorial intervention.[50]

The inhabitants of Baghdad city numbered at present two hundred thousand. The urban population presented a diversity of elements: Arab, Iranian, Kurdish, Jewish, and Christian, variously apportioned. The province of Baghdad returned three members of Chamber of Deputies in İstanbul. Maruf al-Rusafi and Jamil Sidqi al-Zahawi were the two Muslim members of the Chamber of Deputies from 1912; Hesqail Sasson, a Jew, the third member. A few words must be said with regard to Jews and Armenians. In all places in Iraq, Jews were treated tolerantly by the Turks.[51] The Jewish community at Baghdad was, after that of Salonika, the most numerous, important, and prosperous in the Ottoman Empire in 1910. The Jews were particularly interested in trade. They had literally monopolized the local trade, and neither Muslims nor Christians could compete with them. Even the few leading Muslim merchants owed their prosperity to the capable and industrious Jews whom they had for years employed as clerks. The Ottoman government fully realized that the Jews were one of the chief elements in the progress of the country. The Turks had all along regarded the Jews as faithful subjects of the sultan and had placed confidence in them. On the other hand, the Jews of Baghdad had borne feelings of gratitude toward the Ottoman government ever since the immigration of their coreligionists from Spain into the Balkans and Asia Minor hundreds of years previously. The community was anxious to cooperate with the government for the improvement of the country.[52]

There was no massacre of Armenians in Baghdad or in any of the Arabic-speaking provinces. Armenian residents of Baghdad or elsewhere in Iraq had not therefore been molested.[53] The suspicion which Armenian separatism evoked elsewhere in the empire was not felt in Iraq.[54]

Efforts were made to celebrate National Day with unusual fervor and *éclat* on July 23. The principal event was a parade of troops and schoolboys in the morning outside the North Gate, after which Cemal Bey received the foreign consuls and other Europeans informally in a tent on the ground. In the evening there were some illuminations and fireworks in the city. The striking feature of the celebrations was the participation of a huge concourse of armed Arab tribesmen convoked by the governor. The Arabs were collected in a camp outside the city; their number was at least three thousand. The governor's idea, which was no doubt suggested by the Ottoman-Italian war in Tripoli, seemed to have been to demonstrate the strength of the Arab tribes of the province and their attachment to the Ottoman government. A number of shaikhs, each with a fixed number of followers, were invited, but others came in who had not been sent for, even from beyond the bounds of the province, and those who had been invited showed a tendency to increase their importance by bringing retinues larger than those prescribed for them. A parade of troops and Arabs took place in the desert outside the city. The Arabs marched past after the troops and were about twice as numerous. They were nearly all armed, and those who carried rifles, as a large proportion did, wore belts full of cartridges. There were few genuine Bedouins among them: most belonged to settled or semisettled tribes. From first to last, no serious hitch or accident occurred. The governor had frequent interviews with the Arab shaikhs at the *Konak*, in their camp—where at one meeting he bestowed kerchiefs and robes of honor to all of them—and even at his own.[55]

The general reorganization of the Ottoman army, decided on at the end of 1910, was carried into effect in this province. The two new army corps at Baghdad and Mosul (Thirteenth and Twelfth Army Corps) together formed the Fourth Inspectorate-General, which took the place of the old Sixth Army Corps or Baghdad army. The improvement of the army was perhaps the part of Cemal Bey's work which was most congenial to his tastes and for which he was best fitted by his training. It seemed that the discipline and spirit of the troops here, as well as their drill and equipment, were on a higher level now than they were before his arrival, but, in military matters as in tribal management, Cemal Bey was only at the beginning of his work, and no one could say how he would have succeeded in the long term.[56]

It could easily be said in Cemal Bey's favor that he kept crime and disorder within bounds, that he initiated not unpromising military reforms and public works, and that, though greatly feared by many, he was not personally unpopular. He gained the good opinion of the British community in Baghdad, the leaders of whom had all spoken to British consul general John Gordon Lorimer, in his praise.[57]

Baghdad seems to have left little impression on Cemal Bey. This province was in contemporary Ottoman officialdom the epitome of professional isolation. Although seeing this part of the country for the first time proved a memorable experience, he was pleased to return to İstanbul, the center of action and decision making.

Cemal Bey's stint in Baghdad was short. In 1911 there was a split within the CUP and opposition to its rule began to grow. The Unionists therefore dissolved the Chamber of Deputies in January 1912 and held a general election in which all but six of the returned members supported the government. In July a group of officers known as the "Saviour Officers" organized a movement in the army which succeeded in bringing down the Unionist government. Sultan Reşad appointed a new government, ratifying the choice of the "Saviour Officers." On the fall of the CUP Cabinet on July 22 Cemal Bey seemed to feel that his position had become untenable, and on July 27 he asked permission by telegram to resign his appointment. On August 1 he announced that his resignation had been accepted, and he was now in the position of acting as a temporary substitute for his late self, but it was expected that he would shortly be relieved. The newly elected parliament was dissolved on August 5, and an attempt was made to round up the leaders of the CUP: some fled abroad, others hid in the capital.[58]

On the days preceding the fall of the cabinet in İstanbul, various city improvements were under discussion at Baghdad—not for the first time. Among these were the widening of the streets, the introduction of electric tramways, the erection of an iron bridge over the Tigris, and a number of less important projects as the construction of a large race course with great stand outside the North Gate. R. I. Money, the consulting engineer of the National Bank, İstanbul, seemed to be impressed by a scheme of the governor for expropriating strips of lands in the city three or four times as wide as were required for streets and for reselling the side portions to the public at enhanced prices, thus meeting the cost of the changes without any great expenditure unless by way of a temporary advance. He reported the Baghdad Tramways to the bank as a promising scheme. The proceedings in regard to these were stopped by the governor's resignation.[59]

And yet Baghdad might have quite a big future in store; the advent of the railway might work great changes. New banks were establishing themselves. The Eastern Bank opened offices there in May 1912, and a German bank was reported to intend to do the same. The irrigation works originally projected by Sir William Willcocks and now in the hands of Sir John Jackson and company, were being pushed steadily forward and should, when completed, have far-reaching results on the trade and agriculture of the surrounding region. Business was being extended on more modern lines, and if European enterprise would only take a more practical shape and business houses at home were to have their own offices and representatives in Baghdad, instead of leaving everything in the hands of the native agents, there would soon be a marked development in every direction.[60]

Cemal Bey visited John Gordon Lorimer, the British consul general, two days before his departure and told him that, as regards his own future, "he would probably enter Parliament or become Secretary to somebody." He added that "every man in this world could earn his livelihood by some means or another." It was not for Lorimer to remark that his political party might no longer have a sufficiency of parliamentary seats at their disposal, nor that an Ottoman former governor with a military training and no civil experience might face the competition of Armenians and other "despised, but intelligent" classes severe in the struggle for a secretaryship. On Lorimer's observing that the new government would make a great mistake if they were to "pursue," by which Lorimer meant "persecute," the members of the CUP, Cemal Bey hastily proceeded to answer on the assumption that it was a question of "prosecuting" the members of his party. He seemed already to have given some thought to the subject, and his rejoinder was that there was no charge on which he or his colleagues could be prosecuted, for their hands were clean, unlike those of the creatures of Abdülhamid: to take his own case as an instance, his savings would only suffice to carry him to İstanbul.[61]

Lorimer reported that notwithstanding his fall the former governor's departure, which took place in the middle of a hot afternoon, was attended by a huge crowd, some of them personal enemies who feared that Cemal Bey might one day return and remember their absence against them. A reception tent was pitched in a street on the outskirts of the city, and most of the leave-takers assembled in the sultry veranda of a native café nearby. At length Cemal Bey appeared, riding, and dressed like an Arab in kerchief and cloak; he made a speech appropriate to the occasion. Lorimer met him and said goodbye, chiefly for the purpose of showing that, though there had been official disagreements between them, there was no personal ill-feeling. Lorimer and the German consul, Dr. Hesse, rode a little way with Cemal Bey on the Aleppo road and then bade him farewell. When they left Cemal Bey he was still attended by an indefatigable crowd, in carriages straggling across the desert.[62]

The American consul there, Emil Saurer, reported on August 4, 1912, that Cemal Bey had been very well liked there except by the small element of the opposition party (Party of Liberty and Entente), which was particularly indignant over his activity in the elections of the last spring. The Governor was very popular with the foreign element in Baghdad with whom he mixed freely. Saurer considered that important political changes at İstanbul might be looked for shortly and he indicated that the accession of Cemal Bey to great power in the capital was a possibility.[63]

There was a fair amount of truth in American consul's opinion. Cemal Bey's prospects seemed promising. As it happened, more achievements lay ahead of him. This owed much to his talents and his remarkable appetite for hard work. After August 16, 1912, Lütfi Bey, the deputy governor, held charge of the province as acting governor; Mehmet Zeki Paşa, formerly commander of the Erzincan Army, was nominated to Baghdad as head of the Fourth Military Inspectorate and civil governor. Upon his arrival to the capital, Cemal Bey was appointed as acting commander of the Konya Reserve Division on 19 October 1912.

Halidé Edib noted in 1926: "Wherever he [Cemal Bey] sojourned the people still enjoy good roads and good public buildings and have the memory of a period of great security and public order."[64] His record proved it. Indeed Cemal Bey's vision for construction extended beyond Adana and Baghdad. Most revealingly, during his command of the Fourth Army in Syria and Palestine in 1914–1917 Cemal Paşa kept some ten advisers, of whom at least five (those responsible for public health, antiquities, architecture, construction, and water) were Germans. One such officer, Theodor Wiegand, an archaeologist who was in charge of preserving and cataloging antiquities, left a valuable eyewitness account of Cemal Paşa's term in Syria. Dr. Peter Mühlens dealt with public health issues. Maximilian Zürcher, of Swiss origin, was a well-educated architect and urban planner who exerted more influence on Cemal Paşa than the others. Arthur Salz, future professor of political science at Heidelberg University, entered Cemal Paşa's service as late as September 1917 to oversee a reform program. Cemal Paşa and Ottoman experts, surrounded by German advisers, engaged in a comprehensive scheme of construction, urban improvement, and other infrastructural projects, including a historical preservation plan conceived as part of the effort to forge a new self-consciousness and to keep Syria for the Ottoman realm. The projects strengthened Ottoman communications, specifically the physical links of greater Syria with Anatolia, as they provided service to the local population. In the area of urban reconstruction, as in public works, many of the projects supplied utilities necessary to sustain daily life.[65]

In 1914–1917 Palestine underwent a great transformation in the matter of railway communication, improved highways, and better sanitary conditions. Journalists saw the same thing. This was evident from a letter to *Frankfurter Zeitung* from its correspondent in Jaffa, the seaport of Jerusalem. He interviewed Cemal Paşa. "Immediately after my arrival in Syria," said Cemal Paşa, "my first work was to take measures to improve and extend the roads. Many battalions of workmen were organized for the purpose of building important new roads and putting into repair old ones that had become useless. Formerly you could not go farther south in a carriage than Hebron, but already I can ride in my automobile through Hebron and Beersheba out into the desert." Here the correspondent remarked that he spent a whole day last year riding horseback from Hebron to Beersheba, where the distance could now be covered by autumobile in one hour. "Within a short time," Cemal Paşa went on, "we have built over 100 kilometers of railway and have connected Jerusalem with the Hejaz railway (the road that runs south from Aleppo and Damascus, over the plateau to the east of the Jordan, and on southward to Mecca). You doubtless know how anxious the English were to prevent the building of this connection. They refused to give the French, the right to carry this road through Ramléh, because they were determined under any and all circumstances, to prevent a land connection from Syria to Anatolia to Egypt. Now we want to carry these roads still further." The correspondent said that this railway building would prove of epoch-making importance for the development of Palestine.[66]

MUAMMER BEY: THE NEW GOVERNOR OF ADANA

In the fall of 1911 William Nesbitt Chambers noted sadly: "I was sorry on my return [from annual leave] to find His Excellency Djemal Bey gone from Adana. He had much to do still in the reconstruction of the province. The man that succeeds him has a difficult place to fill. We hope the present governor will make good. His action in the present crisis seems to be correct and he gave excellent advice to the people." No little anxiety would be felt throughout Cilicia. It would be a satisfaction to know the situation in different localities. The city Adana remained very calm. In Tarsus there was not a little anxiety and those who were still in the mountains began to prepare to return to the town at once.[67]

The new governor Muammer Bey arrived in Adana on June 26, 1911, and took charge of his post. A civilian, he was only thirty-five years of age and was previously *mutasarrıf* of Kayseri for two years. He came from there with a good reputation and was much liked by the Christian inhabitants whom he governed with impartiality and justice. In Kayseri he carried out certain works of public utility such as school building, road making, and drainage of land.[68]

Muammer Bey appeared to be an example of the right man in the right place. He was singularly well qualified for his difficult task. Since his appointment he gave proofs of ability to govern. He took a remarkably broad view.[69]

Toward the end of November 1911, such a profound feeling of anxiety manifested itself among the Armenians, who feared an attack from the Muslim population, as to induce the acting British vice consul to apply for the protection of a British ship. Upon inquiry in İstanbul, however, and as no reliable facts could be produced, it was not considered necessary that such a step should be taken.[70] To the Armenians, Muammer Bey showed a sympathetic and conciliatory spirit. Needless to add, this step gave rise to satisfaction among the Armenians. He called the leading citizens and cautioned them all—Muslim and Christian alike—to remain calm and maintain tranquility. One passage in his address was quite to the point. Muammer Bey, in his clean, congenial, convincing manner, spoke to the hearts of men. He told the people that the Ottomans were once a conquering people; they ruled large territory; they were strong and virile. They had lost much and were still losing because they had lost in moral fiber. Progress was based on morality. His address was good. The city remained tranquil and there had been no indication of hostility toward foreigners. In fact Muammer Bey urged the people to treat all foreigners with due respect. He was a man of smooth words. Clear-eyed, warm-hearted, with a love for men and a zeal for righteousness, he watched the course of events intently and formed his judgments and opinions on what was transpiring in the province. There seemed to be more anxiety felt in some of the out districts—for instance in Hacin. But this seemed to be more anxiety because of past experiences rather than any real indication of present or future trouble.[71]

Seldom had it been the fortune of Adana to have a governor with so wide a range of interests. Suffering and need appealed to Muammer Bey on all sides. Progressive and energetic, he took hold of affairs here with a will. Such an administration was greatly needed. He took a special pleasure in the city's improvements; against all odds, he proved equal to the task. He was well spoken of by all who knew him, and he brought to this important post many qualifications which ought to ensure his success. His remarkable capacity as an administrator was shown to the whole province and evoked much enthusiasm. Muammer Bey's genial disposition won for him hosts of friends.[72]

A man of great vigor and imagination, his career was studded with positions of responsibility. But as far as he was concerned, they all fell within a single pattern—that of service to his country.[73] Muammer Bey was born in 1875 in İstanbul. After graduating from the Drama middle and Mercan secondary schools, he attended the College of Administrative Sciences and completed his studies in the summer of 1899. Entering the Ministry of the Interior in the autumn of the same year, he served nine years as *kaymakam* in Kangal, Niksar, Vodina, Medina, and Aziziye (Emirdağ). After being promoted and appointed *mutasarrıf* in Kayseri in 1909, with the usual versality of an Ottoman provincial administrator, he was appointed governor in Adana on June 26, 1911, in Konya on February 5, 1912, in Sivas on March

30, 1913, and in Konya, for a second time, on February 8, 1916, until December 14, 1918. On May 28, 1919, he was arrested by the government in İstanbul and on June 11 of the same year he was deported by the British occupation forces to Malta on charges of war crimes, where he was detained with other 143 senior Ottoman statesmen and officials until their acquittal on September 19, 1921. Following his release by the British, Muammer Bey joined the government in Ankara. He became member of the TGNA on July 12, 1923, for Sivas until his death on November 18, 1928. He had a good command of French and was acquainted with Arabic, Persian, and Armenian. He was a permanent and very active member of the CUP. His patriotic credentials were impeccable. Muammer Bey posthumously assumed the surname of Cankardeş. The list of his good deeds and admirable qualities is long, and it is clear that he is remembered fondly. Mustafa Nedim Bey succeeded him on February 26, 1912.[74]

AGRICULTURAL AND INDUSTRIAL DEVELOPMENT OF ADANA ON THE EVE OF THE FIRST WORLD WAR

A letter came to the ABCFM's board in May 1911 from the director of agriculture at Adana. It was written upon government paper, bearing the Ottoman headings and official marks. The striking facts about it were that the official was an Armenian who, after graduating at Robert College in İstanbul, came to the United States, took a full course in at the Massachusetts Agricultural College, and pursued postgraduate work in the experimental station there and at Manhattan, Kan; that returning to his home in Harput as a teacher he left his agricultural books stored at the board, not venturing to take them with him in the hazard of reentering the Ottoman Empire; and that whereas ten years ago this Armenian managed to slip quietly back to his native land, today he was an officer of the Ottoman government in the large and important province of Adana.[75] In 1912 the Municipality of Adana decided to send at its expense Shakin Adjemian to America to study at the Massachusetts Institute of Technology. He was young and enthusiastic and immensely keen to go to America.[76]

The efforts of the agriculturists in the province of Adana were concentrated on cotton cultivation, and, thanks to the iniative they exercised in the introduction of agricultural machinery of a perfected type, and its use on a vast scale, the cotton area was estimated at about four thousand square kilometers. The Egyptian varieties were not cultivated, owing no doubt to climatic conditions, but within last five years an American variety of New Orleans was tried with a certain measure of success. It was estimated that about three thousand bales of this variety would be produced in 1912. After Ottoman ports, Italy (before its attack on the province of Tripolitania) and Austria came in for the larger share of exports of cotton. Cotton cultivation became so important in Adana that the well-known British firm of C. Whittall and Company erected a mill for the making of cotton seed cake, of which the turnout was about twenty tons per day. By 1912, all the cake, about thirty-five hundred tons, was shipped to Britain.[77]

All four banks doing business in Cilicia, the Imperial Ottoman Bank, the Turkish Agricultural Bank, the Deutsche Orient Bank, and the Bank of Athens, enlarged their operations and opened new branches at points in the interior, Ceyhan, Ayas, and Osmaniye. The Imperial Ottoman Bank was especially powerful. In addition to being the principal supplier of state loans, it had invested in major industrial ventures, and, through its delegate on the Ottoman Debt Council, it participated in the administration of official revenues.[78] At the beginning of the twentieth century the Imperial Ottoman Bank was not only by far the largest bank in the Levant, it was also one of the largest anywhere in the world. It was founded in 1863 by a group of British and French financiers as the state bank of the Ottoman Empire.[79]

It is to be reminded here that the *Boston Daily Adviser* of December 4, 1912, commented editorially on the letters of the missionaries from the Ottoman Empire, reassuring their friends as to their personal safety. It said that while American warships were being sent clear across the Atlantic and the Mediterranean the missionaries were sending home the most positive assurances that there need to be no care, uneasiness, nor worry about them, "that they have had convincing assurances from their paynim neighbors that they are safe and will be safe, through everything."

It went on to say:

It is something that may well stir the pride of Americans in the work of the American Board of Commissioners for Foreign Missions, that the representatives of that board in Turkey have lived such lives and done such work, and borne themselves so well, that no amount of religious fanaticism can influence their influence to hurt those workers, or to allow any Mohammedan fanatics to attack them. It is wonderful indeed, in the light of the horrible tales which are coming from the scene of the war,[80] that this is so. But there can be no question as to the facts.[81]

In the British House of Commons on May 8, 1913, Sir Francis Dyke Acland, the undersecretary of state for foreign affairs, declared that a few days previous there was a rumor in some European papers that matters were not as they should be in Adana. Britain had a vice consul in that city who kept the Foreign Office constantly informed, and Acland was glad to say he had been able to report that some hundreds of refugees and families who had come to that part of Asia Minor from Europe had been successfully set down, and work had been found for them, often among Armenian populations. The rumors as to difficulties had been very much exaggerated, and the Armenians up to present had been absolutely safe, and no difficulty had been occurring.[82]

Despite early fears to the contrary, the cereal crops in the province of Adana proved satisfactory in 1913. Plentiful rains in the spring improved the condition of fields which had been greatly affected by a prolonged drought during the whole winter. The result, therefore, exceeded every anticipation, giving an average of production for wheat, barley, and oats of eleven times the seed sown, while the proportion of the preceding season was only seven to one. This unexpected increase was due partly to the favorable climatic conditions and partly to the efficient system of modern plowing recently introduced on a large scale. With the increase of cotton production all industries in connection with this article were also improved and developed. Besides the ginning, spinning, and weaving mills already in existence, in the principal centers of Cilicia, new schemes for the improvement and enlargement of these industries were always contemplated. Two cotton seed oil mills were erected in Mersin in the summer of 1913.[83]

On April 30, 1913, *Tanin* reproduced from *Jamanak* without comment the following letter from Adana. For some days a German warship happened to be before Mersin. Five to six other foreign warships had also arrived there on April 29. For a week, the rumor ran that the Christians were going to be massacred and the Armenian women took refuge in the churches. But thanks to the stringent measures taken by the government, these apprehensions were dissipated. On being informed that certain individuals were going over villages exciting the population, the authorities carried out some arrests and secured order. It was considered that the arrival of these vessels was due to these rumors.[84]

It was in June 1913 William Nesbitt Chambers reached Adana after an absence of a little more than a year. When he arrived the people were slowly recovering from panic—a painful reminder of the days and months succeeding the awful experiences of the massacres. Naturally, shattered nerves tingled with the slightest suggestion of trouble. However the present governor, Emin (Zincirkıran) Bey, Chambers wrote, was alive to the necessity of putting a stop to those remarks or demonstrations calculated to arouse apprehension. It was credibly reported that in some places the Muslims ran in one direction and Christians in the other, both apprehensive of the possible action of the other. Nothing sinister had taken place and tranquility was preserved so that many were already moving out to the vineyards and there appeared to be no apprehension in the minds of the people. There were reported many deserters in hiding in various places making travel unsafe, at least in appearance, and there was less night travel than was customary because of this apprehension. However, Chambers did not hear of any depredations.[85]

In this connection it may be noted that the naval demonstrations made by Germany on the Cilician coast in May 1913, in which Italy joined, was said by Armenians to have prevented a massacre. It was quite possible that the Armenians were overstating the case, and that things were not as bad as they were said to be. Anyhow, the appearance of the powerful *Goeben* off Mersin, with the *Strassburg* and *Geier* and the Italian *Amalfi* and *Etruria*, seemed to have caused memories of Kiao-Chau to arise in some Turkish minds, and to have given the impression that the Germans were making the first step toward the establishment of their sphere of influence in the region between the Taurus and the Euphrates, the "vitals" of their railway construction. *Qui vivra verra*. The idea certainly prevailed among foreigners that the Germans did not go to Mersin merely to show their desire of protecting the Armenians.[86]

Young, tall, and slender, Emin Bey was an impressive figure. Being a particularly good choice for the office of the governor, he had also served in that capacity in İstanbul and Kastamonu provinces, respectively, in October 1911–January 1912 and January–August 1912. He was not ranked among the stars of the Ottoman Ministry of the Interior. Yet this unassuming public administrator was a man of sound judgment and unbiased common sense. He had the province well in hand and did fine work in restraining any element in the region that might be inclined to robbery or other lawlessness. Emin Bey took stern measures. He made all kind of arrangements for keeping order, and he warned the military authorities. His career at Adana had been most creditable. He was a man universally respected for indefatigable hard work and faithfulness and honesty, and his little difference with the government made no material alteration to his career, as he was shortly afterwards appointed to his present post.[87] Emin Bey was an upright, high-minded, and conciliatory man, and he had certainly shown considerable tact and talent during recent months. He left behind a record for clean and honorable dealing. He died in 1963.[88]

During the few weeks in November 1913 that the British journalist and historian Philips Price was in Cilicia, he visited Kozan, Hacin, and Zeytun, the last two places being noted as outlaw retreats for the whole countryside. Situated at the head of rocky gorges, these towns consisted of mud houses, literally piled, like packs of cards, for protection from enemies in the valleys below. At Zeytun Price found a large colony of outlaws and brigands, headed by a bishop who had a closer acquaintance with military lore than with principles of theology. A state of warfare existed on all weekdays between the inhabitants of Zeytun, headed by its bishop and four so-called noblemen, against the Ottoman garrison of a fort lower down the valley. Raids and forays were frequent on the rocks above the town, one of which Price witnessed one evening from the verandah of the bishop's house, between an Ottoman outpost and a gang of outlaws. The Armenians of Zeytun were up in arms against anything which savored of central government control. Nothing would persuade them to pay their taxes or send a soldier to serve in the Ottoman army, while, of course, any caravan of Turkish goods or a flock of sheep passing from one town to the other was in their eyes a lawful object for plunder. In fact, here was an area subdued by the government, in the heart of the Empire, living in a tribal state, and one could hardly wonder at the Young Turks taking some steps to bring these primitive tribesmen to law and order. There was a state of guerilla warfare continually going on in and around Zeytun, with a truce every Sunday.[89]

Price witnessed the comedy of Oriental warfare one Sunday morning in November 1913, when he attended mass in the ancient Gregorian church on the rock at Zeytun. The bishop officiated in full robes, and as Price reached the church who should he find at the entrance but the Ottoman commander of the soldiers with whom the Zeytunlis were at war on weekdays, accompanied by the mufti of the Ottoman forces. Price would not readily forget the sight of that gaunt, bare church, perched up on the cliff, half-fortress like, battered by storm and siege for many a century. Within its walls stood the rude Christian altar with its screen of lattice, behind which went forth the ancient Gregorian chants in shrill, weird Eastern strains, while the incense enveloped the body of the little church in its fragrant haze. It was a display of Oriental Christianity, with all its pomp and mystery. And there, crowded in the nave, were the rude picturesque Armenian highlanders, armed to the teeth with knives and rifles, and standing beside Price the representative of the Ottoman government, commander of the forces, with whom these highlanders were at war on weekdays. All of them, whether Christian or Muslim, were worshipping at the same shrine, and whatever might be said against Islam, this incident was enough to prove that there was no religion which showed more tolerance for the rights and customs of other faiths. After the service, the bishop, the Ottoman officials, and Price, all retired to the vestry, where a spread of rice, mutton, and grease was served with wine and cognac. Speeches of a semipolitical nature were accompanied by uproarious toasts, and finally the bishop became very merry, and the Ottoman *kaymakam* required the assistance of a gendarme to get him out of the room.[90]

Such was the paradox of Eastern life. But no one who visited Cilicia could say that the Armenians were crushed under the heel of a tyrannous Turk. In Zeytun at least, it was the other way. In the area of Göksu river, the principal brigand bands were all Armenian. In fact, Price found just the same state of affairs here as he found further east, in eastern Anatolia, when he visited it in 1913. The only difference was that here Zeytunli Armenians, and to a certain extent Circassians, were the disturbing element, while in eastern Anatolia that function was usurped by the Kurds. Gradually, the Turks were penetrating both these districts, and indeed, considerable progress was made in the last ten years in building roads, and in establishing gendarmerie posts in these highlands. An American missionary, whom Price met at Maraş, who had lived forty years on the borders of this country, told him he had himself witnessed during that time a great improvement in the social state of the populations. Raids on villages by robber bands were less frequent as compared with former times, the power of the tribal chiefs was less, and gradually the Ottoman government was asserting its control.[91]

Ali Seydi Bey was the governor of Adana from December 10, 1913, to March 11, 1914. He had the prestige of long experience. Although his appointment was brief, it was a step in the right direction. Ali Seydi Bey was a man of good will and good purpose. He spoke directly and to the point. His working hours were long. After Adana, his progress continued, and he received the standard decorations and regular promotions.[92] He was succeeded by İsmail Hakkı Bey, who was energetic and had administrative capacity. The general situation in the province improved since his arrival notwithstanding the inferior class of subordinate officials through whom he had to work and the lack of support from İstanbul. He took a promising view of the near future with regard to Adana.[93] During 1913 considerable changes had taken place. The able-bodied prisoners had been used for removal and reconstruction work a good deal. These men, under guard, might be seen working in gangs cleaning up the debris. There was much still to be done in reconstruction.[94]

In 1913, the Germans organized a school in Adana and negotiated for one of the largest houses in the city and paid 400 Turkish liras a year rent for a period of four years. Apparently the German scheme was to organize a central university with affiliated schools in principal cities such as Konya, Adana, Aleppo, etc. The scheme seemed to have been well thought out and intended to be extended in its operation.[95]

In the spring of 1913, there were in Adana two cotton spinning and weaving factories, one with ten thousand spindles and one hundred and eighty looms, and the other with five thousand spindles and fifty looms. Tarsus had two factories, one with twenty thousand spindles and the other with six thousand spindles. These factories had been handicapped during the last three years by the scarcity and increasing cost of labor. The *Deutsche Levantinische Baumwall Gesellschaft* had a cotton pressing and bailing mill at

Adana. A British company established a cotton seed oil mill at Mersin, which it was anticipated would gradually absorb the local supply of cotton seeds.[96]

Adana was undergoing a rapid and fundamental change. This was essentially a socioeconomic progress. In addition to large Armenian and Greek elements, here was the center of Ottoman Turkish life. On January 19, 1914, in a letter filled with insight and candor, Chambers could write the following on the city:

> Every one who visits Adana is impressed with the hustle and drive of this busy, modern city. The streets are filled with a rushing crowd in which young men constitute the large proportion and the number of foreigners is very remarkable. Business is booming. There is a mad rush for money. Prices, values and rents have risen in an incomprehensible way.[97]

Ernest Otto Jacob readily agreed with Chambers:

> To be sure, it [Adana] is not as well-known abroad as Smyrna, Aleppo or Damascus. I never heard of it until it sprang into sad fame in 1909. But three visits have branded it into my memory to stay. This energetic changing city of 75,000 is conscious of a future. Steam plows and threshing machines, cotton mills and railroads make one feel its progressive commercial spirit. Great school buildings loom up all over the city. The Germans have put up a railway plant of which many a European or American city would be proud.[98]

Chambers again wrote on Adana on January 24, 1914:

> The ruins caused by the massacres have been largely obliterated, the streets widened and new ones opened many of which are lined with shops. The whole city is crowded with traffic and the population is steadily increasing. The material prosperity is marvelous. The Baghdad Railway station would grace a European city.[99]

According to Chambers, the agricultural development of the province of Adana by 1914 had been impressive. Large tracts of land had been brought under cultivation producing splendid crops. This growth was indicated by the fact that a score of years ago only the ancient style of farming implements were in use. Now there were two score steamplows, six score steam threshers, and scores of reapers. The seed grill had come to show its superiority over the old style of hand scattering of seed, and other modern implements were asserting themselves. The cotton crop of eighty thousand bales of 1912 was surpassed in 1913 by twenty thousand to twenty-five thousand bales. The principal output consisted of cotton, wheat, barley, oats, and sesame seed. Cotton mills and grist mills were increasing in number and the weaving of cotton cloth was greatly developing. The growth and importance in the autumn of 1914 were indicated by the fact that the population was seventy-five thousand to eighty thousand, about two-thirds being Muslim. Since the massacres of 1909 the burned quarters had been rebuilt and trade had boomed and was booming, attracting a large volume of business. The Imperial Ottoman Bank, the Turkish Agricultural Bank, the Deutsche Orient Bank, and the Bank of Athens were doing a large business in Adana. The shrewdest observers, in the words of Chambers, prophesized a brilliant future for the city.[100]

The province of Adana was opened up and was a battleground for railway expansion. All foreign countries sought and did their utmost to secure for themselves and for their enterprise the right to expand and to open up vast territories, whereby they would gain orders for their industries at home and reap other advantages locally, industrially, and financially. Britain was the oldest trading country with the region. It was earlier established than in any other country in the world, and because of its historic association with it, Britain expected that it should have a fair share in all expansion, railway and otherwise, that was going on.

The Turks, Young and Old alike, realized that their country was keenly coveted by more than one powerful state. They writhed under the grip in which Germany held them by virtue of the railway concessions and colonizing concessions which Emperor Wilhelm coaxed out of his friend Sultan Abdülhamid II. For did not the Baghdad railway concession alone, by granting to Germany mining rights over twenty kilometers on either side of this one thousand-mile line, already place that power in practical possession of a strip of territory, through the heart of Asia Minor, extending over some thirty thousand square miles? A formidable wedge, indeed, and it was being utilized for all it was worth.[101]

The Baghdad railway had shown its estimate of the possibilities by making Adana a principal station on the line. As soon as the tunnels in the Tarsus and Adana mountains were completed Adana would be in railway communication with İstanbul on the west and Aleppo, Baghdad, and the Persian Gulf on the east. It already had two outlets to the Mediterranean, Mersin and İskenderun. The Mersin-Adana railroad had been practically reconstructed and equipped with much new rolling stock.[102]

The annual value of the agricultural machinery imported at Mersin in 1914 was about 100,000 dollars. Steam plows, thrashers, reapers, binders, and plows were the principal kinds in demand. Steam plows and thrashers came almost exclusively from Britain and plows of German make were preferred. Reapers and binders were practically all from the United States.[103]

The changes which had taken place in the appearance of Adana since 1910 were many. According to the United States consul at Mersin, Edward Nathan, the Adana province had had a rapid development of late because of improved transportation facilities. The American official spent eight years in this post and thus came to know the place well. The Mersin-Adana railroad connected with the new Baghdad railway, which extended across the province and linked Mersin with İstanbul and the Persian Gulf as opposite termini. While a large part of the Cilician plain was under cultivation, vast tracts of swamp land could be reclaimed, and a system of irrigation would greatly improve the cotton culture. Plans to this end were being considered for execution in the near future. The farmers of Adana plain had been more enterprising than those of other parts of the Ottoman Empire in regard to the use of modern agricultural implements and machinery.[104]

The Ottoman government very recently had taken up the question of further improvement of the Cilician plain. The irrigation scheme to be undertaken was to cost four million Turkish liras (17,700,000 dollars), and its completion would cover eight to ten years while the first section was intended to be ready for the farmer in one and a half years. Various foreigners made their appearance at Adana and showed interest in the irrigation works.

On the plains of Cilicia, western ideas made greater headway than on the Anatolian plateau. Philips Price thought in February 1914 it would be safe to say that the advent of the Baghdad railway to the Cilician plains, accompanied by the rush of modern improvements and European methods, would prevent any "artificially-organised reprisals between Mohammedan and Christian in future."[105]

Following the calling of mobilization on August 2, 1914, the military government of Adana and the behavior of the troops deserved praise. Seizure of goods and animals and conscription of men were necessities of the situation. But martial law secured uniform quiet and security, and there were no stories of violence or insult of any kind offered to the city by the soldiers. The First World War period was a challenging time for the Ottoman army. Setbacks experienced during the Balkan Wars of 1912–1913 provoked grave concern about the efficiency of the nation's armed forces.

ABCFM had on November 10, 1914, received through the State Department in Washington, DC the following dispatch from William Wheelock Peet of İstanbul, treasurer of all the ABCFM's Ottoman missions: "American Ambassador with hearty cooperation of Turkish officials has situation completely in hand. Missionaries and their work fully safeguarded. Everything proceeding as though normal conditioning prevailed. You may safely reassure all friends." This meant that the ABCFM's 174 missionaries at twenty centers all over the empire, together with their homes, their schools, their seven colleges, and their nine hospitals, were not only safe from injury, but were proceeding with their work as though the Ottoman Empire had not been at war.[106]

EVACUATION OF THE ARMENIANS OF ADANA, OCTOBER–NOVEMBER 1921

By 1914 the Armenians were back and prospering again. The peoples of Adana underwent their full share of the vicissitudes of the First World War and its aftermath. In 1915 the majority of Armenians in the province were relocated to Syria.[107] Upon receiving news of the armistice on October 30, 1918, many were gradually returning to their homes and were beginning to rehabilitate their homes in some measure. At first the Turks were rather friendly to the repatriated Armenians who were expelled from their province, and in some instances Turks gave back to the owners the property they had taken over. A number of Turks also offered to pay back-rent for houses and farms. Armenians were no worse off than the other people. Many had hidden a little material with which they set up shop and carried on. They had supplies and means for building houses, providing cattle and seed, and establishing the various classes of people in productive work.[108] During the relocation Armenians of Adana—thanks to Cemal Paşa—had suffered comparatively less. Zaven Der Yeghiayan, the Armenian patriarch of İstanbul in 1913–1922, said:

> I consider it necessary to state that, in the area's under Jemal Pasha's rule—Syria, Palestine, Cilicia, etc.—the Armenian deportees lived more comfortably than in the other areas. Jemal Pasha had been Governor of Adana, and many people who knew him from that time enjoyed his protection. . . . Armenians within the boundaries of Syria were not massacred. Even the murderers of [Krikor] Zohrab and Vartkes [Serengülyan] were arrested and hanged in Aleppo [sic Damascus].[109]

Cilician Armenians and some of the other relocated Armenians, who were natives of districts other than Adana, also settled in the province. They sided with the French when they occupied Adana, were armed and enlisted by the French, took their revenge on the Turks.[110]

There was sharp dissatisfaction with French occupation rule at Adana. The French went into Adana and occupied the province as if they were annexing it and issued orders and made propaganda along this line. Certain French officers and officials received and expected liberal presents for services rendered by them. The French exploited the province to their own profit, and to the detriment of the Turks.[111]

The French used troops composed, in large majority, of Armenians. These Armenians were tactless and did things that irritated the native population. The French had all Turkish flags hauled down in Adana, and only French and Armenian flags were allowed to be flown. They occupied the government buildings and deposed the government officials. All these acts, which began on November 1, 1919, started agitations that gradually increased. At first there were isolated murders in out-of-the-way places. The Armenian National Union, as it was called, began agitations for their national rights, as they termed them, the organization of militia, and the arming of the Armenian native population. Thus the national antagonistic feeling between the two peoples augmented, and from small affairs they gradually increased.[112]

And when the French were driven out in October and November 1921 from the region almost all the Armenian population went with them. In Adana Armenian merchants quietly packed up their goods and shipped them out of the country. Household furniture was sold at any price. What could not be sold or taken away was burned or broken. Men, women, and children lined the streets trying to sell paltry little things often of no value. Streams of humanity poured down to Mersin. Ordinary passenger trains in no way sufficing, open freight cars were loaded high with baggage, with the owners in families perching on top. Soon thousands of people were camping in the streets of Mersin. Many had started with only a few liras, and almost immediately began to feel the pinch of poverty. Heavy rains and black small pox added to the distress. The American Mission, Near East Relief, and the Young Women's Christian Association came to their aid as far as possible with shelter, free clinic, soup kitchen, and milk for babies.[113]

In a communication dated November 17, 1921, addressed to General Marie de Lamothe, the delegate of the French high commissioner at Aleppo, it appeared to Jesse Jackson, the American consul in that city, that extraordinary excitement had reigned in Cilicia during the past few days among the Christian population, native as well as foreign, due to the news of the approaching evacuation of that region by the French troops of occupation. The communication went on as follows. The panic that was prompted by the reentry of the territory in question by the Turkish forces was so great that the Armenian and Greek inhabitants, especially the well-to-do class, were leaving the country by thousands, selling their property at wretched prices or taking away with them all that they could in their hasty exodus. This emigration inspired an anxiety to American citizens and "protégés," who had already had rather serious experiences in several parts of Cilicia, in connection with their lives as well as their property and interests. The philanthropic institutions; the missions; the relief committees; the Standard Oil, Socony Vacuum, and Singer Sewing Machine companies; and others possessed at Adana, Tarsus, Mersin, Ceyhan, Dörtyol, Kilis, and Ayntab real property and stocks of merchandise of a considerable value, and the interested parties desired to know in a clear and precise manner what guarantees had been taken by the French government in reference to the protection of their lives and property and to whom they should refer for aid and protection in case of danger. France having been entrusted, by the consent of the Allied Powers, with the maintenance of order and the protection of minorities in Cilicia, Jackson was brought to believe that it devolved upon the French government to take such efficacious measures as the creation of the new situation in the said region imposed in order to prevent all arbitrary or inhuman action on the part of the Turkish forces. In consideration of the foregoing, Jackson found himself obliged, in his capacity as consul of the United States, to draw the attention of General de Lamothe, as representative of French High Commissioner for Syria and Lebanon Robert de Caix, to the situation prevailing in Cilicia, as a consequence of the withdrawal of the French troops before peace should have been signed between Turkey and the Allied Powers, and to throw upon whom it might concern the responsibility for the loss of human lives and property that might therefrom to American citizens and "protégés."[114]

Rear Admiral Mark Bristol,[115] the United States high commissioner in İstanbul, gave his impression in regard to one or two statements which appeared in Jackson's communication to General Marie de Lamothe. Bristol was not aware that American officials in the Old Ottoman Empire were authorized to extend protection or to recognize so-called protégés. In fact he did not believe that the State Department authorized such recognition, and he felt that it should be avoided. In his letter to General de Lamothe, Jackson referred to the fact that France in agreement with the Allies had assumed responsibility for the protection of minorities in Cilicia. It was further to be inferred from Jackson's letter that certain obligations rested upon France for American citizens and American "protégés" in Cilicia. In Bristol's opinion it would be well to avoid statements of this nature. As far as Bristol was aware the American government had never recognized that France had political or moral responsibilities in Cilicia which would imply the obligations to which Jackson referred. The United States high commissioner in İstanbul stated he would appreciate any comment on this correspondence which the State Department might be disposed to make.[116]

In reply it was desired to say, with regard to the point Bristol raised concerning the Aleppo Consul's use of the word "protégé," that, in view of Jackson's extended experience in the Near East, the State Department felt he could not have intended to attach to the term the special significance to which Bristol properly took exception. But since in the Levant the word frequently had undesirable implications, the consul had been advised by the State Department to exercise caution in his use of it. As to Bristol's second point, touching the protection of American citizens and interests in Cilicia, the State Department decided that this subject would for practical reasons now fall more directly under the high commissioner's own supervision, the consul had been requested to discontinue his correspondence on this matter with the French authorities.[117]

Olin P. Lee of the Young Men's Christian Association at Adana, Robert Wilson of the American Mission of the Reformed Presbyterian Church at Mersin, and Miss Lowe of the Near East Relief, with whom J. C. Cunnungham, lieutenant commander of the United States ship *Williamson* anchored in Mersin harbor, met on November 18, 1921, and stated that the government of the TGNA had agreed with the French to guarantee the rights and privileges of all Christians including those who had actively opposed them during the French occupation. When asked what would really happen to these people if they remained here and complied with the law, Lee expressed the opinion that the majority would probably not be molested. Lieutenant Commander Cunnungham explained the conditions in İstanbul with reference to the refugees who, due to lack of work, were almost entirely dependent on charity and asked what conditions these people might expect to find upon arriving their destination—whether they would really be better off by remaining or leaving, without actually suggesting it. This was done with the idea of getting the Americans to try to induce at least those who had shown no active hostility to the Turks to remain. However, it appeared that these people were very much alarmed, and a great many had already completed their plans for leaving. Wilson stated that the Armenians and Greeks had chartered three steamers which were due to arrive the following day. Most of the stores and business houses in Adana, Tarsus, and Mersin were closed. The people who were leaving were selling their property for anything they could get for it. A month ago it was almost impossible to rent a house in Adana, but now there were numbers of them for rent.[118]

RESUMPTION OF TURKISH CONTROL OF ADANA, JANUARY 5, 1922

American officials kept a close watch upon the pulse of Armenian sentiment. Lieutenant Commander J. C. Cunningham, cruising in Cilician waters on a flag-showing expedition, reported to Rear Admiral Mark Bristol on November 20, 1921, that he took a walk around Mersin and then went to the railroad station to see a train from Adana and Tarsus come in. There were several thousand Armenians in the town, all churches, church yards, and vacant lots being filled with them. The train consisted of about four box cars filled with baggage and about twelve flat cars with sides two feet high. These flat cars were filled with baggage and the tops of all cars were completely covered with men, women, and children.[119]

As no less a person than Bristol shrewdly confided:

One of the effects of the Franco-Turkish pact, recently signed at Angora, has been the throwing into a condition of panic of the Christian part of the population of Cilicia. This to be turned over to the Turkish Nationalists within a period of two months. Many of these Christians have very closely affiliated themselves with the French against the Turks in many instances, having even gone to the point of bearing arms against the Turks. They fear if they remain in Cilicia they will have revenge in a violent form inflicted on them. However, it would seem the part of wisdom for most of these Christians to remain where they are rather than rushing off into other parts of the world where the difficulty of earning a living will no doubt be very great. It seems a very bad precedent in view of the some two or three million Christians in Anatolia, where no doubt Turkish rule will ultimately be recognized in full force. From private letters from American relief workers at Ismidt it was feared that American and Christians generally, in that area, might be in danger, but from an investigation made by the Commanding Officer of the U.S.S.C. no.96, it appears that there is no visible reason for fears on this score. The government is conducting itself in an orderly manner, and the feeling towards Americans seems very good.[120]

The French statesman Henri Franklin-Bouillon,[121] who signed the Ankara Agreement[122] of October 20, 1921, for the evacuation of Cilicia with the government of the TGNA, assured Lieutenant Commander Cunningham that both Muhittin (Akyüz) Paşa,[123] the new military commander of Cilicia, and Hamid Bey,[124] under secretary of the Ministry of the Interior charged with the administration of the region, were men of proven integrity and that they would assure complete freedom for all persons—Christians and Muslims alike.[125] Muhittin Paşa, in speaking of the armistice, remarked: "I am a soldier by profession but no one desires peace more than I do, for I know how much our soldiers as well as civilians need peace. We are indeed weary of war."[126]

Muhittin Paşa, rotund and genial, was dressed in the green uniform of the Turkish army. He had a suave manner. Hamid Bey was a tall angular man, whose *kalpak* (high astrakhan cap) accentuated his height. Very dark with bristling moustache, his appearance belied his courteous manner. He was straightforward and direct almost to the point of bluntness and gruffness. William Nesbitt Chambers was convinced of his sincerity and good will.[127]

Muhittin Paşa was an earnest and sincere liberal, and showed the strength of his convictions by the fact that not only was he condemned to exile under the rule of Sultan Abdülhamid II, but he was kept in close confinement for a great many years. Apart from his political opinions, he was a thoroughly honest man with the courage of his convictions, and what the Levant required more than anything else just then was honest men who had the courage of their convictions. Muhittin Paşa was of gentlemanly appearance and spoke perfect French, but with an eye which seemed to be taking careful stock of the person with whom he was talking. His manner and talk made a favorable impression on others. He had the reputation of a soldier-diplomat. Hamid Bey was the right man in the right place at this important juncture. He had many qualities which deserved esteem. He did not mince his words, he spoke with force and directness—which was sometimes the only method of talk that carried weight there. Any apologetic tone or sign of weakness would have been fatal. There was no sign of weakness on Hamid Bey's part. He spoke admirably throughout his term of duty. He talked in French without an interpreter.[128]

Hamid Bey was rather a remarkable personality among Turkish governors. Before the First World War he was associated with Colonel Robert Graves and Brigadier General Wyndham Deedes in the organization of the civil inspectorate of the Ottoman Ministry of the Interior, and both these officers spoke highly of his ability, energy, and honesty of purpose.[129] In the autumn of 1914 he was appointed governor of Diyarbekir, where, on the outbreak of war, he did everything in his power to facilitate the journey of the British vice consul and staff to the coast, in spite of instructions to the contrary from İstanbul. In consequence of his opposition to the policy of relocation of Armenians, he was dismissed from the post of governor of Diyarbekir in 1915, and returned to his post in the inspectorate of the Ministry of the Interior. In 1919 at the urgent request of the Minister of the Interior, he accepted the inferior post of *mutasarrıf* of Samsun, as it was felt that the situation there required the presence of an exceptionally capable governor.[130]

The panic caused among the Armenians of Cilicia by the conclusion of the Ankara Agreement spread rather than diminished. As in all such cases, it would be wise to make somewhat wide allowance for exaggeration in these reports, which usually owed their origin to refugees who were, very naturally, hardly in a state to see things in any but the worst light. But even when such allowance was made, it was clear that the panic was widespread. General Henri Gouraud, the French high commisioner for Syria and Lebanon, pointed out to the frightened people that not only the honor of the government of the TGNA, but its interests also were at stake, and that "it cannot be imagined that the Turks will display rancor on account of the past or resort to massacre." The editors of the London weekly *The Near East* believed that the government of the TGNA would do its best to avoid disgracing itself before the Western world. Mustafa Kemal Paşa and his associates naturally realized that for them Ankara Agreement constituted, as General Gouraud put it, halfway house toward peace; if anything untoward should happen, it would surely be against their desires and intention. Yet the rush to escape from the area continued. At least four shiploads of refugees arrived at Alexandria and Port Said at the beginning of December 1921, and so great was the passengers' fear that in one case when they were refused permission to land they seized the ship in order to prevent its return to Mersin, nor would they allow the captain to proceed to Beirut without an official guarantee that they would be allowed to land there.[131]

The British ship *Montaza* brought to İzmir on November 23, 1921, over three hundred Christian refugees from Cilicia, who were escaping before the territory was handed back to the Turks. M. Sterghiades, the governor of this province, refused a landing to them in İzmir, and when a Greek deputation sought to induce him to allow the refugees to land he asked for a guarantee that they would be housed and fed—which was not forthcoming. The steamer took them on to İstanbul, but they were also not allowed to land there, as there were already over fifty thousand refugees in İstanbul.[132]

The archbishop of Canterbury, having received appeals on behalf of the Cilician refugees from the Armenian bishop in Egypt and the Armenian archbishop of İzmir, placed them before Lord Curzon, the British foreign secretary, who sent a reasoned reply which should be studied by all those people who thought that this country could effectively intervene in the matter. Briefly, Lord Curzon pointed out that it was not in the power of Britain to transport the refugees to a place of safety and to take charge of them there. "It is a practical impossibility to accommodate them in Cyprus, Egypt, Mesopotamia, or Palestine," said the British foreign secretary, "and there is no money to defray the very heavy expenses of their maintenance, even if the necessary accommodation were to be made available. Our previous experience in Mesopotamia has shown that they cannot, or will not, support themselves."[133]

On December 9, 1921, General Gouraud addressed to the inhabitants of Cilicia and of Ayntab and Kilis a message regarding France's decision, "in her generous desire to restore peace to Turkey . . . to hand over to the Ottoman Government one of the old provinces and two of the old Turkish towns of the empire, which she occupied in virtue of the additional clauses of the Armistice of Mudros." This message urged the Christian populations of the district to be transferred to remain calm and to have confidence in the Turkish administration. In one passage the general called upon all good citizens, to whatever religion they might belong, to heed his words; to "keep calm, and not to obey a wild impulse that might throw them on the road of exile and misfortune, where they could rely on no adequate help." In another he said: "To leave is to court a disastrous adventure, to which no happy issue is visible. To remain is to keep the fruits of the labor of the ancestors, and revive thereby in peace the prosperity of Cilicia, Killis and Aintab." Unfortunately this eloquent appeal was made in vain, and the earnest assurances it contained were not heeded. Panic seized the Christian population. The captain of a Greek steamer that transported about eight hundred and fifty of these fugitives from Mersin to Cyprus, Jaffa,

Haifa, and Beirut declared that not less than 170,000 Armenians and Greeks swarmed into Mersin from the interior. This estimate might be exaggerated but in Beirut itself there were said to be not less than seventeen hundred Armenians who were given such shelter as was possible in the convents and churches or in the houses of compassionate coreligionists. Some had to camp outside the city. Every available steamer in Syrian and Egyptian waters was rushed to Mersin, thousands were already been transported to various destinations, such as Rhodes, Piraeus, Salonika, and İstanbul, or to Syrian, Palestinian, Cypriot, and Egytian ports. As December 25, 1921, was said to be fixed as the limit of the evacuation period, the fugitives were taking every available means of transport. Wealthy merchants were traveling almost as beggars, with only trifling sums on them in such cash or jewelry as they were able hurriedly to collect and take away with them. The authorities in Beirut, in view of their inability to cope with such a large and sudden influx of refugees (the shortage of houses being already keenly felt by the native population), tried to prevent the landing of refugees who arrived on November 23 on Italian and Khedivial mail steamers, and to redirect them to another destination.[134]

After British and Greek steamers had taken the first installment of these refugees, word came that all ports had been closed to them. Now Cyprus, İzmir, İstanbul, and Egypt had closed their doors. Despair began to settle on them. France opened the ports of Syria, and French steamers came to carry them. At first a ticket to Damascus was 8.50 liras, then 3.50 liras, and finally free steamers were sent to take away all who wished to go. The inhabitants of Osmaniye, Ceyhan, and Dörtyol were allowed to go to İskenderun, the number of refugees there at present being estimated even as high as twenty thousand.[135]

The ruin and loss in the retroceded territory were appalling, and fortunes that survived the war were lost in a few days. When it is remembered that the economic life of Cilicia was constituted to a considerable extent by the Armenian element, the magnitude of the loss to the country would be realized. This loss was bound to react not only on Turkey, but on France as well. Hence the passionate appeal of the high commissioner.[136]

Some idea of the economic location and loss that resulted from the evacuation was given by the fact that out of seventeen industrial establishments at Adana (flour mills, ginning, spinning, and weaving factories), two or three only, owned by Turks, remained working; all the commercial houses of the Greeks and the majority of the Armenian firms were closed down. At Mersin one big flour mill, two ginning factories, and three or four cotton seed oil presses, as well as all the workshops and little foundries run by Armenians, were said to have closed down. At Tarsus one big spinning and weaving works owned by a Greek, and four or five ginning factories were said also to have closed down. The foreign banks in Cilicia were, by the exodus of the Armenian and Greek populations, suddenly faced with the difficulty of the depletion of their staffs, most of their personnel having been recruited from among these two elements, especially the Greeks.[137]

The French and Americans were sincerely trying to induce all Armenians to return to their homes, emphasizing that requisite safeguards were secured for the protection of the Christian minorities that remained under Turkish rule.[138] Henri Franklin-Bouillon, after the signature of the agreement in Ankara, returned to Paris, whence he left, via Marseilles, for Beirut on board the cruiser *Ernest Renan*, and, after conversations there with General Gouraud, went to Adana for about a week, during which time he attempted to allay the fears of the emigrating Christians, and subsequently departed for Konya, where he met Yusuf Kemal, the minister of foreign affairs.[139]

The Turks not only did nothing to cause disturbance, but tried their best to quiet the Armenians and, like the French and Americans, urged them to stay. But the Armenians were adamant: go they would and that immediately, before the last French soldiers left. During the French occupation of Adana many Armenians combined with the French against the Turks and in several instances, engaged in hostilities against the Turks. These people were encouraged by the French to do this. Now with the Turks coming back into power here, these people were terror-stricken in spite of all the assurances that they would not be molested. Adana remained in perfect tranquility. The officials declared they would be glad to have the refugees return at any time.[140]

The government of the TGNA made no general discrimination between Muslims and Christians. It looked upon Ottoman subjects as Turkish subjects, and in its earlier stages it taxed them all alike, taxation which in view of the desperate conditions which prevailed was concurred in by the overwhelming majority of the Anatolian peasantry. In a number of minor matters, however, the government of the TGNA discriminated between Muslims and Christians to the benefit of the latter. It requisitioned numerous smaller and older mosques for military purposes; along the route which the American journalist and historian Clair Price followed across Anatolia—İnebolu, Kastamonu, Çankırı, Ankara, Sarayönü, Konya, Pozantı, Adana, Tarsus, Mersin—he saw no church which was so taken over. It did not conscript Armenians for military service, except in labor battalions, although under the 1908 Reforms it had an undoubted right to do so. It rescinded the 40 percent requisition tax in the case of Cilician Armenians, and upon their refusal to remain in the country voluntarily, it gave them permission to leave. These discriminations were made for local reasons, and the government of the TGNA was not always given credit for them.[141]

The withdrawal from Adana by the French troops and its reentry by the Turkish authorities continued peacefully. The Turkish sanitary service was being installed. The mixed commission to delimit the newly accepted frontier between Turkey and Syria met at İskenderun and commenced its work. Mustafa Kemal Paşa, president of the TGNA, issued a proclamation to the population of Adana and vicinity, exhorting them all to live together in love and harmony.[142]

Very few of the Armenian population elected to stay there, many having crossed over into Syria. Some went to the Sanjak of İskenderun to augment the indigenous Armenian population. Some settled in the cities of Aleppo and Beirut, where other Armenians were found. Or that they ventured further afield and joined the tens of thousands of Syrian Jacobites, Armenians, and Assyrians who had repeopled the great plains of upper Mesopotamia, the Jezireh, in the northeast corner of Syria, whither had come those who since the First World War had fled from Turkey. In İskenderun there were now about twenty thousand, in Beirut two thousand to three thousand. The Catholicos of Sis, Sahak II, took up his residence at Beirut. Very many were heading for the Damascus region. The Armenian exodus was voluntary.[143]

But why did the Armenians risk all this? Could they not trust the spirit of the new Turkey? Was it sheer panic? They said that the trouble was that there had been too much history to make it at all probable that they could be happy in Turkey. They pointed out that the Turks did not trust them, and that, indeed, the Armenians had rebelled against them. They had been working strenuously to keep Cilicia from the Turks. All this they felt the Turks cannot forget. The new Turkish officials were very pleasant and might be doing their best, but fear was rampant, and that it affected other Christians and even some Muslims as well showed that it must be something of which account had to be taken.[144]

On December 16, 1921, in reply to questions in the House of Commons on the subject of Asia Minor by T. P. O'Connor, Aneurin Willims, and one or two other members who wanted information regarding the fate of the Cilician refugees, Undersecretary for Foreign Affairs Hammond declared that he was not at all sure that the Armenians had been well advised to fly from Cilicia. He was definite in stating that the British government had never promised autonomy for Cilicia, and he would not accept Williams's statement that that government had caused the refugees to return there after the Armistice.[145]

The evacuation of the Christian population of Cilicia was practically complete by January 4, 1922. Comte R. De Gontaut-Biron and L. Le Révérend say by February 1, 1922, seven thousand to eight thousand Christians, mostly Greeks, remained in Cilicia. They also contend that according to official French figures ten thousand to twelve thousand of them stayed behind.[146] The

French however estimated that there were five thousand Christians left in the region. Dr. Cyril Haas of the American hospital at Adana thought that there were not more than four hundred to five hundred Christians left in that city. Paul Nilson of Tarsus estimated that fifteen to twenty families, perhaps one hundred persons, were left there. In Mersin there was perhaps a larger proportion of those remaining. There would probably be two thousand Christians left in Mersin.[147]

There were no reports of mistreatment of the Armenians who had not fled. No doubt the watchword of the Turks was caution. On May 22, 1922, the government of the TGNA issued the following statement on the legal rights of the Christians in Anatolia, which mainly ran as follows. (1) By measures taken at the time, and laws elaborated for the purpose, the government of the TGNA has made allotment of the landed property abandoned by Armenians, by following in this operation the same procedure as that in force concerning state property. Sums derived from this allotment are paid into a deposit account opened in the name of proprietors of the above-mentioned properties. Hitherto no requisition concerning these goods has been carried out by the Ankara government. (2) The legal rights of Armenians are safeguarded by the courts. (3) The rights of inheritance of Christian elements are not subjected to any restriction. Christians benefit to the same extent as Muslims from the law of inheritance. Reference to the files of the courts within the limits of the nationalist territory will be sufficient to prove this truth. (4) Male Christians are never imprisoned unless legal necessity requires such a measure. The registers of places of detention contain the substance for the refutation of such an accusation. (5) No Christian woman is employed against her will in Muslim families. Information of this nature is nothing else but the application of a harmful plan intended to discredit Turks in the eyes of the world. (6) No example can be cited of any Turkish official who has made a fortune by pillaging Christians. Turkish officials are suffering privations every day for the realization of our national aspirations and would not soil their conscience and their honor by pillage.[148]

C. E. Mendl from the Foreign Office was invited to luncheon on January 10, 1922, by Howard d'Egville of the British Empire Parliamentary Association to meet Henri Franklin- Bouillon who returned the previous week from Cilicia. In reply to a question as to what value the precautions taken against the massacres of the Christian minorities were worth, he said that the Armenians consisted of two kinds: there were the people who were not indigenous to the soil and were ready to stir up strife as *agents provocateurs*, and it was their behavior which had caused the greatest preoccupation to the French. He quoted the case of three thousand Armenians who had had to be disarmed, having been found near the Syrian frontier with thousands of rifles and cartridges, and he said that the Armenian representatives at İstanbul and elsewhere had asserted that the French would be unable to withdraw their troops without the Armenians on the spot being massacred. The second kind were the indigenous Armenians, only about ten thousand of whom remained in Cilicia, the remainder having emigrated at French expense to Syria. He stated that they did not mind this as they had nothing to lose by being moved and were perfectly willing to go. He brushed against the suggestion that they were only too glad to go anywhere to get away from the Turks.[149]

Dr. Cyril Haas continued his work unmolested. He was constantly busy in the hospital, and his reputation continued to grow. In Adana the hospital was in the heart of the city and so crowded that all longed for the time when it would be possible to build a new hospital outside of the city. Christians and Muslims of all degrees of rank came to share in the advantages offered by the institution. There was room for thirty to thirty-five beds. The men's ward was full, largely of surgical cases. In addition to the inpatient work, Dr. Haas reached a large constituency of the various nationalities in a daily clinic. About one hundred people came each Wednesday to his clinics at Tarsus. The work so increased that one of his trained nurses remained in this town to carry on the work during the week. Hundreds found relief from the eye diseases and malarial fevers that infested the plain.[150]

The hospital served three hundred and eleven sick during 1923–1924. There were sixteen nationalities included in the above number, of whom one hundred and ninety-eight were Turks, two-thirds of all patients. The hospital had always been self-supporting, except during the occupancy of the Near East Relief.[151]

Probably the two areas where the activities of American missionaries in the province of Adana produced the most apparent effects was in the modernization of medical and educational practices.

William Nesbitt Chambers and his wife remained in Adana. Their daughter Dorothea Chambers Blaisdell had always felt that the Turks appreciated keenly this move on her father's part. They knew of his lifelong service and his knowledge of the country. According to Blaisdell, Hamid Bey and Muhittin Paşa were fine progressive individuals. They wished to prove that Turks were not fiends and that the government of the TGNA would be progressive and fair. Chambers's leaving would have shown a lack of confidence in their sincerity and in their ability to carry out their program. He came to feel it was only fair to give them the chance to prove their promises.[152] St. Paul's Institute in Tarsus had not been interfered with. Robert Wilson of the Presbyterian Mission in Mersin went on with his work.[153] The American Girls' School in Adana went forward with its work.[154]

The evangelistic work in Adana centered around an Armenian pastor, Hampartsum Geuvkalajian, who remained in the city when all other Armenian pastors and Gregorian priests fled from the province. He had a regular preaching service on Sunday and mid-week service on Wednesday with an audience of about one hundred and fifty. In this congregation there were perhaps fifty children and young people who led in the singing and responsive reading; the rest were largely Gregorians. The services were entirely in Turkish with the exception of two Gregorian chants which the children sang every Sunday. In September 1923 the Protestant church was taken by the Turkish government; Geuvkalajian was told to hold his services in the Gregorian church building. Here they were treated as guests. Before their services the Gregorian sexton lighted candles on the altar and before the saints, and the most devout Gregorians stood before them and said their prayers.[155]

The reentry of the Turkish army in Adana on December 20, 1921, was celebrated by the Turks of the city with a spontaneous joy and exultation seldom equalled. More prominent than anything else in the celebrations were the display of flags. The whole city was ablaze with flags of red and white, and triumphal arches were erected, decked with leaves, colors, and appropriate mottoes. A huge Turkish crescent and star was flown between the clock tower and the minaret of the Grand Mosque. The Turkish population lined the main street from end to end, the crowd being so dense that progress along the street was very difficult and in places impossible. Street car traffic was suspended for most of the day. The place of honor was given to children from the Turkish orphanages and schools, of whom hundreds were lined up to hail the troops with songs and recitations, each group with its banners. It was a great scene. There was no doubt that Adana had not seen such an imposing national ceremony.[156]

Under the old Ottoman government the Turks thought of themselves as Ottomans and tried to wake Ottoman subjects of other peoples to a similar sense of Ottomanism. But the old concept of Ottomanism ended with the old Ottoman government. New government at Ankara thought of itself as the Turkish government and of its citizens as Turks, and the Turkish national consciousness had run high in consequence. The old concept of Ottomanism was a notion which had no backing among some of the peoples who formed part of the Ottoman Empire. But among the Turks, the concept of the Turkish nation had a distinct historical value, and it was the new concept of Turkish nationalism which found utterance in the government of Ankara. In the eyes of the Turks, it lent a new and forceful meaning to the Turkish crescent and star.

Nationalism in Anatolia was having an effect similar to that which it was having in Syria, in Palestine, and in Egypt. It was proving to be a welding force, tending to draw Muslims and Christians together on the basis of that Eastern civilization which was the common heritage of both. In view of this apparent disposition on the part of Muslims and Christians to discover common ground in nationalism, it was disquietening for Clair Price to return from Ankara to the West in the autumn of 1922 and to find Westerners still urging the Muslim-Christian feud and still insisting on the necessity for "protecting" the Christians from their Muslim compatriots. Price concluded that if the West intended to continue insisting that "minorities" existed in Anatolia, and that guarantees must still be furnished for their safety, the government of the TGNA presumably would agree to such guarantees as the West exacted them from other independent governments (the Greek government, for instance), with the proviso that while asking guarantees from the government for the safety of the "minorities," guarantees be also asked from the "minorities" for their loyalty to the government.[157]

Politically the province of Adana was quiet and with the rising cost of cotton business was beginning. Farmers were carrying on their agricultural work and better days were in sight. Agriculture, aided by modern methods of production and transportation, should be able to nourish an enormous population in that favored land, and should make it more highly prosperous.

In Adana, there were great economic possibilities. Provided capital could be found for experts, new machinery, and more steady labor. They could do great things; they could even grow Egyptian cotton.

LATE REFORM MOVEMENT IN THE OTTOMAN EMPIRE AND CEMAL PAŞA

In a letter he addressed to John Merrill at the Boston headquarters of the ABCFM on December 24, 1921, William Nesbitt Chambers referred to his association with Cemal Paşa when the latter was governor of Adana. The American missionary said the Ottoman statesman gave expression to high ideals and serious purpose and wondered how Cemal Paşa would have developed had not the war came in to change the whole aspect of affairs.[158]

Chambers's argument may well hold validity as a whole, a conjecture that invites further investigation. Cemal Paşa was a man of exceptional gifts who strove to drag his tradition-bound and change-averse country into the modern world. The Young Turks had, of course, done valuable pioneer work and the powerful CUP would, no doubt, have brought a great evolution in the customs and traditions of the country if their work had not been arrested by the series of wars in which the Ottoman Empire found itself so quickly involved.[159]

Administratively the Unionist leadership embarked on such constructive projects as the country required. They established a new system of provincial and local administration. They modernized that of İstanbul itself, through a new municipal organization with an energetic program of public works, equipping it with such amenities as fire brigades and public transport services. They reorganized its police, together with that of the provinces, where the new style gendarmerie, introduced into Macedonia under Sultan Abdülhamid II, was extended to other parts of the empire. In much of this they benefited from the experience of foreign advisers. They tackled judicial reform. They expanded public education at all levels, and for the first time opened the schools and the University of İstanbul to women. This move toward feminine emancipation was to lead, during the years ahead, to their entry into professional life and to new legislation with regard to the rights of the female sex.[160]

The Ottoman government never denied the need of reforms. The Young Turks carried out the revolution precisely so as to put reforms in force. But the reforms needed were purely an internal affair. They were applied with a view to the prosperity and happiness of the country, and to safeguard the union and secure the greater power of the empire. In no country in the world were reforms made for the sake of enfeebling the country or dividing it up, or opening the doors for foreign interference. Any government that would accept reforms of such a character would threaten its own existence and condemn itself to death. The application of reforms was a *sine qua non* for the rejuvenation of the country. The Young Turks had already outlined their course, which was to base the civil, administrative, social, and judicial organization of the country on new foundations, and to give the country thus a new lease of life, to assure the development of all the peoples, but on an Ottoman basis.[161]

There was a time when the entire silk trade of Asia was in the hands of Turks and the caravan routes from China to Levant were the achievements of this nation. The Ottoman Turks, however, had of late years become more and more a people of government officials. This was due in part to a faulty school system and partly owing to the system of military service and capitulations which put the Turks at a great disadvantage economically. Recognizing, however, that the decline of political power was chiefly the result of the loss of economic power, a movement set after the Young Turk revolution of 1908 for the purpose of nationalizing the economic apparatus, heretofore for the most part in the hands of Europeans and native Christians. With this end in view the Turks had recently began directing their attention to commercial pursuits, establishing numerous business houses in their own country and developing and extending their activities to other countries, such as Germany and Italy.

The last four decades of the Ottoman Empire constituted a turbulent and bloody period that saw the Ottoman state, other states great and small, and multiple local actors all join in a struggle for control of what still remained of the polyethnic, multiconfessional, and polyglot Ottoman Empire—namely, the Balkans, Anatolia, and the Arab lands. These territories were the focus of intense competition among the great powers, who, on numerous occasions, dismembered the Ottoman Empire by galvanizing its subjects to rebel under the banner of nationalism and then intervening on their behalf. The Sublime Porte for a host of reasons—technological, military, economic—was hopelessly outclassed, a "sub-peer" competitor playing in the game of nineteenth-century power politics against rivals who were bigger and who hit faster and harder. Try as the Ottoman elites might—and try they did—they could never reform their institutions and society quickly enough. They watched with bitterness as the European powers, sometimes working in concert with former Ottoman subjects, dismantled their once mighty empire from within and without, each loss of territory resulting in a stream of Muslim refugees fleeing lands that in many cases they had lived in for centuries. For the Turks, the high tide of this onslaught came in the eleven years stretching from 1911 to 1922, when the Tripolitanian War (1911–1912), Balkan Wars (1912–1913), the First World War (1914–1918), and the Turkish War of Independence (1919–1922) came one after another.[162]

If the Young Turks had been left to themselves in the course of the years that followed 1908, they might have solved many problems. The development of their policy was one of the riddles of that period of history. But they were not allowed the chance. Foreign intrigues and intervention wrecked all chances of peaceful development.[163] As the Turcologist Ernest Jackh puts it: "To prove successful the Young Turkish Revolution needed ten years of peace: instead it got twelve years of war."[164]

The deterioration of the reform movement in the Ottoman Empire during its last decade of survival must be attributed to a variety of causes. The first was the unwillingness of the non-Muslim peoples of the Empire, after the first flush of enthusiasm, to surrender the special privileges which they had traditionally enjoyed since the days of Sultan Mehmet II (r. 1444–1446 and 1451–1481),[165] and to substitute therefore the constitutional guarantee of a revolutionary administration. The second was a series of wars which provided for less strict observance of the constitution than would have been required in time of peace; the Ottoman-Italian War, the two Balkan Wars, and the First World War subordinated parliamentary experiments to the more pressing problems of national defense. The third was the conflicting interests of the Great Powers, each maneuvering for some special advantage in the Middle East and showing no disposition to assist reform in the Ottoman Empire except insofar as such reform might be expected to serve its own purposes. Finally, the financial difficulties of the Young Turks compelled them to consent to a tightened grip of European financiers and concessionaires on the imperial purse strings.[166]

THE LAST DAYS OF CEMAL PAŞA

If Cemal Paşa had lived to carry out his vision, the flow of Turkish history might have been different. On November 1, 1918, at the age of forty-six, together with six other Unionist leaders, he left İstanbul on board a German ship, which took them to the Crimea. From there they made their way to Berlin.[167] Cemal Paşa would be heard from again. About one year in the Swiss village of Closters, forty to fifty kilometers of Davos, was a time of reflection and writing for him, but he nevertheless continued actively as ever to try to influence the course of national and regional affairs.[168]

While in Europe, he took service with Amanullah Khan, the Emir of Afghanistan, and upon the mediation of Karl Radek, traveled to Russia, where he secured the support of Gyorgy Chicherin, the Soviet commissar of foreign affairs, for his mission of modernizing the Afghan army. The ideals of Cemal Paşa and Mustafa Kemal Paşa should on no account be confused. They both aimed at furthering Turkish nationalism. Cemal Paşa was a whole-hearted supporter of Mustafa Kemal Paşa and the Turkish National Movement in Anatolia.[169] He had been in constant communication by letter and telegram beginning in June 1920 with Ankara; Mustafa Kemal Paşa replied to the correspondence of Cemal Paşa, thanking him for his offers of services. He had on more than one occasion served as an intermediatory between the Turkish leaders and the Soviet rulers which culminated in the Turkish-Soviet Treaty of March 16, 1921.[170]

In 1920 Cemal Paşa proceeded to Kabul and allied himself with the Emir of Afghanistan. He was in Kabul from October 1920 to September 1921 as the head of a Turkish mission, financed by Soviet funds. His aims were the reorganization of the Afghan army and the prosecution of anti-British acts among the tribes of the Indo-Afghan frontier and India. He was not fully recognized by the government of the TGNA, and was suspected by the Soviets of planning independently a Pan-Islamic movement. Toward the end of 1920 the relations between the Soviet envoy in Kabul and Cemal Paşa were strained owing to the latter promising Afghanistan considerable material help, over which he was to have complete control. Cemal Paşa was also to have complete control over all Indian work. In order to carry out this work he proposed the formation of Indian units, improvement of existing defenses, establishment of a young officers school, and to examine the conditions on the frontier. The Emir of Afghanistan approved these steps being taken. The Afghan government agreed to give Cemal Paşa charge of the reorganization of the Afghan army, and to organize, with Soviet help, the Central Committee at Kabul containing representatives of the Khilafat Mussulman League and Congress. Cemal Paşa expressed the opinion that the Afghan-Soviet Treaty of November 22, 1921, would enable a vigorous propaganda campaign to be carried out on the Indian frontier.[171]

Early in 1922 Cemal Paşa visited Germany and France for the purpose of purchasing war material for the Afghan army of which he had become chief of staff. Some time later Mustafa Kemal Paşa himself proposed to send Cemal Paşa to Afghanistan, but difficulties were raised by Moscow, and eventually it was learned that the Emir would only permit him to return as a private individual, subject to a proviso that he would not dabble in politics. In Moscow on July 21, 1922, he was killed by Armenian assassins, Stepan Dzaghigian and his accomplices Bedros Der Boghosian and Artashes Kevorkian, outside secret Cheka (All-Russian Extraordinary Commission for Combating Counter-Revolution, Sabotage and Speculation) headquarters in the Georgian city of Tbilisi. He was fifty years old. He was accompanied by two aides-de-camp, Nusret and Süreyya Beys, who were also shot dead. Cemal Paşa would have been surprised to learn that his murderers were Armenian.[172] It is also claimed that they were murdered by Russians.[173]

Hagop Sarkissian, who had been relocated with his family from Kilis in southeastern Anatolia to Aleppo, was an important eyewitness to the events of his time. He pays tribute and expresses personal token of appreciation to the memory of Cemal Paşa, saying the Ottoman commander was magnanimous toward the Armenians and refers to him as "a great man," who was "responsible for the saving of half-a-million Armenians in the part of Turkey subject to his control; and consequently, for the large Armenian population flourishing today in Syria, Lebanon and Palestine." He further states that also the thousands who later migrated from those regions to Europe and America, himself among them, were indebted to him. Sarkissian came to the conclusion that Cemal Paşa did all that was practically feasible under the circumstances to give as many Armenians as possible a chance to be saved. In those days Armenians hated the man but he said, "If the Armenians knew what I have done for them, they would make my statue of gold and erect it on the top of their Ararat Mountain." Sarkissian now believed he was right. The irony of it was that he was shot by Armenians.[174]

Cavid Bey in his diary entry of one day after Cemal Paşa's death remarked:

> Cemal Paşa is also martyred. He very unjustifiably became a martyr—more unjustifiable than others—by an Armenian bullet. There is perhaps also a British finger in the assassination. But I have no doubt that it was Armenian hand which triggered the gun. Although Cemal Paşa was somewhat involved in the Adana relocation—and that because of his position—should not his effort to preserve the lives of thousands of Armenians in Syria constitute a proof for Armenians to be fair, if not be gratitude, to him? Cemal Paşa had virtues to be a man of administration. He was not of the reactionary opinion; he always wanted to use his exertion and

influence in the path of progress. His arms of protection were wide open toward the youth. He had a special liking for men of culture. And he always wanted to be seen with them. In all these respects he was superior to Enver Paşa.[175]

It is pitiful to think that a man of the eminent qualities of this distinguished officer should not have met with a soldier's death on the battlefield, but should have been foully assassinated by a few infatuated and misguided Armenians. Cemal Paşa was survived by his wife, Seniha; his four sons Ahmet Rüşdi, Hasan Necdet, Mehmet, and Hasan Behçet; and his daughter, Kamran.[176] Seniha Cemal lived to be eighty. After her husband's death, she did not remarry.[177]

The martyrdom of this statesman of rare quality was reported on the front pages of all the Turkish newspapers together with obituaries and photographs of the deceased. News of the death also appeared widely in the world press. Upon his death, the plaudits were no less impressive than those that had been offered when he became minister of marine. The press paid due consideration to his memory and acknowledged his special and distinguishing features as a man and a soldier. Obituary notices lamented the martyrdom of a much venerated personality, invaluable for his wisdom, knowledge, and goodness.[178]

The simplicity and reserve of funeral were in sharp contrast to the public attention generated by the news of his martyrdom. His coffin, covered with Turkish flag, was borne on gun carriage escorted by a squadron of troops and a military band, and followed by mourners. He was buried in Tbilisi and later reburied on the grounds of Kars Kapı military graveyard in Erzurum.[179] It is to be hoped that Cemal Paşa's bones are disinterred and transfered to the Hill of Eternal Liberty in İstanbul where Talat and Enver Paşas are laid to ground.

Cemal Paşa's skill as a commander has been fiercely, and continually, debated by a wide range of commentators, and his role in the First World War has interested a much broader range of investigators and readers than students of military history alone. Interpretations of his command and character commenced soon after the war ended. In the immediate aftermath of a heavy defeat, his generalship was sharply criticized by authors unable to access the full range of primary sources. Soon after his death in 1922, however, others provided a very different interpretation.[180]

In the opinion of the editors of *The Near East* Cemal Paşa had several outstanding virtues. They remarked on August 3, 1922: "He is known to have protected Armenians from massacre, and during the War quite a number of British prisoners owed him their liberty, to say nothing of minor acts of kindness, shown at some risk to himself."[181]

It might be some encouragement and consolation to the friends and associates of Cemal Paşa to know that the sterling worth of their deceased comrade was recognized at all events by many people in the country. True that he was never grand vizier as was Talat Paşa. But he and those who worked with him had no doubt that he could have been so. Upon this Ottoman statesman's death Falih Rıfkı (Atay) wrote the following and it is worth quoting him extensively:

> Cemal Paşa was a great statesman molded by will, faith and resolution. With Cemal Paşa, we are not perhaps losing a supreme politician and a unique soldier. But for the reconstruction of the country and the reformation of the state, we can hardly raise a Turk with such a mental ability and character. There are two dissimilar persons among the chiefs of the CUP that I solely liked. I used to tell myself "I wish these two men were not so much engaged in partisanship, and Cemal Paşa would remain a provincial governor, Ziya Gökalp[182] a scholar." One of them was the arm, the other was the brain of the new generation. Ziya Gökalp has thought and Cemal Paşa has acted. They are the ones who did the best deeds in the country since the Constitutionalism. The other day I met a naval lieutenant colonel and he told me: "He [Cemal Paşa] reactivated the force [marine]" and those in Adana say: "He [Cemal Paşa] built this embankment." I don't know what those in Baghdad said but a foreigner who visited Syria after the armistice has observed: "I meet Cemal Paşa at every step." Those who will come from the middle of Asia tomorrow will say: "Cemal Paşa was one day in Afghanistan."
>
> From the edge of the [Suez] Canal to the Trans-Taurus, in Sinai, Palestine, Syria and Adana, Cemal Paşa's endless traces are visible. This man, toiling from dawn to dawn for four years, was one of those remarkable individuals who knew the method of conquering the nature. In the first [Suez] canal expedition those who crossed the desert while sucking muddy and wormy marshes with their shattered lips, saw on the same route after four years not only thousands of men and camels but also enough water wells and water basins to cultivate gardens and vegetable plants. In these four years, as though walking through roads, he traversed across the mountains and deserts, Jerusalem railway extended up to the centers of the Sinai. Towns such as Pozantı was created from stretch, ruined villages like Beersheba were turned into small cities through their water and lightning networks, and through their streets and buildings.
>
> Some say: "It was Cemal Paşa's greatest mistake to pour Turkish treasure into Syria and Palestine." This was Cemal Paşa's greatest virtue, for he had never thought that Syria could be lost, for he had never forgot that Syria was a province of Turkey.[183]

Cemal Paşa could have been paid no higher compliment. Atay was one of the ablest and best informed of the Turkish publicists of the time. He had risen through the ranks of the grand vizier's offices and come to the attention of the Unionist leadership through his weekly columns in *Tanin*. He covered the Balkan Wars, where he met War Minister Enver Paşa. As minister of the interior, Talat Bey appointed Atay as second secretary in his private cabinet. When Cemal Paşa left İstanbul on November 21, 1914, to become commander of the Fourth Army in Damascus, he specifically requested that Atay be seconded to his staff at the headquarters. Therefore to a very large extent he was entitled to be right on Cemal Paşa. The views expressed by him fairly represented the opinions of the Turkish press as a whole.

Cemal Paşa was decorated with the grand cordon of the order of the *Osmaniye*; the grand cordon of the order of the *Mecidiye* set in brilliants; the silver and gold medals of *İmtiyaz*; the gold medal of *Liyakat*; the medals of Navy, Red Crescent, and Hedjaz railway; the decorations of the Merit, Leopold and Red and Black Eagles of Germany; Merit, Iron, and Red Crosses, Graz Fordavin, and Bavaria of Austria; the grand cross of the Order of St. Alexander of Bulgaria; the order of Chevalier of the Legion of Honor from France; and a decoration from Belgium for his meritorous and distinguished services in the performances of duties of great responsibility.[184]

NEVZAT ARTUÇ'S BIOGRAPHY OF CEMAL PAŞA

One last point must be made to end this chapter. Biography unfortunately is not a field which Turkish historians have cultivated in the twentieth century as intensively as their colleagues in the English-speaking world, no doubt due in part to the influence of the *Annales* school's emphasis on social and economic analysis. Happily, this disposition has been changing of late, and one can hope that Nevzat Artuç's work on Cemal Paşa will inspire others to take up this genre.

In Turkey, around a dozen books have been published wholly or partly about Cemal Paşa. In English, only his memoirs *Memories of a Turkish Statesman 1913–1919* and Talha Çiçek's *War and State Formation in Syria: Cemal Pasha's Governorate during World War I, 1914–1917* exist. No substantial new work in Turkish has appeared for a decade, which is alone sufficient reason to look again at the major Ottoman leader, and an unusually complicated human being, whom the passage of time now allows us to see more clearly than was the case when he lived.

Cemal Paşa's remarkable life clearly warrants a scholarly biography, and Artuç has provided the first such attempt to draw on published and unpublished Ottoman sources. *Cemal Paşa Askeri ve Siyasi Hayatı* represents a revised and enlarged version of Artuç's 2005 doctoral dissertation completed in the Institute of Social Sciences at Süleyman Demirel University, İsparta, under the supervision of Professor Bayram Kodaman. In the years since the dissertation's writing, Artuç has had the opportunity to research and think further about Cemal Paşa's role in the history of the Ottoman Empire. The author has not strayed measurably from any of the conclusions he reached in the dissertation, but he is thankful for the time to have thought in more detail about the questions raised there.

Cemal Paşa Askeri ve Siyasi Hayatı is both chronologically and thematically arranged, a descriptive-analytical account divided into four basic parts. In part one, Cemal Paşa's family background, education, and entry to the military career; his first duties in the army; his entry to the Ottoman Freedom Society and the CUP and his activities there; the proclamation of the Second Constitutionalism and Cemal Bey; the personality of Cemal Paşa and some observations on him; and his publications and the decorations he received are mentioned. The March 31, 1909, incident and Cemal Bey; his provincial governorships in Adana and Baghdad; his participation in the Balkan Wars of 1912–1913; his military governorship in İstanbul; Cemal Bey regarding Edirne's restitution on July 20, 1913, and the question of Western Thrace; abolition of the military governorship of İstanbul and Cemal Bey's appointment to the acting commandership of the First Army Corps; and his post of minister of public works are reviewed in part two. The main emphasis in part three has been laid upon Cemal Paşa's post of minister of marine and entry scenarios to the First World War and Cemal Paşa. Cemal Paşa and Syria and his role vis-à-vis Arab separatist movements are also considered here. Cemal Paşa's departure abroad and its effects, his activities abroad, his endeavors in Europe for Afghanistan, his views on the Turkish Independence Movement, his correspondence with Mustafa Kemal Paşa, and his assassination in Tbilisi are treated in part four. The book contains a number of maps and illustrations. It also includes a wide-ranging bibliography and a good index.

Artuç brought new material about the man, his origins, his upbringing, his military career, and his family life, material which has not to date found its way into coherent form in a biography. We know now much more about his extraordinary personality than before. With 1,782 footnotes, the documentation is exhaustive. Only a native speaker of Turkish could have plumbed the Turkish sources pertaining to Cemal Paşa and the early twentieth century with the thoroughness that Artuç clearly has. For that matter, he has evidently read everything both in Ottoman and modern Turkish relevant to the topic.

Artuç has put all students of Cemal Paşa permanently to his debt. It should be noted, however, that about the time he was finishing his work, the Ottoman archives for the First World War and the Armistice Period (1919–1922) had only begun to become available, and subsequent scholarship on these periods has flourished mightily.

Until now, accounts of this Ottoman statesman's career have been monopolized by muckrakers and friends. Artuç's inquiry supersedes them all by supplying a much more solid evaluation, one that does for Cemal Paşa what most political biographies fail to do for their subjects. The author's portrait is a perfect example of the maxim that a good biographer must empathize with his subject. That Artuç does.

Cemal Paşa should have found a biographer long ago. Such neglect is unjustifiable and almost incomprehensible in view of his contribution to the making of modern Turkey. Biography is a much neglected genre in historical writing on the Ottoman Empire. Artuç's biographical study of Cemal Paşa makes a significant contribution to the literature which seeks to use an individual's life and work as a metaphor for wider political and social realities. All this is achieved through rigorous interrogation of the surviving source material.

Artuç's book is a detailed portrait of an age. It has something for just about everybody concerned with the modern and contemporary Middle East: historians of Turkey interested in the twilight of the Ottoman Empire, students of Armenian nationalism in the Republic of Armenia as well as in the diaspora, and political historians of the Young Turk period and its immediate aftermath. Born in 1872 and deceased in 1922, Cemal Paşa's life could be regarded as representative in many respects of the painful and only partially successful adjustments facing a generation of Turkish military officials who suffered the dislocations and wounds of the passage from the Ottoman Empire to that of the postwar Turkish settlement.

Biographies of major political figures pose particular problems for any author. Such biographies can turn too easily into accounts of the period rather than the person. Artuç addresses this difficulty relatively well. His biography is a detailed and balanced one, both in terms of the respective weight he gives to Cemal Paşa's life as a soldier and as a statesman.

Given the paucity of historical works about Cemal Paşa, Turks and foreigners alike tend to base their view of him upon the unflattering, though admittedly often dramatic, portraits that emerge from autobiographical and memoir accounts by a number of those who suffered from the ravages of the Second Ottoman Constitutional Period. Artuç's study, among other things, redresses the balance to some extent in Cemal Paşa's favor. Certainly it is not intended as an apology for the Ottoman Empire's firm statesman. It is, however, an effort to view Cemal Paşa as his contemporaries saw him and, given the distance of some ninety-six years since his death, to place him and his policies in a more balanced perspective. However, his biography is also problematic. The charges brought against Cemal Paşa after he left Turkey on November 1, 1918, involved allegations of misuse of office, and it is rather surprising to see these passed over lightly. Artuç lists the charges, but makes no attempt to investigate them in detail, despite the fact that there is plenty of surviving evidence to do so. He leaves some stones unturned. This reader gained little sense of what Cemal Paşa's views of the Armenian relocation of 1915 were. The fairness with which Artuç examines the existing literature often means that his own assessments are unclear or are not articulated explicitly. This is reinforced in the early chapters of the monograph which seem too reliant on published work rather than original research.

Artuç's account of Cemal Paşa's personal life may not be accurate in every detail, but it does represent the most careful sifting to date of the evidence readily available. The author has combed the available Ottoman materials with admirable thoroughness. The Ottoman statesman has until now received less attention than he deserved. This biography does him justice. One hopes that there will be an English translation to enhance its accessibility to a wider audience.

NOTES

1. FO 690/33. Monthly Summary for July 1911. J. G. Lorimer (Baghdad) to Sir Gerard Lowther (Istanbul), August 7, 1911.

2. Gökhan Çetinsaya, *Ottoman Administration of Iraq, 1890–1908* (London and New York: Routledge, 2006), pp. 1–2; Stephen Hemsley Longrigg, *Iraq, 1900 to 1950: A Political, Social, And Economic History* (London: Oxford University Press, 1953), pp. 1–2. *Ottoman Administration of Iraq, 1890–1908* marks a great advance over *Iraq, 1900 to 1950* both in accuracy and in completeness. Gökhan Çetinsaya is thoroughly at home with the extensive Ottoman and British sources and has worked up his account from the original materials. His reference book should do much to stimulate further work in the field. Stephen Hemsley Longrigg was the British political officer for Kirkuk in 1919–1922 and a veteran of forty-seven years' service in the Middle East.

3. *Iraq Administration Reports 1914–1932*, Vol. 1: 1914–1918 (Melksham and Oxford: Archive Editions, 1992), p. 11. In May 1909, John Gordon Lorimer was appointed consul general at Baghdad, an unusual distinction, since this post had usually been filled by military officials. During his tenure of office he spent much time and labor in compiling a gazetteer of Mesopotamia, which, in addition to the most minute details, contained information regarding the tribes in this region, their strength, number of horses, cattle, rifles, etc. See "Obituary," *The Near East*, Vol. 6, No. 145 (February 13, 1914), p. 479; "Baghdad Notes," *The Near East*, Vol. 6, No. 151 (March 27, 1914), p. 665.

4. Yücel Güçlü, "Iraq on the Way to Its New Constitution: The Ottoman Experience and Turkish Example," *International Journal of Turkish Studies*, Vol. 11, Nos. 1–2 (Fall 2005), p. 143.

5. Kayalı, "Elections and the Electoral Process in the Ottoman Empire, 1876–1919," pp. 265 and 282. For a fuller discussion of this theme, see idem, *Arabs and Young Turks*.

6. Elie Kedourie, "The Kingdom of Iraq: A Retrospect," in *The Chatham House Version and Other Middle-Eastern Studies* (London: Weidenfeld and Nicolson, reprint, 1984), p. 278.

7. Güçlü, "The Role of the Ottoman-Trained Officers in Independent Iraq," p. 447.

8. Colonel Yate's remark at House of Commons Debate, Vol. 22, cc 1267-300, March 8, 1911.

9. Longrigg, *Iraq, 1900 to 1950*, p. 3. The resident at Baghdad was answerable to the Government of India, the Bombay Government, the Colonial Office, War Office, and Air Ministry.

10. Reader Bullard, *The Camels Must Go* (London: Faber and Faber, 1961), p. 80.

11. FO 195/2369. The Arrival of Djemal Bey at Baghdad. Sir Gerard Lowther (Istanbul) to Sir Edward Grey (FO), September 15, 1911.

12. "Cemal Bey'in Bağdat Vilayetine Tayin Kararnamesi" (Appointment Decree of Cemal Bey to the Province of Baghdad), *Tanin*, August 31, 1911, p. 1.

13. "Cemal Bey'in Nutku" (Speech of Cemal Bey), *Tanin*, August 31, 1911, p. 1.

14. Ibid.

15. Ibid.

16. Çetinsaya, *Ottoman Administration of Iraq, 1890–1908*, pp. 8–10.

17. Ali Haydar Midhat, *The Life of Midhat Pasha: A Record of His Services, Political Reforms, Banishment, and Judicial Murder* (London: John Murray, 1903), pp. 49–50.

18. Ibid., p. 50.

19. Ibid., p. 51.

20. Ibid., pp. 51–52.

21. BOA, DH. MTV, No. 37/8, Enclosures 2 and 3. Baghdad in 1911, July 1, 1911; Çetinsaya, *Ottoman Administration of Iraq, 1890–1908*, pp. 1 and 12–14.

22. Longrigg, *Iraq, 1900 to 1950*, pp. 2–3.

23. BOA, DH. İdare (Administration), No. 63/20. Cemal Bey's Governorship in Baghdad, June 25, 1912; Artuç, *Cemal Paşa*, pp. 88–90.

24. FO 807/38. Summary for September 1911. John Gordon Lorimer (Baghdad) to Sir Gerard Lowther (Istanbul), October 2, 1911.

25. Ibid.

26. Ibid.

27. Longrigg, *Iraq, 1900 to 1950*, p. 36.

28. FO 807/38. Summary of Events in Turkish Iraq for the Month of September 1911. John Gordon Lorimer (Baghdad) to Sir Gerard Lowther (Istanbul), October 2, 1911.

29. On September 29, 1911, Italy went to war with the Ottoman Empire in order to wrest from it its last possession in North Africa, the province of Tripolitania.

30. FO 912/42. Summary of Events in Turkish Iraq for the Month of October 1911. John Gordon Lorimer (Baghdad) to Sir Gerard Lowther (Istanbul), November 6, 1911.

31. Ibid.

32. FO 963/43. Summary of Events in Turkish Iraq for the Month of November 1911. Norman Scott (Baghdad) to Sir Gerard Lowther (Istanbul), December 4, 1911.

33. BOA, MV, No. 159/67. Improvements in the Province of Baghdad, November 29, 1911; BOA, BEO, No. 4120/308990. Cemal Bey's Governorship in Baghdad, December 4, 1912.

34. FO 195/2415. Summary of Events in Turkish Iraq for the Month of January 1912. John Gordon Lorimer (Baghdad) to Sir Gerard Lowther (Istanbul), February 10, 1912.

35. FO 195/2415. Summary of Events in Turkish Iraq for the Month of February 1912. John Gordon Lorimer (Baghdad) to Sir Gerard Lowther (Istanbul), March 6, 1912.

36. BOA, MV, No. 159/67. Improvements in the Province of Baghdad, November 29, 1911; BOA, BEO, No. 4120/308990. Cemal Bey's Governorship in Baghdad, December 4, 1912.

37. Ibid.

38. Ibid.

39. "Sir William Willcocks," *Le Moniteur Oriental*, 29 septembre 1908, p. 2.

40. See further on this point, Morris Jastrow, Jr., "The Turks and the Future of the Near East," *The Annals of the American Academy of Political and Social Science*, Vol. 84 (July 1919), p. 31.

41. FO 195/2415. Summary of Events in Turkish Iraq for the Month of January 1912. John Gordon Lorimer (Baghdad) to Sir Gerard Lowther (Istanbul), February 10, 1912.

42. FO 195/2415. Summary of Events in Turkish Iraq for the Month of February 1912. John Gordon Lorimer (Baghdad) to Sir Gerard Lowther (Istanbul), March 6, 1912.

43. BOA, MV, No. 159/67. Improvements in the Province of Baghdad, November 29, 1911; BOA, BEO, No. 4120/308990. Cemal Bey's Governorship in Baghdad, December 4, 1912.

44. Feridun Kandemir, İbrahim Öztürkçü, ed., *Yakın Tarihten Bir Sahife Cemal Paşa'nın Son Günleri* (A Page From the Recent History: The Last Days of Cemal Paşa) (İstanbul: Yağmur Yayınevi, 2012), p. 131.

45. "Cemal Bey ve Alemdar" (Cemal Bey and *Alemdar*), *Tanin*, September 22, 1911, p. 1.

46. FO 195/2366. Alleged Malpractices of the Late Governor. Ian Smith (Adana) to Sir Gerard Lowther (Istanbul), October 30, 1911.

47. Ibid.

48. Ibid.

49. Ibid.

50. BOA, DH. Muhaberatı Umumi İdaresi Mütenevvi Kısmı (Administration of General Correspondence Miscellaneous Matters) (hencefoth referred to as MTV), No. 18/47, Enclosure 2. Müftüzade Muhammed Kamil Bey's Complaint Petition to the Sublime Porte, August 4, 1912; BOA, DH. MTV, No. 18/47, Enclosure 3, Müftüzade Muhammed Kamil Bey's Complaint Petition to the Sublime Porte, August 5, 1912; Kayalı, "Elections and the Electoral Process in the Ottoman Empire, 1876–1919," p. 274 and fn49.

51. Sadok Masliyah, "Zionism in Iraq," *Middle Eastern Studies*, Vol. 25, No. 2 (April 1989), p. 216.

52. FO 191/10. Account of the Jewish Community in Baghdad. John Gordon Lorimer (Baghdad) to Sir Gerard Lowther (Istanbul), February 27, 1910.

53. *Iraq Administration Reports 1914–1932*, Vol. 1, pp. 16 and 34.

54. Longrigg, *Iraq, 1900 to 1950*, p. 11.

55. BOA, DH. MTV, No. 37/8, Enclosure 9. July 10 Celebrations at Baghdad, July 23, 1911; "Bağdat'ta Iydi Milli Tesidi" (National Day Celebrations at Baghdad), *Tanin*, July 25, 1912, p. 3; FO 195/441-499. Summary of Events in Turkish Iraq During the Month of July 1912. John Gordon Lorimer (Baghdad) to Sir Gerard Lowther (Istanbul), August 5, 1912; "Bedouin in Baghdad," *The Near East*, Vol. 3, No. 69 (August 30, 1912), p. 494.

56. BOA, MV, No. 159/67. Improvements in the Province of Baghdad, November 29, 1911; BOA, BEO, No. 4120/308990. Cemal Bey's Governorship in Baghdad, December 4, 1912.

57. FO 912/42. Relations Between Governor of Baghdad and the British Consul General. John Gordon Lorimer (Baghdad) to Sir Gerard Lowther (Istanbul), April 2, 1912.

58. BOA, DH. MTV, No. 33/1-45, Enclosure 3. Cemal Bey's Resignation, August 8, 1912; BOA, DH. MTV, No. 33/1-46, Enclosure 1/1. Cemal Bey's Resignation, August 12, 1912.

59. FO 195/441. Summary of Events in Turkish Iraq During the Month of July 1912. John Gordon Lorimer (Baghdad) to Sir Gerard Lowther (Istanbul), August 5, 1912.

60. "The Future of Baghdad," *The Near East*, Vol. 4, No. 79 (November 8, 1912), p. 20.

61. FO 195/449. Summary of Events in Turkish Iraq During the Month of August 1912. John Gordon Lorimer (Baghdad) to Sir Gerard Lowther (Istanbul), September 3, 1912.

62. Ibid.

63. USNA, 867.00/399. Cemal Bey's Resignation. Emil Saurer (Baghdad) to William Rockhill (Istanbul), August 4, 1912.

64. Halidé Edib, *Memoirs of Halidé Edib*, p. 390.

65. Hasan Kayalı, "Ottoman and German Imperial Objectives in Syria During World War I: Synergies and Strains Behind the Front Lines," in Hakan Yavuz with Feroz Ahmad, eds., *War and Collapse: World War I and the Ottoman State* (Salt Lake City, UT: University of Utah Press, 2016), pp. 1125–26.

66. "Turks Clean Palestine; Stretching Out Railroads," *The Washington Post*, August 8, 1915, p. 10.

67. "Situation in Cilicia," *The Orient*, Vol. 2, No. 28 (October 25, 1911), p. 3.

68. FO 195/2366. New Governor of Adana. Ian Smith (Adana) to H. A. C. Eyres (Istanbul), July 1, 1911.

69. BOA, DH. MTV, No. 1/37, Enclosure No. 3/1-2. Appointment of Muammer Bey to the Governorship of Adana, June 14, 1911; BOA, DH. MTV, No. 1/38.

On Muammer Bey, June 15, 1911; BOA, DH. MTV, No. 6-2/20. On Muammer Bey, June 24, 1911; BOA, BEO, No. 3996/299627. On Muammer Bey, January 28, 1912.

70. BOA, HR. SYS, No. 83/71. Condition of Christians in Adana. Muammer Bey (Adana) to Celal Bey (İstanbul), December 28, 1911; FO 195/25-40. Quarterly Report. Anatolia, Mesopotamia, Yemen, Syria for the Quarter Ending 31 December 1911. Sir Gerard Lowther (Istanbul) to Sir Edward Grey (FO), January 3, 1912.

71. MAE, NS Turquie, Vol. 85, pp. 136–37. Nouvelles d'Adana. Barré de Lancy (Mersine) à M. Selves (Paris), 27 décembre 1911.

72. BOA, DH. MTV, No. 6-2/41. Reasons for Muammer Bey's Resignation, September 20, 1911; BOA, DH. MTV, No. 6-2/82. Transfer of Muammer Bey to the Governorship of the Province of Konya, February 5, 1912.

73. BOA, Dahiliye Nezareti Siyasi (Ministry of the Interior Political), No. 53/47. On the Resignation of Muammer Bey, July 31, 1911.

74. Çankaya, *Mülkiye Tarihi ve Mülkiyeliler*, Vol. 3, pp. 819–22; Orhun, Kasaroğlu, Belek, Atakul, *Meşhur Valiler*, pp. 309–39; *Türk Parlamento Tarihi* (History of the Turkish Parliament), Vol. 3: *Türkiye Büyük Millet Meclisi İkinci Dönem 1923–1927* (Turkish Grand National Assembly Second Term 1923–1927) (Ankara: Türkiye Büyük Millet Meclisi Basımevi Müdürlüğü, 1995), pp. 712–13; Feridun Kandemir, "Malta Yaranı" (Malta Companions), *Resimli Tarih Mecmuası*, Vol. 5, No. 59 (November 1954), pp. 3492–97; Kuneralp, *Son Dönem Osmanlı Erkan ve Ricali (1839–1922)*, p. 58. On Muammer Bey and the CUP, see Şakir, *İttihat ve Terakki - I Nasıl Doğdu?* p. 175.

75. "Another Sign of New Turkey," *The Missionary Herald*, Vol. 57, No. 5 (May 1911), p. 202.

76. "Turkish Students in America," *Levant Trade Review*, Vol. 1, No. 4 (March 1912), p. 425.

77. "Cultivation in Adana," *The Near East*, Vol. 3, No. 58 (June 14, 1912), p. 185.

78. "Progress in Cilicia," *Levant Trade Review*, Vol. 1, No. 4 (March 1912), p. 442.

79. André Autheman, *La Banque impériale ottomane* (Paris: Comité pour l'histoire économique et financière de la France, 1996); Edhem Eldem, *A History of the Ottoman Bank* (İstanbul: Ottoman Bank Historical Research Center, 1999); Christopher Clay, "The Origins of Modern Banking in the Levant: The Branch Network of the Imperial Ottoman Bank, 1890–1914," *International Journal of Middle East Studies*, Vol. 26, No. 4 (November 1994), p. 590.

80. By war here it is meant the two Balkan Wars of 1912–1913.

81. "Real Christianity," *The Orient*, Vol. 3, No. 52 (December 25, 1912), p. 3.

82. House of Commons Debates, Vol. 52, cc 2298, May 8, 1913.

83. John Debbas, "Crop Conditions in Adana," *Levant Trade Review*, Vol. 3, No. 2 (September 1913), p. 134; Redan, *La Cilicie et le problème ottoman*, p. 115.

84. "Adana'da Fesad" (Sedition in Adana), *Tanin*, April 30, 1913, p. 1.

85. William Nesbitt Chambers, "Letter from Adana," *The Orient*, Vol. 4, No. 21 (May 21, 1913), p. 6.

86. "Constantinople Letter," *The Near East*, Vol. 5, No. 107 (May 23, 1913), p. 59.

87. BOA, DH. MTV, No. 33-2/1. On Emin Bey, December 11, 1912; BOA, Dahiliye Nezareti Umur-ı Mahalliye ve Vilayat Müdiriyeti (Ministry of the Interior Directorate for Local and Provincial Affairs), No. 63/15. On Emin Bey, December 15, 1913.

88. BOA, DH. MTV, No. 7/62. Emin Bey's Tenure of Office, May 26, 1913; BOA, MV, No. 230/117. Dismissal of Emin Bey, November 26, 1913; BOA, BEO, No. 4235/317560. Dismissal of Emin Bey, November 27, 1913.

89. Philips Price, "The Problem of Asiatic Turkey," *The Contemporary Review*, Vol. CV (February 1914), pp. 213–14.

90. Ibid., pp. 214–15.

91. Ibid., p. 215.

92. For Ali Seydi Bey, see Çankaya, *Mülkiye Tarihi ve Mülkiyeliler*, Vol. 3, pp. 465–67; Kuneralp, *Son Dönem Osmanlı Erkan ve Ricali (1839–1922)*, p. 65.

93. Kuneralp, *Son Dönem Osmanlı Erkan ve Ricali (1839–1922)*, p. 84.

94. Chambers, "Letter from Adana," p. 6.

95. BOA, HR. SYS, No. 84/66. The Opening of the German School in Adana, May 22, 1913; William Nesbitt Chambers, "Adana Activities," *The Orient*, Vol. 4, No. 50 (December 10, 1913), p. 7.

96. "Adana Cotton Factories," *The Near East*, Vol. 4, No. 100 (April 4, 1913), p. 627.

97. Chambers, "Letter from Adana," p. 44.

98. Ibid. Ernest Otto Jacob served as the North American Young Men's Christian Association Secretary in the Ottoman Empire in 1910–1917 and 1920–1923.

99. ABCFM Papers, Houghton Library, Harvard University. Unit 5 (16.9.5) Reel 669. Vol. 23 Central Turkey Mission 1910–1919 Letters A-CHA ABC 16: The Near East 1817–1919. Letter from William Nesbitt Chambers (Adana) to Dear Friends (Boston), January 24, 1914.

100. Chambers, "The Possibilities of Adana and the Cilician Plain," pp. 148–49.

101. "Great Britain and Turkey," *The Near East*, Vol. 3, No. 66 (August 9, 1912), p. 413.

102. ATASE, BDHK, Amanus Supply Line Command of the Fourth Army. Supply: Anatolian-Taurus Railway Organization, Folder: 3314, File: 230, January 14, 1918–March 29, 1918.

103. Edward Nathan, "Agricultural Implements and Machinery in Mersina-Adana District," *Levant Trade Review*, Vol. 4, No. 2 (September 1914), p. 146.

104. "Agricultural Machinery in the District of Adana," *Levant Trade Review*, Vol. 5, No. 3 (December 1915), p. 252.

105. Price, "The Problem of Asiatic Turkey," pp. 212–13.

106. "American Missionaries in Turkey Are Safe," *The Boston Globe*, November 10, 1914, p. 4.

107. Armstrong, *Turkey and Syria Reborn*, p. 138.

108. USNA, RG 45 Records Collection of the Office of Naval Records and Library Area File, 1911–1927 Mediterranean Area 6 March 1919–6 May 1919. American Committee for Relief in the Near East Notes, April 25, 1919.

109. Zaven Der Yeghiayan, trans. Ared Misirliyan and ed. Vatche Gazarian, *My Patriarchal Memoirs* (Barrington, RI: Mayreni Publishing, 2002), p. 113.

110. Armstrong, *Turkey and Syria Reborn*, p. 138; Yeghiayan, *My Patriarchal Memoirs*, p. 176.

111. ATASE, İstiklal Harbi Koleksiyonu (Collection of the War of Independence) (henceforth referred to as İSHK), Box: 270, File: 129, No. 10690. Increase in Municipal Taxes in Adana Under French Occupation, November 4, 1919; ATASE, İSHK, Box: 104, File: 43, No. 4678. Increase in Municipal Taxes in Adana Under French Occupation, December 11, 1919; Canbaz and Kılıç, *Kuvayı Milliye Komutanı Sinan Bey'in Günlüğü*, pp. 5, 19, 25–26, 139, 192, 220, 228, 232, 287, and 394.

112. USNA, Naval Records, 27 January 1920–31 December 1920, Box 182, Mark Bristol's Letter of 8 April 1920 to James Barton.

113. "The Evacuation of Cilicia," *The Orient*, Vol. 9, No. 2 (February 1922), p. 5.

114. USNA, 867.00/1458. Evacuation of Cilicia. Rear Admiral Mark Bristol (Istanbul) to Charles Hughes (Secretary of State), 11 January 1922. Enclosure No.3: Copy of Jesse Jackson's Communication of 17 November 1921 Addressed to General Marie de Lamothe. Though a man of intelligence, learning, and insight, Jesse Jackson had not much impact on Washington policy makers and never won a major diplomatic assignment.

115. Rear Admiral Mark Bristol played a major part in winning the friendship of Turkey, a former enemy power. In recognition of the diplomatic work he was called upon to perform, he was appointed United States High Commissioner to Turkey with headquarters in İstanbul in 1919. He won the confidence of the President of the TGNA Mustafa Kemal Paşa and negotiated an agreement to restore Turkish-American trade and to settle claims against both governments by a joint commission. Bristol was the first diplomat of any Western country to open relations with the Turkish government in the new capital at Ankara. Secretary of State Charles Hughes remarked on Bristol's "important services which have been rendered this government." Bristol's papers, some 33,000 items, and diary are in the Manuscript Division of the Library of Congress at Washington, DC. These oft-overlooked documents comprise part of the United States historical record concerning the Armenian rebellion and the Ottoman military response. Any assessment of the Armenian question must take Bristol into accouınt.

116. USNA, 867.00/1458. Evacuation of Cilicia. Rear Admiral Mark Bristol (Istanbul) to Charles Hughes (Secretary of State), 11 January 1922. Enclosure No.4: Copy of Rear Admiral Mark Bristol's Letter of 10 January 1922 Addressed to Jesse Jackson.

117. USNA, 867.00/1480. Evacuation of Cilicia. Charles Hughes (Secretary of State) to Rear Admiral Mark Bristol (Istanbul), 7 April 1922.

118. USNA, 867.00/1477. Evacuation of Cilicia. Rear Admiral Mark Bristol (Istanbul) to Charles Hughes (Secretary of State), 6 January 1922. Enclosure: Copy of the Diary of the Destroyer *Williamson*.

119. Ibid.

120. USNA, 867.00/1456. Report of Operations For Week Ending 20 November 1921. Commander US Naval Detachment in Turkish Waters. Rear Admiral Mark Bristol (Istanbul) to Charles Hughes (Secretary of State), 20 November 1921.

121. Henri Franklin-Bouillon was the French Minister of Propaganda in 1917 and the chairman of the Foreign Affairs Committee of the French Senate in 1921–1922.

122. ATASE, İSHK, Box: 1365, File: 146, No.14477. Circular on the Conclusion of the Ankara Agreement, 22 October 1921; ATASE, İSHK, Box: 1365, File: 166, No.145508. Circular on the Ankara Agreement, 23 October 1921. Although it was not without considerable difficulty that the French envoy to Ankara, Henri Franklin-Bouillon, succeeded after spending three weeks over the final haggle, in persuading the government of the TGNA to sign and ratify a peace agreement, the event was one of the most hopeful signs that had appeared upon the Near Eastern horizon for some time. See "The Franco-Turkish Convention," *The Near East*, Vol.20, No. 547 (November 3, 1921), p. 553.

123. For Muhittin (Akyüz) Paşa, see *Türk Parlamento Tarihi Dördüncü Dönem 1931–1935* (History of the Turkish Parliament Fourth Term 1931–1935), Vol. 2 (Ankara: Türkiye Büyük Millet Meclisi Basımevi Müdürlüğü, 1996), pp. 326–27.

124. On Hamit Bey's life and career, see Halit Eken, *Bir Milli Mücadele Valisi ve Anıları Kapancızade Hamit Bey* (A Governor of the National Struggle and His Reminiscences: Kapancızade Hamit Bey) (İstanbul: Yeditepe Yayınevi, 2008).

125. USNA, 867.00/1477. Evacuation of Cilicia. Rear Admiral Mark Bristol (Istanbul) to Charles Hughes (Secretary of State), 6 January 1922. Enclosure: Copy of the Diary of the Destroyer *Williamson*.

126. ABCFM Papers, Letter from J. C. Martin (Adana) to the "Rooms" (Boston), 14 April 1922. 762 Central Turkey 1920–August 1924, Vol. 1, Documents.

127. Blaisdell, *Missionary Daughter*, pp. 196–97.

128. Eken, *Bir Milli Mücadele Valisi ve Anıları*, pp. 282 and 336–37.

129. See Robert Graves, *Storm Centres of the Near East: Personal Memories 1879–1922* (London: Hutchinson Co., 1933), pp. 289–90; Presland, *Deedes Bey*, p. 126.

130. FO 406/41. Conversation With Hamid Bey on 24 August 1919. Rear Admiral Richard Webb (Istanbul) to Earl Curzon (FO), September 3, 1919.

131. "Flight from Cilicia; Some Consequences," *The Near East*, Vol. 20, No. 552 (December 8, 1921), p. 722.

132. Ibid., p. 727.

133. "The Cilician Refugees," *The Near East*, Vol. 20, No. 553 (December 15, 1921), p. 758.

134. "General Gouraud's Declaration," *The Near East*, Vol. 20, No. 554 (December 22, 1921), p. 801.

135. "The Evacuation of Cilicia," *The Orient*, Vol. 9, No. 2 (February 1922), p. 5.

136. "General Gouraud's Declaration," *The Near East*, Vol. 20, No. 554 (December 22, 1921), p. 801.

137. "The Evacuation of Cilicia," *The Near East*, Vol. 21, No. 559 (January 26, 1922), p. 114.

138. USNA, 867.00/1477. Evacuation of Cilicia. Rear Admiral Mark Bristol (Istanbul) to Charles Hughes (Secretary of State), 6 January 1922. Enclosure: Copy of the Diary of the Destroyer *Williamson*.

139. FO 371/7853. Relations Between French and Turkish Nationalists Since Signature of Angora Agreement. Director of Military Intelligence (WO) to FO, January 16, 1922.

140. USNA, Naval Records, Notes and Information Syrian Coast, 10 December 1921, WT-Turkey, Asia Minor Conditions, Box 831; ABCFM Papers, Letter from William Nesbittt Chambers (Adana) to John Merrill (Boston), 4 January 1922. 763 Central Turkey 1920–August 1924 A-L, Vol. 2, Letters.

141. Clair Price, "The Turkish Nationalist Government," *The Fortnightly Review*, Vol. CXII (July–December 1922), pp. 565–66.

142. Eken, *Bir Milli Mücadele Valisinin Anıları*, pp. 302–4; "Le Gendarmerie Turque Dans Les Territoires Evacués," *Le Temps*, 26 janvier 1922, p. 3.

143. ABCFM Papers, Letter from William Nesbitt Chambers (Adana) to John Merrill (Boston), 4 January 1922. 763 Central Turkey 1920–August 1924 A-L, Vol. 2, Letters; "The Political Situation," *The Orient*, Vol. 9, No. 2 (February 1922), p. 7; Kenneth Waring, "Armenians on the March Again," *The Christian Science Monitor*, September 16, 1939, pp. 5 and 15.

144. Waring, "Armenians on the March Again," pp. 5 and 15.

145. "Parliament and the Refugees," *The Near East*, Vol. 20, No. 555 (December 29, 1921), p. 830.

146. Comte Roger de Gontaut-Biron and L. Le Révérend, *D'Angora à Lausanne: Les Etapes d'une déchéance* (Paris: Plon-Nourrit, 1924), p. 82 and fn1.

147. USNA, 867.00/14.79. Evacuation of Cilicia. Gabriel Bie Ravndal (Istanbul) to Rear Admiral Mark Bristol (Istanbul), 12 January 1922. Enclosure: Copy of Robert Wilson's Reply of 2 January 1922 Furnishing Certain Information Regarding the Situation in Cilicia.

148. "The Angora Government's Defence," *The Near East*, Vol. 21, No. 578 (June 8, 1922), pp. 761–62.

149. FO 371/7853. Conversation with Henri Franklin-Bouillon. FO Minute (C. E. Mendl), January 10, 1922. Also FO 371/7854. Conversation with Franklin-Bouillon. FO Minute (W. J. Childs), January 30, 1922.

150. Charles Riggs, *Dear Friends*, No. 20 (December 23, 1924), p. 1.

151. ABCFM Papers, Near East Mission in Turkey, Annual Station Reports: 1914–1921 to 1925–1926. Brief Report, American Hospital, April 1923–April 1924.

152. Blaisdell, *Missionary Daughter*, p. 196.

153. ABCFM Papers, Letter from J. C. Martin (Alexandretta) to E. W. Riggs (Boston), 11 January 1923. 764 Central Turkey 1920–August 1924 M-Z, Vol. 3, Letters.

154. ABCFM Papers, Letter from J. C. Martin (Suq-el-Gharb/Syria) to E. W. Riggs (Boston), 29 September 1923. 764 Central Turkey 1920–August 1924 M-Z, Vol. 3, Letters.

155. Charles Riggs, *Dear Friends*, No. 12 (October 28, 1924), p. 1.

156. ATASE, İSHK, Box: 600, File: 36–165, No. 51. Reentry of the Turkish Army in Adana, December 20, 1921.

157. Price, "The Turkish Nationalist Government," pp. 566–67.

158. ABCFM Papers, Letter from William Nesbitt Chambers (Adana) to John Merrill (Boston), 24 December 1921. 763 Central Turkey 1920–August 1924 A-L, Vol. 2, Letters.

159. ATASE, BDHK, Headquarters of the Lightning Armies Group Seventh Division. Administrative Matters: General Liman von Sanders's Correspondence Relating to Cemal Paşa, Box: 3754, File: 5, April 2, 1918–April 20, 1918.

160. Lord Kinross, *The Ottoman Centuries*, p. 597.

161. "Anatolian Reforms," *The Orient*, Vol. 5, Vol. 2 (January 14, 1914), p. 17.

162. Michael Reynolds, Echoes of Empire: Turkey's Crisis of Kemalism and the Search for an Alternative Foreign Policy, Brookings Institute Saban Center, Center on the United States and Europe Analysis Paper No. 26, June 2012, p. 6.

163. Philips Price, *A History of Turkey From Empire to Republic* (London: George Allen and Unwin Ltd; New York: The Macmillan Company, 1956), p. 85.

164. Ernest Jackh, *The Rising Crescent-Turkey: Yesterday, Today, and Tomorrow* (New York: Farrar and Reinhard, 1944), p. 96. Ernest Jackh had been made a professor by the Kingdom of Württemberg and was formerly chairman of the German-Turkish Association in Germany and head of the influential Central Office for Foreign Services in the German Ministry of Foreign Affairs.

165. As noted earlier, Christians and Jews in the Ottoman Empire were exempt from jurisdiction of the imperial courts in matters of religion and personal status (including marriage, divorce, legitimacy, inheritance, etc.); they enjoyed ecclesiastical self-government within religious communities; they were permitted to maintain their own schools, conducting instruction in the vernacular. For details, see George Young, *Corps de droit ottoman; recueil des codes, lois, règlements, ordonnaces, et actes les plus importants du droit intéurier, et d'études sur le droit coutumier de l'Empire ottoman*, seven volumes (Oxford: The Clarendon Press, 1905 *et seq.*), especially Vol. 2, chapters 21–29.

166. Earle, "The New Constitution of Turkey," pp. 79–80.

167. BOA, DUİT, No.79-4/176-2-1, Enclosure 2. Departure of Cemal Paşa from İstanbul, November 21, 1918.

168. Feridun Kandemir, "Cemal Paşa'nın Son Günleri" (The Last Days of Cemal Paşa), *Yedi Gün*, Vol. 3, No. 77 (August 29, 1934), p. 16; "Cemal Paşa'nın Son Faaliyetleri" (The Last Activities of Cemal Paşa), *İkdam*, August 17, 1922, p. 4.

169. Kandemir, "Cemal Paşa'nın Son Günleri," Vol. 4, No. 86 (October 31, 1934), p. 15.

170. Hülya Baykal, "Milli Mücadele Yıllarında Mustafa Kemal Paşa ve Cemal Paşa Arasındaki Yazışmalar" (Correspondence Between Mustafa Kemal Paşa and Cemal Paşa During the Years of the National Struggle), *Atatürk Araştırma Merkezi Dergisi*, Vol. 5, No. 4 (March 1989), pp. 379–439. Text of the Turkish-Soviet Treaty of 16 March 1921 in İsmail Soysal, ed., *Türkiye'nin Siyasi Antlaşmaları* (The Political Treaties of Turkey), Vol. 1: 1920–1945 (Ankara: Türk Tarih Kurumu Basımevi, 1983), pp. 32–38; and *British and Foreign State Papers*, Vol. 118, pp. 990–96.

171. India Office Records, British Library, Euston, London (henceforth to be referred to as IO). Political and Secret Department: Annual Files. P 22/1921. War

Office Views As to Jemal Pasha's Mission to Kabul, 1921; Kandemir, "Cemal Paşa'nın Son Günleri," Vol. 3, No. 73 (August 1, 1934), p. 17; ibid, Vol. 4, No. 85 (October 24, 1934), p. 6.

172. Alaattin Uca, "Cemal Paşa'nın Resmi Hal Tercümesi ve Milli Savunma Bakanlığı Arşivindeki Bazı Belgeler" (The Official Curriculum Vitae of Cemal Paşa and Some Documents in the Archive of the Ministry of National Defense), *Atatürk Üniversitesi Türkiyat Araştırmaları Enstitüsü Dergisi*, Vol. 16, No. 41 (2009), pp. 271–305; Fehmi Nuza, "Cemal Paşa'yı Kim Öldürdü veya Öldürttü" (Who Killed or Ordered to Kill Cemal Paşa), *Türk Kültürü*, Vol. 16, No. 243 (July 1983), pp. 454–64; "Cemal Paşa'nın Katilleri" (The Assassins of Cemal Paşa), *Peyamı Sabah*, July 30, 1922, p. 1; "Cemal Paşa Nasıl Şehit Edildi?" (How Cemal Paşa Is Martyred?), *Hakimiyeti Milliye*, August 1, 1922, p. 1; "Cemal Paşa'nın Hadisei Şehadeti" (Cemal Paşa's Act of Martyrdom), *İkdam*, August 8, 1922, p. 1; "Tiflis Cinayeti" (Tbilisi Murder), *İkdam*, August 10, 1922, p. 1; "Cemal Paşa'nın Katline Dair" (On the Assassination of Cemal Paşa), *İkdam*, August 17, 1922, p. 1; "Cemal Paşa'nın Katilleri Hakkında" (On the Assassins of Cemal Paşa), *Vakit*, August 22, 1922, p. 1; Altan Deliorman, *Türklere Karşı Ermeni Komitecileri* (Armenian Revolutionaries Against Turks) (İstanbul: Boğaziçi Yayınları, 1973), pp. 292–94.

173. İsmet Karadoğan, "Cemal Paşa'yı Ruslar Öldürmüştü" (The Russians Had Killed Cemal Paşa), *Yakın Tarihimiz*, Vol. 2, No. 14 (1962), pp. 36–38; Firuz Kesim, "Cemal Paşa Nasıl Katledildi" (How Cemal Paşa Was Assassinated), *Yakın Tarihimiz*, Vol. 2, No. 18 (1962), pp. 131–32. İsmet Karadoğan was the third aide-de-camp of Cemal Paşa, who happened to be in Ankara at the date of assassination. Firuz Kesim was at the time a member of the Turkish mission in Tbilisi.

174. Sutherland, *The Adventures of an Armenian Boy*, pp. 146–48.

175. Cavid Bey, *Meşrutiyet Ruznamesi*, Vol. 4, p. 381.

176. "Esbak Bahriye Nazırı Cemal Paşa Merhumun Tercümei Hali" (The Curriculum Vitae of the Deceased Former Minister of Marine Cemal Paşa), *İkdam*, August 8, 1922, p. 1.

177. Orhan Koloğlu, "Seniha Cemal'in Yaşam Öyküsü" (The Life Story of Seniha Cemal), *Popüler Tarih*, No. 42 (February 2004), pp. 46–51.

178. "Cemal Paşa Katledildi" (Cemal Paşa Is Assasinated), *Peyamı Sabah*, July 26, 1922, p. 1; "Cemal Paşa," *Vakit*, July 26, 1922, p. 1; "Cemal Paşa," *Vakit*, July 27, 1922, p. 1; "Cemal Paşa," *Peyamı Sabah*, July 27, 1922, p. 1; "Cemal Paşa Hakkında" (On Cemal Paşa), *İkdam*, July 27, 1922, p. 1; "Cemal Paşa Hiyanet ve Cinayet Kurbanı" (Cemal Paşa: Victim of Treachery and Murder), *Hakimiyeti Milliye*, July 28, 1922, p. 1; "Assassination of Jemal Pasha," *The Near East*, Vol. 22, No. 588 (August 24, 1922), pp. 249–50; "Djemal Pasha, Fugitive, Assassinated in Tiflis; Condemned as Author of Armenian Massacres," *The New York Times*, July 26, 1922, p. 17; "One After Another," *The New York Times*, July 27, 1922, p. 17.

179. "Cemal Paşa'nın Cenazesi" (The Funeral of Cemal Paşa), *Vakit*, September 30, 1922, p. 1; "Cemal Paşa ve Yaverleri Merasimle Defnedildi" (Cemal Paşa and His Aides-De-Camp Are Buried With Ceremony), *Sabah*, September 30, 1922, p. 1; "Jemal Pasha," *The Near East*, Vol. 22, No. 591 (September 7, 1922), p. 305.

180. IO. Political and Secret Department: Annual Files. P 5111/1922. Movement of Jemal Pasha: Murder of Jemal Pasha at Tiflis, 1922.

181. "Jemal Pasha," *The Near East*, Vol. 22, No. 586 (August 3, 1922), p. 134.

182. Ziya Gökalp taught philosophy at İstanbul University and was active in the Turkish Hearth movement. He introduced the Durkheimian sociology in the Ottoman Empire and became the leading Turkish nationalist ideologist of the Second Constitutional Period. His theories, broadcast in essays, appeared in many İstanbul journals between 1912 and 1919 and stressed that Turkey should conciously become part of Western civilization. With Gökalp the question of how should the Ottoman Empire modernize itself was left behind because he was concerned with Turks rather than Ottomans. He was elected to the TGNA in 1923.

183. Falih Rıfkı (Atay), "Şehid Cemal Paşa" (Martyr Cemal Paşa), *Akşam*, July 30, 1922, p. 1.

184. BOA, DUİT, No. 4/1-2, Enclosure 25. Cemal Paşa's Decorations, June 29, 1918.

Conclusion

Adana was an Ottoman province which was the most southerly portion of Anatolia from the Taurus Mountains down to the Gulf of İskenderun. Its boundary on the north was the Taurus range, and on the east the Amanus range. These are natural boundaries which have known no change for centuries. Both the Taurus and the Amanus rise to over ten thousand feet and are beautifully wooded. The Taurus Mountains have been likened in appearance to the Pyrenees. They consist of a rugged mass rising almost sheer out of the plain of Cilicia.

The Cilician plain, over which the armies of Xerxes, Cyrus, Mithriadates, Alexander the Great, Caesar, Pompey, Harun Reşid, Selahattin, and İbrahim Paşa moved through the centuries of conquest, was very fertile, and, given irrigation, could produce far more than in 1909. The rich black loam plain extends from the towering, snow-covered Taurus Mountains to the sea, and reaches for more than 150 kilometers with only one break of hills. As far as the eye could see, fields of cotton, wheat, barley, oats, and sesame covered the landscape, with here and there green vineyards; groves of mulberry, almond, and apricot trees; meadows brilliant with poppies, daisies, and wild parsley; and thousands of larks singing endlessly. A German irrigation scheme existed before the First World War which was not completed.

The province of Adana is old and haunted by history. This district lying between the Cilician Gates in the Taurus on the west and the Syrian Gates in the Amanus on the east was the way from Mesopotamia and Iran, Syria, and Egypt to the West. Adana had enjoyed periods of great prosperity but it was also time and again dragged under the harrows of war. Alexander and Darius fought their great battle of Issus in this district. Christianity led by Paul of Tarsus had its triumphs here. The last Armenian principality (1080–1393) struggled for three centuries to maintain its existence in Cilicia, but was finally wiped out. In the 1830s Mehmet Ali Paşa of Egypt took possession of the region and held it for some years.

The people in the eastern basin of the Mediterranean are connected with the past by a line that is never quite erased in their thoughts or in their policy. The inhabitants of Adana cross the river Seyhan by a bridge built by Justinian when the place was a station on the Roman military road to the east. They pass day by day the demolished ruins of the castle built by Harun Reşid. The bridge and the memories of the ruin are more solid still than most of the structures of today, and what they recall is as real as anything in the immediate foreground.

The strategic and economic importance of Adana has always been recognized. The new sections of the Baghdad railroad which traversed the province had been opened to traffic and transportation facilities were creating new possibilities. The present section opened up the rich Cilician plain, and connected with the Adana-Mersin route to the Mediterranean.

The city, known as "the one prosperous spot in the Ottoman Empire," was industrial and gave promise of an important future. Three rivers of importance cross the plain from the mountains to the Mediterranean: the Tarsus Çay past Tarsus, the Seyhan through Adana, and the Ceyhan through Misis. These rivers were full of possibilities. There were great forests of pine and cedar in the Taurus, large rafts of which were floated down the rivers. The historic city of Adana is situated on the right bank of the Seyhan river, partly on the plain at its foot. It is only seven meters above sea level and is in the very midst of the great Cilician Plain. With the irrigation of the plain and the draining of many marshy districts new areas would be cultivated and crops of cotton and cereals would increase. Here there existed a great field for the further development of the cotton industry, for agricultural enterprise, and for the importation of machinery. Mersin was the port for the entire province of Adana and had a large import and export trade valued at over 3,000,000 Turkish liras (13,200,000 dollars) in 1913. The province produced annually large crops of cotton and grain and these were in part utilized by local industries. Flour mills, ginning factories, cotton spinning and weaving mills, as well as minor industries required large equipments of machinery. Agricultural machinery and implements of all kinds were also imported. The province of Adana was one of the most progressive in the Ottoman Empire as regards the use of agricultural and industrial machinery.

The Armenians were spread all over the region and they were in close relationship with their Muslim neighbors, whom they resembled in traditions, customs, manners of dress, and whose language they spoke. They used Turkish also in their liturgy. Their women even dressed like Turkish women and went about veiled. The Armenian community of Adana was in a degree more advanced than that of neighboring provinces; there was commerce, more intercourse with the capital and with foreigners, they had larger and better schools. At the beginning of the twentieth century the business of Adana was principally in the hands of the Armenians and they undoubtedly formed the most wealthy proportion of the population. They were also found in telegraph offices, in provincial secretariats, and in the courts. They considered Cilicia, where an Armenian principality had existed from the eleventh to the fourteenth centuries, to be part of the national patrimony.

As of 1830, American Presbyterian missionaries sent by the ABCFM were active in Cilicia. The Bible used in schools was printed in Turkish transcribed with the Armenian script by these. Missionaries were frequently men and women of extraordinary intellectual capacity—witness their accomplishments in linguistics and translation, not to neglect their ingenuity in organization and improvization—but they were handicapped by one divisive factor: it was Christians who accepted their ministrations. Yet when combined with Ottoman, British, French, and American records and used with great care, the ABCFM sources give us a unique perspective on events, personalities, and society in the region.

There was worldwide interest in the Armenian events that transpired in Adana at their hundredth anniversary. If the debate is old, the subject is still fresh—in fact it is fresher and more relevant now than it was twenty or thirty years ago. The changes in our world have altered our perspective on the events of 1909. The origins, course, and the effects of those events retain considerable relevance for the study of present-day conflicts. Despite the passage of time since then, historians, political scientists, and sociologists have unfortunately dealt with only a fraction of the available documentation. The Adana affair of 1909 within the context of late Ottoman history has remained a neglected theme.

After the proclamation of the constitution in 1908, Armenians indulged in oratory of the wildest kind: they talked openly of Armenian independence (possibly of Cilicia as a self-governing principality), and they preached the duty of revenge. The Christians in Cilicia, as in other parts of the Ottoman dominions, bought arms in quantities that were exaggerated by the fears of the Muslims. Reports were circulated that the faith was threatened and that the Christians were preparing to rise against the Muslims. There were plenty of people already to fan the anxieties of the faithful. It was evident that the spirit of antagonism between Muslims and Christians was increasing, and fuel was added to the flame by the open boasts of some Armenians that they were arming themselves and speaking abusively of Muslims.

Two days preceding the outbreak in Adana there had been bitter feud between Muslims and Christians in one of the vineyards. Shooting had begun and hatred had been aroused. On April 12, 1909, an Armenian shot one Turk dead and wounded another, afterward escaping to Mersin, where he took passage by sea. The Turks in the city then assumed a sharp attitude and greatly alarmed the Armenians. The body of the murdered Muslim was dragged into the open square and left there as a challenge. The rumor spread among the Armenians on April 14 that a massacre had already commenced by the Turks, and in panic they fired shots into the air. There was firing in all directions. Turks and Armenians carried on house-to-house fighting. The provincial government could and should have preserved order from the very first, but the governor had abandoned the city to mob violence and to devastation by fire.

The struggle in the province of Adana in 1909 was not a massacre in the sense that the Armenians died unresisting. Many of them were armed and made a strong resistance. They took up positions commanding those streets leading to the Armenian quarter of the city, and held their own well through days. They fought fiercely, and in proportion as they succeeded in slaying the Muslims, the fury of the Turks increased. Yet many Armenians found refuge in Turkish houses. Individual Turks protected the Armenians, the regular soldiers usually did their duty, where they did not do so, it was not always possible to say whether they lacked the power or the desire.

While Adana was the center of the outbreaks, they extended into the neighboring province of Aleppo to such cities and towns as Maraş, Ayntab, Antakya, and Aleppo itself. Those had much the same population elements as those of Adana. In Mersin there was great excitement but Esad Rauf Bey, the *mutasarrıf*, paraded the town at the risk of his life and stopped any outbreak.

The Armenians, with their omnipresent ideas of an Armenian nation and a revolution against Ottoman rule, was responsible for much of the trouble that occurred in Adana in 1909. They calculated that the incidents in the city might bring out the necessity of foreign intervention, in the belief that foreign warships would be forced to land detachments on Ottoman soil. The hope was that Europeans and Americans would intervene on the Armenian side, but they did not.

The Huntchak Society did much to stir up the Armenians and to alarm the Turks. It is certain that Musheg Seropian, the Armenian bishop, was also responsible to a large extent for flaming the passions of his people and the fears of the Turks, for Major Charles Doughty-Wylie, the British vice consul, recognized it to such an extent as to prevent his landing at Mersin on his return to his diocese, in the interests of order. The foremost culprit for most of the period was this prelate. But once the outbreak had taken place, a heavy responsibility fell on the local authorities. The provincial governor and the military commander both showed an entire absence of resolution and courage.

Cevad Bey, who clearly lacked the talent to be governor, and the military commander Mustafa Remzi Paşa, who shared responsibility for the disorders through their paralyzed and criminal inactivity, were dismissed from their posts. The government in İstanbul strongly disapproved of the outbreak. It hastened to make judicial and financial amends for these unfortunate events. Courts martial were established at Adana, Erzin, Kozan, Hacin, Tarsus, and other towns which had been the scene of massacres. A commission of investigation was named by the Chamber of Deputies to inquire into the circumstances of the rising in Adana and of the human losses. It was impossible to form any accurate estimate of the number of those who perished in the massacres. But that it was sufficiently large to inflict a grave pecuniary loss on the Ottoman government is certain.

It is usually easier to see history through the lens of the individual, and there is no better vantage point overlooking the Adana affair than the life of Cemal Paşa. Soldier and administrator, Cemal Paşa was one of the most extraordinary figures in the Ottoman Second Constitutional Period. His achievements cannot properly be understood without taking into account his work as administrator and civil reformer. While a soldier by profession, he was an administrator by preference. He was dispatched to Adana as governor to restore order. As a man of action, he did this with a strong hand. No man in the Ottoman Empire could have been more fitly chosen for this difficult post.

Cemal Bey set with a will to reconstruct the province, where he is still remembered as one of the best governors it has ever had. He took a keen interest in public works, began several roads, and tried to improve the city to the best of his ability. The province was during his governorship firmly and wisely administered. The old residents of Adana said that they had never seen at Adana a governor of his stamp. This is not something that has faded with the passage of time. The people of Adana reserved a warm place in their hearts where Cemal Paşa would forever remain.[1]

During his governorship of the province of Adana in 1909–1911, Cemal Bey took several measures to alleviate distress among the Turks and Armenians. Ruined towns and villages were reconstructed. Many of the burned streets were rebuilt, new streets were opened up, old streets widened, and much of the massacre catastrophe debris removed. Trade boomed, attracting a large volume of business. Orphanages were organized and thousands of parentless children were being cared for under conditions that were better than they had ever before known. Armenians built their lives anew. They were entrusted with high-ranking positions in the administrative council of the province of Adana. Cemal Bey assumed responsibility for the upkeep of Armenians and acquitted himself well in the circumstances. The Ottoman official's benevolent policy toward them was mostly based upon humane intentions. His compassionate deeds were both a pragmatic and principled response to the needs of the moment. In Cemal Bey Adana found a just, liberal-minded, and enlightened governor. Reconstructing Adana was no easy task. His services are underresearched today and deserve serious academic recognition.

Like in Adana, Cemal Bey proved to be a very strong military and civil administrator in Baghdad. He put down with an iron hand cases of robbery and other serious crime in the city and expelled vagabonds and those who had no ostensible means of livelihood and could not furnish security. The province had a territory not only large in extent, but possessed enormous possibilities of development. With irrigation in the land, there were huge areas of cultivation. The inquiries of Cemal Bey showed that it was possible to restore the old irrigation once there and reconvert Mesopotamia into one of the granaries of the world. Certainly Cemal Bey was an imposing figure. Many admired and even venerated him. None could remain indifferent to the force of his personality and the system he developed.

Cemal Bey was proud of his achievements as governor; indeed, he seems to have taken far greater pride in his administration successes than in any other area of his career.

The Young Turks organized a parliament of two hundred and eighty deputies, including a large number of Christians, all chosen by vote of the people, recalled forty thousand exiles, dismissed thirty thousand spies, punished by death many Muslims guilty of reaction and massacre in İstanbul and Adana in 1909, embodied Christian soldiers in the army, and granted freedom of worship in private houses, freedom of public assembly, freedom of travel, freedom of the press, and education for Muslim students. In short, the Young Turks attempted to secure not only the overthrow of autocratic rule, but also the equal civic rights of all Ottoman citizens.

The Young Turk leaders were committed to the concept of Ottomanism, the heritage of the *Tanzimat* era. They aimed principally at the Ottomanization of the empire. That is to say, they wished Greeks, Armenians, Jews, Albanians, Arabs, and all the nationalities of the country to sink their respective national individualities into a single nationality. Much like the Young Ottomans forty years earlier, they believed that the best way to restore the vitality of the empire was through constitutional government that would limit the power of the monarch and guarantee the rights of non-Muslims by incorporating them into the framework of Ottomanism. Stress was placed on the equality of all Ottoman subjects—in civil liberties, in legal rights, in office-holding, as members of the Chamber of Deputies and on patriotism and loyalty to the land.

Talat Bey was recognized as the strongest member of the constitutional government and the chief driving force behind the CUP. Sad memories were left behind the Unionists, though in 1908, when they first came to power, the whole world hailed them with great enthusiasm, as the liberators of the Ottoman Empire. They were surrounded by hostilities of every description, and might not be able to do as much as they wished, but many of them were honest and capable men; they knew their country and understood its requirements; they did not make the fatal error of endeavoring to make too servile a copy of Western institutions.

Armenians served as officers in the Ottoman army, attended the higher academies in İstanbul, and aspired to appointments in the official hierarchy. After August 6, 1908, they were reserved one portfolio in each cabinet. As late as January 1913, the minister of foreign affairs of the Ottoman Empire, Gabriel Noradunghian, was an Armenian. After arranging the Treaty of Ouchy of October 15, 1912, which formalized the loss of the Ottoman province of Tripolitania to the Italians in a bid to concentrate on the danger closer to home, Noradunghian proceeded to conduct the Sublime Porte's diplomacy of the First Balkan War. Oskan Mardikian was minister of posts and telegraphs at the entry of the Sublime Porte in the First World War on October 29, 1914.

The civic model of Ottomanism was founded on expectations of cooperation among Ottomans of all confessions. Yet the events of 1908–1914 called into question the policy of Ottomanism. They showed that the minority people preferred national affiliations to Ottoman citizenship, and they undermined the proposition that Muslim and Christian could share in a common Ottoman bond.

Cemal Paşa's efforts to relieve Armenian suffering in Syria during the First World War must also be added to his credit. As commander of the Fourth Army in Syria and Palestine in 1914–1917, he provided humanitarian protection and assistance to Armenians. He ordered an effective relief effort, as a result of which the vast majority of the relocatees in his zone of command survived. He also took protective measures to keep the Armenians in the city centers. He employed artisans from among the relocatees in army factories and used this opportunity to prevent as many Armenians as possible from being sent to the desert. Cemal Paşa inflicted severe penalties on those who mistreated the Armenians during the displacements. Similarly, robbers who assaulted Armenian relocatees were heavily punished when their attacks were reported to him. All in all, during the removal of Armenians he wholeheartedly strove to improve their conditions. Generally Armenians spoke well of Cemal Paşa. Thanks to him many of them, especially those from Adana, were taken to Damascus and Hama regions and areas further south and were able to live reasonable lives. Individual appeals and requests made to him were often taken into account. Once again, the former governor of Adana had shown generosity toward those he had earlier governed. He was a real statesman, with a grasp of the situation, a wide outlook and a true perspective, whose echoes would reverberate in Middle Eastern politics and historiography for many years to come. The lessons of his life and career still resonate to this day.[2]

NOTES

1. Arıkoğlu, *Hatıralarım*, pp. 45–49; Aktan, *Dünkü ve Bugünkü Adana*, p. 9; Walker, *Armenia*, pp. 182–88.
2. The sources here are numerous. See, for instance, ATASE, BDHK, Box: 1768, File: 206, July 25, 1916; ATASE, BDHK, Box: 533, File: 2084-1-3, May 29, 1917; Muhittin Birgen, Zeki Arıkan, ed., *İttihat ve Terakki'de On Sene* (Ten Years in the Committee of Union and Progress), Vol. 2: *İttihat ve Terakki'nin Sonu* (End of the Committee of Union and Progress) (İstanbul: Kitap Yayınevi, 2006), p. 765; Tunaya, *Türkiye'de Siyasi Partiler*, Vol. 3, pp. 277–78; Dabağyan, *Emperyalistler Kıskacında Ermeni Tehciri I (Türk Ermenileri)*, pp. 290–91; Sarkis Çerkezyan, *Bu Dünya Hepimize Yeter* (This World Suffices For All of Us) (İstanbul: Belge Yayınları, reprint, 2009), p. 37; Enver Konukçu, *Erzurum'da Kars Kapı Şehitliğindeki İki Mezar: Hafız Hakkı ve Cemal Paşalar (1915, 1922)* (Two Graves in the Kars Kapı Military Graveyard in Erzurum: Hafız Hakkı and Cemal Paşas [1915, 1922]) (Erzurum: Atatürk Üniversitesi Yayınları, 2010), pp. 428–31; Çiçek, *War and State Formation in Syria*, pp. 116 and 118–19; Sutherland, *The Adventures of an Armenian Boy*, pp. 146–48; Yervant Odian, trans. Ara Stepan Melkonian, *Accursed Years: My Exile and Return from Der Zor, 1914–1919* (London: Gomidas Institute, 2009), p. 94; Hilmar Kaiser, "Regional Resistance to Central Government Policies: Ahmed Djemal Pasha, the Governors of Aleppo, and Armenian Deportees in the Spring and Summer of 1915," *Journal of Genocide Research*, Vol. 12, No. 3–4 (2010), pp. 173–218.

Bibliography

I. UNPUBLISHED PRIMARY SOURCES

Official

Archives de Ministère des Affaires Etrangères, Courneuve, Paris
Centre des Archives Diplomatiques, Nantes
Department of State Papers, National Archives and Records Administration, College Park, Maryland
Foreign Office Papers, The National Archives, Kew, London
India Office Records, British Library, Euston, London
Prime Minister's Office Ottoman Archive, Kağıthane, İstanbul
Turkish General Staff Military History and Strategic Studies Directorate Archive, Ankara
War Office Papers, The National Archives, Kew, London

Private

American Board of Commissioners for Foreign Missions Papers, Houghton Library, Harvard University
Sir Gerard Lowther Papers, The National Archives, Kew, London
Sir Henry Layard Papers, British Library, Euston, London

II. PUBLISHED PRIMARY SOURCES

Official

Britain

British and Foreign State Papers, Vol. 118.
Great Britain, Admiralty. *A Handbook of Mesopotamia*, four volumes, London: Admiralty War Staff, Intelligence Division, 1916–1917.
Great Britain, Foreign Office. *Correspondence Relating to the Asiatic Provinces of Turkey: Turkey, No.1 (1895), Part 1: Events at Sassoun, and Commission of Inquiry at Moush*, London: His Majesty's Stationery Office, 1895.
Great Britain, Foreign Office. *Correspondence Relating to the Asiatic Provinces of Turkey: Turkey, No.1 (1895), Part 2: Commission of Inquiry at Moush: Procès-Verbaux and Separate Depositions*, London: His Majesty's Stationery Office, 1895.
Lorimer, John Gordon, *Gazetteer of the Persian Gulf, Oman, and Central Arabia*, five volumes, Calcutta: Superintendent Government Printing, 1908–1915.
Parliamentary Command Papers No. 4529, *Correspondence Respecting the Constitutional Movement in Turkey 1908*, London: His Majesty's Stationery Office, 1909.
Parliamentary Papers, House of Commons, 1877, Vol. XCI.
The Treatment of Armenians in the Ottoman Empire 1915–1916: Documents Presented to Viscount Grey of Fallodon, Secretary of State for Foreign Affairs, Parliamentary Papers Miscellaneous No. 31, London: Joseph Causton, 1916; reprinted, Astoria, New York: J. C. and A. L. Fawcett, 1990.

Turkey

Aspirations et Agissements Révolutionnaires des Comités Arméniens Avant et Aprés la Proclamation de la Constitution Ottomane, İstanbul: Matbaai Orhaniye, 1917.
Genç et al., Yusuf İhsan, *Başbakanlık Osmanlı Arşivi Rehberi* (Guide to the Prime Minister's Office Ottoman Archive), Ankara: Başbakanlık Basımevi, reprinted, 2010.
Karakaya et al., Recep, *Osmanlı Belgelerinde 1909 Adana Olayları* (Adana Events of 1909 in Ottoman Documents), two volumes, Ankara: Başbakanlık Basımevi, 2010.
Küçük et al., Mustafa, *Başbakanlık Osmanlı Arşivi Katalogları Rehberi* (Guide to the Catalogs of the Prime Minister's Office Ottoman Archive), Ankara: Başbakanlık Basımevi, 1995.
Meclisi Mebusan Zabıt Ceridesi (Proceedings of the Chamber of Deputies), Vols. 1 and 3, Ankara: Türkiye Büyük Millet Meclisi Basımevi, 1982.
Orhun, Hayri, Celal Kasaroğlu, Mehmet Belek, Kazım Atakul, eds., *Meşhur Valiler* (The Famous Provincial Governors), Ankara: İçişleri Bakanlığı Merkez Valileri Bürosu Yayınları, 1969.
Tableaux Indiquant le Nombre de Divers Eléments de la Population dans l'Empire Ottoman au 1er Mars 1330, İstanbul: Imprimerie Osmanié, 1919.

Toker, Hülya and Nurcan Aslan, eds., *Birinci Dünya Savaşına Katılan Alay ve Daha Üst Kademedeki Komutanların Biyografileri* (Biographies of the Regiment and More Senior Level Commanders Who Participated in the First World War), Vol. 3, Ankara: Genelkurmay Basımevi, 2009.

Türk Parlamento Tarihi (History of the Turkish Parliament), Vols. 1, 2 and 3, Ankara: Türkiye Büyük Millet Meclisi Basımevi Müdürlüğü, 1995, 1997, 1998.

Türkiye Cumhuriyeti Genelkurmay ATASE ve Denetleme Başkanlığı Yayın Kataloğu (Publication Catalog of the Turkish General Staff Directorate of Military History and Strategic Studies and Directorate of Inspection), Ankara: Genelkurmay Basımevi, 2005.

United States

Guide to the National Archives of the United States, Washington, DC: National Archives and Records Service, 1974.

Papers relating to the foreign relations of the United States for the year 1909, Washington, DC: U.S. Government Printing House, 1914.

Private (Memoirs, Correspondences, Statements, Contemporary Studies)

Abbott, G. F., *Turkey in Transition*, London: Edward Arnold, 1909.

Adossidès, Alexandre, *Arméniens et Jeunes-Turcs: les Massacres de Cilicie*, Paris: P. V. Stock, 1910.

Aflalo, Fredrick George, *An Idler in the Middle East*, London: Milne, 1910.

———, *Regilding the Crescent*, London: G. Bell, 1911.

Ahmed Cevdet Paşa, Cavid Baysun, ed., *Tezakir 21–29* (Communications 21–29), Ankara: Türk Tarih Kurumu Basımevi, second edition, 1986.

Ali Cevat, Faik Reşit Unat, ed., *İkinci Meşrutiyetin İlanı ve Otuzbir Mart Hadisesi* (The Proclamation of the Second Constitutionalism and the Incident of March 31), Ankara: Türk Tarih Kurumu Basımevi, reprinted, 1991.

Ali Haydar Mithat, *Hatıralarım 1872–1946* (My Reminiscences 1872–1946), İstanbul: Güler Basımevi, 1946.

———, *The Life of Midhat Pasha: A Record of His Services, Political Reforms, Banishment, and Judicial Murder*, London: John Murray, 1903.

Ali Münif Bey, Taha Toros, ed., *Ali Münif Bey'in Hatıraları* (Reminiscences of Ali Münif Bey), İstanbul: İSİS Yayıncılık, 1996.

Alishan, Léonce, *Sissouan ou L'Arméno-Cilicie: Description Géographique et Histoire*, Venice: S. Lazare, 1899.

Andersen, Rufus, *History of the Missions of the American Board of Commissioners for Foreign Missions to the Oriental Churches*, two volumes, Boston, MA: Congregational Publishing Society, 1872.

Aral, Hamid, ed., *Dışişleri Bakanlığı 1967 Yıllığı* (1967 Annual of the Ministry of Foreign Affairs), Ankara: Ankara Basım ve Ciltevi, 1968.

Arıkoğlu, Damar, *Hatıralarım Milli Mücadele, Çukurova'da Fransız İşgali ve Kanlı Savaşlar, Birinci Büyük Millet Meclisi, Yurtta Çeşitli İsyanlar, Yunanlıların Denize Dökülmesi, Atatürk'ten Hatıralar, Resimler Vesikalar* (My Reminiscences: The National Struggle, The French Occupation of Cilicia and the Bloody Battles, The First Term of the Grand National Assembly, Various Revolts in the Country, Pushing the Greeks into the Sea, Recollections from Atatürk, Pictures Documents), İstanbul: Tan Gazetesi ve Matbaası, 1961.

Ayni, Mehmet Ali, İsmail Dervişoğlu, ed., *Hatıralar* (Memoirs), İstanbul: Yeditepe Yayınevi, reprinted, 2009.

Babacan, Hasan, and Servet Avşar, eds., *Cavid Bey Meşrutiyet Rûznamesi* (Cavid Bey: Agenda of the Constitutionalism), four volumes, Ankara: Türk Tarih Kurumu Basımevi, 2014.

Balakian, Grigoris, trans. Peter Balakian with Aris Sevas, *Armenian Golgotha: A Memoir of the Armenian Genocide, 1915–1918*, New York: Alfred Knopf, 2009.

Bardakçı, Murat, ed., *Mahmud Şevket Paşa'nın Sadaret Günlüğü* (The Grand Vizierial Diary of Mahmud Şevket Paşa), İstanbul: Türkiye İş Bankası Kültür Yayınları, 2014.

Baring, Maurice, *Letters from the Near East, 1909 and 1912*, London: Smith, Elder, 1913.

Barker, William Burckhardt, *Lares and Penates: Or Cilicia and Its Governors*, London: Ingram, Cooke, And Co., 1853.

———, *The Birth Land of St. Paul, Cilicia: Its Former History and Present State*, London and Glasgow: Richard Griffin and Company, 1853.

Barton, James, *Daybreak in Turkey*, Boston, MA: The Pilgrim Press, second edition, 1908.

Biren, Mehmet Tevfik, Fatma Rezan Hürmen, ed., *II. Abdülhamid, Meşrutiyet ve Mütareke Devri Hatıraları* (Reminiscences of the Periods of Abdülhamid II, Constitutionalism and Armistice), two volumes, İstanbul: Arma Yayınları, 1993.

Birgen, Muhittin, Zeki Arıkan, ed., *İttihat ve Terakki'de On Sene* (Ten Years in the Committee of Union and Progress), Vol. 2, İstanbul: Kitap Yayınevi, 2006.

Blaisdell, Dorothea Chambers, *Missionary Daughter: Witness to the End of the Ottoman Empire*, La Vergne, TN: 1st Book Library, 2002.

Bliss, Daniel, *The Reminiscences of Daniel Bliss*, New York and London: Fleming Revell Company, 1920.

Bourne, Kenneth, and Donald Cameron Watt, eds., British Documents on Foreign Affairs: Reports and Papers from the Foreign Office Confidential Print, Part 1: From the Mid-Nineteenth Century to the First World War, Series B The Near and Middle East 1856–1914, Vol. 20: The Ottoman Empire Under the Young Turks 1908–1914, Frederick, MD: University Publications of America, 1985.

Brézol, Georges, *Les Turcs ont passé là . . . Recueil de documents, dossiers, rapports, requêtes, protestations, suppliques et enquêtes, établissant la vérité sur les massacres d'Adana en 1909*, Paris: (en vente chez l'auteur), 1911; republished Yerevan: The Armenian Genocide Museum-Institute, 2010.

Bullard, Reader, *The Camels Must Go*, London: Faber and Faber, 1961.

Buxton, Charles Roden, *Turkey in Revolution*, New York: Charles Scribner's Sons; London: T. Fisher Unwin, 1909.

Buxton, Noel, and Harold Buxton, *Travel and Politics in Armenia*, London: Smith, Elder and Co., 1914.

Cavid Bey, Hasan Babacan, and Servet Avşar, eds., *Meşrutiyet'in Ruznamesi* (Agenda of the Constitutionalism), four volumes, Ankara: Türk Tarih Kurumu Basımevi, 2014.

Chambers, William Nesbitt, *Yoljuluk: Random Thoughts on a Life in Imperial Turkey*, London: Simpkin Marshall Limited, 1928; republished, Paramus, NJ: Armenian Missionary Association of America, 1988.

Childs, W. J., *Across Asia Minor on Foot*, Edinburgh and London: William Blackwood and Sons, 1918.

Cuinet, Vital, *La Turquie d'Asie: géographie administrative, statistique descriptive et raisonnée de chaque province de l'Asie Mineure*, Vol. 2, Paris: Ernest Leroux, 1890–1895.

Çallıyan, Karabet, *Adana Vakası ve Mesulleri* (The Adana Incident and Those Responsible For It), İstanbul: n.p., 1909.

Çalyan, Garabed, "Adana Vakası ve Mesulleri" (Adana Incident and Those Responsible For It), in Ari Şekeryan, ed., *1909 Adana Katliamı: Üç Rapor* (1909 Massacre of Adana: Three Reports), İstanbul: Aras Yayıncılık, 2015.

Çambel, Hasan, *Makaleler Hatıralar* (Articles Recollections), Ankara: Türk Tarih Kurumu Basımevi, 2011.

Çamurdan, Ahmet Cevdet, *Kozan'ı Tanıyalım* (Let Us Know Kozan), Adana: Önder Matbaa, 1973.

Çerkezyan, Sarkis, *Bu Dünya Hepimize Yeter* (This World Suffices For All of Us), İstanbul: Belge Yayınları, reprinted, 2009.

Danişmend, İsmail Hami, *Sadrazam Tevfik Paşa'nın Dosyasındaki Resmi ve Hususi Vesikalara Göre 31 Mart Vakası* (The March 31 Incident According to Official and Private Documents in the Files of Grand Vizier Tevfik Paşa), İstanbul: İstanbul Kitabevi, 1961.

de Gontaut-Biron, Roger, et L. Le Révérend, *D'Angora à Lausanne: Les étapes d'une déchéance*, Paris: Plon-Nourrit, 1924.

Djemal Pasha, *Memories of a Turkish Statesman 1913–1919*, New York: George Doran Company, 1922.

Duru, Kazım Nami, *İttihat ve Terakki Hatıralarım* (My Recollections of the Committee of Union and Progress), İstanbul: Sucuoğlu Matbaası, 1957.

Eddy, David Brewer, *What Next in Turkey: Glimpses of the American Board's Work in the Near East*, Boston, MA: The American Board Press, 1913.

Edib, Halidé, *Memoirs of Halidé Edib*, New York and London: The Century Co., 1926.

Eken, Halit, *Bir Milli Mücadele Valisi ve Anıları Kapancızade Hamit Bey* (A Governor of the National Struggle and His Reminiscences: Kapancızade Hamit Bey), İstanbul: Yeditepe Yayınevi, 2008.

Elgood, Percival George, *Egypt and the Army*, London: Oxford University Press, 1924.

Eliot, Charles (Odysseus), *Turkey in Europe*, London: Edward Arnold, 1900.
Ferriman, Duckett, *The Young Turks and the Truth about the Holocaust at Adana in Asia Minor, during April, 1909*, London: n.p., 1913, republished Yerevan: The Armenian Genocide Museum-Institute, 2009.
Fraser, David, *The Short Cut to India: The Record of a Journey along the Route of the Baghdad Railway*, Edinburgh and London: William Blackwood and Sons, 1909.
Gaillard, Gaston, *The Turks and Europe*, London: Thomas Murby and Co., 1921.
Galitekin, Ahmed Nezih, ed., *Salname-i Nezaret-i Umur-ı Hariciyye* (Annual of the Ottoman Ministry of Foreign Affairs), Vol. 4, İstanbul: İşaret Yayınları, 2003.
Gibbons, Helen Davenport, *The Red Rugs of Tarsus: A Woman's Record of the Armenian Massacres of 1909*, New York: The Century Company, 1917.
Gövsa, İbrahim Alaettin, *Türk Meşhurları Ansiklopedisi* (Encyclopedia of Famous Turks), İstanbul: Yedigün Yayınları, 1946.
Graves, Robert, *Storm Centres of the Near East*, London: Hutchinson and Co., 1933.
Greene, Joseph, *Leavening the Levant*, New York: The Pilgrim Press, 1916.
Grew, Joseph, Walter Johnson, ed., *Turbulent Era: A Diplomatic Record of Forty Years 1904–1945*, two volumes, Boston, MA: Houghton Mifflin Company, 1952.
Gust, Wolfgang, ed., *The Armenian Genocide Evidence from the German Foreign Office Archives, 1915–1916*, New York and Oxford: Berghahn Books, 2014.
Hamlin, Cyrus, *Among the Turks*, New York: Robert Carter and Brothers, 1878.
———, *My Life and Times*, Boston, MA: Congregational Sunday School and Publishing Society, 1893.
Hurewitz, J. C., ed., *Diplomacy in the Near and Middle East: A Documentary Record*, Vol. 1, Princeton, NJ: D. Van Nostrand Company, Inc., 1956.
Hüseyin Kazım Kadri, İsmail Kara, ed., *Meşrutiyetten Cumhuriyete Anılarım* (My Reminiscences from the Constitutionalism to the Republic), İstanbul: Dergah Yayınları, reprinted, 2000.
Iraq Administration Reports 1914–1932, Vol. 1, Melksham and Oxford: Archive Editions, 1992.
İrtem, Süleyman Kani, Osman Selim Kocahanoğlu, ed., *Ermeni Meselesinin İçyüzü Ermeni İsyanları Tarihi, Bomba Hadisesi, Adana Vakası, Meclisi Mebusan Zabıtları* (The True Nature of the Armenian Question: History of Armenian Revolts, Bomb Incident, Adana Event, Proceedings of the Chamber of Deputies), İstanbul: Temel Yayınları, 2004.
———, Osman Selim Kocahanoğlu, ed., *Meşrutiyet Doğarken: 1908 Jön Türk İhtilali* (While the Constitutionalism Was Rising: Young Turk Revolution of 1908), İstanbul: Temel Yayınları, 1999.
———, Osman Selim Kocahanoğlu, ed., *Sultan Abdülhamid ve Yıldız Kamarillası* (Sultan Abdülhamid and the Yıldız Camarilla), İstanbul: Temel Yayınları, 2000.
Jebb, Louisa, *By Desert Ways to Baghdad*, London: T. Fisher Unwin, 1908.
Jernazian, Ephraim, trans. Alice Haig, *Judgment Unto Truth: Witnessing the Armenian Genocide*, New Brunswick, NJ: Transaction Publishers, 1990.
Karabekir, Kazım, Faruk Özerergin, ed., *İttihat ve Terakki Cemiyeti 1896–1909* (The Committee of Union and Progress 1896–1909), İstanbul: Emre Yayınları, reprint, 1993.

Kazanjian, Paren, ed., *The Cilician Ordeal*, Boston, MA: Hye Intentions, 1989.
Klinghardt, Karl, *Denkwürdigkeiten des Marschalls Izzet Pascha. Ein kritischer Beitrag zur Kriegsschuldfrage*, Leipzig: K. F. Koehler, 1927.
Knight, Edward Frederick, *The Awakening of Turkey: A History of the Turkish Revolution*, Philadelphia, PA: J. B. Lippincot Co., 1909.
Kodaman, Bayram, and Mehmet Ali Ünal, eds., *Son Vakanüvis Abdurrahman Şeref Efendi Tarihi: İkinci Meşrutiyet Olayları (1908–1909)* (History of the Last Chronicler Abdurrahman Şeref Efendi: Events of Second Constitutionalism [1908–1909]), Ankara: Türk Tarih Kurumu Basımevi, 1996.
Köker, Osman, ed., *Orlando Carlo Calumeno Koleksiyonundan Kartpostallarla 100 Yıl Önce Türkiye'de Ermeniler* (With Post Cards from the Orlando Carlo Calumeno Collection: Armenians in Turkey 100 Years Ago), İstanbul: Birzamanlar Yayıncılık, 2005.
Kuran, Ahmed Bedevi, *İnkılap Tarihimiz ve Jön Türkler* (Our History of Revolution and the Young Turks), İstanbul: Kaynak Yayınları, reprint, 2000.
———, *Osmanlı İmparatorluğunda İnkılap Hareketleri ve Milli Mücadele* (Revolutionary Movements in the Ottoman Empire and the National Struggle), İstanbul: Türkiye İş Bankası Kültür Yayınları, reprint, 2012.
Lambert, Rose, *Hadjin and the Armenian Massacres*, New York: Fleming H. Revell Co., 1911.
Lengley, Emil, *Turkey*, New York: H. Wolff, 1941.
Massacres d'Adana et nos missionaires, récit de témoins, Lyon: Imprimerie Vve M. Paquet, 1909.
Mayakon, İsmail Müştak, *Yıldız'da Neler Gördüm* (What I Saw in Yıldız), İstanbul: Sertel Matbaası, 1940.
McGilvray, Margaret, *The Dawn of a New Era in Syria*, New York: Fleming H. Revell Company, 1920.
Mehmet Asaf, İsmet Parmaksızoğlu, ed., *1909 Adana Ermeni Olayları ve Anılarım* (1909 Armenian Incidents of Adana and My Reminiscences), Ankara: Türk Tarih Kurumu Basımevi, 1982.
Mevlanzade Rıfat, Ahmet Nezih Galitekin, ed., *İttihat ve Terakki İktidarı ve Türkiye İnkılabının İçyüzü* (The Rule of the Committee of Union and Progress and the Inside Story of the Turkish Revolution), İstanbul: Yedi İklim Yayınları, 1993.
Neyzi, Ali, *Meyzi ile Neyzi* (Meyzi With Neyzi), İstanbul: Karacan Yayınları, 1983.
Neyzi, Nezih, *Osmanlılıktan Cumhuriyet'e Kızıltoprak Anıları* (From the Ottomanness to the Republic: Recollections of Kızıltoprak), İstanbul: Türkiye İş Bankası Kültür Yayınları, second revised and expanded edition, 2016.
Noradounghian, Gabriel Effendi, ed., *Recueil d'actes internationaux de l'Empire ottoman: traités, conventions, arrangements, déclarations, protocoles, procès verbaux, firmans, berats, lettres patentes et autres documents relatifs au droit public extérieur de la Turquie*, four volumes, Paris: Librairie Cotillon, F. Pichon, Successeur, 1897–1903.
Odian, Yervant, trans. Ara Stepan Melkonian, *Accursed Years: My Exile and Return from Der Zor, 1914–1919*, London: Gomidas Institute, 2009.

Oran, Baskın, ed., *"M. K." Adlı Çocuğun Tehcir Anıları 1915 ve Sonrası* (Relocation Reminiscences of a Child Called "M. K.": 1915 and Beyond), İstanbul: İletişim Yayınları, 2005.

Ortaç, Yusuf Ziya, *Portreler* (Portraits), İstanbul: Akbaba Yayınları, reprint, 1963.

Osmanoğlu, Ayşe, *Babam Sultan Abdülhamid* (My Father Sultan Abdülhamid), İstanbul: Timaş Yayınları, third edition, 2015.

Parfit, Canon J. T., *Twenty Years in Baghdad and Syria*, London: Simpkin Marshall Co., 1916.

Patrick, Mary Mills, *Bosporus Adventure: Constantinople Womens College, 1871–1924*, Stanford, CA: Stanford University Press, 1934.

Pears, Edwin, *Forty Years in Constantinople: The Recollections of Sir Edwin Pears 1873–1915*, London: Herbert Jenkins Limited, 1916.

———, *Turkey and Its People*, London: Methuen and Co. Ltd., 1911.

Phillips, Clifton Jackson, *Protestant America and the Pagan World: The First Half Century of the American Board of Commissioners for Foreign Missions, 1810–1860*, Cambridge, MA: Harvard University Press, 1969.

Pope, R. Martin, *Here and There in the Historic Near East*, London: Epworth Press, 1923.

Powell, E. Alexander, *The Struggle for Power in Moslem Asia*, New York and London: The Century Company, 1923.

Ramazanoğlu, Niyazi, *La Province d'Adana Aperçu Historique, Ethnographique et Statistique*, İstanbul: Société Anonyme de Papeterie et d'Imprimerie, 1920.

Ramsay, W. W., *The Revolution in Constantinople and Turkey: A Diary*, London: Hodder and Stoughton, 1909.

Ravndal, Gabriel Bie, *Turkey: A Commercial and Industrial Handbook*, Washington, DC: Government Printing House, 1925.

Redan, Pierre, *La Cilicie et le problème ottoman*, Paris: Gauthier-Villars, 1921.

Richter, Julius, *A History of Protestant Missions in the Near East*, Edinburgh and London: Oliphant, Anderson and Ferrier, 1910.

Riggs, Alice Shepard, *Shepard of Aintab*, New York: Interchurch Press, 1920.

Ryan, Andrew, *The Last of the Dragomans*, London: Geoffrey Bles, 1951.

Selahattin Adil Paşa, *Hayat Mücadeleleri* (Struggles for Life), İstanbul: Zafer Matbaası, 1982.

Sertel, Zekeriya, *Hatırladıklarım* (Those I Remember), İstanbul: Remzi Kitabevi, reprint, 2000.

Simavi, Lütfi, *Osmanlı Sarayının Son Günleri* (The Last Days of the Ottoman Palace), İstanbul: Hürriyet Yayınları, 1970.

Story, Sommerville, ed., *The Memoirs of Ismail Kemal Bey*, London: Constable and Company Ltd, 1920.

Strong, E. E., *Condensed Sketch of the Missions of the American Board in Asiatic Turkey*, Boston, MA: The American Board, 1908.

Strong, William, *The Story of the American Board: An Account of the First One Hundred Years of the American Board of Commissioners for Foreign Missions*, New York: Pilgrim Press, 1910.

Sutherland, James Kay, *The Adventures of an Armenian Boy: An Autobiography and Historical Narrative Encompassing the Last Thirty Years of the Ottoman Empire*, Ann Arbor, MI: Ann Arbor Press, 1964.

Şalvuz, İsmail Ferahim, *Kurtuluş Savaşında Kahraman Çukurovalılar: Adana, Tarsus ve Mersinliler* (Heros of Cilicia in the War of Liberation: Those From Adana, Tarsus and Mersin), Ankara: Türkiye Cumhuriyeti Kültür Bakanlığı Yayınları, 2000.

Şeref, Abdurrahman, *Sultan Abdülhamid-i Sani: Suret-i Hali* (Sultan Abdülhamid II: His Dethronement), İstanbul: Hilal Matbaası, 1918.

Şerif, Ahmet, Çetin Börekçi, ed., *Anadolu'da Tanin* (Tanin in Anatolia), Ankara: Türk Tarih Kurumu Basımevi, 1999.

Tahsin Paşa, *Abdülhamid ve Yıldız Hatıraları* (Abdülhamid and Yıldız Recollections), İstanbul: Muallim Ahmet Halit Kitaphanesi, 1931.

Talat Paşa, *Hatıralarım ve Müdafaam* (My Reminiscences and Defense), İstanbul: Kaynak Yayınları, 2006.

Tepeyran, Ebubekir Hazım, *Hatıralar* (Reminiscences), İstanbul: Türkiye Yayınevi, 1944.

Terzian, Hagop, trans. Ara Stepan Melkonian and Ara Sarafian, ed., *Cilicia 1909: The Massacre of Armenians*, London: Gomidas Institute, 2009.

The Adana Massacres and the Catholic Missionaries: Account of Eye-Witnesses, New York: Society for the Propaganda of Faith, 1910.

Townshend, Arthur FitzHenry, *A Military Consul in Turkey*, London: Seeley, 1910.

Tsapalos, Georges, et Pierre Walter, *Rapport sur le domaine imperial de Tchoucour-Ova (Vilayet d'Adana, Turquie d'Asie)*, Paris: Imp. L'Union Typographie, 1911–1912.

Türkgeldi, Ali Fuad, *Görüp İşittiklerim* (What I Saw and Heard), Ankara: Türk Tarih Kurumu Basımevi, reprint, 2010.

———, *Mesaili Mühimmei Siyasiye* (The Important Political Questions), Ankara: Türk Tarih Kurumu Basımevi, 1957.

Uşaklıgil, Halid Ziya, *Saray ve Ötesi* (The Palace and Beyond), İstanbul: İnkılap Kitabevi, 1940.

Ürgüplü, Ali Suat, ed., *Şeyhülislam Ürgüplü Mustafa Hayri Efendi'nin Meşrutiyet, Büyük Harp ve Mütareke Günlükleri (1909–1922)* (Constitutional Period, Great War and Armistice Diaries of Sheikh-ul-Islam Mustafa Hayri Efendi of Ürgüp [1909–1922]), İstanbul: Türkiye İş Bankası Kültür Yayınları, 2015.

von Sanders, Liman, trans. Carl Reichman, *Five Years in Turkey*, Annapolis, MD: US Naval Institute, 1927; republished Nashville, TN: The Battery Press, 2000.

Werner, Theodor, *Die Türken unter des britischen Faust 1918–1923*, Berlin: Deutsche Informationsstalle, 1940.

Woods, Charles, *The Cradle of the War: The Near East and Pan-Germanism*, Boston, MA: Little, Brown, and Company, 1918.

———, *The Danger Zone of Europe: Changes and Problems in the Near East*, London: T. Fisher Unwin, 1911.

Wratislaw, A. C., *A Consul in the East*, Edinburgh: William Blackwood and Sons, 1924.

Yalçın, Hüseyin Cahit, *Talat Paşa*, İstanbul: Yedigün Neşriyatı, 1943.

——, Cemil Koçak, ed., *Tanıdıklarım* (My Acquaintances), İstanbul: Yapı Kredi Yayınları, reprinted, 2001.

Yeghiayan, Zaven Der, trans. Ared Misirliyan and Vatche Gazarian, ed., *My Patriarchal Memoirs*, Barrington, RI: Mayreni Publishing, 2002.

Yessayan, Zabel, trans. Kayuş Çalıkman Gavrilof, *Yıkıntılar Arasında Tanıklık* (Among the Ruins: Testimony), İstanbul: Aras Yayıncılık, 2014.

Young, George, *Corps de droit ottoman; recueil des codes, lois, règlements, ordonnances, et actes les plus importants du droit intérieur, et d'études sur le droit coutumier de l'Empire ottoman*, seven volumes, Oxford: The Clarendon Press, 1905 et seq.

III. NEWSPAPERS

English: *Asbarez* (Fresno), *Boston Evening Transcript*, *Boston Morning Globe*, *England and the Union* (London), *Haaretz* (Tel Aviv), *Haaretz Weekly* (Tel Aviv), *Los Angeles Herald*, *Morning Advertiser* (London), *The Armenian Weekly* (Watertown), *The Boston Daily Globe*, *The Boston Globe*, *The Chicago Daily Tribune*, *The Christian Science Monitor* (Boston), *The Daily Telegraph* (London), *The Levant Herald* (İstanbul), *The New York Times*, *The Philadelphia Inquirer*, *The Times* (London), *The Wall Street Journal Europe* (London).

French: *Journal de Genève*, *La République* (İstanbul), *Le Monde* (Paris), *Le Petit Temps* (Paris), *Le Temps* (Paris).

Turkish: *Akşam* (İstanbul), *Hakimiyeti Milliye* (Ankara), *İkdam* (İstanbul), *İttihad* (İstanbul), *İttihad ve Terakki* (Salonika), *Peyamı Sabah* (İstanbul), *Sabah* (İstanbul), *Tanin* (İstanbul), *Tasviri Efkar* (İstanbul), *Ulus* (Ankara), *Vakit* (İstanbul), *Vatan* (İstanbul).

IV. SECONDARY SOURCES

Books

A Correspondent, *The Armenian Troubles and Where the Responsibility Lies*, New York: J. J. Little and Co., 1895.

Açıkses, Erdal, *Amerikalıların Harput'taki Misyonerlik Faaliyetleri* (Missionary Activities of the Americans in Harput), Ankara: Türk Tarih Kurumu Basımevi, 2003.

Ahmad, Feroz, *From Empire to Republic: Essays on the Late Ottoman Empire and Modern Turkey*, two volumes, İstanbul: İstanbul Bilgi Üniversitesi Yayınları, 2008.

——, "Special Relationship: The CUP and the Ottoman Jewish Political Elite, 1908–1918," in Avigdor Levy, ed., *Jews, Turks, Ottomans: A Shared History, Fifteenth Through the Twentieth Century*, New York: Syracuse University Press, 2002.

———, *The Young Turks and the Ottoman Nationalities: Armenians, Greeks, Albanians, Jews, and Arabs, 1908–1918*, Salt Lake City, UT: University of Utah Press, 2014.

———, *The Young Turks: The Committee of Union and Progress in Turkish Politics, 1908–1914*, Oxford: Clarendon Press, 1969.

Akbayar, Nuri, Raşit Çavaş, Yücel Demirel, Bahattin Öztuncay, Mete Tunçay, eds., *İkinci Meşrutiyetin İlk Yılı 23 Temmuz 1908–23 Temmuz 1909* (The First Year of the Second Constitutionalism: 23 July 1908–23 July 1909), İstanbul: Yapı Kredi Yayınları, 2008.

Akgündüz, Ahmed, *Arşiv Belgeleri Işığında Tarsus Tarihi ve Eshab-ı Kehf* (History of Tarsus in the Light of Archival Documents and the Cave Dwellers), İstanbul: Tarsus Ticaret ve Sanayi Odası Yayınları, 1993.

Aksüt, Ali Kemali, *Profesör Mehmet Ali Ayni: Hayatı ve Eserleri* (Professor Mehmet Ali Ayni: His Life and Works), İstanbul: Ahmet Sait Matbaası, 1944.

Akşin, Sina, *Jön Türkler ve İttihat ve Terakki* (The Young Turks and the Committee of Union and Progress), Ankara: İmge Yayınevi, reprint, 2001.

———, *31 Mart Olayı* (The March 31 Incident), Ankara: Ankara Üniversitesi Siyasal Bilgiler Fakültesi Yayınları, 1970.

Aktan, Selma, *Dünkü ve Bugünkü Adana* (Adana of Yesterday and Today), Adana: Güney Basımevi, 1967.

Alan, Gülbadi, *Osmanlı İmparatorluğunda Amerikan Protestan Okulları* (American Protestant Schools in the Ottoman Empire), Ankara: Türk Tarih Kurumu Basımevi, 2015.

Alkan, Mehmet, ed., *Prens Sabahattin Gönüllü Sürgünden Zorunlu Sürgüne* (Prince Sabahattin: From Voluntary Exile to Forced Exile), İstanbul: Yapı Kredi Yayınları, 2007.

Anadol, Cemal, *Tarihin Işığında Ermeni Dosyası* (The Armenian File in Light of History), İstanbul: Turan Kitabevi, 1982.

Anderson, Ewan, *The Middle East: Geography and Geopolitics*, London: Routledge, 2000.

Arkun, Aram, "Into the Modern Age, 1800–1913," in Edmund Herzig and Marina Kurkchiyan, eds., *The Armenians Past and Present in the Making of National Identity*, London and New York: Routledge Curzon, 2005.

Armstrong, Harold, *Turkey and Syria Reborn: Records of Two Years of Travel*, London: John Lane The Bodley Head Ltd., 1930.

Artuç, Nevzat, *Cemal Paşa: Askeri ve Siyasi Hayatı* (Cemal Paşa: His Military and Political Life), Ankara: Türk Tarih Kurumu Basımevi, 2008.

Astourian, Stephan, "Testing World-System Theory, Cilicia (1830–1890): Armenian-Turkish Polarization and the Ideology of Modern Historiography," doctoral dissertation, University of California at Los Angeles, 1996.

———, "The Silence of the Land: Agrarian Relations, Ethnicity, and Power," in Ronald Grigor Suny, Fatma Müge Göçek and Norman Naimark, eds., *A Question of Genocide: Armenians and Turks at the End of the Ottoman Empire*, New York: Oxford University Press, 2011.

Atalay, Besim, *Maraş: Tarihi ve Coğrafyası* (Maraş: Its History and Geography), İstanbul: Dizerkonca Matbaası, reprinted, 1973.

Atamian, Sarkis, *The Armenian Community: The Historical Development of a Social and Ideological Conflict*, New York: Philosophical Library, 1955.

Autheman, André, *La Banque impériale ottomane*, Paris: Comité pour l'histoire économique et financière de la France, 1996.

Aydemir, Şevket Süreyya, *Makedonya'dan Ortaasya'ya Enver Paşa* (Enver Paşa: From Macedonia to Central Asia), Vol. 2, İstanbul: Remzi Kitabevi, reprinted, 2010.

Babacan, Hasan, *Mehmet Talat Paşa, 1874–1921*, Ankara: Türk Tarih Kurumu Basımevi, 2005.

Balakian, Peter, *The Burning Tigris: The Armenian Genocide and America's Response*, New York: HarperCollins, 2004.

Bali, Rıfat, *Bir Kıyımın, Bir Talanın Öyküsü Hurdaya (S)Atılan Matbu ve Yazma Eserler, Evrak-ı Metrukeler, Arşivler* (The Story of a Destruction, a Plunder: Printed and Manuscript Works, Abandoned Documents, Archives That Are Sold or Thrown As Waste), İstanbul: Libra Yayıncılık, second revised edition, 2015.

Bardakçı, Murat, *Enver*, İstanbul: Türkiye İş Bankası Kültür Yayınları, 2015.

Bartholomew, Alan Alfred, "Tarsus American School, 1888–1988: The Evolution of a Missionary Institution in Turkey," doctoral dissertation, Bryn Mawr College, 1989.

Bayazıt, Bekir Sami, *1865–1866 Kürtdağı, Cebeli Bereket Kozanoğulları İsyanı ve Güneydeki Aşiretlerin İskanları* (The Revolt of the Kozanoğlu Tribe of Kürtdağı and Cebeli Bereket in 1865–1866 and the Resettlement of the Tribes in the South), Antakya: Kültür Eğitim Tesisleri, 1989.

Bayerle, Gustav, *Pashas, Begs, and Effendis: A Historical Dictionary of Titles and Terms in the Ottoman Empire*, Istanbul: Isis Press, 1997.

Bayındır, Seda, "Adana Ermeni İsyanı (1909)" (Adana Armenian Revolt [1909]), master's thesis, Marmara University, 1997.

Baykara, Tuncer, *Anadolu'nun Tarihi Coğrafyasına Giriş I Anadolu'nun İdari Taksimatı* (Introduction to the Historical Geography of Anatolia I: Administrative Division of Anatolia), Ankara: Türk Kültürünü Araştırma Enstitüsü, 2000.

Bayur, Yusuf Hikmet, *Türk İnkılabı Tarihi* (History of the Turkish Revolution), Vol. 2, Ankara: Türk Tarih Kurumu Basımevi, second edition, 1991.

Bengi, Hilmi, *Gazeteci, Siyasetçi ve Fikir Adamı Olarak Hüseyin Cahid Yalçın* (Hüseyin Cahid Yalçın As Journalist, Politician, and Intellectual), Ankara: Atatürk Araştırma Merkezi, 2000.

Billings, Florence, "The Causes of the Outbreak in Cilicia, Asia Minor, April, 1909," master's thesis, Columbia University, 1927.

Blanche, Lesley, *Pierre Loti: Portrait of an Escapist*, London: Collins, 1983.

Bliss, Edwin Munsell, Henry Otis Dwight, Allen Tupper, eds., *The Encyclopedia of Missions*, Detroit, MI: Gale Research Company, 1975.

Bogle, Emory, *The Modern Middle East: From Imperialism to Freedom, 1800–1958*, Upper Saddle River, NJ: Prentice-Hall, Inc., 1996.

Bogosian, Eric, *Operation Nemesis: The Assasination Plot That Avenged the Armenian Genocide*, New York: Little, Brown and Company, 2015.

Bournoutian, George, *A Concise History of the Armenian People (From Ancient Times to the Present)*, Costa Mesa, CA: Mazda Publishers, Inc., 2006.

Breitman, Richard, *The Architect of Genocide: Himmler and the Final Solution*, Hanover and London: Brandeis University Press, 1991.

Budak, Muzaffer, *Toplumbilimci Prens Sabahattin* (Sociologist Prince Sabahattin), İstanbul: Kurtiş Matbaacılık, 1998.

Burnaby, Frederick, *On Horseback Through Asia Minor*, Oxford and New York: Oxford University Press, second edition, 1996.

Butler, Daniel Allen, *Shadow of the Sultan's Realm: The Destruction of the Ottoman Empire and the Creation of the Modern Middle East*, Washington, DC: Potomac Books, 2011.

Buzanski, Peter Michael, "Admiral Mark L. Bristol and Turkish-American Relations, 1919–1922," doctoral dissertation, University of California at Berkeley, 1960.

Campos, Michelle Ursula, *Ottoman Brothers: Muslims, Christians, and Jews in Early Twentieth-Century Palestine*, Stanford, CA: Stanford University Press, 2010.

Chambers, Frank, *The War Behind the War 1914–1918: A History of the Political and Civilian Fronts*, London: Faber and Faber Limited, 1939.

Clark, Peter, *Marmaduke Pickthall: British Muslim*, London: Quartet Books, 1986.

Cohen, Julia Phillips, *Becoming Ottomans: Sephardi Jews and Imperial Citizenship in the Modern Era*, New York: Oxford University Press, 2014.

Cox, Nicholas, "The Thirty-Year Rule and Freedom of Information: Access to Government Records," in G. H. Martin and Peter Stufford, eds., *The Records of the Nations: The Public Record Office 1838–1988 The British Record Society 1888–1988*, Woodbridge: The Boydell Press, 1990.

Creasy, Edward, Archibald Cary Coolidge, and Harold Claflin, *The History of Nations*, Vol. 14, New York: P. F. Collier and Son Company Publishers, 1928.

Çalık, Ramazan, *Alman Kaynaklarına Göre II. Abdülhamit Döneminde Ermeni Olayları* (According to the German Sources the Armenian Incidents in the Period of Abdülhamit II), Ankara: Kültür Bakanlığı Yayınları, 2000.

Çankaya, Ali, *Mülkiye Tarihi ve Mülkiyeliler* (History of the College of Administrative Sciences and Its Alumni), eight volumes, Ankara: Mars Matbaası, 1968–1969.

Çavdar, Tevfik, *İttihat ve Terakki* (The Committee of Union and Progress), İstanbul: İletişim Yayınları, 1991.

Çiçek, Kemal, ed., *1909 Adana Olayları: Makaleler* (Adana Events of 1909: Articles), Ankara: Türk Tarih Kurumu Basımevi, 2011.

Çiçek, Talha, *War and State Formation in Syria: Cemal Pasha's Governorate during World War I, 1914–1917*, London and New York: Routledge, 2014.

Dabağyan, Levon Panos, *Emperyalistler Kıskacında Ermeni Tehciri I (Türk Ermenileri)* (Armenian Relocation at the Pincer of the Imperialists I [Turkish Armenians]), İstanbul: IQ Kültür Sanat Yayıncılık, 2007.

Dadrian, Vahakn, *The History of the Armenian Genocide: Ethnic Conflict from the Balkans to Anatolia to the Caucasus*, Providence, RI, and Oxford: Berghahn Books, second revised edition, 1997.

———, and Taner Akçam, *Judgment at Istanbul: The Armenian Genocide Trials*, New York and Oxford: Berghahn Books, 2011.

Danişmend, İsmail Hami, *İzahlı Osmanlı Tarihi Kronolojisi* (Annotated Chronology of the Ottoman History), Vol. 4, İstanbul: Türkiye Yayınevi, 1961.

Davison, Roderic, "European Archives as a Source for Later Ottoman History," in Kathleen Brown, ed., *Report on Current Research 1958: Survey of Current Research on the Middle East*, Washington, DC: The Middle East Institute, 1958.

———, *Reform in the Ottoman Empire 1856–1876*, Princeton, NJ: Princeton University Press, 1963.

——— "The *Millets* as Agents of Change in the Nineteenth-Century Ottoman Empire," in Benjamin Braude and Bernard Lewis, eds., *Christians and Jews in the Ottoman Empire: The Functioning of a Plural Society*, Vol. 1, 1982.

Delikoca, Yusuf, *Çukurova Kahramanları* (Heroes of Cilicia), Adana: Çukurova Yayınları, reprint, 2006.

Deliorman, Altan, *Türklere Karşı Ermeni Komitecileri* (Armenian Revolutionaries Against Turks), İstanbul: Boğaziçi Yayınları, 1973.

Demir, Fevzi, "Bir Siyaset Okulu Olarak Meclis-i Mebusan" (The Chamber of Deputies as a School of Politics), in Ferdan Ergut, ed., *İkinci Meşrutiyeti Düşünmek* (Thinking About the Second Constitutionalism), İstanbul: Tarih Vakfı Yurt Yayınları, 2010.

Demirci, Aliyar, *Ayan Meclisi 1908–1912* (The Chamber of Notables 1908–1912), İstanbul: İstanbul Bilgi Üniversitesi Yayınları, 2006.

Demiryürek, Mehmet, *Tanzimat'tan Cumhuriyet'e Bir Osmanlı Aydını: Abdurrahman Şeref Efendi (1853–1925)* (From the *Tanzimat* to the Republic: An Ottoman Intellectual Abdurrahman Şeref Efendi [1853–1925]), Ankara: Phoenix Yayınevi, 2003.

Demoyan, Hayk, "Foreword," *The Young Turks and the Truth about the Holocaust at Adana in Asia Minor*.

Devereux, Robert, *The First Ottoman Constitutional Period: A Study of Midhat Constitution and Parliament*, Baltimore, MD: The Johns Hopkins Press, 1963.

Dickie, John, *The British Consul: Heir to a Great Tradition*, New York: Columbia University Press, 2007.

Divine, Donna Robinson, *Politics and Society in Ottoman Palestine: The Arab Struggle for Survival and Power*, Boulder, CO, and London: Lynne Rienner Publishers, 1994.

Ege, Nezahat Nurettin, *Prens Sabahattin: Hayatı ve İlmı Müdafaaları* (Prince Sabahattin: His Life and Scholarly Defenses), İstanbul: Güneş Neşriyatı, 1977.

Eldem, Edhem, *A History of the Ottoman Bank*, İstanbul: Ottoman Bank Historical Research Center, 1999.

Emiroğlu, Kudret, *Anadolu'da Devrim Günleri* (Days of Revolution in Anatolia), Ankara: İmge Kitabevi, 1999.

Ener, Kasım, *Adana Tarihi ve Tarımına Dair Araştırmalar* (Studies on the History of Adana and Its Agriculture), Adana: Türksözü Matbaası, reprint, 1968.

———, *Tarih Boyunca Adana Ovasına (Çukurova'ya) Bir Bakış* (A Glance at the Adana Plain [Cilicia] Throughout History), Adana: Bugün Matbaası, 1955.

Engin, Vahdettin, *Sultan Abdülhamid ve İstanbul'u* (Sultan Abdülhamid and His İstanbul), İstanbul: Simurg Yayınları, 2001.

Erdeha, Kamil, *Milli Mücadelede Vilayetler ve Valiler* (Provinces and Governors During the National Struggle), İstanbul: Remzi Kitabevi, 1975.

Erickson, Edward, *Ottomans and Armenians: A Study in Counterinsurgency*, New York: Palgrave Macmillan, 2013.

Erim, Nihat, *Devletlerarası Hukuku ve Siyasi Tarih Metinleri* (Texts of International Law and Political History), Vol. 1, Ankara: Türk Tarih Kurumu Basımevi, 1953.

Ersan, Mehmet, "Kilikya Ermeni Krallığı" (Armenian Kingdom of Cilicia) in Erman Artun and Sabri Koz, eds., *Efsaneden Tarihe, Tarihten Bugüne Adana: Köprü Başı* (From Legend to History, From History to Our Day: Bridge Head), İstanbul: Yapı Kredi Yayınları, 2000.

Eryılmaz, Bilal, *Osmanlı Devletinde Gayrımüslim Tebaanın Yönetimi* (The Governance of the Non-Muslim Subjects in the Ottoman State), İstanbul: Risale Yayınları, 1996.

Esin, Taylan, and Zeliha Etöz, *1916 Ankara Yangını Felaketin Mantığı* (Ankara Fire of 1916: The Logic of the Disaster), İstanbul: İletişim Yayınları, 2015.

Farkas, Paul, trans., Kenneth Kronenberg, *Palace and Counterrevolution in Turkey (March–April 1909)*, İstanbul: The Isis Press, 2005.

Fawaz, Leila Tarazi, *A Land of Aching Hearts: The Middle East in the Great War*, Cambridge, MA and London: Harvard University Press, 2014.

Georgeon, François, *Abdulhamid II Le sultan calife (1876–1909)*, Paris: Librairie Arthème Fayard, 2003.

Gidney, James, *A Mandate for Armenia*, Oberlin, OH: Kent University Press, 1967.

Goldstone, Patricia, *Aaronsohn's Maps: The Untold Story of the Man Who Might Have Created Peace in the Middle East*, Orlando, FL: Harcourt, Inc., 2007.

Gough, Mary, *The Plain and Rough Places: An Account of Archaelogical Journeying Through the Plain and the Rough Places of the Roman Province of Cilicia in Southern Turkey*, London: Chatto and Windus, 1954.

Göçek, Fatma Müge, *Denial of Violence: Ottoman Past, Turkish Present, and Collective Violence against the Armenians 1789–2009*, New York: Oxford University Press, 2015.

Gökbel, Ahmet, *Anadolu'da Varsak Türkmenleri* (Varsak Turkomans in Anatolia), Ankara: Atatürk Kültür Merkezi Yayınları, 2007.

Göney, Süha, *Adana Ovaları I* (The Plains of Adana I), İstanbul: İstanbul Üniversitesi Coğrafya Enstitüsü Yayınları, 1976.

Gözübüyük, Abdullah Şeref, and Suna Kili, *Türk Anayasa Metinleri Tanzimattan Bugüne Kadar* (Turkish Constitution Texts: From the *Tanzimat* to the Present), Ankara: Ajans-Türk Matbaası, 1957.

Grabill, Joseph, *Protestant Diplomacy and the Near East*, Minneapolis, MN: University of Minnesota Press, 1973.

Grainger, John, *The Battle for Syria 1918–1920*, Woodbridge, Suffolk: The Boydell Press, 2013.

Gunning, Lucia Patrizio, *The British Consular Service in the Aegean and the Collection of Antiquities for the British Museum*, Farnham, Surrey: Ashgate Publishing Limited, 2009.

Güçlü, Yücel, *Armenians and the Allies in Cilicia 1914–1923*, Salt Lake City, UT: University of Utah Press, 2010.

———, *Historical Archives and the Historians' Commission to Investigate the Armenian Events of 1915*, Lanham, MD: University Press of America, 2015.

———, *The Holocaust and the Armenian Case in Comparative Perspective*, Lanham, MD: University Press of America, 2012.

———, *Zeki Kuneralp and the Turkish Foreign Service*, Newcastle upon Tyne: Cambridge Scholars Publishing, 2015.

Güler, Ali, *Osmanlı'dan Cumhuriyete Azınlıklar* (Minorities from the Ottoman to the Republic), Ankara: Tamga Yayıncılık, 2000.

Güllü, Ramazan Erhan, *Antep Ermenileri (Sosyal-Siyasi ve Kültürel Hayatı)* (Armenians of Antep [Their Social-Political and Cultural Life]), İstanbul: IQ Kültür Sanat Yayıncılık, 2010.

Gürün, Kamuran, *The Armenian File: The Myth of Innocence Exposed*, London, Nicosia, and Istanbul: K. Rustem and Weidenfeld and Nicolson, 1985.

Halaçoğlu, Yusuf, *Onsekizinci Yüzyılda Osmanlı İmparatorluğunun İskan Siyaseti ve Aşiretlerin Yerleştirilmesi* (The Resettlement Policy of the Ottoman Empire and the Placement of the Tribes in the Eighteenth Century), Ankara: Türk Tarih Kurumu Basımevi, 1988.

Hanioğlu, Şükrü, *Preparation for a Revolution: the Young Turks, 1902–1908*, New York and Oxford: Oxford University Press, 2001.

———, *The Young Turks in Opposition*, New York and Oxford: Oxford University Press, 1995.

Hathaway, Jane, "An Agenda for Historical Study of the Ottoman Arab Provinces," in Kemal Çiçek, ed., *Pax Ottomana: Studies in Memoriam—Prof. Dr. Nejat Göyünç*, Haarlem-Ankara: Sota-Yeni Türkiye, 2001.

Haydaroğlu, İlknur Polat, *Osmanlı İmparatorluğunda Yabancı Okullar* (The Foreign Schools in the Ottoman Empire), Ankara: Ocak Yayınları, 1993.

Heller, Joseph, *British Policy towards the Ottoman Empire 1908–1914*, London: Frank Cass, 1983.

Herbert, Aubrey, Desmond MacCarthy, ed., *Ben Kendim: A Record of Eastern Travel*, London: Hutchinson and Company, 1924.

Hoff, Michael, and Rhys Townsend, eds., *Rough Cilicia: New Historical and Archaeological Approaches*, Oxford and Oakville: Oxbow Books, 2009.

Hooson, D., ed., *Geography and National Identity*, Oxford: Blackwell, 1994.

Howell, Georgina, *Daughter of the Desert: The Remarkable Life of Gertrude Bell*, London: Macmillan, 2006.

Hülagü, Metin, *Sultan II. Abdülhamid'in Sürgün Günleri (1909–1918): Hususi Doktoru Atıf Hüseyin Bey'in Hatıratı* (Days of Exile of Sultan Abdülhamid II [1909–1918]: Recollections of His Private Physician Atıf Hüseyin Bey), İstanbul: Pan Yayıncılık, 2003.

İlter, Erdal, *Ermeni Kilisesi ve Terör* (The Armenian Church and Terror), Ankara: Ankara Üniversitesi Osmanlı Tarihi Araştırma ve Uygulama Merkezi Yayınları, 1996.

İnal, İbnülemin Mahmud Kemal, *Osmanlı Devrinde Son Sadrazamlar* (The Last Grand Viziers in the Ottoman Era), Sect. 10, İstanbul: Maarif Matbaası, 1940–1953.

İnalcık, Halil, *Osmanlı İmparatorluğunun Ekonomik ve Sosyal Tarihi (1300–1600)* (Economic and Social History of the Ottoman Empire [1300–1600]), Vol. 1, İstanbul: Eren Yayınları, 2000.

İstepenyan, Torkom, *Atatürk'ün Doğumunun 100. Yılında Türk-Ermeni İlişkileri* (Turkish-Armenian Relations at the Hundredth Birthday Anniversary of Atatürk), İstanbul: Murat Ofset, 1984.

Jackh, Ernest, *The Rising Crescent-Turkey: Yesterday, Today, and Tomorrow*, New York: Farrar and Reinhard, 1944.

Kaligian, Dikran Mesrob, *Armenian Organization and Ideology Under Ottoman Rule 1908–1914*, New Brunswick, NJ, and London: Transactions Publishers, 2009.

———, "The Armenian Revolutionary Federation in Constantinople, 1908–1914," in Richard Hovannisian and Simon Payaslian, eds., *Armenian Constantinople*, Costa Mesa, CA: Mazda Publishers, 2010.

Kandemir, Feridun, İbrahim Öztürkçü, ed., *Yakın Tarihten Bir Sahife Cemal Paşa'nın Son Günleri* (A Page From the Recent History: The Last Days of Cemal Paşa), İstanbul: Yağmur Yayınevi, 2012.

Kansu, Aykut, *Politics in Post-Revolutionary Turkey 1908–1913*, Leiden: E. J. Brill, 2000.

———, *The Revolution of 1908*, Leiden: E. J. Brill, 1997.

Kara, İsmail, "Müsavat Yahut Müslümanlara Eşitsizlik: Bir Kavramın Siyaseten/ Dinen İnşası ve Dönüştürücü Güçü" (Equality or Unequality Toward Muslims: Political/Religious Construction of a Concept and Its Transformatory Force), in Azmi Özcan, ed., *Osmanlı Devletinde Din ve Vicdan Hürriyeti* (Freedom of Religion and Conscience in the Ottoman State), İstanbul: Ensar Neşriyat, 2000.

Karal, Enver Ziya, *Osmanlı Tarihi* (Ottoman History), Vols. 5, 6, 8 and 9, Ankara: Türk Tarih Kurumu Basımevi, reprinted, 1988, 1995, and 1996.

Karpat, Kemal, *Ottoman Population, 1830–1914: Demographic and Social Characteristics*, Madison, WI: University of Wisconsin Press, 1982.

———, *Studies on Ottoman Social and Political History: Selected Articles and Essays*, Leiden: Brill, 2002.

Kasbarian-Bricout, Béatrice, *L'Arméno-Cilicie, royaume oublié*, Paris: Editions Astrid, 1982.

Kaşgarlı, Mehlika Aktok, *Kilikya Tabi Ermeni Baronluğu Tarihi* (History of the Cilician Vassal Armenian Barony), Ankara: Köksav Yayınları, 1990.

Katz, Steven, *Historicism, the Holocaust and Zionism: Critical Studies in Modern Jewish Thought and History*, New York and London: New York University Press, 1992.

———, *Post-Holocaust Dialogues: Critical Studies in Modern Jewish Thought*, New York and London: New York University Press, 1983.

———, *The Holocaust in Historical Context*, Vol. 1, New York and Oxford: Oxford University Press, 1994.

———, "The Uniqueness of the Holocaust: The Historical Dimension," in Alan Rosenbaum, ed., *Is the Holocaust Unique? Perspectives on Comparative Genocide*, Boulder, CO: Westview Press, 1996.

Kayalı, Hasan, *Arabs and Young Turks: Ottomanism, Arabism, and Islamism in the Ottoman Empire, 1908–1918*, Berkeley and Los Angeles, CA: University of California Press, 1997.

———, "Ottoman and German Imperial Objectives in Syria During World War I: Synergies and Strains Behind the Front Lines," in Hakan Yavuz with Feroz Ahmad, eds., *War and Collapse: World War I and the Ottoman State*, Salt Lake City, UT: University of Utah Press, 2016.

Kedourie, Elie, "The Impact of the Young Turk Revolution in the Arabic-Speaking Provinces of the Ottoman Empire," in Elie Kedourie, ed., *Arabic Political Memoirs and Other Studies*, London: Frank Cass, 1974.

Kévorkian, Raymond, "Traductions d'Extraits du Livre Adanayı Hayots Badmoutiun, de Puzant Yeghiyayan, Antélias 1970," in Raymond Kévorkian, Mihran Minassian, Lévonian Nordiguian, Michel Paboudjian, Vahé Tachjian, *Les Arméniens de Cilicie Habitat, mémoire et identité*, Beyrouth: Presses de Université de Saint-Joseph, 2012.

———, *The Armenian Genocide: A Complete History*, London and New York: I. B. Tauris, 2011.

———, "The Cilician Massacres, 1909," in Richard Hovannisian and Simon Payaslian, eds., *Armenian Cilicia*, Costa Mesa, CA: Mazda Publishers, 2008.

Kévorkian, Raymond et Paul Paboudjian, *Les Arméniens dans l'Empire ottoman à la veille du génocide*, Paris: Editions d'Art et d'Histoire, 1992.

Kieser, Hans-Lucas, *Der verpasste Friede: Mission, Ethnic und Staat in den Ostprovinzen der Türkei, 1839–1938*, Zürich: Chronos, 2010.

Kirakossian, Arman, *British Diplomacy and the Armenian Question, from the 1830s to 1914*, Princeton, NJ: Gomidas Institute Books, 2003.

Kırmızı, Abdulhamit, *Abdülhamid'in Valileri Osmanlı Vilayet İdaresi 1895–1908* (The Governors of Abdülhamid: Ottoman Provincial Administration 1895–1908), İstanbul: Klasik, 2007.

———, *Avlonyalı Ferid Paşa Bir Ömür Bir Devlet* (Ferid Paşa of Avlonya: State Service Throughout a Whole Life), İstanbul: Klasik, 2014.

Kocabaşoğlu, Uygur, *Anadolu'daki Amerika Kendi Belgeleriyle 19. Yüzyılda Osmanlı İmparatorluğundaki Amerikan Misyoner Okulları* (America in Anatolia: American Missionary Schools in Nineteenth-century Ottoman Empire in Their Own Documents), İstanbul: İmge Kitabevi Yayınları, 1989.

———, *"Hürriyeti" Beklerken İkinci Meşrutiyet Basını* (Waiting for the "Liberty": Press of the Second Constitutionalism), İstanbul: İstanbul Bilgi Üniversitesi Yayınları, 2010.

———, *Majestelerinin Konsolosları, İngiliz Belgeleriyle Osmanlı İmparatorluğundaki İngiliz Konsoloslukları (1580–1900)* (Consuls of Their Majesties, British Consulates in the Ottoman Empire in British Documents [1580–1900]), İstanbul: İletişim Yayınları, 2004.

Kocahanoğlu, Osman Selim, "Önsöz" (Preface), in İrtem, *Meşrutiyet Doğarken*.

Koloğlu, Orhan, *1908 Basın Patlaması* (Press Explosion of 1908), İstanbul: Türkiye Gazeteciler Cemiyeti Yayınları, 2005.

Konukçu, Enver, *Erzurum'da Kars Kapı Şehitliğindeki İki Mezar: Hafız Hakkı ve Cemal Paşalar (1915, 1922)* (Two Graves in the Kars Kapı Military Graveyard in Erzurum: Hafız Hakkı and Cemal Paşas [1915, 1922]), Erzurum: Atatürk Üniversitesi Yayınları, 2010.

Krikorian, Mesrob, *Armenians in the Service of the Ottoman Empire, 1860–1908*, Boston, MA: Routledge and Kegan Paul, 1978.

Kuneralp, Sinan, *Son Dönem Osmanlı Erkan ve Ricali (1839–1922) Prosopografik Rehber* (The Late Ottoman Period Statesmen and Officialdom [1839–1922]: Prosopographical Guide), İstanbul: İSİS, 1999.

Kurt, Yılmaz, *Çukurova Tarihinin Kaynakları I: 1525 Tarihli Adana Sancağı Mufassal Tahrir Defteri* (Sources of the Cilician History I: Detailed Tax Register of the Sanjak of Adana Dated 1525), Ankara: Türk Tarih Kurumu Basımevi, 2004.

Kurt, Yılmaz and M. Akif Erdoğru, *Çukurova Tarihinin Kaynakları IV, Adana Evkaf Defteri* (Sources of Cilician History IV: Religious Endowments Register of Adana), Ankara: Türk Tarih Kurumu Basımevi, 2000.

Küçük, Cevdet, *Osmanlı Diplomasisinde Ermeni Meselesinin Ortaya Çıkışı 1878–1897* (The Emergence of the Armenian Question in the Ottoman Diplomacy 1878–1897), İstanbul: Türk Dünyası Araştırmaları Vakfı, 1986.

Landau, Jacob, and Mim Kemal Öke, "Ottoman Perspectives on American Interests in the Holy Land," in Moshe Davis, ed., *With Eyes Toward Zion: Themes and Sources in the Archives of the United States, Great Britain, Turkey and Israel*, Vol. 2, Westport, CT: Praeger Publishers, 1986.

Landen, Robert, *The Emergence of the Modern Middle East: Selected Readings*, New York: D. Van Nostrand Company, 1970.

Lewis, Bernard, *The Emergence of Modern Turkey*, London: Oxford University Press, second edition, 1968.

Longrigg, Stephen Hemsley, *Four Centuries of Modern Iraq*, Oxford: Clarendon Press, 1925.

———, *Iraq, 1900 to 1950: A Political, Social, And Economic History*, London: Oxford University Press, 1953.

Lord Kinross, *The Ottoman Centuries: The Rise and Fall of the Turkish Empire*, New York: Morrow Quill, 1977.

Lüdke, Tilman, *Jihad Made in Germany: Ottoman and German Propaganda and Intelligence Operations in the First World War*, Münster: Lit Verlag, 2005.

Maksudyan, Nazan, "New 'Rules of Conduct' for State, American Missionaries, and Armenians: 1909 Adana Massacres and Ottoman Orphanage (Dârü'l-Eytâm-ı Osmânî)" in François Georgeon, ed., *Livresse de la Liberté: La Revolution de 1908 dans l'Empire Ottoman*, Paris: CNRS, 2012.

Mango, Andrew, *Atatürk: The Biography of the Founder of Modern Turkey*, London: John Murray, 1999.

Matossian, Bedross Der, *Shattered Dreams of Revolution: From Liberty to Violence in the Late Ottoman Empire*, Stanford, CA: Stanford University Press, 2014.

McCarthy, Justin, *Muslims and Minorities: The Population of Ottoman Anatolia and the End of the Empire*, New York: New York University Press, 1983.

———, *The Arab World, Turkey and the Balkans (1878–1914): A Handbook of Historical Statistics*, Boston, MA: G. K. Hall and Company, 1982.
McCarthy, Justin, Ömer Turan, and Cemalettin Taşkıran, *Sasun: The History of an 1890s Armenian Revolt*, Salt Lake City, UT: University of Utah Press, 2014.
McMeekin, Sean, *The Ottoman End Game: War, Revolution, and the Modern Middle East, 1908–1923*, New York: Penguin Press, 2015.
Mennecke, Martin, "The Crime of Genocide and International Law," in Barbara Boender and Wichert ten Have, eds., *The Holocaust and Other Genocides: An Introduction*, Amsterdam: Amsterdam University Press, 2012.
Minassian, Anahide Ter, "The Role of the Armenian Community in the Foundation and Development of the Socialist Movement in the Ottoman Empire and Turkey: 1876–1923," in Mete Tunçay and Erik Jan Zürcher, eds., *Socialism and Nationalism in the Ottoman Empire 1876–1923*, London: British Academic Press, 1994.
Moumdjian, Garabet, "From Millet-i Sadıka to Millet-i Asiya," in Hakan Yavuz with Peter Sluglett, eds., *War and Diplomacy: The Russo-Turkish War of 1877–1878*, Salt Lake City, UT: University of Utah Press, 2011.
Mutafian, Claude, et Catherine Otten-Froux, *Le royaume arménien de Cilicie: XIIe-XIVe siècle*, Paris: CNRS Editions, 1993.
Mutlu, Şamil, *Osmanlı Devletinde Misyoner Okulları* (Missionary Schools in the Ottoman State), İstanbul: Gökkubbe Yayınları, 2005.
Mühlmann, Carl, *Deutschland und die Türkei, 1913–1914*, Berlin-Grunewald: Walther Rothschild, 1929.
Naimark, Norman, *Fires of Hatred: Ethnic Cleansing in Twentieth-Century Europe*, Cambridge, MA: Harvard University Press, 2001.
Nalbandian, Louise, *The Armenian Revolutionary Movement*, Berkeley and Los Angeles, CA: University of California Press, 1963.
Nassibian, Akaby, *Britain and the Armenian Question, 1915–1923*, London and Sydney: Croom Helm, 1984.
Okday, İsmail Hakkı Tevfik, *Adana Vilayeti Matbuatı* (The Press of the Province of Adana), Ankara: Hariciye Vekaleti, 1932.
Onar, Mustafa, *Hacın Dosyası* (The Hacin File), Adana: Önder Matbaa, 1984.
Oppenheim, Lassa Francis Lawrence, ed., Ronald Roxburgh, *International Law: A Treatise*, Vol. 1: *Peace*, London: Longmans, Green and Company, third edition, 1920.
Oral, Haluk, and Erol Şadi Erdinç, *Meclis-i Mebusan Birinci Seçim Dönemi 1908–1911* (Chamber of Deputies First Legislative Term 1908–1911), İstanbul: Türkiye İş Bankası Kültür Yayınları, 2008.
Ortaylı, İlber, *İmparatorluğun En Uzun Yüzyılı* (The Longest Century of the Empire), İstanbul: Timaş Yayınları, reprinted, 2013.
———, *Osmanlı Barışı* (Pax Ottomana), İstanbul: Timaş Yayınları, 2007.
———, *Osmanlı İmparatorluğunda Alman Nüfuzu* (German Influence in the Ottoman Empire), İstanbul: Timaş Yayınları, reprint, 2015.
Oshagan, Vahe, "Modern Armenian Literature and Intellectual History from 1700 to 1915," in Richard Hovannisian, ed., *The Armenian People from Ancient to Modern Times*, New York: St. Martin's Press, 1977.

Özçelik, Ayfer, *Sahibini Arayan Meşrutiyet (Meclisi Mebusan'ın Açılışı, 31 Mart ve Adana Olayları)* (The Constitutionalism Seeking Its Owner [The Opening of the Chamber of Deputies, the March 31 and Adana Incidents]), İstanbul: Tez Yayınları, 2001.

Özdemir, Bülent, "Being Part of the Cinderalla Service: Consul Charles Blunt at Salonica in the 1840's," in Colin Imber, Keiko Kiyotaki and Rhoads Murphy, eds., *Frontiers of Ottoman Studies*, Vol. 2, London and New York: I. B. Tauris, 2005.

Özdemir, Hikmet, *Cemal Paşa ve Ermeni Göçmenler: 4. Ordu'nun İnsani Yardımları* (Cemal Paşa and the Armenian Emigrants: Humanitarian Assistance of the Fourth Army), İstanbul: Remzi Kitabevi, 2009.

———, *Üç Jöntürk'ün Ölümü (Talat-Cemal-Enver)* (The Death of the Three Young Turks [Talat-Cemal-Enver]), İstanbul: Remzi Kitabevi, 2007.

Öztürk, Necdet, and Murat Yıldız, *İmparatorluk Tarihinin Kalemli Muhafızları: Osmanlı Tarihçileri* (The Penned Guardians of the Imperial History: Ottoman Historians), İstanbul: Bilge Kültür Sanat, 2013.

Paboudjian, Michel, "Zeytoun la Singulière," in Kévorkian, Minassian, Nordiguian, Paboudjian, Tachjian, *Les Arméniens de Cilicie*.

Pakalın, Mehmet Zeki, *Osmanlı Tarih Deyimleri ve Terimleri Sözlüğü* (Dictionary of Ottoman Historical Expressions and Terms), İstanbul: Milli Eğitim Bakanlığı Yayınları, 2004.

Pamukcıyan, Kevork, *Ermeni Kaynaklarından Tarihe Katkılar* (Contributions to the History from the Armenian Sources), Vol. 4, İstanbul: Aras Yayıncılık, 2003.

Panossian, Razmik, *The Armenians: From Kings and Priests to Merchants and Commissars*, New York and London: Columbia University Press, 2006.

Parker, Geoffrey, *Geopolitics. Past, Present and Future*, London: Pinter, 1998.

Platt, D. C. M., *The Cinderella Service: British consuls since 1825*, Hamden, CT: Archon Books, 1971.

Prens Sabahattin, Ahmet Zeki İzgöer, ed., *İttihat ve Terakki'ye Açık Mektuplar, Türkiye Nasıl Kurtulabilir ve İzahlar* (Open Letters to the Committee of Union and Progress, How Can Turkey Be Saved and the Explanations), İstanbul: Dün Bugün Yarın Yayınları, 2013.

Presland, John (pseud. for Gladys Skelton), *Deeds Bey. A Study of Sir Wyndham Deeds, 1883–1923*, London: Macmillan, 1942.

Price, Clair, *The Rebirth of Turkey*, New York: Thomas Seltzer, 1923.

Price, Philips, *A History of Turkey From Empire to Republic*, London: George Allen and Unwin Ltd; New York: The Macmillan Company, 1956.

Prousis, Theophilus, *British Consular Reports From the Ottoman Levant in an Age of Upheaval, 1815–1830*, İstanbul: The Isis Press, 2008.

Quataert, Donald, *Social Disintegration and Popular Resistance in the Ottoman Empire, 1881–1908: Reactions to European Penetration*, New York: New York University Press, 1983.

Ramsaur, Ernest Edmondson, *The Young Turks: Prelude to the Revolution of 1908*, Princeton, NJ: Princeton University Press, 1957.

Robbins, Keith, *Sir Edward Grey: A Biography of Lord Grey of Fallodon*, London: Cassell, 1971.

Rodogno, Davide, *Against Massacre: Humanitarian Interventions in the Ottoman Empire 1815–1914*, Princeton, NJ: Princeton University Press, 2012.

Roshwald, Aviel, *Ethnic Nationalism and the Fall of Empires: Central Europe, Russia and the Middle East, 1914–1923*, London and New York: Routledge, 2001.

Sachar, Howard, *The Emergence of the Middle East 1914–1924*, New York: Alfred Knopf, 1969.

Sahara, Tetsuya, *What Happened in Adana in April 1909?* İstanbul: The İsis Press, 2013.

Sanjian, Avedis, *The Armenian Communities in Syria under Ottoman Dominion*, Cambridge, MA: Harvard University Press, 1965.

Sarınay, Yusuf, and Recep Karakaya, *1909 Adana Ermeni Olayları* (Armenian Events of Adana in 1909), İstanbul: İdeal Kültür Yayıncılık, 2012.

Sert, Selahattin, *Haçlıların Son Kurbanı Ermeniler* (The Last Victim of the Crusaders: Armenians), Vol. 1, İstanbul: Kum Saati Yayınları, 2005.

Shaw, Stanford, and Ezel Kural Shaw, *History of the Ottoman Empire and Modern Turkey*, Vol. 2: *Reform, Revolution, and Republic: The Rise of Modern Turkey 1808–1975*, Cambridge: Cambridge University Press, second edition, 1977.

Shrikian, Gorun, "Armenians Under the Ottoman Empire and the American Mission's Influence On Their Intellectual and Social Renaissance," doctoral dissertation, Concordia Seminary in Exile (Seminex) in Cooperation with Lutheran School of Theology at Chicago, 1977.

Simonyan, Hrachik, trans. Melissa Brown and Alexander Arzumanian, *The Destruction of Armenians in Cilicia, April 1909*, London: Gomidas Institute, 2012.

Sohrabi, Nader, *Revolution and Constitutionalism in the Ottoman Empire and Iran*, Cambridge: Cambridge University Press, 2011.

Sousa, Nasim, *The Capitulary Regime of Turkey: Its History, Origin, and Nature*, Baltimore, MA: Johns Hopkins University Press, 1933.

Soysal, İsmail, ed., *Türkiye'nin Siyasi Antlaşmaları* (The Political Treaties of Turkey), Vol: 1920–1945, Ankara: Türk Tarih Kurumu Basımevi, 1983.

Sönmez, Erdem, *Ahmed Rıza Bir Jön Türk Liderinin Siyasi-Entelektüel Portresi* (Ahmed Rıza: Political-Intellectual Portrait of a Young Turk Leader), İstanbul: Tarih Vakfı, 2012.

Stackelberg, Roderick, *Hitler's Germany: Origins, Interpretations, Legacies*, London and New York: Routledge, 1999.

Stevens, Marcia, and Malcolm, *Against the Devil's Current: The Life and Times of Cyrus Hamlin*, Lanham, MD: University Press of America, 1988.

Suny, Ronald Grigor, *A History of the Armenian Genocide*, Princeton and Oxford: Princeton University Press, 2015.

Şakir, Ziya, *İttihat ve Terakki—I Nasıl Doğdu?* (The Committee of Union and Progress—I How Was It Born?), İstanbul: Akıl Fikir Yayınları, 2014.

———, *İttihat ve Terakki—II Nasıl Yaşadı?* (The Committee of Union and Progress—II How Did It Live?), İstanbul: Akıl Fikir Yayınları, 2014.

———, *Sultan Abdülhamid*, İstanbul: Akıl Fikir Yayınları, reprint, 2010.

Şişman, Adnan, *Yirminci Yüzyıl Başlarında Osmanlı Devletinde Yabancı Devletlerin Kültürel ve Sosyal Müesseseleri* (Cultural and Social Institutions of the Foreign

States in the Ottoman State at the Beginning of the Twentieth Century), Ankara: Atatürk Araştırma Merkezi.

Tachjian, Vahé, *La France en Cilicie et en Haute-Mésopotamie: Aux confins de la Turquie, de la Syrie et de l'Irak, 1919–1933*, Paris: Karthala, 2004.

Taylor, P. J., *Political Geography. World-Economy, Nation-State and Locality*, Harlow: Longman, 1989.

Terzian, Mary Mangigian, *The Armenian Minority Problem 1914–1934: A Nation's Struggle for Security*, Atlanta, GA: Scholars Press, 1992.

The Records of the Foreign Office 1782–1939, London: Her Majesty's Stationery Office, 1969.

Thobie, Jacques, "Les intérêts économiques, financiers, et politiques français dans la patrie asiatique de L'Empire Ottoman, de 1895 à 1914," Thèse de doctorat d'état, Université de Paris, 1973.

Thomas, Lewis, and Richard Frye, *The United States and Turkey and Iran*, Cambridge, MA: Harvard University Press, 1951.

Thomassian, Levon, *Summer of '42: A Study of German-Armenian Relations During the Second World War*, Atglen, PA: Schiffer Publishing Ltd., 2012.

Toksöz, Meltem, "Adana Ermenileri ve 1909 İğtişaşı" (Armenians of Adana and the Revolt of 1909), in Fahri Aral, ed., *İmparatorluğun Çöküş Döneminde Osmanlı Ermenileri: Bilimsel Sorumluluk ve Demokrasi Sorunları* (Ottoman Armenians in the Decline Period of the Empire: Scholarly Responsibility and the Questions of Democracy), İstanbul: Bilgi Üniversitesi Yayınları, 2011.

———, *Nomads, Migrants and Cotton in the Eastern Mediterranean: The Making of the Adana-Mersin Region 1850–1908*, Leiden and Boston, MA: E. J. Brill, 2010.

Toksöz, Meltem, and Emre Yalçın, "Modern Adana'nın Doğuşu ve Günümüzdeki İzleri" (The Birth of Modern Adana and Its Present-Day Traces), in Çiğdem Kafesçioğlu and Lucienne Thys-Şenocak, eds., *Essays in Honor of Aptullah Kuran*, İstanbul: Yapı Kredi Yayınları, 1999.

Toriguian, Shavarsh, *The Armenian Question and International Law*, Beirut: Hamaskaine Press, 1973.

Tosun, Mehmet, ed., *Osmanoğulları ve Aydınların Anlatımıyla İmparatorluğun Yüzük Taşı II. Abdülhamid* (The Ring Stone of the Empire Abdülhamid II As Narrated By the Royal Ottoman Family and the Intellectuals), İstanbul: Yeditepe Yayınevi, 2009.

Toumani, Meline, *There Was and There Was Not: A Journey Through Hate and Possibility in Turkey, Armenia, and Beyond*, New York: Mark Smith/Metropolitan Books, 2014.

Tuathail, G. O., S. Dalby, and P. Routledge, *The Geopolitics Reader*, London: Routledge, 1998.

Tunaya, Tarık Zafer, *Hürriyet'in İlanı* (Proclamation of the Liberty), İstanbul: İstanbul Bilgi Üniversitesi Yayınları, 2004.

———, *Türkiye'de Siyasi Partiler* (Political Parties in Turkey), three volumes, İstanbul: İletişim Yayınları, third edition, 2000 and 2009.

Tunçer, Polat, *İttihatçı Cavit Bey* (The Unionist Cavit Bey), İstanbul: Yeditepe Yayınevi, 2010.

Turan, Ömer, *Avrasya'da Misyonerler* (Missionaries in Euroasia), Ankara: ASAM Yayınları, 1992.

———, "Lozan Konferansında Amerikan Misyonerleri" (American Missionaries in the Lausanne Conference), in Yusuf Halaçoğlu, ed., *80. Yılında 2003 Pencer-esinden Lozan Sempozyum Bildirileri 6 Ekim 2003, Ankara* (Communications of the Lausanne Symposium at Its Eightieth Anniversary from the 2003 Window 6 October 2003, Ankara), Ankara: Türk Tarih Kurumu Basımevi, 2005.

Turfan, Naim, *Rise of the Young Turks: Politics, the Military and Ottoman Collapse*, London and New York: I. B. Tauris Publishers, 2000.

Tusan, Michelle, *Smyrna's Ashes: Humanitarianism, Genocide, and the Birth of the Middle East*, Berkeley and Los Angeles, CA: University of California Press, 2012.

Umar, Bilge, *Kilikia Bir Tarihsel Coğrafya Araştırması ve Gezi Rehberi* (Cilicia: A Historical Geography Research and Travel Guide), İstanbul: İnkılap Kitabevi, 2000.

Uras, Esat, *Tarihte Ermeniler ve Ermeni Meselesi* (Armenians in History and the Armenian Question), İstanbul: Belge Yayınları, second revised edition, 1987.

Uzunçarşılı, İsmail Hakkı, *Osmanlı Tarihi* (Ottoman History), Vol. 2, Ankara: Türk Tarih Kurumu Basımevi, 1949.

Ünal, Ahmet, and Serdar Girginer, *Kilikya-Çukurova: İlk Çağlardan Osmanlı Döne-mine Kadar Kilikya'da Tarihi Coğrafya, Tarih ve Arkeoloji* (Cilicia-Çukurova: Historical Geography, History and Archaelogy in Cilicia From the Early Ages to the Ottoman Era), İstanbul: Homer Kitabevi, 2007.

Üngör, Uğur Ümit, and Mehmet Polatel, *Confiscation and Destruction: The Young Turk Seizure of Armenian Property*, London and New York: Continuum, 2011.

Ünlü, Tülin Selvi, and Tolga Ünlü, eds., *İstasyon'dan Fener'e Mersin* (Mersin: From the Station to the Lighthouse), Mersin: Mersin Ticaret ve Sanayi Odası Yayınları, 2009.

Ürgenç, Orhan, *Büyük Adana Vilayeti (Kizzuwatna-Kilikya) Çukurova'nın 4000 Yıllık Tarihi* (The Great Adana Province [Kizzuwatna-Cilicia]: 4000-Year History of Cilicia), Adana: Adana Büyükşehir Belediyesi Yayınları, 2013.

van den Boogert, Maurits, *The Capitulations and the Ottoman Legal System: Qadis, Consuls, and Beraths in the 18th Century*, Leiden: Brill, 2005.

———, and Kate Fleet, eds., *The Ottoman Capitulations: Text and Context*, Rome: Istituto per l'Oriente C. A. Nallino, 2003.

von Mikusch, Dagobert, trans. John Linton, *Mustafa Kemal: Between Europe and Asia*, London: William Heinemann Ltd, 1931.

Walker, Christopher, *Armenia: The Survival of a Nation*, New York: St. Martin's Press, revised second edition, 1980.

Waugh, Telford, *Turkey Yesterday, To-day and To-morrow*, London: Chapman and Hall's, 1930.

Weitz, Eric, *A Century of Genocide: Utopias of Race and Nation*, Princeton, NJ and Oxford: Princeton University Press, 2003.

———, "Germany and the Ottoman Borderlands," in Omer Bartov and Eric Weitz, eds., *Shatterzone of Empires: Coexistence and Violence in the German, Habsburg,*

Russian, and Ottoman Borderlands, Bloomington and Indianapolis, IN: Indiana University Press, 2013.

Willcocks, W. W., *The Irrigation of Mesopotamia*, London: E. and F. N. Spoon, 1911.

Winstone, H. V. F., *Gertrude Bell: A Biography*, London: Barzan Publishing, second revised edition, 2004.

Yetkiner, Cemal, "After Merchants, Before Ambassadors: Protestant Missionaries and Early American Experience in the Ottoman Empire, 1820–1860," in Nur Bilge Criss, Selçuk Esenbel, Tony Greenwood, and Louis Mazzari, eds., *American Turkish Encounters: Politics and Culture, 1830–1989*, Newcastle upon Tyne: Cambridge Scholars Publishing, 2011.

———, "At the Center of the Debate: Bebek Seminary and the Educational Policy of the American Board of Commissioners for Foreign Missions (1840–1860)," in Mehmet Ali Doğan and Heather Sharkey, eds., *American Missionaries and the Middle East: Foundational Encounters*, Salt Lake City, UT: University of Utah Press, 2011.

Yıldız, Aytaç, *Üç Dönem Bir Aydın: Burhan Asaf Belge (1899–1967)* (Three Periods One Intellectual: Burhan Asaf Belge [1899–1967]), İstanbul: İletişim Yayıncılık, 2011.

Yıldız, Özgür, *Anadolu'da Amerikan Misyonerleri* (American Missionaries in Anatolia), İstanbul: Yeditepe Yayınları, 2015.

Yılmaz, Coşkun, ed., *II. Abdülhamid Modernleşme Sürecinde İstanbul* (Abdülhamid II: İstanbul in the Process of Modernization), İstanbul: 2010 Avrupa Kültür Başkenti, 2010.

Yılmaz, Ömer Faruk, *Belgelerle Sultan İkinci Abdülhamid Han* (Sultan Abdülhamid Han II With Documents), İstanbul: Osmanlı Yayınevi, 1999.

Young, Robert, *French Foreign Policy, 1918–1945. A Guide to Research and Research Materials*, Wilmington, DE: Scholarly Resources Inc., second and revised edition, 1991.

Yurtsever, Cezmi, *Atatürk ve Çukurova Kahramanları* (Atatürk and the Heroes of Cilicia), Adana: Çukurovalı Yayınları, 2010.

———, *1915 Sahibini Arayan Belgeler* (1915: Documents Looking for Their Owner), Adana: Çukurovalı Yayınları, 2009.

———, *Çukurova Tarihi* (The History of Cilicia), Adana: Çukurovalı Yayınları, 2008.

———, *Çukurova Tarihi Valiler, Derebeyler, Eşkiyaların Bitmeyen Kavgaları* (The History of Cilicia: Unending Fights of Provincial Governors, Feudal Lords and Brigands), Adana: Çukurovalı Yayınları, reprinted, 2011.

———, *Ermeni Terör Merkezi: Kilikya Kilisesi* (Center of Armenian Terror: Church of Cilicia), İstanbul: Alper Yayınları, 1983.

———, *Hacin Bir Yangının Külleri* (Hacin: Ashes of a Fire), Adana: Çukurovalı Yayınları, 2010.

———, "Hamparsum Boyacıyan veya "Haçinli Murat'ın" Tarihi Yol Hikayesidir" (Hamparsum Boyacıyan or the Historical Road Story of "Murat of Haçin"), Hasan

Celal Güzel, ed., *Yeni Türkiye Ermeni Meselesi Özel Sayısı*, Vol. 3, Ankara: Yeni Türkiye Stratejik Araştırma Merkezi Yayınları, 2014.

———, *Müftüyü İdam Ettiler* (They Executed the Mufti), Adana: Çukurovalı Yayınları, 2013.

Zeidner, Robert Farrer, "The Tricolor Over the Taurus: The French in Cilicia and Vicinity, 1918–1922," doctoral dissertation, University of Utah, 1991.

Articles

"A Man to the Rescue," *The Missionary Herald*, Vol. 105, No. 11 (November 1909).

"A Turkish Correspondent's Views," *The Orient*, Vol. 1, No. 2 (April 27, 1910).

"Adana Cotton Factories," *The Near East*, Vol. 4, No. 100 (April 4, 1913).

"Adana Widows and Orphans," *The Orient*, Vol. 2, No. 41 (January 25, 1911).

"Agricultural Machinery in the District of Adana," *Levant Trade Review*, Vol. 5, No. 3 (December 1915).

Ahmad, Feroz, "Ottoman Perceptions of the Capitulations 1800–1914," *Journal of Islamic Studies*, Vol. 11, No. 1 (2000).

———, "The Young Turk Revolution," *Journal of Contemporary History*, Vol. 3, No. 3 (July 1968).

Ahmad, Feroz, and Dankwart Rustow, "İkinci Meşrutiyet Döneminde Meclisler 1908–1918" (Chambers in the Period of Second Constitutionalism 1908–1918), *Güney-Doğu Avrupa Araştırmaları Dergisi*, Nos. 4–5 (1976).

Ahmed Reşit, İbnüzziya, "Memleketimizde Ecnebi Postahaneleri" (Foreign Post Offices in Our Country), *İstişare*, No. 16 (1908).

"Ahmed Rıza Bey, Senator," *The Orient*, Vol. 3, No. 5 (January 31, 1912).

"Alexandretta," *Levant Trade Review*, Vol. 6, No. 1 (June 1916).

Ali Rıza Bey, "Adana ve Havalisi Hakkında İktisadi Tedkikat" (Economic Studies on Adana and Its Vicinity), *Ayın Tarihi*, Vols. 10–11, Nos. 29–34 (September 1926–1927).

"An Ottoman Ideal," *The Missionary Herald*, Vol. 105, No. 12 (December 1909).

"Anatolian Reforms," *The Orient*, Vol. 5, Vol. 2 (January 14, 1914).

Andersen, Margaret Lavinia, Michael Reynolds, Hans-Lukas Kieser, Peter Balakian, A. Dirk Moses, and Taner Akçam, "Taner Akçam, The Young Turks' Crime Against Humanity: The Armenian Genocide and Ethnic Cleansing in the Ottoman Empire (Princeton, NJ: Princeton University Press, 2012)," *Journal of Genocide Research*, Vol. 15, No. 4 (December 2013).

"Armenian Massacre," *Muslim Outlook*, No. 24 (April 1, 1920).

Armstrong, Harold, "Turkey," *Royal Central Asian Society Journal*, Vol. 15, Part 4 (1928).

Arpee, Leon, "A Century of Armenian Protestantism," *Church History*, Vol. 5, No. 2 (June 1936).

"Assassination of Jemal Pasha," *The Near East*, Vol. 22, No. 587 (August 10, 1922).

Baer, Marc David, "An Enemy Old and New: The Dönme, Anti-Semitism, and Conspiracy Theories in the Ottoman Empire and Turkish Republic," *The Jewish Quarterly Review*, Vol. 103, No. 4 (Fall 2013).

"Baghdad Notes," *The Near East*, Vol. 6, No. 151 (March 27, 1914).
Barker, Ellis, "Future of Asiatic Turkey," *The Nineteenth Century and After*, Vol. CCCLXXII (June 1916).
———, "The Future of Turkey," *The Fortnightly Review*, Vol. LXXXIV (July–December 1908).
Barton, James, "New Turkey and Modern Education: The Influence of American Colleges and Schools," *The Delta Upsilon Quarterly*, Vol. 15 (September 15, 1909).
Bashking, Orit, "Roundtable Jewish Identities in the Middle East, 1876–1956: The Middle Eastern Shift and Provincializing Zionism," *International Journal of Middle East Studies*, Vol. 46, No. 3 (August 2014).
Baykal, Hülya, "Milli Mücadele Yıllarında Mustafa Kemal Paşa ile Cemal Paşa Arasındaki Yazışmalar" (Correspondence Between Mustafa Kemal Paşa and Cemal Paşa During the Years of the National Struggle), *Atatürk Araştırma Merkezi Dergisi*, Vol. 5, No. 4 (March 1989).
"Bedouin in Baghdad," *The Near East*, Vol. 3, No. 69 (August 30, 1912).
Bilinski, Alfred de, "The Turkish Revolution," *The Nineteenth Century and After*, Vol. 114, No. CCCLXXVIII (August 1908).
Birinci, Ali, "Hatırat Türünden Kaynakların Tarihi Araştırmalardaki Yeri ve Değeri" (The Place and Value of Sources Like Memoirs in Historical Research), *Atatürk Araştırma Merkezi Dergisi*, Vol. 14, No. 40 (March 1998).
Bliss, Frederick, "Djemal Pasha: A Portrait," *The Nineteenth Century and After*, Vol. DXIV (December 1919).
Bloxham, Donald, "The Armenian Genocide of 1915–1916: Cumulative Radicalization and the Development of a Destruction Policy," *Past and Present*, No. 181 (November 2003).
Cavendish, Lucy, "The Peril of Armenia," *The Contemporary Review*, Vol. CIII (January 1913).
Chambers, William Nesbitt, "Adana Activities," *The Orient*, Vol. 4, No. 50 (December 10, 1913).
———, "Letter from Adana," *The Orient*, Vol. 4, No. 21 (May 21, 1913).
———, "The Ambassador at Adana," *The Orient*, Vol. 5, No. 19 (May 13, 1914).
———, "The Possibilities of Adana and the Cilician Plain," *Levant Trade Review*, Vol. 4, No. 2 (September 1914).
Charlton, Zeeneb, "Six Ottoman Patriots," *The Nineteenth Century and After*, Vol. 124, No. CCCCXLII (December 1913).
Chester, Arthur Tremaine, "History's Verdict on New Turkey's Rise to Power," *Current History*, Vol. 19, No. 1 (October 1923).
Chester, Colby Mitchel, "Turkey Reinterpreted," *Current History*, Vol. 16, No. 6 (September 1922).
Clay, Christopher, "The Origins of Modern Banking in the Levant: The Branch Network of the Imperial Ottoman Bank, 1890–1914," *International Journal of Middle East Studies*, Vol. 26, No. 4 (November 1994).
Cohen, Julia Philips, "Between Civic and Islamic Ottomanism: Jewish Imperial Citizenship in the Hamidian Era," *International Journal of Middle East Studies*, Vol. 44, No. 2 (May 2012).

Creelman, James, "After the Great Massacre," *Pearson's Magazine*, Vol. 22, No. 4 (October 1909).
———, "The Moslem Answer to Christendom," *Pearson's Magazine*, Vol. 22, No. 2 (August 1909).
———, "The Turks, the Christians and the Holy Sepulchre," *Pearson's Magazine*, Vol. 22, No. 5 (November 1909).
———, "Will Christendom Remain Silent?" *Pearson's Magazine*, Vol. 22, No. 3 (September 1909).
"Cultivation in Adana," *The Near East*, Vol. 3, No. 58 (June 14, 1912).
Çalık, Ramazan, "Alman Kaynaklarına Göre Cemal Paşa" (Cemal Paşa According to German Sources), *Osmanlı Araştırmaları Dergisi*, No. 19 (1999).
Dadrian, Vahakn, "The Armenian Genocide: Review of Its Historical, Political, and Legal Aspects," *University of St. Thomas Journal of Law and Public Policy*, Vol. 5 (April 2011).
———, "The Circumstances Surrounding the 1909 Adana Holocaust," *The Armenian Review*, Vol. 41, No. 4 (Winter 1988).
Davison, Roderick, "Turkish Attitudes Concerning Christian-Muslim Equality in the Nineteenth Century," *The American Historical Review*, Vol. 59, No. 4 (July 1954).
———, "Westernized Education in Ottoman Turkey," *The Middle East Journal*, Vol. 15, No. 3 (Summer 1961).
Debbas, John, "Crop Conditions in Adana," *Levant Trade Review*, Vol. 3, No. 2 (September 1913).
"Decentralisation in Turkey," *The Near East*, Vol. 6, No. 140 (January 1914).
Dillon, E. J., "The First Pacific Struggle of Nationalities and Creeds," *The Contemporary Review*, Vol. XCV (January–June 1909).
———, "The Opening of the Turkish Parliament," *The Contemporary Review*, Vol. XCV (January–June 1909).
———, "The Person and Work of Mahmud Shefket Pasha," *The Contemporary Review*, Vol. CIV (July 1913).
———, "The Unforeseen Happens as Usual," *The Contemporary Review*, Vol. XCIV (July–December 1908).
Earl, Edward Mead, "The New Constitution," *Political Science Quarterly*, Vol. 40, No. 1 (March 1925).
"Editorial," *The Orient*, Vol. 6, No. 19 (May 12, 1915).
"Empire News," *The Orient*, Vol. 6, No. 48 (December 1, 1915).
Enginün, İnci, "Cemal Paşa'nın Hatıraları" (Cemal Paşa's Memoirs), *Hisar*, Vol. 17, No. 171 (March 1978).
Erdinç, Erol Şadi, "(Mehmet) Cavid Bey Hakkında Küçük Notlar" (Brief Notes on [Mehmet] Cavid Bey), *Bilgi ve Bellek*, No. 4 (Summer 2005).
Farhi, David, "The Şeriat as a Political Slogan—or the 'Incident of the 31st,'" *Middle Eastern Studies*, Vol. 7, No. 3 (October 1971).
"Fifty Moslems Hanged," *The Missionary Herald*, Vol. 106, No. 1 (January 1910).
"Flight from Cilicia; Some Consequences," *The Near East*, Vol. 20, No. 552 (December 8, 1921).

Foss, Clive, "Armenian History As Seen By Twentieth Century Turkish Historians," *The Armenian Review*, Vol. 45, No. 1–2 (Spring–Summer 1992).

Freeman, Michael, "The Theory and Prevention of Genocide," *Holocaust and Genocide Studies*, Vol. 6, No. 2 (1991).

Fujinami, Nobuyoshi, "Decentralizing Centralists, or the Political Language on Provincial Administration in the Second Constitutional Period," *Middle Eastern Studies*, Vol. 49, No. 6 (November 2013).

Gardner, Harold, "A High Commission of Embroidery," *The Missionary Herald*, Vol. 106, No. 3 (March 1910).

"General Gouraud's Proclamation," *The Near East*, Vol. 20, No. 554 (December 22, 1921).

Ginio, Alisa Meyuhas, "Review of Julia Philips Cohen's *Becoming Ottomans*," *International Journal of Turkish Studies*, Vol. 21, Nos. 1 and 2 (Fall 2015).

Goetze, Albrecht, "Cilicians," *Journal of Cuneiform Studies*, Vol. 16, No. 2 (1962).

"Great Britain and Turkey," *The Near East*, Vol. 3, No. 66 (August 9, 1912).

Güçlü, Yücel, "Review of Edward Erickson's *Ottomans and Armenians: A Study in Counterinsurgency*," *Journal of Muslim Minority Affairs*, Vol. 34, No. 2 (June 2014).

———, "Review of Hasan Kayalı's *Arabs and Young Turks: Ottomanism, Arabism, and Islamism in the Ottoman Empire, 1908–1918*," *Perceptions*, Vol. 4, No. 4 (December 1999–February 2000).

———, "Review of Julia Philips Cohen's *Becoming Ottomans*," *Middle East Policy*, Vol. 22, No. 4 (Winter 2015).

———, "The Role of the Ottoman-Trained Officers in Independent Iraq," *Oriente Moderno*, Vol. 21 (132), No. 2 (December 2002).

———, "Will Untapped Ottoman Archives Reshape the Armenian Debate?" *Middle East Quarterly*, Vol. 16, No. 2 (Spring 2009).

Günay, Nejla, "1909 Adana Olaylarından Sonra Yapılan Yardım Çalışmaları" (Relief Work Done After the Adana Events of 1909), *Akademik Bakış*, Vol. 2, No. 4 (Summer 2009).

Haim, Sylvia, "Aspects of Jewish Life in Baghdad under the Monarchy," *Middle Eastern Studies*, Vol. 12, No. 2 (May 1976).

Hamilton, Angus, "Turkey: The Old Régime and the New," *The Fortnightly Review*, Vol. LXXXIV (July–December 1908).

Hanilçe, Murat, "İkinci Meşrutiyet Dönemine Dair Hatırat Bibliyografyası Denemesi" (Essay on the Memoir Bibliography Relating to the Second Constitutional Period), *Bilig*, No. 47 (Fall 2008).

Hanioğlu, Şükrü, "Review of Selim Deringil's *The Well-Protected Domains: Ideology and the Legitimation of Power in the Ottoman Empire, 1876–1909*," *The American Historical Review*, Vol. 105, No. 1 (February 2000).

Harbord, James, "Investigating Turkey and Trans-Caucasia," *The World's Work*, Vol. 15 (May 1920–October 1920).

———, "Mustapha Kemal Pasha and His Party," *The World's Work*, Vol. 15 (May 1920–October 1920).

Harford, Frederic, "Old Caravan Roads in the East," *The Nineteenth Century and After*, Vol .CCCXCVII (July 1918).

Herlt, Günter, "Aus Zeitschriften und Zeitungen," *Der Neue Orient*, Vol. 5, No. 1 (Oktober 1918).

Hovannisian, Armen, "The United States Inquiry and the Armenian Question, 1917–1919 The Archival Papers," *The Armenian Review*, Vol. 37, Vol. 1 (Spring 1984).

"Irrigation in Anatolia," *Levant Trade Review*, Vol. 1, No. 1 (June 1911).

Iseminger, G. L., "The Old Turkish Hands: The British Levantine Consuls, 1856–76," *The Middle East Journal*, Vol. 22, No. 3 (Summer 1968).

Jastrow, Jr., Morris, "The Turks and the Future of the Near East," *The Annals of the American Academy of Political and Social Science*, Vol. 84 (July 1919).

"Jemal Pasha," *The Near East*, Vol. 22, No. 586 (August 3, 1922).

"Jemal Pasha," *The Near East*, Vol. 22, No. 591 (September 7, 1922).

"Journalism in Constantinople," *The Orient*, Vol. 3, No. 45 (November 6, 1912).

Kaiser, Hilmar, "Regional Resistance to Central Government Policies: Ahmed Djemal Pasha, the Governors of Aleppo, and Armenian Deportees in the Spring and Summer of 1915," *Journal of Genocide Research*, Vol. 12, No. 3–4 (2010).

Kandemir, Feridun, "Cemal Paşa'nın Son Günleri" (The Last Days of Cemal Paşa), *Yedi Gün*, Vols. 3 and 4, Nos. 73 (August 1, 1934), 77 (August 29, 1934), 85 (October 24, 1934), and 86 (October 31, 1934).

———, "Cemal Paşa'yı Kimler, Nasıl Öldürmüşlerdi?" (How Had Cemal Paşa Been Assassinated by Some People?), *Dün ve Bugün Mecmuası*, No. 32 (June 1956).

———, "Malta Yaranı" (Malta Companions), *Resimli Tarih Mecmuası*, Vol. 5, No. 59 (November 1954).

Kaligian, Dikran Mesrob, "A Prelude to Genocide: CUP Population Policies and Provincial Insecurity, 1908–1914," *Journal of Genocide Research*, Vol. 10, No. 1 (March 2008).

Kara, Abdulvahap, "Yeni Bilgi ve Belgeler Işığında Cemal Paşa'nın Son Günleri ve Ölümü" (The Last Days and the Assassination of Cemal Paşa in Light of New Information and Documents), *Türk Dünyası Araştırmaları*, No. 156 (June 2005).

———, "75 Yıllık Tarihi İfşaat" (Historical Revelations of 75 Years), *Tarih ve Düşünce*, No. 58 (May 2005).

Karacakaya, Recep, "Meclis-i Mebusan Seçimleri ve Ermeniler 1908–1914" (Chamber of Deputies Elections and the Armenians 1908–1914), *Yakın Dönem Türkiye Araştırmaları*, No. 3 (2003).

Karadoğan, İsmet, "Cemal Paşa'yı Ruslar Öldürmüştü" (The Russians Had Killed Cemal Paşa), *Yakın Tarihimiz*, Vol. 2, No. 14 (1962).

Karpat, Kemal, "Ottoman Population Records and the Census of 1881/82–1893," *International Journal of Middle East Studies*, Vol. 9, No. 2 (May 1978).

———, "The Memoirs of N. Batzaria: The Young Turks and Nationalism," *International Journal of Middle East Studies*, Vol. 6 (1975).

———, "The Social, Economic and Administrative Situation of the Sanjak of Kayseri in 1880: The Report of Lieutenant Ferdinand Bennet, British Vice-Consul of Anatolia (October, 1880)," *International Journal of Turkish Studies*, Vol. 1, No. 2 (Autumn 1980).

Kasımov, Musa, "Yeni Arşiv Belgeleri Esasında Cemal Paşa'nın Öldürülmesi" (The Assassination of Cemal Paşa in Light of New Archival Documents), *Orkun*, No. 63 (June 2003).
Katz, Steven, "The Unique Intentionality of the Holocaust," *Modern Judaism*, Vol. 1, No. 2 (September 1981).
Kayalı, Hasan, "Elections and the Electoral Process in the Ottoman Empire, 1876–1919," *International Journal of Middle East Studies*, Vol. 27, No. 3 (August 1995).
Kedourie, Elie, "Young Turks, Freemasons and Jews," *Middle Eastern Studies*, Vol. 7, No. 1 (January 1971).
Kern, Karen, "Review of Julia Phillips Cohen's *Becoming Ottomans*," *International Journal of Middle East Studies*, Vol. 47, No. 1 (February 2015).
Kesim, Firuz, "Cemal Paşa Nasıl Katledildi" (How Cemal Paşa Is Assassinated), *Yakın Tarihimiz*, Vol. 2, No. 18 (1962).
Koloğlu, Orhan, "Mayıs-Eylül 1908 Belgelerine Göre İttihatçılarda Osmanlı Birliği Arayışı-I" (The Quest For Ottoman Unity By the Unionists According to the Documents of May–September 1908-I), *Toplumsal Tarih*, No. 55 (July 1998).
———, "Seniha Cemal'in Yaşam Öyküsü" (The Life Story of Seniha Cemal), *Popüler Tarih*, No. 42 (February 2004).
Korff, S. A., "Review of Djemal Pasha's *Memories of a Turkish Statesman 1913–1919*," *The American Historical Review*, Vol. 28, No. 4 (July 1923).
Kuyaş, Salih, "Posta Tarihi ve Kapitülasyon Postahaneleri I" (History of Postal Services and the Post Offices of the Capitulations I), *Tarih ve Toplum*, No. 1 (1984).
Kütükoğlu, Mübahat, "Osmanlı İktisad Tarihi Bakımından Konsolosluk Raporlarının Ehemmiyet ve Kiymeti" (The Importance and Value of the Consular Reports Regarding the Ottoman Economic History), *İstanbul Üniversitesi Edebiyat Fakültesi Güney-Doğu Avrupa Araştırmaları Dergisi*, Vol. 11–12 (1983).
Leipnik, Ferdinand, "The Future of the Ottoman Empire," *The Contemporary Review*, Vol. XCVI (March 1910).
Lewis, Bernard, "The Ottoman Empire in the Mid-Nineteenth Century: A Review," *Middle Eastern Studies*, Vol. 1, No. 3 (April 1965).
Lybyer, Albert Howe, "America's Missionary Record in Turkey," *The Current History Magazine*, Vol. 19, No. 5 (February 1924).
Lydiardopoulos, Demosthenes, "News from Mersine," *Levant Trade Review*, Vol. 1, No. 3 (December 1911).
Maksudyan, Nazan, "Cemal Bey'in Adana Valiliği ve Osmanlıcılık İdeali" (The Adana Governorship of Cemal Bey and His Ideal of Ottomanism), *Toplumsal Tarih*, No. 176 (August 2008).
Manachy, Lorenzo, "Report from Aleppo," *Levant Trade Review*, Vol. 1, No. 3 (December 1911).
Margoliouth, D. S., "Constantinople at the Declaration of the Constitution," *The Fortnightly Review*, Vol. LXXXIV (July–December 1908).
Matossian, Bedross Der, "From Bloodless Revolution to Bloody Counterrevolution: The Adana Massacres of 1909," *Genocide Studies and Prevention*, Vol. 6, No. 2 (August 2011).

———, "The Genocide Archives of the Armenian Patriarchate of Jerusalem," *The Armenian Review*, Vol. 52, No. 3–4 (Fall–Winter 2011).
McCullagh, Francis, "The Constantinople Mutiny of April 13th," *The Fortnightly Review*, Vol. LXXXVI (July–December 1909).
Meyer, Willy, "Djemal Pascha," *Germania*, No. 49 (February 1923).
Midhat Pasha, "The Past, Present, and Future of Turkey," *The Nineteenth Century* (January–June 1878).
"Motive of the Adana Massacres," *The Literary Digest*, Vol. 39, No. 1 (June 3, 1909).
Mutlu, Servet, "Late Ottoman Population and Its Ethnic Distribution," *Turkish Journal of Population Studies*, Vol. 25 (2003).
Nathan, Edward, *Levant Trade Review*, Vol. 2, No. 2 (September 1912).
———, "Aerial Cargo Railway at Turkish Port," *Levant Trade Review*, Vol. 2, No. 3 (December 1912).
———, "Agricultural Implements and Machinery in Mersina-Adana District," *Levant Trade Review*, Vol. 4, No. 2 (September 1912).
———, "Agricultural Implements and Machinery in Mersina-Adana District," *Levant Trade Review*, Vol. 5, No. 3 (December 1915).
"Notes," *The Orient*, Vol. 1, No. 3 (May 4, 1910).
"Notes," *The Orient*, Vol. 1, No. 4 (May 11, 1910).
Nuza, Fehmi, "Cemal Paşa'yı Kimler Öldürdü veya Öldürttü" (Who Killed or Ordered to Kill Cemal Paşa), *Türk Kültürü*, Vol. 16, No. 243 (July 1983).
Okandan, Recai Galip, "Amme Hukukumuz Bakımından Tanzimat, Birinci ve İkinci Meşrutiyet Devirlerinin Önemi" (The Importance of the Periods of the *Tanzimat*, First and Second Constitutionalism Regarding Our Public Law), *İstanbul Üniversitesi Hukuk Fakültesi Mecmuası*, Vol. 15, No. 1 (1949).
Öke, Mim Kemal, "Hukuk-Tarih-Siyaset Üçgeninde Kilikya Ermeni Krallığı Polemiği" (Polemics of the Cilician Armenian Kingdom in the Triangle of Law-History-Politics), *Türk Dünyası Araştırmaları Dergisi*, No. 46 (February 1987).
Özalay, Eren, "Adana ve Çevresi Toplumsal ve Ekonomik Tarihi Konferansı" (Social and Economic History Conference on Adana and Its Vicinity), *Toplumsal Tarih*, No. 180 (December 2008).
"Parliament and the Refugees," *The Near East*, Vol. 20, No. 555 (December 29, 1921).
"Parliamentary Elections," *The Orient*, Vol. 3, No. 5 (March 6, 1912).
Pears, Sir Edwin, "Developments in Turkey," *The Contemporary Review*, Vol. XCVII, No. 6 (June 1911).
———, "The Situation in Turkey," *The Contemporary Review*, Vol. CI (June 1912).
———, "The Turkish Revolution," *The Contemporary Review*, Vol. XCIV (July–December 1908).
———, "Turkey and the War," *The Contemporary Review*, Vol. CVI, No. 5 (November 1914).
———, "Turkey: Developments and Forecasts," *The Contemporary Review*, Vol. XCV, No. 6 (June 1909).
Pickthall, Marmaduke, "Armenian Atrocities," *The New Age*, Vol. 18, No. 7 (December 16, 1915).
———, "The Black Crusade," *The New Age*, Vol. 12, No. 1 (November 7, 1912).

Price, Clair, "The Turkish Nationalist Government," *The Fortnightly Review*, Vol. CXII (July–December 1922).
Price, Philips, "The Problem of Asiatic Turkey," *The Contemporary Review*, Vol. CV (February 1914).
"Progress in Armenian National Affairs," *The Orient*, Vol. 1, No. 33 (November 30, 1910).
"Progress in Cilicia," *Levant Trade Review*, Vol. 1, No. 4 (March 1912).
"Provinces," *The Orient*, Vol. 1, No. 31 (November 16, 1910).
"Provinces," *The Orient*, Vol. 2, No. 35 (December 13, 1911).
"Real Christianity," *The Orient*, Vol. 3, No. 52 (December 25, 1912).
Reed, Howard, "Perspectives on the Evolution of Turkish Studies in North America Since 1946," *The Middle East Journal*, Vol. 51, No. 1 (Winter 1997).
Reid, James, "The Armenian Massacres in Ottoman and Turkish Historiography," *The Armenian Review*, Vol. 37, No. 1–145 (Spring 1984).
Sarafian, Ara, "Génocide arménien et la Turquie," *Nouvelles d'Arménie*, septembre 2008.
———, "Study the Armenian Genocide with Confidence, Ara Sarafian Suggests," *The Armenian Reporter* (December 20, 2008).
Schmitt, Bernadotte, "Review of Djemal Pasha's *Memories of a Turkish Statesman 1913–1919*," *Political Science Quarterly*, Vol. 38, No. 1 (March 1923).
Shaw, Stanford, "Christian Anti-Semitism in the Ottoman Empire," *Belleten*, Vol. 54, No. 68 (1991).
———, "Ottoman Population Movements During the Last Years of the Empire, 1885–1914," *Journal of Ottoman Studies*, Vol. 1, No. 1 (1980).
———, "Review of Benjamin Braude and Bernard Lewis's, eds., *Christians and Jews in the Ottoman Empire: The Functioning of a Plural Society*, 2 Vols.," *The American Historical Review*, Vol. 94, No. 4 (October 1989).
———, "The Ottoman Census System and Population, 1831–1914," *International Journal of Middle East Studies*, Vol. 9, No. 3 (October 1978).
Shepard, F. D., "Personal Experience in Turkish Massacres and Relief Work," *Journal of Race Development*, Vol. 1 (January 1910).
———, "Undeveloped Resources of Northern Syria," *Levant Trade Review*, Vol. 5, No. 2 (September 1915).
"Sir Edwin Pears on Turkey," *The Contemporay Review*, Vol. C (November 1911).
Sir, İhsan Nuri, "Cemal Paşa İstanbul Muhafızlığından Nasıl İstifa Etmişti?" (How Had Cemal Paşa Resigned From the Office of İstanbul Military Governor?), *Tarih Konuşuyor*, Vol. 2, No. 17 (December 1950).
"Situation at Adana," *The Orient*, Vol. 3, No. 43 (February 8, 1911).
"Situation in Cilicia," *The Orient*, Vol. 2, No. 28 (October 25, 1911).
Sohrabi, Nader, "Global Waves, Local Actors: What the Young Turks Knew About Other Revolutions and Why It Mattered," *Comparative Studies in Society and History*, Vol. 44, No. 1 (January 2002).
Sonyel, Salahi, "Turco-Armenian 'Adana Incidents' in the Light of Secret British Documents (July 1909–December 1909)," *Belleten*, Vol. 51, No. 201 (December 1987).

Strong, William, "Things That Remain in Turkey," *Envelope Series*, Vol. 19, No. 1 (April 1916).
Sümer, Faruk, "Çukurova Tarihine Dair Araştırmalar (Fetihten Onaltıncı Yüzyılın İkinci Yarısına Kadar)" (Research on the History of Cilicia [From the Conquest to the Second Half of the Sixteenth Century]), *Tarih Araştırmaları Dergisi*, Vol. 1, No. 1 (1963).
Swenson, Victor, "The Military Rising in Istanbul 1909," *Journal of Contemporary History*, Vol. 5, No. 4 (October 1970).
"Tales of Adana," *The Literary Digest*, Vol. 39, No. 5 (July 31, 1909).
Thain, A. R., "Cyrus Hamlin D.D., LL. D. Missionary, Statesman, Inventor: A Life Sketch," *The Envelope Series*, Vol. 10, No. 2 (July 1907).
"The Angora Government's Defence," *The Near East*, Vol. 21, No. 578 (June 8, 1922).
"The Athena Party in Adana," *The Orient*, Vol. 1, No. 19 (August 24, 1910).
"The Baghdad Railway," *The Near East*, Vol. 5, No. 105 (May 9, 1913).
"The Cilician Refugees," *The Near East*, Vol. 20, No. 553 (December 15, 1921).
"The Conflict in the Provinces," *The Missionary Herald*, Vol. 105, No. 6 (June 1909).
"The Constantinople Letter," *The Near East*, Vol. 5, No. 107 (May 23, 1913).
"The Economic Future of the Near East," The Editorial, *The Near East*, as cited in "Turkey's Resources," *The Orient*, Vol. 4, No. 15 (April 9, 1913).
"The Evacuation of Cilicia," *The Near East*, Vol. 21, No. 559 (January 26, 1922).
"The Evacuation of Cilicia," *The Orient*, Vol. 9, No. 2 (February 1922).
"The Franco-Turkish Convention," *The Near East*, Vol. 20, No. 547 (November 3, 1921).
"The Future of Baghdad," *The Near East*, Vol. 4, No. 79 (November 8, 1912).
"The Government Relief in Adana," *The Orient*, Vol. 1, No. 1 (April 20, 1910).
"The Hadjin Problem," *The Orient*, Vol. 3, No. 34 (August 21, 1912).
"The Latest from Adana," *The Missionary Herald*, Vol. 105, No. 12 (December 1909).
"The Massacres of Cilicia and the Young Turks," *The Armenian Herald* (February 1918).
"The New Rule in Turkey," *The Literary Digest*, Vol. 38, No. 19 (May 8, 1909).
"The New Turkey: Interesting Interview with Halid Halid Bey," *The Near East*, Vol. 2, No. 19 (November 5, 1909).
"The Provinces," *The Orient*, Vol. 1, No. 10 (June 22, 1910).
"The Provinces," *The Orient*, Vol. 1, No. 12 (July 6, 1910).
"The Provinces," *The Orient*, Vol. 1, No. 21 (September 7, 1910).
"The Provinces," *The Orient*, Vol. 1, No. 31 (November 16, 1910).
"The Sultan's Desire for Peace," *The Near East*, Vol. 5, No. 123 (September 12, 1913).
"The 22 Days of Marash: Papers on the Defense of the City Against Turkish Forces Jan.-Feb., 1920," Part I, *The Armenian Review*, Vol. 30, No. 4 (Winter 1977).
Thobie, Jacques, "La France a-t-elle une politique culturelle dans l'Empire ottoman à la veille de la première guerre mondiale?" *Relations internationales*, Vol. 25 (1981).

Toprak, Zafer, "Bir Hayal Ürünü: İttihatçıların Türkleştirme Politikası" (A Figment of Imagination: The Turkification Policy of the Unionists), *Toplumsal Tarih*, No. 146 (February 2006).

Trowbridge, Stephen van, "Letters from the Scene of the Massacre, Adana, Asia Minor," *The Missionary Review of the World*, Vol. 22 (January–December 1909).

"Turkey in England: The Visit of the Delegates from Constantinople," *The Near East*, Vol. 2, No. 16 (July–August 1909).

"Turkish Students in America," *Levant Trade Review*, Vol. 1, No. 4 (March 1912).

Uca, Alaattin, "Cemal Paşa'nın Resmi Hal Tercümesi ve Milli Savunma Bakanlığı Arşivindeki Bazı Belgeler" (The Official Curriculum Vitae of Cemal Paşa and Some Documents in the Archive of the Ministry of National Defense), *Atatürk Üniversitesi Türkiyat Araştırmaları Enstitüsü Dergisi*, Vol. 16, No. 41 (2009).

Uzunçarşılı, İsmail Hakkı, "1908 Yılında İkinci Meşrutiyetin Ne Suretle İlan Edildiğine Dair Vesikalar" (Documents on How the Second Constitutionalism Was Proclaimed in 1908), *Belleten*, Vol. 20, No. 77 (January 1956).

Ümit, Devrim, "The American Protestant Missionary Network in Ottoman Turkey, 1876–1914," *International Journal of Humanities and Social Science*, Vol. 4, No. 6 (1) (April 2014).

Viator, "The Turkish Revolution," *The Fortnightly Review*, Vol. LXXXIV (July–December 1908).

von Herbert, F. W., "Kamil Pasha and the Succession in Turkey," *The Fortnightly Review*, Vol. LXXXIV (July–December 1908).

von Kressenstein, Friedrich Freiherr Kress, "Ahmed Djemal Pascha als Soldat," *Mitteilungen des Bundes des Asienkampfers*, Vol. 4, No. 9 (1922).

Wasti, Syed Tanvir, "Ahmed Rüstem Bey and the End of an Era," *Middle Eastern Studies*, Vol. 48, No. 5 (September 2012).

———, "Süleyman Nazif—A Multi-Faceted Personality," *Middle Eastern Studies*, Vol. 50, No. 3 (May 2014).

Webb, Elizabeth, "Report of Adana Seminary 1909–1910," *The Orient*, Vol. 1, No. 14 (July 18, 1910).

Weiker, Walter, "The Ottoman Bureaucracy: Modernization and Reform," *Administrative Science Quarterly*, Vol. 13, No. 3 (December 1968).

"Where Turk and Christian Cooperate," *The Missionary Herald*, Vol. 107, No. 2 (February 1911).

"Who Will End the Armenian Killing?" *The Literary Digest*, Vol. 38, No. 23 (June 5, 1909).

Wigran, W. A., "Enver Pasha," *The Near East*, Vol. 22, No. 588 (August 24, 1922).

Woods, Charles, "The Capitulations and Christian Privileges in Turkey," *The Contemporary Review*, Vol. CXXII (December 1922).

———, "The Internal Situation in Turkey and the Effect of the War Upon It," *The Fortnightly Review*, Vol. XCI (January–June 1912).

Yapp, M. E., "Review of Salahi Sonyel's *The Great War and the Tragedy of Anatolia: Turks and Armenians in the Maelstrom of Major Powers*," *Middle Eastern Studies*, Vol. 37, No. 1 (January 2001).

Yazıcı, Nesimi, "Osmanlı İmparatorluğunda Yabancı Postalar ve Atatürk Türkiye'sinde Postacılık" (Foreign Mail Posts in the Ottoman Empire and Postal Services in Atatürk's Turkey), *İletişim*, No. 3 (1981).

Zamir, Meir, "Population Statistics of the Ottoman Empire in 1914 and in 1919," *Middle Eastern Studies*, Vol. 17, No. 1 (January 1981).

Index

Photo section images are identified as p*1*, etc.

Abalıoğlu, Yunus Nadi, 301
abandoned property, 405
ABCFM. *See* American Board of Commissioners for Foreign Missions
Abdülhamid II (sultan), 10, 217;
  against Christians, 224, 226;
  conspiracy of, 225;
  Constitution (1908) and, 98;
  deposition of, 237n27, 238n31;
  documents from, 104–6;
  estates of, 51;
  Lobanoff and, 69;
  opinions on, 220–21;
  to parliament, 121–22;
  responsibility of, 219–28;
  restrictions for, 118;
  secret societies and, 119;
  ulema on, 238n31
Abdurrahman (Paksoy), 148
Abdurrahman Şeref Efendi, 9
Abidin Paşa, 46–47
accusations, 376–79, 417–18
Acland, Francis Dyke, 387–88
Adam, Herbert:
  on Cemal Bey, 313–14;
  Doughty-Wylie and, 260
Adana:
  Ali Seydi Bey in, 391;
  anxiety in, 314–15, 384–85, 388–89;
  Bahri Paşa and, 116–17;
  Constitution Day in, 346;
  CUP in, 131;
  evacuations from, 402;
  French occupation of, 395–96, 402–3;
  governors of, 391;
  missionaries in, 84–85, 115–16;
  Mixed Commercial Court, 217;
  Muammer Bey in, 384–86;
  natural resources near, 46–52;
  political liberalization in, 128;
  restoration of Constitution in, 114, 346;
  Turkish army arrival in, 407–8;
  Turkish control resumption of, 399–408.
  See also Cilicia
"Adana 1909: History, Memory, and Identity from a Hundred Year Perspective," 288
Adana affair. *See* Adana clashes
Adana affair 2009 centenary, 287–89, 433
Adana Armenians:
  abandoned property of, 405;

475

advancement of, 432–33;
arms of, 138–39, 215, 266–67;
boasting of, 140–42, 216, 224–25, 227, 234;
Christianity of, 76;
after Constitution proclamation, 136–38;
in crafts, 77;
in education, 77;
Fedayee, 146–48;
in government service, 77–78;
in health services, 77;
houses of, 74, 191;
influx of, 144–45;
in judiciary, 76;
labor of, 74–75, 214, 249;
language of, 73;
location of, 71–72;
missionary schools of, 73–74;
Muslims and, 138;
origin of, 71;
political committees of, 137;
positions of, 75–77;
propaganda of, 145;
Reformed Huntchak Party of, 137;
as refugees, 404;
relocation of, 395;
schools of, 73–74, 391;
seasons for, 72;
Seropian and, 137–38;
in technical field, 76–77;
theater for, 145;
usury and, 78–79;
wealth of, 75
Adana city, 432;
buildings in, 52;
labor shortages in, 47, 214, 249, 252;
seasons in, 52;
site of, 45;
wealth of, 47
Adana clashes:
Adil Bey on, 183–84;
April 16–24, 175–82;
April 16 end of, 173–74;
April 25 resumption of, 189–91;
beginning of, 165–67, 185, 248, 266–67, 433–34;
Cevad Bey and, 165–66, 248–52;
Chambers, W. N., and, 165, 173–74;
commercial failures after, 202;
concessions after, 180–81;
deaths from, 169, 174, 186–88, 190, 192, 249;
displaced persons after, 182;
Doughty-Wylie in, 167–73, 250;
dragomans in, 167–68, 203n16;
explosives in, 251;
Fedayee and, 165–67, 174;
fires in, 166, 186–87, 191, 232, 255;
foreigners in, 174;
insurance related to, 254–56;
in market place, 165–66, 249;
military in, 189, 201–2, 250;
misinterpretations of, 184–85, 188–90;
relief work after, 202, 241;
restoration after, 201–2;
telegrams before, 217–18.
See also responsibility
Adana demography, 59n58;
from Armenian Patriarchate of İstanbul, 53–54;
census and, 53, 59n52;
Turkish majority in, 52–54
Adana economic recovery, 435;
Adana plain in, 337–38;
Baghdad railway and, 337;
cotton in, 344;
German colony in, 337–39;
Shepard, F. D., and, 348–49;
voyage for, 340–43;
widows and, 345
Adana events. *See* Adana clashes
The Adana Massacres and the Catholic Missionaries: An Account by Eye Witnesses, 5
Adana plain, 337–38
Adana province, 57n25;
Armenian businesses in, 49;
boundaries of, 45–46;

coal in, 49;
cotton from, 47–48, 344, 386–88, 391–92, 402–3;
deforestation in, 49–50;
fertility of, 44–48;
history of, 431–32;
marshes of, 46–47;
Mersin in, 44;
rivers of, 44;
sanjaks of, 43;
textile industry in, 48;
weather in, 49–50
Adana question. *See* Adana clashes; responsibility
Adana Turks:
nobility of, 195–97;
protection by, 195–96
Adil Bey, 183–84, 256–57
Adıvar. *See* Edib, Halidé
Adjemian, Shakin, 386
Administrative Council of Adana, 236n4
Afghanistan, 411–12
Afghan-Soviet Treaty (November 22, 1921), 411–12
Aflalo, F. G., 170, 234
Agricultural Bank, 76, 258
agricultural college, 337, 378
agricultural machinery, 51, 393
agriculture, 329, 369, 375, 386–87, 432;
Chafy and, 315–16;
Chambers, W. N., on, 392–93;
grain, 388;
usury related to, 79.
See also cotton
Ahmad, Feroz, 149n5, 233
Ahmed Cevdet Paşa, 14, 25, 31n24
Ahmed Rıza Bey, 124–25, 259, 263
Ahmed Vefik Efendi/Paşa, 14, 31n25, 106
Akyüz. *See* Muhittin Paşa (Akyüz)
Alai Bey, 169–70
Aleppo, 404;
April 16–24 clashes in, 176–78, 185;
CUP and, 113–14;
fertility around, 50–51;
irrigation near, 50;
restoration of Constitution in, 112–14
Alexander the Great, 41–42
Ali Cevat Bey, 121, 156n98
Ali Kemal Bey, 100
Ali Paşa, 109
Ali Rıza Paşa, 370–71
Ali Seydi Bey, 391
Alkan, Mehmet, viii
Amanullah Khan, 411
ambassadors, 18
Amending Act of 1967, 16
America, 362n209, 398–99
American Board of Commissioners for Foreign Missions (ABCFM), 12–13, 21–22, 30n22, 387;
Armenian schooling and, 2, 84–85;
Cemal Bey and, 301–2;
handicap of, 433;
responsibility and, 227–28;
wars and, 394
American College (Beirut), 351–52
American Embassy, 111
American Girls' School, 406
American hospital, 321–22, 405–6
American missionaries:
deaths of, 169, 186–88;
effects of, 406;
Mustafa Zihni Paşa against, 257;
opposition to, 244;
weaving and, 325.
See also Chambers, William Nesbit; van Trowbridge, Stephen
American mission schools, 21;
Armenian nationalism and, 81–82;
Armenian schooling, 80–82;
evangelization and, 81;
history of, 81;
language and, 81
American Red Cross, 351, 354n34
American Research Institute, 22
Amerikan Bord Heyeti, 22
amnesty, political, 100

Anadolu'da Tanin (Tanin in Anatolia), 360n164
anarchism, 63–64
Anatolia, 1, 29nn1–2, 97, 360n164, 431; nationalism in, 407–8
Anatolian Armenians, 82, 84
Ankara Agreement, 399–400, 425n122
Anstruther-Gray, Major, 198–99
anti-Semitism, 233
anxiety, 328;
  in Adana, 314–15, 384–85, 388–89;
  of Armenians, 326–27, 398;
  of Christians, 317–18, 345–46, 348
Apelian, Soghomon, 177
appeasement, 215
April 13, 1909, 226, 237n27
April 16–24 clashes:
  in Aleppo, 176–78, 185.
  See also Adana clashes
April 25 resumption, of Adana clashes, 189–91
Arabism, 135
Arabs, 416;
  authority of, 365;
  Cemal Bey and, 371–72;
  in Cilicia, 42;
  on National Day, 380;
  Ottomanism and, 364
Aram I (Catholicos), 287
archives, vii
Arıkoğlu, Damar, 58n49, 190;
  on arms, 139;
  on bazars, 75;
  on moneylenders, 79
Arkun, Aram, 213–14
Armenian archives, 22–23
Armenian Church, 61–62
Armenian Diaspora, 70
Armenian events of 1909. *See* Adana clashes
Armenian historians, 213–14
Armenian movement:
  Boyacıyan in, 77–78;
  Hamlin in, 65–66;
  rebellions in, 62–63.
  See also Huntchak Committee
Armenian National Assembly, 184, 258–59
Armenian nationalism, 265;
  American mission schools and, 81–82;
  liberty and, 128;
  Young Turks and, 127
Armenian National Union, 396
Armenian Patriarchate in Jerusalem, 22, 23, 35n48
Armenian Patriarchate of İstanbul, 84, 346;
  Adana demography from, 53–54;
  on Cemal Bey, 395;
  statistics from, 59n58
Armenian principality, 61–63
Armenian Revolutionary Federation, 23, 220, 272–73
Armenians:
  America on, 398–99;
  Anatolian, 82, 84;
  anxiety of, 326–27, 398;
  appointments of, 437;
  arms of, 138–39, 215, 266–67, 405–6;
  businesses of, 49;
  Cemal Paşa and, 437;
  Dashnak Party of, 22, 127–28, 138;
  deserters among, 71;
  with French military, 403;
  on genocide, 275–77;
  Greeks against, 196;
  in Maraş, 40;
  memoirs of, 23;
  relocation of, 274–75, 395;
  responsibility of, 211–12;
  Young Turks with, 101.
  See also Adana Armenians
Armenian schooling, 2, 73–74, 391;
  American mission schools, 80–82;
  Anatolian Armenians and, 84;
  Catholicism in, 83–85;
  freedom in, 213;
  French mission schools and, 83;
  Gregorian Armenians, 84–85

Armenian separatists, 268–72
Armenian societies, 119, 155n79
Armenian viewpoint, 23–24
Armistice Period (1919–1922), 416
arms:
　of Adana Armenians, 138–39, 215, 266–67;
　of Armenians, 138–39, 215, 266–67, 405–6;
　from Russia, 273–74;
　Seropian for, 137, 139–42, 144, 160n156
Armstrong, Harold, 78, 232
army reorganization, 380
Artin, Sinyor, 77
Artuç, Nevzat, 9, 415–18
Asaf Bey (Belge), 176, 248, 252–53
Ashmead-Bartlett, Ellis, 66–70
Asia Minor, 1, 29n1
Aspirations et Agissements Révolutionnaires des Comités Arméniens Avant et Aprés la Proclamation de la Constitution Ottomane, 5
assassination:
　of Cemal Paşa, 412–13;
　of Talat Bey, 300
Astourian, Stephan, 58n35, 79
Atamian, Sarkis, 213
ATASE. *See* Turkish General Staff Military History and Strategic Studies Directorate's Archive
Atay. *See* Rıfkı, Falih
autocracy, 116–17
autonomy, 96–97
Avlonyalı. *See* Ferid Paşa
Aydemir, Şevket Süreyya, 9
Ayni, Mehmet Ali, 177–78
Ayntab, 40, 181, 329

Babacan, Hasan, 9
Babanzade İsmail Hakkı, 134–35, 297
Babanzade Mustafa Zihni Paşa, 200–1, 297, 320;
　against American missionaries, 257;
　order restoration by, 246–47
Babikian, Agop, 223–24, 228, 256, 261;
　commission of inquiry and, 261;
　order restoration and, 261
Bağdadizade Abdülkadir, 148;
　punishment of, 268
Baghdad, 372;
　Britain related to, 365–66;
　Constitution (1908) and, 364;
　importance of foreign policy in regard to, 370;
　India and, 365–66, 419n9;
　Jewry in, 379;
　prominence of, 363;
　Thirteenth Army Corp of, 370–71
Baghdad Company, 338–39
Baghdad railway, 315, 322, 394;
　accusations about, 378;
　Adana economic recovery, 337;
　Germany and, 318, 393
Bahçe, 306
Bahri Paşa, 113, 116–17, 155n73, 265
Balakian, Grigoris, 253
Balakian, Peter, 275
Balkans, 97
Balkan Wars (1912–1913), 8, 173, 293–94, 394, 422n80
Balph, James, 177
banks, 76, 258, 304, 338, 387
banquet, 319–21
Barnum, Dr., 329
Barton, James, 89n28
bazars, 75
Becoming Ottomans: Sephardi Jews and Imperial Citizenship in the Modern Era (Cohen), 131, 153n48
Behiç, Hakkı (Bayiç), 315
Beirut:
　American College of, 351–52;
　refugees in, 402
Belen, 259
Belen (Beilan) Pass, 38
Belge. *See* Asaf Bey
berat (official warrant of approval), 19
Berlin Treaty (July 13, 1878), 80

Bernstein, Herman, 244–45
Bezdikian, Zachariah, 1, 146–48, 174
Bezdikyan, Artin, 77
Billings, Florence, 34n45
biography, 415–18
Blaisdell, Dorothea Chambers, 195, 206n64, 406
Blue Books, 66–68, 87n14
BOA. See Prime Minister's Office Ottoman Archive
boasting, 235;
    of Adana Armenians, 140–42, 216, 224–25, 227, 234
Bölükbaşı. See Tevfik, Rıza
Bompard, Maurice, 304
Boşo, Yorgi (Boussios), 126
The Bosphorus News, 93n81
Bournoutian, George, 61
Boussios. See Boşo, Yorgi
Boyacıyan, Hamparsum, 77–78, 256
Braude, Benjamin, 98
Bristol, Mark:
    on Franco-Turkish pact, 399;
    Mustafa Kemal Paşa and, 424n115;
    "protégés" and, 397–98
Britain:
    Baghdad related to, 365–66;
    Cemal Bey and, 302–3, 309–10, 313–14, 350, 366;
    Currie related to, 67–70;
    Curzon of, 401;
    debates in, 66;
    economic loss and, 254–56;
    House of Commons, 198, 201–2, 404;
    Turks and, 173;
    voyage to, 341–42
British consuls, 20
British records, 15–16, 18
Bryce, Lord, 230
Bryce reports, 11
Büge, Eugen, 320, 338
von Bülow, Bernhard, 120
Burg, Yosef, 278
Buzpınar, Tufan, 2

Cahid, Hüseyin (Yalçın), 7, 25, 36n55, 298, 301, 315;
    on responsibility, 222–24
de Caix, Robert, 397
calendars, 59n52, 237n27
Çallıyan, Karabet, 131
Campos, Michelle Ursula, 136, 160n148
Çankaya, Ali, 11
capitulation agreements, 18–19, 32n34, 198
Carasso, Emmanuel, 130–31, 298
Cardashian, Vahan, 126–27
casualties, 265;
    estimates of, 263–64;
    genocide related to, 276.
    See also deaths
Catholicism, 5, 287;
    in Armenian schooling, 83–85
Catoni, Joseph, 180
Cavid Bey, 233, 295–96;
    on Cemal Paşa, 412–13;
    diaries of, 24–25, 135;
    on reconstruction, 337
Çavuş, Hacı. See Hacı Mehmet Ağa
Cebelibereket, 252–53
Cemal, Seniha, 413
Cemal Bey/Paşa, 2, 8–9, 11, 138, 289, 437;
    appointments of, 291–94, 296–97;
    Arabs and, 371–72;
    assassination of, 412–13;
    biography of, 415–18;
    Britain and, 302–3, 309–10, 313–14, 350, 366;
    on casualties, 265;
    in CUP, 291–93, 295–96;
    education of, 290–91;
    Enver Paşa and, 295–96;
    family of, p12, 290, 413;
    France and, 294–95, 304;
    Germany and, 293–94;
    honors of, 415;
    last days of, 411–12;
    memoirs of, 24, 141–42, 145–46, 212–13;

missionaries and, 21;
  as *mutasarrıf*, 292–93;
  von Oppenheim and, 274–75;
  in Palestine, 383–84, 414;
  photos of, p*1–11*;
  summary about, 416;
  tributes to, 413–15
Cemal Bey/Paşa Adana governorship:
  ABCFM and, 301–2;
  Adana affair 2009 centenary and, 287–89;
  Adana arrival, 296–98, 302–3;
  Adana economic recovery, 337–45, 348–49, 435;
  anxiety and, 314–15, 317–18, 326–27, 345–46, 348;
  Armenians and, 437;
  Babanzade Mustafa Zihni Paşa and, 297;
  banquet of, 319–21;
  come-back, 335–37;
  criticism about, 318–19, 324, 337;
  energy of, 303–7, 313;
  funding and, 308–12, 321, 328–29, 334–36;
  gendarmerie and, 307, 309, 325–26;
  in İstanbul, 342–43;
  local and general politics, 349–52;
  order restoration, 312–19, 331–32, 435;
  orphanages and, 310–11, 315, 331–32, 335;
  personal life, 289–91;
  professional life, 291–96, 352n7, 353n9;
  reconciliation, 310, 319–31;
  reconstruction and, 305–7, 310, 435–36;
  relief committees, 308–12;
  relief work and, 304–5, 321;
  women and girls industrial relief, 332–35
Cemal Bey/Paşa Baghdad governorship, 365, 384, 436;
  accusations against, 376–79, 417–18;
  agriculture and, 369;
  Ali Rıza Paşa and, 370–71;
  appointment decree for, 366;
  army reorganization in, 380;
  departure from, 382;
  drainage and, 369;
  equality in, 368;
  feelings related to, 366–67;
  on foreigners, 371–72;
  Lorimer and, 363–64, 366, 372–73, 382;
  Midhat Paşa and, 368–69;
  municipalities in, 375;
  National Day in, 380;
  navigation and, 369;
  newspapers and, 371–72;
  policy of, 368;
  potential in, 367–68;
  prospects after, 382–83;
  reforms and, 368–70;
  resignation of, 381;
  successes in, 374–76, 380;
  taxation in, 375;
  unification in, 367–68;
  weakness in, 367.
  See also Baghdad
Cemaleddin, Efendi, 121
Cemal Paşa Askeri ve Siyasi Hayatı (Artuç), 415–18
census, 53, 59n52
Center of Armenian Studies of Yerevan State University, 3
central Asia natives, 95
Çetinsaya, Gökhan, viii, 2, 418n2
Cevad Bey:
  Adana clashes and, 165–66, 248–52;
  appointment of, 143–44;
  background of, 143;
  incompetence of, 148–49, 166, 168, 191–95, 248, 435;
  on order restoration, 248–52;
  orders of, 167;
  punishment of, 267;
  replacement of, 200–1;
  reports of, 182–83, 248–52;

warnings from, 144–45
Chafy, R. E. W., 302–4, 309–11;
   agriculture and, 315–16;
   dragomans and, 314
Chamber of Deputies, 10, 12–13, 300, 381;
   Adana clashes and, 183–84;
   Ahmed Rıza Bey in, 124–25;
   Babanzade İsmail Hakkı Bey in, 134–35;
   Cemal Bey and, 379;
   crack in, 129;
   elections for, 119–21;
   funding from, 257–58;
   opening of, 106;
   on order restoration, 256–59;
   parliamentary commission from, 257;
   recommendations of, 185, 256–57;
   on responsibility, 256–59
Chamber of Notables, 119, 123
Chambers, Lawson, 165, 168, 171, 194
Chambers, Miss, 340
Chambers, William Nesbitt, 21, 84–85, 148, 161n168, 206n64, 301–2, 306, 309, 388, 399;
   Adana clashes and, 165, 173–74;
   on agriculture, 392–93;
   Cemal Bey and, 308, 311–12, 323–24, 330–31, 384, 408;
   on Christians, 115–16;
   on education, 351;
   loyalty of, 406;
   Mehmet Ali Bey and, 335;
   on peacefulness, 347–48;
   on reception, 348–49;
   women and girls industrial relief and, 332–34
Charlton, Zeeneb, 352
Chartier, Charles, 309, 311
Chermside, Herbert, 46, 53
Chester, Arthur Tremaine, 231, 239n62
Chester, Colby Mitchel, 231–32, 239n62
Chicherin, Gyorgy, 411
Childs, W. J., 232–34

Christianity, 42, 115–16;
   of Adana Armenians, 76;
   Jesuit Mission, 327;
   Jesus Christ, 243, 245
Christians, 398, 423n98;
   Abdülhamid II against, 224, 226;
   anxiety of, 317–18, 345–46, 348;
   attacks on, 190;
   Chambers, W. N., on, 115–16;
   friendship with, 262;
   in gendarmerie, 326;
   houses of, 320–21;
   jurisdiction of, 427n165;
   landownership of, 79;
   in military, 133;
   Muslims and, 148, 221–22, 242–44;
   panic of, 401–5;
   Protestant Armenians, 65–66, 81–82, 85
Christians and Jews in the Ottoman Empire: The Functioning of a Plural Society (Braude and Lewis), 98
Christie, Thomas Davidson, 21, 53, 82, 175;
   on Hacin, 324–25;
   on responsibility, 218–19;
   on unrest, 347
Çiçek, Kemal, 5–6
Çiçek, Talha, 9, 292–93, 415
Cicero, 41–42
Cilicia (Çukurova), 233–34;
   Arabs in, 42;
   Armenian principality in, 61–63;
   banks in, 387;
   Belen Pass in, 38;
   Berlin Treaty and, 80;
   boundaries of, 39–40;
   Cicero in, 41–42;
   demographics of, 53–54;
   economic loss in, 402–3;
   European enterprise in, 51;
   French occupation of, 396–98;
   Greeks in, 41–42;
   Gulf of İskenderun in, 38–39, 55n6;

history of, 40–43, 56n16, 61–62;
importance of, 40;
irrigation, 52;
lack of writings about, 40;
location of, 38–40, 45, 55n6, 55n9, 57n25;
name of, 39;
products of, 39;
"protégés" in, 397;
rivers in, 51–52;
Romans in, 41–42;
sanjaks in, 39–40, 55n9;
Syria and, 38;
trade of, 39, 55n6;
Turkomans in, 42–43;
USNA on, 56n16;
Yurtsever on, 41
Cilicia 1909: The Massacre of Armenians (Terzian), 5
Cilician plain, 42, 394, 431–32
Cilix (prince), 39
Circassians, 251;
generosity of, 179–80;
as refugees, 195, 404
coal, 49
Cochin, Denis, 270
Cohen, Julia Phillips, 131, 153n48
collective identity, 160n148
commercial failures, after Adana clashes, 202
commercial voyage, 341–42
commission of inquiry:
on order restoration, 259–63;
representatives of, 259
Committee of National Defense, 373
Committee of Seven, 292
Committee of Union and Progress (CUP), 10, 24–25, 109;
in Adana, 131;
Aleppo and, 113–14;
in Baghdad, 371;
Cemal Bey in, 291–93, 295–96;
diversity of, 130;
equality and, 132;
Hüseyin Hilmi Paşa and, 163n187;
moderation of, 102;
origins of, 130;
Ottomanization and, 134;
parliament elections and, 120;
patriotism of, 129–30;
responsibility related to, 228–31;
Sabahattin and, 128;
"Saviour Officers" and, 381;
Unionists and, 436–37;
vigilance of, 132;
Young Turk-Dashnak cooperation and, 272–73;
Young Turks and, 130, 132
Committee on Building and Relief, 335
The Congregationalist (Hamlin), 65–66
conspiracy, 225
Constitution (1876):
CUP and, 109;
equality in, 107–8;
fraternity under, 111;
legal system in, 108;
parliament and, 106–8;
reforms and, 109–10;
regulations and, 106–8, 112, 152nn37–38;
rights in, 104–7
Constitution (1908):
against autocracy, 116–17;
Baghdad and, 364;
equality and, 101, 212;
fraternity and, 99, 101–3, 112;
freedom of press and, 99–100;
joy about, 112, 114;
nationalism and, 125–26, 433;
without parliament, 101;
political amnesty and, 100;
reception for, 112–19;
restoration of, 98–104, 112–15, 346;
Sheikh-ul-Islam Sahib Molla on, 110–11;
Young Turks and, 101–4, 109–10
Constitution Day, 346
Constitution proclamation, Adana Armenians after, 136–38

consuls, 18, 171–72;
  informants of, 20;
  local governments and, 20;
  in Mersin, 45–46;
  reports of, 19–20;
  subdistrict governors and, 19.
  See also Doughty-Wylie, Charles
The Contemporary Review, 150n15
cotton:
  in Adana economic recovery, 344;
  from Adana province, 47–48, 344, 386–88, 391–92, 402–3;
  economic loss related to, 402–3;
  exports of, 47–48, 344, 386–87
Council of Justice, 105
Council of Ministers, 106–7, 142–43
Council of State, 106–7
county (sanjak), 39–40, 43, 55n9
des Coursous, (viscomte), 63–64
court martial, 246, 248, 266–67;
  causes of troubles in, 265
crafts, 77, 325, 345
Creelman, James, 89n38, 213, 221, 241;
  Ahmed Rıza Bey and, 263;
  Hüseyin Hilmi Paşa and, 262–63;
  order restoration and, 242–44;
  on responsibility, 225
criticism:
  of Baghdad Company, 339;
  about Cemal Bey/Paşa Adana governorship, 318–19, 324, 337;
  from Muslims, 146
Çukurova. *See* Cilicia
Cunningham, J. C., 399;
  on Armenian anxiety, 398
CUP. *See* Committee of Union and Progress
Currie, Philip, 67–70
Curzon, Lord, 401

Dadrian, Vahakn, 277–78
Dağlı, Tuğba, viii
Daim, Hüseyin, 196
Dalyan, Kamil, viii

Dashnak Party/Society, 22, 124, 127–28, 138;
  Young Turk-Dashnak cooperation, 272–73
Daudet, Justin, 48
Davison, Roderic, 152n38
Daybreak in Turkey (Barton), 89n28
deaths:
  from Adana clashes, 169, 174, 186–88, 190, 192, 249;
  of American missionaries, 169, 186–88;
  executions, 64, 267, 316–17
decentralization, 128–29
Deedes, Wyndham, 294, 400
deforestation, 49–50
Demolins, Edmond, 128
"denial of justice," 256
Department of State, US, 17–18
von Der Goltz, Colmar Freiherr, 133, 291
Deschanel, Paul, 103–4
The Destruction of Armenians in Cilicia, April 1909 (Widespread Massacres of Armenians in Cilicia (April 1909)) (Simonyan), 3–4
diaries, 24–25, 135
Dillon, E. J., 103
Dinçer, Sinan, 289
diplomats, 14–15.
  See also consuls
Directorate General of the Turkish State Archives, 6–7
displaced persons, 182.
  See also refugees
Dıblanoğlu, 168
documentation lack, 1–2
Dörtyol, 180;
  kaymakam of, 199;
  order restoration in, 259;
  rumors about, 326–27
Doughty-Wylie, Charles, 139–40, 147;
  in Adana clashes, 167–73, 250;
  Cemal Bey and, 312;
  on commission of inquiry, 260–61;

as consul, 172;
  Daim and, 196;
  dispersions by, 167–70, 192;
  honors for, 172;
  Lowther and, 199–200;
  in military, 172–73;
  order restoration and, 247;
  orders from, 170–71;
  on renewed unrest, 317;
  against Seropian, 188–89, 434;
  wounding of, 170, 198, 250
dragomans, 239n61;
  in Adana clashes, 167–68, 203n16;
  Chafy and, 314;
  duties of, 366, 374;
  non-Muslims as, 14
Dufferin, Earl of, 46
Duman, Özkan, viii

Earle, Edward Mead, 19, 33n37, 118
economic loss:
  Britain and, 254–56;
  in Cilicia, 402–3;
  in order restoration, 253–56
Edhem Paşa, 183
Edib, Halidé (Adıvar), 101, 151n22;
  on Cemal Bey, 383;
  on responsibility, 219
education, 236n14;
  Adana Armenians in, 77;
  agricultural college, 337, 378;
  of Cemal Paşa, 290–91;
  Chambers, W. N., on, 351;
  at orphanages, 351;
  in Ottoman Empire, 220–21;
  for women and girls industrial relief, 333;
  Young Turks and, 133–34
Eldem, Vedat, viii
elections:
  for Chamber of Deputies, 119–21;
  CUP and, 120;
  for parliament, 119–21, 123–24;
  standards from, 364
Eler, Ayten, viii

Elgood, Percival George, 294
Eliot, Charles, 97
Emin Bey (Zincirkıran), 388–89
Endricks, Herr, 339
Enver Bey/Paşa, 9, 112, 121, 295–96, 413–14
equality:
  in Cemal Bey/Paşa governorship Baghdad, 368;
  in Constitution (1876), 107–8;
  Constitution (1908) and, 101, 212;
  CUP and, 132;
  in orphanages, 332;
  of religions, 245;
  TGNA and, 404;
  for Young Turks, 132–33.
  See also Muslim-Non-Muslim equality
Erickson, Edward, viii, 2, 23, 36n51
Ermeni Terör Merkezi: Kilikya Kilisesi (Yurtsever), 41
Erzurum, 68–69
Esad Rauf Bey, 175, 247, 260, 322, 434
European enterprise, in Cilicia, 51
evacuations, 402
evangelization, 81
executions, 64, 267, 316–17
exoneration, 252–53
explosives, 251
exports, of cotton, 47–48, 344, 386–87
eyewitnesses, 12

Fahri Paşa, 340
Faroqhi, Suraiya, 2
Fawaz, Leila Tarazi, 134
Fedayee:
  Adana clashes and, 165–67, 174;
  from Huntchak Committee, 146–48
Ferid Paşa (Avlonyalı), p*14*, 150n11, 167, 203n14;
  order restoration from, 245–46
Ferriman, Duckett, 3
fertility:
  of Adana province, 44–48;
  around Aleppo, 50–51

Fihri, Ihsan, 197
Fikri, İhsan:
  leader of the local CUP, 114;
  order restoration and, 261;
  punishment of, 267–68;
  responsibility and, 266
fires, 166, 186–87, 191, 232, 255
First World War, 7–8, 394–95, 437;
  Cemal Paşa in, 413
FO. *See* Foreign Office
Föllner, 275
Fontana, Raphael, 71, 340
food, 335–36
foreign agents, 211, 266
foreign battleships, 198–99
foreign citizenship, 19
"foreign dependency," 363
foreigners, 371–72, 383;
  in Adana clashes, 174
Foreign Office (FO), 12, 15–16, 141
foreign policy, in regard to Baghdad, 370
foreign post offices, 46
foreign subjects, 254
foreign warships, 180, 190, 323, 434;
  anxiety over, 388;
  at İskenderun, 198–99;
  in Mersin, 197–202
France:
  Adana occupation by, 395–96, 402–3;
  Cemal Bey and, 294–95, 304;
  Cilicia occupation by, 396–98;
  missionaries from, 83;
  responsibility and, 230.
  See also French military
Franco-Turkish pact, 399
Franklin-Bouillon, Henri, 399, 403, 405–6, 425n122
fraternity:
  under Constitution (1876), 111;
  Constitution (1908) and, 99, 101–3, 112
freedom:
  in Armenian schooling, 213;
  of press, 99–100

French military, 189–90;
  Armenians with, 403
French Ministry of Foreign Affairs archives, 16–17
French mission schools, 83
French occupation:
  of Adana, 395–96, 402–3;
  of Cilicia, 396–98
Fuad Paşa, 109
funding:
  Cemal Bey/Paşa Adana governorship and, 308–12, 321, 328–29, 334–36;
  from Chamber of Deputies, 257–58

Gabriel, Simbad, 264
Gaillard, Gaston, 62, 232
Gasparian, Aristakes, 255
gendarmerie, 307, 309, 325–26;
  Christians in, 326
genocide, 275–79
geography, 37–38
German colony, 337;
  hospital and, 338–39
German press, 102
Germany, 120;
  Baghdad railway and, 318, 393;
  Cemal Bey and, 293–94;
  economic loss and, 254;
  naval demonstrations from, 389;
  Ottoman War Academy and, 290–91;
  responsibility of, 229;
  school from, 391;
  Talat Bey and, 299, 301;
  voyage to, 342
Geuvkalajian, Hampartsum, 406–7
Gibbons, Helen Davenport, 139, 161n163
Gibbons, Herbert Adams, 168, 192–94
girls. *See* women and girls industrial relief
Gökalp, Ziya, 148, 429n182
Gökdereliyan, Garabet, 201, 218–19, 240, 248, 317
Göksun, 179–80
de Gontaut-Biron, R., 404
Gooch, George, 201–2

Goodell, Wiliam, 213
Goulbenkian, Avedis, 378
Gouraud, Henri, 400–1
government, 20;
   Hamidian regime, 62, 108–9, 130, 220, 367;
   order restoration by, 241–48
Government Industrial Commission, 325
government land graft, 378–79
government records, 12–13
government service, 77–78
governors (*Vali*), 142–43, 153n53;
   of Adana, 391.
   See also Cemal Bey/Paşa; *kaymakam*
Grabowski, M., 304–5, 309;
   accusations related to, 377–78
grain, 388
Graves, Philip, 190–91, 222
Graves, Robert, 68–69, 400
Great Powers, 410
Greeks:
   against Armenians, 196;
   Cemal Bey and, 350;
   in Cilicia, 41–42;
   elections related to, 120;
   Herodotus, 39
Gregorian Armenians, 62, 145;
   Armenian schooling, 84–85;
   Geuvkalajian and, 406–7;
   guerilla warfare and, 390
Gregorian calendar, 59n52
Grey, Edward, 198–99, 201–2, 256, 270
Güçlü, Yücel, 159n138
guerilla warfare, 389–91
Guide to the National Archives of the United States, 32n33
Gulf of İskenderun, 38–39, 55n6
Gülhane, 152n39

Haas, Cyril, 405–6
Hacı Halil Bey, 317
Hacin, 179, 251;
   Cemal Bey in, 324;
   Christie on, 324–25;
   poverty in, 330

Hacıefendioğlu, Elvan, viii
Hacı Mehmet Ağa (Hacı Çavuş), 181–82
Hairig, Khirimian. *See* Khirimian, Mekertitch
Halid, Halil, 132
Halid Efendi, 178
Hallaçyan, Bedros, 130–31
Hamid Bey, 399–400, 406
Hamidian regime, 62, 108–9, 130, 220, 367
Hamilton Books, vii
Hamlin, Cyrus, 65–66, 82
Hanioğlu, Şükrü, 86n5
Harbord, James, 328, 359n146
Harput, 329
Hattı Hümayun, 365
Hattı Hümayun (Reform Edict) (1856), 14, 104–6
Hattı Şerif (Sacred Edict) (1839), 104–5
health services, 77;
   hospitals, 321–22, 338–39, 405–6
Henderson, Patrick, 46
Herodotus, 39
Hikmet, Arif, 256
Hırlakyan, Agop, 78
historians, 10–11, 26;
   genocide related to, 275–77;
   values of, 27
historiography:
   without context, 3;
   document declassification in, 6–7;
   gaps in, 2–3;
   interpretations in, 7–9, 26–27;
   memoirs in, 4–5;
   Simonyan in, 3–4
history:
   of Adana province, 431–32;
   of American mission schools, 81;
   of Cilicia, 40–43, 56n16, 61–62
Holocaust, 3, 275–78, 285n112
hospitals, 321–22, 338–39, 405–6
House of Commons, 198, 201–2;
   Cilician refugees and, 404
houses, 322;
   of Adana Armenians, 74, 191;

of Christians, 320–21;
funding for, 335–36;
in Hacin, 325
Huntchak Committee (Huntchak
   Society), 63;
   executions from, 64;
   Fedayee from, 146–48;
   plots of, 200–1, 434;
   Russia and, 65, 69
Huntchak Party, 77–78;
   Reformed Huntchak Party, 137, 140,
   146, 189–90
Hüseyin Bey, 309
Hüseyin Hilmi Paşa, p*13*, 144–45,
   163n187, 257, 267, 298;
   Creelman and, 262–63;
   Jewry and, 229–30;
   on Muslim-Non-Muslim equality,
   262–63;
   order restoration and, 259–60;
   responsibility of, 260
Hüseyin Kazım Bey, 185

İbrahim Paşa, 43
identity:
   collective, 160n148;
   of Ottomanism, 135–36
İkdam, 25, 128
Imperial Ottoman Bank, 304, 338
imperium in imperio, 96–97
İnal, İbnülemin Mahmud Kemal, 31n25,
   173n187
İnalcık, Halil, 2
India, 365–66, 419n9
Indo-Afghan frontier, 411
industries, 48, 325, 332–35, 432
inheritance, law of, 405
insurance, 254–56
International Committee, 304–5
international courts, 276
international law, 287–88
International Relief Commission
   (International Relief Committee),
   298, 308, 321;
   appeals from, 328–30

international workshop, 288
Iran (Persia), 33n40
Iraq:
   as "foreign dependency," 363;
   Young Turk revolution and, 364.
   See also Baghdad; Cemal Bey/Paşa
   Baghdad governorship
irrigation, 50, 52, 337, 381, 394, 432
İskenderun, 180;
   foreign warships at, 198–99;
   Gulf of, 38–39, 55n6;
   violence at, 176, 274
İslahiye, 181–82
İsmail Hakkı Efendi, 316–17
İsmet Bey (İnönü), 293, 300, 301
İstanbul, 293;
   April 13, 1909 in, 226, 237n27;
   Cemal Bey in, 342–43;
   September 30, 1895, riot in, 67, 69
Italian press, 102
Italy, 373;
   economic loss and, 254;
   naval demonstrations from, 389;
   against Ottoman Empire, 419n29;
   Tripolitania and, 378, 437
İtidal (newspaper), 214–15
İzmirliyan, Mateos (patriarch), 241

Jackh, Ernest, 410, 427n164
Jackson, Jesse, 396–97, 424n114
Jacob, Ernest Otto, 392, 423n98
Jemal Bey. *See* Cemal Bey/Paşa
Jernazian, Ephraim, 89n30
Jerusalem Patriarchate, 22–23, 35n48
Jesuit Mission, 5, 327
Jesus Christ, 243, 245
Jewry, 96, 131;
   anti-Semitism against, 233;
   in Baghdad, 379;
   on Committee of National Defense,
   373;
   Holocaust of, 275–78, 285n112;
   Hüseyin Hilmi Paşa and, 229–30;
   jurisdiction of, 427n165;
   World Jewish Congress, 278

Joure (Père), 304, 309
judiciary, 76;
　law of inheritance, 405;
　legal system, 108;
　Mixed Commercial Court, 217;
　Ottoman Civil Code, 31n24
Justinian, 45, 432

Kabul, 411
Kadri, Tevfik (Ramazanoğlu), 147–48, 164n203, 196–97, 209n122
Kaligian, Dikran Mesrob, 264, 326
Kambour, Rupen, 63
Kamil Paşa, 121–22
Karabekir, Kazım, 153n56
Karacagil, Kürşad, viii
Karacakaya, Recep, 6–7
Karadoğan, İsmet, 428n173
Karayan, Stepan, 258, 298
Karpat, Kemal, 2, 20, 59n53
Katiba, Kamar. *See* Patkanian, Rafael
Katz, Steven, 277
Kayalı, Hasan, 159n138, 364
Kaygusuz, Ayhan, viii
kaymakam (lower district governor), 180;
　Asaf Bey as, 253;
　of Belen, 259;
　consuls and, 19;
　of Dörtyol, 199;
　of Göksun, 179;
　of Jissr, 340;
　Muammer Bey as, 385;
　of Zeytun, 71
Kayseri, 100, 384
Kedourie, Elie, 233
Kemal, Mustafa (Atatürk), 291, 301
Kemal, Namık, 121
Kemal, Yusuf (Tengirşek), 260–61, 298, 320, 403
Kennaway, John, 66, 68
Kennedy, Samuel H., 180;
　on funding, 329
Kesim, Firuz, 428n173
Kessab:
　economic recovery in, 340;
　violence at, 176–77
Kévorkian, Raymond, 313
Khilafat Mussulman League, 411
Khirimian, Mekertitch (Khirimian Hairig), 70
Kiliades Efendi, 180–81
Kirsch, Julie, vii
Kırmızı, Abdulhamit, 288
Knight, Edward Frederick, 120, 133
knitting, 345
Koran, 242–44;
　Sheikh-ul-Islam Sahib Molla on, 261–62
Kot, James, 48
Kozan, 177–78
Kozlovski, Stanislas, 309, 315, 377–78;
　accusations related to, 377–78
Kudret Bey, 373
Kundakçıyan, Esther, 340
Kuneralp, Sinan, viii
Kurt, Yılmaz, 57n25

labor, 74–75
labor shortages, 47, 214, 249, 252
Lambert, Rose, 179
de Lamothe, Marie, 396–97, 424n114
de Lancy, Barré, 308, 339–40
landownership, 80;
　of Christians, 79;
　nomad tribes and, 368–69
languages:
　of Adana Armenians, 73;
　American mission schools and, 81;
　French, 83;
　in methodology, 28–29;
　of newspapers, 117–18;
　Turkish, 133–34
Lanzoni, Dr., 373–74
law of inheritance, 405
Law of Nations, 287–88
Lawrence, Thomas Edward, 231
Layard, Henry, 264
Lazkiye, 177
League for Personal Initiative and Decentralization, 128

Lee, Olin P., 398
legal system, 108
Leishman, John, 188, 262
Lemkin, Raphael, 275
Lengyel, Emil, 140–41
Leo II (king), 42
Leslie, Francis, 51
Letchilian, Garabet, 1, 146, 165–67
Levant Trade Review, 55n6
Lewis, Bernard, 2, 98, 233;
    on genocide, 278–79
liberalization, political, 128
libraries, vii
"Little Paris" (Salonika), 100, 113,
    116–17, 151n20, 291–92
Lobanoff (prince), 69
local governments, 20;
    municipalities, 375, 408–9
Longrigg, Stephen Hemsley, 418n2
Longworth, H. Z., 68, 112
Lorimer, John Gordon, 380, 418n3;
    Cemal Bey/Paşa Baghdad
    governorship and, 363–64, 366,
    372–73, 382
lower district governor. *See kaymakam*
Lowther, Gerard, 123–24, 141, 190,
    228, 233;
    Doughty-Wylie and, 199–200;
    on Hüseyin Hilmi Paşa, 260
lunar calendar, 59n52
Lybyer, Alfred H., 152n44

Macallum, Frederick W., 206n74
Macedonia, 101–2, 262, 291–92;
    gendarmerie and, 309
Magavourian, Nishan, 63
Magie, David, 53
Mahmud II (sultan), 108
Mahmud Şevket Paşa, p*15*, 133, 221–22,
    245, 293
Mallet, Louis, 299;
    on Cemal Bey, 323
Manyasizade Refik Bey, 122
Maraş, 179;
    Armenians in, 40;

poverty of, 330;
sanjak of, 39–40;
site of, 40
Mardikian, Oskan, 437
marketplace, 165–66, 249
marshes, 46–47
Matossian, Bedross Der, 114, 214
Matossian, Lou Ann, 289–90
Maurer, Henry, 186–88
McCarthy, Justin, 54
McGilvray, Margaret, 354m34
Meclisi Mebusan Zabıt Ceridesi
    (Proceedings of the Chamber of
    Deputies), 27
Mehmet Ali Bey, 200–1, 246–47, 303,
    315;
    Cemal Bey and, 309–10;
    Chambers, W. N., and, 335;
    power of, 317–18
Mehmet Ali Paşa, 432
Mehmet II (sultan), 32n34, 410
memoirs: of Armenians, 23;
    of Cemal Paşa, 24, 141–42, 145–46,
    212–13;
    in historiography, 4–5
*Memories of a Turkish Statesman
    1913–1919* (Cemal Paşa), 415
Mendl, C. E., 405–6
Merrill, John, 408
Mersin:
    American Reformed Presbyterian
    Church in, 85, 398, 406;
    consuls in, 45–46;
    footholds in, 19;
    foreign post offices in, 46;
    foreign warships in, 197–202;
    railway of, 44;
    refugees to, 398, 401–2;
    restoration of Constitution in, 114–15;
    trade in, 49, 432;
    unrest in, 175, 345–46
methodology, 26;
    chronology in, 27–28;
    languages in, 28–29;
    note references in, 28;

omissions in, 28–29;
punctuation in, 28
Middle East, 33n40
Midhat Paşa, 101, 106–7, 109, 121, 368–69
military:
in Adana clashes, 189, 201–2, 250;
Christians in, 133;
to Dörtyol, 259;
Doughty-Wylie in, 172–73;
French, 189–90, 403;
non-Muslims in, 326;
Roumelian soldiers, 190, 307
Military Council, 105
military rebellion. *See* Adana clashes
millet system, 96–98, 149n2;
Protestants and, 81
minorities, 437;
in Russia, 95, 97, 195
missionaries, 21;
ABCFM, 30n22;
in Adana, 84–85, 115–16;
from France, 83;
Leslie as, 51;
Paul of Tarsus, 42–43.
See also American missionaries
The Missionary Herald, 154n58, 348
missionary schools, 73–74, 83.
See also American mission schools
Mixed Commercial Court, 217
Mohammed (prophet), 243–45
Molla, 327.
See also Sheikh-ul-Islam Sahib Molla
money, Ottoman, 58n37
moneylenders, 78–79
Mordtmann, Herr, 339
Morgenthau, Henry, 311
Muammer Bey, 377, 384–86
Muhittin Paşa (Akyüz), 399–400, 406
Mülkiye Tarihi ve Mülkiyeliler, 11
municipalities, 375;
Unionists and, 408–9
Münir Bey, 217
Muslihittin Adil Bey, 183–84, 247, 256

Muslim-Non-Muslim equality, 107, 115–16, 242, 245;
at banquet, 319–20;
Hüseyin Hilmi Paşa on, 262–63;
Koran on, 261–62;
law of inheritance and, 405;
on tour, 340–42
Muslims:
Adana Armenians and, 138;
in Adana clashes, 165–67;
Christians and, 148, 221–22, 242–44;
criticism from, 146;
executions of, 316–17;
Ramazan of, 323, 358n130;
responsibility of, 212.
See also non-Muslims
Mustafa Hayri Efendi, 111
Mustafa Kemal Paşa:
Ankara Agreement and, 400;
Bristol and, 424n115;
Cemal Paşa and, 411–12;
encouragement from, 404
Mustafa Remzi Paşa, 168, 191–93, 195, 248, 267, 435
Mustafa Reşid Paşa, 109
mutasarrıf, 385;
Asaf Bey as, 176;
Ayni as, 177;
Cemal Paşa as, 292–93

Naimark, Norman, 75
Nalbandian, Mikael, 70
Nalbantyan, Matyos, 78
Nasır Paşa, 339–40
Nathan, Edward, 216, 309, 393–94
National Archives (TNA), 15–16
National Day, 380
nationalism, 417;
in Anatolia, 407–8;
Constitution (1908) and, 125–26, 433;
Young Turk revolution and, 409.
See also Armenian nationalism
"national" languages, 81
natural resources, 46–52
naval demonstrations, 389

navigation, 369
Nazis, 277–78
Nazım Paşa, 371, 373, 375
Near East, 33n40
Nebuchadennazar II (king), 41
newspapers, 214–16, 307;
  in Baghdad, 371–72;
  contemporary, 25–26;
  of France, 230;
  incitement by, 252;
  languages of, 117–18;
  Tanin, 25, 110, 134–35, 222–23, 246
1909 Adana Ermeni Olayları
  (Karacakaya and Sarınay), 7
1909 Adana Olayları: Makaleler, 5–6
Nilson, Paul, 405
Niyazi Bey, 112, 121
nomad tribes, 325;
  landownership and, 368–69
non-Muslims:
  as dragomans, 14;
  foreign citizenship of, 19;
  in military, 326;
  in parliament, 125;
  rights of, 436
Noradounghian, Gabriel, 99, 437
Nossing, Alfred, 299
Nurdan, Semiha, viii

Ocak, Ahmet Yaşar, 2
Odian, Krikor, 109
official warrant of approval (*berat*), 19
"Oğul" (son), 147, 164n203
Onaner, Ali, viii
Oppenheim, Lassa Francis Lawrence, 287–88
von Oppenheim, Max, 272–75
Oran. *See* Ahmed Cevdet
order restoration, 201–2;
  Cemal Bey/Paşa Adana governorship and, 312–19, 331–32, 435;
  Cevad Bey on, 248–52;
  Chamber of Deputies on, 256–59;
  commission of inquiry on, 259–63;
  court martial in, 246, 248, 265–67;
  in Dörtyol, 259;
  economic loss in, 253–56;
  exoneration in, 252–53;
  by government, 241–48;
  judgments in, 246;
  von Oppenheim and, 273–75;
  punishment in, 267–68;
  separatism in, 268–72;
  stolen goods in, 247–48, 250;
  trials in, 259;
  ulema and, 242–44;
  Young Turk-Dashnak cooperation in, 272–73
The Orient, 93n81
orphanages, 331, 335;
  education at, 351;
  equality in, 332;
  plans for, 310–11, 315
Ortaylı, İlber, 126
Osman, Tekelizade, 197
Osmanlı Belgelerinde 1909 Adana Olayları (Karacakaya et al.), 6–7
Ottoman Administration of Iraq, 1890–1908 (Çetinsaya), 418n2
Ottoman Civil Code, 31n24
Ottoman Constitution, 3, 10, 84
Ottoman Empire, 419n29;
  competition over, 409–10;
  diversity of, 95–96;
  education in, 220–21;
  extent of, 37;
  Iraq in, 363;
  millet system in, 96–98;
  misinformation about, 11;
  products of, 37;
  sources about, 2
Ottomanism:
  Arabs and, 364;
  identity of, 135–36;
  minorities and, 437;
  old and new, 407;
  of Young Turks, 135–36, 436
Ottomanization, 134
Ottoman Jewry, 131
Ottoman Ministry of Foreign Affairs, 13

Ottoman Ministry of the Interior, 400
Ottoman money, 58n37
Ottoman nation, 135–36
Ottoman national citizenship, 129
Ottoman Protestant church, 81
Ottoman Second Constitutional Period, 435
Ottoman Turkish, 3–4
Ottoman War Academy, 290–91
Özdemir, Hikmet, 9
Özler. *See* Safa, İsmail

Paksoy (Abdurrahman), 148
Palestine:
    Cemal Paşa in, 383–84, 414;
    Jerusalem Patriarchate, 22–23, 35n48
von Papen, Franz, 300–1
parade, 121
parliament, 101, 106–8;
    Abdülhamid II to, 121–22;
    Chamber of Notables in, 119, 123;
    elections for, 119–21, 123–24;
    inauguration of, 121–22;
    Kamil Paşa in, 121–22;
    meetings of, 118;
    non-Muslims in, 125;
    parade before, 121;
    representation within, 123;
    voters for, 119.
    See also Chamber of Deputies
parliamentary commission, 257
Pastırmacıyan, Karekin, 156n101
Patkanian, Rafael (Kamar Katiba), 70
patriotism:
    CUP, 129–30;
    of Young Turks, 132
Paul of Tarsus (saint), 42–43
peacefulness, 347–48
Pears, Edwin, 111, 133, 171, 298;
    on responsibility, 224–25, 228, 234
Pearson's Magazine, 161n157
Peet, William, 347–49, 394
Pichon, Stéphane, 104, 258, 270
Pickthall, Marmaduke, 133, 230–31
Pinon, René, 45

Pivet, Rear-Admiral, 144
police force, 252
political amnesty, 100
political committees, 137
political liberalization, 128
post offices, foreign, 46
poverty, 330
Powell, Edward Alexander, 229
press, 102;
    freedom of, 99–100.
    See also newspapers
Price, Clair, 403;
    disquiet for, 407–8
Price, Philips, 389–91, 394
Prime Minister's Office Ottoman Archive (BOA), vii, 4, 6–7, 12–13, 27
prisoners, 322–23
propaganda, 64;
    of Adana Armenians, 145
prosperity. *See* wealth
"protégés," 397–98
Protestant Armenians, 65–66, 81–82, 85
provincial administration, 142–49
Public Debt Administration, 90n46
Public Records Act of 1958, 16
punishment, in order restoration, 267–68

Radek, Karl, 411
railway, 44.
    See also Baghdad railway
Ramazan, 323, 358n130, 366
Ramazanoğlu. *See* Kadri, Tevfik
Ramsay, W. M., 234
Ravndal, Gabriel Bie, 55n6;
    on responsibility, 216–18
Rawlins, G. C. Donaldson, 319, 322, 340;
    on Cemal Bey, 349–50;
    on Christians, 320–21;
    on gendarmerie, 326;
    on hospital, 338–39;
    on rumors, 328;
    on voyage, 342
rebellions, 62–63

494 Index

reconciliation, 310, 330–31;
  American hospital and, 321–22;
  banquet in, 319–21;
  funding for, 328–29;
  gendarmerie in, 325–26;
  Hacin and, 324–25;
  prisoners, 322–23;
  rumors and, 326–28
reconstruction, 305–7, 310, 337, 435–36
Reformed Huntchak Party, 137, 140, 146, 189–90
Reform Edict (*Hattı Hümayun*) (1856), 14, 104–6
Reformed Presbyterian church, 84
reforms, 109–10;
  Cemal Bey/Paşa Baghdad governorship and, 368–70;
  Young Turks and, 409
refugees, 194, 208n106;
  Adana Armenians as, 404;
  in Beirut, 402;
  Circassians as, 195, 404;
  to Mersin, 398, 401–2
Régie Administration, 91n48
Reid, James, 110
relief commissions, 298, 308, 321, 328–30
relief committees, 308–12
relief work, 202, 241, 298;
  Cemal Bey and, 304–5;
  Cemal Bey/Paşa Adana governorship and, 304–5, 321;
  from Chamber of Deputies, 257–58
religions, 245.
  See also Christianity; Jewry; Muslims
relocation, 274–75, 395
Reorganization (*Tanzimat*), 106–8, 112, 152nn37–38
reparations, 287–88
Reşad (sultan), p*19*, 121, 126, 322, 349, 381;
  as constitutional sovereign, 241–42
Reşad Efendi (prince), 121
resources, natural, 46–52
responsibility, 264–65, 385;

ABCFM and, 227–28;
  of Abdülhamid II, 219–28;
  Armenian historians on, 213–14;
  of Armenians, 211–12;
  Chamber of Deputies on, 256–59;
  Christie on, 218–19;
  contemporary observations about, 231–35;
  CUP related to, 228–31;
  executions related to, 267, 316–17;
  of foreign agents, 211, 266;
  France and, 230;
  of Germany, 229;
  Halidé Edib on, 219;
  of Hüseyin Hilmi Paşa, 260;
  of Muslims, 212;
  Nathan on, 216;
  Özler on, 214–16;
  Pears on, 224–25, 228, 234;
  politics as, 225–27, 262;
  Ravndal on, 216–18;
  in reports, 251–52;
  of Russia, 232–33;
  of Seropian, 188–89, 212–13, 434;
  Woods on, 225–26, 228–29;
  Young Turks and, 228–31
Reuter's, 67–68
revenge, 215
Reynolds, Michael, vii, 2, 277
Richard, Emma, vii
Rickards, Henry, 174
rights, 104–7;
  of non-Muslims, 436
rivers, 44, 51–52
Rıza Bey, 259
Rıfkı, Falih (Atay), 414–15
roads, 383–84
Robert, Christopher, 82
Rodogno, Davide, 270
Rogan, Eugene, 80
Rogers, Daniel Miners, 186–88
Roman Catholic Church, 83;
  Anatolian Armenians and, 84;
  in Maraş, 85
Romans, 41–42

Rooshbazian, Hamayak, 63
Roque-Ferrier, M., 178, 196
Rosetti, M., 377–78
Roumelian soldiers, 190, 307
Rupen (prince), 42, 71
Rupenian kingdom, 217
al-Rusafi, Maruf, 364, 379
Russia, 295;
   Afghan-Soviet Treaty, 411–12;
   arms from, 273–74;
   Cemal Bey and, 350–51, 411;
   Huntchak Committee and, 65, 69;
   minorities in, 95, 97, 195;
   responsibility of, 232–33
Rüstem, Ahmed, 151n24
Ryan, Andrew, 313

Sabahattin (prince), 128
Sacred Edict (*Hattı Şerif*) (1839), 104–5
Safa, İsmail (Özler), 214–16, 236n14, 268
Sahak II, 404
Sahara, Tetsuya, 7, 139, 189
Sahib Molla, 111, 242–45;
   on Koran, 261–62
Said Halim Paşa, 298–300
Said Paşa, 98, 102, 122–23, 150n11, 241
St. Paul's Institute (College) at Tarsus, 82–83, 406
Şakir Efendi, 306–7
Salonika ("Little Paris"), 100, 113, 116–17, 151n20, 291–92
Salt, Jeremy, viii
Salz, Arthur, 383
von Sanders, Otto Liman, 294
sanjak (county, subdistrict), 39–40, 43, 55n9
Sanjian, Avedis, 214
Saraçoğlu, Şükrü, 300–1
Sarınay, Yusuf, 7
Sarkissian, Hagop, 196, 213;
   on Cemal Paşa, 412
Sarper, Selim Rauf, 175–76
Sassoun atrocities, 66–67, 184;
   casualties of, 264

Saurer, Emil, 382–83
"Saviour Officers," 381
schools, 73–74, 83, 391, 406.
   See also American mission schools;
   Armenian schooling
seasons, 52
"Second Constitutionalism 1908–1918," 99
Second Ottoman Constitutional Period, 9, 24, 143, 417
secret societies, 119
Selim I (sultan), 42, 71
separatism, 268–72
Serengülyan, Vartkes, 156n101
Şerif, Ahmet, 336, 360n164
Seropian, Musheg, 138, 252, 266;
   for arms, 137, 139–42, 144, 160n156;
   responsibility of, 188–89, 212–13, 434
Sevian Efendi, 372–73
Shahnazarian, Karapet Vardabet, 70
Shalev, Avner, 278
Shalmaneser (king), 41
Shaw, Stanford, 2, 95–96
Sheikh-ul-Islam Sahib Molla, 111, 242–45;
   on Constitution (1876), 110–11
Shepard, Elliott, 82
Shepard, Frederick Douglas, 227, 306–7;
   Adana economic recovery and, 348–49;
   on executions, 316–17;
   on funding, 329
Shepard, Mrs., 333, 335
Sherif Hüseyin, 135
Shipley, Hammond Smith, 124, 156n101
Simonyan, Hrachik, 39, 73, 170, 214, 275;
   in historiography, 3–4;
   on oppression, 97–98
Sipahi, Mustafa, viii
Sisliyan, Avedis, 249
Sisters of Saint Joseph, 5

Smith, Ian, 376–79
Society for the Propagation of the Faith, 5
son ("Oğul"), 147, 164n203
Souine, Sarkis, 344–45
sources:
  Armenian archives, 22–23;
  bias of, 14;
  British records, 15–16, 18;
  civil society agencies, 12;
  closure of, 16–18;
  contemporaneous documents, 12;
  diplomats, 14–15;
  eyewitnesses, 12;
  French records, 16–17;
  government records, 12–13;
  memoirs, 23–24;
  newspapers, 25–26;
  unpublished materials, 27;
  USNA, 17–18, 21–22, 32n33, 56n16;
  Western records, 14–18, 21–22, 26
Spanish Jews, 96
Sterghiades, M., 401
stocking knitting, 345
stolen goods, 247–48, 250
subdistrict (sanjak), 39–40, 43, 55n9
Subhi Paşa, 196–97, 209n122, 309
subject matter, 11;
  complexity of, 8–9;
  how in, 9;
  purpose in, 8;
  scholarship in, 9;
  summary in, 9–10;
  themes in, 8
Sublime Porte, 18, 24, 33n35, 80
Suez Canal, 414
Süleyman the Lawgiver (sultan), 32n34
Suny, Ronald Grigor, 98, 135, 231, 277
Syria:
  Cemal Paşa and, 414;
  Cilicia and, 38;
  refugees to, 402

Talat Bey/Paşa, 9, p*16–18*, 268, 272, 295, 413–14;
  Armenian patriarchate and, 346;
  assassination of, 300;
  humility of, 300;
  personality of, 298–99;
  professional life of, 299–301, 355n44
Tanin (newspaper), 25, 110, 246;
  Babanzade İsmail Hakkı in, 134–35;
  Hüseyin Cahid in, 222–23
Tanin in Anatolia (*Anadolu'da Tanin*), 360n164
Tanzimat (Reorganization), 104, 106–9, 112, 152nn37–38, 436
Tarsus:
  economic loss in, 402–3;
  gendarmerie in, 325–26;
  poverty in, 330;
  St. Paul's Institute at, 83, 406;
  violence in, 175
taxation, 375
technical field, 76–77
Tehlirian, Soghomon, 300
telegrams, 217–18
telegraph line, 322
terror, 64
Terzian, Hagop, 5
Tevfik, Rıza (Bölükbaşı), 211–12, 235n2, 298
textile industry, 48
TGNA. *See* Turkish Grand National Assembly
theater, 145, 235, 308
theocracy, 244
Thursby, C. F., 199–200
Timaksiyan, Hmayag, 258
The Times (London), 165, 202n1
Tittoni, Tommaso, 104
TNA. *See* National Archives
Tobacco Régie or Monopoly, 91n47, 311
Tokay, Gül, vii
Toker, Mustafa, viii
Toynbee, Arnold, 230
Trabzon, 68
trade:
  of Cilicia, 39, 55n6;
  cotton, 47–48, 344, 386–87;

in Mersin, 49, 432
Translation Bureau, 162n180
transportation, 393–94;
   roads, 383–84.
   See also Baghdad railway; railway
treaties:
   Afghan-Soviet Treaty, 411–12;
   Berlin Treaty, 80;
   Turkish-Soviet Treaty, 411
Treaty of Amity and Commerce of 1535, 32n34
Treaty of Ouchy (October 15, 1912), 437
trials, 259;
   court martial in, 246, 248, 265–67
Tripani, Constantine, 167–69, 239n61
Tripani Brothers (Constantine and Manolli), 48–49
Tripolitania, 378, 437
Troshag, 140, 146
van Trowbridge, Stephen, 169, 186–87, 194, 197
Tunaya, Tarık Zafer, 9, 126, 292
Turkey in Europe (Eliot), 97
Turkish army arrival, in Adana, 407–8
Turkish control resumption, of Adana, 399–408
Turkish exactions, 63
Turkish General Staff Military History and Strategic Studies Directorate's Archive (ATASE), 4, 13
Turkish Grand National Assembly (TGNA), 425n122, 429n182;
   discrimination of, 403;
   equality and, 404;
   Franklin-Bouillon and, 399;
   Muammer Bey in, 386
Turkish language, 133–34
Turkish majority, 52–54
Turkish-Soviet Treaty (March 16, 1921), 411
Turkomans, 42–43
Turks:
   Britain and, 173.
   See also specific topics

ulema, 106, 112;
   on Abdülhamid II, 238n31;
   authority of, 242;
   definition of, 152n43;
   order restoration and, 242–44;
   Sheikh-ul-Islam from, 110–11
UNCG. *See* United Nations Convention on the Prevention and Punishment of the Crime of Genocide
Underwood, Herbert, 227–28, 234
Unionists, 62, 293;
   CUP and, 436–37;
   Great Powers and, 130;
   Kamil Paşa and, 122;
   municipalities and, 408–9;
   non-Muslims and, 125;
   Sheikh-ul-Islam and, 110–11
United Church Board for World Ministries, 12
United Nations Convention on the Prevention and Punishment of the Crime of Genocide (UNCG), 276
United States National Archives and Records Administration (USNA), 17–18, 32n33, 56n16
usury, 78–79

Vahdettin Efendi (prince), 121
Vali. *See* governors
Vambery, Herman, 103
Van province, 273–75
Vartges, Ohannes, 256
Varzhabedian, Nerses, 70
vigilante groups, 64
voters, 119
voyage, 340–43

Walker, Christopher, 234
Wallace, Miss, 186–87, 206n73
War and State Formation in Syria: Cemal Pasha's Governorate during World War I, 1914–1917 (Çiçek, T.), 415
wars, 362n209, 410;
   ABCFM and, 394;

Balkan, 173, 293–94, 394, 422n80;
First World War, 394–95, 413, 437;
guerilla warfare, 389–91
wealth, 244;
of Adana Armenians, 75;
of Adana city, 47;
of Young Turks in Adana, 195
weather, 49–50
weaving, 325
Webb, Elizabeth, 84–85, 192–93
Webb, Mary, 84
Weitz, Eric, 235
Wendland, 226–27
Western Insurance Company, 254–56
What Happened in Adana in April 1909? (Sahara), 7
widows, 345
Wiegand, Theodor, 383
Wilhelm II (Kaiser), 299, 393
Williams, Aneurin, 404
Wilson, Charles, 46, 96–97
Wilson, Robert, 398, 406
Winkler, Herr, 338–39
women, 345;
emancipation of, 409
women and girls industrial relief:
administration for, 332–35;
advisor for, 333, 335;
funding for, 334–35
Woods, Admiral, 53
Woods, Charles, 135, 297;
on Cemal Bey, 351;
on responsibility, 225–26, 228–29
World Jewish Congress, 278
World War II, 362n209

Yad Vashem Holocaust Museum, 278
Yalçın. *See* Cahid, Hüseyin
Yalman, Ahmet Emin, 301
Yeğena, Ali Münif, 62, 86n3
Yeghiayan, Zaven Der, 395
Yessayan, Zabel, 310
Young Men's Christian Association, 85, 398, 423n98

Young Turk-Dashnak cooperation, 272–73
Young Turk revolution, 360n164;
Iraq and, 364;
nationalism and, 409
Young Turks, 10, 62, 86n5, 100, 109, 417;
Armenian nationalism and, 127;
Armenian societies and, 119, 155n79;
Armenians with, 101;
Bahri Paşa and, 117;
CUP and, 130, 132;
education and, 133–34;
equality for, 132–33;
intention of, 118, 155n76;
Ottomanism of, 135–36, 436;
patriotism of, 132;
policy of, 410;
reforms and, 409;
responsibility and, 228–31;
wealth of, 195
The Young Turks and the Truth about the Holocaust at Adana in Asia Minor, during April, 1909 (Ferriman), 3
The Young Turks in Opposition (Hanioğlu), 86n5
The Young Turks: The Committee of Union and Progress in Turkish Politics, 1908–1914 (Ahmad), 149n5
Yükseltan, İbrahim, viii
Yurtsever, Cezmi, 41
Yusuf İzzettin Efendi (prince), 121

al-Zahawi, Jamil Sidqi, 364, 379
Zarzecki, M., 308
Zeidner, Robert Farrer, 235
Zeytun, 62–63, 71;
guerilla warfare in, 389–91;
violence in, 274
Zincirkıran. *See* Emin Bey
Ziya Paşa, 127
Zohrab, Krikor, 211–13, 258

About the Author

Yücel Güçlü is associate professor of political history in Ankara, Turkey. His previous publications include *The Question of the Sanjak of Alexandretta: A Study in Turkish-French-Syrian Relations* (Ankara, 2001); *Eminence Grise of the Turkish Foreign Service: Numan Menemencioğlu* (Ankara, 2002); *The Life and Career of a Turkish Diplomat: Cevat Açıkalın* (Ankara, 2002); *The Turcomans and Kirkuk* (Philadelphia, Pennsylvania, 2007); *Armenians and the Allies in Cilicia 1914–1923* (Salt Lake City, Utah, 2010); *The Holocaust and the Armenian Case in Comparative Perspective* (Lanham, Maryland, 2012); *Zeki Kuneralp and the Turkish Foreign Service* (New Castle upon Tyne, 2015); *Historical Archives and the Historians' Commission to Investigate the Armenian Events of 1915* (Lanham, Maryland, 2015); and numerous articles on Turkish diplomatic history which appeared in the United States, Canada, Britain, Italy, Hungary, and Turkey. He was the winner of the Afet İnan Historical Studies Prize in 1996. He is currently engaged in research on Turkey, the Holocaust, and the West.

www.ingramcontent.com/pod-product-compliance
Lightning Source LLC
Chambersburg PA
CBHW052045290426
44111CB00011B/1624